WORLD WAR II IN ASIA AND THE PACIFIC AND THE WAR'S AFTERMATH, WITH GENERAL THEMES

World War II in Asia and the Pacific and the War's Aftermath, with General Themes

A Handbook of Literature and Research

Edited by Loyd E. Lee

Foreword by Carol N. Gluck
Robin Higham, Advisory Editor

Greenwood Press
WESTPORT, CONNECTICUT • LONDON

Library of Congress Cataloging-in-Publication Data

World War II in Asia and the Pacific and the war's aftermath, with
  general themes : a handbook of literature and research / edited by
  Loyd E. Lee ; foreword by Carol N. Gluck.
    p. cm.
  Includes bibliographical references and index.
  ISBN 0–313–29326–0 (alk. paper)
  1. World War, 1939–1945—Asia. 2. World War, 1939–1945—Pacific
Area. 3. World War, 1939–1945—Historiography. 4. History,
Modern—1945– —Historiography. I. Lee, Loyd E., 1939– .
D767.W67 1998
940.54'25—dc21   98-5348

British Library Cataloguing in Publication Data is available.

Library of Congress Catalog Card Number: 98-5348
ISBN: 0–313–29326–0

First published in 1998

Greenwood Press, 88 Post Road West, Westport, CT 06881
An imprint of Greenwood Publishing Group, Inc.

Printed in the United States of America

The paper used in this book complies with the
Permanent Paper Standard issued by the National
Information Standards Organization (Z39.48-1984).

10 9 8 7 6 5 4 3 2 1

This book is Emily's

Contents

Part VI. World War II and Postwar International Relations

Foreword

Carol N. Gluck

In the late 1990s, more than half a century after it ended, World War II is the subject of intense debate in many societies. Issues of history and memory generate political heat both within nations and between them. France focuses obsessively on its Vichy past. The United States challenges Switzerland over the spoils of Nazi gold. Serbs evoke Croatian wartime fascism to justify new violence. China confronts Japan over its failure to remember and acknowledge the Rape of Nanjing. Others chastise the United States for its postwar coverup of Japanese biological warfare. And the list continues. Far from bringing either commemorative closure or scholarly consensus, the fiftieth anniversary of the end of the war in 1995 launched a new round of attention to, and contention about, the nature and meaning of the twentieth century's most deadly global war.

Historians have not been idle. Their customary work of revising existing interpretations, rummaging through newly opened archives, and revisiting the past through the lens of the present has only intensified since the end of the Cold War. The sheer volume of scholarly material on World War II in different languages around the world is astonishing, and, as this book shows, the works in English alone amount to a vast literature on everything from airplanes to advertising, wartime planning to postwar poetry, presidents to POWs. To study the war is to learn the twentieth century and also to see the world.

The world, of course, has been less well represented in English-language scholarship than our own particular corners of it. We know far more about the war against the Nazis, and in the United States, about the war against Japan, than we do about the war in Asia or, for that matter, in countries other than the great powers or the major belligerents. But this volume attests to the fact that recent work has begun to remedy these habits of inattention. Asia is the subject of a growing scholarly literature, which reveals both the commonalities and differences among the nations embroiled in bitter conflict in different parts of the globe. Easy analogies of the sort that once equated Germany and Japan, or Hitler and Hirohito, no longer serve to explain Japan's aggressive war against China. Notions of collaboration and resistance meant something different in the colonial contexts of Japanese-occupied Southeast Asia than they did in sovereign European states under Nazi occupation.

And yet, such distinctions between the war in Europe and Asia should not obscure the historical geometry of global war. Events in a single country, or a single region, did not unfold in a vacuum. It was the cross-connections that made the war global, and they cannot necessarily be traced in national or binational terms alone. Japanese-American relations, for example, do not in themselves explain "the road to Pearl Harbor"; for that one needs Hitler's invasion of the Soviet Union, the fall of France, the China quagmire, and so on. Each country saw—and continues to see—the war in its own terms: the Greater East Asia War for Japan was the Anti-Japanese War of Resistance for China, the Pacific War for the United States, and the Far Eastern War for Britain; for years the Soviets commemorated the Great Patriotic War while the East Germans remembered the Antifascist War. But the historian is obliged to investigate the ways in which these seemingly separate wars connected in a global geometry of conflict. This process of connection, now underway, remains one of the important scholarly tasks for the future.

The fruits of another scholarly task are already apparent in the sections in this volume devoted to the cultural aspects of war. No longer is war the sole province of statesmen and generals, national politics, and international battles. For just as World War II was a global war, it was also a total war. It mobilized society totally and operated on totalistic world-views that gave no quarter to the other side. From high art to popular music, culture went to war in the same way that Hollywood did. And, in the broader sense of the term, the cultures of gender and ethnicity, of religion and class, affected, and were affected by, the winds of war. The essays here also reveal the conflict in values and the dilemmas of morality posed by atrocities, civilian bombing, and genocide, and the responses—or non-responses—to them. Even at a distance of over fifty years, history offers no easy judgment here.

The value of these essays, with their extensive references, lies in pointing the way to greater complexity, wider connections, and deeper comprehension of the war that left so profound an imprint on history and memory in the twentieth century.

Introduction

Loyd E. Lee

There probably is no best time for a historiographical evaluation of the issues and literature of the Second World War, though the conclusion of the recent spate of fiftieth-year anniversaries makes as much sense as any other. Publications on the war have been rather steady since it came to an end, though the rate has accelerated in recent years. Our understanding of the war, however, has not remained fixed. The opening of archives, first in the West, then in Eastern Europe and the former Soviet Union, the rethinking of old questions, and research into new areas previously not thought central to understanding the war years have all enriched our knowledge of this momentous era.

There is, surprisingly, no comprehensive historiographic survey of the Second World War, due, in part, to specialization in the study of the war but also due to the massive amount of literature on the many aspects of the conflict. This volume presents a reevaluation of basic aspects of the war in Asia and the Pacific, as well as themes relating to societies at war, culture, the arts, science, and technology as well as international relations and the postwar world.

To limit the scope of the work to a manageable length, primary emphasis is given to English-language material. Even this limitation leaves out mountains of material. Here we strike a balance between the best-informed scholarship and an introduction of the reader to a broad variety of issues not reviewed elsewhere and not under the unified rubric of the Second World War.

Many bibliographies of the Second World War have appeared in English and other languages; these are discussed in a companion volume, *World War II in Europe, Africa, and the Americas, with General Resources* published in 1997. No bibliography is complete. Indeed, given what scholars consider to be the proper content of the topic "World War II," the vastness of the primary material, the multitude of publications and the large amount of nonprint material, artifacts in museums, photographs, films, and sound recordings, there may never be a single reference listing all that is available. There will likely never be a complete annotated bibliography.

This is the first comprehensive historiographic reference work on the topics covered by authorities in the main areas of scholarly and popular interest in the history of the war. The chapters will interest experts of the respective topics as well as scholars and college teachers who want to know the historiography of the many war-related topics. It will also aid advanced students and serious amateurs who wish insight into the history of the war and its literature, whether on controversial topics (whether resolved or still contended), those areas where our knowledge has been expanded, or those needing further research.

Included are not only grand strategy, military and naval campaigns and operational history, and related matters of diplomacy but also resistance, collaboration, and the broad topics of the "home front." There are also chapters on gender issues, film, literature, popular culture, prisoners of war, science, propaganda, and war crimes.

The contributors, regardless of their topic, were asked to include, when possible, several common elements in their chapters. First, they were asked to describe the state of knowledge on the topic and to prepare a selected bibliography of the most significant books, articles, dissertations, memoirs, and other material. Narrative essays discuss various aspects of each topic, relating each bibliographic reference to its themes and issues. Recent original scholarship is incorporated if it aids new understanding, and older works of enduring value find a place. Finally, contributors point out areas of needed research or topics yet poorly understood. Each chapter concludes with a bibliography.

In the course of devising a workable scheme to organize this handbook and recruit twenty-seven contributors, I relied on the expertise and helpful suggestions of several hundred scholars from around the world. Though unnamed here, their publications are cited in the following pages and in the companion volume. I am very appreciative and thank them. During the past few years I have also had the pleasure of the advice and guidance of Robin Higham, Advisory Editor, without whose extraordinary knowledge of the literature, research, and scholars of the war this endeavor would not have been possible.

Various libraries in the New York area were indispensable for planning and carrying out the project, especially the vast collections of the New York Public Library and its special World War II holdings and the Library of the U.S. Military Academy at West Point. Particular appreciation goes to the librarians of the Sojourner Truth Library at the State University of New York, College at New Paltz.

A NOTE ON ABBREVIATIONS AND CITATIONS

The following abbreviations are used in citing publishers:

HMSO   His (Her) Majesty's Printing Office
GPO   Government Printing Office
NIP   Naval Institute Press
UP   University Press

The words "Press," "Publisher," "Company," "Limited," and "Books" are omitted. For titles that have been frequently reprinted, the earliest and latest dates of publication are included. When the same work is published under different titles, that is noted.

Western and Eastern (Asian) names are all listed in bibliographies in Western order. A comma is placed after the surname in all cases to avoid confusion.

ASIA AND THE PACIFIC

PART I

International Background to the War in Asia

1 International Relations and the Origins of the War in Asia and the Pacific War

Michael A. Barnhart

Scholars studying the origins of the Second World War in Asia are almost universally agreed on two points. A new synthesis is required to cover new work, especially new work for players besides the United States and Japan. (For this very reason, a more satisfactory name for the conflict would be in order, since "Pacific War" seems inadequate.) Unfortunately, this agreement exists despite international efforts at scholarly cooperation and exchange spanning decades and unparalleled in comparison to any other topic in the history of American foreign relations.

In fact, the first generation of scholarship on the war's origins was itself characterized by team studies. William Langer and Everett Gleason's classic two-volume *Challenge to Isolation* has stood the test of time. On the Japanese side, a team of scholars collaborated to produce the five-volume *History of the Pacific War*, edited by Rekishigaku kenkyukai, a deliberate attempt at a broad synthesis of the origins and course of the war in terms of the social, economic, and political conditions that resulted from Japan's incomplete adjustment to the challenges of Western capitalism. Both of these broad syntheses, perhaps because they were such, focused on the global environment of the path to Pearl Harbor. Both portrayed a United States and a Japan that considered each other distinctly secondary to more pressing concerns, America's in Europe and Japan's in Asia. In addition, both were written at a time when it was hardly clear that Japan would emerge from deep economic difficulties or that a Japanese–American partnership would amount to much in the coming decades, so attention to the Pacific conflict, while certainly present, was indirect.

Unhappily, the first burst of direct attention to that conflict was concerned with anything but wider issues. The controversy over the American disaster at Pearl Harbor generated a publishing industry unto itself, one with a remarkably long life span. These books fall into two groups, those blaming Roosevelt (or, in the case of Rusbridger and Nave's *Betrayal at Pearl Harbor*, Churchill) for engineering a "back door" to war at a frightful cost of American lives in Hawaii and those blaming anyone but Roosevelt for incompetence, pettiness, and plain stupidity. The latter may be passed over with scant loss. They apportion blame differently but, read as a whole, argue sufficiently well that there was plenty of blame to apportion. None are greatly interested in placing American unpreparedness at Pearl Harbor, much less Japan's decision to attack Hawaii, within the context of the origins of the Pacific War. Rather more surprisingly, none bother to illustrate the relevance of the "Pearl Harbor syndrome" that dominated a great deal of American strategic thought throughout the postwar era. Two useful "Pearl Harbor" studies that avoid these shortcomings have been prepared by Stephan, *Hawaii under the Rising Sun*, and Conroy and Wray's *Pearl Harbor Reexamined*.

The "backdoor" books are another matter, for they take as their central premise the secondary nature of the Pacific War, at least on the American side. Several of these, works by Beard and Barnes, for example, are thinly veiled attacks against Roosevelt's supposed tendency to tyranny. But Schroeder's *The Axis Alliance* stood the "backdoor" thesis on its head, provoking an extended debate on the true reasons for America's refusal to come to terms, at least temporarily, with Japan over Asian and Pacific issues. Schroeder argued that the United States' chief interests were, indeed, in Europe and that Roosevelt and Cordell Hull, his secretary of state, were rightly concerned with the Tripartite Alliance that Japan had signed with Germany and Italy in September 1940. But this concern ought to have been short-lived. It should have been clear that by the summer of 1941 Japan was prepared to abandon whatever obligations it might have had under that alliance to intervene in the European War if the United States engaged German forces. Further, by that time Japan was ready to forswear any further advance into British or Dutch possessions in the Southwest Pacific, another matter of European concern to Washington. Roosevelt and Hull easily could have had peace with Japan, but they foolishly elected to discard their chance by insisting upon a Japanese evacuation of China, a primary concern to Tokyo to which its leaders could not possibly agree. Why did their American counterparts insist upon the impossible and make war unavoidable? Schroeder's answer is an American obsession with morality and principle that could not see China abandoned, even if abandonment was in America's true interests. Bitterly, he concluded that America saved China from Japan only to preserve it for the more despicable forces of international communism nearly a decade later.

Whatever else one might think of Schroeder's essay, it had the virtues of placing the central issues of the origins of the war in the Pacific and Asia on the table. Washington's primary interest clearly was in Europe.

Roosevelt and Hull surely were correct to become alarmed when the Axis alliance and Japan's moves to the south endangered America's de facto allies in Europe. But Schroeder maintained that the United States was sufficiently tied to China, albeit with ropes of morality and delusion, to justify a war with Japan under this independent compulsion. The next task appeared obvious enough: to gauge the strength of America's commitments to China before the final months of 1941.

Studies of this subject had their own intellectual baggage under which to labor. If an examination of American–Japanese relations before the Pacific War strained to see through the smoke of Pearl Harbor, studies of Sino-American ties were seldom allowed to forget the collapse of Republican China and the bloodletting in Korea that followed, events that deflected attention from the seemingly less vital years of the mid-1920s to the start of the Pacific War. This relative inattention was remedied by the appearance of two lengthy studies by Borg and the first of many influential works by Iriye. Borg found an American government quite cautious in its commitments to China, even within the context of the new Pacific and Asian system forged at the Washington conference of 1921–1922, a position reinforced by Iriye's rich study in American, Chinese, Japanese, and other sources. The principles of international conduct embodied in that system were important to Washington but, for global reasons, not anything specific to China. Borg's study of the 1930s, as respect for those principles waned, portrayed a United States even less willing to extend even slight commitments to China at Japan's expense. Although Borg was reluctant to extend her analysis past 1938, it seems clear from her work that if America was willing to go to war with Japan in 1941, China could not have been the sole, or even primary, cause.

In Japan, however, scholarly work in the early 1960s demonstrated just how important China had become—to Japan—as a sufficient cause to justify war with America. Unsurprisingly, the keystone of this work came in a multivolume series, *The Road to the Pacific War [Taiheiyō sensō e no michi]*, authored by leading Japanese scholars and appearing in English in several volumes under the editorship of Morley.

Despite the series' title, its volumes, especially the earlier ones, focused upon continental questions. Japan's treaty rights in Manchuria, the legacy of the victory over Russia in 1905, had become of critical importance not to Japan at large but to an Imperial Japanese Army that had emerged, certainly by 1931, as the key player in Japan's continental policy. Within that army, the garrison force along the South Manchurian Railway, by 1919 known as the Kwantung Army, had become powerful enough to enforce its militant version of maintaining those treaty rights. The rise of the Chinese Nationalists posed the most immediate threat to those rights. But, as the authors of *Taiheiyō sensō e no michi* made clear, the Imperial Army viewed them as essential not in preventing the eventual reunification of Chinese territory but in containing the growing power of the Soviet Union. China was to be enlisted into the anticommunist cause if possible—a theme of Japanese diplomacy throughout the interwar period—but suborned into it otherwise. Some recruiters were to be Japanese business leaders, either in the semipublic South Manchurian Railway Company or in other enterprises in China, and Chinese who had been educated in Japan.

But the spearhead was always the army. The authors of *Taiheiyō sensō e no michi* presented the first glimpses of the debates within the army that pitted those desiring a consolidation of Japan's dominance of all north China before confronting the Soviet Union against others who felt that the time for confrontation had arrived in the mid-1930s.

The findings of *Taiheiyō sensō e no michi* and of another American-trained Japanese scholar, Asada, also discovered militants inside the Imperial Navy. In many respects, this was more interesting, at least in terms of the origins of the Pacific War, because the navy had good reason to find the United States the source of its torments and justification for its budgets for nearly two decades. Indeed, one of the central contributions of Asada's early work and a core idea of his later writings has been the existence of a bitterly anti-American "Fleet Faction" in the navy long before the explosive debates over the ratification of the London Naval Treaty in 1930. A decade later, that faction had come to dominate the navy so completely that that service, far from acting as a brake upon Japan's eventual collision with the United States, actually served as an accelerator, especially during the crucial high-level discussions of the summer of 1941, despite the reservations of Admiral Isoroku Yamamoto.

The recognition that there were extreme militants inside the Japanese military was hardly a discovery of the early 1960s, of course. The multiple assassinations of moderate political and business leaders in the early 1930s were quite public at the time and well covered by early histories of Japan's road to war, such as Storry's *The Double Patriots*. But the naval side was new. So also was an argument, raised most directly by Crowley in *Japan's Quest for Autonomy*, that the assassins did not represent the entirety of army opinion, or even very much of it. Crowley agreed that the army favored an aggressive foreign policy, but its senior officers were more interested in alliance with civilian elites to ensure its success. Moreover, the army's ideas were entirely reasonable, given Japan's difficult position as it entered the 1930s; it was hardly the by-product of an atavistic and irrational death wish on the part of young fanatics who had managed to intimidate their seniors, civilian and military alike.

Such findings set the stage for the next multivolume synthesis of *Pearl Harbor as History*, edited by Borg and Okamoto. The product of a 1969 conference at Lake Kawaguchi, this collection provided sets of mirrored studies: of the role of the Imperial Japanese Navy and U.S. Navy, of the

Foreign Ministry and State Department, and so on, all focused on the decade prior to the Hawaiian attack. The chapters on Japan extended the arguments of *Taiheiyō sensō e no michi*, not surprising since some of the authors had participated in that earlier project, but also broke new ground. Asada's chapter on "The Japanese Navy and the United States" contributed to the overall assessment of most Japanese authors that their government had chosen courses that made war with America difficult to avoid by 1941. Yamamura's "The Role of the Finance Ministry," Naka-mura's on "The Activities of the Japan Economic Federation" (*Nihon Kei-zai Renmeikai*), and a joint chapter by Misawa and Ninomiya on "The Role of the Diet and Political Parties" showed how weak the opposition was (when it existed) to the aggressive programs of the army and its civilian allies. In "The Role of the Japanese Army," Fujiwara pointed out that the army barely considered the United States in its calculations before 1939, and not very much thereafter.

The American chapters often represented new ways of thinking about Washington's role in the origins of the Pacific War. Weigley in "The Role of the War Department and the Army" and Heinrichs in "The Role of the United States Navy" made clear how little influence the American army and navy had over foreign policy making prior to Pearl Harbor. In "The Role of the Department of States," Thomson authored an excellent study of internal divisions within the department, concluding that its most senior adviser, Stanley Hornbeck, misunderstood many fundamental features and workings of the Japanese government. A common theme, in fact, of nearly all the American essays was ignorance, and the American authors tended to blame Washington for permitting a drift toward war until collision became unavoidable.

Despite its outstanding scholarship, original contributions, and binational representation and archival research, *Pearl Harbor as History* drew criticism, especially in Japan. Ironically, the chief point of attack was that the studies were much too binational, making the war in Asia and the Pacific appear entirely too narrow. What of Great Britain, the Soviet Union, or Germany, much less China? How could historians assess the influence of Japan's drive to the south without examining British, French, and even Dutch archives? How could it be possible to determine the role of the Axis alliance without an inspection of German and Italian records? How could a reasoned examination of the role of China be completed without Chinese studies? A truly comprehensive synthesis appeared more distant than ever to these critics.

Yet much of the scholarship in the decade that followed ignored these calls for unity and built on *Pearl Harbor as History*, usually in studies on Japan or the United States. This turned out to be no bad thing, for a comprehensive synthesis appeared to be emerging, unforced, from these specialized works. Herzog's *Closing the Open Door* reinforced Thomson's

view that senior policymakers were rarely in thrall to their East Asian specialists and that those specialists did not always hold sophisticated views
of Japan, though Herzog's institution was the navy, not the State Department. A delightfully innovative book by Anderson examined the role of
multinational oil companies, primarily Standard-Vacuum, in American–
Japanese relations. It is regrettable that no one has pursued his focus in
other industries, and doubly so that new scholarship appearing in the mid-
1990s in the field of political economy does not extend itself very often
to Asian concerns.

On the Japanese side, Shillony's *Revolt in Japan* provided a detailed examination of the fanatical young officers during their abortive coup of
26 February 1936. Their antiliberal—hence, anti-Western—sentiments
emerge with great clarity, but it is not so certain whether or not those
sentiments would have led to war with the United States. Such a connection is much more apparent in the excellent study by Peattie of that driven
eccentric Kanji Ishiwara. Ishiwara was a young officer in 1931, a crucial
cog in the Kwantung Army's decision to force the Manchurian issue that
year. He was nearly unique in the Imperial Army in arguing that the
United States was the army's real enemy and that it, not Asia, should be
the focus of army attention, a stance that baffled his fellow officers. It was
also a stance that led to Ishiwara's vigorous, unsuccessful, and ultimately
career-ending attempts to block the expansion of fighting with China after
the Marco Polo Bridge Incident of July 1937. Ishiwara was finished, but
his Pan-Asianist ideas would survive long after the war they had helped
foster had concluded.

Appearing shortly after Peattie's book was *Parties out of Power in Japan,
1931–1941* by Berger. Japan's political parties, it turns out, were not so
far out of power as earlier accounts had supposed, nor were they uniformly composed of civilian moderates anxious to prevent the military's
aggressive actions abroad. Instead, Berger paints a much more complex
mural of the army's repeatedly unsuccessful efforts to create a broad civil–
military consensus in favor of aggression abroad, which most party leaders
were willing to tolerate, and fundamental economic and political change
within Japan in order to sustain that aggression, which they were not. No
account is better in showing the terrific ambivalence of prince and frequent prime minister Fumimaro Konoe, upon whom the army pinned so
much of its hopes only to be disappointed time after time, last and most
famously in Konoe's resignation of mid-October 1941.

Also in the mid-1970s came two genuinely multinational studies. Both
were written along the lines of *Pearl Harbor as History*'s cross-institutional
comparison instead of attempting a new grand synthesis. In many respects,
Butow's exhaustive *The John Doe Associates* is a tale of institutional confu-
sions, if not outright breakdowns. Butow's judgments are harsh but well
grounded. Bishop James E. Walsh and Father James M. Drought were well-

intentioned amateurs whose efforts for peace made real diplomatic solutions less likely. Ambassador Nomura failed in the most basic respects of his office. Hull is faulted for not putting his "Four Principles" and a reasonable proposal on the table long before he managed only the former.

Race to Pearl Harbor incorporates Britain into a three-way examination of naval rivalry. Its author, Pelz, maintains somewhat ironically that the Royal Navy was not a great factor in the Pacific by the start of the war but that it and its American counterpart might have helped avoid that conflict if they had built with more steadiness in the mid-1930s and less panic as they entered the new decade. The American program of 1940, in turn, led to desperation in the Imperial Navy. In this fashion, the naval race contributed to the cause and timing of the Pacific War.

The British connection itself led to a London conference of Japanese and British scholars in 1979 on the theme of *Anglo-Japanese Alienation,* edited by Nish. Although most of the papers dealt with wartime and postwar aspects of that alienation, many provide key insights into the origins of the Pacific War. Hosoya and Watt had hoped to sponsor studies that would de-emphasize the Tokyo–Washington connection in order to provide a more international view of those origins. In fact, Watt went so far as to term much American scholarship on the subject the result of American fixations upon contemporary American concerns, from the height of the Cold War to the depths of Vietnam. He joined Hosoya in arguing that the Pacific War was, at base, a war between Japan and Britain. The United States intervened only because the Imperial Navy believed that the American fleet had to be neutralized to permit victory over Britain in Asia and because Roosevelt viewed such a victory as possibly leading to Britain's collapse in Europe. Apparently, Schroeder had been right all along, at least from the American angle.

Then again, most of the chapters were considerably more ambiguous on this count. Every Japanese study emphasized the long-term connection between London and Washington in the eyes of Japan's leaders, dating at least from Prince Fumimaro Konoe's famous public article of 1918, "Down with the Anglo-American Peace Principles." No mere strategic consideration of 1940 here. As Watt himself pointed out, it was not so much Britain's colonies as its Commonwealth that compelled it, year after year and decade after decade, to ignore the tactical advantages of arrangements with Japan that might offend the Commonwealth and, by the same token, the Americans. In so doing, Watt ensured that no true synthesis of the origins of the Pacific War would be complete without an understanding of how Canada, the Antipodes, or even South Africa influenced relations between London and Washington. For good measure, he reminded scholars that there still were no studies on the role of economics and finance, certainly from the European side. What effect did growing British imperial protectionism have upon Japan in the early and middle 1930s? What of the rift between the sterling and dollars blocs during those same years?

Some of these questions were addressed by yet another international group of scholars meeting in the early 1980s. One result of their collaboration was *American, Chinese, and Japanese Perspectives on Wartime Asia, 1931–1949*, edited by Iriye and Cohen. Three chapters discuss economic and business affairs at considerable length. Wang Xi, elaborating upon an argument first broached by Borg, noted how America's silver purchasing policy of mid-decade benefited the Imperial Army's scheming in north China. Washington swiftly cast aside the vaunted Open Door principles whenever domestic considerations required it. The ubiquitous and prolific Hosoya sounded a similar tune. He maintained that an opportunity to improve American–Japanese relations existed after the crises of 1931–1933 but was quashed by a hastily conceived, but much debated, cotton and wheat loan from Washington to Nanjing. The result was further dismay among moderates in Japan's Foreign Ministry, who believed that America had undercut their position against the fire-eaters. Cochrane boldly asserted that "war in China" was the "main event" in East Asian–American relations for the two decades after 1931 and that private business organizations greatly affected American policy, from Chinese business leaders who strongly supported the cotton and wheat loan to the South Manchurian Railway's struggle to limit the encroachments of the Kwantung Army upon its domain and Standard-Vacuum's vigorous defense of its market and market rights on the Asian mainland with Washington's steady, if not always strong, support. Stanvac also made an appearance in Gary R. Hess' consideration of American influence in Southeast Asia, though Hess is inclined to discount much importance for that region in the coming of the Pacific War. In his view, Roosevelt sought to "stabilize" the region without sacrificing "priorities elsewhere" (195).

Institutional studies proliferated in the 1980s, proving that a good deal could be learned about the broad questions of war origins from narrowly focused examinations of key players. One of the best on the American side was Utley's *Going to War with Japan*. Utley establishes that the State Department, particularly Cordell Hull, quite firmly kept control of American policy toward Japan, with the rather crucial exception of oil. Dismissing the Schroeder–realist critique, Utley argues that neither Hull nor his senior advisers were idealists. They were perfectly aware that words alone would not restrain Japan. But they did want Japan restrained. Hull believed precisely what he said he believed in his memoirs: Japan was untrustworthy because it was in the hands of ruthless militarists aiming for hegemony over all East Asia by use of force whenever necessary. These militarists intended to create a self-sufficient trading bloc that would be a mockery of the American principles of the Open Door. As importantly, that creation would make it very nearly impossible for the Open Door— free international trade—to exist anywhere in the world. All nations, including the United States, would have to pass up the chance for shared prosperity in exchange for an existence less vulnerable to foreign interference, to be sure, but far less commodious as a result. Militarist Japan, therefore, had to be restrained because it sought to impose poverty upon all and to do so using the tools of violence. Both invited a return to the scabrous carnage of 1914–1917 and further deterioration of the human condition everywhere.

These certainly seemed strong grounds for opposing Japan, but public memories of that carnage ruled out any military means for doing so. Roosevelt intermittently toyed with the idea of using America's economic leverage over Japan as a tool, or at least as a threat. Utley makes clear, however, that Hull fended off such exercises as much too provocative, even in the aftermath of Japan's unprovoked attack on the *Panay* and the Stanvac barges it was escorting on the Yangtze River. By the same token, Hull was disinclined to appease. After Ambassador Joseph C. Grew obtained, or believed he had obtained, a meaningful concession from the Japanese military concerning rights to navigate the Yangtze River, Hull refused to reciprocate with any goodwill gesture of his own. He and most of his advisers in Washington felt that Japan could not defeat China. In its failure, its military leaders would be discredited and fall from power without any active American opposition. On the other hand, American encouragement of the militarists had to be avoided. Better to let them overreach themselves.

But what if, in overreaching, they reached for Southeast Asia? A Japanese declaration of interest in continuing oil shipments from the Netherlands East Indies triggered marathon sessions for Hull and his staff and a shift in the American fleet's base for Pacific operations from California to Hawaii. Utley makes clear that this new attention had more to do with the new crisis in Europe than the intrinsic value of Southeast Asian resources to the United States. But resources were not completely irrelevant. To Hull and Roosevelt, the crises in Europe and East Asia were increasingly of one piece, one threat to the liberal world order that they saw as critical to American well-being. Japan would not be provoked, but its leaders would be shown the stick.

As it turned out, Japan was shown two sticks, one not fully within Hull's control. A central theme, an original contribution, of Utley's study is his careful examination of the evolution of an economic control bureaucracy arising from the July 1940 passage of the National Defense Act, itself a direct result of Germany's stunning triumphs in Europe. This bureaucracy, embodied in such agencies as the Office of Production Management, was primarily concerned with conserving materials for America's rearmament, exactly the materials that Japan required to continue its military efforts. As well, it provided fertile ground for hard-liners, both outside the State Department, such as Henry Morgenthau and Harold Ickes, and inside, such as Hornbeck and Herbert Feis, to put the screws on Tokyo inch by inch.

Hull resisted these efforts, remaining the central figure in Utley's account. The secretary of state entered 1941 certain that he wanted no confrontation with Japan over China or Southeast Asia until the situation in Europe had improved. Unfortunately, Hull was also certain, it seems, that American entry into the war against Germany would be necessary for that improvement and that for Japan to encroach further upon British and Dutch possessions in Southeast Asia would lead instead to deterioration in the mother countries. A further complication was Tokyo's alliance with Berlin, which might require Washington to fight on two fronts if it acted against Germany.

The preferred solution was obvious. Hull wanted to nullify the alliance and stop any encroachment. How to do either eluded him, as concessions to Japan remained repulsive. At this juncture Utley introduces the John Doe Associates. In his interpretation, Hull and Roosevelt were nearly as skeptical of the associates' claims as the chorus of doubters in the State Department but elected to proceed on a gamble that at least some time might be purchased (as Roosevelt emphasized) or that a genuine and comprehensive settlement might be reached (as Hull desired). So the Hull–Nomura discussions began.

Utley forcefully shows that they were Hull's discussions all the way. Hull wanted the German alliance nullified and Japan to leave Indochina and China (but not necessarily Manchuria). Yet these demands were only means, not ends, Utley argues. Hull sought nothing less than his primary goal all along: to "regenerate" Japan by shaking militarism to its core. That goal emerged most clearly in his "Four Principles" of mid-April and virtual insistence, two months later, that pro-German elements such as Foreign Minister Matsuoka Yōsuke be purged from the Japanese government.

Hull's problem was Germany's success. So long as Berlin's star was rising, it would be difficult to weaken those pro-German elements in Japan. There was not much Hull could do to influence Germany's latest attack against the Soviet Union. But he was willing to show Japan the two sticks after learning that the Imperial Army would occupy the remaining, southern half of French Indochina in late July. American reinforcements were moved to the Philippines, and the United States froze all Japanese assets, a move that quickly escalated into a full embargo, including oil.

At this point Hull begins to fade from Utley's account. Hull himself was taking a badly needed vacation. He was not on hand for implementing the freeze. That task fell to Welles, who, in turn, entrusted it to Dean Acheson. Welles loosened Acheson's tough initial procedures regarding export licenses for goods bound for Japan but was unable to moderate the Treasury Department's insistence upon exceedingly strict conditions for the unfreezing of funds to pay for those goods. The implications of this hard freeze dawned upon Prime Minister Fumimaro Konoe by early August, leading him to propose a summit meeting with Roosevelt. According to Utley, Hull opposed the summit because he feared a loss of control over American relations with Japan. This motive cannot be discounted, though it seems as likely that Hull feared that Roosevelt would sacrifice his overarching goal of regenerating Japan in favor of an informal agreement to buy more time, the sort of improvisation that the president was occasionally partial toward. Hull also believed that Konoe was untrustworthy, all the more reason to insist upon a fundamental and comprehensive agreement, or at least agreement in principle, before any summit. Hull would receive such a proposal in late November, labeled "Plan A." Again differing with the thrust of Schroeder's analysis, Utley maintains that Hull saw little that was attractive or even new in that proposal, and he successfully dismissed "Plan B," a modest modus vivendi, as a betrayal of China.

Utley concludes with a somewhat startling attack upon the fundamentals of Hull's diplomacy as he examines the actual origins of the Pacific War. The United States was foolish to permit "its diplomatic goals [to exceed] its military means, thus forcing it to depend too much upon China" (177). This dependence was created by America's need to protect Southeast Asia out of European concerns and thus America's need to keep China in the fight to protect Southeast Asia. But it was also created by Hull's stubborn insistence on a comprehensive settlement with Japan. A temporary understanding would probably not have led to a Chinese collapse; it almost certainly would have bought invaluable time for the United States. Finally, Hull's inability to control the rearmament bureaucrats ultimately led to his inability to control America's drift toward war.

These are stinging indictments of American diplomacy, and Utley is hardly alone in making them. Yet they raise the obvious question of whether or not an understanding, along the lines of "Plan B" or any other, really would have been acceptable to Japan, which is to say, whoever was in control in Japan. Shortly after Utley's book, two studies of Japan's most powerful institution, the Imperial Army, appeared, Coox's *Nomonhan* and Barnhart's *Japan Prepares for Total War.*

Both are cautionary tales for those who would believe that even a temporary solution to American–Japanese differences was possible by 1940–1941, much less as even likely. Coox's massive study is highly focused upon the intense war (a lesser term for that struggle would be incorrect) between the Soviet Union and the Imperial Army in the summer of 1939. As such, it was not written to address directly the origins of the Pacific War. Nevertheless, Coox provides a devastating portrait of an Imperial

Army led by remarkably inflexible senior officers determined to have their way in the most irrational of circumstances. Some officers, appalled at the army's slaughter at the hands of the Red Army, openly wondered how their service could even consider conflict with the even better armed West. They were ignored. Perhaps worse, the army permitted its experience at Nomonhan to incline it to oppose an attempt against the Soviet Union in the summer of 1941. Instead, it would move south to take on the West!

This author's book is more broadly based but likewise places the Imperial Army at its center. Many officers, middle-level and senior, had concluded shortly after the First World War that Japan could not cope with a second. The country had an impossibly slim base of resources and was not much better off in terms of its industry, yet both materials and the means to make them into engines of war were crucial to any nation's survival. These "total war" officers dedicated themselves to a two-pronged program of reform: securing resources in Manchuria, northern China, and possibly the Southwest Pacific and constructing a broad, modern industrial economy for Japan under the army's direct or indirect control. Only in this way—the way of autarky—could Japanese security be guaranteed.

As Berger's and other prior studies, such as Fletcher's *The Japanese Business Community*, have noted, the officers encountered few obstacles to their program outside Japan and very substantial ones in it, especially to their mechanisms for controlling the economy. The result was swift difficulty when the "total war" officers proved completely unable to control their hotheaded counterparts in the field during the summer of 1937. Ironically, Ishiwara of 1931 fame led the "total war" officers six years later in arguing that any escalation of the fighting around the Marco Polo Bridge would simply sap Japan's strength and render it more dependent on the West, especially the United States. They lost their fight but lived to see their dire predictions fulfilled all too well. The army was experiencing difficulties supplying its campaign by the spring of 1938. At the same time, the advocates of autarky hoped to use civilian allies such as Konoe to overthrow the existing political and economic order now that wartime needs and, presumably, fervor, were at high pitch. Konoe was disappointed in 1938 and again two years later, by which time it is fair to say that the Japanese economy overall was in quite serious trouble. Then came Germany's great successes in Europe.

Those successes offered twin rescue to a beleaguered Imperial Army. First, the colossal drain of the China "incident" might at last be ended by an occupation of French Indochina that would nearly sever the remaining flow of Western aid to Chiang Kai-shek. Second, the fall of Holland and besieging of the British home islands might open access, by diplomatic or military routes, to their rich colonies to the south. It was a perversion of the "total war" officers' original attempt to achieve autarky, of course. That attempt had relied on good relations with the West while Japan acquired the wherewithal finally to ignore and, if necessary, confront the Anglo-American powers. This new one required immediate confrontation in order to solve outstanding problems in China and then create conditions of relative self-sufficiency after the confrontation had been resolved in Japan's favor.

The obvious finesse was to assume that any "Southward Advance," even by force, would not involve the United States. Not surprisingly, that is exactly what the army argued for until early August 1941. This exercise in fantasy was checked only by the Imperial Navy's insistence that America had to be involved, in fact, attacked, as part of any "Southward Advance." But the navy's argument was not based on any sounder understanding of Washington's disposition. Instead, the navy insisted upon the United States as an opponent to ensure itself adequate funding and materials for warship construction even as Japan was beginning to run short of iron, steel, alloys, and practically everything else needed for such construction.

The lone exception was oil. Washington's cutoff of early August compelled the army to agree to a "Southward Advance" of the navy's design, ensuring American belligerency by deliberate act of Japan. Utley's book makes clear that Roosevelt's attempt to fine-tune the flow of oil to Tokyo went awry, but Heinrichs' most recent book, *Threshold of War*, maintains that the asset freeze was a carefully considered part of a global plan of the administration, one that, in the end, worked rather well for American interests.

Heinrichs' study centers squarely on a Roosevelt who had an outstanding grasp of the global diplomatic situation and the intricacies of power politics. Not surprisingly, Roosevelt followed Germany's wartime fortunes in extraordinary detail. Putting relations with Japan within the global context of Roosevelt's policies provides insights that are new and persuasive. Moreover, those insights make clear that Japan was an important, but secondary, consideration in Roosevelt's calculations. For example, Hull informed Nomura of his "Four Principles" just as Yugoslavia was collapsing under German attack and Roosevelt was moving to extend the hemispheric defense zone to include Greenland and the Azores. Defense of the Americas grew more urgent through May, as German successes in North Africa and a coup in Iraq triggered fears about the future of French West Africa, Portugal, Spain, and eventually Iceland.

Yet Roosevelt and Hull were reluctant to permit the weakening of the Pacific Fleet and quite adamant about maintaining a very hard line with Japan. Neither was prepared to break off Hull's discussions with Nomura, hoping that the talks themselves would irritate Berlin (as they did) without dismaying London and Chungking (but they did). Hull's message of 21 June came quite close to a break, however. He remained determined to regenerate Japan, even after the first days of Germany's attack on the

Soviet Union convinced nearly everyone that the Russians were doomed. Roosevelt agreed with Hull's stance, Heinrichs reminds us. But the president also moved to restore balance in July. He increased American assistance to China just enough, he noted, to replace aid lost from the Soviet Union and to counter defeatist sentiment in Chiang's latest capital. He pressed hard for more and faster help for the Russians. He met with Churchill and agreed to warn Japan away from the Southwest Pacific. But, aware of the Japanese buildup in Manchuria along the Soviet border, he did not warn Tokyo too much against moving southward, and he supported the asset freeze and sharp reduction of oil shipments to Japan at least, in part, to frustrate any plans to attack the Russians.

The Russian angle colors Heinrichs' subsequent discussion of American–Japanese relations. The Americans (quite wrongly) read Tōjō's appointment as prime minister in mid-October as a sign of renewed Japanese interest in attacking the Soviet Union, as Germany launched its offensive against Moscow. Washington increased its military presence in the Philippines, and London its in Singapore, in response. As the Soviet defenses stiffened, Roosevelt became more interested in a temporary understanding with Japan, since a northern attack had become less likely, and peace with Tokyo would buy time to aid the Soviet Union and Britain.

Why did Roosevelt, in the end, reject Japan's "Plan B" and refuse to offer a modus vivendi of his own? Heinrichs supplies three answers. American code-breaking operations, known as MAGIC, reinforced already strong impressions of Japanese bad faith. Apparently, Hull's suspicions had been right all along. Germany recommenced a push to Moscow in mid-November, just as "Plan B" was under consideration, with solid initial success. Roosevelt had fresh worries about a possible northward attack if he consented to any temporary accord in the south. Finally, Britain and China were wary of any American–Japanese deal. To damage relations with Britain was unthinkable to Roosevelt, who, on 1 December, at last assured London that the United States would intervene even if Japan avoided American territory. Permitting defeatism to triumph in China would almost certainly permit the Japanese assault against Russia that Roosevelt had tried so hard to prevent since July. Heinrichs reminded his readers that Roosevelt had had very few cards in his hand for much of 1941, but he played them quite well. America entered the war, globally, with an international coalition built, in no small part, by Roosevelt and capable of victory if maintained, as he so well understood.

In Tokyo, by contrast, there was little appreciation of the usefulness of coalitions. In part, this myopia was the result of the "total war" officers' desire for autarky, which hardly lent itself to alliance building. But Akira Iriye's 1987 overview of the origins of the war in Asia and the Pacific demonstrates that that war was the result of Japan's failure to prevent its conflict with China from escalating into a wider struggle and, conversely,

China's diplomatic success in precisely this regard. As well, Iriye traces the roots of that conflict to Japan's initial challenge to the Washington treaty system in 1931, not simply to the outbreak of widespread fighting six years later.

At first, Japan enjoyed the fruits of its bilateral approach to differences with China as the West shied from a direct challenge to Tokyo, although the Soviet Union, closer and thus more concerned, moved to align itself with Chinese resistance. By mid-1935, Moscow's Comintern was showing keen interest in containing the fascist powers. The resulting Anti-Comintern Pact of 1936 might have signaled Japan's end of isolation in the global arena. Instead, Japan so badly misplayed its position that when war commenced in Europe in 1939, it was utterly alone and virtually without compass. The stunning Nazi–Soviet Pact was only the most obvious indication that Japan was adrift. Iriye comments that the Russians signed it—deciding to meet Germany halfway (or more) in Europe—even as their army was ripping Japanese forces to shreds at Nomonhan. As for the West, Nomura, the new foreign minister who inherited the war in Europe and disaster at Nomonhan, understood that Japan's dickering with Germany and burned bridges to accommodation with China limited options rather severely. Under these circumstances, it was no surprise that Konoe and the army thought themselves and their country rescued by German successes the next spring and a neutrality pact, though more had been hoped for, with the Soviets a year later.

In fact, both of these initiatives badly backfired. The Axis alliance was a godsend to China and instrumental in forming a grand anti-Japanese "ABCD" coalition. The neutrality pact was useless within months as Germany attacked the Soviet Union. By that time, Iriye judges, only a Japanese renunciation of the "southward advance" or an American betrayal of ABCD could have avoided a Pacific war. Konoe was strong enough to oust the newly anti-Soviet Matsuoka Yōsuke as his foreign minister, but he could not prevent the army and navy from agreeing to proceed minimally with the advance by occupying the remainder of French Indochina. Iriye argues at length that Konoe would have required substantial concessions at any summit with Roosevelt and that Roosevelt, had he yielded at all over China, would have dissolved ABCD as a whole. Tōjō emerges in this account as a prime minister dedicated to his emperor's wish to make a final try for peace, a portrait reinforced by recent studies of Hirohito himself by Stephen Large and Masanori Nakamura. But the facts were that both Plans A and B aimed to break up ABCD and, for that very reason, were unlikely to succeed. Iriye closes with the observation that Japan's war plans, while brilliant for a brief campaign, were completely inadequate for anticoalition warfare, much less war termination.

These new studies emphasized the importance of coalitions and the roles of China and the Soviet Union in forming them. Suitably, yet an-

other conference of scholars gathered at Lake Yamanaka in 1991 to consider the origins and course of the war in Asia and the Pacific, with
Chinese, Russians, Koreans, Germans, British, Japanese, and Americans
all in attendance. Perhaps at last a truly comprehensive synthesis of the
war's beginnings was at hand.

Such hopes would have proven premature. The conference papers, thus
far published only in Japanese as *Taiheiyō sensō* under the editorship of
Hosoya and others, have gone some distance in providing answers, but
only at the price of raising some new and not so new questions. China
bulks large in four chapters of this thick volume. Sumio Hatano traces the
debate within the army over whether to continue to insist upon a bilateral
solution to the China Incident or turn to Washington for help in ending
that conflict. Konoe and influential officers in the Army Ministry felt that
the Americans were deeply involved in Europe and would be willing to
appease Japan over China. The General Staff officers were more cautious.
They appeared vindicated in late June 1941. Hull's proposal hardly
seemed appeasing, and the Americans apparently not only had known of
the impending Nazi–Soviet war but actually welcomed it and now plotted
to force Japan into a "southward advance," not a northern one. Clearly,
a Washington so inclined was not going to let Japan off the Chinese hook.
For this reason, the General Staff vehemently opposed Konoe's idea of a
summit with Roosevelt. Although the German alliance might be finessed,
Konoe would have no choice but to accept humiliation over China, which
the army could not permit. For that same reason, the army strongly opposed "Plan B," because it would do nothing to resolve the China affair,
but viewed "Plan A" as a significant and major concession, because it
would limit Japan's presence in China. Its officers felt vindicated when
the United States rejected B, dashing hopes in the Foreign Ministry that
American acceptance would have permitted a return to a bilateral path
with the Chinese.

Warren Cohen's chapter provides a historiographical overview of China
as an issue in American–Japanese relations for the entire decade before
Pearl Harbor. Cohen concludes that Schroeder was right and wrong.
China was not important to the United States for moral or idealistic reasons (nor for its economic value), but it was a symbol for more important
concerns, such as restraining Japan directly and forging a global coalition
against Germany. This latter was the key. Only after Japan's southward
advance and alliance with Germany were American partisans for China
such as Roger Greene (explored in another of Cohen's works) able to
persuade Washington to offer assistance. Schroeder was correct to see that
Roosevelt switched tactics in the summer of 1941, but the president's objectives had not changed.

Tetsuya Sakai and Waldo Heinrichs placed the Soviet Union at the center of their studies in the Hosoya volume. Sakai chronicles a success story for Soviet diplomacy, from obtaining recognition from Washington as a by-product of Japan's actions in Manchuria to diverting Tokyo's attention from any northward advance in 1941. Heinrichs does not count Soviet–American relations as overly friendly at any point. Washington was displeased by Moscow's neutrality pact with Tokyo but unwilling to appease Japan in the south if the result was a northward advance. Still, he would not dissent from Sakai's high marks (at least in the Pacific) for Stalin's diplomacy.

Hitler's statecraft does not fare so well, nor Ribbentrop's. Nobuo Tajima demonstrates that Ribbentrop used the Anti-Comintern Pact and subsequent collaboration with Japan almost entirely as a way to shore up his own power base within the Third Reich. He argued strongly for a northward advance in the summer of 1941, but more for increased personal influence than out of any appreciation for the wider realities involved. Bernd Martin comments that the German–Japanese alliance was an empty instrument. German war planning seldom considered Japan. Hitler openly dismissed the idea of a northward advance, preferring that Tokyo attack the British at Singapore. Although he wavered briefly, when his own intelligence reported stiffened Soviet resistance, he openly welcomed an October confirmation of Japan's decision to strike south, confident that he could finish Stalin swiftly.

One of Martin's most interesting points concerns Germany's declaration of war upon the United States on 11 December. The alliance with Japan did not require the declaration, and Japan requested one only on 18 November. Germany was amenable, so long as Japan agreed to no separate peace with the Americans. Japan consented on 11 December; the German declaration immediately followed. In this way the two wars were merged completely.

The components of *Taiheiyō sensō* point to an emerging consensus of the origins of the war in Asia and the Pacific. That view emphasizes the construction of coalitions, one successful, one not. While it would not tolerate a return to a strictly American–Japanese focus on those origins, this new synthesis does reemphasize the central roles of Washington and Tokyo in the coalition-making process. It also serves to refocus attention on leaders. The United States was blessed with one of the best, a president who combined tactical flexibility with a firm vision of what he wanted to accomplish. Japan was riven with factions pursuing their own narrow agendas. Only two of these had any long-range goals. One, the army's "total war" officers, lost their battle for eventual autarky in the summer of 1937. The other, Hull's "moderates," would restore Japan to the Western universe only after Allied military power had obliterated the other contestants by 1945. A new synthesis on the origins of the war in Asia and the Pacific will comprehend internal politics in Tokyo and Washington and how those politics blocked or permitted successful coalition building and, ultimately, military victory for the Allies.

NOTE

The author gratefully acknowledges Professor Michael J. Hogan's permission to reprint this work, which appeared in longer form and with full citations in Michael A. Barnhart, "The Origins of the Second World War in Asia and the Pacific: Synthesis Impossible?," *Diplomatic History* 20 (1996): 241–260.

BIBLIOGRAPHY

Agawa, Hiroyuki. *The Reluctant Admiral: Yamamoto and the Imperial Navy.* New York: Hill and Wang, 1994.

Anderson, Irvine H., Jr. *The Standard-Vacuum Oil Company and the United States East Asian Relations, 1933–1941.* Princeton: Princeton UP, 1975.

Asada, Sadao. "Japan and the United States, 1915–1925." Ph.D. diss., Yale, 1962.

———. "The Japanese Navy and the United States." In Dorothy Borg and Shumpei Okamoto, eds., *Pearl Harbor as History*, 225–260. New York: Columbia, UP, 1973.

———. *Ryō taisenkan no Nichi-Bei kankei: Kaigun to seisaku kettei katei [Japanese–American Relations between the War: Naval Policy and the Decision Making Process].* Tokyo: Tokyo Daigaku Shuppankai, 1993.

Barnes, Harry E. *Perpetual War for Perpetual Peace: A Critical Examination of the Foreign Policy of Franklin Delano Roosevelt and Its Aftermath.* Caldwell, ID: Caxton, 1953; Westport, CT: Greenwood, 1969.

Barnhart, Michael A. *Japan Prepares for Total War: The Search for Economic Security, 1919–1941.* Ithaca, NY: Cornell UP, 1987.

Beard, Charles A. *President Roosevelt and the Coming of the War, 1941: A Study in Appearances and Realities.* New York: Yale UP, 1948.

Berger, Gordon M. *Parties Out of Power in Japan, 1931–1941.* Princeton: Princeton UP, 1977.

Borg, Dorothy. *American Policy and the Chinese Revolution, 1925–1928.* New York: Macmillan, 1947.

———. *The United States and the Far Eastern Crisis of 1933–1938: From the Manchurian Incident through the Initial Stage of the Undeclared Sino-Japanese War.* Cambridge: Harvard UP, 1964.

Borg, Dorothy, and Shumpei Okamoto, eds., with the assistance of Dale K. A. Finlayson. *Pearl Harbor as History: Japanese–American Relations, 1931–1941.* New York: Columbia UP, 1973.

Boyle, John H. *China and Japan at War, 1937–1945: The Politics of Collaboration.* Stanford, CA: Stanford UP, 1971.

Butow, Robert J. C. *The John Doe Associates: Backdoor Diplomacy for Peace, 1941.* Stanford, CA: Stanford UP, 1974.

———. "Marching Off to War on the Wrong Foot: The Final Note Tokyo Did *Not* Send Washington." *Pacific Historical Review* 63 (1994): 67–79.

Cohen, Warren R. *The Chinese Connection: Roger S. Greene, Thomas W. Lamont, George E. Sokolsky and American–East Asian Relations.* New York: Columbia UP, 1978.

Conroy, Hilary, and Harry Wray, eds. *Pearl Harbor Reexamined: Prologue to the Pacific War.* Honolulu: University of Hawaii, 1990.

Coox, Alvin D. *Nomonhan: Japan against Russia, 1939.* 2 vols. Stanford, CA: Stanford UP, 1985.

Crowley, James B. *Japan's Quest for Autonomy: National Security and Foreign Policy, 1930–1938.* Princeton: Princeton UP, 1966.

Fletcher, William Miles, III. *The Japanese Business Community and National Trade Policy, 1920–1942.* Chapel Hill: University of North Carolina, 1989.

Fujiwara, Akira. "The Role of the Japanese Army." In Dorothy Borg and Shumpei Okamoto, eds., *Pearl Harbor as History,* 189–196. New York: Columbia UP, 1973.

Haslam, Jonathan. *The Soviet Union and the Threat from the East, 1933–41.* Pittsburgh: University of Pittsburgh, 1992.

Hata, Ikuhiko. "Going to War: Who Delayed the Final Note?" *Japan Echo* 19 (Spring 1992): 53–65.

Heinrichs, Waldo H., Jr. "The Role of the United States Navy." In Dorothy Borg and Shumpei Okamoto, eds., *Pearl Harbor as History,* 197–224. New York: Columbia UP, 1973.

Herzog, James. *Closing the Open Door: American–Japanese Diplomatic Negotiations, 1936–1941.* Annapolis, MD: NIP, 1973.

Hosoya, Chihiro, Nagayo Homma, Akira Hatano, and Sumio Iriye, eds. *Taiheiyō sensō.* Tokyo: University of Tokyo, 1993.

Humphreys, Leonard A. *The Way of the Heavenly Sword: The Japanese Army in the 1920's.* Stanford, CA: Stanford UP, 1995.

Iriye, Akira. *After Imperialism: The Search for a New Order in the Far East, 1921–1931.* Cambridge: Harvard UP, 1965.

———. *The Origins of the Second World War in Asia and the Pacific.* London and New York: Longman, 1987.

Iriye, Akira, and Warren Cohen, eds. *American, Chinese, and Japanese Perspectives on Wartime Asia, 1931–1949.* Wilmington, DE: Scholarly Resources, 1990.

Krebs, Gerhard. "Deutschland und Pearl Harbor." *Historische Zeitschrift* 253 (1991): 313–369.

Langer, William L., and S. Everett Gleason. *The Challenge to Isolation, 1937–1940.* New York: Harper, 1964.

———. *The Undeclared War, 1940–1941.* New York: Harper, 1953.

Large, Stephen. *Emperor Hirohito and Showa Japan: A Political Biography.* New York: Routledge, 1992.

Marshall, Jonathan. *To Have and Have Not: Southeast Asian Raw Materials and the Origins of the Pacific War.* Berkeley: University of California, 1995.

Matsuda, Takeshi. "The Coming of the Pacific War: Japanese Perspectives." *Reviews in American History* 14 (1986): 629–652.

Misawa, Shigeo, and Saburo Ninomiya. "The Role of the Diet and Political Parties." In Dorothy Borg and Shumpei Okamoto, eds., *Pearl Harbor as History,* 321–340. New York: Columbia UP, 1973.

Morley, James William. *The China Quagmire: Japan's Expansion on the Asian Continent, 1933–1941.* New York: Columbia UP, 1983.

————. *Deterrent Diplomacy: Japan, Germany, and the U.S.S.R., 1935–1941.* New York: Columbia UP, 1976.

————. *The Final Confrontation: Japan's Negotiations with the United States, 1941.* New York: Columbia UP, 1994.

Nakamura, Hideichiro. "The Activities of the Japan Economic Federation." In Dorothy Borg and Shumpei Okamoto, eds., *Pearl Harbor as History*, 411–420. New York: Columbia UP, 1973.

Nakamura, Masanori. *The Japanese Monarchy: Ambassador Joseph Grew and the Making of the "Symbol Emperor System," 1931–1939.* Armonk, NY: M. E. Sharpe, 1992.

Nihon kokusai sieji gakkai, ed. *Taiheiyō sensō e no michi.* 7 vols. Tokyo: Asahi shinsbunsha, March 1962.

Nish, Ian. *Anglo-Japanese Alienation 1919–52: Papers of the Anglo-Japanese Conference on the History of the Second World War.* Cambridge and New York: Cambridge UP, 1982.

Oka, Yoshitake. *Konoe Fumimaro. A Political Biography.* Tokyo: University of Tokyo, 1983.

Peattie, Mark R. *Ishiwara Kanji and Japan's Confrontation with the West.* Princeton: Princeton UP, 1975.

Pelz, Stephen E. *Race to Pearl Harbor: The Failure of the Second London Naval Conference and the Onset of World War II.* Cambridge: Harvard UP, 1974.

Prange, George W. *At Dawn We Slept: The Untold Story of Pearl Harbor.* New York: McGraw-Hill, 1981, 1988, 1991.

Prange, Gordon W., with the collaboration of Donald M. Goldstein and Katherine V. Dillon. *Pearl Harbor: The Verdict of History.* New York: McGraw-Hill, 1981; Penguin, 1991.

Rekishigaku kenkyukai, ed. *Taiheiyō sensōshi.* 5 vols. Tokyo: Toyo keizai shimposha, 1953.

Rusbridger, James, and Eric Nave. *Betrayal at Pearl Harbor: How Churchill Lured Roosevelt into World War II.* New York: Summit, 1991.

Schroeder, Paul W. *The Axis Alliance and Japanese-American Relations, 1941.* Ithaca, NY: Cornell University Press, 1958.

Shillony, Ben Ami. *Revolt in Japan: The Young Officers and the February 26, 1936 Incident.* Princeton: Princeton UP, 1973.

Stephan, John G. *Hawaii under the Rising Sun.* Honolulu: University of Hawaii, 1984.

Sun, Youli. *China and the Origins of the Pacific War, 1931–1941.* New York: St. Martin's, 1993.

Thomson, James C., Jr. "The Role of the Department of States." In Dorothy Borg and Shumpei Okamoto, eds., *Pearl Harbor as History*, 81–106. New York: Columbia UP, 1973.

Utley, Jonathan G. *Going to War with Japan, 1937–1941.* Knoxville: University of Tennessee, 1985.

————. "Upstairs, Downstairs at Foggy Bottom: Oil Exports and Japan, 1940–1941." *Prologue* 8 (Spring 1976): 17–28.

Weigley, Russell F. "The Role of the War Department and the Army." In Dorothy Borg and Shumpei Okamoto, eds., *Pearl Harbor as History*, 165–188. New York: Columbia UP, 1973.

Yamamura, Katsuro. "The Role of the Finance Ministry." In Dorothy Borg and Shumpei Okamoto, eds., *Pearl Harbor as History*, 287–302. New York: Columbia UP, 1973.

PART II

The Asian and Pacific Theaters

2 The Second Sino-Japanese War, 1931–1945

Thomas Marvin Williamsen

The Second Sino-Japanese War, 1931–1945, falls into three distinct phases. The 1931 Japanese invasion of the northeast Chinese provinces, Manchuria in the dated parlance, opened six years of aggressive, piecemeal Japanese military penetrations into contiguous Chinese territory and ill-considered probing actions against Russian forces on China's northern frontier. This first period also included continuous military violence among Chinese armies, both Nationalist and communist, and warlords. This was prologue to phase two, the campaign of the Imperial Japanese Army to conquer China beginning in 1937. Late in 1941 the third phase opened with Japanese attacks on Pearl Harbor and virtually all of the Western colonial bastions in East Asia; this joined the war in Asia to the war in Europe as Japanese war aims assumed more grandiose dimensions.

THE PROBLEM OF THE REGIONAL MILITARY SEPARATISTS, 1931–1937

During the Second Sino-Japanese War substantial military forces not effectively integrated into the evolving national army of the Chinese Kuomintang government remained under local, more or less autonomous control. These are often labeled "warlord" formations, the units of "regional military separatists." The government faced additional problems in this deadly and destructive factionalism, which divided China into virtual satrapies. The 1926–1928 campaigns of the "Northern Expedition" of Kuomintang revolutionary forces, on the eve of the Second Sino-Japanese War, provided abundant evidence of Chinese military realities.

Jordan's *Northern Expedition* tells the complete story on the basis of solid scholarship; political alignments of all the factions are detailed along with the tactical encounters and fluid, internecine alliances. Wilbur eschewed the theoretically crude term "warlord" in favor of the more explicative "regional military separatist" in his landmark "Military Separatism and the Process of Reunification" and sorted out the extreme complexity of the military-political morass through which Chiang Kai-shek maneuvered to become leader of the Republic in time to confront Japanese aggression. Wilbur brought to bear decades of learning in his admirably succinct "The Nationalist Revolution," which traced military and political events from the Russian advisory missions to the restricted military success of the revolutionary forces in 1928. He included a useful bibliographic essay and comprehensive list of all major sources available by the early 1980s in English, Chinese, Japanese, and Russian.

Sheridan's *Feng Yu-hsiang* and Gillin's *Warlord: Yen Hsi-shan* definitively interpreted the two individuals and the systems and institutions subject to their command. Lary's *Warlord Soldiers* depicted common soldiers as a unique social group with distinct tribulations. She defined major armies, local armies, petty armies, militias, bandit gangs, irregular units, mass units, stragglers, and local bullies as divisions of the military-like organizations inflicted upon Chinese citizens as the Second Sino-Japanese War began.

Other studies of warlords includes McCormack's *Chang Tso-lin*, which traced this Manchurian's rise and the creation of his powerful Fengtien Army. McCormack portrayed the continuous campaigns and shifting alliances of Chang Tso-lin amid the dangerous imperialist challenges from Russians and Japanese, demonstrated conclusively with the assassination of Chang by the Japanese in 1928. The best study of the educated and presumptive Wu Pei-fu is in Wou's *Militarism*, which ably detailed the campaigns of militarist Wu and his prowess both as tactician and as extortionist, skills equally useful to China's military separatists. Kapp, *Szechwan*, explicated with clarity and often graceful writing the peculiarities of provincial warlordism in Szechwan. Once Yunnan forces were driven out, local garrisons managed to hold their own pieces of the province in something like stability well into the 1930s.

One more important analysis of provincial military forces is Lary's history of the powerful and influential Kwangsi clique, *Region and Nation*. The Kwangsi forces centered around two of China's most competent fighting generals, Li Tsung-jen and Pai Chung-hsi. Lary's work highlights the generally effective political administration that made possible the fielding of a successful army and the role played by this military formation.

The most useful of all warlord studies attempt to analyze and understand the era in general as a system of military politics. Chief among these is Chi's reliable and comprehensive *Warlord Politics*, an important study listing the intricate military factions and determining how and why they came into being, thereby explaining much about the cultural dimensions of militarism in China. He explained recruitment and training mechanisms, economic practices, and the nature of the despoliation that followed defeat on the battlefield. Chi contrasted the vicissitudes of warlord formations with the reformed organizations of the revolutionary Kuomintang on campaign in this early period. Another fine general treatise born of decades of research on military separatism is *The Military-Gentry* by Chen, distinguished by deep and sympathetic understanding of China's malaise. Chen emphasized the costs of extreme factionalism and the subsequent impossibility of uniting to solve China's great problems and observed that military and gentry elites were equally self-aggrandizing and conservatively resistant to any change that might cost profit or privilege. The only modernization the militarists might consistently value was new military hardware.

THE COMMUNIST THREAT

By 1931 the communist Red Army had become strong enough in the Kiangsi Soviet to compel Chiang Kai-shek to military action. Elimination of the communists in their most significant base was the objective of five military campaigns fought from 1930 to 1934. The best study is Wei's *Counter Revolution*. Wei noted the loss of Kuomintang revolutionary spirit and sense of direction as the Kiangsi campaigns produced a militarization of Nationalist policy. Factionalism and residual warlordism were only part of the causes of military failure prior to 1934. Wei unearthed a wealth of persuasive detail about the Nationalist government programs to pacify the countryside and failure to be concerned with winning the hearts and minds of the peasantry. He believed the Kiangsi campaigns were the critical turning point toward a military-civil bureaucracy that would fail the Nationalists over the long-term struggle against abundant opponents.

A second useful source is Whitson's *Chinese High Command*, which also interprets the history of the encirclement campaigns, analyzing the communist military forces in terms of the evolution of military elites and the large unit formations from 1927 to 1971.

Most recently, Dreyer used both Whitson and Wei in his valuable and terse overview of twentieth-century Chinese military history, *China at War*. The chapter including the Kiangsi combat episodes borrows Chiang Kai-shek's metaphor of the communists as a disease of the heart, while the Japanese were a disease of the skin. Dreyer commendably encapsulated and reliably condensed the terribly complex histories of Kuomintang conflicts and alliances with the great variety of regional military separatists whom Chiang was gradually eliminating or integrating into Nationalist formations. Dreyer also included in his survey Liu's *Military History of Modern China*, which has served a generation of American historians admirably as the principal interpretation of Republican China's military history. Liu wrote with an inside informant's understanding of the Kuomintang and its military forces with judicious impartiality.

The role of the German military advisory missions to Chiang Kai-shek between 1927 and 1938 is told well and reliably in three histories, in addition to Liu's *Military History*. Wei carefully weighed the evidence unearthed in Taiwan in his judicious appraisal of German influence on strategic decisions in the encirclement campaigns. The most comprehensive examination of the German missions, including detailed scrutiny of German documentation, is in Seps' dissertation, "German Military Advisers and Chiang Kai-shek." The military missions are but only a part of Kirby's general history of relations between *Germany and Republican China*. Not one of the three sets of foreign military advisers—Russian, German, or American—successfully bridged the cultural chasm separating its national military traditions and the Chinese morass in which Chiang Kai-shek survived as the last warlord and the first national commander in chief in the twentieth century.

The most useful collection of Mao's military writings was published as *Selected Military Writings*. All of the most famous essays appear here, including "Problems of Strategy in China's Revolutionary War," "Problems of Strategy in Guerrilla War against Japan," and "On Protracted War." Griffith's *The Chinese People's Liberation Army* is a broad-ranging study of the entire history of the communist army, with only three chapters on the second war era. But the interested aficionado will include General Griffith's analysis of Mao's military thought and certainly his critique of China's martial spirit.

THE MANCHURIAN INCIDENT AND THE JAPANESE THREAT, 1931–1937

The study everyone turns to first for the events of 1931 is Yoshihashi, *Conspiracy at Mukden*, the standard English-language treatment of the Mukden Incident, set within the larger story of Japanese military politics. Ogata's *Defiance in Manchuria* concentrated on the development of Japanese foreign relations but leads the reader to understand the unique power exercised within government by the Japanese militarists. Crowley's widely respected *Japan's Quest for Autonomy* considers, in addition to his analysis of the Mukden Incident, the wider realm of diplomatic issues and difficulties the Japanese faced. More recent studies of high reliability and excellent scholarship exploited archival and other materials not available previously. Morley edited eminent Japanese scholarship about the war in *The China Quagmire: Japan's Expansion*. Included in this excellent volume is "Designs on North China" by Shimada, translated by Crowley, who also provided a helpful introduction highlighting the significance of this interpretation. Shimada emphasized the Japanese army and described the encroachments into Chinese provinces adjacent to the Manchukuo puppet state. This is an informed, impartial indictment of the military system led by senior field commanders who were beyond political control in the years 1932 to 1937.

Shinkichi compressed the history of the emergence of Japanese military power in Manchuria in "China's International Relations 1911–1931." The military arm of Japanese expansion, the Kwantung Army, was only a part of the aggressive and very effective imperial apparatus led in the early years of the twentieth century by the South Manchurian Railway Company, which administered territory in a manner not totally dissimilar from that of the British East India Company of the Raj era but in the total absence of accountability to civilian authority.

By the time of the incident at Mukden on 18 September, 1931 a long series of hostile conflicts and confrontations had inflamed the passions of Chinese and Japanese in northeast China. These are ably summarized by Iriye, "Japanese Aggression and China's International Position 1931–1949," citing current Japanese scholarship defining the emerging integration of Manchuria into the Chinese Republic's economy amid rising nationalistic fervor intensely hostile to Japanese. Iriye's other books, *After Imperialism* and *Power and Culture*, provide much greater detail and are among the most important secondary sources. Iriye's work, like most described here, is not standard military history and does not analyze operations; this is military history in the comprehensive sense, which must include the grand strategic maneuvering of diplomacy as well as consideration of force as a form of directed political policy.

Military dimensions of the Japanese presence in China prior to open warfare were explored in *The Japanese Informal Empire in China*, edited by Duus, Myers, and Peattie. In the chapter "Kwantung Army" Coox provided a clearly written, succinct description of these Japanese forces on the East Asian mainland. He briefly traced the history of these units and portrayed the early militaristic adventurism that would eventually drag the Japanese into full-scale war in China. Coox's chapter stands as an authoritative précis of the Japanese military administration in Manchuria, replete with highlights of major historical episodes involving Japan's aggressive, military superpatriots. Kitaoka's excellent overview of "China Experts in the Army" delineates the career patterns of serving officers in the several key agencies. He also surveyed the variety of plots and conspiracies in which Japanese military leaders were engaged with local Chinese militarists, most especially Chang Tso-lin. Coble's *Facing Japan* placed the events of the early 1930s within the context of the longer crisis presented to the Chinese by aggressive Japanese designs.

The previous studies shed light on the Manchurian Incident and on the Japanese military role in China during the early 1930s from the per-

spective of Japanese sources. On the basis of a comprehensive review of
Chinese materials, Sun put the Manchurian Incident in the wider context
of the Chinese weltanschauung and portrayed the eventual Chinese decisions for war in a historical matrix that delineates the Chinese cultural
environment, historical understanding, and international experience of
the 1930s. In *China and the Origins of the Pacific War* Sun interpreted Chinese policy for the 1931 crisis to be an internationalist approach based
on hopeful expectations of concerted international containment of Japanese aggression. The author reviewed the dilemmas that resulted in a
decision for war in 1937 and the renewed desperate search for support
from other nations, principally Stalin's USSR and then the United States.
In spite of the foreign powers' unwillingness to come to China's aid prior
to Pearl Harbor, Sun believes the patient Chinese leadership was sustained
by their belief that both Russia and the United States would, in the end,
have to go to war with Japan.

Japanese marines invaded Shanghai on 28 December 1932 and met
stunning resistance, courtesy of the nineteenth Route Army of Ts'ai T'ing-
k'ai. Ts'ai's army was fresh from the first encirclement campaign against
the communist Kiangsi Soviet and had remained loyal to Nanking even
when other southern Chinese comrades-in-arms established a rebel government in Canton. Sparse details are available in Boorman's invaluable,
four-volume *Biographical Dictionary of Republican China* (1967–1971). A major scholarly enterprise of the late 1960s, these volumes include data on
every major military and political figure of the Nationalist era, contributed
by a galaxy of contemporary scholars and China specialists.

THE JAPANESE INVASION, 1937–1941

The most important, really the only, detailed study of ground combat
operations of the Japanese invasion is Dorn's *The Sino-Japanese War*, a masterful and standard American treatment of the first four years of the Japanese invasion. Dorn was a practiced author, a professional soldier who
had served in China with the fifteenth Infantry at Tientsin, and a language
officer in Beijing. He was on the ground for some of the combat he reported, and his firsthand information and wide-ranging knowledge informed his book continuously. Dorn's research was enhanced by his
personal experience, his professional knowledge, and extensive work in
the Modern Military Records, U.S. National Archives, and in Japanese
operation reports compiled after the war for U.S. Army historians.

The *Japanese Monographs* (U.S. Department of the Army) produced after
October 1945 exploited information surviving in the demobilized Japanese War Ministry and Japanese General Staff. Although many records
were lost during combat and in the destruction of air raids, these valuable
historical tools were fashioned by U.S. Army historians working with senior

Japanese officers and translators. One hundred eighty-five monographs were written as well as additional studies of night combat and operations in Manchuria. In the absence of the missing daily strength reports, unit combat journals, and other standard, official records, these monographs are a valuable historical collection. Japanese scholars, using new documents, are improving them, but until their work is translated into Western languages, *Monographs* is the best.

One controversy that bedeviled conscientious and impartial historians after 1937 was, Who fired first at the Lu-Kou-Ch'iao (Marco Polo Bridge)? In Western nations already alienated by Japanese belligerence and aggression, the tendency was to accept the Chinese government's official denial of culpability as most likely true. However, as early as 1946 the U.S. Strategic Bombing Survey reported credible Japanese denials from authoritative sources, the same interpretation offered in the *Japanese Monographs* and recent Japanese scholarship. Some of the most solidly documented and judicious works have been translated into English. Lu's explanatory introduction to Hata's "The Marco Polo Bridge Incident" established for the Western reader the authority of Hata's work. Hata's meticulous scholarship advanced the thesis generally developed in Japan that the Japanese military high command were not intending on 7 July to invade and conquer the whole of China. Hata persuasively argued that even the generalized goal of separating north China from the administrative control of the Nationalist government was not a military objective at that critical moment. Japanese units in the area were engaged in night maneuvers, but only an infantry company was in the vicinity of the bridge that night, and it was heavily outnumbered.

The publication most closely resembling an official history of the war by the Military History Bureau, Ministry of National Defense, Republic of China was published serially in the early 1960s in 101 small volumes. A greatly abridged translation, *History of the Sino-Japanese War, 1937–1945* by Hsu and Chang, is useful for gaining some idea about the official Republic of China view, but the complete absence of modern scholarly standards weakens its utility significantly. Dreyer's *China at War* accepts Crowley's 1966 "revisionist" interpretation that the Japanese troops were not to blame. General Dorn, who was present in Beijing, refers in *Sino-Japanese War* to the Japanese attributions without judging their accuracy. What was important to Dorn was that the entire Japanese military establishment in north China, Manchuria, and Korea was soon advancing in large-scale troop movements, undeniably preplanned. No matter which soldier fired the first round, Japanese forces were ready to exploit the opportunity and launch their full-scale penetration into the rest of China. Unlike the Manchurian Incident of 1931, uncertainty remains justified about the first shot in July 1937.

Comparing warfare south of the Great Wall with Japan's humbling encounter much farther north at the borders of the Soviet Union at the same time (1938–1939) demonstrates why the southern operations were a juggernaut but not blitzkrieg. Coox, in the most reliable studies of Russo-Japanese conflict at this time, explains the difference between the modern army of the Soviets and that of Japan. The combined-arms teams, standard in the industrialized West, were far more powerful than Japan's infantry divisions, light in artillery, armor, and airpower. His *Anatomy of a Small War* presents the 1938 warfare on the commanding terrain at Changku-feng, where poorly defined borders of Korea, northeast China, and Russia meet. Division-size forces fought this first time for only two weeks; the Japanese were heavily engaged farther south, and the Russians watched Europe anxiously.

Coox's second study, the two-volume *Nomonhan,* is arguably the best military history written about Asia. For thirty years Coox was intrigued by the little-known miniwar fought on the border of puppet regimes, Mongolia of the USSR and Manchukuo for Japan. Coox brought to life the desperate deprivations of the soldiers as he also provided a thorough examination of tactics, strategy, command and control, logistics, and leadership. This was no minor event for the soldiers who fought and died on the desolate plain. The Japanese suffered nearly 20,000 casualties, relying on spiritual strength displayed in mass infantry assaults against the industrial tools of modern war, but then they had not experienced the failure of élan in the trenches of Western Europe. This is the definitive study of a brief, but deadly, war at Nomonhan in 1939. Zhukov won his spurs here; the Japanese were spared a return match until 1945.

Utilizing predominantly Japanese materials, Li, *Japanese Army in North China,* diagnosed the political and economic problems facing the Japanese military forces and detailed the occupying army's attempts to solve them. Li identified the serious lack of manpower inhibiting Japanese control but did not utilize Chinese or other materials to flesh out Chinese dimensions of his narrative. Li's account is useful in comparison with the officially sanctioned histories from the Republic of China, which tend to omit any reference to Japanese difficulties or shortages.

China's Bitter Victory, edited by Hsiung and Levine, comprehensively covers the many dimensions of Chinese life during the eight-year war. Chapters by twelve authors consider diplomacy and foreign relations, domestic politics, the Chinese communists, economic issues, science, literature, and judicial reform as well as two chapters on military events. Williamsen's "Political Training and Work at the Whampoa Military Academy" on the first four years of the conflict traced the Japanese campaigns and assessed the state of modernization of the Chinese forces in a brief review of the medical service. Chi considered the campaigns of 1942 to 1945, analyzing China's wartime performance in terms not only of military factors but also of China's historic resistance to foreign imperialism. Chi's chapter should be viewed as an addendum to his excellent and comprehensive *Nationalist China at War*. Chi demonstrated conclusively that the militarized Kuomintang had by 1937 lost track of Sun Yat-sen's plan for political tutelage and democratization. Chiang and his loyal supporters were unable to escape the dilemma posed by the dual urgencies of military pacification and political reform. The singular concentration on achieving military dominance to the total neglect of political reform doomed the regime. The terrible political and social strain of the war became unbearable in spite of Allied support after 1941.

THE CHINA THEATER, 1942–1945

After Pearl Harbor Americans viewed the ground war in East Asia differently. In their reporting, young American observers on the scene, who had lived, traveled, and worked in China, reacted against the romanticized illusions of the stateside media. The heroic image of Chiang Kai-shek and the Nationalists in their resistance to the brutal Japanese was less impressive for Americans who witnessed in person the Kuomintang dictatorship. Their informed reporting established long-lasting interpretations of the Sino-Japanese dimension of World War II. Principal among them are Snow, White, Peck, and Belden. Of a different order, even more reliable and valuable, were the dispatches of John Stewart Service and his professional colleagues in the Foreign Service, *The Amerasia Papers*, written for official U.S. government consumption.

Snow's time-honored, highly regarded reporting from the communist headquarters and base camp at Yenan, *Red Star over China*, was finished in Beijing as the guns announced the expansion of Japan's war in the summer of 1937. *Red Star* informs about military matters, the growth of the Red Army, and the typical linking of land reform and community building with military expansion that came to be the Communist Party's system among the poverty and debasement of the local peasant survivors of famine, warlords, and rapacious absentee landlords. Snow recorded interviews and commentaries about numbers of communist leaders and units when the Red Army of Workers and Peasants began to refit and rebuild in the Shensi-Kansu-Ninghsia Soviet. The contrasts he drew between Nationalists and communists were quite revealing to an unsuspecting and uninformed stateside readership. Snow was on the scene during a lull in the combat with the Kuomintang that culminated in the "kidnapping" of Chiang by his not-so-subordinate Manchurian general, Chang Hsueh-liang.

The abduction of Chiang became the internationally famous "Sian (Xian) Incident," which resulted in the second of the fragile united front alliances of communists and Nationalists, this time in the face of the advancing military threat from Japan. There are three superior portrayals of this complex episode. Bertram was on the scene, and his account, *First*

Act in China, offers the immediacy and local color of the period. Two other books, by distinguished American historians, complement each other. Wu's *The Sian Incident* and his updated "New Materials on the Xi'an (Sian) Incident: A Bibliographic Review" make up the conclusive history until new data are unearthed. The second united front should have produced patriotic cooperation against the national enemy, a phenomenon analyzed by Van Slyke in *Enemies and Friends*. In 1937 no one could predict the future of the announced Kuomintang-communist alliance, but the Japanese militarists had reason to take alarm.

When full-scale war began six months later, adventurous Americans were on the ground to record what they witnessed. Theodore White went to China and found work with the information service of the Kuomintang government. Tiring of life as, in his view, a propagandist, he next wrote for *Time* magazine. His interpretations of life in China are collectively available in *Thunder Out of China*, coauthored with Annalee Jacoby. They provide a synopsis of the war years, beginning in Chungking in 1939. Chapter titles indicate their approach and their sympathies: "The Peasant," "Stalemate," "Chiang Kai-shek—The People's Choice?" "Doomed Men—The Chinese Army," and "Stilwell's War."

Graham Peck, *Two Kinds of Time*, written in the late 1940s, sympathized with the hapless Chinese trapped under a rapacious government fighting desperately for its survival amid the destruction of traditional Chinese society. John Fairbank, doyen of American China scholars, believed Peck described the Chinese in more human terms than any Western contemporary and found no heroes and many victims. In *China Shakes the World*, Jack Belden wrote about the civil war following World War II, but his observations about the ruling Kuomintang extended back to the Sino-Japanese conflict. Like the others this influential book helped communicate the overriding interpretation of Kuomintang corruption, ineptitude, and dictatorship, as well as remarkable military ineffectiveness. These American authors were basically sympathetic to General Stilwell and understood the enormous difficulties facing Chiang's American subordinate.

Belden accompanied Stilwell on the heroic trek from the failed operations in Burma in 1942 to India, recounted in *Retreat with Stilwell*. Just as descriptively powerful and more authoritative is Dorn's *Walkout*.

Writing for a different audience, Foreign Service officers reported what they saw and what they thought it meant. Those contemporary documents helped establish a historical interpretation of events in China, even if the audience was the official community. Normally available only in archival repositories or in foreign relations documentary collections, a major set of those contemporary documents is available for the China theater. Particularly important are Esherick's *Lost Chance in China: The World War II*

Despatches of John S. Service and Service's monograph *The Amerasia Papers: Some Problems in the History of U.S.–China Relations.*

Service was born in China and learned about China first through the missionary life and world of his parents. Intellectually astute, his acute observations are key evidence for understanding military realities in China, even if military events were only a small portion of Service's observation and analysis. *The Amerasia Papers: A Clue to the Catastrophe of China* (no author) is a massive, two-volume collection of documents, including much of substantial value to the military historian. A prelude to McCarthyism, the *Amerasia* spy case itself highlights the disastrous course of anticommunist hysteria in the government of the United States during the postwar era.

In 1987 thirty-five veteran journalists of the China theater met with twenty scholars of the period to review the journalism of the war years. If journalism is the first draft of historiography, their purpose was to critique that draft. Their richly reminiscent and sagacious discussion is recorded in *China Reporting*, edited by MacKinnon and Friesen.

Of equal significance and even greater status among military readers in the 1940s was the field report of Captain Evans Carlson, U.S. Marine Corps. His observations and travels on raids with the communist eighth Route Army, published as *Twin Stars of China*, gave a positive and enthusiastic account of communist success with irregular tactics.

Three volumes of the official U.S. Army history by Romanus and Sunderland quickly became and remain the standard reference for studying and writing about the American role in the East Asian land war. Major differences distinguish the carefully researched and heavily documented official histories from contemporary reporting, but volumes on the China, Burma, and India theater (CBI) tend to corroborate the negative perspectives advanced from the theater about corruption, venality, repressive government, and a definite lack of will and capacity to fight the Japanese. They document in detail the manifold difficulties and complexities faced by the Chinese in their struggle with the Japanese invaders and, to this degree, back up the field reports of the 1930s and 1940s.

Volume 1, *Stilwell's Mission to China*, recounts his experience from early 1942 until late 1943. Included are the ill-fated first Burma campaign and the early attempts to sort out the extremely complex relationships among Chinese, American, and other Allies with a common enemy. *Stilwell's Command Problems* continues the narrative to October 1944, when Stilwell was recalled by President Roosevelt at the request of Chiang. It includes the second and successful Burma campaign as well as the Japanese Ichigo operations to neutralize the air bases of Chennault's fourteenth Air Force and the Service of Supply (SOS) personnel. American politics were at center stage with Chennault's politicking with the president and Special

Presidential Envoy Patrick Hurley's taking sides with Chiang against Stilwell. Romanus and Sunderland's third volume, *Time Runs Out in CBI*, studies the two theaters, China and India, that resulted from the command reorganization and the assignment of Wedemeyer to replace Stilwell.

Other official histories are also very valuable. Air operations in China, much more limited than in other theaters, are included in the *The Army Air Forces in World War II*, edited by Craven and Cate. The low priority assigned to the China-India-Burma theater is apparent in the official volumes focused on global planning, strategy, and logistics. Among the Technical Services volumes, two are particularly useful for the war in China. Dod's *The Corps of Engineers* includes the herculean engineering triumphs of the Ledo Road and airfield construction in the primitive economic conditions of China. Condon-Rall and Cowdrey's *Medical Department* concentrates more on the South and Southwest Pacific campaigns, because the number of Americans assigned in CBI was much smaller, but includes the desperately needy troops of Nationalist China, assorted guerrilla units, and injured civilians, along with U.S. military personnel in exacting conditions. Other volumes of the Technical Services will be of substantial interest to research specialists.

Tuchman's Pulitzer Prize-winning *Stilwell and the American Experience in China* became immensely popular in the United States. On one hand, *Stilwell* popularized CBI issues to the American public and the world at large; Tuchman educated masses of people who knew little or nothing of General Stilwell, the outrageous complexity of command in CBI, the awe-inspiring tragedies of war on the ground, or the complicated, cross-cultural difficulties Americans and their Chinese allies encountered. On the other hand, some historians and military officers had reservations. The review literature became a useful guide to the importance of Tuchman's work and surviving controversies. Her major interpretations are those of the Romanus and Sunderland official histories, and she did not distance herself from Stilwell's antagonistic views of the British. In the end her excellent popularization did not deliver on its title's implied dual promise of a comprehensive biography of General Stilwell and an inclusive history of relations between the United States and China.

White's *The Stilwell Papers* contains the unexpurgated views of General Stilwell's personal journal and letters to his wife: 300 pages of pure Stilwell, honest, dedicated, compassionate, and vitriolic. Writing originally for himself, the general told it the way he saw it. Opponents of the Nationalist regime applaud his acidic expression, while Stilwell's opponents mark his hostility as evidence of his inappropriateness for the mission in China.

Stilwell's former subordinate as military attaché in Beijing, the eminently qualified China expert Colonel David D. Barrett, later wrote a valuable footnote for the American military record *Dixie Mission*, a brief, superlative memoir. His military critique of communist forces provides authoritative insight. His work is one more painful reminder of first-rate reporting from the field in China that failed to persuade higher-level authorities.

The British author and China specialist Wilson explicitly aimed *When Tigers Fight* at the general reader, thus asserting no responsibility for comprehensive documentation. The book is extraordinarily interesting for the gritty details and first-person accounts of the horrid, barbaric cruelty abundant throughout the war. Wilson used an eclectic collection of sources, missing some of the best from the American side of the Atlantic, including others not well known or frequently cited. Wilson combined excellent analytical insight with bitter judgments about Stilwell equal to Stilwell's hostility toward Wilson's countrymen a generation ago.

Not all the political controversies, petty conspiracies, and mutual abrasions belonged to Chinese actors. The most passionate of the controversies and certainly the one with the longest historical tail was that between Chennault and Stilwell. The Stilwell perspective is well presented in works cited earlier. Chennault's memoir *Way of a Fighter* is the best known and most popular of many first-person accounts from ex-AVG (American Volunteer Group) fliers. Chennault and the "Flying Tigers" are the subject of dozens of books in the past fifty years. Chennault's story is told best in Byrd's excellent *Chennault*, a meticulously documented and judiciously balanced interpretation of a complex human being. She accurately portrayed him as heroic and visionary, if also capable of disloyalty to professional superiors and contentious to a fault. Byrd, ever the impartial historical adjudicator, avoided taking sides in the passionate controversies surrounding the two American leaders Chennault and Stilwell, and gave sound, reliable descriptions of battle, air tactics, and the impossible political-military morass in which the war was fought.

Ford's *Flying Tigers* is more narrowly focused on the American Volunteer Group and has less to say about the later controversies. He included informative detail about Japanese equipment, formations, and air combat and incorporated Japanese sources effectively in a first-rate, sparsely documented, military history. Samson's partisan account, *Chennault*, was written for a general public. The terrible difficulties of mounting the air war against the Japanese are presented from Chennault's perspective. Samson clearly sided with the anti-Stilwell cohort who became steadfastly supportive of Chiang and the Kuomintang well beyond World War II, when the divisions between Americans in China turned into Cold War antagonisms. Included in their ranks were Joseph Alsop, Commodore Merry Miles, the naval attaché John McHugh, and even Ambassador Patrick Hurley.

An excellent analysis of American–Chinese interactions, Schaller's *The U.S. Crusade in China*, is a cautious and discerning analysis of the American leadership's ignorance of Chinese realities and the tangled conflicts of personality and obscure military missions. This account is lucid, colorful, and ultimately fascinating. Schaller demonstrated clearly the extreme advantage of scholarly ability and impartiality in comparison with mere personal recollection and hagiography.

JAPANESE WAR CRIMES

Japanese atrocities and war crimes are part of the experience of the ground war in China. Japanese scholars have faced honestly the issues of responsibility for both initiating hostilities and extreme and heinous cruelties visited upon the Chinese. Political leaders have been less forthcoming, and thus matters of historical interpretation are certain to achieve continuing notoriety. Exemplary was Tsuneishi's *"Research Guarded by Military Secrecy."* Tsuneishi uncovered for both Japanese and Western readers the extensive experimentation using human subjects for excruciating and despicable scientific tortures.

More recently, two Western studies have exploited source materials originating with all belligerent nations and extended our understanding even deeper. Williams and Wallace, *Unit 731: Japan's Secret Biological Warfare in World War II*, concentrated on the Manchurian research centers, which were death camps for the hapless Chinese and foreign prisoners of war upon whom Japan's soldier scientists were unleashed. They also take up Japanese employment of bacteriological and chemical agents in the prosecution of their war against the Chinese in a fine and frightening book. Harris' *Factories of Death: Japanese Biological Warfare 1932–45 and the American Cover-up* goes over some of the same ground on the basis of deeper and wider documentation. *Factories of Death* is a comprehensive investigation of the American willingness not to prosecute war crimes in order to protect intelligence information. Both books emphasize the achievements of Japan's equivalent of Josef Mengele, Lieutenant General Shiro Ishii, a medical doctor of a different sort. Finally, the most extensive account of Japanese atrocities to date, although focused on the wider range of Japanese military forces than just the China theater, is by Tanaka, a research fellow at the Australian National University. He carefully documented the *Hidden Horrors: Japanese War Crimes in World War II* and includes a useful bibliography.

BIBLIOGRAPHY

Amerasia Papers: A Clue to the Catastrophe of China. 2 vols. Subcommittee to Investigate the Administration of the Internal Security Act and Other Internal Security Laws of the Committee on the Judiciary of the United States Senate. Washington, DC: GPO, 1970.

Barrett, David D. *Dixie Mission: The United States Army Observer Group in Yenan, 1944.* Berkeley: University of California, 1970.

Belden, Jack. *China Shakes the World.* New York: Harper, 1949.

———. *Retreat with Stilwell.* New York: Knopf, 1943.

Bertram, James. *First Act in China: The Story of the Sian Mutiny.* New York: Viking, 1938.

Boorman, Howard L., ed. *Biographical Dictionary of Republican China.* 4 vols. New York: Columbia UP, 1967–1971.

Byrd, Martha. *Chennault: Giving Wings to the Tiger.* Tuscaloosa: University of Alabama, 1987.

Carlson, Evans Fordyce. *Twin Stars of China.* New York: Dodd, Mead, 1941.

Chen, Jerome. *The Military-Gentry Coalition.* Toronto: Toronto UP, 1979.

Chennault, Claire L. *Way of a Fighter: The Memoirs of Claire Lee Chennault.* Edited by Robert Hotz. New York: Putnam, 1942.

Chi, Hsi-Sheng. "The Military Dimension, 1942–1945." In James C. Hsiung and Steven I. Levine, eds., *China's Bitter Victory,* 157–184. Armonk, NY: M. E. Sharpe, 1992.

———. *Nationalist China at War: Military Defeats and Political Collapse, 1937–1945.* Ann Arbor: University of Michigan, 1982.

———. *Warlord Politics in China, 1916–1928.* Stanford, CA: Stanford UP, 1976.

Coble, Parks M. *Facing Japan: Chinese Politics and Japanese Imperialism, 1931 to 1937.* Cambridge: Harvard UP, 1991.

Condon-Rall, Mary Ellen, and Albert E. Cowdrey. *The Medical Department: Medical Service in the War against Japan.* Washington, DC: Center for Military History, 1994.

Coox, Alvin D. *Anatomy of a Small War: The Soviet-Japanese Struggle for Changkufeng/Khasan, 1938.* Westport, CT: Greenwood, 1977.

———. "Kwantung Army Dimension." In Peter Duus, Ramon H. Myers, and Mark R. Peattie, eds., *The Japanese Informal Empire in China, 1895–1937,* 395–428. Princeton: Princeton UP, 1989.

———. *Nomonhan: Japan against Russia, 1939.* 2 vols. Palo Alto, CA: Stanford UP, 1985.

Craven, Wesley Frank, and James Lea Cate, eds. *The Army Air Forces in World War II.* 7 vols. Chicago: University of Chicago, 1948–1958.

Crowley, James B. *Japan's Quest for Autonomy: National Security and Foreign Policy, 1930–1938.* Princeton: Princeton UP, 1966.

Dod, Karl C. *The Corps of Engineers: The War against Japan.* Washington, DC: Center for Military History, 1966, 1982.

Dorn, Frank. *The Sino-Japanese War, 1937–41.* New York: Macmillan, 1971.

———. *Walkout with Stilwell in Burma.* New York: Pyramid, 1971.

Dreyer, Edward L. *China at War 1901–1949.* New York: Longman Group, 1995.

Duus, Peter, Ramon H. Myers, and Mark R. Peattie, eds. *The Japanese Informal Empire in China, 1895–1937.* Princeton: Princeton UP, 1989.

Esherick, Joseph W. *Lost Chance in China: The World War II Despatches of John S. Service.* New York: Random House, 1974.

Fairbank, John K., ed. *The Cambridge History of China.* Vol. 13. London: Cambridge UP, 1986.

Ford, Daniel. *Flying Tigers: Claire Chennault and the American Volunteer Group.* Washington, DC: Smithsonian Institute, 1991.

Gillin, Donald G. *Warlord: Yen Hsi-shan in Shansi Province, 1911–1949.* Princeton: Princeton UP, 1967.

Griffith, Samuel B. *The Chinese People's Liberation Army.* New York: McGraw-Hill, 1967.

Harris, Sheldon. *Factories of Death: Japanese Biological Warfare 1932–45 and the American Cover-up.* New York: Routledge, 1994.

Hata, Ikuhiko. "The Marco Polo Bridge Incident, 1937." In James William Morely, ed., *The China Quagmire: Japan's Expansion on the Asian Continent 1933–1941,* 243–288. New York: Columbia UP, 1983.

Hsiung, James C., and Steven I. Levine, eds. *China's Bitter Victory: The War with Japan 1937–1945.* Armonk, NY: M. E. Sharpe, 1992.

Hsu, Long-hsien, and Ming-kai Chang, eds. *History of the Sino-Japanese War, 1937–1945.* Taipei: Chung Wu, 1971.

Iriye, Akira. *After Imperialism: The Search for a New Order in the Far East, 1921–1931.* Cambridge: Harvard UP, 1965.

———. "Japanese Aggression and China's International Position 1931–1949." In John K. Fairbank and Albert Feuerwerker, eds., *The Cambridge History of Modern China,* vol. 13, part 2, 492–546. Cambridge: Cambridge UP, 1986.

———. *Power and Culture: The Japanese–American War, 1941–1945.* Cambridge: Harvard UP, 1981.

Jordan, Donald A. *The Northern Expedition: China's National Revolution of 1926–1928.* Honolulu: UP of Hawaii, 1976.

Kapp, Robert. *Szechwan and the Chinese Republic: Provincial Militarism and Central Power 1911–1938.* New Haven, CT: Yale UP, 1973.

Kirby, William. *Germany and Republican China.* Stanford CA: Stanford UP, 1984.

Kitaoka, Shin'ichi. "China Experts in the Army." In Peter Duus, Ramon H. Myers, and Mark R. Peattie, eds., *The Japanese Informal Empire,* 330–368. Princeton: Princeton UP, 1989.

Lary, Diana. *Region and Nation: The Kwangsi Clique in Chinese Politics, 1925–1937.* Cambridge: Cambridge UP, 1974.

———. *Warlord Soldiers: Chinese Common Soldiers, 1911–1937.* Cambridge: Cambridge UP, 1985.

Li, Lincoln. *Japanese Army in North China, 1937–1941: Problems of Political and Economic Control.* Tokyo: Oxford UP, 1975.

Liu, F. F. *A Military History of Modern China, 1924–1949.* Princeton: Princeton UP, 1956.

MacKinnon, Stephen R., and Oris Friesen, eds. *China Reporting: An Oral History of American Journalism in the 1930's and 1940's.* Berkeley: University of California, 1987.

Mao, Tse Tung. *Selected Military Writings of Mao Tse Tung.* Beijing: Foreign Language, 1967.

McCormack, Gavan. *Chang Tso-lin in Northeast China, 1911–1928: China, Japan, and the Manchurian Idea.* Stanford, CA: Stanford UP, 1977.

Morley, James William, ed. *The China Quagmire: Japan's Expansion on the Asian Continent 1933–1941.* New York: Columbia UP, 1983.

Ogata, Sadako. *Defiance in Manchuria: The Making of Japanese Foreign Policy, 1931–1932.* Berkeley: University of California, 1964.

Peck, Graham. *Two Kinds of Time: A Personal Story of China's Crash into Revolution.* Boston: Houghton Mifflin, 1950.

Romanus, Charles F., and Riley Sunderland. *Stilwell's Command Problems.* Washington, DC: GPO, 1955.

———. *Stilwell's Mission to China.* Washington, DC: GPO, 1953.

———. *Time Runs Out in CBI.* Washington, DC: GPO, 1959.

Samson, Jack. *Chennault.* New York: Doubleday, 1987.

Schaller, Michael. *The U.S. Crusade in China, 1938–1945.* New York: Columbia UP, 1979.

Seps, J. Bernard. "German Military Advisers and Chiang Kai-shek, 1927–1938." Ph.D. diss., University of California, 1972.

Service, John S. *The Amerasia Papers: Some Problems in the History of U.S.–China Relations.* Berkeley: University of California, 1971.

Sheridan, James E. *Chinese Warlord: The Career of Feng Yu-hsiang.* Stanford, CA: Stanford UP, 1966.

Shimada, Toshihiko. "Designs on North China." In James William Morley, ed., *The China Quagmire: Japan's Expansion on the Asian Continent, 1933–1941,* 11–230. New York: Columbia UP, 1983.

Shinkichi, Eto. "China's International Relations 1911–1931." In *The Cambridge History of China,* vol. 13, part 2, 74–115. Cambridge: Cambridge UP, 1986.

Snow, Edgar. *Red Star over China.* New York: Random House, 1938.

Storry, Richard. *The Double Patriots: A Study of Japanese Nationalism.* Boston: Houghton Mifflin, 1956; London: Chatto and Windus, 1957; Westport, CT: Greenwood, 1973.

Sun, Youli. *China and the Origins of the Pacific War, 1931–1941.* New York: St. Martin's, 1993.

Tanaka, Toshiyuki. *Hidden Horrors: Japanese War Crimes in World War II.* Boulder, CO: Westview, 1996.

Tsuneishi, Keiichi. "The Research Guarded by Military Secrecy: The Isolation of the E. H. F. Virus in Japanese Biological Warfare Unit." *Historia Scientarium* (Japan) 30 (1986): 79–92.

Tuchman, Barbara. *Stilwell and the American Experience in China.* New York: Macmillan, 1970.

U.S. Department of the Army. *Japanese Monographs.* Washington, DC: Office of the Chief of Military History, 1945–1960.

Van Slyke, Lyman P. *Enemies and Friends: The United Front in Chinese Communist History.* Stanford, CA: Stanford UP, 1967.

Wei, William. *Counter Revolution: The Nationalists in Jiangxi During the Soviet Period.* Ann Arbor: University of Michigan, 1985.

White, Theodore, ed. *The Stilwell Papers.* New York: William Sloane, 1948.

White, Theodore, and Annalee Jacoby. *Thunder Out of China.* New York: William Sloane, 1946.

Whitson, William H., with Hung Chien-hsia. *The Chinese High Command: A History of Communist Military Politics, 1927–1971.* New York: Macmillan, 1973.

Wilbur, C. Martin. "Military Separatism and the Process of Reunification under the Nationalist Regime, 1922–1937." In Ping-ti Ho and Tang Tsou, eds., *China in Crisis*, vol. 1, 203–263. Chicago: University of Chicago, 1968.

———. "The Nationalist Revolution: From Canton to Nanking, 1923–28." In John K. Fairbank, ed., *Republican China, 1912–1949*, vol. 12, part 1, 527–720. *The Cambridge History of China*. Cambridge: Cambridge UP, 1986.

Williams, Peter, and David Wallace. *Unit 731: Army's Secret of Secrets*. London: Hodder and Stoughton, 1989. Also published as *Unit 731: Japan's Secret Biological Warfare in World War II*. New York: Free Press, 1989.

Williamsen, Thomas Marvin. "Political Training and Work at the Whampoa Military Academy Prior to the Northern Expedition." Ph.D. diss., Duke University, 1975.

Wilson, Dick. *When Tigers Fight: The Story of the Sino-Japanese War, 1937–1945*. New York: Viking, 1982.

Wou, Odoric Y. K. *Militarism in Modern China: The Career of Wu P'ei-fu, 1916–1939*. Canberra: Australian National UP, 1978.

Wu, Tien-wei. "New Materials on the Xi'an (Sian) Incident: A Bibliographic Review." *Modern China* 10 (1984): 115–141.

———. *The Sian Incident: A Pivotal Point in Modern Chinese History*. Ann Arbor: University of Michigan, 1976.

Yoshihashi, Takehiko. *Conspiracy at Mukden: The Rise of the Japanese Military*. New Haven, CT: Yale UP, 1963.

3 The Japanese Attack on Pearl Harbor

Eugene L. Rasor

Few issues have provoked more ongoing debate and controversy in the United States and elsewhere than the surprise Japanese carrier, airborne attack on the major American base at Pearl Harbor, Hawaii, early on Sunday morning, 7 December 1941. A spectrum of all of the positions of the controversy is presented in this chapter.

The conflict over Pearl Harbor began long before the war. Early in the twentieth century, a number of prognosticators presented virtual blueprints of future events. Didactically, they stressed defense, security, and timely preparation. In the 1920s and 1930s other vocal and powerful elements, including respected and prestigious historians and political international isolationists, opposed involvement of the United States in any war. They provided background, foundation, and continuity for later accusations of conspiracy and cover-up made against President Franklin Roosevelt and high-ranking members of his administration, especially in the State, War, and Navy Departments. The increasingly stringent diplomatic measures aimed at Japan, these critics contended, were implemented for the purpose of forcing America into joining the war in Europe.

Many saw the Japanese attack without a formal declaration of war as a dastardly and horrendous outrage. Nothing unified the American public more than the determination for revenge and retaliation. The controversy over who among American officials, including those at the highest levels, was "guilty" for the debacle has led to some extreme positions and vicious accusations.

The matter of "scapegoats" has generated much heat and little light. The essential need for wartime secrecy meant that much important information regarding communications and intelligence was not available to investigators and researchers until decades after the war. Perceived and alleged failures in those matters are yet another factor. What did the United States know, and when did it know it? Finally, there are ongoing and extensive historiographical and bibliographical surveys of the literature. That literature is extensive. Four of the contributors to the debate have been presidents of the American Historical Association: Charles Beard, William Langer, Samuel Eliot Morison, and Akira Iriye.

First there were the prognosticators. Decades before the attack, prescient writers came forward. Honan's *Visions of Infamy* is a comprehensive biography of Hector Bywater, the best-known example. Bywater, a British journalist-spy, wrote prophetic analyses, *Sea Power in the Pacific* and *The Great Pacific War* in the 1920s, which apparently influenced American and Japanese war planners. He died under unusual circumstances in London in 1940.

Even earlier, in 1908, German novelist Grautoff wrote *Banzai!*, incorporating an early Japanese victory over General MacArthur, commander of American forces. A year later Lea, an American who became a general in the Chinese revolutionary army, produced a scenario of Japanese attacks on American territory, *The Valor of Ignorance*. General Billy Mitchell, an air enthusiast, conducted an inspection tour of Pacific bases in 1923 and, in his unpublished *Report*, warned that Pearl Harbor was vulnerable to surprise attack. In 1937, Bienstock warned the United States and Great Britain to prepare to wage *The Struggle for the Pacific* against Japan in Japanese territory. That would require extraordinary weaponry, which must be sustained over long distances and for lengthy periods. In *War in the Pacific* Denlinger and Gary urged naval preparations in 1936.

Even during the period prior to American entrance in World War II, a large, vocal, and distinguished group of critics persisted in campaigns to prevent American involvement. The America First Committee and several leading scholars led the opposition, formulating revisionist ideas, devil theories, conspiracy theories, and the "back door" to war, that is, that Roosevelt and a cabal of officials such as Cordell Hull, Henry Stimson, Franklin Knox, and George Marshall knowingly conspired to lure the Japanese into an attack so as to precipitate American entry in the war in the Pacific and in Europe and then conducted a systematic cover-up of all evidence.

Stenehjem studied the "New York Chapter of the America First Committee." Schneider's *Should America Go to War?* analyzes public opinion in the greater Chicago area. Among early critics of the Roosevelt administration were well-known academics Charles A. Beard (*President Roosevelt and the Coming of the War*) and Harry Elmer Barnes (*Perpetual War for Perpetual Peace*). In their view historians such as Samuel Eliot Morison in *Rising Sun in the Pacific*, Walter Millis in *This Is Pearl!*, Basil Rauch in *Roosevelt from Munich to Pearl Harbor*, and Herbert Feis in *The Road to Pearl Harbor* were apologists, "Court Historians," "ballyhoo racketeers," and

"Whitewashers." Other critics from the wartime period include Flynn, *As We Go Marching*; Morgenstern, *Pearl Harbor: The Story of the Secret War*; Cole, *America First*; Tansill, *Back Door to War*; Sanborn, *Design for War*; and Theobald, *The Final Secret*.

Immediately following the attack, a series of ever more elaborate official investigations was conducted. They focused on defense and security preparations, readiness, warnings, communications, intelligence, and war planning. Of these topics, intelligence has provoked the greatest debate. As a result of the early investigations, punitive measures taken were limited to the local naval and army commanders in Hawaii, Admiral Husband Kimmel and General Walter Short. Kimmel defended his role in *Admiral Kimmel's Story*. More recently, a vocal element has arisen depicting Kimmel and Short as "scapegoats" in need of rehabilitation.

Official American investigations concerning preparation and readiness proliferated: first came the Roberts Commission, then the Hart Inquiry, an Army Board, and a Navy Court of Inquiry in 1944, and the Clarke, Clausen, and Hewitt investigations in 1945, culminating with the U.S. Congress' Joint Congressional Committee, November 1945–May 1946, with seventy days of hearings published in thirty-nine volumes. The latter concluded with majority (six members) and minority (two members) reports. The only punitive measures were censure of Kimmel and Short. The records of the joint committee incorporated data from the seven previous inquiries. There is an extensive *Index* compiled by Smith. Melosi reviewed the history of the investigations in *The Shadow of Pearl Harbor*. The best and most comprehensive study of the intelligence failure that led to the surprise attack remains Wohlstetter's *Pearl Harbor: Warning and Decision*. One of the investigators, Clausen, wrote a fiftieth-anniversary reappraisal with Lee, *Pearl Harbor: Final Judgment*.

The story of American strategic war planning during four decades before the attack is clearly and brilliantly told in *War Plan Orange* by Miller. At the time of Pearl Harbor Kimmel was to be the leading "thruster," that is, commander of the American battle fleet charged to take the naval war directly and aggressively to Japanese territory. His predecessor as Pacific fleet commander, James Richardson, in his *Memoirs*, criticized basing the fleet at Pearl Harbor in the first place.

Personalities are the focus of some studies. Among the better biographies of Roosevelt is Freidel's *Franklin D. Roosevelt*, originally in a four-volume edition and later abridged in one volume. Kimball's *The Juggler* is a sympathetic attempt to decipher the enigmatic president. *Franklin Roosevelt, Cordell Hull, and Sumner Welles* is the subject of Gellman's survey. For the chief of naval operations, the highest position in the U.S. Navy in December 1941, see Simpson's *Admiral Harold R. Stark*.

The role of the Showa emperor, Hirohito, is the subject of much debate and controversy. Most extreme is Bergamini's *Japan's Imperial Conspiracy*, which contends Hirohito aimed to rid the Far East of the white man from the beginning and that he personally ordered preparation for a Pearl Harbor raid in 1940. After a recent study of diaries and memoirs of imperial advisers, Bix in "Japan's Delayed Surrender" concluded that the emperor sanctioned the move toward war and the Pearl Harbor attack.

Recent advocates of conspiracy theories include Utley in *Going to War with Japan*; Layton in *"And I Was There"*; Bartlett in *Cover-up*; Costello in *Days of Infamy*. Toland in *The Rising Sun* followed the nonconspiracy view about surprise. However, in *Infamy*, written a decade later, he claimed to have conducted the tenth and definitive investigation of Pearl Harbor. He indicted Roosevelt, high cabinet members, and military officials based on two charges: the Japanese task force was clearly tracked using radio intercepts, and Dutch intelligence, if not others, had warned of a carrier task force attack.

In more comprehensive detail in *Days of Infamy*, with a sensationalized subtitle half a page long, Costello touted "a vital, monumental revision of one of the most important chapters in modern history." His thesis linked the debacle in the Philippines with that at Pearl Harbor, claiming the former was more disastrous and debilitating and that MacArthur was the most culpable of all. Instead of "Remember Pearl Harbor!" the slogan should be "Remember the Philippines!" Not only was there no investigation of that disaster, but also Roosevelt never acknowledged that attack as "the greatest military defeat in U.S. history" (2–4). Churchill withheld vital information from Roosevelt, who entered the Pacific War to protect the British empire, an unconstitutional act by the president. The bill of particulars continued. Costello relies heavily on the account of an American naval intelligence officer during the war, Edwin Layton, *"And I Was There."* Costello admitted there has yet to be produced a "smoking gun" proving the conspiracy theory, but when the British records are released under a seventy-five-year rule, he believed that will be forthcoming. At the moment, even Toland's accusations are "an empty holster" (352).

Gordon Prange's several monumental books, published posthumously from even more extensive notes, respond to the revisionists and conspiracy theorists, often point by point. These include *At Dawn We Slept*, *Pearl Harbor: The Verdict of History*, *December 7, 1941*, and *God's Samurai*, the story of Nitsuo Fuchida, commander of the air attack. All were published in collaboration with, or by, two of Prange's students, Goldstein and Dillon. They have continued to publish from Prange's notes *The Pearl Harbor Papers*, original Japanese planning documents, the *Diary of Admiral Matome Ugaki*, and *The Way It Was*. Prange spent four decades in research and conducted over 200 oral interviews. Prange led what might be called the "war-is-inevitable" school and attributed Japanese success to brilliant preparation, daring, and competence.

In 1969 Dorothy Borg hosted a conference of distinguished scholars who thoroughly assessed the question of Pearl Harbor, published as *Pearl Harbor as History* with Okamoto as coeditor. In *Threshold of War* Heinrichs placed American foreign policy in 1940–1941 in a global perspective. Dallek's prizewinning general review of *Franklin D. Roosevelt and American Foreign Policy* is available in several editions. For more recent appraisals that have uncovered no provable conspiracy, see Conroy and Wray, *Pearl Harbor Reexamined.*

Among Japanese historians and observers tactical factors associated with the raid have become controversial, particularly the decision by the naval task force commander, Admiral Nagumo, not to deploy a third attack later in the day. Nagumo's assistants, Captains Genda and Fuchida, urged a third wave to search out and destroy the American carriers and to destroy the huge oil reserve tank farm. Albright's *Pearl Harbor* elaborates on this issue. "A fatal flaw" is how Barker assessed this inaction in *Pearl Harbor.*

Admiral Isoroku Yamamoto was the initiator, planner, and executioner of the attack. There are studies from the Japanese perspective, Agawa's *The Reluctant Admiral,* and a hagiographic biography by Hoyt, *Yamamoto.* One problem for the Japanese planners concerned launching airborne torpedoes in shallow water. The British Mediterranean fleet demonstrated in its carrier air attack on the Italian naval base of Taranto in November 1940 that torpedoes could be used effectively in shallow water.

Pertinent parts of the fifteen-volume diary of Admiral Matome Ugaki, chief of staff to Yamamoto, are particularly enlightening on Japan's decision for war and for the Pearl Harbor attack. The diary was another discovery of Gordon Prange. Goldstein and Dillon edited a condensed English version. Ike documents a series of decision-making government conferences in *Japan's Decision for War.*

In the last two decades an increasingly vocal group demands rehabilitation and restitution. "Scapegoats" is the most frequently used term by critics, especially when describing Kimmel and Short; see Bartlett's *Cover-up.* Without formal courts-martial, they were found to have been derelict in their duties and were forced to retire at a reduced rank. The objective of the current petitioners is to officially reinstate them at their highest attained ranks. They are led by Edward Beach, a naval officer and submariner. Beach's *Scapegoats* touts eminent scholarship with the objective "to right a wrong of 50 years." Earlier apologists included Kimmel himself in his *Story* and Brownlow, *The Accused,* who stressed insufficiency of resources, for example, the lack of reconnaissance aircraft and experienced personnel, and exclusion from key information (the Hawaii commands were not "in the loop" of MAGIC and other intelligence decrypts). Gannon in "Reopen the Kimmel Case" cited numerical factors: to adequately cover all directions for reconnaissance, a total of 250 long-range aircraft would be necessary; the Hawaii command had 49 such aircraft in December 1941.

Critics cite other instances of questionable action. Roosevelt sent out decoys to entice the Japanese to attack and create an incident that would precipitate war, an accusation of Bartlett in *Cover-up* and Tolley in *Cruise of the Lanikai*. The so-called Winds Execute Message is another bone of contention. Much was made of it in the joint committee investigation. A communications officer insisted he had intercepted a message, "East Wind, Rain, West Wind, Clear," which indicated the Japanese would attack south and remain at peace to the north, the Soviet Union. No copy of the "Winds Execute" message could be found. Costello declared the entire issue a "red herring." Prange agreed.

Matters concerning intelligence and communications, now called MAGIC and ULTRA, were kept secret at first. Release for access to researchers was delayed. The most recent analysis of American communications intelligence matters by Andrew has concluded that if Signals intelligence (SIGINT) had been given higher priority in the years before the attack, the Japanese plans for Pearl Harbor would have been detected and that, unlike Winston Churchill, who favored SIGINT information, Roosevelt was partial to what is now deemed to be inferior, Human Intelligence (HUMINT). Also, in the 1990s, Parker in *Pearl Harbor Revisited*, officially, and Kahn, in "The Intelligence Failure of Pearl Harbor," unofficially, reviewed technical details of American intelligence developments prior to the attack to discount prior knowledge of the attack. MAGIC intercepts related to Pearl Harbor were published in eight volumes by the U.S. Department of Defense.

Bratzel and Rout twice reviewed the espionage case of Dusko Popov, a German agent with links to British intelligence and J. Edgar Hoover, the Federal Bureau of Investigation (FBI) director. See "Pearl Harbor, Microdots, and J. Edgar Hoover" and "Once More."

The British story is told in Best's monograph *Britain, Japan and Pearl Harbor.* How much did the British prime minister Winston Churchill know, and when did he know it? Rusbridger and Nave, *Betrayal at Pearl Harbor,* answer that question. They claim Churchill was well informed from British Signals Intelligence about details and timetables but that he purposely refrained from informing Roosevelt so as to ensure American entry into the war. Few have taken them seriously. Chapman, an Australian intelligence agent, contended there is no evidence in Anglo-Australian secret files to implicate Churchill. The secret British documents are not yet released.

There are a number of standard reviews of the controversy: Bachrach's *Pearl Harbor: Opposing Viewpoints,* Slackman's *Pearl Harbor in Perspective,* Thompson's *A Time for War,* and Weintraub's *Long Day's Journey into War.* Also see Coox's "Repulsing the Pearl Harbor Revisionists." Smith has compiled a new bibliography, *Pearl Harbor, 1941: A Bibliography.*

Among commemorative publications are a collection of 430 photographs assembled by Goldstein and Dillon, *The Way It Was;* a profusely illustrated history by Kimmett and Regis, *The Attack on Pearl Harbor*; forty eyewitness accounts edited by LaForte and Marcello, *Remembering Pearl Harbor*; and thirty-eight paintings especially commissioned and published in Freeman and Delgado's *Pearl Harbor Recalled*. The role of the Marine Corps is commemorated by Cressman and Wenger in *Infamous Day*. The Pearl Harbor Survivors Association sponsored a fortieth-anniversary pictorial review, Cohen's *East Wind Rain*.

Personal accounts and recollections of attack experiences can be found in Satterfield's *The Day the War Began*, Young's *Trapped at Pearl Harbor*, and Stillwell's *Air Raid, Pearl Harbor!* Stillwell also published a history of *Battleship Arizona: An Illustrated History*. The process of salvaging sunken ships at Pearl Harbor is recounted by Wallin in *Pearl Harbor*.

AREAS FOR FUTURE RESEARCH

It is time for another solid, comprehensive, and definitive study of Pearl Harbor. The work by Toland is too extreme. The efforts of Prange and of Goldstein and Dillon are unimaginative and obsolete. The agenda of Costello has diverted the focus from where it should be. More literature for younger readers is needed.

BIBLIOGRAPHY

Agawa, Hiroyuki. *The Reluctant Admiral: Yamamoto and the Imperial Japanese Navy*. Tokyo: Kodansha, 1965, 1979, 1992; New York: Hill and Wang, 1994.

Albright, Harry. *Pearl Harbor: Japan's Fatal Blunder: The True Story behind Japan's Attack on December 7, 1941*. New York: Hippocrene, 1988.

Andrew, Christopher. *For the President's Eyes Only: Secret Intelligence and the American Presidency from Washington to Bush*. New York: HarperCollins, 1995.

Bachrach, Deborah. *Pearl Harbor: Opposing Viewpoints*. San Diego: Greenhaven, 1989.

Barker, A. J. *Pearl Harbor. Ballantine's Illustrated History of World War II*. New York: Ballantine, 1969.

Barnes, Harry E., ed. *Perpetual War for Perpetual Peace: A Critical Examination of the Foreign Policy of Franklin Delano Roosevelt and Its Aftermath*. Caldwell, ID: Caxton, 1953; Westport, CT: Greenwood, 1969.

Bartlett, Bruce R. *Cover-up: The Politics of Pearl Harbor, 1941–1946*. New York: Arlington, 1978.

Beach, Edward L. *Scapegoats: A Defense of Kimmel and Short at Pearl Harbor*. Annapolis, MD: NIP, 1995.

Beard, Charles A. *President Roosevelt and the Coming of the War, 1941: A Study in Appearances and Realities*. Hamden, CT: Archon, 1948, 1968.

Bergamini, David. *Japan's Imperial Conspiracy*. New York: Morrow, 1971, 1972.

Best, Antony. *Britain, Japan and Pearl Harbor: Avoiding War in East Asia, 1936–1941*. London: Routledge, 1995.

Bienstock, Gregory. *The Struggle for the Pacific*. Port Washington, NY: Kennikat, 1970; London: Allen and Unwin, 1937.

Bix, Herbert P. "Japan's Delayed Surrender." *Diplomatic History* 19 (1991): 197–226.

Borg, Dorothy, and Shumpei Okamoto, eds. *Pearl Harbor as History: Japanese–American Relations, 1931–1941.* New York: Columbia UP, 1973.

Bratzel, John F., and Leslie B. Rout. "Once More: Pearl Harbor, Microdots, and J. Edgar Hoover." *American Historical Review* 88 (1983): 953–960.

———. "Pearl Harbor, Microdots, and J. Edgar Hoover." *American Historical Review* 87 (1982): 1342–1351.

Brownlow, Donald G. *The Accused: The Ordeal of Rear Admiral Husband Edward Kimmel, USN.* New York: Vantage, 1968.

Bywater, Hector C. *The Great Pacific War.* New York: St. Martin's, 1925, 1942, 1991.

———. *Sea Power in the Pacific: A Study of the American–Japanese Naval Problem.* Boston: Houghton, 1921.

Chapman, John W. M. "Pearl Harbor: The Anglo-Australian Dimension." *Intelligence and National Security* 4 (1989): 451–460.

Clausen, Henry C., and Bruce Lee. *Pearl Harbor: Final Judgment.* New York: Crown, 1992.

Cohen, Stan. *East Wind Rain: A Pictorial History of the Pearl Harbor Attack.* Missoula: Pictorial, 1981.

Cole, Wayne S. *America First: The Battle against Intervention, 1940–1941.* Madison: University of Wisconsin, 1953.

Conroy, Hilary, and Harry Wray, eds. *Pearl Harbor Reexamined: Prologue to the Pacific War.* Honolulu: Hawaii, 1990.

Coox, Alvin D. "Repulsing the Pearl Harbor Revisionists: The State of Present Literature on the Debacle." *Military Affairs* 50 (January 1986): 29–31.

Costello, John. *Days of Infamy: MacArthur, Roosevelt, Churchill.* New York: Pocket, 1994.

———. *The Pacific War.* New York: Rawson, 1981, 1982.

Cressman, Robert J., and J. Michael Wenger. *Infamous Day: Marines at Pearl Harbor, 7 December 1941.* Washington, DC: GPO, 1992.

Dallek, Robert. *Franklin D. Roosevelt and American Foreign Policy, 1932–1945.* New York: Oxford UP, 1979, 1981, 1995.

Denlinger, Sutherland, and Charles B. Gary. *War in the Pacific: A Study of Navies, Peoples and Battle Problems.* New York: Arno, 1936, 1970.

Feis, Herbert. *The Road to Pearl Harbor: The Coming of the War between the U.S. and Japan.* Princeton: Princeton UP, 1950, 1962, 1963.

Flynn, John T. *As We Go Marching.* New York: Doubleday, 1944, 1973.

Freeman, Tom, and James Delgado. *Pearl Harbor Recalled: New Images of the Day of Infamy.* Annapolis, MD: NIP, 1991.

Freidel, Frank B. *Franklin D. Roosevelt.* 4 vols. Boston: Little, Brown, 1952–1973.

———. *Franklin D. Roosevelt: A Rendezvous with Destiny.* Boston: Little, Brown, 1990.

Gannon, Michael. "Reopen the Kimmel Case." *Naval Institute Proceedings* 121 (December 1994): 51–56.

Gellman, Irwin F. *Secret Affairs: Franklin Roosevelt, Cordell Hull, and Sumner Welles.* Baltimore: Johns Hopkins UP, 1995.

Goldstein, Donald M., and Katherine V. Dillon, eds. *Fading Victory: The Diary of Admiral Matome Ugaki, 1941–1945.* Pittsburgh: Pittsburgh UP, 1991.

———. *The Pearl Harbor Papers: Inside the Japanese Plans.* Washington, DC: Brassey, 1993.

———. *The Way It Was: Pearl Harbor: The Original Photographs.* Washington, DC: Brassey, 1991.

Grautoff, Ferdinand H. *Banzai!* New York: Arno, 1908, 1975.

Heinrichs, Waldo H., Jr. *Threshold of War: Franklin D. Roosevelt and American Entry into World War II.* New York: Oxford UP, 1988.

Honan, William H. *Visions of Infamy: Hector C. Bywater.* New York: St. Martin's, 1991.

Hoyt, Edwin P. *Yamamoto: The Man Who Planned Pearl Harbor.* New York: McGraw-Hill, 1990.

Ike, Nobutaka, ed. *Japan's Decision for War: Records of the 1941 Policy Conferences.* Stanford, CA: Stanford UP, 1967.

Kahn, David. "The Intelligence Failure of Pearl Harbor." *Foreign Affairs* 70 (Winter 1991–1992): 138–152.

Kimball, Warren F. *The Juggler: Franklin Roosevelt as Wartime Statesman.* Princeton: Princeton UP, 1991, 1994.

Kimmel, Husband E. *Admiral Kimmel's Story.* Chicago: Regnery, 1955.

Kimmett, Larry, and Margaret Regis. *The Attack on Pearl Harbor: An Illustrated History.* Seattle: Navigator, 1992.

LaForte, Robert S., and Ronald E. Marcello, eds. *Remembering Pearl Harbor: Eyewitness Accounts by U.S. Military Men and Women.* New York: Scholarly Resources, 1991.

Layton, Edwin T. *"And I Was There": Pearl Harbor and Midway—Breaking the Secrets.* New York: Morrow, 1985.

Lea, Homer. *The Valor of Ignorance.* New York: Harper, 1909, 1942.

Melosi, Martin V. *The Shadow of Pearl Harbor: Political Controversy over the Surprise Attack, 1941–1946.* College Station: Texas A&M UP, 1977.

Miller, Edward S. *War Plan Orange: The U.S. Strategy to Defeat Japan, 1897–1945.* Annapolis, MD: NIP, 1991.

Millis, Walter. *This Is Pearl!: The U.S. and Japan, 1941.* New York: Morrow, 1947.

Mitchell, William. *Report of Inspection Tour, Pacific Ocean Area.* Unpublished report, files of the National Archives, 1924.

Morgenstern, George. *Pearl Harbor: The Story of the Secret War.* New York: Devin-Adair, 1947.

Morison, Samuel Eliot. *Rising Sun in the Pacific.* 15 vols. Vol. 3: *History of United States Naval Operations in World War II.* Boston: Little, Brown, 1947–1962.

Parker, Frederick D. *Pearl Harbor Revisited: U.S. Navy Communications Intelligence, 1924–1941.* Washington, DC: GPO, 1994.

Prange, Gordon W., Donald M. Goldstein, and Katherine V. Dillon. *At Dawn We Slept: The Untold Story of Pearl Harbor.* New York: Mcgraw-Hill, 1981, 1988, 1991.

———. *December 7, 1941: The Day the Japanese Attacked Pearl Harbor.* New York: McGraw-Hill, 1987, 1988.

———. *God's Samurai: Lead Pilot at Pearl Harbor.* Washington, DC: Brassey, 1990.

———. *Pearl Harbor: The Verdict of History.* New York: McGraw-Hill, 1986; Penguin, 1991.

Rauch, Basil. *Roosevelt from Munich to Pearl Harbor: A Study in the Creation of a Foreign Policy.* New York: Creative, 1950.

Richardson, James O. *On the Treadmill to Pearl Harbor: Memoirs.* Washington, DC: GPO, 1973.

Rusbridger, James, and Eric Nave. *Betrayal at Pearl Harbor.* New York: Simon and Schuster, 1991.

Sanborn, Frederic R. *Design for War: A Study of Secret Power Politics, 1937–1941.* New York: Devin-Adair, 1951.

Satterfield, Archie. *The Day the War Began.* Westport, CT: Praeger, 1992.

Schneider, James C. *Should America Go to War?: The Debate over Foreign Policy in Chicago, 1939–1941.* Chapel Hill: North Carolina UP, 1989.

Simpson, B. Mitchell, III. *Admiral Harold R. Stark: Architect of Victory, 1939–1945.* Columbia: University of South Carolina, 1989.

Slackman, Michael, ed. *Pearl Harbor in Perspective.* Honolulu: Arizona Memorial, 1986.

———. *Target: Pearl Harbor.* Honolulu: University of Hawaii, 1990.

Smith, Myron J., Jr. *Pearl Harbor, 1941: A Bibliography.* New York: Greenwood, 1991.

Smith, Stanley H., comp. *Investigations of the Attack on Pearl Harbor: Index to Government Hearings.* New York: Greenwood, 1990.

Stenehjem, Michele Flynn. "John Thomas Flynn and the New York Chapter of the America First Committee: Noninterventionism in the Northeast, 1940–1941." Ph.D. diss., State University of New York, Albany, 1975.

Stillwell, Paul, ed. *Air Raid, Pearl Harbor!: Recollections of a Day of Infamy.* Annapolis, MD: NIP, 1981.

———. *Battleship Arizona: An Illustrated History.* Annapolis, MD: NIP, 1991.

Tansill, Charles C. *Back Door to War: The Roosevelt Foreign Policy, 1933–1941.* Westport, CT: Greenwood, 1952, 1975.

Theobald, Robert A. *The Final Secret of Pearl Harbor: The Washington Contribution to the Japanese Attack.* New York: Devin-Adair, 1954.

Thompson, Robert S. *A Time for War: Franklin Delano Roosevelt and the Path to Pearl Harbor.* New York: Prentice-Hall, 1991.

Toland, John. *Infamy: Pearl Harbor and Its Aftermath.* New York: Doubleday, 1982.

———. *The Rising Sun: The Decline and Fall of the Japanese Empire, 1936–1945.* 2 vols. New York: Random House, 1970.

Tolley, Kemp. *Cruise of the Lanikai: Incitement to War.* Annapolis, MD: NIP, 1973.

U.S. Congress. *Joint Committee on the Investigation of the Pearl Harbor Attack, 79th Congress, Second Session.* 39 vols. Washington, DC: GPO, 1946; 20 vols. New York: AMS, 1972.

———. *Report of the Pearl Harbor Attack, 79th Congress, Second Session.* Washington, DC: GPO, 1946.

U.S. Department of Defense. *The MAGIC Background of Pearl Harbor.* 8 vols. Washington, DC: GPO, 1978.

Utley, Jonathan G. *Going to War with Japan, 1937–1941.* Knoxville: University of Tennessee, 1985.

Wallin, Homer N. *Pearl Harbor: Why, How, Fleet Salvage and Final Appraisal.* Washington, DC: GPO, 1968.

Weintraub, Stanley. *Long Day's Journey into War: December 7, 1941.* New York: Penguin, 1991, 1992.

Wohlstetter, Roberta. *Pearl Harbor: Warning and Decision.* Stanford, CA: Stanford UP, 1962.

Young, Stephen Bower. *Trapped at Pearl Harbor: Escape from Battleship Oklahoma.* Annapolis, MD: NIP, 1991.

4 Japanese Strategy and Campaigns in the Pacific War, 1941–1945

Mark R. Peattie

While the Pacific War in its entirety constitutes a vast historical literature in English, works devoted to the specific Japanese strategies and campaigns in the war have a far narrower historiography, and the treatment of those activities from a Japanese perspective using Japanese sources constitutes an even narrower range of study. The most obvious reason for this situation is that so little of the literature on the war in Japanese has been translated into English, given the paucity of Western scholars and researchers with the necessary language competence. Yet it is not often realized in the West that, even in Japan, the span of archival and primary sources concerning the activities of the former Imperial Japanese Army and Navy is quite modest compared to the bountiful archival collections on Allied strategies and combat operations that exist in the West. Even scholarly studies on these subjects are few.

The causes of this situation are manifold: the wholesale and purposeful destruction of a sizable portion of army and navy historical documents at the end of the war; the peculiarities of prewar Japanese military culture, which did not encourage detailed exploration of the processes of decision-making; the aversion of that same culture to the recording of strategic or operational debate; the general rejection of military concerns in Japan after its humiliating defeat; the indifference, if not outright hostility, of postwar civilian scholarship in Japan toward operational history; and the reluctance of most of those who served in responsible positions to speak their minds. This general problem, as it has affected the state of Japanese naval and maritime history in the postwar period, has been dealt with in greater detail in "Japan" by Peattie and Evans.

PRIMARY SOURCES

One major Japanese-language source should be mentioned in this summary of English-language materials since it relies so greatly on the largest collection of primary documentation in Japan and because it will increasingly become the essential source for any study of Japanese strategy in the Pacific War that claims to be authoritative. This is the 104-volume collection known as the "War History Series" (*Senshi sosho*) (Japan, 1966–1980), covering the period 1937–1945 and compiled by the research staff of the Japanese Defense Academy's Defense Research Center, 1966–1980. While it has a number of deficiencies (described by Peattie and Evans in "Japan"), the series comprises the most detailed, most complete, and most authoritative record of the plans, organization, armaments, strategy, and tactics of the Japanese armed forces in the Pacific War.

A lesser, but often useful, English-language source of primary documentation is the series of studies known as the *Japanese Monographs* (U.S. Department of the Army, 1945–1960). Compiled at the direction of the U.S. Army in the decade after the war, 185 monographs on the operations of Japanese armed forces in the China and Pacific Wars were drafted by former officers of both services and translated into English. Many of the studies were later used in preparation of the U.S. Army's own official histories of World War II. Available in microfilm through the Library of Congress, the monographs are of uneven quality, as explained in the *Guide to the Japanese Monographs*, also available through the Library of Congress.

In 1980 a selection of the best of these studies was published by Detwiler and Burdick in a fifteen-volume set entitled *War in Asia and the Pacific.* Also useful are the records of the postwar interrogations of various Japanese army and navy officers that were published as part of the U.S. Strategic Bombing Survey, though researchers using the volumes must understand the environment in which these depositions were undertaken. In the years immediately following the war many of those questioned either were sullen in defeat or had reason to believe that they might be brought before the International Military Tribunal for the Far East, conditions hardly conducive to a frank and complete accounting of the plans and campaigns in which they participated.

GENERAL STUDIES

There are four major and interrelated historical issues in regard to Japanese strategy in the Pacific War: Japan's decision to go to war; how Japan hoped to win in the face of overwhelming Allied industrial might and latent military strength; whether or not there was any prospect for Japan to win the war or at least to have postponed defeat; and the reasons for the actual defeat.

While there is no book-length, scholarly, English-language survey of Japanese strategy and campaigns for the entire course of the war or one that explores all these issues, a number of excellent shorter studies provide great insight in that regard. At the top of the list of such studies one should put the individual essays of Ikeda ("Japanese Strategy") and Rosinski ("The Strategy of Japan"). Ikeda, a former naval officer, offers a finely honed summary of Japan's major strategic decisions of the war and illuminates the thinking behind each. While sparing in his commentary, Ikeda concludes that the basic error in Japanese strategic planning was a narrowness of vision that had little conception of "total war" and that mistakenly assumed that a war with the Anglo-American naval powers could be limited in ways that were to Japan's advantage. Rosinski, in an essay that retains its acuity after fifty years, sounds much the same theme and argues that Japan's defeat in the Pacific War lay, in large part, in its erroneous assumption that the carefully limited wars against China in 1894–1895 and Russia in 1904–1905 could collectively serve as a model for a struggle against the two greatest naval powers on earth. In his summary of "Japanese Strategic Decisions" that he sees as particularly damaging to the Japanese cause, Kennedy sees Japan's two greatest blunders as the army's obsessive concern with the continent of Asia, which blinded it to the weakness of Japan's Pacific flank, and the series of failures at Coral Sea, Midway, and Guadalcanal, which gave the United States breathing space to mobilize its enormous industrial might behind a series of unstoppable counteroffensives. Other generalized overviews of Japanese strategy in the Pacific have been provided by James in "American and Japanese Strategies" and Barlow in "World War II," each of whom compares and contrasts it with American strategy in the war.

Viewing Japanese strategy in the Pacific through a historical perspective, Reynolds in "The Continental Strategy of Imperial Japan" argued that, despite Japan's being an island nation, its history and traditions were fundamentally continental, rather than maritime, a fact that complicated Japan's conduct of the Pacific War. In "Interception" Hirama of the Japanese Self-Defense Academy narrowed that historical perspective somewhat in his exploration of the origins of the navy's Pacific strategy in the period between the world wars, a strategy that counted on Japanese interception and attrition of a westward-moving American naval force in the Pacific.

Boyd's analysis of "Japanese Military Effectiveness" during the interwar period offers a useful complement to the Reynolds and Hirama pieces and notes the limitations in the operational doctrines of Japan's armed services once Japan's strategic context began to change in the 1930s. Boyd's thesis is logically followed by Coox's analysis of the "Effectiveness of the Japanese Military Establishment," in which Coox notes the appalling disparity between Japanese ends and means. While giving Japanese morale and fighting spirit the highest marks, Coox concludes that the Japanese armed forces were anachronistic in outlook. A similar judgment, focused on the navy, has been sounded in Parillo's *The Japanese Merchant Marine*, though in sifting through the causes of the navy's defeat, he exaggerates the importance of the navy's feudal outlook.

Not surprisingly, since the war in the Pacific was, in large part, a naval war, most of the major studies of the Japanese side of the war have to do with naval campaigns. First among them is *The Japanese Navy in World War II*, edited by Evans, which is itself the second and expanded edition of an earlier work of the same title edited by O'Connor. The Evans volume comprises an invaluable collection of essays on specific Japanese naval operations by former officers of the Imperial Japanese Navy, many of whom were involved in the planning and conduct of the operations described. Equally important is Dull's operational history of the Japanese navy for the entire course of the Pacific War, *A Battle History of the Imperial Japanese Navy*. Dull based his thorough, balanced survey, in great part, on the "War History" series mentioned earlier. Ito's *The End of the Imperial Japanese Navy*, long out of print and less reliable as a factual history because of its absence of documentation, is nevertheless valuable because of its critical insights on the navy's conduct of the war by one of postwar Japan's most respected military commentators. The English translation of Hayashi's survey of the army's operations in the war, *Kogun*, which appeared about the same time, needs a scholarly and more analytical successor. Nevertheless, it still serves as an objective, though less overtly critical, outline of army operations by a knowledgeable former army staff officer.

It is important also to mention two multivolume histories that concentrate on U.S. armed forces but that have relevance to a study of Japanese strategy and campaigns in the Pacific. The first is the official history series *The U.S. Army in World War II*. Eleven volumes of this series deal with the U.S. Army's plans and operations in the Pacific, and two of these, Miller's study of the *Guadalcanal* campaign and Morton's work on *The Fall of the Philippines* to Japan in 1942, contain sufficient detail on Japanese plans and operations to warrant their citation. The second multivolume work is Morison's superb *History of United States Naval Operations in World War II*. All volumes dealing with the Pacific in each of these histories include at least some information and analysis of Japanese strategy and operations based on extant Japanese documentation and interviews with, and testimony of, former members of the Japanese army and navy.

SPECIALIZED STUDIES

For obvious reasons, Japan's decision to go to war has been the particular concern of World War II historians. Two outstanding sets of scholarship are relevant here. The first comprises the two volumes of the late Arthur Marder's magisterial study of the naval relations between Japan and Great Britain, *Old Friends, New Enemies.* Based on a significant number of Japanese-written sources and extensive interviews with Japanese naval officers for their treatment of the Japanese side, these two volumes trace the shift in the relationship from peacetime amity, to enmity, to wartime hostility. The first volume views the Japanese turn to war largely as a product of extremism within the navy, combined with opportunism by both services in planning the conquest of Southeast Asia at a time of extreme Western vulnerability there. Perhaps Marder's greatest contribution, however, is his discussion of the interrelationship of matériel, tactics, and strategy in the navy as it evolved in the interwar period, one of the most informative treatments of the subject to appear in print so far.

Though it depends largely on English-language secondary works, an even more insightful analysis is provided in the two volumes of a projected trilogy on the Pacific War by Willmott, *Empires in the Balance* and *The Barrier and the Javelin.* While the volumes concentrate on the early months of the war itself, the first volume provides an extensive strategic background. Willmott discusses, inter alia, the ambiguities of the Japanese strategic outlook on the eve of war as its leaders confronted both glittering opportunity and appalling risk in their plans to seize Southeast Asia and its treasure-house of resources. His perspective places less emphasis on American economic pressures in the Japanese decision to go to war than do many American historians, but in his revision of the conventional view of the causes of the war he did not go as far as Barnhart's detailed *Japan Prepares for Total War* on Japanese decision making in the immediate prewar years. Making full use of Japanese sources, Barnhart broke new ground by arguing that Japan's internal political dynamics, especially the bitter rivalry between its army and navy, played a far greater role in propelling the nation into war with the United States than did its economic condition or even pressure from Washington.

Earlier studies of Japan's decision to go to war had also assumed that as late as midautumn 1941 the Japanese navy was hesitant about entering into hostilities. But this view has been challenged in the recently published last volume of the English-language version of the *Taiheiyō sensō e no michi* [*Japan's Road to the Pacific War*], a remarkable collection of essays by Japanese scholars undertaken over thirty years ago for the Japan Association on International relations and the most richly documented account of the Japanese origins of the Pacific War. Edited by Morley but written largely by Jun Tsunoda, aide to Premier Konoe before the war, this last volume, *The Final Confrontation,* makes it clear that the navy, particularly its bellicose middle echelon, was the most critical element in the decision to open hostilities with the West. In part, this belligerent stance by the navy appears to have been based on incredible optimism and complacency about the prospects for success in any war with the United States.

These outlooks, in turn, stemmed from supremely unrealistic intelligence assessments made by the Japanese armed forces on the eve of the war. In his essay on prewar "Japanese Intelligence" Barnhart illuminates the thinking behind Japan's reluctance to appraise rationally America's vast economic predominance and how assessments of projected operations usually rested on "best case" analyses. That the thinking of Japan's military leadership paralleled such assessments is amply demonstrated by the collected records of the 1941 policy conferences—some held in the emperor's presence—which have been translated and annotated by Ike in *Japan's Decision for War*. These documents provide a unique, ringside view of Japan's decision makers as they argued and deliberated the policies and strategies that were to take Japan into war and, once in it, that were to frame its initial operations. As Ike points out in his introduction, the records show both the optimism and fatalism of the Japanese military leadership in undertaking the great strategic risks involved in planning for hostilities against the Allies. The assumption by this leadership, particularly in the navy, was that Japan could launch a lightning conquest of the great resource area of Southeast Asia, and, once having gained it, Japan could then construct an impregnable barrier against all Allied efforts to retake it, a situation that would enhance the prospects for a negotiated peace in which Japan could bargain for its conquests. In the year before the war, only one responsible official, Admiral Shigeyoshi Inoue, administrative head of Japanese naval aviation, challenged the assumptions underlying that strategy by providing a sweeping, prescient, and unheeded analysis of what a naval war with the United States would be like and offering a series of radical departures from conventional Japanese strategies that might at least narrow the odds in a Japan–United States conflict.

Obviously, the Pearl Harbor operation forms the most dramatic element in Japanese strategic conduct of the war. In comparison to the mountain of English-language works that focus on the stunning shock registered by the attack and on the search for the locus of responsibility of American unpreparedness to meet it, far smaller is the quantity of materials based on Japanese sources that concentrate on the Japanese planning and execution of the operation. Prange's detailed and ever-popular *At Dawn We Slept* remains the standard work on the attack—its planning, its execution, and its consequences. It is included here because of Prange's detailed attention to the Japanese, as well as the American, side and because of his extensive use of interviews with former Japanese naval officers with personal knowledge of the operation. Goldstein and Dillon have recently collected and published many of the Japanese documents used in Prange's earlier works—the secret plans and battle group histories, as well as letters and diaries of those Japanese officers involved. It is worth mentioning that these records prove that the Japanese task force approaching Hawaii did *not* break radio silence and thus did not serve to alert the American high command to its movements, as some American revisionists have asserted. In "The Hawaii Operation," Fukudome, who at the time was chief of the Operations Division of the Navy General Staff, sets forth the premises behind the attack and defends its execution in the light of various criticisms that have been made of it by Morison and others.

In his biography of Admiral Isoroku Yamamoto, architect of the plan, Agawa provides a good deal of interesting color and anecdotal background to Yamamoto's formulation of the plan, though he offers fewer analytic insights. The influence of the navy's intraservice politics and of interservice antagonisms is the focus of Barnhart's still useful insight on the opposition to Yamamoto's scheme for the Pearl Harbor attack, "Planning the Pearl Harbor Attack." Koda's "A Commander's Dilemma" explored the difficulties encountered by Yamamoto in shifting the navy's outlook from its traditional "gradual attrition" strategy to a new offensive strategy envisioned in the navy's projected operations against Hawaii and Southeast Asia. In a similar fashion, Hata analyzed Yamamoto's Pearl Harbor plans and their bold defiance of the navy's traditional doctrine of strategic defense in "Yamamoto's Surprise Attack." In doing so, Hata rates as "phenomenal" the success of the attack in gaining its original objectives: the destruction of the U.S. battle fleet and the consequent prevention of American naval interference in the Japanese drive on Southeast Asia. American commentators have not been so generous to Yamamoto's concept. Prange, in his *Verdict of History*, tends to agree with Morison that the operation was a "strategic imbecility," given the trade-off between the destruction of a few overage warships and the outraged and unified response of the American public.

The initial Japanese offensives of 1941–1942 have had reasonably good coverage in English-language literature, though much of it has been largely based on other English-language secondary sources. Morison's third volume was an important early exception to that generalization, though it has been superseded by newer works. Among these, none are better for the early Japanese naval triumphs than the second volume of Marder's superb study of the Royal Navy and the Imperial Japanese Navy, *The Pacific War, 1942–1945*. Based, like the first volume, on significant documentation and extensive interviews with former Japanese naval officers, the study provides more detailed information on the navy's campaigns in the East Indies and the Indian Ocean in early 1942 than is available anywhere else. Lundstrom's earlier *First South Pacific Campaign*, which surveys Japanese as well as American fleet strategies in the South Pacific, December 1941–June 1942, made use of the relevant studies from the *Japanese Monographs* mentioned earlier and took particular note of Japan's vacillation between the search for decisive battle and the acquisition of strategic positions.

Far more comprehensive and sophisticated in their analysis of the early phases of the war are Willmott's volumes mentioned earlier. In the first volume Willmott describes the unfolding of Japan's offensives on the ground, sea, and air in the first months of the war and ends the work with an excellent analysis of Japanese options in April 1942 and an insightful critique of the Japanese muddling of those options in the plans for a campaign covering both the South and Central Pacific that spring. Taking full measure of that ill-considered campaign, which began to fall apart at the Coral Sea and ended in disaster four weeks later at Midway, Willmott's second volume illuminates Japan's strategic weaknesses even at the flood tide of its conquests, centering on the flaws in the Japanese decision-making process that prevented the formulation of a coherent strategy. Morton's *Fall of the Philippines* in the U.S. Army official history contains a good deal of information on Japanese plans and operations in the conquest of the Philippines in 1942. Dull's *Battle History* includes a useful survey of the Japanese naval campaigns during this early period in the war.

Despite its intriguing title and its supposed use of selections from the *Japanese Monograph* series, Thomas' *Japan's War at Sea*, which treats Japan's naval war up to the Coral Sea, is disappointing because of its outdated partisan tone and because it provides no specific documentation for many of its more provocative assertions. The Evans volume contains two excellent and more specialized studies of the Japanese navy's triumphs in the Indian Ocean in this early period of the war: Shimada's chapter on "The Opening Air Offensive against the Philippines" (also in the earlier O'Connor edition) in the first days of the war, whose success he attributes to the superlative performance of the navy's Zero fighters based on Taiwan, and Ohmae's essay on "Japanese Operations in the Indian Ocean" in April 1942, which could have been a catastrophe for the Allies in South Asia had it been coordinated with a victorious German offensive in the Middle East. One of the most fascinating insights into Japanese strategic plans following Pearl Harbor is Stephan's study, *Hawaii under the Rising Sun*, which details the abortive Japanese plans for the occupation of those islands.

Because of its dramatic importance in stemming the tide of the Japanese advance, the Battle of Midway is given prominent treatment and careful analysis by Dull in *Battle History*, by Willmott in *The Barrier and the Javelin*, and by Morison in *The Coral Sea, Midway and Submarine Actions*. Prange's *Miracle at Midway*, like his earlier volume on the Pearl Harbor attack, is a popular account but based on solid evidence from Japanese sources. But the most authoritative treatment from the Japanese side is still *Midway: The Battle That Doomed Japan* by Fuchida and Okumiya, both naval aviators who participated in the battle. Of particular interest is the final chapter, in which the authors enumerate the reasons for the Japanese defeat as being an outdated confidence in the battleship, a mistaken personnel policy for Japanese naval aviation, and arrogant overconfidence by the Japanese naval high command. A condensed account, "The Battle of Midway" by the same authors, is available in the Evans volume.

But if Midway was the battle that halted the Japanese offensive in the Central Pacific, it may be argued that the Solomon Islands campaign, centered on the struggle for Guadalcanal in the second half of 1942, began the irreversible decline of Japanese fighting power: the exhaustion of the Japanese army and the grinding down of the Japanese navy. The process was first described by Morison in *The Struggle for Guadalcanal* and Miller in *Guadalcanal* and, more recently, in admirable detail by Richard Frank in his *Guadalcanal*. In between, there have appeared two first-rate Japanese perspectives, both of which are included in the Evans volume: "The Struggle for Guadalcanal," an overview of the campaign by former admiral Raizo Tanaka (also in the O'Connor edition), one of the most tenacious and resourceful of the Japanese commanders and one who gave as good as he got for most of the campaign, and Toshikazu Ohmae's account of "The Battle of Savo Island," the greatest Japanese surface victory of the war.

Relevant to the naval war in this 1942–1943 period is a major work by Evans and Peattie. While the focus of *Kaigun: Strategy, Tactics, and Technology* concerns the evolution of strategy, tactics, and technology in the navy prior to December 1941, the concluding chapter provides a detailed analysis of the causes of the navy's defeat in the Pacific War, with particular attention to the first year and a half of the conflict.

By 1943, as we know, Japan was forced on the defensive. The strategic implications of the decision that year by the Japanese high command to pull back to an "absolute defense barrier" have been analyzed by Dull in *A Battle History* and by Hayashi in *Kogun*, as well as in the Ikeda and Rosinski essays mentioned earlier. There are as yet few English-language histories of the subsequent and futile Japanese defense of its island bases in the Central Pacific in late 1943 and early 1944. This is due, one suspects, to the fact that few Japanese survived the American amphibious offensives, and hence there is little firsthand evidence on which to base postwar accounts of this resistance. Piecing together what evidence is available, Peattie, in " 'Crushed Jewels' and Destitute Garrisons," a chapter in his study of the Japanese in Micronesia, attempted to take a Japanese perspective in telling the story of the immolation of Japan's Micronesian bases. But if 1943 marked the annihilation of the navy's land-based garrisons in the Pacific, it was also a time of relative quiet for the navy's major fleet units. Nomura in his "Ozawa in the Pacific: A Junior Officer's Experience" in the Evans volume (also in the O'Connor edition) provides a glimpse of the comparatively calm period for the Japanese carrier fleet as it went about its business of refitting and training.

The major Japanese defeats on land and at sea in the Philippines in 1944 have had better coverage. Field's account of *The Japanese at Leyte Gulf* was the first major study of that great sea and air battle and, despite its age, retains significant value because of its emphasis on the Japanese side. This cannot be said of most later treatments, though Morison's *Leyte* provides important analysis of the Japanese miscalculations and disasters in the Philippines. Koyanagi's "The Battle of Leyte Gulf" demonstrates how badly Japanese forces in the Philippines were served by the decision of the Japanese high command to commit the remaining Japanese naval strength to the dual mission of the disruption of the American amphibious invasion and the destruction of major components of the American fleet. It also provides a multiple explanation of Admiral Kurita's long-debated decision to break off action and discontinue the pursuit and destruction of the American escort carrier force. More recently, Prados' work, *Combined Fleet Decoded*, on the critical role of American intelligence in the defeat of the Japanese navy, gives ample space to the Japanese reverses at Leyte Gulf.

By late 1944, so badly reduced in surface strength had the Japanese navy become that it was forced to resort to desperate alternatives to attempt to halt the inexorable tide of the American counteroffensives in the Pacific. Chief among these was the formation of the kamikaze groups of naval air units, which traded the certain death of their air crews for the possibility of destroying Allied fleet units. The standard history here is still the account *The Divine Wind* by Inoguchi and Nakajima, former naval officers who were both involved in the formation of these "special attack groups," though it offers little in the way of an analysis as to the effectiveness of the horrendous and heroic efforts involved. A shorter account by the same authors, "The Kamikaze Attack Corps," is available in the Evans volume, which also contains Yokoi's "Kamikazes in the Okinawa Campaign" (both are also in the O'Connor edition), an account that is very critical of the tactic. But air units were not the only forces to employ this ultimately futile suicide effort, as Denis and Peggy Warner have recounted in *The Sacred Warriors*, an overall survey of the Japanese death squadrons of aircraft, submarines, and small surface craft. Even the last remaining major Japanese fleet unit, the superbattleship *Yamato*, was sent to its destruction in this fashion, as recounted in the Evans volume by Mitsura Yoshida in "The Sinking of the *Yamato*."

But the ultimate defeat of Japan was not due to the loss of set-piece battles or failed efforts of sacrifice. Indeed, one can argue that the most important maritime campaign that Japan lost in the war involved the destruction of its merchant fleet, largely at the hands of American submarine forces. Without freighters and transports to bring to the home islands the essential strategic resources from its conquered territories, Japan was doomed to strangulation in any event. The reasons for the destruction of the Japanese merchant marine have been expertly and thoroughly explored in Parillo's *The Japanese Merchant Marine* and in Evans' *Japanese Navy*.

Conversely, the Japanese submarine campaign against the Allies was surprisingly ineffective, given the size of the force at the beginning of the war, as Mochitsura Hashimoto, himself a former submarine commander, first recounted many years ago in his popular *Sunk*, a history of the Japanese submarine fleet. The reason, provided by Boyd in a more recent, scholarly treatment of "The Japanese Submarine Force," largely had to do with the faulty doctrine worked out by the navy in the interwar period. Japanese submarine strategy and operations in the Pacific have also been recently treated by Carpenter and Polmar in *Submarines*, a volume largely devoted to submarine technology. The use of the so-called human torpedoes is the focus of "Submarine Tactics and the *Kaiten*" by Kennosuke Torisu, a former submarine commander. Still serviceable for the purpose of comparing U.S. and Japanese submarine strategies is Holmes' *Undersea Victory*, which devotes some attention to Japanese submarine operations in the Pacific based on Japanese sources.

While a comprehensive and scholarly study of Japanese naval air campaigns in the Pacific has yet to be written, Brown's *Carrier Operations* does deal with Japanese carrier operations up to February 1943. Japanese amphibious operations have had only minor treatment in English, the best available study being a brief overview, "Japanese Landing Operations in World War Two" by Lehman. The failure of Japan and Germany to coordinate their strategies in World War II still awaits an in-depth analysis that uses Japanese documentation, but until such a study is completed, scholars will have to be content with the German side of the story as analyzed by Rahn's "Japan and Germany."

Of English-language biographies of Japanese military and naval officers who shaped the strategy of the Pacific War, only three are worth mentioning. While reliable, all are on the popular, rather than the scholarly, level: the Agawa biography of Admiral Yamamoto mentioned earlier; Coox's brief study of General Hideki *Tojo*; and Barker's similarly short biography of General Tomoyuki *Yamashita*. More valuable as a sourcebook for the day-to-day operations of the navy is the detailed diary of Admiral Matome Ugaki, *Fading Victory*, translated by Masataka Chihaya and expertly edited and annotated by Donald Goldstein and Katherine Dillon.

Of particular relevance to the intelligence side of Japan's naval war in the Pacific is Prados' sweeping *Combined Fleet Decoded*, based on a wide array of archival and secondary sources. While the work deals largely with the role of American intelligence in the destruction of the Japanese Combined Fleet, it also incorporates a great deal of information on Japanese naval intelligence before and during the war, based on the considerable primary material that exists in English translation.

Scholarly treatment of the strategic (as opposed to the political) situation behind the Japanese decision to surrender in World War II—as distinct from the vast literature on the Allied efforts to bring it about—is limited to only several works. Still valuable after forty years is Robert Butow's fine study of the tortured process behind the surrender decision. The Pacific War Research Society's exploration of the minds and emotions of the Japanese leadership at the end of the war at least touches upon some of the strategic issues involved. Yokoi's "Thoughts on Japan's Naval Defeat" (in Evans) argues that, at least for the conduct of the naval war, Japan did not really have a grand strategy, relying instead on obsolete concepts from the Russo-Japanese War. Similar criticisms of the Japanese strategic conduct of the war have been leveled by Rosinski and Ikeda in articles cited earlier. The second volume by Marder, *The Pacific War*, sums up the Japanese difficulties as resting on a set of strategic assumptions and attitudes that could be called "the Japanese way in warfare": the tactical obsession with decisive battle to the exclusion of most other considerations, the overemphasis on moral and spiritual qualities, the priority given to short-term strategic interests over long-term political ones, and, above all, the failure to address the necessities of protracted, total war. The most curious (and, to this writer, a mistaken) critique is provided in the Fuchida and Okumiya account of *Midway*, which finds the cause of the Japanese defeat in the entire war as lying deep in the Japanese national character.

AREAS FOR FUTURE RESEARCH

The broad outlines of Japanese strategy and campaigning in the Pacific have long been known. There are, of course, questions and issues that may never be resolved—such as the exact origins of Admiral Yamamoto's scheme for the attack on Pearl Harbor—and information that may never come to light—such as details concerning the preparation and conduct of the Japanese navy's fleet maneuvers and map exercises before the war—because of the difficulties alluded to at the outset of this chapter. Yet the quantity of Japanese-language sources is sufficient to undertake a far greater range of serious studies than currently available in English, and it only awaits exploitation by scholars with the necessary language skills. Among the most obvious subjects for treatment: a detailed history of the key decisions undertaken by Japanese Imperial General Headquarters during the war; a book-length survey of the army's campaigns in the Pacific to match the work on the navy by Dull; a major study of the Pearl Harbor operation entirely from the Japanese perspective; a history of Japanese naval air combat in the war; the interrelationship between strategy, tactics, and technology in the development of all three in each of the two services before the war; a study of Japanese command and leadership during the war; monographs on some of the military and naval officers who were in command during the more important campaigns or who played a major role in the shaping of strategy; a truly analytical study of the Japanese submarine force during the war; and a detailed study of Japanese preparations for the defense of the homeland in the summer of 1945. Most of these topics could be researched largely from the "War History" series mentioned early on in this chapter. Indeed, one might argue that the most important place to start would be to translate the more important volumes of the series, beginning with the volume on the Hawaiian operation.

BIBLIOGRAPHY

Agawa, Hiroyuki. *The Reluctant Admiral: Yamamoto and the Imperial Navy.* Tokyo, New York, and San Francisco: Kodansha International, 1979.

Barker, A. J. *Yamashita.* New York: Ballantine, 1973, 1983.

Barlow, Jeffrey G. "World War II: U.S. and Japanese Naval Strategies." In Colin S. Gray and Roger Barnett, eds., *Seapower and Strategy,* 245–272. Annapolis, MD: NIP, 1989.

Barnhart, Michael A. "Japanese Intelligence before the Second World War: 'Best Case' Analysis." In Ernest R. May, ed., *Knowing One's Enemies: Intelligence Assessment before the Two World Wars.* Princeton: Princeton UP, 1986, 1996.

———. *Japan Prepares for Total War: The Search for Economic Security, 1919–1941.* Ithaca, NY: Cornell UP, 1987.

———. "Planning the Pearl Harbor Attack: A Study in Military Politics." *Aerospace Historian* 29:4 (Winter 1982): 246–252.

Brown, David. *Carrier Operations in World War II. Vol. 2: The Pacific Navies, December 1941–February 1943.* Annapolis, MD: NIP, 1974.

Boyd, Carl. "Japanese Military Effectiveness: The Interwar Period." In Allan R. Millett and Williamson Murray, eds., *Military Effectivenesss. Vol. 2: The Interwar Period,* 131–168. Boston: Unwin Hyman, 1988.

Boyd, Carl, and Akihiko Yoshida. *The Japanese Submarine Force and World War II.* Annapolis, MD: NIP, 1995.

Butow, Robert. *Japan's Decision to Surrender.* Stanford, CA: Stanford UP, 1954.

Carpenter, Dorr, and Norman Polmar. *Submarines of the Imperial Japanese Navy.* Annapolis, MD: NIP, 1986.

Coox, Alvin D. "Effectiveness of the Japanese Military Establishment in the Second World War." In Allan R. Millett and Williamson Murray, eds., *Military Effectiveness. Vol. 3: The Second World War,* 1–44. Boston: Unwin Hyman, 1988.

———. *Tojo.* New York: Ballantine, 1975.

Detwiler, Donald S., and Charles Burdick, eds. *War in Asia and the Pacific.* 15 vols. New York and London: Garland, 1980.

Dull, Paul S. *A Battle History of the Imperial Japanese Navy (1941–1945).* Annapolis, MD: NIP, 1978.

Evans, David C., ed. *The Japanese Navy in World War II: In the Words of Former Japanese Naval Officers.* Annapolis, MD: NIP, 1986.

Evans, David C., and Mark R. Peattie. *Kaigun: Strategy, Tactics, and Technology in the Imperial Japanese Navy, 1887–1941.* Annapolis, MD: NIP, 1997.

Field, James A., Jr. *The Japanese at Leyte Gulf: The Sho Operation.* Princeton: Princeton UP, 1947.

Frank, Richard. *Guadalcanal. The Definitive Account of the Landmark Battle.* New York: Random House, 1990.

Fuchida, Mitsuo, and Masatake Okumiya. *Midway: The Battle That Doomed Japan.* Annapolis, MD: NIP, 1955.

Fukudome, Shigeru. "The Hawaii Operation." In David C. Evans, ed., *The Japanese Navy in World War II*, 1–38. Annapolis, MD: NIP, 1986.

Goldstein, Donald M., and Katherine V. Dillon, eds. *The Pearl Harbor Papers: Inside the Japanese Plans.* New York: Brassey's, 1993.

Hashimoto, Mochitsura. *Sunk: The Story of the Japanese Submarine Fleet, 1941–1945.* Translated by E. H. M. Colegrove. New York: Henry Holt, 1954.

Hata, Ikuhiko. "Admiral Yamamoto's Surprise Attack and the Japanese Navy's War Strategy." In Saki Dockrill, ed., *From Pearl Harbor to Hiroshima: The Second World War in Asia and the Pacific, 1941–45*, 55–71. New York: St. Martin's, 1994.

Hayashi, Saburo. *Kogun: The Japanese Army in the Pacific War.* Quantico, VA: U.S. Marine Corps, 1959.

Hirama, Yoichi. "Interception—Attrition Strategy: The Sun against the Eagle." *Journal of the Pacific Society* 11:4 (January 1989): 9–22.

Holmes, W. J. *Undersea Victory: The Influence of Submarine Operations in the War in the Pacific.* Garden City, NY: Doubleday, 1966.

Hosoya, Chihiro, Nagayo Homma, Akira Hatano, and Sumio Iriye, eds. *Taiheiyō sensō.* Tokyo: University of Tokyo, 1993.

Ike, Nobutaka, ed. *Japan's Decision for War. Records of the 1941 Policy Conferences.* Stanford, CA: Stanford UP, 1967.

Ikeda, Kiyoshi. "Japanese Strategy and the Pacific War, 1941–5." In Ian Nish, ed., *Anglo-Japanese Alienation, 1919–1952: Papers of the Anglo-Japanese Conference of the History of the Second World War*, 125–145. Cambridge, U.K.: Cambridge UP, 1982.

Inoguchi, Rikihei, and Tadashi Nakajima. *The Divine Wind: Japan's Kamikaze Force in World War II.* Annapolis, MD: NIP, 1958, 1994.

Ito, Masanori. *The End of the Imperial Japanese Navy.* New York: W. W. Norton, 1962.

James, D. Clayton. "American and Japanese Strategies in the Pacific War." In Peter Paret, ed., *Makers of Modern Strategy from Machiavelli to the Nuclear Age*, 703–732. Princeton: Princeton UP, 1986.

Japan, Self-Defense Agency, Self-Defense Research Center, War History Office. *War History Series [Senshi sosho].* 102 vols. Tokyo: Asagumo Shimbun Sha, 1966–1980.

Kennedy, Paul. "Japanese Strategic Decisions, 1939–45." In Paul Kennedy, ed., *Strategy and Diplomacy, 1870–1945*, 181–195. London: Allen and Unwin, 1983.

Koda, Yoji. "A Commander's Dilemma: Admiral Yamamoto and the 'Gradual Attrition' Strategy." *Naval War College Review* 44 (Autumn 1993): 63–74.

Koyanagi, Tomiji. "The Battle of Leyte Gulf." In Raymond O'Connor, ed., *The Japanese Navy in World War II*, 106–117. Annapolis, MD: NIP, 1982. Also in David C. Evans, ed., *The Japanese Navy in World War II: In the Words of Former Japanese Naval Officers*, 355–384. Annapolis, MD: NIP, 1986.

Lehman, Hans G. Von. "Japanese Landing Operations in World War Two." In Merrill Bartlett, ed., *Assault from the Sea: Essays on the History of Amphibious Warfare*, 195–201. Annapolis, MD: NIP, 1983.

Lundstrom, John B. *The First South Pacific Campaign: Pacific Fleet Strategy, December 1941–June 1942*. Annapolis, MD: NIP, 1976.

Marder, Arthur. *Old Friends, New Enemies: The Royal Navy and the Imperial Japanese Navy*. Vol. 1: *Strategic Illusions, 1936–1941*; vol. 2: *The Pacific War, 1942–1945*. Oxford: Clarendon, 1981–1990.

Miller, John, Jr. *Guadalcanal, The First Offensive*. Washington, DC: Office of the Chief of Military History, Department of the Army, 1949.

Morison, Samuel Eliot. *A History of United States Naval Operations in World War II*. 15 vols. Boston: Little, Brown, 1947–1962. In particular vol. 3: *The Rising Sun in the Pacific*; vol. 4: *The Coral Sea, Midway and Submarine Actions*; vol. 5: *The Struggle for Guadalcanal*; and vol. 12: *Leyte*.

Morley, James William. *The Final Confrontation: Japan's Negotiations with the United States, 1941*. New York: Columbia UP, 1994.

Morton, Louis. *The Fall of the Philippines*. Washington, DC: Office of the Chief of Military History, Department of the Army, 1953.

O'Connor, Raymond G. *The Japanese Navy in World War II*. Annapolis, MD: NIP, 1982.

Pacific War Research Society, eds. *Japan's Longest Day*. Tokyo: Kodansha International, 1968.

Parillo, Mark P. "The Imperial Japanese Navy in World War II." In James J. Sadkovich, ed., *Re-evaluating Major Naval Combatants of World War II*, 61–77. Westport, CT: Greenwood, 1990.

———. *The Japanese Merchant Marine in World War II*. Annapolis, MD: NIP, 1993.

Peattie, Mark R. " 'Crushed Jewels' and Destitute Garrisons: The Nan'yo Conquered, 1941–1945." Chapter 9 of *Nan'yo: The Rise and Fall of the Japanese in Micronesia, 1885–1945*. Honolulu: University of Hawaii, 1988.

Peattie, Mark R., and David C. Evans. "Japan." In John B. Hattendorf, ed., *Ubi Sumus? The State of Maritime and Naval History*, 213–221. Newport, RI: Naval War College, 1994.

Prados, John. *Combined Fleet Decoded: The Secret History of American Intelligence and the Japanese Navy in World War II*. New York: Random House, 1995.

Prange, Gordon. "A Strategic Imbecility." In Gordon Prange, *Pearl Harbor: The Verdict of History*, 553–572. New York: McGraw-Hill, 1986.

Prange, Gordon, with Donald Goldstein and Katherine Dillon. *At Dawn We Slept: The Untold Story of Pearl Harbor*. Harmondsworth, U.K.; New York: Penguin, 1981.

———. *Miracle at Midway*. Harmondsworth, U.K.; New York: Penguin, 1982.

———. *Pearl Harbor: Verdict of History*. New York: McGraw-Hill, 1986, 1991.

Rahn, Werner. "Japan and Germany, 1941–1943: No Common Objective, No Common Plans, No Basis of Trust." *Naval War College Review* 46:3 (Summer 1993): 47–68.

Reynolds, Clark. "The Continental Strategy of Imperial Japan." *United States Institute Proceedings* (August 1983): 65–71.

Rosinski, Herbert. "The Strategy of Japan." In B. Mitchell Simpson, ed., *The Development of Naval Thought: Essays by Herbert Rosinski*, 102–120. Newport, RI: Naval War College, 1977.

Seno, Sadao. "A Chess Game with No Checkmate: Admiral Inoue and the Pacific War." *Naval War College Review* (January–February 1974): 26–39.

Stephan, John. *Hawaii under the Rising Sun: Japan's Plans for Conquest after Pearl Harbor.* Honolulu: University of Hawaii, 1984.

Thomas, David. *Japan's War at Sea: Pearl Harbor to the Coral Sea.* London: Deutsch, 1978.

Torisu, Kennosuke. "Japanese Submarine Tactics and the *Kaiten.*" In David C. Evans, ed., *The Japanese Navy in World War II: In the Words of Former Japanese Naval Officers*, 440–452. Annapolis, MD: NIP, 1986.

Ugaki, Matome. *Fading Victory: The Diary of Admiral Matome Ugaki.* Translated by Masataka Chihaya. Edited by Donald M. Goldstein and Katherine V. Dillon. Pittsburgh: University of Pittsburgh, 1991.

U.S. Army in World War II. Official History. 78 vols. Washington, DC: GPO, 1949–1993.

U.S. Department of the Army. *Japanese Monographs.* Washington, DC: Office of the Chief of Military History, 1945–1960.

———. *Guide to Japanese Monographs and Japanese Studies on Manchuria.* Washington, DC: Office of Military History, 1980, 1962.

U.S. Strategic Bombing Survey (USSBS). *Report 72: Interrogation of Japanese Officials.* 2 vols. Washington, DC: Military Analysis Division, USSBS, 1946.

Warner, Denis, and Peggy Warner, with Sadao Seno. *The Sacred Warriors: Japan's Suicide Legions.* New York: Avon, 1982.

Willmott, H. P. *The Barrier and the Javelin: Japanese and Allied Strategies, February to June 1942.* Annapolis, MD: NIP, 1983.

———. *Empires in the Balance: Japanese and Allied Strategies to April 1942.* Annapolis, MD: NIP, 1982.

5 American and Allied Strategy and Campaigns in the Pacific War, 1941–1945

Jeffrey G. Barlow

In the years since 1945, books and articles concerning various aspects of the fighting in the Pacific during World War II have appeared in a seemingly unending stream. They have ranged the gamut from individual accounts of combat by men who fought in Pacific battles to large-scale, official histories produced by the service historical offices of the several Allied countries that waged the war.

This chapter discusses books and articles that pertain to two major aspects of the Pacific War—the Allied strategy of the war and the conduct of military and naval campaigns and operations.

Depending on how it is used, the term "strategy" can have one of several distinct meanings. As used here, it refers to both national (or grand) strategy, which is the assembling and employment of all skeins of national power—political, economic, military, technological, and psychological—in an attempt to achieve a country's wartime objectives, and military strategy, which is national strategy's dominant subset. Where national strategy is the realm of a country's political leaders, working in conjunction with their military, economic, scientific, and technological advisers, military strategy is (or should be) the domain of that nation's highest-ranking generals and admirals.

The links between strategic thought and action at the national level are the existing state organizational structures that enable governmental policies to be executed. For the purposes of this chapter both a country's senior civilian leaders and its wartime decision-making and implementation structures are taken to be components of "the high-level direction of war."

ROOSEVELT AND CHURCHILL

For the Pacific War, the two principal, Allied, national-level actors were President Franklin D. Roosevelt of the United States and Prime Minister Winston Churchill of Great Britain. During the First World War, both men had occupied senior civilian positions in their respective navies—Roosevelt serving as assistant secretary of the navy and Churchill serving as first lord of the Admiralty until May 1915, when he was forced to resign in the aftermath of the Dardanelles debacle. The two men began corresponding in 1939, following a letter that Roosevelt sent to Churchill congratulating him on his return to the Admiralty as first lord and suggesting that Churchill should keep in touch with him on matters of interest. Churchill, who, after becoming prime minister in May 1940, liked to refer to himself in his messages to Roosevelt as "Former Naval Person," soon accepted the president's offer to establish a personal channel for communications between the two men. Both Roosevelt and Churchill have been individual subjects of considerable interest to biographers and historians since 1945. Their personal and professional interactions during the Second World War also have received extensive examination.

For all of the scrutiny he has received, however, Roosevelt remains, in many ways, an enigmatic individual. While president, he liked to keep his decision-making options open by rarely allowing staffers to keep substantive records of his meetings with advisers or his conversations with the numerous official and unofficial visitors to the Oval Office. Accordingly, for the wartime period, we have limited authoritative information on how and why Roosevelt made the specific decisions he did regarding Pacific strategy.

This being said, however, there are a number of useful studies of Roosevelt's wartime leadership. In Burns' *Roosevelt: The Soldier of Freedom*, the second volume of his biography, the president emerges as both a man of principle and a realist politician. A more recent study that relies on the new primary material that has been released in the quarter century since Burns completed his study is Kimball's *The Juggler*, a collection of essays on various aspects of Roosevelt's wartime foreign policy. An earlier article by Emerson, "Franklin Roosevelt as Commander-in-Chief," deals insightfully with Roosevelt's wartime role as head of the army and navy. An article that discusses Roosevelt's role in assessing and anticipating the emerging Axis threat to United States' interests, although too favorably, in this author's estimation, is Christman's "Franklin D. Roosevelt and the Craft of Strategic Assessment." Another study on Roosevelt that covers the wartime period in considerable detail is Sherwood's early, but still authoritative, book *Roosevelt and Hopkins*. Finally, a work that examines Franklin Roosevelt's month-by-month movement toward war during 1941 is Heinrichs' *Threshold of War*.

Books on Winston Churchill's role as wartime prime minister abound. A good starting place is his own six-volume *History of the Second World War*. Despite its evident cheerleading and special pleading, this series retains a freshness and pungency of expression common to Churchill's best writing. The two wartime volumes of Churchill's authorized biography by Gilbert, *Finest Hour* and *Road to Victory*, are also very good and, in addition, make use of certain Churchill documents still unavailable to other historians. *Fringes of Power*, the published diaries of Sir John Colville, one of the prime minister's assistant private secretaries during the war, provides an unusual, insider's look at Churchill's prime ministry.

In recent years, a number of books have appeared that examine Roosevelt's and Churchill's wartime interactions in some detail. Of first importance in this regard is Kimball's three-volume *Churchill and Roosevelt: The Complete Correspondence*, which reprints all of the letters and messages that the two leaders exchanged with each other, while also providing detailed editorial commentary. An interesting British perspective on the two men's wartime leadership is provided by Sainsbury in *Churchill and Roosevelt at War: The War They Fought*. Kimball in his 1997 *Forged in War* provides the most recent analysis of the two leaders' wartime relationship, based on a detailed examination of the extensive documentation now available.

THE CHIEFS

The other aspect of the high-level direction of war consists of each country's strategic decision making and implementation structures. In the United States from February 1942 onward the principal military organization consisted of the Joint Chiefs of Staff (JCS) and its subsidiary committees. It reported directly to the president as commander in chief. Its British counterpart—the Chiefs of Staff Committee—was actually a subcommittee of the British War Cabinet, but Churchill's domination of the process as both prime minister and defense minister made this distinction largely moot. Throughout the war, the military chiefs of the two Allies sat together periodically as the Combined Chiefs of Staff to decide on matters of common strategy. Day-to-day dealings between the American and British chiefs were handled primarily through the British Joint Staff Mission— a group of senior British representatives headquartered in Washington.

There exists no overall official history of the Joint Chiefs of Staff during World War II. Immediately after the war, historians assigned to the Joint Staff began a series of JCS histories. The history dealing with the war against Germany and its satellites was never completed and consists today only of various manuscript drafts of particular chapters found in the holdings of the National Archives and Records Administration. Fortunately, historian Hayes completed her official volume *The War against Japan*, which examines in substantial detail the byplay in the Joint Chiefs of Staff over strategy for the Pacific War. Originally issued as a security-classified study in 1953, it was published by the Naval Institute Press in 1982. A dissertation by Brower, "The Joint Chiefs of Staff and National Policy," investigates the development in the JCS of strategy for the Pacific during the last two years of the war, particularly from the army's perspective. Two army official histories that examine American wartime strategic planning are Matloff and Snell's chronological volumes on *Strategic Planning for Coalition Warfare.*

The Chiefs, a recent study by General Sir William Jackson and Field Marshal Lord Bramall, analyzes the wartime British Chiefs of Staff in two chapters of a work covering the entire history of the Chiefs of Staff Committee. Thoroughly grounded in a reading of solid secondary works, their chapters provide a useful account of the interaction between the British officers and their American colleagues. The performance of the wartime British Joint Staff Mission in Washington is explored in abundant detail in Parker's 1984 dissertation, "Attendant Lords." For the American chiefs, the most important British member of the Joint Staff Mission until his unexpected death was Field Marshal Sir John Dill, the former chief of the Imperial General Staff. His invaluable service to the wartime Allied effort is skillfully examined in Danchev's book *Very Special Relationship.* Danchev has also edited the wartime diaries of Brigadier Vivian Dykes, one of the mission's key staffers, in a volume entitled *Establishing the Anglo-American Alliance.*

The wartime interaction between the British Chiefs of Staff and the prime minister is exceedingly well covered in Butler's six-volume official history entitled *Grand Strategy.* This series covers the development of British strategy chronologically from the period of rearmament in the second half of the 1930s through the war's end in September 1945. Each of the later volumes contains several chapters having to do with wartime events in the Far East. Noted British military historians who wrote the individual volumes in this series include Norman H. Gibbs, J. R. M. Butler, John Ehrman, J. M. A. Gwyer, and Michael Howard. Although Australia did not have a seat at the top table when it came to establishing the Allies' strategy for the war against Japan, it did what it could to influence decisions. Australian officer-author Horner's *High Command* examines his nation's role in Allied wartime strategy.

To better understand the byplay over strategy that took place in these high-level military committees, it is necessary to know something about the individuals on these committees. The senior army member of the U.S. Joint Chiefs of Staff was General (later General of the Army) George C. Marshall. The definitive biography of Marshall (in four volumes) was written over a thirty-year span by Pogue. The two middle volumes of the series, *Ordeal and Hope* and *Organizer of Victory*, examine Marshall's life during the war years. For those desiring a less detailed audit, Cray has produced a useful, one-volume biography entitled *General of the Army*.

During the first weeks of its existence, the navy member of the JCS was Admiral Harold R. Stark, the chief of Naval Operations (CNO), who had helped to mobilize the navy for war during 1940 and 1941. Simpson's biography of Stark, *Architect of Victory*, is reliably grounded in research drawn from Stark's own papers, held at the Naval Historical Center's Operational Archives, and the substantial official files of the office of Commander, Naval Forces Europe—the wartime position Stark held after being relieved as CNO.

The man who took Stark's place as chief of Naval Operations, while retaining his duties as commander in chief, U.S. Fleet (COMINCH), was Admiral (later Fleet Admiral) Ernest J. King. Just as Marshall was the key figure on the JCS in matters relating to Europe, King was the dominant strategist on the JCS for the Pacific War. *A Naval Record*, the autobiography that King wrote with Walter Whitehill, while useful, fails to capture both the admiral's incisive mind and his dreaded, caustic personality, which were so well known to those who served under him during the war. Buell's biography of King, *Master of Sea Power*, is particularly good on King's personality, his private life, and his career up to the time he became COMINCH. "Ernest Joseph King, 26 March 1942–15 December 1945," the lengthy chapter by Love on King as COMINCH/CNO, furnishes vital detail on his wartime thinking and decisions. Love's thorough familiarity with the wartime documentation on King's role dates back to the research he conducted for his dissertation on the working relationship between King and his chief wartime planner, Charles M. "Savvy" Cooke.

General (later General of the Army) Henry H. "Hap" Arnold, the commanding general, Army Air Forces (AAF), served as the air member on the JCS, even though he remained Marshall's subordinate. Unfortunately, he still lacks a first-rate biography. Arnold's ghost-written autobiography, *Global Mission*, is short on substance, while *Hap*, the 1982 biography of Arnold by Thomas Coffey, is not nearly as well researched as it should have been.

The fourth and last member of the wartime JCS from mid-1942 onward was Admiral (later Fleet Admiral) William D. Leahy, the chief of staff to the commander in chief (Roosevelt). Leahy, a former CNO, had been brought into the Joint Chiefs of Staff at Marshall's suggestion to serve as its chairman (and also to help balance its existing composition of one navy and two army officers). He never assumed the role in the Chiefs that Marshall had hoped he would, however, because Roosevelt preferred to use Leahy largely as his personal staff officer and liaison with the JCS. Leahy, like Arnold, is still in need of a really good biography. Leahy's autobiography, *I Was There*, is a workmanlike volume based primarily on his wartime diaries, but it fails to tell us much about Leahy the man.

Witness to Power, the 1985 biography of the admiral written by Adams, is disappointing in its overall level of research.

The senior member of the British Chiefs of Staff for most of the war was Field Marshal Alan Brooke (later Lord Alanbrooke of Brookeborough), the chief of the Imperial General Staff and (from 1942) chairman of the Chiefs of Staff Committee. He has been well served by two accounts of his wartime experiences. The first of these is a two-volume study of the war years based on Brooke's diaries, *Turn of the Tide* (for 1939–1943) and *Triumph in the West* (for 1943–1945), written by Bryant. The second is a single-volume biography, concisely titled *Alanbrooke*, by General Fraser. The portrait of the man that emerges in the latter biography is a better-rounded one because Fraser was not constrained, as Bryant had been, by having to stick to Brooke's diaries in painting his picture. The Fraser volume has the additional benefit of showing us more of Alanbrooke's formidable side by providing an even fuller airing of some of his negative assessments of people and events than did Bryant, who was writing at a time when many of these men were still alive.

Britain's senior service, the Royal Navy, was represented on the wartime Chiefs of Staff Committee by two admirals who served as first sea lord and chief of the Naval Staff. The first was Admiral of the Fleet Sir Dudley Pound. Although he lacks a complete biography, Pound is discussed in two useful, article-length studies: Kemp's "Admiral of the Fleet Sir Dudley Pound" and a recent article by Broadhurst, "Admiral Sir Dudley Pound." Broadhurst is completing a full-length biography of the admiral. The Royal Navy's other senior wartime admiral was Admiral of the Fleet (later Viscount of Hyndhope) Andrew B. Cunningham, the heroic commander of the Mediterranean Fleet during the hard-fought years from 1939 through 1942. Cunningham is well served by his autobiography, *A Sailor's Odyssey*, and, in addition, has been the subject of a useful chapter by Michael Simpson in *The First Sea Lords*.

The third member of the British military triumvirate was Marshal of the Royal Air Force (RAF) (later Viscount of Hungerford) Charles Portal. Though less colorful than some of the other RAF senior officers of the time, notably Bomber Command's Sir Arthur Harris, Portal proved a staunch supporter of air-related strategy on the Chiefs of Staff Committee. Unfortunately, in his 1977 study *Portal of Hungerford*, Richards produced a biography of this senior airman that comes close to hagiography, ignoring the very real conflicts that existed among senior RAF air marshals and absolving Portal of all errors of judgment.

INTELLIGENCE

A vital component of strategy that received short shrift in earlier studies of the war is intelligence. Although most official documentation relating to prewar and wartime intelligence gathering and utilization was released to the public much more slowly than was material on military operations, nothing at all was released on communications intelligence, the most important source of Anglo-American wartime secret information (designated ULTRA) until the latter half of the 1970s. The publication of Group Captain F. W. Winterbotham's short study *The Ultra Secret* in 1974 first informed the public of Allied communications intelligence successes in the European War, but it took the U.S. National Security Agency's 1977 decision to release communications intelligence material to the National Archives to finally open up this last great source of new material on the war. The starting point for a general understanding of the art and science of code making and code breaking remains David Kahn's seminal 1967 book *The Codebreakers*, which has been recently republished.

For the Pacific War, unfortunately, there is nothing comparable to the five-volume series *British Intelligence in the Second World War* by F. H. Hinsley et al., which examines in great detail the influence of the British (and American) breaking of German and Italian codes and machine ciphers on Allied naval operations in the Atlantic and military operations in the European and Mediterranean theaters. Although America's prewar success in cracking Japan's high-level diplomatic cipher designated "Purple" had been known in a more general way since the 1945–1946 congressional hearings into the Pearl Harbor attack, the full extent of this coup was not known until the U.S. Department of Defense published an eight-part study in 1978 entitled *The "MAGIC" Background of Pearl Harbor*, which printed a large number of the deciphered 1940–1941 Japanese messages for the first time. In the 1988 volume *Listening to the Enemy*, Spector provided a short, edited collection of communications intelligence research histories (designated SRHs) originally released by the National Security Agency.

The best introduction to the wealth of Pacific War-related communications intelligence material available at the National Archives and Records Administration is Drea's "Ultra and the American War against Japan." Drea is also the author of *MacArthur's ULTRA*, a superb study of the use (and misuse) of communications intelligence in General Douglas MacArthur's Southwest Pacific theater. Much research still remains to be done, however, with regard to the U.S. Navy's wartime use of intelligence derived from breaking into JN-25, the Imperial Japanese Navy's General Purpose code. The best study now available is Prados' 1995 book *Combined Fleet Decoded*. On a related issue, Herbig wrote a useful article about the U.S. Navy's Pacific deception operations entitled "American Strategic Deception in the Pacific." Finally, a very solid and readable account of the overall intelligence efforts in Admiral Chester Nimitz's Pacific Ocean Areas theater is Holmes' *Double-Edged Secrets*. Although the Army Air Forces did not have as prominent a role in communications intelligence matters in the Pacific as did the army and navy, it did play a necessary part. The recent official history edited by Kreis, *Piercing the Fog*, contains several valuable chapters on AAF intelligence gathering and analysis during the Pacific War.

The British government to date has not been forthcoming about its prewar and wartime code-breaking efforts against the Japanese. A few individual British code breakers, though, have written useful reminiscences of their efforts. See, for example, Stripp's memoir *Codebreaker in the Far East*. The 1993 volume *Codebreakers*, edited by Hinsley and Stripp, presents a variety of personal accounts by people who served during the war at Britain's highly secret Government Code and Cypher School (GC&CS) at Bletchley Park. The book contains several articles on the code-breaking efforts against Japan. Horner's "Special Intelligence in the South-West Pacific Area" discusses Australia's role in the wartime communications intelligence effort. Finally, a piece that examines the infighting over intelligence between the British and American Allies in Asia is Aldrich's 1988 "Imperial Rivalry."

CAMPAIGNS AND OPERATIONS—OFFICIAL HISTORIES

The number of books and articles on American and Allied campaigns and operations during the Pacific War is so vast that no attempt will be made to discuss more than a representative number of the better ones. For the interested reader, though, the starting place must be the official histories produced by the various Allied countries. The most complete listing of these is found in Higham's *Official Histories*.

The U.S. Army's volumes on the Pacific War in its superb series of "Green Books" are absolutely essential reading for a detailed understanding of the army's Pacific operations. Of special note for its masterful explication of the initial American strategy for the Pacific War is Morton's *Strategy and Command*. Other volumes in the army's *War in the Pacific* series include Morton's *The Fall of the Philippines*, Milner's *Victory in Papua*, Miller's *Cartwheel: The Reduction of Rabaul*, Crowl and Love's *Seizure of the Gilberts and Marshalls*, Crowl's *Campaign in the Marianas*, Smith's volumes *The Approach to the Philippines* and *Triumph in the Philippines*, Cannon's *Leyte: The Return to the Philippines*, and the multiauthor effort by Appleman et al. entitled *Okinawa: The Last Battle*. Although some of the earlier volumes have begun showing their age, all of them are notable for their exhaustive research and solid writing.

The U.S. Navy never put the resources into its postwar historical writing program that the army did. Nonetheless, it is well represented by the semiofficial series *History of United States Naval Operations in World War II*, written by the Harvard historian Samuel Eliot Morison, who had been fortunate enough in 1942 to be named historian of naval operations by Roosevelt. Nine of the fifteen volumes published from 1947 through 1962 deal with the Pacific War. All of the books in the series display Morison's uniquely interesting and informative writing style.

The U.S. Marine Corps published its *History of U.S. Marine Corps Operations in World War II* in five volumes from 1958 to 1971. Four of the five volumes were coauthored by Henry Shaw, who eventually served as the Marine Corps Historical Center's senior historian. Thoroughly researched and drawing upon work done for well-written monographs of individual Pacific operations published in the 1950s by the Marine Corps, these volumes stand up well today.

The U.S. Army Air Forces's official history, *The Army Air Forces in World War II*, edited by Craven and Cate, was published in seven volumes from 1948 through 1958. It is, unfortunately, the most dated of the U.S. official histories, both because it was written too soon after the war to benefit from access to a number of important primary sources and because the space limitations imposed on the individual chapters of the volumes required their authors to leave out a great deal of substantive material. Accounts of tactical air (as opposed to strategic bombardment) operations seem to have been especially shortchanged in this series. Accordingly, the history of the Army Air Forces in World War II is a particularly fruitful area for new scholarship.

For most of the war, the British army's fight against the Japanese was in Burma, on the Indian subcontinent, rather than in the Pacific. Accordingly, only the first, fourth, and last books of the five-volume official army history *The War against Japan* by Kirby et al. cover fighting in areas of the Pacific in any detail. The three-volume official history of the Royal Navy in World War II, *The War at Sea*, by Captain S. W. Roskill is very well done, being both accurate in particulars and objective in its assessments. The second and third volumes contain coverage of the Royal Navy's operations in the Indian Ocean and the Pacific. One very useful official study of the Royal Navy's operations in the Pacific War published in 1995 by Great Britain's Ministry of Defence, entitled *War with Japan* (Great Britain), had been issued originally as a Confidential Naval Staff History in the mid-1950s. The three-volume popular, official history of the Royal Air Force in World War II by Richards and Saunders was published in 1953 and 1954. Although the second and third volumes contain several slim chapters relating to RAF efforts in the Pacific War, the overwhelming concentration in this series is on the air war in Europe. As is the case with the U.S. Army Air Forces, the history of the wartime RAF, particularly in the Far East, remains a productive field for research.

Australia's official history program during the 1950s and 1960s benefited from the continuing presence of its general editor, Gavin Long. The army's World War II official history series appeared in seven substantial volumes from 1952 to 1966. The last four of these books, written, respectively, by historians Wigmore, McCarthy, Dexter, and Gavin Long, deal with the fighting in the Pacific War. It is not surprising, given Australia's heavy commitment of troops to the desperate fighting on New Guinea, that two of the four examine the battles on that huge island in substantial detail. The two-volume history of the wartime Royal Australian Navy by Gill is both well done and comprehensive. It should be noted, though, that on particular issues of disagreement among Allied historical accounts he tends to side, perhaps not surprisingly, with Royal Navy views rather than those of the U.S. Navy. The first two books in the four-volume, official history on the Royal Australian Air Force (RAAF) examine the air war against Japan. Gillison's volume covers the swift defeats it suffered at Japanese hands in late 1941 and early 1942, while Odgers details the RAAF's successful comeback during the final years of the war.

New Zealand's part in the Pacific fighting is examined in Gillespie's official history *The Pacific.* The efforts of all three of its military services are recounted in the expanse of this single volume. Gillespie pays particular attention to the fighting in and around the Solomons, where New Zealand's sea, land, and air forces were actively committed for much of the war.

Six Years of War, the first book of the Canadian army's three-volume official history by Stacey, details the army's combat in the Pacific. Stacey recounts the heroic fighting of the Winnipeg Grenadiers and the Royal Rifles during Japan's capture of Hong Kong in December 1941. He also provides a solid narrative on the thirteenth Infantry Brigade's training for, and actions during, the Allies' disappointing invasion of Kiska in August 1943. Joseph Schull's official history of Canadian naval operations in World War II, *Far Distant Ships,* provides only a few, sparsely sketched pages recounting the service of the cruiser *Uganda* in the final months of the Pacific War. Although *Crucible of War,* by Greenhous et al., the third of the three official volumes published to date on the Royal Canadian Air Force (RCAF), is focused primarily on Europe, it briefly discusses the RCAF's limited operations in the Aleutians.

CAMPAIGNS AND OPERATIONS—OTHER WORKS

The United States was propelled into the war in December 1941 by the Japanese surprise attack on the American fleet berthed at Pearl Harbor. During the past half century, matters relating to this attack have provided a cottage industry not only for military and diplomatic historians but also for hundreds of enthusiastic amateurs. Although debate still rages in some quarters over the issue of whether or not President Roosevelt (or, in some versions, Winston Churchill) knew about the impending Japanese attack and let it occur as planned in order to bring the United States into the

European War, the best current historical writing argues against such conspiratorial theories. The most accurate and complete account of the attack
remains Prange's magisterial *At Dawn We Slept*.

Early American and Allied operations in the Pacific were marked by
desperate heroism against seemingly unbeatable Japanese military and naval forces. *Old Friends, New Enemies* by Marder examines in great detail the
interaction of the Royal Navy and Japan's Imperial Japanese Navy from
1936 through the first few days of the Pacific War in 1941. The U.S. Marines' stand at Wake Island is best told in Cressman's recent *"A Magnificent
Fight."* Leutze discusses the Asiatic Fleet's struggle against odds in the
Philippines and the Dutch East Indies in the context of the life of its
commander, Admiral Thomas Hart, in *A Different Kind of Victory*. The Army
Air Forces' losing battle against the Japanese air forces in the Philippines
is superbly recounted by Edmonds in his recently republished book *They
Fought with What They Had*.

The outcome of the battle of Midway in June 1942 provided a major
turning point in the Pacific War. It checked Japan's further military expansion and enabled the Allies to move gradually to the offensive. The
most interesting account of the tactical decision making related to the
battle is in *The Quiet Warrior*, Buell's biography of Admiral Spruance. *"A
Glorious Page in Our History,"* a jointly written effort directed by Cressman,
provides a wealth of new material on the battle itself.

The U.S. Navy began its initial offensive in the South Pacific with the
invasion of the island of Guadalcanal. Frank's *Guadalcanal* examines the
land, sea, and air fighting there in substantial detail. *The First Team and
the Guadalcanal Campaign*, a recent book by Lundstrom, provides important new information from both Japanese and American sources on air
combat over the island.

The U.S. Navy began its major offensive in the Central Pacific in the
fall of 1943. Marine Colonel Joseph Alexander's *Utmost Savagery* thoroughly examines the desperate battle for Tarawa. By the spring of 1944,
the Central Pacific offensive was moving ever closer to the Japanese home
islands. Gailey's *Howlin' Mad Smith vs. the Army* recounts the epic battle
for Saipan in the context of marine–army command problems.

The movement by General MacArthur's Southwest Pacific troops into
the Philippines served as the southern wing closing in on Japan. It sparked
the battle of Leyte Gulf in October 1944, which proved the final defeat
for the Imperial Japanese Navy's Combined Fleet; thereafter it never ven-
tured out in force to fight the ever-encroaching U.S. Navy. *The Battle for
Leyte Gulf* by Woodward retains its value despite having been written half
a century ago. The Royal Navy had a difficult time adapting its forces to
the realities of combat in the vastness of the Pacific, but by early 1945 it
had a task force ready to serve with the U.S. Navy's Fifth Fleet. Two books

of value that deal with the evolution of the British Pacific Fleet are the second volume of Marder's *Old Friends, New Enemies* (completed after his death by two former graduate students) and *Graves of a Dozen Schemes*, the published version of Willmott's doctoral dissertation.

A number of useful books detail the development of particular components of the fighting forces. Blair's *Silent Victory* is an excellent account of U.S. submarine warfare in the Pacific, despite having been written before material on ULTRA intelligence was released. The wartime development of U.S. and Japanese carrier aviation is thoroughly examined in *The Fast Carriers* by Reynolds. Amphibious warfare was a form of combat that the U.S. Navy and Marines had raised to the level of a true military art by war's end. Iseley's and Crowl's *The U.S. Marines and Amphibious War* remains a superb account of its development. Lorelli's 1995 *To Foreign Shores* discusses American amphibious operations both in Europe and in the Pacific but with more of an emphasis on the navy's role.

There are a number of valuable biographical studies of Allied senior officers who served in the Pacific. The second book of James' magisterial, three-volume *The Years of MacArthur* provides a well-rounded wartime portrait of that enigmatic general. *Nimitz* by Potter is an interesting account of the U.S. Navy's senior admiral in the Pacific. Biographical chapters on important U.S. and British admirals who fought during the Pacific War can be found in Howarth's excellent *Men of War*. Solid biographical accounts on MacArthur's commanders are present in Leary's edited volume *We Shall Return!* Shorter biographical sketches of some of the British generals who served in the war against Japan are in *Churchill's Generals*, edited by Keegan. Finally, biographical chapters on some of Australia's wartime generals, including Lieutenant General Sir Vernon Sturdee and Field Marshal Sir Thomas Blamey, are contained in the book *The Commanders*, compiled by historian David Horner.

BIBLIOGRAPHY

Adams, Henry H. *Witness to Power: The Life of Fleet Admiral William D. Leahy.* Annapolis, MD: NIP, 1985.

Aldrich, Robert. "Imperial Rivalry: British and American Intelligence in Asia, 1942–46." *Intelligence and National Security* 3 (January 1988): 5–55.

Alexander, Joseph H. *Utmost Savagery: The Three Days of Tarawa.* Annapolis, MD: NIP, 1995.

Appleman, Roy E., et al. *Okinawa: The Last Battle.* United States Army in World War II Series. *The War in the Pacific.* Washington, DC: Historical Division, Department of the Army, 1948, 1991.

Arnold, Henry H. *Global Mission.* New York: Harper Brothers, 1949.

Blair, Clay. *Silent Victory: The U.S. Submarine War against Japan.* Philadelphia: J. B. Lippincott, 1975.

Broadhurst, Robin. "Admiral Sir Dudley Pound (1939–1943)." In Malcolm H. Murfett, ed., *The First Sea Lords. From Fisher to Mountbatten*, 185–200. Westport, CT: Praeger, 1995.

Brower, Charles F., IV. "The Joint Chiefs of Staff and National Policy: American Strategy and the War with Japan, 1943–1945." Ph.D. diss., University of Pennsylvania, 1987.

Bryant, Arthur. *Triumph in the West: A History of the War Years Based on the Diaries of Field-Marshal Lord Alanbrooke, Chief of the Imperial General Staff.* Garden City, NY: Doubleday, 1959.

———. *The Turn of the Tide: A History of the War Years Based on the Diaries of Field-Marshal Lord Alanbrooke, Chief of the Imperial General Staff.* Garden City, NY: Doubleday, 1957.

Buell, Thomas B. *Master of Sea Power: A Biography of Fleet Admiral Ernest J. King.* Boston: Little, Brown, 1980.

———. *The Quiet Warrior: A Biography of Admiral Raymond A. Spruance.* 2d ed. With an introduction and notes by John B. Lundstrom. Annapolis, MD: NIP, 1987. (Original edition: Boston: Little, Brown, 1974.)

Burns, James MacGregor. *Roosevelt: The Soldier of Freedom, 1940–1945.* New York: Harcourt Brace Jovanovich, 1970.

Butler, James R. M. *Grand Strategy.* Vol. 2: *September 1939–June 1941. History of the Second World War.* United Kingdom Military Series. London: HMSO, 1957.

———. *Grand Strategy.* Vol. 3, part 2: *June 1941–August 1942. History of the Second World War.* United Kingdom Military Series. London: HMSO, 1964.

Cannon, M. Hamlin. *Leyte: The Return to the Philippines.* United States Army in World War II Series. *The War in the Pacific.* Washington, DC: Office of the Chief Of Military History, Department of the Army, 1954.

Christman, Calvin L. "Franklin D. Roosevelt and the Craft of Strategic Assessment." In Williamson Murray and Allan R. Millett, eds., *Calculations: Net Assessment and the Coming of World War II*, 216–257. New York: Free, 1992.

Churchill, Winston. *History of the Second World War.* 6 vols. Boston: Houghton Mifflin, 1948–1953.

Coffey, Thomas M. *Hap: The Story of the U.S. Air Force and the Man Who Built It: General Henry H. "Hap" Arnold.* New York: Viking, 1982.

Colville, John. *The Fringes of Power: 10 Downing Street Diaries 1939–1955.* New York: W. W. Norton, 1985.

Craven, Wesley F., and James L. Cate, eds. *The Army Air Forces in World War II.* 7 vols. Chicago: University of Chicago, 1948–1958.

Cray, Ed. *General of the Army: George C. Marshall, Soldier and Statesman.* New York: W. W. Norton, 1990.

Cressman, Robert J. *"A Magnificent Fight": The Battle for Wake Island.* Annapolis, MD: NIP, 1995.

Cressman, Robert J., Steve Ewing, Barrett Tillman, Mark Horan, Clark Reynolds, and Stan Cohen. *"A Glorious Page in Our History": The Battle of Midway 4–6 June 1942.* Missoula, MT: Pictorial Histories, 1990.

Crowl, Philip A. *Campaign in the Marianas.* United States Army in World War II Series. *The War in the Pacific.* Washington, DC: Office of the Chief of Military History, Department of the Army, 1960.

Crowl, Philip A., and Edmund G. Love. *Seizure of the Gilberts and Marshalls.* United

States Army in World War II Series. *The War in the Pacific.* Washington, DC: Office of the Chief of Military History, Department of the Army, 1955.

Cunningham, Andrew. *A Sailor's Odyssey.* London: Hutchinson, 1951.

Danchev, Alex. *Establishing the Anglo-American Alliance: The Second World War Diaries of Brigadier Vivian Dykes.* London: Brassey's (U.K.), 1990.

———. *Very Special Relationship: Field-Marshal Sir John Dill and the Anglo-American Alliance 1941–44.* London: Brassey's Defence, 1986.

Dexter, David. *The New Guinea Offensives.* Australia in the War of 1939–1945 Series. Canberra: Australian War Memorial, 1961.

Drea, Edward J. *MacArthur's ULTRA: Codebreaking and the War against Japan, 1942–1945.* Lawrence: UP of Kansas, 1992.

———. "Ultra and the American War against Japan: A Note on Sources." *Intelligence and National Security* 3 (1988): 195–204.

Edmonds, Walter D. *They Fought with What They Had: The Story of the Army Air Forces in the Southwest Pacific, 1941–1942.* Boston: Little, Brown, 1951; reprint, Washington, DC: Center for Air Force History, 1992.

Ehrman, John. *Grand Strategy.* Vol. 5: *August 1943–September 1944. History of the Second World War.* United Kingdom Military Series. London: HMSO, 1956.

———. *Grand Strategy.* Vol. 6: *October 1944–August 1945. History of the Second World War.* United Kingdom Military Series. London: HMSO, 1956.

Emerson, William R. "Franklin Roosevelt as Commander-in-Chief in World War II." *Military Affairs* 22 (Winter 1958–1959): 181–207.

Frank, Richard B. *Guadalcanal: The Definitive Account of the Landmark Battle.* New York: Random House, 1990.

Fraser, David. *Alanbrooke.* With a Prologue and Epilogue by Arthur Bryant. New York: Atheneum, 1982.

Gailey, Harry A. *Howlin' Mad vs. the Army: Conflict in Command, Saipan 1944.* Novato, CA: Presidio, 1986.

Gilbert, Martin. *Winston S. Churchill.* Vol. 6: *Finest Hour: 1939–1941.* Boston: Houghton Mifflin, 1983.

———. *Winston S. Churchill.* Vol. 7: *Road to Victory: 1941–1945.* Boston: Houghton Mifflin, 1986.

Gill, G. Herman. *Royal Australian Navy 1939–1942.* Canberra: Australian War Memorial, 1957.

———. *Royal Australian Navy 1943–1945.* Canberra: Australian War Memorial, 1968.

Gillespie, Oliver A. *The Pacific. Official History of Zealand in the Second World War 1939–45.* Wellington, New Zealand: War History Branch, Department of Internal Affairs, 1952.

Gillison, Douglas. *Royal Australian Air Force, 1939–42.* Canberra: Australian War Memorial, 1962.

Great Britain, Naval Historical Branch, Ministry of Defence. *War with Japan.* 6 vols. in 4. London: HMSO, 1995.

Greenhous, Brereton, Stephen Harris, William Johnson, and William G. P. Rawling. *The Official History of the Royal Canadian Air Force.* Vol. 3: *Crucible of War.* Toronto: Department of National Defence and University of Toronto, 1994.

Gwyer, J. M. A. *Grand Strategy.* Vol. 3, part 1: *June 1941–August 1942. History of the Second World War.* United Kingdom Military Series. London: HMSO, 1964.

Hayes, Grace P. *The History of the Joint Chiefs of Staff in World War II: The War against Japan.* Annapolis, MD: NIP, 1982.

Heinrichs, Waldo, Jr. *Threshold of War: Franklin D. Roosevelt and American Entry into World War II.* New York: Oxford UP, 1988.

Herbig, Katherine L. "American Strategic Deception in the Pacific, 1942–44." *Intelligence and National Security* 2 (July 1987): 260–300.

Higham, Robin, ed. *Official Histories: Essays and Bibliographies from around the World.* Manhattan: Kansas State University Library, 1970.

Hinsley, F. H., and Alan Stripp, eds. *Codebreakers: The Inside Story of Bletchley Park.* Oxford: Oxford UP, 1993.

Hinsley, F. H., E. E. Thomas, C. F. G. Ransom, R. C. Knight, C. A. G. Simpkins, and Michael Howard. *British Intelligence in the Second World War: Its Influence on Strategy and Operations.* 5 vols. in 6. London: HMSO; New York: Cambridge UP, 1979–1990.

Holmes, W. J. *Double-Edged Secrets: U.S. Naval Intelligence Operations in the Pacific during World War II.* Annapolis, MD: NIP, 1979.

Horner, D. M. *The Commanders: Australian Military Leadership in the Twentieth Century.* Sydney, Australia: Allen and Unwin, 1984.

———. *High Command: Australian and Allied Strategy 1939–1945.* Sydney, Australia: Allen and Unwin, 1982.

———. "Special Intelligence in the South-West Pacific Area in World War II." *Australian Outlook* 32 (December 1978): 310–327.

Howard, Michael. *Grand Strategy.* Vol. 4: *August 1942–September 1943. History of the Second World War.* United Kingdom Military Series. London: HMSO, 1972.

Howarth, Stephen, ed. *Men of War: Great Naval Leaders of World War II.* New York: St. Martin's, 1993.

Isely, Jeter A., and Philip A. Crowl. *The U.S. Marines and Amphibious War: Its Theory, and Its Practice in the Pacific.* Princeton: Princeton UP, 1951.

Jackson, William, and Lord Bramall. *The Chiefs: The Story of the United Kingdom Chiefs of Staff.* London: Brassey's (U.K.), 1992.

James, D. Clayton. *The Years of MacArthur.* Vol. 2: *1941–1945.* Boston: Houghton Mifflin, 1975.

Kahn, David. *The Codebreakers: The Story of Secret Writing.* New York: Macmillan, 1967.

Keegan, John, ed. *Churchill's Generals.* New York: Grove Weidenfeld, 1991.

Kimball, Warren F., ed. *Churchill and Roosevelt: The Complete Correspondence.* 3 vols. Princeton: Princeton UP, 1984.

———. *Forged in War: Roosevelt, Churchill, and the Second World War.* New York: William Morrow, 1997.

———. *The Juggler: Franklin Roosevelt as Wartime Statesman.* Princeton: Princeton UP, 1991.

King, Ernest J., and Walter M. Whitehill. *Fleet Admiral King: A Naval Record.* New York: W.W. Norton, 1952.

Kirby, S. Woodburn, C. T. Addis, J. F. Meiklejohn, G. T. Wards, N. L. Desoer, and M. R. Roberts. *The War against Japan.* 5 vols. *History of the Second World War.* United Kingdom Military Series. London: HMSO, 1958–1969.

Kreis, John F., ed. *Piercing the Fog: Intelligence and Army Air Forces Operations in World War II.* Washington, DC: Air Force History and Museums Program, 1996.

Leahy, William D. *I Was There: The Personal Story of the Chief of Staff to Presidents*

Roosevelt and Truman, Based on His Notes and Diaries Made at the Time. New York: Whittlesey House, 1950.

Leary, William M., ed. *We Shall Return! MacArthur's Commanders and the Defeat of Japan 1942–1945.* Lexington: University of Kentucky, 1988.

Leighton, Richard M., and Robert W. Coakley. *Global Logistics and Strategy, 1940–1943.* United States Army in World War II Series. *The War Department.* Washington, DC: Office of the Chief of Military History, Department of the Army, 1955.

Leutze, James R. *A Different Kind of Victory: A Biography of Admiral Thomas C. Hart.* Annapolis, MD: NIP, 1981.

Long, Gavin. *The Final Campaigns.* Australia in the War of 1939–1945 Series. Canberra: Australian War Memorial, 1963.

Lorelli, John A. *To Foreign Shores: U.S. Amphibious Operations in World War II.* Annapolis, MD: NIP, 1995.

Love, Robert W., Jr. "Ernest Joseph King, 26 March 1942–15 December 1945." In Robert W. Love, Jr., ed., *The Chiefs Of Naval Operations,* 136–179. Annapolis, MD: NIP, 1980.

Lundstrom, John B. *The First Team and the Guadalcanal Campaign: Naval Fighter Combat from August to November 1942.* Annapolis, MD: NIP, 1994.

The "Magic" Background of Pearl Harbor. 5 vols. in 8. Washington, DC: Department of Defense, 1978.

McCarthy, Dudley. *South-West Pacific Area. First Year: Kokoda to Wau.* Australia in the War of 1939–1945 Series. Canberra: Australian War Memorial, 1959.

Marder, Arthur J. *Old Friends, New Enemies: The Royal Navy and the Imperial Japanese Navy, vol. 1 Strategic Illusions, 1936–1941.* Oxford: Clarendon, 1981.

Marder, Arthur J., Mark Jacobsen, and John Horsfield. *Old Friends, New Enemies: The Royal Navy and the Imperial Japanese Navy.* Vol. 2: *The Pacific War, 1942–1945.* Oxford: Clarendon, 1990.

Matloff, Maurice. *Strategic Planning for Coalition Warfare, 1943–1944.* United States Army in World War II Series. *The War Department.* Washington, DC: Office of the Chief of Military History, Department of the Army, 1959.

Matloff, Maurice, and Edwin M. Snell. *Strategic Planning for Coalition Warfare, 1941–1942.* United States Army in World War II Series. *The War Department.* Washington, DC: Office of the Chief of Military History, Department of the Army, 1953.

Miller, John, Jr. *Cartwheel: The Reduction of Rabaul.* Washington, DC: Office of the Chief of Military History, Department of the Army, 1959.

———. *Guadalcanal: The First Offensive.* Washington, DC: Office of the Chief of Military History, Department of the Army, 1949.

Milner, Samuel. *Victory in Papua.* Washington, DC: Office of the Chief of Military History, Department of the Army, 1957.

Morison, Samuel Eliot. *History of United States Naval Operations in World War II.* 15 vols. Boston: Little, Brown, 1947–1962.

Morton, Louis. *The Fall of the Philippines.* Washington, DC: Office of the Chief of Military History, Department of the Army, 1953.

———. *Strategy and Command: The First Two Years.* Washington, DC: Office of the Chief of Military History, Department of the Army, 1962.

Murfett, Malcolm R., ed. *The First Sea Lords: From Fisher to Mountbatten.* Westport, CT: Praeger, 1995.

Odgers, George. *Air War against Japan, 1943–45.* Canberra: Australian War Memorial, 1957.

Parker, Sally Lister. "Attendant Lords: A Study of the British Joint Staff Mission in Washington, 1941–1945." Ph.D. diss., University of Maryland, 1984.

Pogue, Forrest C. *George C. Marshall: Ordeal and Hope, 1939–1942.* New York: Viking, 1966.

———. *George C. Marshall: Organizer of Victory 1943–1945.* New York: Viking, 1973.

Potter, Elmer B. *Nimitz.* Annapolis, MD: NIP, 1976.

Prados, John. *Combined Fleet Decoded: The Secret History of American Intelligence and the Japanese Navy in World War II.* New York: Random House, 1995.

Prange, Gordon, in collaboration with Donald M. Goldstein and Katherine V. Dillon. *At Dawn We Slept: The Untold Story of Pearl Harbor.* New York: McGraw-Hill, 1981.

Reynolds, Clark G. *The Fast Carriers: The Forging of an Air Navy.* New ed. Annapolis, MD: NIP, 1992.

Richards, Denis. *Portal of Hungerford: The Life of Marshal of the Royal Air Force Viscount Portal of Hungerford KG, GCB, OM, DSO, MC.* London: Heinemann, 1977.

Richards, Denis, and Hilary St. George Saunders. *Royal Air Force 1939–1945.* 3 vols. London: HMSO, 1953–1954.

Roskill, S. W. *The War at Sea 1939–1945.* 3 vols. in 4. *History of the Second World War.* United Kingdom Military Series. London: HMSO, 1954–1961.

Sainsbury, Keith. *Churchill and Roosevelt at War: The War They Fought and the Peace They Hoped to Make.* New York: New York UP, 1994.

Schull, Joseph. *Far Distant Ships: An Official Account of Canadian Naval Operations in World War II.* Ottawa: Edward Cloutier, King's Printer, 1950; reprint, Toronto: Stoddart for NIP, 1987.

Sherwood, Robert. *Roosevelt and Hopkins: An Intimate History.* Rev. ed. New York: Grosset and Dunlap, Universal Library, 1950.

Simpson, B. Mitchell, III. *Admiral Harold R. Stark: Architect of Victory, 1939–1945.* Columbia: University of South Carolina, 1989.

Simpson, Michael. "Admiral Viscount Cunningham of Hyndhope." In Malcolm H. Murfett, ed., *The First Sea Lords: From Fisher to Mountbatten,* 201–216. Westport, CT: Praeger, 1995.

Smith, Robert R. *The Approach to the Philippines.* United States Army in World War II Series. *The War in the Pacific.* Washington, DC: Office of the Chief of Military History, Department of the Army, 1953.

———. *Triumph in the Philippines.* United States Army in World War II Series. *The War in the Pacific.* Washington, DC: Office of the Chief of Military History, Department of the Army, 1963.

Spector, Ronald H., ed. *Listening to the Enemy: Key Documents on the Role of Communications Intelligence in the War with Japan.* Wilmington, DE: Scholarly Resources, 1988.

Stacey, C. P. *Six Years of War: The Army in Canada, Britain and the Pacific.* Vol. 1: *Official History of the Canadian Army in the Second World War.* Ottawa: Edmond Cloutier, Queen's Printer, 1955.

Stripp, Alan. *Codebreaker in the Far East.* With an introduction by Christopher An-
    drew. London: Frank Cass, 1989.

U.S. Marine History and Museums Division. *History of U.S. Marine Corps Operations
    in World War II.* 5 vols. Washington, DC: GPO, 1958–1971.

Wigmore, Lionel. *The Japanese Thrust.* Australia in the War of 1939–1945 Series.
    Canberra: Australian War Memorial, 1957.

Willmott, H. P. *Graves of a Dozen Schemes: British Naval Planning and the War against
    Japan, 1943–1945.* Annapolis, MD: NIP, 1996.

Winterbotham, Frederick W. *The Ultra Secret.* New York: Harper and Row, 1974.

Woodward, C. Vann. *The Battle for Leyte Gulf.* New York: Macmillan, 1947.

6 Burma and Southeast Asia, 1941–1945

Mark P. Parillo

World War II in Burma and Southeast Asia had implications with which the world is still dealing today, and it has generated a literature as rich and varied as the lands and peoples of that vast and populous corner of the world. The Malaya/Singapore and Burma campaigns have received copious consideration, much of it tied to the strategic conceptions underlying them. Historians have used the campaign in Malaya as an avenue for examining British naval and overall imperial policy.

Operations in Burma have received similar attention, although often with an eye toward the larger issues of China's wartime and postwar roles and status. While there is a reasonably comprehensive literature on the economic, political, and diplomatic consequences of the Japanese occupation of the rest of East and Southeast Asia, the limited military operations outside Malaysia and Burma have not provoked Western writers to spill much ink on the topic. Thus, despite the growing, present-day significance of the war for this region of the world, World War II in Southeast Asia is perhaps the least-known aspect of the global conflict.

"Singapore has fallen," wrote Admiral Sir Herbert Richmond in an article that appeared scarcely a month after the event described (see Gwynn, "Singapore"). "It is the greatest disaster that we have suffered since the collapse of France." So begins the vast body of historical writing on the question of why Singapore fell with such apparent ease to an enemy inferior in numbers and, it had been assumed by Westerners, in military capabilities. Richmond went on to attribute the catastrophe to the loss of command of the sea, which he blamed on collective British and imperial forgetfulness about the fundamental principles of strategy. This interpretation has scarcely been contested in the succeeding half century, although it has certainly been probed and refined.

For the next quarter of a century, the historiography of the Malaya/

Singapore campaign consisted mostly of official histories, general works on the war or strategy, and personal accounts from the memoirs of the high and mighty to the reminiscences of front-line soldiers. Three outstanding official histories appeared in 1957: Kirby's *The Loss of Singapore*, Hermon's *Royal Australian Navy, 1939–42*, and Wigmore's *The Japanese Thrust*. These volumes feature detailed narratives of unit operations and excellent visual materials.

But in the late 1960s a number of monographs devoted to the campaign began to appear. In *A Sinister Twilight*, Barber wove the individual stories of several participants into a compelling narrative of Singapore's fall. More analytical is Leasor's *Singapore*, although befuddling in spots and lacking scholarly documentation. Swinson provided a short, but solid, narrative in his *Defeat in Malaya*.

Publication of the classic *Singapore: The Chain of Disaster* after author Kirby's death initiated a new era of scholarship on the topic. This volume appeared in 1971 and remained for years the best overall work on the strategic situation and the campaign itself. Falk added an admirable history of the fighting in Malaya with *Seventy Days to Singapore*, which utilized newly released U.S. intelligence summaries. Allen followed with *Singapore, 1941–42*, based partly on Japanese sources. The organization is weak, but it furnished the first extensive commentary in English from the Japanese point of view. The author concluded that in their very moment of triumph, the Japanese were setting the stage for their ultimate defeat by military overextension with their raids into the Indian Ocean and by political shortsightedness with their cruelty toward the expatriate Chinese community, thus ensuring Chinese noncooperation throughout Southeast Asia.

Callahan furthered the dialogue with *The Worst Disaster*, a study of the Singapore question in Great Britain's strategic thinking. He argued forcefully that British prime minister Winston Churchill's strategic inclination to limit commitments to East Asia in order to underwrite a Mediterranean campaign doomed Singapore but was nevertheless the correct decision in the larger view. McIntyre followed in 1979 with *The Rise and Fall of the Singapore Naval Base, 1919–1942*, which examines the entire interwar period for the roots of Singapore's fall. Neidpath produced a similar study two years later, *The Singapore Naval Base and the Defence of Britain's Eastern Empire, 1919–1941*.

Another general account soon followed, *The Bitter End* by Holmes and Kemp, providing one more cogent narrative of the campaign and also including additional firsthand accounts. The lack of notes beyond textual references and a disappointingly terse bibliography are offset by useful historiographical essays in both the introductory and concluding chapters, in which the authors agree with previous assessments that the genesis of Singapore's vulnerability was in the insoluble twentieth-century dilemma of the British empire: defense of a worldwide empire with shrinking economic and military resources. But the authors go on to consider the personal responsibility of the principal political and military leaders involved, and they agree with the earlier appraisals by Kirby and others that, while better leadership might have improved the situation, it probably would not have altered the eventual outcome. Murfett has contributed a recent perspective with "Living in the Past: A Critical Reexamination of the Singapore Naval Strategy, 1918–1941," and his article on recent research on the subject in *Neue Forschungen zum Zweiten Weltkrieg* will bring the reader up-to-date.

Scholars interested in the non-British perspective on Singapore's strategic role should consult Hamill, *The Strategic Illusion*, which argues that the failure of plans to safeguard the Antipodes does not give credence to earlier accusations that the defense of Australia and New Zealand was incoherent or nonexistent. Barclay explores U.S. views in "Singapore Strategy." Brailey studies the impact of the campaign on one of the indigenous peoples of Southeast Asia in *Thailand and the Fall of Singapore.*

Although participants' memoirs fall outside the purview of this chapter, two such accounts are worth mentioning. In *Singapore: Too Little, Too Late,* by Malaya Command's chief engineer Ivan Simson, the author acknowledges the difficulties imposed on the defense by the strategic situation but maintains that interservice rivalry was a major factor in the debacle. Masanobu Tsuji, chief of staff for Japan's victorious twenty-fifth Army, contributed his account to the literature in 1951, and an English translation appeared nine years later. Tsuji was notorious for both his hard-line political views and his wartime conduct (there is evidence that he supervised and personally committed some of the atrocities of the Bataan Death March, for instance), and readers must bear this in mind when studying his description of events. Nevertheless, a version of the campaign by a highly placed Japanese participant holds not a little interest and value.

There is yet another type of source for studying the Malayan campaign and other aspects of the war in Southeast Asia: prisoner of war (POW) accounts. The focus of these works naturally tends to be on the terrible ordeal of imprisonment and forced labor, but many also include descriptions of their actions before capture. Particularly noteworthy in this regard is Harrison's *The Brave Japanese*, which conveys his experiences as an antitank gunner in the defense of Malaya. What is remarkable about Harrison's recollections is that they are told without any bitterness and with genuine admiration for the fighting qualities of his captors. In *Out in the Midday Sun,* Caffrey amalgamated numerous POW accounts with carefully selected secondary works to produce a narrative of the campaign and the subsequent captivity.

A fascinating sidelight of the Singapore story is the issue of Japanese intelligence methods and effectiveness. Bridges wrote about the British response in "Britain and Japanese Espionage in Pre-War Malaya: The Shinozaki Case," while Allen's "Japanese Intelligence Systems" is a more general assessment of Japan's overall intelligence effort. Allen concluded that Allied beliefs about an extensive Japanese spy network and Japanese confessions of inferiority on the intelligence front are equally exaggerated. Fuller appreciation of this aspect of hostilities awaits further scholarship, especially detailed case studies of Japanese espionage, cryptanalysis, and the like.

Allied intelligence efforts in Southeast Asia, as distinct from the much-discussed success in general cryptanalysis and radio traffic analysis, have elicited some coverage in the journals. Trenowden tells the story of one of the British Special Operations Executive units in Malaya in *Operations Most Secret*, written in conjunction with the unit commander and without access to many classified documents, while De Graaff analyzes the slipshod Dutch attempts at espionage. Dommen and Dalley point out the occasional usurpation of policy-making prerogatives by U.S. intelligence agencies in the recent "The OSS in Laos," as had Spector in an earlier article. Spector also traced the initial and eventually neglected contacts with exiled Vietnamese nationalists in " 'What the Local Annamites Are Thinking.' "

The fighting in Burma has attracted attention as much for its policy implications as for the military operations, although combat narratives are not lacking. Volumes 2–5 of *The War against Japan* series, team-written under Kirby's direction, constitute the British official histories. The United States Army in World War II "green" series devoted three volumes by Romanus and Sunderland to the China–Burma–India theater. There are also four volumes on the Burma campaigns in Prasad's *Official History of the Indian Armed Forces in the Second World War (1939–1945)*.

Independent scholars have added several general histories of the various campaigns in Burma. Callahan offers a concise version of events in *Burma, 1942–1945*. He is effusive in his praise of General William Slim but contends that lack of clear political objectives robbed the Allies' military victory in Burma of much of its potential meaning. Smith provides a similarly brief, but sweeping, account in his *Battle for Burma*, in which he highlights the national differences and inconsistencies among the Allies and also makes special mention of Slim as the architect of victory. For an in-depth study, consult *Burma: The Longest War, 1942–45*, by Allen, doyen of scholars of World War II in Southeast Asia. His interpretation of the theater's ultimate significance is only slightly less skeptical than Callahan's. An excellent bibliography further enhances the book's value.

Monographs on individual battles and campaigns are surprisingly sparse. Carew provides the British perspective on the disastrous 1942 campaign in *The Longest Retreat*, still useful after a quarter century. Lunt has added some depth with journal articles on the campaign, particularly the insightful " 'A Hell of a Licking,' " and Dorn's *Walkout* captures the dramatic feel of General Joseph Stilwell's retreat from Burma, but it is from a participant's, rather than an analyst's, perspective. Monographs on the indecisive Arakan campaigns are scarce outside the official histories. For the defense of India against the 1944 Japanese invasion, one should consult *The Siege* by Campbell and *Kohima* by Swinson. Both are workmanlike narratives penned before 1970. Dating from the same era and also more descriptive than analytical is Evans and Brett-James' *Imphal.* Aside from the attention devoted to the activities of General Orde Wingate's Long Range Penetration Group, there are few works specifically devoted to the victorious Commonwealth campaigns in central Burma in 1944–1945. Allen traces the Japanese twenty-eighth Army's epic struggle to escape after the final Japanese collapse in Burma in *Sittang: The Last Battle.*

Chindit operations, by way of contrast, have generated a number of personal accounts and a few general histories. For instance, Fergusson related his experiences as commander of Number Five column in the 1943 Chindit expedition in *Beyond the Chindwin* and followed this with *The Wild Green Earth.* The best of the general histories is *The Chindit War,* in which Bidwell praises the élan and stoicism of the Chindits while decrying the differences in national strategic orientation that neutralized their accomplishments. In "The Chindits' Operations in Burma," Lewis also argued that, due to training and morale, the Chindits had performed very successfully as light infantry. The American version of the Long Range Penetration Group, the 5,307th Provisional Regiment, but better known as "Merrill's Marauders," had their story told in Ogburn's *The Marauders.* Ogburn expanded on his own experiences with the unit by interviewing other Marauders and consulting memoirs to produce a lively account.

But controversy still exists over the ultimate value and cost-effectiveness of the Chindit operations. Not surprisingly, Orde Wingate, the eccentric creator and first commander of the Long Range Penetration Group, also stands as a controversial figure. The official histories tend to question his personal stability and judgment. In the official biography, undertaken by Sykes in 1959, Wingate emerges as an enigmatic figure more concerned with concepts and principles than with fellow human beings. Sykes asserts that the Chindit adventures in 1944 garnered few direct military benefits but so unsettled the Japanese that they committed errors that presented the Allies with the chance for victory in central Burma. Mead and Bidwell resumed the debate in the pages of the *Journal of Contemporary History* in 1979–1980, with the former asserting that Wingate had far better strategic sense than the official histories allow, while Bidwell claimed that Wingate's strategic talents were good but not exceptional. Rooney and Royle have contributed to the controversy in the last few years, with the former defending Wingate in two separate monographs and portraying the Chindit conception as critical to Slim's eventual success, and the latter producing a copiously researched biography that is a model of objectivity.

The Indian National Army (INA) was another of the forces engaged in the battle for Burma, and it has also drawn special attention in the literature. One of the principals in the Japanese effort to recruit Indian prisoners for the INA, General Iwaichi Fujiwara, told his story in *F. Kikan*, which must naturally be read with some reservations. Roughton described the failed First Indian Army in "The Sangu River, 1943." In his study based on Indian sources, Ghosh concludes that the postwar courts-martial of INA leaders mark the real contribution of the group to Indian independence. Corr agreed that the Indian National Army accomplished in defeat what it had hoped to achieve through victory on the battlefield. Lebra's uneven, but useful, *Jungle Alliance* depicts the affair as the result of the intersection of conflicting political agendas pursued by dedicated Japanese and Indian patriots. Lebra followed this study with a broader examination of the phenomenon of Japanese harnessing of Asian nationalism in *Japanese-Trained Armies in Southeast Asia*, in which she notes a direct connection between the military training program and the political evolution of postwar Southeast Asia. Yoon echoes that interpretation in "Military Expediency" but avers that Japanese motives were self-serving all along.

One of the more intriguing aspects of the INA was the inclusion of an all-female combat unit, the Rani of Jhansi Regiment. Composed of about a thousand Indian, Thai, and Burmese women, the regiment produced many of the outstanding leaders of the new Indian nation. In a recent article, "Nationalism and Colonialism," Hills credits the Indian nationalist leader Subhas Chandra Bose's political skill, particularly his organizational talents and his ability to manipulate Indian mythology to create new images of female heroism, for the creation of the unit.

Bose was a critical figure in the organization and employment of the entire INA, and his biographers pay due tribute to his role in the war in Asia. Jog's flattering portrait in *In Freedom's Quest* ranks Bose with Mohandas Gandhi as a coarchitect of the new nation. Similarly favorable is the biography by journalist Hayashida, which depicts Bose as a Pan-Asianist and anticolonial martyr. Much more balanced and scholarly is Gordon's *Brothers against the Raj*, which concludes that Bose was a true nationalist who dealt with the fascist powers out of a sincere, if misguided, belief that such machinations were necessary for the liberation of India.

Discussion of figures such as Wingate and Bose underscores a fundamental aspect of the historical literature on the war in the China–Burma–India theater (CBI), namely, that often the most extensive treatment of operations and strategic thinking appears in biographies of those who commanded in the theater. Even biographical sketches, as found in Swinson's *Four Samurai*, contain some discussion of the relevant campaigns. In this case, Swinson's aim is to discuss the samurai ethic as translated into World War II conditions, and two of his four subjects, Renya Mutaguchi and Masaki Honda, fought in Burma, while a third, Tomoyuki Yamashita, directed the conquest of Malaya and Singapore.

But English-language sources naturally concentrate on Allied figures, and there are several whose biographies shed light on the campaigns in Burma. Viscount Wavell was the theater commander when war erupted, and he presided over the disastrous early campaigns in Malaysia and Singapore as well as in Burma. Lewin's compact *The Chief*, written in 1980, depicts Wavell as a noble, cerebral warrior whose unfortunate fate was to be the most competent individual available to command in some situations that promised defeat. Much more detailed is *Wavell: Supreme Commander*, the second of Connell's intended three-volume biography of the man, completed after his death. Told as much as possible with Wavell's own dispatches, the work offers a detailed overview of the fall of Singapore and the campaigns in Burma in 1942–1943, including a fine treatment of the 1943 Arakan offensive and the first Chindit adventure. Lord Louis Mountbatten, who served as theater commander from October 1943 until the war's end, is the subject of several biographies, although some focus more on his duties as the last viceroy of India than on his military career. Shortly after Mountbatten's death in 1979, Hough penned an informal look at the man's life, *Mountbatten*, but in 1985 Ziegler published the far more thorough and scholarly official biography. Ziegler's treatment of Mountbatten's stint as theater commander in Southeast Asia emphasizes the admiral's role in the Allies' formulation of grand strategy over descriptions of the military operations.

If there is any one common theme in the literature on the war in Southeast Asia, it is the universally high regard for the professional and personal qualities of General Sir William Slim, who suffered through the dark days of the retreat out of Burma but returned to conquer it at the helm of the fourteenth Army. Lewin's *Slim: The Standardbearer* supplies balanced and lucid accounts of all the viscount's campaigns and makes a convincing case for Slim as the person most responsible for the Allied victory in Burma. Equally complimentary toward his subject is Evans in *Slim as Military Commander*, based on official records and personal interviews. Both biographies provide superb maps, another reason that they stand as two very fine sources on the campaigns in Burma.

But ultimately, the war in Burma was about access to China. Anders' *The Ledo Road* concludes that constructing the overland link to China proved worthwhile despite growing Allied disenchantment with Chiang Kai-shek and Chinese military potential, because the capture of the Myitkina airfields, the employment of Chinese forces against the Japanese in Burma, and the pipelines that accompanied road construction all eased the pressure on the supply flights over the Himalayan "Hump." The challenges of the airlift itself are the focus of *The Hump,* a personal account by Thorne. However, while many histories and biographies of the war in CBI comment on the theater's various military transport operations, there exist as yet no in-depth studies of the cost-effectiveness and ultimate worth of the diverse routes to China.

China's value as a military ally, as opposed to the alternative methods of supporting Chiang's regime, was actually the subject of much wartime controversy, and that controversy swirled relentlessly around the figure of another of CBI's remarkable characters, General Joseph W. Stilwell. Victory over Japan did not end the debate. Romanus and Sunderland in *China–Burma–India* are supportive of Stilwell's position that an overland link to China was a sine qua non of meaningful Chinese participation in the war against Japan and that Stilwell's nemesis, Generalissimo Chiang Kai-shek, was more concerned with the postwar showdown with the Chinese communists than he was with defeating the Japanese. Tuchman's study defended Stilwell as an intelligent, experienced soldier forced into an untenable position by Roosevelt's unrealistic expectations for Chinese military success. This version is unfair to Roosevelt, who was neither as unsophisticated nor as superficial as Tuchman suggests, but otherwise it provides a convincing analysis of the failures of America's China policy. Shephard's 1989 article, based on much primary research, also depicts Roosevelt as vacillating. Liang's *General Stilwell in China* offers a Chinese interpretation, which holds that Stilwell's problems were nothing more than symptoms of the general American failure to understand the true nature of Chiang and his regime. Perhaps the best single-volume overview of the U.S. effort in China is Schaller's *The U.S. Crusade in China, 1938–1945.* Schaller is critical of American policymakers, from Roosevelt and Truman on down, for their failure to accept the reality of the hopelessness of supporting the Nationalist regime after 1942. This echoed Varg's conclusions in his *The Closing of the Door,* a more narrowly diplomatic history. Wakeman pointed out in a recent article that even before the war American naïveté was evident in U.S. assistance with police training, as there was no appreciation that Chiang's government might use the police for political purposes.

The debate over the U.S. role in the war in China does not end with the colorful Joseph Stilwell. General Claire Chennault, the American who helped build Chiang's air force and then rejoined the U.S. Army after Pearl Harbor, is scarcely less controversial, if not quite as central to U.S. policy in China. *Ding Hao,* by Cornelius and Short, is a comprehensive, but nonscholarly, history of the U.S. air campaigns in China that is highly complimentary of Chennault's tactical expertise and personal qualities. Byrd's well-researched and familiar biography depicts Chennault as an old-fashioned gentleman who persevered because of his loyalty to his personal code of conduct. In the evenhanded *The Maverick War*, Schultz presents Chennault's strategic misperceptions as well as his strengths as a commander.

Although the Soviet Union officially entered the war against Japan only in the closing weeks of World War II, friction between the two powers had been evident for years and had occasionally erupted into hostilities well before 1945. Coox details one of the first significant confrontations between the Soviets and the Imperial Japanese Army, which occurred at Changkufeng, Korea, in 1938, in *The Anatomy of a Small War*. Even more extensive was the fighting the following year at Nomonhan in Mongolia, which has generated some outstanding scholarship. Sella's "Khalkin-Gol: The Forgotten War" presents a brief overview, and Bellamy and Lahnstein discuss the Soviets' study of the battle in the 1980s. Drea has contributed an excellent monograph, *Nomonhan*, on the tactical aspects of the battle. Nyman looked at its political implications for the postwar domination in "Sinkiang, 1934–1943." But the work likely to remain the standard reference for years to come is Coox's two-volume *Nomonhan: Japan against Russia, 1939*. The author used numerous interviews and his impressive familiarity with Japanese sources to turn an examination of a battle into a profound analysis of the Kwantung Army and, through it, the Imperial Japanese Army, in all its strengths and weaknesses. Subsequently, Coox discussed Japanese army strategic thinking about the Soviet Union as well as the problems researchers of these topics face in two lectures published as *The Unfought War*. Garver has contributed an article on Chiang Kai-shek's efforts to induce the Soviet Union to enter the war against Japan sooner. For a refreshing perspective, one should consult the articles by Iur'ev ("China") and Vladimirov ("The USSR's Role") on the value of the Red Army's participation in the war on Japan. Equally strident in asserting the primacy of the Soviet Union's role in the defeat of Japan is "China's War of National Liberation" by Achkasov and Iur'ev.

Despite the low level of purely military activity in Indochina during World War II, there has been ample consideration of how the war affected the Vietnamese nationalist movement and the subsequent struggle for independence. In an essay for the anthology *Aspects of Vietnamese History*, Lam claimed that there was no connection between the Japanese occupation forces and the Vietnamese nationalists. But Smith disputed that conclusion, as did Nitz in the same journal a few years later. Nitze offered a look at the Japanese motivation behind the formal ousting of the French colonial administration in March 1945. In "The Vietnamese August Revolution," Khanh praises the political skills of the Viet Minh for converting the opportunities presented by the Japanese occupation into an ultimately successful independence movement, while Chieu attributes the successful transition, in part, to the brief period of empire (March–August 1945). The periodical literature has also supplied some studies of the French,

British, and American diplomatic responses to Japan's presence in Indochina.

The reader will have gleaned from the preceding that World War II in Burma and Southeast Asia was a diverse and multifaceted ordeal with consequences that are still emerging now, a half century after Japan's defeat. Historical scholarship reflects this depth and complexity, and yet only recently has it begun to explore all the dimensions of this little-known but endlessly fascinating sphere of World War II.

BIBLIOGRAPHY

Achkasov, V. I., and M. F. Iur'ev. "China's War of National Liberation and the Defeat of Imperialist Japan: The Soviet Role." *Soviet Studies in History* 24 (1985–1986): 39–68.

Allen, Louis. *Burma: The Longest War, 1941–45.* London: Guild, 1984.

———. *The End of the War in Asia.* London: Hart-Davis, MacGibbon, 1976.

———. "Japanese Intelligence Systems." *Journal of Contemporary History* 22 (1987): 547–562.

———. *Singapore, 1941–42.* Newark: University of Delaware, 1979.

———. *Sittang: The Last Battle.* New York: Ballantine, 1973.

Anders, Leslie. *The Ledo Road: General Joseph W. Stilwell's Highway to China.* Norman: University of Oklahoma, 1965.

Barber, Noel. *A Sinister Twilight: The Fall of Singapore, 1942.* Boston: Houghton Mifflin, 1968.

Barclay, Glen St. John. "Singapore Strategy: The Role of the United States in Imperial Defense." *Military Affairs* 39 (1975): 54–59.

Bellamy, Christopher, and Joseph S. Lahnstein. "The New Soviet Defensive Policy: Khalkhin Gol 1939 as Case Study." *Parameters* 20 (1990): 19–32.

Bidwell, Shelford. *The Chindit War: Stilwell, Wingate, and the Campaign in Burma, 1944.* New York: Macmillan, 1979.

———. "Wingate and the Official Historians: An Alternate View." *Journal of Contemporary History* 15 (1980): 245–256.

Bidwell, Shelford, and Peter Mead. "Orde Wingate—Two Views." *Journal of Contemporary History* 15 (1980): 401–404.

Brailey, Nigel J. *Thailand and the Fall of Singapore: A Frustrated Asian Revolution.* Boulder, CO, and London: Westview, 1986.

Bridges, Brian. "Britain and Japanese Espionage in Pre-War Malaya: The Shinozaki Case." *Journal of Contemporary History* 21 (1986): 23–35.

Byrd, Martha. *Chennault: Giving Wings to the Tiger.* Tuscaloosa: University of Alabama, 1987.

Caffrey, Kate. *Out in the Midday Sun: Singapore 1941–45—The End of an Empire.* New York: Stein and Day, 1973.

Callahan, Raymond. *Burma, 1942–1945.* London: Davis-Poynter, 1978.

———. *The Worst Disaster: The Fall of Singapore.* Newark: University of Delaware, 1977.

Campbell, Arthur. *The Siege: The Story from Kohima.* New York: Macmillan, 1956.

Carew, Tim. *The Longest Retreat: The Burma Campaign, 1942.* London: Hamish Hamilton, 1969.

Chieu, Vu Ngu. "The Other Side of the 1945 Vietnamese Revolution: The Empire of Viet-Nam (1945)." *The Journal of Asian Studies* 45 (1986): 293–328.

Connell, John. *Wavell: Supreme Commander, 1941–1943.* London: Collins, 1969.

Coox, Alvin D. *The Anatomy of a Small War: The Soviet–Japanese Struggle for Changkufeng-Khasan, 1938.* Westport, CT: Greenwood, 1977.

———. *Nomonhan: Japan against Russia, 1939.* 2 vols. Stanford, CA: Stanford University, 1985.

———. *The Unfought War: Japan 1941–1942.* San Diego: San Diego State UP, 1992.

Cornelius, Wanda, and Thayne Short. *Ding Hao: America's Air War in China, 1937–1945.* Gretna: Pelican, 1980.

Corr, Gerard H. *The War of the Springing Tigers.* London: Osprey, 1975.

De Graaf, Bob. "Hot Intelligence in the Tropics: Dutch Intelligence Operations in the Netherlands East Indies during the Second World War." *Journal of Contemporary History* 22 (1987): 563–584.

Dommen, Arthur J., and George W. Dalley. "The OSS in Laos: The 1945 Raven Mission and American Policy." *Journal of Southeast Asian Studies* 22 (1991): 327–346.

Dorn, Frank. *Walkout: With Stilwell in Burma.* New York: Crowell, 1971.

Drea, Edward J. "Missing Intentions: Japanese Intelligence and the Soviet Invasion of Manchuria, 1945." *Military Affairs* 48 (1984): 66–73.

———. *Nomonhan: Japanese–Soviet Tactical Combat, 1939.* Fort Leavenworth, KS: Combat Studies Institute, U.S. Army Command and General Staff College, 1981.

Evans, Geoffrey. *Slim as Military Commander.* London: B. T. Batsford, 1969.

Evans, Geoffrey, and Antony Brett-James. *Imphal: A Flower on Lofty Heights.* London: Macmillan, 1962.

Falk, Stanley L. *Seventy Days to Singapore: The Malayan Campaign, 1941–1942.* New York: G. P. Putnam's Sons, 1975.

Fergusson, Bernard. *Beyond the Chindwin.* London: Collins, 1945, 1962.

———. *The Wild Green Earth.* London: Collins, 1946.

Fujiwara, Iwaichi. *F. Kikan: Japanese Army Intelligence Operations in Southeast Asia during World War II.* Translated by Yoji Akashi. Hong Kong: Heinemann Asia, 1983.

Garver, John W. "Chiang Kai-shek's Quest for Soviet Entry into the Sino-Japanese War." *Political Science Quarterly* 102 (1987): 295–316.

Ghosh, Kalyan Kumar. *The Indian National Army: Second Front of the Indian National Movement.* Meerut: Meenakshi Prakashan, 1969.

Gordon, Leonard A. *Brothers against the Raj: A Biography of Indian Nationalists Sarat and Subhas Chandra Bose.* New York: Columbia UP, 1990.

Gwynn, Charles, and Herbert Richmond. "Singapore." *The Fortnightly* n.s. 903 (1942): 238–244.

Hamill, Ian. *The Strategic Illusion: The Singapore Strategy and the Defence of Australia and New Zealand, 1919–1942.* Singapore: Singapore UP, 1981.

Harrison, Kenneth. *The Brave Japanese.* Adelaide: Rigby, 1967.

Hayashida, Tatsuo. *Netaji Subhas Chandra Bose: His Great Struggle and Martyrdom.* Edited by Biswanath Chatterjee. Calcutta: Allied, 1970.

Hermon, Gill G. *Royal Australian Navy, 1939–42.* Australian Series 2 (Navy). Canberra: Australian War Memorial, 1957.

Hills, Carol. "Nationalism and Colonialism in Late Colonial India: Rani of Jhansi Regiment, 1943–1945." *Modern Asian Studies* 27 (1993): 741–760.

Holmes, Richard, and Anthony Kemp. *The Bitter End.* Chichester: Anthony Bird, 1982.

Hough, Richard. *Mountbatten: Hero of Our Time.* London: Weidenfeld and Nicolson, 1980.

Iur'ev, M. "China: The Year 1945." *Far Eastern Affairs* (1986): 127–139.

Jog, N. G. *In Freedom's Quest: A Biography of Netaji Subhas Chandra Bose.* New Delhi: Orient Longmans, 1969.

Khanh, Huynh Kim. "The Vietnamese August Revolution." *Journal of Asian Studies* 30 (1971): 761–781.

Kirby, S. Woodburn. *The Loss of Singapore.* London: HMSO, 1957.

———. *Singapore: The Chain of Disaster.* New York: Macmillan, 1971.

———. *The War against Japan.* Vols. 1–5. London: HMSO: 1957–1969.

La Forte, Robert S., and Ronald E. Marcello. *Building the Death Railway: The Ordeal of American POWs in Burma, 1942–1945.* Wilmington, DE: Scholarly Resources, 1993.

Lam, Truong Buu. "Japan and the Disruption of the Vietnamese Nationalist Movement." In Walter F. Vella, ed., *Aspects of Vietnamese History,* 237–269. Honolulu: University of Hawaii, 1973.

Leasor, James. *Singapore: The Battle that Changed the World.* London: Hodder and Stoughton, 1968.

Lebra, Joyce C. *Japanese-Trained Armies in Southeast Asia.* New York: Columbia UP, 1977.

———. *Jungle Alliance: Japan and the Indian National Army.* Singapore: Asia Pacific, 1971.

Lewin, Ronald. *The Chief: Field Marshal Lord Wavell, Commander-in-Chief and Viceroy, 1939–1947.* London and Melbourne: Hutchinson, 1980.

———. *Slim: The Standardbearer.* London: Leo Cooper, 1976.

Lewis, Robert D. "The Chindits' Operations in Burma." *Military Review* 6 (1988): 34–43.

Liang, Chin-tung. *General Stilwell in China, 1942–1944: The Full Story.* New York: St. John's UP, 1972.

Lunt, James D. " 'A Hell of a Licking': Some Reflections on the Retreat from Burma, December 1941–May 1942." *Journal of the Royal United Services Institute for Defence Studies* 130 (1985): 55–58.

McIntyre, W. David. *The Rise and Fall of the Singapore Naval Base, 1919–1942.* London: Macmillan, 1979; Hamden, CT: Archon, 1979.

Mead, Peter. "Orde Wingate and the Official Historians." *Journal of Contemporary History* 14 (1979): 55–82.

Morley, James, ed. *The Fateful Choice: Japan's Advance into Southeast Asia, 1939–1941.* New York: Columbia UP, 1980.

Murfett, Malcolm H. "Living in the Past: A Critical Reexamination of the Singapore Naval Strategy, 1918–1941." *War and Society* 11 (1993): 73–103.

———. "New Research on the Second World War in Singapore." In Jürgen Rohwer and Hildegard Muller, eds., *Neue Forschungen zum Zweiten Weltkrieg*, 427–432. Koblenz: Bernard and Graefe 1990.

Neidpath, James. *The Singapore Naval Base and the Defence of Britain's Eastern Empire, 1919–1941.* Oxford: Oxford UP, 1981.

Nitz, Kiyoko Kurusu. "Independence without Nationalists? The Japanese and Vietnamese Nationalism during the Japanese Period, 1940–1945." *Journal of Southeast Asian Studies* 15 (1984): 108–133.

Nitze, Paul. "Japanese Military Policy towards French Indochina during the Second World War: The Road to the Meigo Sakusen (9 March 1945)." *Journal of Southeast Asian Studies* 14 (1983): 328–353.

Nyman, Lars-Erik. "Sinkiang 1934–1943: Dark Decade for a Pivotal Puppet." *Cahiers du Monde Russe et Sovietique* 32 (1991): 97–105.

Ogburn, Charles. *The Marauders.* New York: Harper, 1959.

Prasad, B., ed. *Official History of the Indian Armed Forces in the Second World War (1939–1945).* Delhi: Orient Longmans, 1954–.

Romanus, C. F., and Richard Sunderland. *China–Burma–India Theater.* 3 vols. *United States Army in World War II* Series. Washington, DC: GPO, 1953–1959.

Rooney, David. *Burma Victory: Imphal, Kohima and the Chindit Issue.* London, New York: Arms and Armour, 1992.

———. *Wingate and the Chindits: Redressing the Balance.* London: Arms and Armour, 1994.

Roughton, J. "The Sangu River, 1943." *Army Quarterly and Defence Journal* 114 (1984): 436–442.

Royle, Trevor. *Orde Wingate: Irregular Soldier.* London: Weidenfeld and Nicolson, 1995.

Schaller, Michael. *The U.S. Crusade in China, 1938–1945.* New York: Columbia UP, 1979.

Schultz, Duane. *The Maverick War: Chennault and the Flying Tigers.* New York: St. Martin's, 1987.

Sella, Amnon. "Khalkhin-Gol: The Forgotten War." *Journal of Contemporary History* 18 (1983): 651–687.

Shephard, John E., Jr. "Warriors and Politics: The Bitter Lesson of Stilwell in China." *Parameters* 19 (1989): 61–75.

Simson, Ivan. *Singapore: Too Little, Too Late; Some Aspects of the Malayan Disaster in 1942.* London: Leo Cooper, 1970.

Smith, E. D. *Battle for Burma.* London: B. T. Batsford, 1979.

Smith, Ralph. "The Japanese Period in Indochina and the Coup of 9 March 1945." *Journal of Southeast Asian Studies* 9 (1978): 268–301.

Spector, Ronald. "Allied Intelligence and Indochina, 1943–1945." *Pacific Historical Review* 51 (1982): 23–50.

———. " 'What the Local Annamites Are Thinking': American Views of Vietnamese in China, 1942–1945." *Southeast Asia: An International Quarterly* 3 (1974): 741–751.

Swinson, Arthur. *Defeat in Malaya: The Fall of Singapore.* New York: Ballantine, 1970.

———. *Four Samurai: A Quartet of Japanese Army Commanders in the Second World War.* London: Hutchinson, 1968.

———. *Kohima.* London: Cassell, 1966.

Sykes, Christopher. *Orde Wingate.* London: Collins, 1959.

Tarling, Nicholas. "The British and the First Japanese Move into Indo-China." *Journal of Southeast Asian Studies* 21 (1990): 35–65.

Thorne, Bliss K. *The Hump: The Great Military Airlift of World War II.* Philadelphia and New York: Lippincott, 1965.

Trenowden, Ian. *Operations Most Secret: SOE, the Malayan Theatre.* London: William Kimber, 1978.

Tsuji, Masanobu. *Singapore: The Japanese Version.* London: Constable, 1960.

Tuchman, Barbara. *Stilwell and the American Experience in China, 1911–1945.* New York: Macmillan, 1970.

Varg, Paul A. *The Closing of the Door: Sino-American Relations, 1936–1946.* East Lansing: Michigan State UP, 1973.

Vladimirov, O. "The USSR's Role in the Creation of the Bridgehead of China's Revolutionary Forces in Manchuria." *Far Eastern Affairs* (1986): 16–25.

Wakeman, Frederic, Jr. "American Police Advisers and the Nationalist Chinese Secret Service, 1930–1937." *Modern China* 18 (1992): 107–137.

Wigmore, Lionel. *The Japanese Thrust.* Australia in the War of 1939–1945, Series 1 (Army). Canberra: Australian War Memorial, 1957.

Yoon, Won Z. "Military Expediency: A Determining Factor in the Japanese Policy regarding Burmese Independence." *Journal of Southeast Asia Studies* 9 (1978): 248–267.

Ziegler, Philip. *Mountbatten: The Official Biography.* London: Collins, 1985.

7 The Air War against Japan and the End of the War in the Pacific

Conrad C. Crane

Of all the areas of research and writing concerning World War II, none are filled with more contention and controversy than the end of the war in the Pacific. This was clearly demonstrated during the intense debate over the content of the Smithsonian's 1995 *Enola Gay* exhibit commemorating the fiftieth anniversary of the dropping of the atomic bomb on Hiroshima. As we move further away from the atmosphere of 1945, the actions taken by the Allied powers to force Japanese surrender appear more extreme, and the victors are more easily portrayed as villains by the vanquished or questioned by a newer generation about the motivations leading to the obliteration of enemy cities.

The air war against Japan marked the culmination of the slide to total war that characterized World War II, but the literature on the aerial campaigns in the Pacific is not as extensive as that concerning the European theater. The standard comprehensive operational summary remains the official history, Craven and Cate's *The Army Air Forces in World War II*, primarily volumes 4 and 5. Another useful, official source is *The United States Strategic Bombing Survey*, a comprehensive, immediate postwar study of the effects of airpower on Germany and Japan by specially selected military and civilian experts. The tone of each separate report tends to reflect the individual biases of different authors, and the claims trumpeted in the summary volumes (written by those most committed to the decisiveness of airpower) are not always matched by the individual reports describing actual targets, but the analysis of bombing results is very detailed. MacIsaac's somewhat biased study of the survey can provide a reader more background on its conduct, and Gentile's "Advocacy or Assessment" covers the biases and contradictions inherent in its reports.

An invaluable official source that really gives a reader an authentic feel for combat and has terrific pictures is the Historical Times eight-volume reprint of *Impact: The Army Air Forces "Confidential" Picture History of World War II*. These magazines were published by the AAF (Army Air Force) intelligence bureau to keep units in the field updated on enemy tactics and friendly actions, and they provide the best pictorial record of the air war a reader can find. Coverage is also very comprehensive, with articles on every obscure area of operations. Useful, official Allied views of the Pacific air war can be gleaned from Odgers' *Air War* and Gillison's *Royal Australian Air Force*, as well as from Ross' *Royal New Zealand Air Force*.

Beginning in 1941, U.S. air operations were spread all over the Pacific theater. The early days of American involvement are best covered in Caidin's *The Ragged, Rugged Warriors*. Robert Scott's *God Is My Co-Pilot* and Claire Chennault's *Way of a Fighter* are memoirs that provide insight into the famous Flying Tigers and operations in China, and Saburo Sakai's *Samurai!* furnishes a firsthand recollection from the premier surviving Japanese ace. Another source on Japanese air operations is *Zero!* by Okumiya and Horikoshi. Glines' *Doolittle's Tokyo Raiders* is the best account of the daring 1942 raid in which the AAF first bombed the Japanese homeland, and that coverage should be supplemented with Jimmy Doolittle's autobiography and Ted Lawson's *Thirty Seconds over Tokyo*. In *Attack on Yamamoto*, Glines has also written about the controversial mission to shoot down the plane carrying that important Japanese leader. For books describing General George Kenney's Fifth Air Force and its support of General Douglas MacArthur's drive in the Southwest Pacific, readers should refer to Birdsall's *Flying Buccaneers* and Kenney's own memoirs. He was an outstanding and resourceful commander who, like his air force, usually gets unjustly overshadowed by more glamorous leaders or campaigns. Sunflower University Press has done a series of aviation books relying heavily on firsthand accounts of the varied facets of the Pacific air war. Among the best examples are Yoshino's *Lightning Strikes* on the 475th Fighter Group of the Fifth Air Force and Kissick's *Guerrilla One* covering the seventy-fourth Fighter Squadron of Chennault's Fourteenth Air Force. Naval air operations are covered in Morison's multivolume *History of United States Naval Operations*, and highlights of marine actions are described in Mersky's official *Time of the Aces*.

The most important and most controversial air operations against Japan were conducted by B-29s of the Twentieth Air Force, operating from China and the Marianas Islands. The greatest gap in the historical literature of the Pacific air war involves good memoirs of the common airmen in this campaign. Though there are some published collections of observations or quotes, only Morrison in *Hellbirds* and Herbert in *Maximum Effort* have really provided extensive accounts of their personal experiences. Morrison has also written a one-volume history of twentieth Air Force operations entitled *Point of No Return*, as has Kerr in *Flames over Tokyo*. Kerr focuses more on the development of incendiary weapons and their application in the great fire raids that devastated Japan's cities. The deadliest air attack of the war was the 9–10 March night bombing that burned out sixteen square miles of Tokyo and killed between 90,000 and 100,000 people. Caidin's *Torch to the Enemy* and Cortesi's *Target: Tokyo* give popular accounts that convey the horrors and effectiveness of that mission, while Edoin has covered it from the Japanese side in *The Night Tokyo Burned.* Werrell's *Blankets of Fire* is the best one-volume history of the development of the B-29 and its role in World War II.

The incendiary campaign was conceived and executed by the most innovative tactical and operational air commander of World War II and the AAF's supreme problem solver, General Curtis LeMay. He discusses his decision process and actions in his revealing memoir written with Kantor, *Mission with LeMay.* Coffey's fine biography, *Iron Eagle,* is a must-read for anyone trying to understand this complex and gifted leader who did so much to shape the modern U.S. Air Force, as well as to bring Japan to its knees. He argued that his B-29s alone could bring surrender without invasion or the atomic bomb by 1 October 1945, since by then he would have destroyed every Japanese city. (A similar argument was advanced by the *Strategic Bombing Survey.*) General Haywood Hansell, LeMay's predecessor, who was relieved because of the ineffectiveness of his precision bombing of Japan, has done a provocative analysis of their actions and possible alternative air strategies in *Strategic Air War against Japan.* Hansell argues that an attack of the Japanese power system would have been more efficient than the fire raids with fewer civilian casualties, though he realizes that such a precision campaign would have probably taken longer to be effective, and "time pressures" on LeMay might have mitigated against such a course of action. Hansell also thinks the B-29s could have caused an enemy collapse eventually without the atomic bomb but believes that its use was essential to convince both the Japanese to surrender and the U.S. Army that it did not need to invade.

Hansell hints and LeMay scoffs at concerns about the morality of the high civilian casualties caused by the incendiary campaign, which set an important precedent for the eventual use of the atomic bomb. Ethical issues of American bombing are discussed in great detail by three recent books. Sherry in his broad study, *The Rise of American Air Power,* sees the air war against Japan as the culmination of American "technological fanaticism," organizational and professional drives built on faith in technology to overcome any difficulty and win the war. Schaffer looks at more operational details than Sherry in *Wings of Judgment* but is also very critical of the morality of AAF bombing. Schaffer blames groupthink and vague definitions of "military necessity" for the slide to total war and does a detailed analysis of varying American perceptions about targeting for aerial bombardment.

Crane gives the most sympathetic treatment to the AAF in *Bombs, Cities, and Civilians.* He argues that U.S. airmen were committed to precision bombing and generally did the best they could with the technology and conditions of World War II to limit civilian casualties. The strategic bombing of Japan was an exception, however, though Crane blames special conditions in the theater and LeMay's unique personality for the evolution of B-29 operations, rather than more impersonal forces. While Kerr claims that the fire raids were motivated by ordnance experts, and Sherry and Schaffer blame leaders in Washington and vagaries in bombing doctrine, Crane argues that the incendiary campaign was the product of LeMay's operations analysts and his own penchant for problem solving. Since precision bombing would not work because of problems with technology and weather, the twentieth Air Force could destroy Japanese industry by burning down the urban areas around the factories. The objectives of the campaign were later expanded to exploit civilian terror and dislocation, and the B-29s eventually burned out 180 square miles in sixty-seven cities. For Crane, the leap from precision bombing to the fire raids was more critical in the slide to total war than the resort to the atomic bomb. It was farther from Schweinfurt to Tokyo than from Tokyo to Hiroshima, both literally and figuratively.

More people died in the fire raids than from the atomic bombs, but the terrible devastation and horrible casualties described so vividly in Hersey's *Hiroshima* have commanded much more attention. The best source concerning the Manhattan project, which produced the new weapons, is Rhodes' Pulitzer Prize-winning *The Making of the Atomic Bomb.* General Leslie Groves' memoir of the program he headed, *Now It Can Be Told: The Story of the Manhattan Project,* is also very useful. *Enola Gay* by Thomas and Witts, focusing on the 509th Composite Group that dropped both "Little Boy" and "Fat Man," describes the training and preparations that led to Hiroshima and the men who performed the mission. Contrary to the stories that have surfaced over the years, no members of the crews of the planes who dropped either bomb have suffered nervous breakdowns or come out against their use. (Thomas and Witts explain that an alcoholic pilot of a weather plane later did blame his problems on the bomb.) The airmen's sentiments are best expressed by the comment a crewman on the Nagasaki raid penned in his journal, "Those poor Japs, but they asked for it." While they felt compassion for their victims, they also were and remain morally confident that their actions were justified.

That position is not acceptable for critics of the Hiroshima and Nagasaki missions, troubled by what we now know in hindsight about the terrible suffering and death that resulted. The most intense controversy about the end of the war in the Pacific revolves around the question of whether or not the B-29s needed to cap the air war against Japan by dropping the atomic bombs in order to bring surrender. Some historians question the real motivations for using nuclear weapons, whether or not other approaches might have brought an early surrender, and why President Harry Truman did not pursue these so-called alternatives.

This spirited debate over the morality and utility of these weapons is a relatively recent phenomenon. In a *Fortune* magazine poll taken in December 1945, fewer than 5 percent of those queried thought the bombs should not have been dropped. Anyone who wants to study or research the decision to use the atomic bomb should start by getting a feel for the atmosphere of the Pacific War in 1945, especially the increasing carnage of ground combat as American forces approached Japan. Feifer's *Tennozan: The Battle of Okinawa and the Atomic Bomb* is a graphic description of a campaign that claimed 30,000 American, 110,000 Japanese, and 150,000 Okinawan lives. This heightened the fears, which Feifer thinks were bona fide, of leaders all the way up to Truman of even higher casualties in any invasion of the home islands and inspired the sentiments in servicemen so eloquently expressed in Fussell's *Thank God for the Atomic Bomb*. These emotions were shared by Allies in the theater, as revealed by Harper in *Miracle of Deliverance: The Case for the Bombing of Hiroshima and Nagasaki*. He was a British soldier slated for Operation ZIPPER, the British invasion scheduled for September 1945 to retake Malaya. Lord Mountbatten insisted that it be conducted as planned even after the surrender, and despite no enemy resistance the landings turned into a muddy debacle. In addition to the heavy casualties a contested ZIPPER would have produced, Harper also emphasizes the thousands of Allied POWs who would have been massacred or starved to death if the war had not ended so abruptly and early. Home-front attitudes as V-J Day approached are covered by Chappell in *Before the Bomb*, especially the combination of belligerence and war weariness that sometimes produced confused and contradictory inclinations.

The plans of each side concerning the invasions of Kyushu and Honshu are covered in great detail in Skates' *The Invasion of Japan: Alternative to the Bomb*. He believes that American firepower would have kept U.S. casualties relatively low for the invasion of Kyushu and eventually made the second phase landings on Honshu unnecessary. Allen and Polmar have looked at the same information in *Code-Name Downfall* and come to the opposite conclusion, arguing that the excuse of the atomic bomb gave the emperor a way to avoid the decisive battle desired by his military leaders that would have cost both sides hundreds of thousands of casualties.

Brower's dissertation, "The Joint Chiefs of Staff," which is being crafted into a book, provides the best coverage of the deliberations of the American Joint Chiefs of Staff (JCS) concerning the conflicting options of assault or siege to defeat Japan.

Haunted by fears of war weariness at home and the specter of intensifying enemy resistance, the Navy and Army Air Forces supported a sea blockade and aerial bombardment, while the army insisted that only an invasion would accomplish military and political goals in a timely manner. In the end the JCS pursued these objectives and more. As Brower concludes:

> The JCS understood that Japan's defeat would result from the increasing application of military, psychological and political pressures upon the island nation. Their strategy clearly reflected that understanding. The JCS gradually tightened the blockade, bombed Japan relentlessly with conventional and atomic weapons, contributed to efforts to induce an early Japanese capitulation through a clarification of the unconditional surrender formula, and strongly urged two presidents to secure early Soviet entry into the war. (296)

For Brower, it took the whole series of shocks to finally bring Japanese surrender; B-29 operations and the atomic bomb, diplomatic pressure, the inexorable island-hopping advance toward Japan, Russian entry, and the naval air and submarine campaign strangling the home islands are described in more detail in Morison's volumes and Blair's *Silent Victory*.

The best description of actual conditions in Japan under the strains of this sophisticated strategy is Havens' *Valley of Darkness*. He agrees with Allen and Polmar that civilians and soldiers alike would have resisted right to the very end, primarily because of "a basic fear of what would happen if people stopped" (191). Though the public was exhausted, it did not choose peace, and Havens speculates that Operations OLYMPIC and CORONET could have been "the bloodiest invasion by sea in history" (188).

The theme of avoiding such a result and saving lives by ending the war speedily with the help of the atomic bombs dominates official explanations about the decision to use them. There were some critics of the U.S. action soon after the war; radical Macdonald in "The Bomb" attacked the use of the bomb on moral grounds and expressed fear about the power of the nation-state to use it, while some others suggested that the bombs might have been directed at the Russians as much as the Japanese. Though such opinions were rare, many of the key leaders involved in the decision crafted essays in its defense.

The most effective response was Secretary of War Henry Stimson's "The Decision to Use the Atomic Bomb," which he wrote with the help of key subordinates and published in *Harper's* in 1947. He argued that policymakers dropped the bomb after careful consideration because it was a legitimate weapon that held some hope of shortening the war and saving American lives. There were no sure alternatives available to bring Japanese surrender as quickly and maybe end the war in 1945. In his memoirs Stimson expanded on his arguments and emphasized that "the least abhorrent choice" (633) of many unpleasant alternatives was to drop the

bomb and hopefully avoid a bloody invasion. Always troubled by the civilian casualties from air attacks, Stimson also saw an additional benefit of
Hiroshima and Nagasaki: the Japanese surrender stopped the fire raids.

President Truman justified the use of the bomb on what he defined as
military targets in his *Memoirs* by claiming that General George Marshall
had advised him that "it might cost half a million American lives to force
the enemy's surrender on his home grounds" (417). The source and reliability of this figure have caused considerable controversy, and Miles
("Hiroshima") and Bernstein ("The Dropping of the A-Bomb" and
"Seizing the Contested Terrain") have argued that Truman never received any casualty estimates that high from his military advisers, though
Giangreco's "Casualty Projections" reveals that planners' predictions covered quite a wide range.

Many critics cite a June Joint War Plans Committee report that estimated casualties of 40,000 dead with 193,500 total and claim that this
somehow lessens the justification for the use of the bomb. As Maddox
pointed out in "The Biggest Decision," the idea that saving a million
casualties justifies the use of the bomb but that 200,000 does not is "bi-
zarre." Allen and Polmar have a fine discussion in *Code-Name Downfall* of
the fluctuations in invasion casualty estimates in the summer of 1945.

While Douglas MacArthur appears to have lowered his predictions to
the president to soothe Truman's fears about the general's leadership in
Operation DOWNFALL, members of the Joint Chiefs of Staff feared losses
might be unacceptably high, and MacArthur's own medical planners were
preparing for 395,000 army casualties alone in the first 120 days of combat. In a memorandum pleading for a negotiated end to the war that
circulated past Truman, Herbert Hoover actually did use the figure of a
million casualties that could be saved. Bernstein has done considerable
research into the writing of both Stimson's and Truman's memoirs. While
he gives Stimson credit for seizing the "moral high ground" for future
debates about the bomb, he also speculates that Truman's ardent attempts
to justify his actions demonstrate some ambivalence and sense of guilt
about Hiroshima and Nagasaki.

Bernstein is the most thorough and objective of all the revisionists who
have come to reexamine the atomic bomb decision, and his edited collection, *The Atomic Bomb: The Critical Issues*, provides readers with a sampling of all the major schools of thought that had appeared by the
mid-1970s. Another source for those trying to get a handle on the extensive literature is Walker's historiographical essay "The Decision to Use the
Bomb," which generally takes up where Bernstein ended. They both agree
that the first real scholarly effort to use primary sources and provide a
definitive evaluation of the subject was provided by Herbert Feis in 1961
in *Japan Subdued*. While he concurred with the argument that the bomb
was dropped to end the war and save lives, Feis agreed with the *Strategic*

Bombing Survey that LeMay could have ended the war with conventional bombing by the close of 1945. While he believed the bomb's use was not essential, it was justified by the desire to win the war as quickly as possible. Some other noteworthy contributions to atomic bomb scholarship of the early 1960s include Batchelder's *The Irreversible Decision, 1939–1950*, a moral-ethical response to Hiroshima, and Giovannitti and Freed's *The Decision to Drop the Bomb*, a book that grew out of an NBC television documentary with some particularly good quotes and firsthand accounts from participants on both sides.

Feis did imply in one paragraph that decision makers might have perceived that an added benefit of the bomb would be to impress and restrain the Russians, but it took the release in 1965 of Alperovitz's *Atomic Diplomacy: Hiroshima and Potsdam*, one of the most influential books of Cold War revisionism, to really give that argument some credibility. He went much further than Feis, arguing that the atomic bombs were used for political reasons, not military ones. Alperovitz agreed with Feis that Japan was already defeated but argued that policymakers were not willing to pursue any alternative approaches to surrender, including a negotiated settlement, because they wanted to use the bomb to intimidate the Soviets and secure a better peace with fewer concessions to communism. This was done by Harry Truman, under the influence of Secretary of State James Byrnes, in an effort to reverse Franklin Roosevelt's more conciliatory policies toward Russia. The bomb was intended to start the Cold War, not to end World War II.

Alperovitz's book was very much a product of the revisionist atmosphere of Vietnam and the 1960s, and while his arguments were embraced by many eager to question official explanations and policies, scholars from both right and left attacked his position for, among other problems, his questionable use of evidence. Alperovitz has since published two updates of his work, including *The Decision to Use the Atomic Bomb*. While his scholarship has improved, his main arguments have not changed, and the number of his supporters has declined. His position still must be dealt with by anyone writing on this issue, however.

The best exposition of the strengths and flaws in Alperovitz's arguments is in a spirited exchange between himself, Bernstein, and Messer in *International Security*. As Bernstein sums up in *The Atomic Bomb*,

Whether anti-Soviet purposes constituted the *primary* reason for using the bomb (as Alperovitz's book also argues), or a *secondary but necessary* reason (as some others think), or a *confirming but not essential* reason (as I contend) is the general range of the ongoing dispute about why the bombs were used. (219)

He should have added that some scholars also still support the official position, giving even less credence to any political motivation. For instance, McCullough in his Pulitzer-Prize winning biography *Truman* emphasizes that the president relied mainly on General Marshall and Secretary Stimson for advice on such matters, not Secretary Byrnes, and the decision was, indeed, based on military factors. Truman dropped what he saw as a "terrible" weapon to save American lives, to avoid a repeat of the bloody ground combat he knew from World War I on Kyushu or Honshu.

Revisionists agree with Alperovitz that there were other viable alternatives to the use of the bomb, and the question then becomes why they were not pursued. The official position is that no one was looking for ways to avoid using the bomb, but, instead, everyone was trying to avoid an invasion. Both Bernstein and Sherwin have proposed that modifying the terms of unconditional surrender might have made the bombing of Hiroshima unnecessary. In *A World Destroyed*, Sherwin agrees that military factors dominated the decision to use the bomb, though diplomatic leverage did give it political advantages. He also argues that the bombing of Nagasaki was indefensible, since inadequate time was allowed for the impact of the first bomb to take effect on Japanese decision makers.

Since the publication of his book, Sherwin has become even more adamant that if unconditional surrender terms could have been modified to guarantee the status of the emperor, the war could have ended even sooner, but concerns about domestic politics as well as a desire for diplomatic leverage prevented Truman from considering such an option. Bernstein has pursued similar themes, though he is more understanding of the perceptions and constraints policymakers faced.

Unlike Alperovitz, Bernstein has been willing to reshape his arguments based on new evidence. In "Understanding the Atomic Bomb" he examined the alternatives available to using the bomb—a demonstration in an isolated location, a modification of surrender demands, an exploration of Japanese peace feelers, waiting for Soviet entry into the war, and allowing LeMay to continue his campaign—and concluded that none by itself seemed likely to end the war quickly, either in the opinion of leaders in 1945 or in hindsight today. He speculates that perhaps a combination of alternative approaches, such as the JCS was trying, might have been successful without the bomb but admits that while such a result seems likely, it is "far from definite." Bernstein has forged a middle ground between the more radical revisionist and traditional schools, arguing that the bomb's use was unethical and had some perceived peripheral benefit in intimidating the Russians but that it was considered a legitimate weapon in 1945 with a primary purpose to help end the war and avoid a costly invasion.

The release of much new material in the last decade or so has helped keep the debate over the use of the bomb fresh and lively. Truman's papers and letters have been interpreted in a number of ways, but they have provided new perspectives on his decision. McGeorge Bundy, who helped Stimson write his memoirs, has produced his own, *Danger and Survival.* While lamenting the fact that the administration did not pursue alternative options more seriously, he denies that the impact on the Soviet Union had any real bearing on the use of the bomb. One of Bundy's more interesting suggestions is that the United States should have invited neutral observers to the atomic test explosion in New Mexico, who then could have conveyed a convincing warning to the Japanese.

Most useful of recent revelations has been the release of ULTRA and MAGIC intercepts. Though revisionists have seized upon individual messages to show that American leaders should have known that Japan was on the verge of defeat and looking for a face-saving way to surrender, the total picture available was much more ambiguous. In *Marching Orders*, Lee covers the daily intelligence summaries and shows that whenever a Japanese diplomat considered alternatives to fighting on, military leaders adamantly resisted. As Drea writes in *MacArthur's ULTRA*, "As far as Allied military intelligence was concerned, the Japanese civil authorities might be considering peace, but Japan's military leaders, who American decision makers believed had total control of the nation, were preparing for war to the knife" (214).

Descriptions of the process leading to Japanese surrender support this view. Butow wrote *Japan's Decision to Surrender* in 1954, but it remains the standard work. He gives much credit to the atomic bomb for creating conditions that allowed the emperor to intercede successfully for surrender. Craig's *The Fall of Japan* and Toland's *The Rising Sun* also provide graphic descriptions of the tortuous Japanese path to capitulation and how close it came to being detoured at the last minute. The Pacific War Research Society's *Japan's Longest Day* is another valuable source, especially for its interviews. The respected historian Iriye is especially critical in *Power and Culture* of the Japanese government's decision to send peace feelers to the Soviet Union. He argues that this failure to deal directly with the United States needlessly prolonged the war.

The most original recent treatment of war termination in the Pacific is *Fighting to a Finish* by Sigal. A political scientist, Sigal looks at the end of the war through the lens of bureaucratic politics, and while his research is not as extensive as in most of the books by historians, he does have some provocative arguments. For Sigal, American and Japanese actions were less a result of rational calculation than of domestic politics and organizational processes. He contends that the lesson for modern war termination is that leaders must make careful political preparations at home before they can secure desired peace abroad.

While revisionists have tended to dominate writings about the atomic bomb over the last thirty years, some recent literature aims to reverse that trend, usually inspired by the perceived revisionism of the Smithsonian

Enola Gay exhibit. The most original is Newman's *Truman and the Hiroshima Cult.* Not only does he support the traditional position and argue for the necessity and morality of dropping the bomb on Japan, but he also claims that attacking the United States for using the atomic bomb has become a secular "cult of atonement" where the guilt for later sins by the U.S. government and its agencies, such as Vietnam, is heaped upon Hiroshima. Newman is also disturbed by portrayals of the Japanese that emphasize their image as innocent victims of a terrible weapon and discourage discussion of their own wartime brutality and transgressions.

In "Why America Dropped the Bomb" Kagan has done a very incisive job summarizing and countering the main revisionist arguments, and Maddox's *Weapons for Victory: The Hiroshima Decision Fifty Years Later* pursues the same themes, returning to the arguments of the official explanation emphasizing the military necessity for using the bomb. As Kagan answers those who decry America's failure to confront its "moral failings" about Hiroshima,

An honest examination of the evidence reveals that their leaders, in the tragic predicament common to all who have engaged in wars that reach the point where every choice is repugnant, chose the least bad course. Americans may look back on that decision with sadness, but without shame. (23)

The atomic bomb was not the only secret project designed to shorten the war in the Pacific theater. *Bat Bomb* by Couffer is an informative and sometimes hilarious, firsthand account of a project to have Mexican free-tailed bats burn down Japanese cities with small incendiary bombs. Project X-RAY actually showed some promise before it was terminated in early 1944 in favor of the Manhattan project. Like Rhodes' book on the atomic bomb, this one also reveals a lot about how scientific research and development are conducted in wartime. More sobering is *Unit 731* by Williams and Wallace. They describe Japanese programs in China to develop chemical and biological weapons, which often involved experiments on Chinese victims. The war ended before a plan could be attempted to deliver biological agents to the United States in balloons released into prevailing winds. Mikesh's *Japan's World War II Balloon Bomb Attacks* explains how hundreds of paper balloon bombs were launched with conventional explosives, however, and Webber describes how Japanese submarines also launched seaplanes to drop incendiaries on forests in the American Northwest. Allen and Polmar have a fine description in their book of the extreme means on both sides that might have been used if the war had continued, and Crane covers American plans to use gas and destroy the Japanese rice crop. In doing research on early ideas for the tactical use of nuclear weapons, Bernstein found that Marshall had even considered using nine atomic bombs to support landings in Kyushu. No one can dispute that the war would have, indeed, become even more terrible if it had continued. This was very evident to people on both sides who were alive in 1945. Historians today, however, will continue to debate whether the war could have been ended differently than with the nuclear destruction of Hiroshima and Nagasaki and the shadow those mushroom clouds cast over the future.

BIBLIOGRAPHY

Allen, Thomas B., and Norman Polmar. *Code-Name Downfall: The Secret Plan to Invade Japan and Why Truman Dropped the Bomb*. New York: Simon and Schuster, 1995.

Alperovitz, Gar. *Atomic Diplomacy: Hiroshima and Potsdam*. New York: Simon and Schuster, 1965.

———. *The Decision to Use the Atomic Bomb*. New York: Knopf, 1995.

Alperovitz, Gar, Robert L. Messer, and Barton Bernstein. "Correspondence: Marshall, Truman, and the Decision to Drop the Bomb." *International Security* 16 (Winter 1991/1992): 204–221.

Batchelder, Robert C. *The Irreversible Decision, 1939–1950*. Boston: Houghton Mifflin, 1962.

Bernstein, Barton J. "Eclipsed by Hiroshima and Nagasaki: Early Thinking about Tactical Nuclear Weapons." *International Security* 15 (1991): 149–173.

———. "Seizing the Contested Terrain of Nuclear History: Stimson, Conant, and Their Allies Explain the Decision to Use the Atomic Bomb." *Diplomatic History* 17 (1993): 35–72.

———. "The Dropping of the A-Bomb: How Decisions Are Made When a Nation Is at War." *The Center Magazine* (March/April 1983): 7–15.

———. "The Perils and Politics of Surrender: Ending the War with Japan and Avoiding the Third Atomic Bomb." *Pacific Historical Quarterly* 46 (1977): 1–27.

———. "Understanding the Atomic Bomb and the Japanese Surrender: Missed Opportunities, Little-Known Near Disasters, and Modern Memory." *Diplomatic History* 19 (1995): 227–273.

———, ed. *The Atomic Bomb: The Critical Issues*. Boston: Little, Brown, 1976.

Birdsall, Steve. *Flying Buccaneers: The Illustrated History of Kenney's Fifth Air Force*. New York: Doubleday, 1977.

Blair, Clay, Jr. *Silent Victory: The U.S. Submarine War against Japan*. New York: Bantam, 1975.

Brower, Charles F., IV. "The Joint Chiefs of Staff and National Policy: American Strategy and the War with Japan, 1943–1945." Ph.D. diss., University of Pennsylvania, 1987.

Bundy, McGeorge. *Danger and Survival: Choices About the Bomb in the First Fifty Years*. New York: Random House, 1988.

Butow, Robert. *Japan's Decision to Surrender*. Stanford, CA: Stanford UP, 1954.

Caidin, Martin. *The Ragged, Rugged Warriors*. New York: Bantam, 1979.

————. *A Torch to the Enemy.* New York: Bantam, 1960.

Chappell, John D. *Before the Bomb: How America Approached the End of the Pacific War.* Lexington: UP of Kentucky, 1997.

Chennault, Claire Lee, with Robert Hotz, eds. *Way of a Fighter.* New York: G. P. Putnam's Sons, 1949.

Coffey, Thomas M. *Iron Eagle: The Turbulent Life of General Curtis LeMay.* New York: Crown, 1986.

Cortesi, Lawrence. *Target: Tokyo.* New York: Zebra, 1983.

Couffer, Jack. *Bat Bomb: World War II's Other Secret Weapon.* Austin: University of Texas, 1992.

Craig, William. *The Fall of Japan.* New York: Dial, 1967.

Crane, Conrad C. *Bombs, Cities, and Civilians: American Airpower Strategy in World War II.* Lawrence: UP of Kansas, 1993.

Craven, Wesley Frank, and James Lea Cate, eds. *The Army Air Forces in World War II.* 7 vols. Chicago: University of Chicago, 1948–1953.

Doolittle, James H., with Carroll V. Glines. *I Could Never Be So Lucky Again.* New York: Bantam, 1991.

Drea, Edward J. *MacArthur's ULTRA: Codebreaking and the War against Japan, 1942–1945.* Lawrence: UP of Kansas, 1992.

Edoin, Hoito. *The Night Tokyo Burned.* New York: St. Martin's, 1987.

Feifer, George. *Tennozan: The Battle of Okinawa and the Atomic Bomb.* New York: Ticknor and Fields, 1992.

Feis, Herbert. *The Atomic Bomb and the End of the War in the Pacific.* Princeton: Princeton UP, 1966.

————. *Japan Subdued: The Atomic Bomb and the End of World War II.* Princeton: Princeton UP, 1961.

Ferrell, Robert H., ed. *Dear Bess: The Letters from Harry to Bess Truman, 1910–1959.* New York: W. W. Norton, 1983.

————. *Off the Record: The Private Papers of Harry S. Truman.* New York: Harper and Row, 1980.

"Fortune Survey: Use of the Atomic Bomb." *Fortune* 37 (December 1945): 305–306, 309.

Fussell, Paul. *Thank God for the Atomic Bomb and Other Essays.* New York: Summit, 1988.

Gentile, Gian Peri. "Advocacy or Assessment: The United States Strategic Bombing Survey of Germany and Japan." *Pacific Historical Review* 66 (1997): 53–79.

Giangreco, D. M. "Casualty Projections for the U.S. Invasions of Japan, 1945–1946: Planning and Policy Implications." *The Journal of Military History* 61 (1997): 521–581.

Gillison, Douglas. *Royal Australian Air Force, 1939–1942.* Canberra: Australian War Memorial, 1962.

Giovannitti, Len, and Fred Freed. *The Decision to Drop the Bomb.* New York: Coward-McCann, 1965.

Glines, Carroll V. *Attack on Yamamoto.* New York: Orion, 1990.

————. *The Doolittle Raid: America's Daring First Strike against Japan.* New York: Orion, 1988.

————. *Doolittle's Tokyo Raiders.* New York: Arno, 1980.

Groves, Leslie R. *Now It Can Be Told: The Story of the Manhattan Project.* New York: Harper, 1962.

Hansell, Haywood, Jr. *Strategic Air War against Japan.* Washington: GPO, 1980.

Harper, Stephen. *Miracle of Deliverance: The Case for the Bombing of Hiroshima and Nagasaki.* London: Sidgwick and Jackson, 1985.

Havens, Thomas R. *Valley of Darkness: The Japanese People and World War II.* New York: W. W. Norton, 1978.

Herbert, Kevin. *Maximum Effort: The B-29s against Japan.* Manhattan, KS: Sunflower UP, 1983.

Hersey, John. *Hiroshima.* New York: A. A. Knopf, 1946, 1985.

Impact: The Army Air Forces' "Confidential" Picture History of World War II. 8 books. Reprint of 1943–1945 periodicals. Harrisburg: Historical Times, 1982.

Iriye, Akira. *Power and Culture: The Japanese-American War 1941–1945.* Cambridge: Harvard UP, 1981.

Kagan, Donald. "Why America Dropped the Bomb." *Commentary* 100 (September 1995): 17–23.

Kenney, George C. *General Kenney Reports: A Personal History of the Pacific War.* Washington, DC: Office of Air Force History, 1949, 1987.

Kerr, E. Bartlett. *Flames over Tokyo: The U.S. Army Air Forces' Incendiary Campaign against Japan, 1944–1945.* New York: Donald I. Fine, 1991.

Kissick, Luther C., Jr. *Guerrilla One: The 74th Fighter Squadron behind Enemy Lines in China, 1942–45.* Manhattan, KS: Sunflower UP, 1983.

Lawson, Ted. *Thirty Seconds over Tokyo.* New York: Random House, 1943.

Lee, Bruce. *Marching Orders: The Untold Story of World War II.* New York: Crown, 1995.

LeMay, Curtis, with MacKinley Kantor. *Mission with LeMay.* Garden City, NY: Doubleday, 1965.

Macdonald, Dwight. "The Bomb." *Politics* 2 (September 1945): 257–260.

MacIsaac, David. *Strategic Bombing in World War II: The Story of the United States Strategic Bombing Survey.* New York: Garland, 1976.

Maddox, Robert James. "The Biggest Decision: Why We Had to Drop the Atomic Bomb." *American Heritage* 46 (May/June 1995): 70–77.

———. *Weapons for Victory: The Hiroshima Decision Fifty Years Later.* Columbia: University of Missouri, 1995.

McCullough, David. *Truman.* New York: Simon and Schuster, 1992.

Mersky, Peter B. *Time of the Aces: Marine Pilots in the Solomons, 1942–1944.* Washington, DC: Marine Corps Historical Center, 1993.

Messer, Robert L. "New Evidence on Truman's Decision." *Bulletin of the Atomic Scientists* 41 (August 1985): 50–56.

Mikesh, Robert C. *Japan's World War II Balloon Bomb Attacks on North America.* Washington, DC: Smithsonian, 1973.

Miles, Rufus E., Jr. "Hiroshima: The Strange Myth of Half a Million Lives Saved." *International Security* 10 (Fall 1985): 121–140.

Morison, Samuel Eliot. *History of United States Naval Operations in World War II.* 15 vols. Boston: Little, Brown, 1947–1962.

Morrison, Wilbur H. *Hellbirds: The Story of the B-29s in Combat.* New York: Duell, Sloan, and Pearce, 1960.

———. *Point of No Return.* New York: Times, 1979.

Newman, Robert P. *Truman and the Hiroshima Cult.* East Lansing: Michigan State UP, 1995.

Odgers, George. *Air War against Japan, 1943–45.* Canberra: Australian War Memorial, 1957.

Okumiya, Masatake, and Jiro Horikoshi, with Martin Caidin. *Zero!* New York: E. P. Dutton, 1956.

Pacific War Research Society. *Japan's Longest Day.* New York: Ballantine, 1972.

Rhodes, Richard. *The Making of the Atomic Bomb.* New York: Simon and Schuster, 1986.

Ross, John Macaulay Sutherland. *Royal New Zealand Air Force.* Wellington: Department of Internal Affairs, RNZAF, 1955.

Sakai, Saburo, with Martin Caidin and Fred Saito. *Samurai!* New York: E. P. Dutton, 1958.

Schaffer, Ronald. *Wings of Judgment: American Bombing in World War II.* New York: Oxford UP, 1985.

Scott, Robert L. *God Is My Co-Pilot.* New York: Charles Scribner's Sons, 1944.

Sherry, Michael S. *The Rise of American Air Power: The Creation of Armageddon.* New Haven, CT: Yale, 1987.

Sherwin, Martin J. *A World Destroyed: The Atomic Bomb and the Grand Alliance.* New York: Knopf, 1975.

Sigal, Leon V. *Fighting to a Finish: The Politics of War Termination in the United States and Japan, 1945.* Ithaca, NY: Cornell UP, 1988.

Skates, John Ray. *The Invasion of Japan: Alternative to the Bomb.* Columbia: University of South Carolina, 1994.

Stimson, Henry L. "The Decision to Use the Atomic Bomb." *Harper's* 194 (February 1947): 54–56.

Stimson, Henry L., with McGeorge Bundy. *On Active Service in Peace and War.* New York: Harper and Brothers, 1948.

Thomas, Gordon, and Max Morgan Witts. *Enola Gay.* New York: Pocket, 1978.

Toland, John. *The Rising Sun: The Decline and Fall of the Japanese Empire, 1936–1945.* 2 vols. New York: Random House, 1970.

Truman, Harry. *Memoirs: Year of Decisions.* Garden City, NY: Doubleday, 1955.

U.S. Strategic Bombing Survey. *The United States Strategic Bombing Survey.* 10 vols. New York: Garland, 1976.

Walker, J. Samuel. "The Decision to Use the Bomb: A Historiographical Update." *Diplomatic History* 14 (Winter 1990): 97–114.

Webber, Bert. *Retaliation: Japanese Attacks and Allied Countermeasures on the Pacific Coast in World War II.* Corvallis: Oregon State UP, 1975.

Werrell, Kenneth P. *Blankets of Fire: U.S. Bombers over Japan during World War II.* Washington, DC: Smithsonian, 1996.

Williams, Peter, and David Wallace. *Unit 731: Japan's Secret Biological Warfare in World War II.* New York: Free, 1989.

Yoshino, Ronald W. *Lightning Strikes: The 475th Fighter Group in the Pacific War, 1943–1945.* Manhattan, KS: Sunflower UP, 1988.

PART III

War and Society in the Asian and Pacific Theaters

8 Japanese Occupation, Resistance, and Collaboration in Asia

Shigeru Sato

HISTORICAL BACKGROUND

In Asia, as in Europe, many people resisted or collaborated with the invading and occupying forces. Their reactions ranged from determined armed resistance in China, to general welcome in Java, with many variations in between.

Conroy's essay "Thoughts on Collaboration" suggests that the Western concepts of resistance and collaboration cannot readily be applied to Asia. This can be illustrated by comparing the fates of the collaborators and resisters in Europe and Asia. Many well-known collaborators in Western and Northern Europe, such as Laval of France, Mussert of the Netherlands, and Quisling of Norway, were executed for treason after the war, while the Resistance, marked by a capital R, came to assume a near mythological magnitude and aura in people's minds. In contrast, a number of Asian collaborators, such as Sukarno of Indonesia, Phibun of Thailand, and Roxas of the Philippines, became heads of state. Some others, such as Aung San of Burma and Subhas Chandra Bose of India, failed to become heads of state due to their early tragic deaths but are widely considered in their own countries as national heroes. As for those who conducted anti-Japanese guerrilla warfare, such as the Hukbalahaps (People's Anti-Japanese Army) in the Philippines and the communist guerrillas in Malaya, they often continued their antiestablishment campaigning into the postindependence period and came to be branded as rebels.

The difference between Europe and Asia as well as the variations within Asia itself need to be understood in terms of the historical background of each area and nation. The European concepts of resistance and collaboration derived from its nation-state history. In prewar Asia, with the exception of Japan, national sovereignty was either completely lacking or severely curtailed by foreign powers. All of Southeast Asia, except Thailand, was colonies of the United States, France, Britain, the Netherlands, or Portugal. Thailand was independent, but its sovereignty had been heavily undermined through many political and economic concessions wrought by Britain and other foreign powers. As for China, it had become, to borrow Sun Yatsen's term, a hypocolony of the Western powers after the Opium War (1839–1842). Moreover, Japan annexed Taiwan in 1895 and Korea in 1910. It also occupied Manchuria in 1931 and the following year created a satellite state, Manchukuo, with the deposed last emperor of China, Puyi, as the titular ruler. The Second Sino-Japanese War broke out in July 1937, and the Japanese invaded northern and central China and created several more puppet governments, which ultimately consolidated in a single collaborationist regime headed by Sun Yatsen's disciple and Chiang Kai-shek's rival, Wang Jingwei, with its seat at Nationalist China's former capital, Nanjing. The Nationalist Party, Guomindang, headed by Chiang Kai-shek, formed the internationally recognized government of China, while the Chinese Communist Party had been challenging its authority and came to control many enclaves in northern and central China behind the Japanese lines, constituting a state within a state.

Another related factor that contributed to the European concepts of resistance and collaboration was the perception of the war's being a struggle between democracy and fascism. Again, this dichotomy does not apply in Asia. China and Thailand had never had a democratic government. In other parts of Southeast Asia, the British, the Dutch, the French, and the Portuguese governments represented "colonialism" rather than "democracy." Only the Americans in the Philippines were seriously preparing their colony for future independence. Organized nationalist movements had been gathering strength all over Asia from around the turn of the century, but only after World War II did a number of nation-states emerge.

In Europe, the Nazi collaborators were often members of the local fascist parties, many of whom were of German descent, feeling alienated in their host countries and sympathetic to Hitler's cause. In Asia, well-known collaborators were nationalists who were more concerned with achieving their own national independence rather than helping the Japanese expansionists. In a number of cases in Southeast Asia, those who collaborated with the Japanese considered their former colonial authorities as their primary enemy, and Japan was their enemy's enemy.

After the Japanese surrender, the former colonial authorities attempted to restore the status quo ante. It was often these returning powers that branded the nationalists as collaborators. In Asia as well, the term "collaborator" was therefore not free from negative connotations, but the degree of negativity depended largely on the degree of compatibility of collaboration with nationalism. In the countries where compatibility was low, collaboration became an issue. It is for this reason that important academic works with collaboration or similar terms in their titles all concern themselves with China and the Philippines.

THE TREND IN HISTORIOGRAPHY

Soon after the war a number of writers, both Western and Asian, who were believers in the *mission civilisatrice* of the Western colonialism, wrote about the Japanese occupation of Southeast Asia from the perspective of democracy versus fascism and lamented the destruction of the Western colonial achievements. A typical example is Aziz, *Japan's Colonialism and Indonesia.* This awkwardly held, rather Eurocentric perspective soon came to be replaced by another, more Asia-centric perspective "from colonialism to independence," which dominated the historiography of the Second World War in Southeast Asia from the 1950s to the 1970s. In this perspective, which is clearly sympathetic toward Asian nationalism, Japanese fascism was considered a virulent, but highly effective, catalyst for decolonization. Both resistance and collaboration came to be considered as means through which independence could be achieved; thus, the pejorative connotation of the latter was substantially reduced. The war period came to be viewed in a longer historical perspective, and emphasis was shifted to the dramatic transformation in the political structure during the war. Elsbree's *Japan's Role in Southeast Asian Nationalist Movements* is a pioneering work. Pluvier, some twenty years later, wrote a more detailed survey, *Southeast Asia from Colonialism to Independence.* Benda's *Continuity and Change* is a collection of this influential scholar's journal articles that theorized about the significance of the war. Silverstein's introductory chapter in his *Southeast Asia in World War II* also summarizes how the impact of the war transformed the societies in Southeast Asia.

From around the early 1980s, however, scholars became more aware that the newly independent nations have inherited a great deal from their colonial and precolonial pasts, and thus they came to reexamine the period, paying closer attention to the continuity aspects. McCoy's introductory chapter in *Southeast Asia under Japanese Occupation* is a challenge to the transformation thesis. Political history tends to focus on a handful of elite activists and affiliated organizations and treat socioeconomic aspects as only the backdrop. In reality, people in all walks of life by various means either resisted, ignored, or cooperated with the occupation government. To obtain a holistic understanding of the social dynamics of the era, we need to have a closer look at the social and economic fabric of the communities in which local people made a living, because the motivations for their behavior were closely connected to the concrete social reality. This trend in historiography is currently gaining some momentum. The following sections survey the political aspect first, followed by military, social, and economic aspects.

ASIAN NATIONALISM AND THE ISSUE OF RESISTANCE AND COLLABORATION

From around the turn of the century, Japan had been a constant stimulant for Asian nationalism. Because of its rapid modernization, the formation of the Anglo-Japanese Alliance in 1902, and the victory over Russia in 1905, many Asians came to regard Japan as a model and the champion of Asian nationalism. Japan's expansionist ambition, however, became increasingly visible, particularly after the occupation of Manchuria and the full-scale invasion of China. Left-wing nationalists had never been deceived by Japan's propaganda about Asia for Asians, but many others considered Japan as the key to their own "liberation." During the war nationalists throughout Asia collaborated with the Japanese to promote their own cause. However, as the Japanese military administration proved oppressive, and the tide of war turned in favor of the Allies, some nationalists swapped sides, without jeopardizing their political integrity. The cases of Aung San of Burma and Phibun of Thailand illustrate this point.

In the 1930s, Aung San was the leader of the Burmese nationalist group the Thakin Party, which consisted mainly of Rangoon University students. In 1940, he fled Burma to escape British persecution, and, with the help of the Japanese officer Colonel Suzuki, he underwent military training and formed the Burma Independence Army. Totaling about 300 men, it led the Japanese invasion from Thailand. After occupying Rangoon, the Japanese decided to implement a military administration instead of granting independence. Within a year, however, as the war situation deteriorated, Tokyo authorities decided to grant independence to Burma to secure stronger cooperation. Independence was thus proclaimed on 1 August 1943, but it soon became clear that the independence that was granted was only nominal. Aung San and many other nationalists, bitterly disappointed, formed a clandestine organization, the Anti-Fascist Organization. This organization contacted the British army while ostensibly cooperating with the Japanese. Obtaining weapons from both sides, the Anti-Fascist Organization brought its resistance out into the open in March 1945 and continued its fight until the Japanese surrendered. Aung San formed the first postwar administration and negotiated with the British and signed an agreement in January 1947 in London that led to Burma's independence the following year. However, in July 1947 at the age of thirty-two, he was assassinated by his political opponent.

The first chapter of Aung San Suu Kyi's *Freedom from Fear*, entitled "My Father," is a biography by his renowned daughter. Silverstein's *The Political Legacy of Aung San* is a collection of Aung San's own writings, with an introductory essay by the editor. Both Aung San Suu Kyi and Silverstein tend to idealize Aung San as a champion of democracy and overlook his authoritarian aspects, which are evident in his writings. Ba Maw's *Break-*

through in Burma is a memoir of the politician who was prime minister (1937–1939) and headed the Japanese-sponsored regime (1942–1945). He views his own and other people's collaboration in the context of Burmese nationalist movements and is highly appreciative of Japan's role in Asian decolonization. Maung Maung's *Burmese Nationalist Movements* deals with more diverse groups and personalities from broader social and political perspectives. Guyot's "The Political Impact of the Japanese Occupation," which admires the Burma Independence Army's ability to form a unified, independent country, is widely considered a standard study. Taylor's chapter in McCoy, *Southeast Asia,* challenges this and argues that the Japanese occupation exacerbated the interethnic conflicts and created the conditions for the civil war. Taylor, *Marxism and Resistance,* contains a translation of an autobiography of a leading Marxist. In his introductory essay, Taylor explores shifting political alliances and the eventual communist eclipse. Studies of the reactions of Burma's ethnic minorities and the British role in developing guerrilla movements among the hill tribes can be found in Guyot's chapter in McVey, *Southeast Asian Transitions,* and Selth, *The Anti-Fascist Resistance.* Yoon's *Japan's Scheme* researches the Japan–Burma relationship mainly from Japanese sources. Concerning Colonel Suzuki's role, see Izumiya, *The Minami Organ.*

Thailand provides another example of a nation's changing sides according to the war situation. Phibun was prime minister at the outbreak of the war. He had used Japanese influence in May 1941 and resolved the territorial disputes with French Indochina to Thailand's advantage. When the Pacific War broke out, he let the Japanese forces pass through his country to attack Burma and Malaya and on 25 January declared war against the United Kingdom and the United States. In 1943, he pushed the national boundaries farther into Malaya and Burma. As the war situation changed, however, Phibun resigned from his office, six days after the Japanese premier Tojo's resignation on 8 July 1944. His government was replaced by a more pro-Allied one, which conducted intense maneuvering to repair Thailand's relationship with the Allies while maintaining its relationship with Japan.

After the war, as a result of British pressure, Phibun and seven other political leaders were arrested and charged with war crimes, while the territories taken from the British colonies through irredentist claims were returned. The Thai Supreme Court, however, ruled in 1946 that the 1945 War Criminal Acts were unconstitutional, and the collaboration charges were consequently dropped. Phibun's actions during the war did not damage his reputation or influence greatly. In 1948 he again became prime minister and dominated Thai politics until 1957.

Those who are interested in Phibun's long and winding political career and the Thai international and interfactional politics can begin with Kobkua, *Thailand's Durable Premier, Phibun.* Phibun's motivation behind the collaboration is still a controversial area. His enigmatic moves during the crucial period of early December 1941 are explored in Batson, *The Tragedy*, which is based on a memoir of a Japanese diplomat stationed in Thailand. There were also those who opposed the collaborationist policy and sought contact with British and American forces. They formed the Free Thai Movement, which is dealt with in Haseman, *The Thai Resistance Movement*. Jayanama, *Siam and World War II*, offers unique insight into these events by the Thai author who has inside knowledge of Thai politics. Reynolds, *Thailand and Japan's Southern Advance*, is the most recent and the most comprehensive political history. The socioeconomic impact of the war and its relations with the resistance movement are analyzed in Numnonda, *Thailand and the Japanese Military Presence*. Concerning the long-term significance, Brailey, *Thailand and the Fall of Singapore*, argues that, unlike most other Southeast Asian countries that could reap the benefit of decolonization, Thailand's involvement in the war reversed the political developments in that country for a quarter century.

In the Netherlands Indies and British Malaya, the nationalists' collaboration with the Japanese lasted throughout the occupation. The nationalists in the prewar Netherlands Indies consisted broadly of two groups: the militant nationalists who refused to cooperate with the Dutch authorities and those who sought to achieve their political goals through cooperation with the Dutch. The noncooperating nationalists were mostly imprisoned or exiled by the Dutch, while the cooperating nationalists became increasingly more disappointed in the latter part of the 1930s due to the Dutch refusal to make any political concessions. The cooperating nationalists thus gradually turned away from the Dutch and came to expect more from the Japanese. Abeyasekere's *One Hand Clapping* analyzes aspirations and frustrations of the cooperating nationalists.

When the Japanese invaded Java in 1942, some cooperating nationalists offered to work with the Japanese and started a mass movement called the Triple A Movement with the slogan "Light of Asia, Japan; Protector of Asia, Japan; Leader of Asia, Japan." Meanwhile, the Japanese released the noncooperating nationalists from prison or recalled them back from places of exile and used them for anti-Allied propaganda and mass mobilization campaigns. The Japanese held tight reins on them, but as the war situation deteriorated, they granted more and more political concessions, including the promise of independence in the future. Two days after the Japanese surrender, Sukarno, under pressure from young activists, declared the independence of Indonesia. The Dutch who attempted to recover their colony, as well as some of Sukarno's critics, accused him of being a Japanese collaborator (see Mangkupradja, "The Peta"), but the issue of collaboration never became a serious challenge to his political authority. When Sukarno's collaboration with the Japanese was criticized, the criticism was directed mainly toward his assistance in the Japanese labor mobilization, rather than toward a political betrayal. Sukarno's awareness of these criticisms and his defense are presented in Adams' *Sukarno.*

Kahin's *Nationalism and Revolution,* published in 1952, is the first major work that examined the occupation in the perspective from colonialism to independence and has come to be considered a classical work. The most comprehensive treatment of the Nationalist–Japanese relationship can be found in Kanahele's "The Japanese Occupation." Anderson's *Some Aspects* and *Java in a Time of Revolution* focus on the last one and one-half years of the occupation, particularly the revolutionary fervor gradually building up among the youth. Kanahele, Anderson, and many others have considered the entire occupation as prelude to independence. Sato, however, in his *War, Nationalism and Peasants* puts the nationalists' activities in a different perspective and examines their roles in the formation of the occupation policies that affected the people's day-to-day lives during the occupation. The Japanese also tried to utilize the Muslim influence. Benda, *The Crescent and the Rising Sun,* studies how the Muslims consolidated themselves while ostensibly cooperating with the Japanese. Not all Indonesians were, of course, cooperative with the invaders. Resistance movements were, however, few, and mostly they remained clandestine. Legge's *Intellectuals and Nationalism* focuses on Sutan Sjahrir, the first prime minister of Indonesia, who chose not to collaborate. Lucas, *Local Opposition and Underground Resistance,* describes communist activities based on their memoirs. Most major works are concerned about Java. However, the situation in northern Sumatra can be found in Reid, *The Blood of the People.*

Political allegiance in British Malaya was divided mainly along ethnic lines. Due to unrestricted immigration of Chinese and Indian labor until 1921 for the tin mines and rubber estates, migrants and their descendants came to constitute the majority of the population in Malaya. These migrants were politically oriented more toward their home countries than to Malaya. By 1930, Malaya had a branch of the Guomindang Party as well as a Communist Party affiliated with the Chinese Communist Party (CCP). The members were strongly anti-Japanese due to Japan's aggression in China. Indians had the Central Indian Association of Malaya, which tried to consolidate and mobilize ethnic Indians for the Indian independence movement. Malay nationalists formed the Kesatuan Melayu Muda (Young Malay Union) and sought to create an independent Malayan state by joining forces with the nationalists in the Netherlands Indies, who were also ethnic Malays.

Prior to the war, both the British and the Japanese tried to utilize the power of these groups. The British, on one hand, helped the Chinese form anti-Japanese guerrilla forces. The Japanese, on the other hand, established links with the Malay nationalists. When Singapore fell, the Japanese rounded up thousands of suspected anti-Japanese Chinese in Singapore and summarily executed them. Nonetheless, anti-Japanese guerrillas were active throughout the occupation. The Japanese created a local defense force, Giyugun, and appointed the Malay nationalist leader, Ibrahim Yaacob, as the commander. Ibrahim hoped to use the Giyugun to fight against the British to achieve independence, but it was mainly used for combating Chinese guerrillas. Thus, the Japanese occupation exacerbated interethnic tension.

Chin, *Malaya Upside Down*, and Chapman (a British officer who stayed to work with the guerrillas), *The Jungle Is Neutral*, present vivid, firsthand accounts of the political and social situations in Malaya. Lebra's *Jungle Alliance* is a study of the Indian National Army, which the Japanese created mainly by recruiting from Indians in Malaya. As regards to Chandra Bose's involvement in this army, see Mihir Bose, *The Lost Hero*, and Bhargava, *Netaji Subhas Chandra Bose*. Cheah, *Red Star over Malaya*, sees in the war era the origin of the interethnic conflict in present-day Malaysia. Akashi has written "Japanese Cultural Policy," "Japanese Military Administration," and "Japanese Policy towards the Malayan Chinese" on aspects of Japanese policies toward the Chinese and the Malays.

Within Southeast Asia, it was in the Philippines that the collaboration issue was discussed most seriously, not so much because many prominent Filipinos chose to collaborate with the Japanese but because they did so in spite of the fact that the Philippines could not hope to obtain many positive results from collaboration. Most privileged Filipinos were keenly aware that their country's prosperity in general and their own comfortable lifestyle in particular depended on the close relationships with the United States, particularly its sugar market. With regard to its political status, the constitution of 1935 provided the Philippines a large measure of self-government and a plan to obtain Commonwealth status in 1946. Few Filipino leaders therefore took the Japanese propaganda of coprosperity seriously. Those who collaborated with the Japanese did so from fear of the consequences of noncollaboration, rather than out of any positive prospect. Moreover, President Manuel Quezon, before he left for the United States to form a government in exile, instructed his aide, Jorge Vargas, and others to cooperate with the Japanese in order to protect civilian lives.

Abaya's *Betrayal in the Philippines*, published in 1946, attacks collaborators and criticizes America's postwar role in returning collaborators to power. Thereafter, the issue of collaboration has remained at the core of major scholarly works. Malay, *Occupied Philippines*, and Agoncillo, *The Burden of Proof*, examine the role of Vargas, both sympathetically. Steinberg's *Philippine Collaboration* is a more comprehensive treatment of the issue and examines why the Japanese, although successful in cajoling the ruling oligarchy to retain power, were unable to mobilize support among the population at large.

Popular resistance was widespread in the Philippines more than anywhere else in Southeast Asia. After MacArthur left, and the U.S. forces surrendered in May 1942, many Filipino officers and soldiers retreated into mountains and continued guerrilla operations. Many villagers joined the communist-led Hukbalahap resistance. Chinese migrants also formed numerous loosely organized resistance groups. Consequently, as Agoncillo puts it in his well-balanced account of the period, *The Fateful Years* (ix), the number of these guerrilla units and the amount of information available on them are so staggering that it will take a lifetime to write even half of the history of that movement. Lear's *The Japanese Occupation* is the most detailed local study of resistance. Kerkvliet's *The Huk Rebellion* is based on intensive fieldwork in one village and tries to see the rebellion from the villagers' own perspective. The Chinese resistance movements are surveyed in Tan, *The Chinese in the Philippines*.

Most writers focused on the moral implications of collaboration and resistance. McCoy's chapter in McCoy, *Southeast Asia*, however, warns against the simplistic collaboration-resistance dichotomy. Based on his study in the western Visayas, he argues that the conflicts between the collaborators and resisters derived largely from the prewar conflicts within Philippine society. The occupation provided certain politicians opportunities to brand their political rivals as collaborators and eliminate them. Similarly, he sees in the Hukbalahap movement a class conflict. Tenant farmers joined the communist-led rebellion, while landlords sought protection in towns under Japanese occupation.

The situation in French Indochina was closely related to the events in Europe. When France was invaded by the Germans, and Pétain formed the collaborationist government at Vichy, the colonial authorities in Indochina recognized it. The Japanese capitalized on this situation and, in agreement with the French, advanced their troops into north Indochina in September 1940, to south Indochina in July 1941. Therefore, the French first collaborated with the Japanese.

The awkward modus vivendi between the French and the Japanese came to an end soon after de Gaulle formed a new government in Paris in August 1944, and the Vichy government ceased to exist. In the Pacific, U.S. forces landed on Leyte in November 1944, and an American attack on Indochina appeared imminent. In the West, Burma, Malaya, and Thailand were under threat by the British. Among the French residents in Indochina, Gaullist sympathizers gained force, and anti-Japanese incidents instigated by them erupted with increasing frequency. At this juncture, the Japanese decided to disarm and intern the French garrisons, which they did on 9 March 1945. The Japanese then persuaded Emperor Bao

Dai of central Vietnam, King Sihanouk of Cambodia, and King Sisavong-vong of Laos to declare independence of their countries under the Japanese aegis.

When the French were removed, the Viet Minh (Vietnam Independence League) led by Ho Chi Minh advanced from China into northern provinces and established its own administration. When Russia declared war against Japan, and the Japanese defeat became imminent, the Viet Minh quickly spread its influence. After the Japanese surrender, Hanoi fell into Viet Minh hands. Bao Dai abdicated soon after, and on 2 September, Ho Chi Minh declared the independence of the Democratic Republic of Vietnam.

Much has been written about the Indochinese communists' struggle for independence, but most works see it in a long perspective because of the Vietnam War and only briefly touch upon the period 1940–1945. Huynh, *Vietnamese Communism, 1925–1945*, explains the communist success in August 1945 in terms of grafting of patriotic nationalism with Marxist-Leninist internationalism. Tønnesson, *The Vietnamese Revolution*, in contrast, attributes the reason to the power vacuum fortuitously created by the removal of the French authorities in March and the Japanese in August 1945. He suggests that Roosevelt engineered an anti-French ploy. Apart from the Communist Party there were various pro-Japanese or pro-Allied groups. Marr's chapter in McCoy, *Southeast Asia*, provides the best summary to these groupings. The main thrust of his *Vietnam 1945* is, however, on the communists' deal with the French and the Japanese in their quest for power. Hammer, *The Struggle for Indochina*, and Chieu, "The Other Side of the 1945 Vietnamese Revolution," also focus on noncommunist groups. McAlister, *Vietnam*, provides more detailed accounts of the era based mainly on French sources. Concerning Cambodia, see Chandler, "The Kingdom of Kampuchea."

In China, war started earlier than elsewhere. Some historians argue that the Manchurian Incident of 1931 marks the beginning of Japan's "Fifteen-Year War." Others see a clear break between the Manchurian Incident and the China Incident of 1937 and consider the latter to mark the true beginning of the war. In either case, Japanese aggression lasted for eight years after 1937. The Guomindang and the Communist Party formed an anti-Japanese united front, and China was thus divided into anti-Japanese and pro-Japanese camps. Within this division, however, it exhibited a bewildering complexity in political alignments. The united front was brittle, and the two parties fought over the spheres of influence. While the Guomindang retreated, the CCP remained behind Japanese lines and rapidly increased the territory under its control. Within the Japanese-occupied area, the puppet regimes, provincial warlords, secret societies, and underground criminal organizations formed a complex and ever-shifting network of power relations with one another, as well as with the Japanese, the CCP, and the Guomindang. Wang Jingwei died in November 1944, the Japanese were removed from the scene in August 1945, and the battle between the Guomindang and the CCP rekindled and raged until 1949.

Most studies of the era revolve around the following three questions. Why did Wang Jingwei collaborate with the Japanese? Why did the Guomindang nearly collapse? How did the CCP achieve phenomenal growth? Boyle, *China and Japan at War*, and Bunker, *Peace Conspiracy*, both published in 1972, attempt to answer the first question. Both consider Wang Jingwei a sincere patriot whose attempt to save the nation through negotiation and compromise was frustrated due to a host of reasons. As regards the second question, Chi's *Nationalist China at War* attributes the Guomindang's decline to its excessive preoccupation with military power and negligence of the tasks of the socioeconomic and political restructuring of China. Eastman, *Seeds of Destruction*, examines the party's structural weakness that engendered intraparty feud, corruption, and precarious relationship with the provincial warlords. The third question has been the most controversial. Johnson, *Peasant Nationalism and Communist Power*, suggests that the Japanese invasion galvanized the peasants into patriotic resistance, and the CCP successfully provided anti-Japanese leadership, which the peasants were searching for. Selden, *The Yenan Way*, was written during the heyday of the Cultural Revolution by a committed populist and attributes the CCP's success to its ability to revitalize the war-aggravated socioeconomic life of the village through popular participation. Kataoka, *Resistance and Revolution*, maintains that the united front was a means for the CCP to engage the Nationalists fully with the Japanese and make them abandon the civil war; meanwhile, the CCP, in the protection offered by the war, could combine the anti-imperialist war with the revolutionary war. Chen's *Making Revolution* and Wou's *Mobilizing the Masses* are more recent studies. Both demonstrate limitations of the previous monocausal explanations and present complex interactions between the party and the peasants, including not only the successes of the party but also its frustrations, intraparty conflicts, and continuous adjustment and readjustment of strategies to local needs. Fu, *Passivity, Resistance, and Collaboration*, examines diverse reactions of Chinese intellectuals in occupied Shanghai, relying mainly on these intellectuals' own writings published during the occupation.

The preceding survey shows that, although the people's reactions varied, we can recognize certain patterns and identify reasons for such variation. Friend, *The Blue-Eyed Enemy*, explains the difference between Java and Luzon in terms of the prewar relationships between the colonies and the suzerains: the Dutch economy depended heavily on the revenue from its colony, while the Philippine economy depended on access to the American market. Indonesians therefore wished to rid themselves of the Dutch and welcomed the Japanese as liberators. Filipinos, in contrast, maintained their loyalty toward the United States and considered the Japanese as invaders. The choice between resistance and collaboration was not simply a moral issue but was based on the historical experience of each nation. Similar analytical methods could, and should, be applied to the entire area invaded by the Japanese, but comparative studies are still few. Thorne, *The Issue of War*, attempts to interpret diverse perceptions of the war in Asia by combining global, regional, and local perspectives, but unfortunately it is not based on solid local studies.

MILITARY, SOCIAL, AND ECONOMIC ASPECTS

At various stages during the war, the Japanese created the Burma Independence Army (BIA), the Indian National Army (INA), and various other defense forces in Java, Sumatra, Borneo, Malaya, Indochina, the Philippines, and the Pacific islands. Lebra, *Japanese Trained Armies*, presents an overview of these armies. Unlike most political collaborators who were well established before the war, the people recruited into these armies were youths in their late teens or early twenties. The INA and the BIA fought against the Allies together with the Japanese, but the other defense forces did not engage in actual combat. Nonetheless, many of these young men came to play important military and political roles in the postwar era. Notosusanto, *The Peta Army*, is a detailed study of the army created in Java.

The Japanese trainers of these armies put emphasis on what they called *seishin*, or mental strength, even more than on military skills. The *seishin* consisted of such aspects as Oriental identity, self-reliance, anticolonialism, fighting spirit, service to the nation, and emperor worship. Besides these armed forces, the Japanese also created a range of mass organizations such as youth corps, vigilance corps, women's associations, and neighborhood associations in most of the Japanese-occupied areas. In these organizations as well, semimilitary training, mass rallies, and so on were conducted in order to inculcate the *seishin* into the masses. A number of historians have argued that, in this way, the political transition from colonialism to independence was accompanied or driven by spiritual transformation. Anderson, *Java*, and Akashi's chapter "Japanese Cultural Policy in Malaya and Singapore" in Goodman, *Japanese Cultural Policies*, are typical examples. Some others, such as Frederick, *Visions and Heat*, however, point out that revolutionary fervor preexisted and gained further momentum during the occupation.

With regard to socioeconomic changes and the ordinary people's reactions, certain parts of China and the Philippines, where communists were active, have received scholarly attention. About other areas, passing references abound, but solid analyses are few. In these areas as well, the war and the occupation affected the people's day-to-day lives, and they responded in various ways. The sudden change in international trade created, on one hand, serious shortages of import commodities and, on the other, surpluses of export commodities and massive unemployment. Partly as countermeasures and partly for their own war effort, the Japanese mobilized local labor and conducted extensive economic reorganization programs, including establishment of local self-sufficiency in food. They used Chinese traders for economic control, which provided the latter with opportunities to conduct war profiteering, often in the face of starving masses. In Malaya, these Chinese became the targets of the guerrillas during the occupation, while in Java and Sumatra, widespread assaults took place after the Japanese surrender. Cheah, *Red Star*, focuses on Malaya during and after the war.

The most important body that the Japanese utilized for control and mobilization was, however, the government bureaucracy. The Japanese removed the colonial authorities and promoted local officials. As the occupation policy became increasingly repressive, some of these bureaucrats resisted by encouraging the villagers to evade the policies, but many acted more like Japanese than the Japanese themselves (Indonesian communist leader Tan Malaka). In the Philippines, Malaya, and Burma, these officials became guerrilla targets due to their collaboration. In Indonesia, sporadic riots took place during the occupation, but it was mainly after the Japanese surrender that ordinary villagers assaulted the local officials. Kurasawa, "Forced Delivery of Paddy," and Lucas, *One Soul One Struggle*, examine peasant riots that broke out in Java in 1944 and 1946.

Another group the Japanese utilized was the nationalists. When the Japanese granted independence to Burma and the Philippines, they also granted political participation to Java, Sumatra, and Malaya and created advisory councils. Creation of these quasi parliaments was ostensibly a political concession, but, in reality, political participation meant that local leading figures, mainly nationalists, took part in the formation of the oppressive occupation policies. After the war, the returning British and the Dutch accused the nationalists of collaboration, while villagers, knowing little about the nationalists, attacked Chinese traders and the local officials who came into close contact with them. The Japanese occupation greatly exacerbated the social conflicts, many of which, latently or manifestly, preexisted the war. An overview of the economic situation in Indonesia can be found in Sutter, *Indonesianisasi*. An effort to bring the social, economic, and administrative aspects to the forefront of analysis can be found in Sato, *War, Nationalism and Peasants*. These aspects, however, require much more thorough investigations.

BIBLIOGRAPHY

Abaya, Hernando J. *Betrayal in the Philippines*. Quezon City, Philippines: Malaya, 1946.

Abeyasekere, Susan. *One Hand Clapping: Indonesian Nationalists and the Dutch, 1939–*

1942. Clayton, Victoria, Australia: Monash Papers on Southeast Asia no. 5, 1976.

Adams, Cindy. *Sukarno: An Autobiography as Told to Cindy Adams*. New York: Bobbs-Merrill, 1965.

Agoncillo, Teodoro. *The Burden of Proof: The Vargas–Laurel Collaboration Case, with Jorge B. Vargas' Sugamo Diary*. Quezon City, Philippines: University of the Philippines, 1984.

———. *The Fateful Years: Japan's Adventure in the Philippines, 1941–1945*. Quezon City, Philippines: R. P. Garcia, 1965.

Akashi, Yoji. "Japanese Cultural Policy in Malaya and Singapore, 1942–45." In Grant K. Goodman, ed., *Japanese Cultural Politics in Southeast Asia during World War 2*, 117–172. London and New York: Macmillan, 1991.

———. "Japanese Military Administration in Malaya: Its Formation and Evolution in Reference to the Sultans, the Islamic Religion, and the Moslem Malays." *Asian Studies* (Manila) 7 (1969): 81–110.

———. "Japanese Policy towards the Malayan Chinese." *Journal of Southeast Asian Studies* 1:2 (1970): 61–89.

Anderson, Benedict R. O'G. *Java in a Time of Revolution: Occupation and Resistance, 1944–1946*. Ithaca, NY, and London: Cornell UP, 1972.

———. *Some Aspects of Indonesian Politics under the Japanese Occupation, 1944–1945*. Ithaca, NY: Modern Indonesia Project, Southeast Asia Program, Department of Far Eastern Studies, Cornell University, 1961.

Aung, San Suu Kyi. *Freedom from Fear*. New York: Penguin, 1991; rev. ed., 1995.

Aziz, Mohammad Abdul. *Japan's Colonialism and Indonesia*. The Hague: Martinus Nijhoff, 1955.

Ba, Maw. *Breakthrough in Burma, Memoirs of a Revolution, 1939–1946*. New Haven, CT: Yale UP, 1968.

Batson, Benjamin A., and Shimizu Hajima. *The Tragedy of Wanit: A Japanese Account of Wartime Thai Politics*. Singapore: Journal of Southeast Asian Studies Special Publication Series, 1990.

Benda, Harry J. *Continuity and Change in Southeast Asia*. New Haven, CT: Yale University Southeast Asia Studies' 1972.

———. *The Crescent and the Rising Sun*. The Hague: W. Van Hoeve, 1958.

Bhargava, Moti Lal. *Netaji Subhas Chandra Bose in Southeast Asia and India's Liberation War 1943–45*. New Delhi: Vishwavidya, 1984.

Bose, Mihir. *The Lost Hero: A Biography of Subhas Bose*. London: Quartet, 1982.

Boyle, John H. *China and Japan at War, 1937–1945: The Politics of Collaboration*. Stanford, CA: Stanford UP, 1972.

Brailey, Nigel J. *Thailand and the Fall of Singapore: A Frustrated Asian Revolution*. Boulder, CO: Westview, 1986.

Bunker, Gerald E. *Peace Conspiracy: Wang Ching-Wei and the China War, 1937–1941*. Cambridge: Harvard UP, 1972.

Chandler, David P. "The Kingdom of Kampuchea: Japanese Sponsored Independence in Cambodia in World War II." *Journal of Southeast Asian Studies* 17: 1 (1986): 80–93.

Chapman, F. Spencer. *The Jungle Is Neutral*. London: Chatto and Windus, 1950.

Cheah, Boon Kheng. *Red Star over Malaya: Resistance and Social Conflict during and after the Japanese Occupation of Malaya, 1941–1946.* Singapore: Singapore UP, 1983.

Chen, Yung-fa. *Making Revolution: The Communist Movement in Eastern and Central China, 1937–1945.* Berkeley: University of California, 1986.

Chieu, Vu Ngu. "The Other Side of the 1945 Vietnamese Revolution: The Empire of Vietnam." *Journal of Asian Studies* 45 (1986): 293–328.

Chi, Hsi-sheng. *Nationalist China at War: Military Defeats and Political Collapse, 1937–45.* Ann Arbor: University of Michigan, 1982.

Chin, Kee Onn. *Malaya Upside Down.* Singapore: Jitts, 1946.

Conroy, F. Hilary. "Thoughts on Collaboration." *Peace and Change* 1 (February 1972): 43–46.

Eastman, Lloyd E. *Seeds of Destruction: Nationalist China in War and Revolution 1937–1949.* Stanford, CA: Stanford UP, 1984.

Elsbree, Willard H. *Japan's Role in Southeast Asian Nationalist Movements, 1940–1945.* Cambridge: Harvard UP, 1953.

Frederick, William H. *Visions and Heat: The Making of the Indonesian Revolution.* Athens: Ohio UP, 1989.

Friend, Theodore. *The Blue-Eyed Enemy; Japan against the West in Java and Luzon, 1942–1945.* Princeton: Princeton UP, 1988.

Fu, Poshek. *Passivity, Resistance, and Collaboration: Intellectual Choices in Occupied Shanghai, 1937–1945.* Stanford, CA: Stanford University, 1993.

Goodman, Grant K., ed. *Japanese Cultural Politics in Southeast Asia during World War 2.* London and New York: Macmillan, 1991.

Guyot, Dorothy Hess. "The Political Impact of the Japanese Occupation of Burma." Ph.D. diss., Yale University, 1966.

Hammer, Ellen J. *The Struggle for Indochina, 1942–1955.* Stanford, CA: Stanford UP, 1966.

Haseman, John B. *The Thai Resistance Movement during the Second World War.* Dekalb: Northern Illinois University Center for Southeast Asian Studies, 1978.

Huynh, Kim Khanh. *Vietnamese Communism 1925–1945.* Ithaca, NY: Cornell UP, 1982.

Izumiya, Tatsuro. *The Minami Organ.* Translated by Tun Aung Chain. Rangoon: Universities, 1981.

Jayanama, Direk. *Siam and World War II.* Translated by Jane Godfrey Keyes. Bangkok: Social Science Association of Thailand, 1978.

Johnson, Chalmers A. *Peasant Nationalism and Communist Power: The Emergence of Revolutionary China, 1937–1945.* Stanford, CA: Stanford UP, 1963.

Kahin, George McTurnan. *Nationalism and Revolution in Indonesia.* Ithaca, NY: Cornell UP, 1952.

Kanahele, George Sanford. "The Japanese Occupation of Indonesia: Prelude to Independence." Ph.D. diss., Cornell University, 1967.

Kataoka, Tetsuya. *Resistance and Revolution in China: The Communists and the Second United Front.* Berkeley: University of California, 1974.

Kerkvliet, Benedict J. *The Huk Rebellion: A Study of Peasant Revolt in the Philippines.* Berkeley: University of California, 1977.

Kobkua, Suwannathat-Pian. *Thailand's Durable Premier, Phibun through Three Decades 1932–1957.* Kuala Lumpur: Oxford UP, 1995.

Kurasawa, Aiko. "Forced Delivery of Paddy and Peasant Uprising in Indramayu:

Japanese Occupation and Social Change." *Developing Economies* 21:1 (March 1983): 52–72.

Lear, Elmer. *The Japanese Occupation of the Philippines: Leyte, 1941–1945.* Ithaca, NY: Cornell University, 1961.

Lebra, Joyce C. *Jungle Alliance, Japan and the Indian National Army.* Singapore: Asia Pacific, 1971.

———, ed. *Japanese Trained Armies in Southeast Asia: Independence and Volunteer Forces in World War II.* New York: Columbia UP, 1977.

Legge, John David. *Intellectuals and Nationalism in Indonesia: A Study of the Following Recruited by Sutan Sjahrir in Occupied Jakarta.* Ithaca, NY: Cornell Modern Indonesian Project, 1988.

Lucas, Anton. *One Soul One Struggle: Region and Revolution in Indonesia.* Sydney: Allen and Unwin, 1991.

———, ed. *Local Opposition and Underground Resistance to the Japanese in Java 1942–1945.* Clayton, Victoria, Australia: Monash Papers on Southeast Asia no. 13, Centre of Southeast Asian Studies, Monash University, 1986.

Malay, Armando J. *Occupied Philippines: The Role of Jorge B. Vargas during the Japanese Occupation.* Manila: Filipiniana Book Guild, 1967.

Mangkupradja, Gatot. "The PETA and My Relationship with the Japanese." *Indonesia* 5 (April 1968): 105–34.

Marr, David G. *Vietnam 1945: The Quest for Power.* Berkeley: University of California, 1995.

———. "World War II and the Vietnamese Revolution." In Alfred W. McCoy, ed., *Southeast Asia under Japanese Occupation,* 104–131. New Haven: Yale University Southeast Asian Studies, 1980.

Maung, Maung. *Burmese Nationalist Movements, 1940–48.* Gartmore, Scotland: Kiscadale, 1989; Honolulu: University of Hawaii, 1990.

McAlister, John T., Jr. *Vietnam: The Origin of Revolution* (1885–1946). Garden City, NY: Doubleday, 1968; New York: Alfred A. Knopf, 1969; London: Allen Lane, 1969.

McCoy, Alfred W., ed. *Southeast Asia under Japanese Occupation.* New Haven, CT: Yale University Southeast Asian Studies, 1980.

McVey, Ruth T., ed. *Southeast Asian Transition: Approaches through Social History.* New Haven, CT: Yale UP, 1978.

Notosusanto, Nugroho. *The Peta Army during the Japanese Occupation of Indonesia.* Tokyo: Waseda UP, 1979.

Numnonda, Thamsook. *Thailand and the Japanese Military Presence, 1941–1945.* Singapore: Institute of Southeast Asian Studies, 1977.

Pluvier, Jan. *Southeast Asia from Colonialism to Independence.* Kuala Lumpur: Oxford UP, 1974.

Reid, Anthony. *The Blood of the People.* Kuala Lumpur: Oxford UP, 1979.

Reynolds, E. Bruce. *Thailand and Japan's Southern Advance, 1940–1945.* New York: St. Martin's; Basingstoke, Hampshire, UK: Macmillan, 1994.

Sato, Shigeru. *War, Nationalism and Peasants: Java under the Japanese Occupation 1942–1945.* Sydney: Allen and Unwin; New York: M. E. Sharpe, 1994.

Selden, Mark. *The Yenan Way in Revolutionary China.* Cambridge: Harvard UP, 1971.

Selth, Andrew. *The Anti-Fascist Resistance in Burma, 1942–1945: The Racial Dimension.*

Nathasn, Australia: James Cook University of Northen Queensland, Centre for Southeast Asian Studies, 1985.

Silverstein, Josef, ed. *The Political Legacy of Aung San.* Rev. ed. Ithaca, NY: Southeast Asia Program, Cornell University, 1993.

————. *Southeast Asia in World War II: Four Essays.* New Haven, CT: Southeast Asia Studies, Monograph Series no. 7, Yale University, 1966.

Steinberg, David Joel. *Philippine Collaboration in World War II.* Ann Arbor: University of Michigan, 1967.

Sutter, John O. *Indonesianisasi: Politics in a Changing Economy 1940–1955.* Ithaca, NY: Southeast Asia Program, Cornell University, 1959.

Tan, Antonio S. *The Chinese in the Philippines during the Japanese Occupation, 1942–1945.* Quezon City, Philippines: University of the Philippines for the Asian Center, 1981.

Taylor, Robert H. *Marxism and Resistance in Burma, 1942–1945.* Southeast Asia Translation Series, vol. 4. Athens: Ohio UP, 1984.

Thorne, Christopher. *The Issue of War: States, Societies, and the Far Eastern Conflict of 1941–1945.* New York: Oxford UP; London: Hamish Hamilton, 1985. Also published as *The Far Eastern War: States and Societies, 1940–45.* London: Unwin, 1986.

Tønnesson, Stein. *The Vietnamese Revolution of 1945: Roosevelt, Ho Chi Minh and de Gaulle in a World at War.* London: Sage, 1991.

Wou, Odoric Y. K. *Mobilizing the Masses: Building Revolution in Henan.* Stanford, CA: Stanford UP, 1994.

Yoon, Won Z. *Japan's Scheme for the Liberation of Burma: The Role of the Minami Kikan and the Thirty Comrades.* Athens: Southeast Asia Series no. 27, Ohio University, 1973.

9   The Domestic Impact of War and Occupation on Japan

William M. Tsutsui

THE SECOND WORLD WAR IN JAPANESE HISTORY

The relevance of the wartime experience to the ongoing process of social, economic, and cultural change in twentieth-century Japan has long been a topic of considerable interest on both sides of the Pacific.

To Japanese scholars (especially those of a conservative bent) and to the Japanese public, the war years are almost invariably conceived as a "dark valley" (*kurai taniwa*), a period so trying and painful as to preclude close historical scrutiny. This view, convenient for those Japanese disinclined to confront their nation's war responsibility and their individual complicity, was also echoed by many American historians in the first postwar decades. According to scholars of the "modernization school"—and notably to the American doyen of Japanese studies, Edwin Reischauer—World War II was an anomalous deviation in Japan's remarkable path to industrial might and democratic maturity. As Reischauer intimated in some of his most important writings (including *The United States and Japan* and "What Went Wrong?"), the war era, while impossible to forget or deny, was best viewed as a catastrophic divergence in an otherwise auspicious developmental trajectory from the "liberal" 1920s to the "New Japan" born after 1945. Likewise, postwar Prime Minister Yoshida Shigeru described the war in his 1962 *Memoirs* as "a historic stumble," while political scientist Nobutaka Ike in 1968 dismissed Japan's wartime course as a "blind alley," with reorientation and redemption coming only with defeat.

In recent years, however, scholars have reassessed this selectively amnesic approach and its marginalization of Japan's wartime experience. Historians increasingly regard the years 1937–1945 as a formative period for the Japanese bureaucratic state and as a crucible in which the prototypes of postwar socioeconomic and political arrangements were cast. Stressing continuities with both the interwar era and the postwar order, historians have now thrown light into the "dark valley," revealing (as Dower has suggested in *Empire and Aftermath*) that the war was "a profound catalyst of structural transformation, accelerated social change, and alteration of popular consciousness" (280).

Among the first and most trenchant expositions of this revised view was that provided by Johnson in *MITI and the Japanese Miracle*. Charting the rise of Japan's "developmental" state, Johnson identified the war years as a crucial phase in extending bureaucratic influence and constructing the institutional apparatus for industrial policy. Comparable changes also took place in the capital–labor relationship, as documented in Gordon's *Evolution of Labor Relations in Japan*. Under a spreading web of state control, a new employment relationship (based on permanent jobs and seniority wages) was tentatively established. As further demonstrated by Garon's *State and Labor in Modern Japan* and Notar's "Japan's Wartime Labor Policy," the government's wartime strategy on labor and welfare issues was, by no means, an aberration but was continuous with interwar precedents as well as postwar developments.

Kasza's *The State and Mass Media in Japan* underscores the profound significance of wartime changes in Japanese state–society relations. Working from the premise that "the most distinctive political characteristic of the twentieth century is an unprecedented expansion of the power of states over their subjects" (xi), Kasza highlighted the accelerated expansion of bureaucratic control over the press, film, and radio in wartime Japan. In this light, wartime developments appeared less a "historic stumble" than a bold step forward: as Kasza argued, the technocratic "New Order" movement of 1940–1941 brought about an "administrative revolution" comparable in scale and import to the Meiji Restoration. Extrapolating from this conclusion and synthesizing much of the recent literature on Japan's wartime experience, Dower observed in "The Useful War" that the managed capitalism and brokered democracy of postwar Japan can trace their heritage directly to the turbulent war years.

Although scholars agree that state power reached unprecedented levels during the war, no consensus exists on how repressive Japan's wartime government actually was, either in comparison to past and future Japanese regimes or in an international context. Debates over whether Japan was "fascist," "totalitarian," "authoritarian," or "none of the above" have long characterized the literature yet have frequently degenerated into semantic arguments. Maruyama (*Thought and Behaviour in Modern Japanese Politics*) and Gordon (*Labor and Imperial Democracy*) are prominent supporters of the tag "fascist," yet both acknowledge unique elements in "Japanese fascism," and Gordon argues for a broader comparative definition of the term. Among those rejecting the usefulness of the "fascist" label and thus stressing the differences between the Japanese and European experiences are Wilson ("A New Look at the Problem of 'Japanese Fascism' ") and Duus and Okimoto ("Fascism and the History of Pre-War Japan"). Most American scholars fall somewhere between these poles or sidestep the "fascism" issue altogether; for example, Fletcher in his treatment of technocratic intellectuals, *The Search for a New Order*, indicated that European fascist ideas were rife in Japanese ruling circles but that the Japanese state itself was not "fascist."

Irrespective of nomenclature, many scholars have stressed the extreme repressiveness of the wartime Japanese government. In seeking an explanation for why there was so little public resistance to Japan's rising militarism—and, in particular, why so few progressive, Westernized intellectuals spoke out against the war effort—historians have frequently placed the blame on a tyrannical state and its apparatus of social control. In analyzing the collapse of the communist movement in the 1930s, Beckmann and Okubo (*The Japanese Communist Party*) emphasized the "absolute power of the state, especially in its rawest form—the police and the military" (270). The prominent historian Ienaga Saburō described the Japanese people as being in a "powerful vise" and concluded in *The Pacific War* that "it is no exaggeration to call the 'Greater Japanese Empire' a Kafkaesque state dedicated to the abuse of human rights" (52).

Yet, as Ienaga and others have recognized, the authority of Japan's wartime state and the submissiveness of the Japanese people did not rest solely on jackbooted government repression. Noting long-standing patterns of censorship, indoctrination through the educational system, glorification of the military, and ideological manipulation by the state, many observers have stressed the insidious subtlety, rather than the oppressive brutality, of the wartime regime. In Maruyama's evocative description, the Japanese state's power was based on "psychological coercion," with the imperial ideology of self-sacrificing nationalism "spreading like a many-layered, though invisible, net over the Japanese people" (1–2). The weaving of this "net" in the decades between the Meiji Restoration and the Pacific War has been documented from several angles. Among the most revealing treatments are Mitchell's *Thought Control in Prewar Japan* and Garon's "State and Religion in Imperial Japan." Both detail the means by which the bureaucracy defined and progressively narrowed the limits of orthodox thought and sanctioned political dissent. As Mitchell concluded in his most recent study, *Janus-Faced Justice*, wartime Japan was a curious synthesis, a "paternalistic police state" equipped with the complete arsenal of physical oppression but exhibiting benevolence as well as brutality, securing public obedience "through persuasion rather than fear" (xiv).

Although the notion of wartime Japan as an "embryonic Gulag" (to borrow Mitchell's tag) is well entrenched on both sides of the Pacific, not all historians have endorsed the vision of an oppressive state and a passive populace. For instance, in detailing conflicts in Japan's industrial mobilization efforts, Cohen (*Japan's Economy in War and Reconstruction*) and Rice ("Economic Mobilization in Wartime Japan") have highlighted tensions both within the state structure and between public-and private-sector actors. Drea, in a detailed study of parliamentary politics (*The 1942 Japanese General Election*), concluded that Japan remained a "pluralistic political system" (154) and was never thoroughly transformed into a monolithic national defense state. Other scholars have sought out rare instances of defiance and faint undercurrents of resistance in the war years. Dower, for example, in a fascinating study of wartime graffiti ("Sensational Rumors, Seditious Graffiti"), posited considerable popular discontent and noted the tenacity of a Marxist idiom of protest, even in the midst of patriotic delirium. Maruyama and Ienaga, on the other hand, argued that Japan's liberal intellectuals, by not *actively* supporting the war effort, participated in a kind of "passive resistance" against ultranationalism and authoritarian control. Although lacking a firm historical basis, such retrospective amnesty for inaction has, understandably, been of considerable appeal to Japanese audiences.

To Western scholars, however, exercises in expiation have held little attraction, and, in recent years, more nuanced accounts of wartime society—which de-emphasize the top-down assertion of absolute state power and seek new explanations for the striking dearth of protest—have proliferated. For example, Shillony and Havens both underscored the durability of core social values in accounting for the docility and endurance of Japan's wartime populace. In *Politics and Culture*, Shillony suggested that traditional cultural forms ensured consensus and obviated the need for a totalitarian dictatorship. Havens, meanwhile, in *Valley of Darkness*, argued that "the deep, underlying structures of society" (like the family and communitarian groupism) gave the Japanese people resilience in the face of unimaginable suffering (204).

Taking a less culturalist approach (yet reaching broadly consistent conclusions), other historians have demonstrated that Japan's wartime course was endorsed by many elements in Japanese society and was not fabricated solely by an elite military-bureaucratic clique. Barshay, for example, argued in *State and Intellectual in Imperial Japan* that "public men"—educators, popular intellectuals, journalists—saw no alternative but to cleave to the state in a time of crisis and war. "It is unhistorical," Barshay declared, "to assume that there should have been wholesale resistance among public men to the trend of the times" (31). In *Parties Out of Power in Japan*, Berger demonstrated that Diet politicians, frequently assumed to be the standard-bearers of liberal democracy, pragmatically accommodated themselves to military expansionism and the circumscription of individual rights. Moreover, while close collaboration between big business interests and the wartime state has long been assumed, several studies (notably Samuels' *Business of the Japanese State* and Fletcher's *Japanese Business Community*) suggest that the state did not dictate to industry so much as negotiate with private interests and compromise to meet business demands. In short, scholars have increasingly recognized that the Japanese people were, after all, participants in the Second World War and should be regarded as more than the passive victims of a militarist, totalitarian state.

If, however, there is any aspect of Japan's wartime experience that is considered uncontroversial by historians, it is that the Japanese people on the home front suffered profoundly, yet stoically, from the material wants, psychological pressures, and physical destruction of war. The best secondary account of the lives of "ordinary" Japanese during the hostilities is surely Havens' *Valley of Darkness*, although Shillony's *Politics and Culture* and shorter treatments by Daniels ("The Great Tokyo Air Raid") and Nish ("Japan") are also valuable overviews.

Regrettably, few memoirs detailing individual experiences of the war years in Japan are available in English. The reminiscences of Aikawa Takaaki and Kodama Yoshio are absorbing and informative, although most of the "inside stories" of the war told from a Japanese perspective seem strangely detached and bloodless. Some interesting insights are provided in accounts written by Western journalists living in wartime Japan, notably Robert Guillain's *I Saw Tokyo Burning* and Otto Tolischus' *Tokyo Record*. An invaluable recent addition to the literature is Haruko and Theodore Cook's *Japan at War*, a rich and compelling oral history collection documenting the varied experiences of dozens of Japanese men and women.

At least to date, Western research on the domestic impact of World War II in Japan has been characterized by an institutionalist approach and has been dominated by intellectual and political historians. Consequently, some aspects of Japan's wartime experience, particularly in the areas of social and cultural history, are not well documented. For instance, although it is widely assumed that the lives of Japanese women were greatly affected by the war, few detailed studies of women's experiences or wartime gender politics are available. The contributions of Havens in "Women and War" and Miyake in "Doubling Expectations" provide suggestive starting points for future study of the mobilization of female labor, changes in the wartime family, and shifts in gender ideology. Similarly, despite Weiner's important research in *Race and Migration in Imperial Japan*, little attention has been given to the position of ethnic minorities (especially Koreans) in wartime Japan. Local histories and demographic studies are also sadly lacking, as is research on the social impact of mass mobilization, the grassroots implementation of health and welfare policies, and changes in the educational system. Popular culture during the Second World War is another subject deserving further scholarly examination. As the provocative writings of Dower (*War without Mercy* and "Japanese Cinema Goes to War") and Silverberg ("Remembering Pearl Harbor") indicate, Japan's wartime propaganda, film, mass print culture, and material life should prove rich areas for future research.

In short, even though the English-language literature has exhaustively treated the nature of the wartime state, the fate of intellectuals under authoritarianism, and the perennial question of fascism, detailed "bottom-up" studies of Japan's war at home remain surprisingly scarce. Scholars of Japanese politics, labor, and economic development have, over the past fifteen years, increasingly adopted a "transwar" perspective, focusing new attention on wartime change and integrating the war experience into longer historical trajectories. Yet social and cultural historians have only begun to incorporate the "dark valley" into their narratives of prewar and postwar Japan. At least in Western scholarship, we are still far from being able to assess fully the complex domestic ramifications of the Second World War in Japan.

THE AMERICAN OCCUPATION IN JAPANESE HISTORY

In striking contrast to the paucity of English-language materials on Japan's war at home, historical studies of the American Occupation period (1945–1952) are available in almost overwhelming profusion. Over the past half century and especially since the 1970s, a large and diverse body of work on the American "interlude" in Japan has appeared, and this rich historiography has been suffused by spirited and highly politicized interpretive debates.

Fortunately, for those seeking an intellectual road map through the welter of historical research on the Occupation era, several bibliographic essays and historiographical reviews are available. Notably, Dower's "Occupied Japan as History" and "Occupied Japan and the Cold War" and Moore's "The Occupation of Japan as History" provide lucid overviews of the major trends. Another invaluable source is Gluck's "Entangling Illusions," an elegant, comprehensive review of both Japanese and American research on the Occupation experience.

For almost twenty-five years after the San Francisco Peace Treaty, Western scholarship on America's achievement in Occupied Japan was overwhelmingly celebratory in tone. Early historical accounts of the Occupation, written, in large part, by American veterans of MacArthur's headquarters, emphasized the extent of the "revolution" wrought under U.S. stewardship and testified to the remarkable success of the American forces in creating a democratic, demilitarized Japan. Gluck acutely tagged this first generation of Occupation historiography the "heroic narratives," and fine examples of this approach include Ward's "Reflections on the Allied Occupation" and the essays in Goodman's *American Occupation of Japan*. Reischauer's influential writings, although less effusive than the appraisals of some former "occupationaires," also supported the initial American proclivity toward self-congratulation. In *The Japanese* and a fascinating 1983 essay, "The Allied Occupation: Catalyst Not Creator," Reischauer suggested that the Americans laid only a light and benevolent hand on Occupied Japan, gently encouraging indigenous trends rather than unilaterally imposing Western constructs of democracy.

Even in recent years, many authors continue to sing the praises of America's proconsulship in Japan, particularly the Occupation's accomplishments in political reform. Prominent among these latter-day "heroic narratives" are Williams' *Japan's Political Revolution under MacArthur*, Perry's *Beneath the Eagle's Wings*, and Finn's *Winners in Peace* (1992). As Perry resolutely concluded, echoing the sentiments of many American observers, "the Occupation of Japan was extraordinarily successful, a landmark in human history" (215).

Despite the enduring appeal of such comforting evaluations, the "heroic narrative" was subjected to wholesale reappraisal by a new generation of scholars in the 1970s and 1980s. These "revisionists"—profoundly affected by the experience of Vietnam, too young to have served in MacArthur's bureaucracy, and enjoying unprecedented access to declassified archival materials—refigured the Occupation as a revolution thwarted, a triumph for conservatism rather than reform. According to this new narrative, the Japanese people and their desire for change were cynically sacrificed by American overlords who proved more committed to political stability, military security, and the preservation of capitalism than they were to meaningful democratization or sweeping socioeconomic reform. Thus, rather than retelling the Occupation as an uplifting story of success, the revisionists delineated a darker tale of betrayal and frustration.

Among the seminal works of the revisionist scholarship is Dower's *Empire and Aftermath*, a detailed study of the influential diplomat and politician Yoshida Shigeru. By tracing Yoshida's career through war and occupation, Dower documented the tenacity of Japan's conservative "old guard" and revealed the conditional nature of American reformism. These themes are developed further in Schaller's *American Occupation*, a broad analysis of the Occupation experience from the perspective of Cold War diplomacy. Schaller outlined how Japan was politically and economically rehabilitated as a "bulwark of democracy" in East Asia and how, in the process, Washington policymakers orchestrated the neutering of the Occupation's reform agenda. Another important survey of revisionist thought is Schonberger's *Aftermath of War*, a collective biography of eight "occupationaires" that underlines the significance of class interests, anticommunism, and American business lobbying in the making of the "reverse course."

Although debates over the Occupation and its legacy in Japan remain active, the fire of revisionist invectives and the dogmatism of the "heroic narratives" have abated over the past decade. One reason lies in the appearance of a more balanced, scholarly consensus on the achievements and deficiencies of the Occupation, a perspective made apparent in two major essay collections, Wolfe's *Americans as Proconsuls* and Ward and Sakamoto's *Democratizing Japan*. As Gluck concluded, "Recent research has scaled the [heroic] narratives down, and complicated but not demolished them" (179). A formal elaboration of this evolving synthesis has yet to be written, but historians are well aware of the need for an approach that tempers the celebratory tone of early Occupation scholarship, while simultaneously avoiding the self-righteous stridency of much revisionist historiography.

Remarkably enough, virtually all major aspects of Occupation policy in Japan have been treated monographically in English. On political reform and the writing of the 1946 "MacArthur Constitution," for example, detailed narratives from the occupiers' vantage point are provided by Williams' *Political Revolution* and Kades' 1989 essay "The American Role in Revising Japan's Imperial Constitution." An engaging account of American attempts to modify the Japanese legal system is given in Oppler's *Legal Reform in Occupied Japan*. Another crucial aspect of the American program, the purge of public officials implicated in the war effort, is described in Baerwald's *Purge of Japanese Leaders under the Occupation*.

The media, censorship, and popular culture in Occupied Japan, although long overlooked by historians, have recently received considerable scholarly attention. American censorship policies in Japan, whose stringency seemingly belied the democratizing mission of MacArthur's forces, are analyzed in Rubin's "From Wholesomeness to Decadence" and in Braw's *The Atomic Bomb Suppressed*. Hirano's *Mr. Smith Goes to Tokyo* and the varied contributions to Burkman's *The Occupation of Japan: Arts and Culture* hint tantalizingly at the Occupation's impact on both high culture and mass entertainments. Nevertheless, the "Americanization" of Japanese popular culture during the Occupation is a topic that has yet to be fully explored in the English-language literature.

Educational policy, which the Americans considered essential to the thorough "democratization" of Japanese society, has been the focus of extensive scholarly research. Nishi's *Unconditional Democracy* emphasizes the contradictions in the U.S. educational agenda, particularly the dissonance created between the Occupation's autocratic methods and its democratic ideals. Tsuchimochi's *Education Reform in Postwar Japan* makes the provocative argument that Occupation-era changes were guided as much by Japanese initiative as by unilateral American direction.

A substantial body of work has also been generated on the economic aspects of the Occupation. The essays in Redford's *The Occupation of Japan: Economic Policy and Reform* provide a broad introduction to the various American initiatives. The Occupation land reform and its consequences are masterfully recounted in Dore's *Land Reform in Japan*. The standard work on the rise and fall of the zaibatsu [banking and industrial combines] dissolution policy is Hadley's *Anti-trust in Japan*. The fate of the Japanese financial sector under Occupation—and the failure of the American authorities to effect meaningful change—is detailed in Tsutsui's *Banking Policy in Japan*. Foreign trade programs, specifically the process by which the United States sponsored Japan's reentry into international commerce, are described by Borden in *The Pacific Alliance*. Hein's *Fueling Growth* is a sophisticated examination of debates over economic policy and industrial structure during the Occupation. Important accounts of the early postwar union movement are Moore's *Japanese Workers and the Struggle for Power* and Gordon's *Evolution of Labor Relations*.

In addition to the extensive secondary literature, a number of American participants in the Occupation have published memoirs and diaries. Although many concentrate on high politics and diplomacy, some detail the domestic consequences of reform and the labyrinthine workings of MacArthur's bureaucracy. Cohen's *Remaking Japan* is a revealing look at policy making within the American headquarters, told from the perspective of one of the reformist "New Dealers" in the Occupation's Labor Division. A unique view of operations on a local level is provided by Jacob van Staaveren, a "civil information and education officer" in rural Yamanashi prefecture, in *An American in Japan*. Furthermore, many contemporary accounts of Occupied Japan still remain fresh and provocative today. Notable in this regard are journalist Mark Gayn's perceptive *Japan Diary* and Harry Emerson Wildes' *Typhoon in Tokyo*, a lively and opinionated memoir by a midlevel Occupation functionary. A compelling fictional account of the Occupation that poignantly captures the moral ambivalence of the American mission in Japan is *Where Are the Victors?* by noted film critic and *Stars and Stripes* correspondent in Occupied Tokyo Donald Richie. Unfortunately, none of the many fine reminiscences of the Occupation era written by Japanese intellectuals and public figures are yet available in English translation.

Above all, what remains lacking in the voluminous scholarship on the Occupation is a clear sense of what impact American reformism and the tempest in MacArthur's headquarters had on that crucial, but so frequently overlooked, constituency, the Japanese people. To date, the lion's share of historical research has focused on upper-echelon policy making and the American role, with few authors considering the Occupation's record at the local level, the contributions of Japanese actors in the making (and unmaking) of reform, or popular responses to American visions of change. In recent years, however, some scholars have begun to address this deficiency in the literature. For example, the essays collected in Nimmo's *The Occupation of Japan: The Grass Roots* provide a solid starting point for future "bottom-up" appraisals of the American proconsulship. Inoue's linguistic study of the making of the 1946 Constitution, *MacArthur's Japanese Constitution*, shows the extent to which both occupiers and occupied participated in the process of reform. Furthermore, Koshiro's suggestive work "The U.S. Occupation of Japan as a Mutual Racial Experience" serves as a much-needed reminder of the importance of race relations in the Occupation. In short, American scholarship is finally beginning to acknowledge that the Japanese people were active participants—and not simply the passive objects of reform—in the Occupation's program of change.

Thus, despite the wealth of materials available and despite the dynamism of historiographical debate in the field, much work remains to be done on the domestic impact of the American Occupation. As with the English-language scholarship on Japan's war at home, the traditional emphasis on institutional reform and high politics in studies of the Occupation has left conspicuous gaps in the areas of social and cultural history. Moreover, due to the long-standing tendency of American observers to focus on the work of the U.S. occupiers—and to deny implicitly the agency of the Japanese occupied—the domestic consequences of the Occupation have received scant attention. Historians are still struggling to live up to the challenge posed by Moore more than a decade ago in his "Reflections on the Occupation of Japan": "[T]he Occupation should not be seen merely as the story of Americans doing things in Japan, but as Japanese history, with Japanese participants, objectives, and ideas influencing events. . . . We have to remind ourselves that defeated Japan, however great the physical destruction, was not an empty blackboard on which Americans wrote a series of reforms" (723). Only when American scholars fully embrace this charge, can an accurate assessment of the Occupation's impact on Japan and its people be made.

BIBLIOGRAPHY

Aikawa, Takaaki. *Unwilling Patriot*. Tokyo: Jordan, 1960.

Baerwald, Hans. *The Purge of Japanese Leaders under the Occupation*. Berkeley: University of California, 1959.

Barshay, Andrew. *State and Intellectual in Imperial Japan*. Berkeley: University of California, 1988.

Beckmann, George, and Genji Okubo. *The Japanese Communist Party, 1922–1945*. Stanford: Stanford UP, 1969.

Berger, Gordon M. *Parties Out of Power in Japan, 1931–1941*. Princeton: Princeton UP, 1977.

Borden, William. *The Pacific Alliance*. Madison: University of Wisconsin, 1984.

Braw, Monica. *The Atomic Bomb Suppressed: American Censorship in Occupied Japan*. Armonk, NY: M. E. Sharpe, 1991.

Burkman, Thomas, ed. *The Occupation of Japan: Arts and Culture.* Norfolk, VA: General Douglas MacArthur Foundation, 1988.

Cohen, Jerome. *Japan's Economy in War and Reconstruction.* Minneapolis: University of Minnesota, 1949.

Cohen, Theodore. *Remaking Japan: The American Occupation as New Deal.* New York: Free, 1987.

Cook, Haruko Taya, and Theodore Cook. *Japan at War: An Oral History.* New York: New, 1992.

Daniels, Gordon. "The Great Tokyo Air Raid." In W. G. Beasley, *Modern Japan.* Berkeley: University of California, 1975.

Dore, Ronald. *Land Reform in Japan.* Oxford: Oxford UP, 1959.

Dower, John W. *Empire and Aftermath: Yoshida Shigeru and the Japanese Experience, 1878–1954.* Cambridge: Council on East Asian Studies, Harvard University, 1979.

———. "Japanese Cinema Goes to War." In John Dower, *Japan in War and Peace: Selected Essays,* 101–154. New York: New, 1993.

———. "Occupied Japan and the Cold War in Asia." In John Dower, *Japan in War and Peace: Selected Essays,* 155–207. New York: New, 1993.

———. "Occupied Japan as History and Occupation History as Politics." *Journal of Asian Studies* 34 (February 1975): 485–504.

———. "Sensational Rumors, Seditious Graffiti, and the Nightmares of the Thought Police." In John Dower, *Japan in War and Peace: Selected Essays,* 33–54. New York: New, 1993.

———. "The Useful War." *Daedalus* 119 (Summer 1990): 49–70.

———. *War without Mercy.* New York: Pantheon, 1986.

Drea, Edward J. *The 1942 Japanese General Election.* Lawrence: Center for East Asian Studies, University of Kansas, 1979.

Duus, Peter, and Daniel Okimoto. "Fascism and the History of Pre-War Japan: The Failure of a Concept." *Journal of Asian Studies* 39 (February 1979): 65–76.

Finn, Richard. *Winners in Peace: MacArthur, Yoshida and Postwar Japan.* Berkeley: University of California, 1992.

Fletcher, William Miles, III. *The Japanese Business Community and National Trade Policy, 1920–1942.* Chapel Hill: University of North Carolina, 1989.

———. *The Search for a New Order: Intellectuals and Fascism in Prewar Japan.* Chapel Hill: University of North Carolina, 1982.

Garon, Sheldon. *The State and Labor in Modern Japan.* Berkeley: University of California, 1987.

———. "State and Religion in Imperial Japan, 1912–1945." *Journal of Japanese Studies* 12 (1986): 273–302.

Gayn, Mark. *Japan Diary.* New York: William Sloane, 1948.

Gluck, Carol. "Entangling Illusions—Japanese and American Views of the Occupation." In Warren Cohen, ed., *New Frontiers in American–East Asian Relations.* New York: Columbia UP, 1983.

Goodman, Grant, ed. *The American Occupation of Japan: A Retrospective View.* Lawrence: Center for East Asian Studies, University of Kansas, 1968.

Gordon, Andrew. *The Evolution of Labor Relations in Japan: Heavy Industry, 1853–1955.* Cambridge: Council on East Asian Studies, Harvard University, 1985.

————. *Labor and Imperial Democracy in Prewar Japan.* Berkeley: University of California, 1991.

Guillain, Robert. Translated by William Byron. *I Saw Tokyo Burning.* Garden City, NY: Doubleday, 1981.

Hadley, Eleanor. *Anti-trust in Japan.* Princeton: Princeton UP, 1970.

Havens, Thomas R. *Valley of Darkness: The Japanese People and World War II.* New York: Norton, 1978.

————. "Women and War in Japan, 1937–1945." *American Historical Review* 80 (1975): 913–934.

Hein, Laura. *Fueling Growth: The Energy Revolution and Economic Policy in Postwar Japan.* Cambridge: Council on East Asian Studies, Harvard University, 1990.

Hirano, Kyoko. *Mr. Smith Goes to Tokyo: Japanese Cinema under the American Occupation.* Washington, DC: Smithsonian Institution, 1992.

Ienaga, Saburō. *The Pacific War: World War II and the Japanese, 1931–1945.* Translated by Frank Baldwin. New York: Pantheon, 1978.

Ike, Nobutaka. "War and Modernization." In Robert E. Ward, ed., *Political Development in Modern Japan,* 189–211. Princeton: Princeton UP, 1968.

Inoue, Kyoko. *MacArthur's Japanese Constitution: A Linguistic and Cultural Study of Its Making.* Chicago: University of Chicago, 1991.

Johnson, Chalmers A. *MITI and the Japanese Miracle: The Growth of Industrial Policy, 1925–1975.* Stanford, CA: Stanford UP, 1982.

Kades, Charles. "The American Role in Revising Japan's Imperial Constitution." *Political Science Quarterly* 104 (1989): 215–247.

Kasza, Gregory. *The State and the Mass Media in Japan, 1918–1945.* Berkeley: University of California, 1988.

Kodama, Yoshio. *I Was Defeated.* Translated by Fukuda Taro. Tokyo: Radiopress, 1959.

Koshiro, Yukiko. "The U.S. Occupation of Japan as a Mutual Racial Experience." *Journal of American-East Asian Relations* 3 (1994): 299–323.

Maruyama, Masao. *Thought and Behaviour in Modern Japanese Politics.* Translated and edited by Ivan Morris. London: Oxford UP, 1963.

Mitchell, Richard. *Janus-Faced Justice.* Honolulu: University of Hawaii, 1992.

————. *Thought Control in Prewar Japan.* Ithaca, NY: Cornell UP, 1976.

Miyake, Yoshiko. "Doubling Expectations: Motherhood and Women's Factory Work under State Management in Japan in the 1930s and 1940s." In Gail Bernstein, ed., *Recreating Japanese Women, 1600–1945,* 267–295. Berkeley: University of California, 1991.

Moore, Joe. *Japanese Workers and the Struggle for Power, 1945–1947.* Madison: University of Wisconsin, 1983.

Moore, Ray A. "The Occupation of Japan as History." *Monumenta Nipponica* 36 (1981): 317–328.

————. "Reflections on the Occupation of Japan." *Journal of Asian Studies* 38 (1979): 721–734.

Nimmo, William, ed. *The Occupation of Japan: The Grass Roots.* Norfolk, VA: General Douglas MacArthur Foundation, 1992.

Nish, Ian. "Japan." In Jeremy Noakes, ed., *The Civilian in War,* 93–103. Exeter, England: University of Exeter, 1992.

Nishi, Toshio. *Unconditional Democracy: Education and Politics in Occupied Japan.* Stanford, CA: Hoover Institution, 1982.

Notar, Ernest. "Japan's Wartime Labor Policy." *Journal of Asian Studies* 44 (1985): 311–328.

Oppler, Alfred. *Legal Reform in Occupied Japan.* Princeton: Princeton UP, 1976.

Perry, John Curtis. *Beneath the Eagle's Wings: Americans in Occupied Japan.* New York: Dodd, Mead, 1980.

Redford, Lawrence, ed. *The Occupation of Japan: Economic Policy and Reform.* Norfolk, VA: MacArthur Memorial, 1980.

Reischauer, Edwin. "The Allied Occupation: Catalyst Not Creator." In Harry Wray and Hilary Conroy, eds., *Japan Examined,* 335–342. Honolulu: University of Hawaii, 1983.

———. *The Japanese.* Cambridge: Harvard UP, 1977.

———. *The United States and Japan.* Rev. ed. Cambridge: Harvard UP, 1957.

———. "What Went Wrong?" In James Morley, ed., *Dilemmas of Growth in Prewar Japan,* 489–510. Princeton: Princeton UP, 1971.

Rice, Richard. "Economic Mobilization in Wartime Japan: Business, Bureaucracy and Military in Conflict." *Journal of Asian Studies* 38 (1979): 689–706.

Richie, Donald. *Where Are the Victors?* Rutland, VT: Charles Tuttle, 1986. Reprint of *This Scorching Earth,* 1956.

Rubin, Jay. "From Wholesomeness to Decadence: The Censorship of Literature under the Allied Occupation." *Journal of Japanese Studies* 11 (1985): 71–103.

Samuels, Richard. *The Business of the Japanese State.* Ithaca, NY: Cornell UP, 1987.

Schaller, Michael. *The American Occupation of Japan.* New York: Oxford UP, 1985.

Schonberger, Howard. *Aftermath of War: Americans and the Remaking of Japan, 1945–1952.* Kent, OH: Kent State UP, 1989.

Shillony, Ben-Ami. *Politics and Culture in Wartime Japan.* Oxford: Oxford UP, 1981.

Silverberg, Miriam. "Remembering Pearl Harbor, Forgetting Charlie Chaplin, and the Case of the Disappearing Western Woman: A Picture Story." *Positions* 1 (Spring 1993): 24–76.

Tolischus, Otto. *Tokyo Record.* New York: Reynal and Hitchcock, 1943.

Tsuchimochi, Gary. *Education Reform in Postwar Japan: The 1946 U.S. Education Mission.* Tokyo: University of Tokyo, 1993.

Tsutsui, William. *Banking Policy in Japan: American Efforts at Reform during the Occupation.* London: Routledge, 1988.

van Staaveren, Jacob. *An American in Japan, 1945–1948.* Seattle: University of Washington, 1994.

Ward, Robert. "Reflections on the Allied Occupation and Planned Political Change in Japan." In Robert Ward, ed., *Political Development in Modern Japan,* 477–535. Princeton: Princeton UP, 1968.

Ward, Robert, and Yoshikazu Sakamoto, eds. *Democratizing Japan.* Honolulu: University of Hawaii, 1987.

Weiner, Michael A. *Race and Migration in Imperial Japan: The Limits of Assimilation.* London: Routledge, 1994.

Wildes, Harry Emerson. *Typhoon in Tokyo.* New York: Macmillan, 1954.

Williams, Justin. *Japan's Political Revolution under MacArthur.* Athens: University of Georgia, 1979.

Wilson, George. "A New Look at the Problem of 'Japanese Fascism.' " *Comparative Studies in Society and History* 10: 4 (1968):401–412.

Wolfe, Robert, ed. *Americans as Proconsuls.* Carbondale: Southern Illinois UP, 1984.

Yoshida, Shigeru. Trans. Yoshida Kenichi. *The Yoshida Memoirs.* London: Heinemann, 1961.

10 European Reconquest and Neocolonialism in Southeast Asia

Dieu Thi Nguyen

European colonies in Southeast Asia existed for more than a hundred years when the Second World War and the rise of Japan ended the illusion they would last forever. By 1942, Japan's vast empire encompassed former British, French, and Dutch territories. The return of Europeans to their colonies in 1945, their attempts to rule as in the past, and their eventual withdrawal, as well as the informal network of ties that continue to bind colonies to metropoles, are the phenomenon of European reconquest and neocolonialism or decolonization.

THE HISTORIOGRAPHY

Decolonization has been scrutinized from three angles, which often intersect thematically and in periodization: decolonization of empires in general; nationalism and struggle for independence; and, as part of the Cold War, Vietnam War in the early phase of U.S. involvement. Each has a rich bibliography in English, French, and Dutch, though this chapter and its bibliography are limited to English-language literature.

Since the 1950s major studies have been conducted, but, to quote Darwin in *Britain and Decolonisation*, "decolonization" as a theme and concept "is still a Dark Continent" where passionate opinions often hinder sound research. At its narrowest, but most commonly used, definition it means the "transfer of power and sovereignty from the colonial powers to the successor state" (55), although it should also include colonial legacies. Some historians emphasize the First World War, others the Second World War, in triggering a chain reaction resulting in imperial retreat; others prefer to see decolonization as a phase in the readjustment of empires after the Second World War. Most count nationalism as a fundamental factor leading to decolonization; others completely reject it.

Holland's *European Decolonization* and Chamberlain's *Decolonization* present clear summaries of events, chronology, and interpretations. There are comparative studies of Western empires and their demises, such as Grimal's *Decolonization*, Ansprenger's *The Dissolution of the Colonial Empires*, Smith's *European Imperialism*, Betts' *Uncertain Dimensions*, and Albertini's *Decolonization* and *European Colonial Rule*.

Colonial administration and economic, political, and occasionally cultural aspects of empires at their height are at the center of Albertini's, Betts', and Smith's works. Albertini and Smith, using the time frame 1880–1940, looked at colonial empires through the lens of modernization theory; to a certain extent, because of their vast topic, they tended to reduce a complex phenomenon to linear, unidimensional interpretations, arguing that nationalism (Albertini) is an inherent presence in all societies that can be awakened by colonialism. Betts, following a similar structural analysis, shifted emphasis by concentrating on the cultural aspect of colonialism manifested in education and urban architecture. Decolonization is given but a cursory treatment by Albertini and Smith. Nonetheless, they are useful panoramas allowing historians to draw parallels between different regions and cultures under a single colonial entity and their diverse and different evolutions.

Grimal, Albertini, and Ansprenger each approached decolonization from a different perspective. Their massive works, emphasizing the British and French empires, delineate the differences between the two in terms of colonial philosophy and policies. Historians of empire, among whom Ansprenger and Albertini loom large, often remark about the differences between the French and British professed convictions concerning the equality (French) or inequality (British) of races and social classes and how such convictions are reflected in their imperial policies and attitudes. Ansprenger argued that the British, paradoxically, showed more flexibility in allowing for diverse social systems and cultures to exist side by side, facilitating the processes of independence, and prepared for a smooth, almost bloodless transition. The French, on the other hand, adamantly applied a uniform, centralized, and rigid Gallic system that did not tolerate the vagaries of diverse and different cultures. Such rigid insistence on the uniformity of all peoples and all cultures bound together by indissoluble ties to the greater French empire—what Marshall referred to as the *French Colonial Myth*—resulted in long, costly, and bloody wars of decolonization from Indochina to Algeria.

In *Decolonization*, Grimal emphasized the impact of the First World War and Wilson's Fourteen Points on the later processes of decolonization. The Second World War furthered the cause of the colonies by forcing European powers to formulate the Atlantic Charter, which affirmed the principle of self-determination; both charter and principle were quoted by nationalist leaders in their independence struggles.

Darwin in *Britain and Decolonisation* and Betts in *France and Decolonisation* focused on particular empires or "imperial systems" and their dismantling after 1945. Darwin's shorter time frame is the Second World War, to which he ascribed much importance in the imperial retreat. He found reasons multiple and multidimensional; he dissected each interpretation (economic, geostrategic, political, etc.), showing that no monocausal explanation can fully explain why, at the end of the war, when Britain emerged victorious, still considered a world power, and with a Labor government that was as "patriotic" as that of the previous Tory, the empire was rapidly fading.

Nationalism is an insufficient cause; nationalist movements of Africa and Asia were divided ethnically, and, with persistence, Britain could have won. Indeed, Darwin, denying widely accepted interpretations, rejected nationalism as the driving force; it was a myth, "an extraordinary delusion." He even contended that the British played "fairy godmother" to nationalist parties, agreeing to independence out of mutual interest, as in Malaya.

Betts traced the rise and fall of the French empire from the Third to the Fourth Republics, showing how it was put together, piece by piece, in a haphazard way by adventurers, geographers, politicians, and businessmen, with the people of France knowing or caring little about these distant lands. Yet for this imperial jigsaw born at random but representing the splendor of Greater France, French governments spent millions of francs and countless lives to retain it. Unlike Darwin, Betts counted nationalism as a main force leading to French imperial demise, crediting the likes of Ho Chi Minh in forcing the French to withdraw from Indochina.

Clayton's *Wars of French Decolonization* specifically addressed the military aspect of decolonization. In his book set in the background of French Cabinets from the Fourth to the Fifth Republics, he showed that France, stubbornly, almost desperately, refused to let go. Covering all corners of the empire, the author devoted the longest section to Vietnam, with which the French had a "love-hate relationship" that did not end in 1954 but continues to this day. Others, like Fitzgerald, asked, "Did France's Colonial Empire Make Economic Sense?" Among voices advocating the retention of empire, some contended that France needed all its resources, its colonies included, to start rebuilding and modernizing. Fitzgerald demonstrated that such an argument is inaccurate. In reality, "rapid decolonization would have been a more economically rational choice" (374) because of the long and costly wars of empire and because the colonies were more an economic burden than an asset.

Decolonization is inseparable from other phenomena, most noticeably nationalism. Yet few specialists are familiar with that field; fewer still are familiar with Asian nationalism. Most studies of decolonization are one-directional, from the viewpoint of European metropoles; nationalism is seen as but one concomitant product of colonialism. Conversely, one finds historians examining decolonization as a reaction to, and result of, the demands and initiatives of nationalist movements, viewing nationalism as a causal phenomenon of decolonization. Thus, European reconquest and neocolonialism are treated as a minor and transitional phase that tidily ended in the year of independence, without paying attention to the lingering effects of colonialism and neocolonialism on the newly independent nation-states. Works treating decolonization as the main theme generally see neocolonialism as an offshoot of empire.

SOUTHEAST ASIA

The historiography of Southeast Asia divides into precolonial, colonial, and postcolonial periods, with particular emphasis on postindependence. Events are then fitted into each compartment, observed as offsprings of a particular period and not in their continuity over the *longue durée.* Among many examples are Pluvier's *Southeast Asia* and Cady's *Post-war Southeast Asia.* Each has chapters dealing with European decolonization as a transitional phase within the evolution of former colonies into independent states.

Pluvier's analysis (more complete concerning decolonization and ending in the 1950s) uniquely emphasized the economics of colonial capitalism, stressing the role played by "economically interested pressure groups" and their preponderance in colonial decision making. He briefly analyzed the Allied occupation and compared and contrasted the French and Dutch attempts at "colonial restoration." Pluvier contended that the less intransigent British saved themselves long, costly wars by acknowledging the ineluctable while maintaining influence long after independence was gained—in Malaya and Singapore at least.

Cady's *Post-war Southeast Asia* chronologically continued his *Southeast Asia,* which spans the period from its origins to the Japanese occupation, down to early 1970. Cady spent little time on decolonization, preferring to emphasize the postindependence period, or the time of "Revolution, Communist and Otherwise," and the Cold War phase with the explosion of the Vietnam War. Both books barely touch upon the developments in the metropoles, an aspect that had an impact on regional events yet is one seldom explored.

Steinberg's *In Search of Southeast Asia,* Osborne's *Southeast Asia,* and Jeffrey's *Asia: The Winning of Independence* adopted the same approach and mentioned only in passing European reconquest and decolonization. *In Search of Southeast Asia,* a survey of ten countries with contributions from many postwar Southeast Asian specialists, begins in the eighteenth century and ends in the 1970s–1980s with "Transforming Southeast Asia." All three works consider decolonization as one result of the struggle for independence flaring up everywhere in 1945–1946. Osborne and Jeffrey viewed the roads to independence as bifurcating between revolution and evolution or other paths. They dissected the complex relationships that bind colonial governments to colonized societies, leading the Dutch and the French to reject the inevitable by going to war against the Indonesians and Vietnamese, Laotians, and Cambodians, while the British shaped Malaysia and Singapore into statehood and completely withdrew from Burma.

Recent historiographic trends indicate viewing nations of Southeast Asia as entities that are the sums of their precolonial and colonial past. This "refocusing," anticipated by Benda in the 1950s with his prophetically entitled "Decolonization in Indonesia" in *Continuity and Change*, stressed both "continuity and change," leading to studies taking a closer look at colonial and neocolonial influences in the construction of Southeast Asian identities. Recently published works like Dixon's *Southeast Asia in the World-Economy*, McCloud's *Southeast Asia*, Christie's *A Modern History of Southeast Asia*, and Stockwell's "Southeast Asia in War and Peace" either integrate Southeast Asia as a macroregion into the world's economy in a continuation from the past to the future or look at the legacy of decolonization as leading to the emergence not only of nation-states with economies shaped by their colonial past but also of separatist movements.

McCloud, for instance, has a "global" approach to integrating the region within a wider framework, placing it along "bipolar" and "multipolar" axes. He skipped decolonization, dealing with British neocolonialism in Malaysia and Singapore in two paragraphs. Dixon's *Southeast Asia* briefly follows the region's economic development from precolonial, through colonial, to postindependence. Nevertheless, Dixon's work is more satisfying in linking past economic phases to present integration into the world economy in a logical continuity, enabling the reader to grasp the evolution of the countries' economies in toto. Thus, Dixon treats decolonization as part of the chain of events and succinctly deals with economic neocolonialism and unequal development. The only regret is that his book is much too short and relies greatly on secondary sources.

Christie's *Modern History* seeks to analyze "decolonization . . . from the perspective of the separatist movements," thus bringing into the foreground a sensitive topic neglected or avoided because of its perceived role in fragmenting centralizing nation-states. Christie approached decolonization from the point of view of the returning powers' treatment of ethnic or religious minorities, that is, how the European colonial powers handled the question of the Moluccans, the Montagnards, or the Karens, a process strengthening them against the soon-to-be independent nation-states. This much-needed study shows the evolution of some separatist movements of

Southeast Asia, which have often been treated as "problems" rather than legitimate historical actors. Stockwell's "Southeast Asia" is a most satisfactory treatment of the question of European reconquest and, to a lesser extent, neocolonialism. Tarling's excellent *The Fall of Imperial Britain* surveyed the rise and fall of the British empire in Southeast Asia over a century and a half through phases of primacy and crises, to conclude with post–Second World War decolonization. Following Ronald E. Robinson and John Gallagher, early proponents of the economic motivation interpretation of imperialism, Tarling demonstrated that Britain acquired informal and formal empires not so much out of territorial greed but because of a commercial necessity, that of free trade.

There is no English-language study concerning the French empire in Southeast Asia. Murray, adopting a Marxist framework in *The Development of Capitalism in Colonial Indochina*, documented the introduction of the capitalist system from France into French Indochina, forever transforming the traditional world of villages and their economies. He scrutinized almost every aspect of the colonial economy in detail but did not extend his analysis beyond the 1940s. There is an inexplicable lack of Anglo-American scholarship concerning the French empire in Southeast Asia— outside of the plethora of works dealing with the First and Second Indochina Wars.

THE INDOCHINA WARS

A score of works incidentally analyze decolonization as part of the French Indochina War, the opening act to America's Vietnam conflict, a field in which American historians predominate. Such studies attempt to locate the roots of the American war in the 1940s, often by focusing on the United States–France–Indochina triangle. Prime examples are Gardner's *Approaching Vietnam*, Irving's *First Indochina War*, Tønnesson's superb *The Vietnamese Revolution of 1945*, Dreifort's detailed *Myopic Grandeur*, and Short's *The Origins of the Vietnam War*. Another common focus is on United States–Britain policies relating to Indochina or Southeast Asia during the Pacific War: Louis' *Imperialism at Bay* or Thorne's magnificent *Allies of a Kind*, which scrutinizes British-American relations during the conflict, and his *The Issue of War*.

Gardner, Louis, Dreifort, Tønnesson, and Hess are considered "Roosevelt historians," as they stress his role, his anti-imperialist stance, his proposals of trusteeship for Indochina, his distrust of the French, and, in particular, his contentious relationship with De Gaulle. Some also made much of Roosevelt's pragmatic attitude toward the end of the war, which placed maintaining the Western alliance above idealistic concerns for colonized people, all elements that weighed heavily in European wartime colonial planning and return to the region.

Tønnesson's introduction usefully describes the evolution in the inter-pretations of Roosevelt's policy, also known as "the lost opportunity school." Other works examine U.S. diplomatic history in the region and the complicated relationships among the United States, Britain, France, and the Netherlands: Fifield's *The Diplomacy of Southeast Asia*, Colbert's *Southeast Asia in International Politics*, and Hess' *The United States' Emergence as a Southeast Asian Power*. Both Colbert and Hess, continuing Fifield's tradition, analyzed a crucial period, 1940s–1950s, which encompassed de-colonization and the Cold War era. Developing themes previously broached—the role of Roosevelt (who, according to Colbert, was ignorant of Southeast Asia), De Gaulle, and the notion of trusteeship—Colbert placed decolonization within the framework of international politics, whereas Hess established the United States as the diplomatic locus around which revolved European powers and regional states. Like Pluvier's com-parison of decolonization in Indochina and Indonesia, Colbert and Hess underlined the differences between French and Dutch policies as well as the paradoxical U.S. and British attitudes vis-à-vis the two metropoles: sup-portive of the French (after Roosevelt's death) to the point of providing military and financial means to wage the war of reconquest and neutral and even hostile toward the Dutch by using threats of withholding eco-nomic aid and the fomenting of international disapproval.

POST-OCCUPATION FORCES AND SEAC

France, Great Britain, and Holland regarded the loss of empires, hu-miliating as it was, as a temporary phenomenon. As Louis and Thorne demonstrated, the wartime European governments never contemplated relinquishing their colonial empires, the better to erase the memory of defeat and to rebuild the metropoles with the contributions of colonized peoples and the natural wealth of their lands. Dennis' *Troubled Days of Peace*, focusing on French Indochina and the Netherlands East Indies, analyzed the difficulties faced by Admiral Lord Louis Mountbatten, in charge of Southeast Asia Command (SEAC), with insufficient forces and logistics at his disposal, having to rely mostly on the Indian army at a time when India itself was demanding independence. Singh's *Post-war Occupa-tion Forces* described (with a number of inaccuracies, however) the tasks undertaken by the Indian army under the command of Lord Mountbatten after the Japanese army's surrender.

FRENCH PLANNING, RECONQUEST, AND NEOCOLONIALISM

France's return to Indochina was complicated by the Petainist govern-ment of Admiral Decoux and De Gaulle's Committee for National Liberation. Dreifort's *Myopic Grandeur,* a rare English-language study of the French role in Asia between the 1920s and 1945, argues that France, lacking the military capacity to protect its possessions in Southeast Asia, resorted to diplomacy, trying to fend off Japanese expansion through negotiations while searching for allies—all to no avail. Like Tønnesson's *Vietnamese Revolution,* Dreifort emphasized Roosevelt and De Gaulle's relations and, to a certain extent Churchill's with De Gaulle, as crucial to Indochina's fate. Dreifort and Tønnesson showed the byzantine efforts by De Gaulle's forces, whose preparations for return were crushed on March 9, 1945. "Operation Blue Moon" destroyed in one swoop all that the Decoux administration had preserved of the French presence in Indochina.

Decoux's role has been hotly debated, many accusing him of collaborating with the Japanese, while others deny this, countering that his acquiescence preserved Indochina from a much harsher Japanese regime. Dreifort asserted that the sight of imprisoned Frenchmen and the lamentable debacle of Frenchmen and their flight in March 1945 had a profounder impact on the nationalist movements than the defeat of 1940.

Unlike most historians, Tønnesson endeavored to prove that Roosevelt never forsook his anticolonialism. On the contrary, Roosevelt put together a campaign meant to deceive the Japanese into overthrowing the French, thus placing Indochina under the category of occupied nations to be liberated by the Allies and placed under the mandate system. This scheme, Tønnesson asserted, directly or indirectly allowed Ho Chi Minh to carry out the August Revolution and, ultimately, the creation of the Democratic Republic of Vietnam on September 2, 1945.

The events leading to the First Indochina War are well known. The basic issues, however, remain problematic. Was the movement led by Ho Chi Minh and the Indochina Communist Party (ICP) a truly nationalist one representative of all the Vietnamese people and their will? Were the events of the summer of 1945, the Democratic Republic of Vietnam (DRV), the result of a fortuitous convergence of factors or determined by the ICP's farsighted planning? In what ways did France's policies and the United States' attitude contribute to the party's success and to the First Indochina War? Which actors (the Free French, the ICP, the Vietnamese Royalists, the sects, China, the Soviet Union, etc.) played key roles at the local, national, regional, and international levels, and to what extent did their actions influence the course of the First and eventually the Second Indochina Wars?

The first studies on Indochina in the 1950s were by French authors, either witness-participants or Indochina experts. Several were translated into English and are often quoted, for example, Devillers, *End of a War,* and Bodard, *The Quicksand War,* which, though lively, lacks the rigor and documentation of Devillers' works.

Early English-language works were scarce and journalistic in nature, with the exception of the remarkable publications by a French-born scholar, Bernard Fall. In works such as *Street without Joy* and *The Two Vietnams*, Fall thoroughly analyzed the political and military aspects of the First and Second Indochina conflicts. Among works by Anglophone authors, Lancaster's *Emancipation of French Indochina*, Hammer's *Struggle for Indochina*, and McAlister's *Vietnam: The Origins of Revolution* are classics on the First Indochina War that analyze its colonial roots, the return of the French in 1945, and the catastrophic turn of events that led to conflict in 1946.

From the perspective of international politics, 1945 is a pivotal year. McAlister's *Vietnam* laid the groundwork for an assessment of the August Revolution of 1945. Toward the end of his study, McAlister analyzed the "French views on colonial reoccupation," arguing that they never wavered and were clearly articulated at the Brazzaville conference in 1944. As noted by Kent in "Anglo-French Colonial Co-operation," France's answer to nationalist demands was to inscribe the French Union within the 1946 Constitution, which allowed former colonies to acquire "Associated States" status.

American explorations of that critical phase understandably view the events in the light of U.S. attitudes concerning France, Britain, and Indochina. Whereas most accounts—Kahin's detailed *Intervention*, for instance—are critical of the British role, British interpretations are sympathetic to the actions of British officers and soldiers and tend to be critical of the "naive anticolonialism" of the Americans.

Scores of historians have criticized Major General Gracey's actions during SEAC's takeover in allowing the situation to degenerate into an armed conflict between the French and the Vietnamese forces in Saigon. Dunn's *The First Vietnam War* defended Gracey by making the unusual argument that, given his limited forces and the necessity of reliance on the Japanese army and his mandate to maintain law and order and to turn over control to the French by "virtue of their historical position in the country," he did the best he could and is, in fact, an unrecognized patron of the soon-to-be-born, anticommunist Republic of Vietnam!

Irving's *First Indochina War* does not analyze the conflict; rather, it is an original study of its impact on each country's politics from 1946 to 1954, the attitudes of the political parties, and how domestic events influenced the choice of the (wrong) French negotiators and generals. The French concluded more than a hundred years' presence by a hasty military withdrawal; in part, because, as Kahin pointed out in *Intervention*, troops were needed for another imperial war in Algeria. The United States then took over. As Post noted in his four-volume *Revolution, Socialism and Nationalism in Vietnam*, French economic interests in the form of plantations, mining concessions, export-import companies, and so on were soon overwhelmed by giant American companies.

Standing apart, a monument to itself, is Marr's magnum opus *Vietnam 1945*, which revisits many essential questions concerning the August Revolution. Marr approached these events from the perspectives of China, France, the United States, and Vietnam; from high-powered figures to the humble "*instituteur*"; from ICP cadres to Royalists; and from Free French to Japanese officers. Marr wove thousands of threads into a tapestry telling a complicated story leading to the rise of the Democratic Republic of Vietnam on September 2, 1945—not quite the simplistic interpretation that made the ICP and Ho Chi Minh the deus ex machina of its birth and the Bao Dai government a mere puppet without will or soul and Decoux not quite the Petainist, but not quite the French patriot. Marr's work will likely remain for many years the definitive work on 1945.

French influence lingered longer in Laos and Cambodia; their historiography is understandably dominated by French scholars. Anglo-American research on their colonial and immediate postwar period is almost nonexistent. Recent publications concerning Cambodia are plentiful and of scholarly interest but concentrate mostly on the question of the Khmer Rouge and the role played by that perennial figure of Cambodian history King Sihanouk. A partial exception is Lancaster's *Emancipation*, an early attempt at appraising French decolonization while placing it within the precolonial and colonial background. The unique and pioneering work by the Indian historian Reddi, *The Cambodian Independence Movement*, carefully assessed Cambodian politics in the 1940s–1950s and the French role but has unfortunately not been elaborated on by later historians. In *Cambodia, a Shattered Society*, French anthropologist Martin analyzed society from protectorate to the present, criticizing the French role in maintaining the "Cochinchinese" provinces within the Vietnamese territory over the protest of Cambodian delegates. The preeminent English-language author is Chandler, whose *History of Cambodia* and *The Tragedy of Cambodian History* made that history accessible and coherent to the general public. Chandler surveyed the French period but only as far as it relates to later Cambodian political events. Decolonization received little emphasis.

Most English-language publications on Laos deal almost exclusively with the rise of communism under the Pathet Lao and the American involvement (a remark also applicable to Cambodia). However, within that framework, a few exceptions scrutinize the French period and influence during and after the Second World War as part of the later communist equation: Dommen, *Conflict in Laos*, and Toye, *Laos*. Both devoted attention to the decades of the 1940s to the 1970s, presenting a more detailed incursion into the Franco-Lao phase of the Indochina War and its aftermath as well as France's lingering influence in Laos. Halpern in *Govern-*

ment, Politics, and Social Structures in Laos noted that French military advisers continued to train the Royal Lao Army, and French aid in education, health care, and infrastructure in the 1950s–1960s was still important.

BRITISH PLANNING, RECONQUEST, AND NEOCOLONIALISM

For Britain, Malaya and Singapore, while precious, were not as vital as India and Burma. In " 'A New and a Better Cunning,' " Tarling mentioned that British planners envisioned Britain's return to Burma as a period of direct rule in order to rebuild the country along British lines, preparing it for eventual autonomy within the Commonwealth. Yet, by 1948, the British withdrew. Burma's relatively rapid and easy accession to independence has stimulated much scholarly analysis. Some ascribe it to the unity and determination of the nationalist movement, some to military factors, others to the Indian factor. Still others attribute it to Burma's lack of economic assets. Some have argued that the postwar British empire contracted territorially as a deliberate process of adapting to new realities and not as a consequence of an uncontrollable decline. Others look at a variety of unpredictable factors, among which is the "military dimension."

Immediately after the war, as Tinker's "The Contraction of Empire in Asia" pointed out, it became necessary to demobilize the conscripts in the British armed services. Heavy demands were thus put on the Indian army, which had been called upon to police the fringes of the British empire as well as to accept the Japanese army's surrender and its repatriation under SEAC.

In August 1945, when Burma was recaptured, the campaign was largely carried out by the Indian army with the cooperation of Burmese forces led by the Anti-Fascist Organization (AFO). When it became clear that the internal situation was evolving toward lawlessness and a mass uprising, it was quickly perceived that the Indian army could not be trusted to reestablish order because of India's parallel demand for independence. As Taylor's "Burma in the Anti-Fascist War" emphasized, "The Indian Army had always been the main force used to hold Burma and without it Britain's future in Burma was sealed" (134). Consequently, Attlee announced a change in the policy. Taylor's "Burma" argues that decisions relating to Burma were influenced by those concerning India since one reason for annexation of Burma was its proximity to India.

When the Labor government decided in 1947 to part ways with India, Burma ceased to matter. Burma, impoverished by the war, had lost its economic appeal, and its ethnic and political mosaic was determined to resist British rule. Faced with this uncommonly united front dominated by the Anti-Fascist People's Freedom League's leader, Aung San, along with the rise of a communist threat, the British agreed to Burma's independence, formally acknowledged in January 1948. Aung San Suu Kyi's biography of her father, *Aung San of Burma*, traces a sympathetic portrait of the man; Maung's edited collection, *Aung San of Burma*, conveys a more complex vision. A score of accounts by British participants was published in the late 1950s, the most important being Donnison's *British Military Administration* and Collis' *Last and First*, based on former governor Sir Reginald Dorman-Smith's papers.

Tinker's edited collection of documents entitled *Burma: The Struggle for Independence* shows how eager Lord Mountbatten was to negotiate with the most powerful parties and leaders. Excerpts of memoirs of participants, the old "Burma Hands," can be found in this monumental collection of documents released by the government.

Taylor in *The State in Burma* examined how British colonial rule, by abolishing the Burmese monarchy and treating Burma as an appendage of India, had disrupted its historical identity. Even with independence in 1948 and before the military coup of 1962, the state nearly vanished and was not replaced by any viable equivalent. In Burma British interests did not linger and could not extend into a neocolonialist phase as elsewhere in the region.

In Malaya and Borneo, the picture was totally different. Both Stockwell in "Southeast Asia" and Lau in *The Malayan Union Controversy* remarked that the Colonial Office was determined to centralize the different states under a single British authority and to address the question of ethnic plurality in Malay society. The plan acknowledged non-Malays' citizenship rights, thus indirectly breaking that tacit entente between the British and the Malays that had given the latter predominance in the Malay world.

Malaya is often cited as welcoming the British back without much opposition. Overall, the British held out the longest in Malaya (and Singapore), exerting influence long after most former colonial powers departed. The reasons advanced are many: Malaya's being necessary for Britain's recovery because of its tin and rubber (exported to the United States) and its dollar-earning capacity; and its geostrategic importance as Britain's base of power. Yet, by August 1957, an independent Federation of Malaya was born.

What, then, were the causes? As demonstrated by Stockwell, Stubbs, and others, the scheme met unexpected resistance from Malay leaders and particularly from the newly formed nationalist party, United Malays National Organization (UMNO), in 1946. Consequently, the Malayan Union scheme was replaced by a more pro-Malay "Federation of Malaya" within the British Commonwealth and the promise of independence. The next stage, the state of emergency declared in July 1948, amply documented and debated in Short's, *The Communist Insurrection*, O'Ballance's *The Communist Insurgent War*, and Stubbs' *Hearts and Minds*, moved Malaya straight into the Cold War era with the Malay Communist Party (MCP) launching an armed struggle against the colonial administration. Clutterbuck's *Conflict and Violence* studied the British monitoring of the MCP's activities with a particular focus on Singapore. Based on classified documents, he revealed how Malay leaders like Tunku Abdul Rahman, by allying themselves to the British governor of Singapore, David Marshall, prevented the MCP's participation in independence discussions and how British policy crushed any communist move, opening the way for a noncommunist, self-governing, and finally independent Singapore in 1965.

Many comparisons (Clutterbuck, *The Long, Long War*, and Stubbs, *Hearts and Minds*) made between the Malayan insurgency and the Vietnamese insurgency attempt to comprehend the success of the Briggs plan and the failure of the strategic hamlets in Vietnam. Stubbs explained that the Malayan emergency's policy succeeded because it took into account the socioeconomic roots of the problem and aimed at winning the population's "hearts and minds." The debate concerning this has centered on a number of issues: the extent of the insurgency on the British decision to withdraw, the international factor of the Cold War and particularly of the Korean War, and the weariness of the British public. Which weighed most in the British decision to leave? Or had Britain always meant to grant independence and merely intended to guide Malaysia toward an acceptable—by British standards—future?

The postindependence period since 1957 has been characterized by students like Nonini in *British Colonial Rule* as one of "neocolonial capitalist development . . . with continued high levels of foreign investment and economic influence" (143). Others (Stockwell or Chin's *Defence of Malaysia and Singapore*) stressed the continued British legacy and involvement in Malaysian affairs after independence.

DUTCH RECONQUEST AND NEOCOLONIALISM

As demonstrated by Kahin's *Nationalism and Revolution* and elaborated by new archival research in McMahon's *Colonialism and Cold War*, the Netherlands, though falling to Germany, considered holding the East Indies as an absolute political and economic necessity for it to retain its great empire-nation status. As Van Der Eng pointed out in "Marshall Aid as a Catalyst," the islands provided almost 14 percent of the Dutch national income in 1938. The Dutch government-in-exile in London was unwilling to consider any plan of autonomy, declaring in December 1942 that the East Indies should remain within a Dutch Commonwealth, in which there would be, however, "complete self-reliance," "partnership," and "freedom of conduct," platitudes meant to please the American ally, which did not oppose the Dutch return.

Several students of Indonesia have remarked on the different behavior of British forces in Indonesia under General Christison of SEAC and those forces in Indochina under General Gracey. The nearly unanimous resistance by Indonesians convinced the British to pressure the Dutch to negotiate. Stockwell brought in the international dimension by placing the Dutch–British relationships within the European framework. While eager to assist in the recovery of the Netherlands, Britain had no intention of getting involved in a costly financial and diplomatic conflict; with great relief the British withdrew in November 1946. For an in-depth analysis, Kahin's *Nationalism* remains unequaled, an impassioned analysis of the nationalist movement, its different expressions and leaders (Sukarno, Tan Malaka, Sjahrir, et al.), their policies of diplomacy versus confrontation, and its struggle against the Dutch attempt at reconquest during 1945–1950.

Kahin's study has been updated by more recent (and Java-centered) works like Anderson's *Java in a Time of Revolution*, which takes Kahin's counterpoint by emphasizing Tan Malaka's uncompromising stand in the revolution, Reid's *Indonesian National Revolution*, and McMahon's *Colonialism and Cold War*. The latter was the first to show in depth the parts played by the United States and the United Nations organization and to emphasize the role of Third World nations like India, which protested the use of Indian troops in repressing a country struggling for independence. Looking at the metropole, Grimal highlighted the influence of the Catholics and Calvinists in Dutch adamant refusal to acknowledge the Republic; Van der Eng, by contrast, advanced economic necessity as the crucial factor in explaining the Netherlands' will to hang on to one of its major sources, the East Indies. Kahin remarked in *Nationalism* that the Dutch (much like the French with their associated states), while conducting military actions, frantically attempted to create a federal structure of states "based on Dutch police and Dutch bayonets" in order to weaken the Republic and to protect those peoples of Indonesia who had been closely associated with the Netherlands.

A number of historians, including McMahon, argue that the United States initially had scant interest in Indonesian nationalism. In 1948, after the Indonesian Republic crushed a communist insurrection, the United States, with Congress and public opinion—and American investors, as pointed out in Kahin and Kahin's *Subversion as Foreign Policy*—increasingly demanding curtailing aid, began to support decolonization. It stepped up pressure by threatening to withhold Marshall aid. A number of historians argued that this led the Dutch to yield. Others, like Van der Eng, asserted that The Hague came to realize that a free East Indies would be economically more beneficial. More importantly, independence would save the Netherlands having to underwrite Indonesia's debts of 1.2 billion guilders, while also avoiding a costly and protracted guerrilla war. As Kahin and McMahon observed, it was upon the American insistence during the negotiations that Indonesia agreed to shoulder that debt itself. All these savings allowed the Netherlands to make a quick economic recovery in the 1950s.

This pragmatic acceptance of economic reality did not mean the Dutch did not suffer a blow to their national psyche. The territory of West New Guinea proved to be The Hague's last colonial hurrah. In a neocolonialist action, the Netherlands stubbornly held on to a remaining fragment of its tattered empire, Parliament voting in 1952 to incorporate it into its territory. Only in the 1960s did the Dutch relinquish this apparently worthless wilderness. Lijphart's *The Trauma of Decolonization* shows that it was not for the usual economic reasons, since the oil potential proved utterly disappointing, nor as an outlet for Holland's surplus labor, since the initial colonizers had all returned home. From the strategic value standpoint, West New Guinea did not attract any Great Power's interest. Lijphart argued the Netherlands clung to this last territory out of an irrational urge to show the world that it was not just another insignificant nation by the North Sea. The author's argument counters the perennial image of Dutch pragmatism in emphasizing that, in this matter, subjective factors won out. Nevertheless, the Dutch were not willing to pay the ultimate price of a war of attrition. West New Guinea came under the Republic of Indonesia in 1963 and was renamed Irian Jaya.

In *Subversion as Foreign Policy*, a fascinating dissection of the Eisenhower administration's involvement in Indonesian affairs, Kahin and Kahin demonstrated that the question of Irian Jaya was a thorn in the side of the Republic, which attempted to present its side of the issue at the United Nations. As a result, it provoked President Sukarno to order "the departure of most of the 46,000 Netherlanders living in Indonesia." Crouch in *The Army and Politics* pointed out that the anger thus generated led nationalist Indonesians to take over Dutch enterprises and manage them. The issue lingered on into the 1960s, a contentious aspect that influenced America's Cold War policy toward Indonesia.

From the theoretical standpoint of the decolonization debate, one may note, as does Wesseling in "The Giant That Was a Dwarf," "the absence of the Dutch in the international debate on imperialism" in contrast to the British, French, Germans, and Italians. Curiously, Dutch intellectuals and politicians denied the existence of Dutch imperialism in the case of the Netherlands East Indies. The Dutch historian Kuitenbrouwer conversely argued in *The Netherlands and the Rise of Modern Imperialism* that there was such a thing as "preemptive imperialism" as proven by the case of the Netherlands East Indies. In any case, Wesseling argued in "The Giant That Was a Dwarf," while the Dutch were anxious to keep their empire, they lacked the political and military means to be an imperial power. The Netherlands were "a colonial giant but a political dwarf."

CONCLUSION

The European reconquest of Southeast Asia in the post–Second World War era and withdrawal from the region along with the lingering legacies of decolonization were a process that took place in Asia and in other parts of the world. As such, decolonization has been studied within the framework of "empires," be they British, French, Dutch, Iberian, or American. It has also been located in the context of nationalist and independence movements that spread worldwide during the same period, and, as such, it was considered a transitory and even minor phase by students of indigenous histories. Decolonization also stretched into the years when the Cold War spread its shadow over continents, setting the United States and the Soviet Union on a collision course.

For Southeast Asia, anticommunism played an important part in American involvement in the later phase of decolonization. The historiography that covers these different topics and fields is abundant—in the case of the Vietnam War, almost encyclopedic; well researched and documented, it uses sources in the relevant languages and has benefited from recent declassification or availability of documents. Nevertheless, the historiography of decolonization in Southeast Asia suffers from a lack of interest on the part of scholars, who tend to see it as a component of larger, more interesting themes and have thus failed to pay due attention to its possible contribution to an understanding of an essential phase of modern history. Decolonization has not been fully analyzed in its continuity as a link between the colonial past and an independent present and future. More importantly, historians have generally failed to examine the multiple legacies of European colonial rule in the new nation-states. Too often, scholars have been content to end their studies on the "independence day"— as if ties forged over centuries could be broken in a matter of days, months, or years! Only by expanding our understanding of the complexity and continuities implied by "decolonization" can we do justice to the true impact of national independence on both the metropoles and the former colonies.

BIBLIOGRAPHY

Albertini, Rudolf von. *Decolonization; the Administration and Future of the Colonies, 1919–1960.* New York: Doubleday, 1971.
———. *European Colonial Rule, 1880–1940: The Impact of the West on India, Southeast Asia, and Africa.* Westport, CT: Greenwood, 1982.
Anderson, Benedict Richard O. *Java in a Time of Revolution: Occupation and Resistance, 1944–1946.* Ithaca, NY: Cornell UP, 1972.
Ansprenger, Franz. *The Dissolution of the Colonial Empires.* London: Routledge, 1989.

Aung, San Suu Kyi. *Aung San of Burma*. Edinburgh: Kiscadale, 1991.

Benda, Harry J. *Continuity and Change in Southeast Asia*. New Haven, CT: Yale University Southeast Asia Studies, 1972.

Betts, Raymond F. *France and Decolonisation, 1900–1960*. New York: St. Martin's, 1991.

———. *Uncertain Dimensions: Western Overseas Empires in the Twentieth Century*. Minneapolis: University of Minnesota, 1985.

Bodard, Lucien. *The Quicksand War*. Boston: Little, Brown, 1967.

Cady, John F. *The History of Post-war Southeast Asia*. Athens: Ohio UP, 1974.

———. *Southeast Asia: Its History and Development*. New York: McGraw-Hill, 1961.

Chamberlain, Muriel Evelyn. *Decolonization, the Fall of the European Empires*. New York: Blackwell, 1985.

Chandler, David P. *A History of Cambodia*. Boulder, CO: Westview, 1992.

———. *The Tragedy of Cambodian History: Politics, War, and Revolution since 1945*. New Haven, CT: Yale UP, 1991.

Chin, Kee Wah. *The Defence of Malaysia and Singapore: The Transformation of a Security System, 1957–1991*. New York: Cambridge UP, 1983.

Christie, Clive J. *A Modern History of Southeast Asia: Decolonization, Nationalism and Separatism*. London: Tauris Academic Studies, 1996.

Clayton, Anthony. *The Wars of French Decolonization*. New York: Longman, 1994.

Clutterbuck, Richard L. *Conflict and Violence in Singapore and Malaysia, 1945–1983*. Boulder, CO: Westview, 1985.

———. *The Long, Long War: Counterinsurgency in Malaya and Vietnam*. New York: Praeger, 1966.

Colbert, Evelyn. *Southeast Asia in International Politics, 1941–1956*. Ithaca, NY: Cornell UP, 1977.

Collis, Maurice. *Last and First in Burma, 1941–1948*. London: Faber and Faber, 1956.

Crouch, Harold. *The Army and Politics in Indonesia*. Ithaca, NY: Cornell UP, 1978.

Darwin, John G. *Britain and Decolonisation: The Retreat from Empire in the Postwar World*. New York: St. Martin's, 1988.

Dennis, Peter. *Troubled Days of Peace: Mountbatten and South East Asia Command, 1945–1946*. New York: St. Martin's, 1987.

Devillers, Philippe. *End of a War: Indochina, 1954*. New York: Praeger, 1969.

Dixon, Chris. *Southeast Asia in the World-Economy*. Cambridge: Cambridge UP, 1991.

Dommen, Arthur J. *Conflict in Laos, the Politics of Neutralization*. New York: Praeger, 1971.

Donnison, F. S. W. *British Military Administration in the Far East, 1943–1946*. London: HMSO, 1956.

Dreifort, John E. *Myopic Grandeur: The Ambivalence of French Foreign Policy toward the Far East, 1919–1945*. Kent, OH: Kent State UP, 1991.

Dunn, Peter. *The First Vietnam War*. London: Hurst, 1985.

Fall, Bernard. *Street without Joy, Insurgency in Indochina, 1946–1963*. Harrisburg, PA: Stackpole, 1963.

———. *The Two Vietnams, a Historical and Military Analysis*. New York: Praeger, 1967.

Fifield, Russell. *The Diplomacy of Southeast Asia: 1945–1958*. New York: Harper, 1958.

Fitzgerald, Edward Peter. "Did France's Colonial Empire Make Economic Sense?

A Perspective from the Postwar Decade, 1946–1956.'' *The Journal of Economic History* 48 (1988): 373–385.

Gardner, Lloyd C. *Approaching Vietnam: From World War II through Dien Bien Phu.* New York: Norton, 1988.

Grimal, Henri. *Decolonization: The British, French, Dutch, and Belgian Empires, 1919–1963.* Boulder, CO: Westview, 1978.

Halpern, Joel. *Government, Politics, and Social Structure in Laos, a Study of Tradition and Innovation.* New Haven, CT: Southeast Asia Studies, Yale UP, 1964.

Hammer, Ellen J. *The Struggle for Indochina, 1940–1955.* Stanford, CA: Stanford UP, 1966.

Hess, Gary R. *The United States' Emergence as a Southeast Asian Power, 1940–1950.* New York: Columbia UP, 1987.

Holland, Roy Fraser. *European Decolonization 1918–1981: An Introductory Survey.* Houndsmills, U.K.: Macmillan, 1985.

Irving, Ronald Eckford Mill. *The First Indochina War: French and American Policy, 1945–1954.* London: Helm, 1975.

Jeffrey, Robin, ed. *Asia: the Winning of Independence: The Philippines, India, Indonesia, Vietnam, Malaya.* London: Macmillan, 1981.

Kahin, Audrey R., and George McT. Kahin. *Subversion as Foreign Policy, the Secret Eisenhower and Dulles Debacle in Indonesia.* New York: New, 1995.

Kahin, George McTurnān. *Intervention: How America Became Involved in Vietnam.* New York: Alfred A. Knopf, 1986.

———. *Nationalism and Revolution in Indonesia.* Ithaca, NY: Cornell UP, 1952.

Kent, John. "Anglo-French Colonial Co-operation, 1939–1949.'' *Journal of Imperial and Commonwealth History* 17 (1988): 55–82.

Lancaster, Donald. *The Emancipation of French Indochina.* London: Oxford UP, 1961.

Lau, Albert. *The Malayan Union Controversy 1942–1948.* Singapore; New York: Oxford UP, 1991.

Lijphart, Arend. *The Trauma of Decolonization: The Dutch and West New Guinea.* New Haven, CT: Yale UP, 1966.

Louis, William Roger. *Imperialism at Bay 1941–1945: The United States and the Decolonization of the British Empire.* Oxford: Oxford UP, 1977.

Marr, David G. *Vietnam 1945, the Quest for Power.* Berkeley: University of California, 1995.

Marshall, D. Bruce. *The French Colonial Myth and Constitution-Making in the Fourth Republic.* New Haven, CT: Yale UP, 1973.

Martin, Marie Alexandrine. *Cambodia, a Shattered Society.* Berkeley: University of California, 1994.

Maung, Maung U., ed. *Aung San of Burma.* The Hague: Martinus Nijhof, 1962.

McCloud, Donald G. *Southeast Asia: Tradition and Modernity in the Contemporary World.* Boulder, CO: Westview Press, 1995.

McAlister, John T., Jr. *Vietnam: The Origins of Revolution* (1885–1946). New York: Doubleday Anchor, 1968, 1971; London: Allen Lane, 1969.

McMahon, Robert J. *Colonialism and Cold War: The United States and the Struggle for Indonesian Independence, 1945–1949.* Ithaca, NY: Cornell UP, 1981.

Murray, Martin J. *The Development of Capitalism in Colonial Indochina, 1870–1940.* Berkeley: University of California, 1980.

Nonini, Donald Macon. *British Colonial Rule and the Resistance of the Malay Peasantry, 1900–1957.* New Haven, CT: Yale University Southeast Asia Studies, 1992.

O'Ballance, Edgar. *Malaya: The Communist Insurgent War, 1948–1960.* Hamden, CT: Archon, 1966.

Osborne, Milton. *Southeast Asia, an Illustrated Introductory History.* Singapore: Allen and Unwin, 1992.

Pluvier, Jan. *Southeast Asia from Colonialism to Independence.* Kuala Lumpur: Oxford UP, 1971.

Post, Ken. *Revolution, Socialism and Nationalism in Vietnam.* 4 vols. Belmont, CA: Wadsworth, 1989.

Reddi, V. M. *The History of the Cambodian Independence Movement, 1863–1955.* Tirupati, Cambodia: Sri Venkateswara UP, 1970.

Reid, Anthony. *The Indonesian National Revolution, 1945–1950.* Hawthorn, Victoria, Australia: Longman, 1974.

Robinson, Ronald E., and John Gallagher. *Imperialism: The Robinson and Gallagher Controversy* New York: New Viewpoints, 1976.

Short, Anthony. *The Communist Insurrection in Malaya, 1948–1960.* New York: Crane, Russak, 1975.

———. *The Origins of the Vietnam War.* London: Longman, 1974, 1989.

Singh, Rajendra. *Post-war Occupation Forces: Japan and Southeast Asia.* Combined Inter-services Historical Section, India and Pakistan; distributors: Orient Longmans, 1958.

Smith, Woodruff D. *European Imperialism in the Nineteenth and Twentieth Centuries.* Chicago: Nelson-Hall, 1982.

Steinberg, David Joel, ed. *In Search of Southeast Asia: A Modern History.* Honolulu: University of Hawaii, 1987.

Stockwell, A. J. "Southeast Asia in War and Peace." In Nicholas Tarling, ed., *The Cambridge History of Southeast Asia,* 329–385. Cambridge: Cambridge UP, 1992.

Stubbs, Richard. *Hearts and Minds in Guerrilla Warfare: The Malayan Emergency, 1948–1960.* Singapore: Oxford UP, 1989.

Tarling, Nicholas. *The Fall of Imperial Britain in Southeast Asia.* Singapore: Oxford UP, 1993.

———. " 'A New and a Better Cunning': British Wartime Planning for Post-war Burma." *Journal of Southeast Asian Studies* 13 (1982): 33–59.

———, ed. *The Cambridge History of Southeast Asia.* 2 vols. Cambridge: Cambridge UP, 1992.

Taylor, Robert H. *The State in Burma.* London: Hurst, 1987.

———. "Burma in the Anti-Fascist War." In Alfred McCoy, ed., *Southeast Asia under Japanese Occupation,* 132–157. New Haven: Yale University Southeast Asian Studies, 1980.

Thorne, Christopher. *Allies of a Kind: The United States, Britain and the War against Japan, 1941–1945.* New York: Oxford UP, 1978.

———. "Burma in the Anti-Fascist War," in Alfred W. McCoy, ed., *Southeast Asia Under Japanese Occupation,* 132–157. New Haven, CT: Yale UP, 1985.

———. *The State in Burma.* London: Hurst, 1987.

Tinker, Hugh. "The Contraction of Empire in Asia, 1945–1948: The Military Dimensions." *Journal of Imperial and Commonwealth History* 16 (1988): 218–233.

————, ed. *Burma: The Struggle for Independence, 1944–1948: Documents from Official and Private Sources.* 2 vols. London: HMSO, 1983, 1984.

Tønnesson, Stein. *The Vietnamese Revolution of 1945.* London: Sage, 1991.

Toye, Hugh. *Laos, Buffer State or Battleground.* London: Oxford UP, 1968.

Van der Eng, Pierre. "Marshall Aid as a Catalyst in the Decolonization of Indonesia, 1947–1948." *Journal of Southeast Asian Studies* 19 (1988): 335–352.

Wesseling, H. L. "The Giant That Was a Dwarf, or the Strange History of Dutch Imperialism." *The Journal of Imperial and Commonwealth History* 16 (1988): 58–70.

11 Prisoners of War and Civilian Internees: The Asian and Pacific Theaters

S. P. MacKenzie

The literature on prisoners of war and civilian internees in the war against Japan is a study in contrasts. Most of the secondary works—and, indeed, memoirs—dealing with captivity in Japanese hands concern prisoners of war. Most of the literature on captivity in Allied hands—especially in American camps—deals with civilian internees.

This dichotomy is, in part, due to the varying scale of the problem. Only a few thousand Japanese servicemen were ever incarcerated until the final surrender in 1945, while several hundred thousand British, Commonwealth, American, and other Allied troops endured the rigors of captivity in camps scattered throughout the Japanese empire. Conversely, the number of Japanese civilians in internment and relocation camps in the United States and Canada (both first-and second-generation Japanese immigrants) was far greater than the number of Allied civilians in Japanese camps. The attention given to the fate of Japanese internees in Allied hands, however, has also been due to a growing sense of guilt. The mass relocation and internment of full-fledged U.S. citizens of Japanese descent as well as enemy aliens are seen, almost without exception, as a huge mistake fueled more by racial paranoia than by legitimate calculation of potential danger. In North America, then, violation of civil rights at home has tended to take precedence over the fate of the fewer Allied civilians (all enemy aliens) in Japanese hands.

PRISONERS OF WAR

As with the large number of relevant memoirs in English—numbering in the high hundreds—the secondary literature on Allied POWs in Japanese hands tends to focus on capture, survival amid extreme privation and brutality, and eventual liberation. It has been calculated that more than one in four Allied prisoners of war captured by the Japanese died between 1942 and 1945 due to overwork, disease, malign neglect, and deliberate murder, a statistic that gives a clear idea of just how bad Japanese POW camps and their rulers really were and helps explain the focus and tone of both primary and secondary works on the subject.

A brief popular introduction to life—and death—in Japanese hands can be found in Garret's *P.O.W.*, which has a chapter devoted to (primarily) British and Commonwealth prisoners; and also, in the relevant sections, Baily's *Prisoners of War*, which focuses, to a greater extent, on the American experience. Both are based, to a great extent, on memoir material—as, indeed, are most studies of Japanese prisons (though often supplemented by interviews) due to lack of documents and the inability of most (military) historians to read Japanese. Insight into what this means in terms of narrative structure in memoirs—and by implication the many histories that imitate this structure—can be found in Doyle's *Voices from Captivity*.

The latest work devoted to Allied POWs in Japanese hands is Daws' popular history *Prisoners of the Japanese*. Though less than objective and often highly emotional in tone, as the author himself admits—understandable in view of the appalling conditions prisoners were forced to endure—the book uses the experiences of individual POWs to highlight the fate of the prisoner population as a whole in highly readable style. The serious student, however, should also consult the selection of personal narratives, statistics, documents, and useful bibliographical references contained in Van Waterford's rather more detached and scholarly study *Prisoners of the Japanese in World War II*.

British prisoners in Japanese hands, oddly enough, lack their own history (though memoir accounts are plentiful). The general studies mentioned before, however, all deal, in part, with the fate of captured British and Commonwealth forces—not least in reference to the notorious Burma-Siam railway project, in which 16,000 of a total POW workforce of 40,000 died (and which is also the specific subject of Kivig's *River Kwai Railway* [1992]). Unlike Britain, however, New Zealand, Australia, and Canada do have a few secondary works that deal with life in Japanese camps.

Treatments of POWs from New Zealand, often mixed together with British and other Commonwealth POWs and therefore fairly typical, can be found in the relevant chapters of Mason's excellent study *Prisoners of War*, part of the New Zealand official history series, and in an earlier volume, *Prisoners of Japan* by Hall. POWs from the Australian forces are dealt with, though somewhat superficially, in Adam-Smith, *Prisoners of War*, and Nelson, *Prisoners of War*, the latter based on interviews taken from an Australian radio documentary, while the lives of captured Australian army nurses have been chronicled in Kenny's *Captives*. Even more superficial is a popular history by Weisbord and Mohr (derived, in turn, from a Canadian Broadcasting Corporation documentary), with a section devoted to Canadian POWs taken at Hong Kong, entitled *The Valour and the Horror* (1991). Luckily, the Canadian experience has recently been covered by a professional historian, Vance, in a section of *Objects of Concern: Canadian Prisoners of War through the Twentieth Century.*

American POWs taken in the war against Japan have, for some reason, been better served by historians than other nationalities. By no means eclipsed by Daws' treatment—in which American POWs usually take pride of place—is Kerr's *Surrender and Survival,* a detailed and solid examination of surrender, endurance, and eventual liberation among American POWs in Japanese hands. *Death March,* a compilation of oral accounts by Donald Knox, very effectively evokes the appalling forced march POWs endured in the immediate aftermath of the U.S. surrender in the Philippines in 1942. One of the more spectacular instances of final liberation, a raid by U.S. Rangers in the Philippines at the end of January 1945 to rescue about 500 American POWs, is chronicled in Breuer's *The Great Raid on Cabanatuan.*

The dynamics of POW life under extreme stress, the subject of orthodox historical narratives, have been studied from a physiological, psychological, and sociological perspective as well. Charles G. Roland, for example, a historian of medicine, has written an interesting article—"Stripping away the Veneer"—that outlines some of the factors influencing whether prisoners survived or perished.

The largely futile efforts of the International Red Cross to send aid to Allied prisoners in Japanese hands are laid out in Durand, *From Sarajevo to Hiroshima,* the second volume of a semiofficial history. Somewhat more detail is provided in the postwar report of the International Committee of the Red Cross (ICRC), *Report of the International Committee.* A rather more personal view of the accompanying frustrations can be found in Junod, *Warrior without Weapons.*

Supplementing the story from the ICRC angle, attempts by national Red Cross societies on the Allied side to get food and medical supplies to prisoners in Japanese hands are briefly chronicled in Dulles, *The American Red Cross,* and, for the British, in Cambray and Briggs, *Red Cross and St. John.* The failure of the Japanese Red Cross to fulfill its obligations and aid Allied POWs is dealt with sympathetically in Checkland's recently published book *Humanitarianism and the Emperor's Japan.* Efforts by Western governments to try to force the Japanese to behave more in accordance with the Geneva and Hague Conventions regarding prisoners of war are summarized briefly in the latter section of MacKenzie, "Treatment of Prisoners of War."

One of the most problematic issues surrounding Allied POWs is why the Japanese behaved so appallingly toward their captives. Memoir accounts and official analyses written during or soon after the war usually tend to assume implicitly or explicitly that race and/or culture (the so-called Bushido tradition) lay at the heart of the matter, a trend critically examined by Dower in his groundbreaking study *War without Mercy*. That those who suffered at Japanese hands continue to view their experience in an overtly racial light is made clear in Daws' book, but such explanations are not entirely satisfactory. Quite apart from the spurious nature of most of the older, supposedly scientific assumptions concerning racial differences, there is the puzzling fact that the Japanese had become famous for how well they treated enemy prisoners captured during the Russo-Japanese War and the First World War.

The Japanese themselves have studiously avoided the issue of POW atrocities; indeed, for the most part, they have refused to accept that the Imperial Japanese Army committed any war crimes at all, as Bosworth summarizes in *Explaining Auschwitz and Hiroshima*. In recent years, however, traditional Western racial and cultural views have been supplanted, to some degree, by rather more subtle and less obviously racist explanations, interpretations that concentrate on shifts in the shape and focus of Japanese nationalism and army culture. Meirion and Susie Harries, to take a recent example, have constructed an interesting hypothesis in *Soldiers of the Sun*, suggesting that Western cultural values only recently assumed were just as easily cast off when their usefulness had passed. This explanation is supported by Checkland in her study of the Japanese Red Cross, whose Western-based value system was overwhelmed by older, more brutal Japanese attitudes to surrender and captivity dating back to the pre-Meiji period. Roland, however, in "Allied POWs, Japanese Captors, and the Geneva Convention" (1991) argues against sweeping generalizations concerning both the roots and nature of captor behavior and suggests—cautiously—that at least some Japanese officers sought to live up to the Geneva Convention.

The extent to which individual commanders and political leaders should or should not have been held responsible for atrocities against Allied POWs—among other war crimes—has been the subject of much agonizing since the 1970s. A number of works have appeared that grapple with issues such as command responsibility and the legal basis of international law and that illuminate—to a greater or lesser extent—the nature of atrocities committed against POWs and other war victims and the overall question of accountability.

Richard H. Minear suggested over twenty years ago that the major Japanese leaders, such as Tojo, sentenced to death in the Tokyo trials were, in fact, victims of *Victors' Justice*, a position recently endorsed on legalist grounds by the Dutch international lawyer Röling in *The Tokyo Trial and Beyond*. The justness of some of the trials of the Class B and C war criminals charged with crimes against POWs and civilians has also been questioned, particularly that of General Yamashita—the subject of Lael's *The*

Yamashita Precedent and Taylor's *A Trial of Generals.* The trials, however, are not unanimously condemned as travesties of justice. John L. Ginn (a participant) in *Sugamo Prison, Tokyo* and Piccigallo in *The Japanese on Trial* seek to keep the trials in proper perspective. Daws, like many of the ex-prisoners whose wartime experience he chronicles, firmly believes that sentences were, if anything, too lenient and trials too few. This is also the view of Peter Williams and David Wallace, authors of a study of Japan's wartime biological warfare experiments in Manchuria conducted on (among others) Allied POWs (*Unit 731*).

Studies of ordinary Japanese POWs in Allied hands are few in number, though especially interesting in light of the prevailing Japanese view that to surrender was shameful. Lewis and Mewha cover the structure of U.S. camp life in their official study *History of Prisoner of War Utilization by the United States Army.* A more rounded approach is taken by Arnold Krammer, best known for his work on German POWs, in an article, "Japanese Prisoners of War in America." The attitudes and behavior of Japanese POWs in the Antipodes, where two prisoner revolts occurred, are dealt with in two studies: *Japanese Prisoners of War in Revolt,* an excellent account by Carr-Gregg, and the recently expanded edition of Gordon's *Voyage from Shame.* Though memoirs in English by former Allied POWs are legion, Aida's *Prisoner of the British* provides a unique—and, in some respects, rather disturbing—view of the mind-set of a captured Japanese soldier.

Though much has been written on POWs in Japanese hands, there is still much to be done. British and Commonwealth POWs, usually mixed together by the Japanese, deserve a comprehensive, scholarly treatment (for which published and unpublished memoir material exists in abundance). As for Japanese prisoners, policies toward, and the lives of the vast number of surrendered enemy personnel who went into temporary captivity in the wake of the 1945 surrender have yet to be properly examined.

Even more pressing, however, is the need for a thorough examination of POW policy formulation and implementation by the Imperial Japanese Army, a task made more challenging, but by no means impossible, by the language barrier and the destruction of many relevant documents in the immediate aftermath of the Japanese surrender. A related area that requires further exploration concerns the efforts by the Allies to improve conditions for POWs and the Japanese responses to these efforts (especially the differing approaches of the foreign ministry and war ministry). These matters have been touched on in a number of works, including Roy, et al., *Mutual Hostages* (1990), and P. S. Corbett's *Quiet Passages,* but mostly in connection with enemy aliens rather than POWs.

CIVILIAN INTERNEES

Work on enemy aliens and other "suspect" civilians taken into captivity is somewhat lopsided. There are memoirs of Allied civilian internees in Japanese hands (though smaller in number than POW memoirs), a small section devoted to the subject in Waterford, and a still-valuable sociological study of a civilian camp in the Philippines—*Community under Stress*—written by a former internee, Elizabeth H. Vaughan. Interested readers may also wish to consult an oral compilation by Onorato, *Forgotten Heroes*, which deals with internees in the Philippines as well. The daring rescue of over 2,000 American civilians in the Los Baños internment camp in the Philippines by elements of the Eleventh Airborne Division, in advance of the arrival of MacArthur's main force in February 1945, is the subject of two books, *The Los Baños Raid* by Flanagan and *Deliverance at Los Baños* by Arthur. Internee life and exchanges are dealt with in the works by Roy (Canada–Japan) and Corbett (United States–Japan) listed earlier. The vast majority of the literature in English on civilians behind barbed wire, however, concerns the approximately 140,000 enemy aliens, naturalized citizens, and American- and Canadian-born citizens of Japanese descent (Nisei) who were removed from their homes on the West Coast of North America and interned inland.

All studies of the relocation programs undertaken in the United States and Canada are more or less united in arguing that the policy was a bad idea pursued ineptly, driven more by racial paranoia than by legitimate security needs. The tone, however, does vary depending on the author's perspective.

Though many books have appeared since its publication, the standard work on the American side remains the impressive, multivolume study produced by a team of Berkeley scholars led by Dorothy Swaine Thomas entitled *Japanese American Evacuation and Resettlement* (1946–1954). Working through field observations made during the war and aiming to examine developments from a sociological, psychological, economic, and policy perspective, the University of California team divided their study into three parts. Volume 1, *The Spoilage*, deals with the alienation caused among Japanese Americans by forced relocation and life in confinement, concentrating on the Thule Lake camp. Volume 2, *The Salvage*, examines the adaptation of the majority to their new conditions and successful efforts to overcome adversity during and after confinement. Volume 3, written by TenBroek, Barnhart, and Matson, *Prejudice, War and the Constitution*, explores the legal and political dimensions of evacuation policy.

As might be expected with an episode so clearly tinged by racial paranoia and involving the suppression of constitutional civil rights (at least in the case of American citizens), the wholesale relocation and internment of Japanese families living on the West Coast have not always been treated with the detachment displayed in the University of California study. An early example of what would become a general trend toward reassessment and forceful condemnation was Grodzin's *Americans Betrayed*. Particularly since the 1960s and 1970s, when governmental authority was being questioned by the postwar generation throughout the Western world, Japanese internment has been presented as a moral outrage requiring some form of material redress.

The titles of many published works speak for themselves: *America's Concentration Camps* by Bosworth; *The Great Betrayal* by Girdner and Loftis; Weglyn's *Years of Infamy*; Nagata's *Legacy of Injustice*; and, for Canada, Adachi's *The Enemy That Never Was*. Even the 1,800 Peruvian Japanese deported to America and then interned are chronicled in Gardiner's *Pawns in a Triangle of Hate*.

Memoir accounts both individual and compiled, such as Yoshiko's *Desert Exile* and Tateishi's *And Justice for All*, tend—naturally enough—to support the view that relocation was an unjust and unnecessary upheaval for Japanese Americans.

Secondary works that have taken a more moderate approach, such as *Uprooted Americans* by the former director of the War Relocation Authority, Dillon S. Myer, have been somewhat defensive in tone in light of the prevailing view condemning internment root and branch. Perhaps only an enemy alien, such as Kiyoaki Murata, could cheerfully disregard the U.S. racial legacy and entitle his internment memoir—published in Japan—*An Enemy among Friends*.

The growing strength of postwar public opposition to wartime internment policy and the ultimately successful drive by ex-internees and others to obtain compensation through the courts in the United States are chronicled in *Righting a Wrong* by Hatamiya and *Repairing America* by Hohri.

The understandable sense of outrage that permeates much of the literature on Japanese internment does not mean, however, that such works should be disregarded. The use of an emotionally loaded term such as "concentration camp," though technically correct, is perhaps inappropriate in this context, given that neither mass death nor genocide, the hallmarks of the Nazi *Konzentrationslager* system, was a feature of what were officially titled relocation centers. Most general secondary studies, however, do succeed in providing the reader with a more or less accurate picture of what happened and why (though Adachi's book, for one, definitely needs to be read in conjunction with several of the more scholarly essays in Roy et al.).

Alongside the more general works that have been published on the subject of Japanese internment over the past thirty years are a number of noteworthy studies that focus on the internment experience through the prism of a discipline other than traditional narrative history. These include Yatsushiro's *Politics and Cultural Values*, a sociological study of the relocation centers; Spicer et al., *Impounded People*, an anthropological examination; and *Removal and Return* by Broom and Riemer, which examines the upheaval from a socioeconomic perspective.

As expected, now that so much work has been done on internment policy in general, interest has begun to shift toward particular camps (Taylor's *Jewel of the Desert*, for instance, which looks at Topaz, wartime home for the Japanese from the San Francisco Bay Area) and the compilation of personal narratives. Aside from a number of memoirs and collections, some of which have already been mentioned, there exists the extensive and scholarly two-volume *Japanese American World War II Evacuation Oral History Project* compiled by Hansen.

While there is no such thing as the last word, it would appear that—especially in light of official apologies and restitution efforts—there is little to be added in the immediate future to the story of Japanese internment in North America (other than at the local level). The internment of Allied civilians, however, in terms of both captor policy and the dynamics of internee life, remains largely untapped as a source of study, as does—though rather more problematic in terms of sources—the story of Asian slave laborers conscripted by the Japanese.

BIBLIOGRAPHY

Also see Bibliography for Chapter 29 on war crimes.

Adachi, Ken. *The Enemy That Never Was.* Toronto: McClelland and Stewart, 1990.
Adam-Smith, Patsy. *Prisoners of War: From Gallipoli to Korea.* New York: Viking, 1992.
Aida, Yugi. *Prisoner of the British: A Japanese Soldier's Experience in Burma.* Edited by Louis Allen. London: Cresset, 1966.
Arthur, Anthony. *Deliverance at Los Baños.* New York: St. Martin's, 1985.
Baily, Robert H. *Prisoners of War.* Alexandria, VA: Time-Life, 1983.
Bosworth, Allan R. *America's Concentration Camps.* New York: Bantam, Norton, 1968.
Bosworth, R. J. B. *Explaining Auschwitz and Hiroshima: History Writing and the Second World War, 1945–1990.* London: Routledge, 1993.
Breuer, William B. *The Great Raid on Cabanatuan: Rescuing the Doomed Ghosts of Bataan and Corregidor.* New York: John Wiley, 1994.
Broom, Leonard, and Ruth Riemer. *Removal and Return: The Socioeconomic Effects of the War on Japanese Americans.* Berkeley: University of California, 1949, 1973.
Cambray, P. G., and G.G.B. Briggs, comps. *Red Cross and St. John: The Official Record of the Humanitarian Services of the British Red Cross Society and the Order of St. John of Jerusalem, 1939–1947.* London: Red Cross, 1949.
Carr-Gregg, Charlotte. *Japanese Prisoners of War in Revolt: The Outbreaks at Featherstone and Cowra during World War II.* St. Lucia, Queensland: University of Queensland, 1978.
Checkland, Olive. *Humanitarianism and the Emperor's Japan, 1877–1977.* London: St. Martin's, 1994.

Corbett, P. Scott. *Quiet Passages: The Exchange of Civilians between the United States and Japan during the Second World War.* Kent, OH: Kent State UP, 1987.

Daws, Gavan. *Prisoners of the Japanese: POWs of World War II in the Pacific.* New York: William Morrow, 1994.

Dower, John. *War without Mercy: Race and Power in the Pacific War.* New York: Pantheon, 1986.

Doyle, Robert C. *Voices from Captivity: Interpreting the American POW Narrative.* Lawrence: UP of Kansas, 1994.

Dulles, Foster Rhea. *The American Red Cross: A History.* New York: Harper, 1950.

Durand, André. *From Sarajevo to Hiroshima: History of the International Committee of the Red Cross.* Geneva: ICRC, 1984.

Flanagan, Edward M. *The Los Baños Raid: The 11th Airborne Jumps at Dawn.* Novato, CA: Presidion, 1986.

Gardiner, C. Harvey. *Pawns in a Triangle of Hate: The Peruvian Japanese and the United States.* Seattle: University of Washington, 1981.

Garrett, Richard. *P.O.W.* Newton Abbot (U.K.): David and Charles, 1981.

Ginn, John L. *Sugamo Prison, Tokyo: An Account of the Trial and Sentencing of Japanese War Criminals in 1948, by a U.S. Participant.* Jefferson, NC: McFarland, 1992.

Girdner, Audrey, and Anne Loftis. *The Great Betrayal: The Evacuation of the Japanese-Americans during World War II.* London: Macmillan, 1969.

Gordon, Harry. *Voyage from Shame: The Cowra Breakout and Aftermath.* St. Lucia, Queensland: University of Queensland, 1994.

Grodzin, Morton. *Americans Betrayed: Politics and the Japanese Evacuation.* Chicago: University of Chicago, 1949.

Hall, David O. W. *Prisoners of Japan.* Wellington, NZ: War History Branch, Department of Internal Affairs, 1949.

Hansen, Arthur H. *Japanese American World War II Evacuation Oral History Project.* 2 vols. Westport, CT: Meckler, 1991.

Harries, Meirion, and Susie Harries. *Soldiers of the Sun: The Rise and Fall of the Imperial Japanese Army.* New York: Random House, 1991.

Hatamiya, Leslie T. *Righting a Wrong: Japanese Americans and the Passage of the Civil Liberties Act of 1988.* Stanford, CA: Stanford UP, 1993.

Hohri, William Minoru. *Repairing America: An Account of the Movement for Japanese-American Redress.* Pullman: Washington State UP, 1988.

International Committee of the Red Cross. *Report of the International Committee of the Red Cross on Its Activities during the Second World War (September 1, 1939–June 30, 1947).* 2 vols. Geneva: ICRC, 1948.

Junod, Marcel. *Warrior without Weapons.* Translated by Edward Fitzgerald. London: Macmillan, 1951.

Kenny, Catherine. *Captives: Australian Army Nurses in Japanese Prison Camps.* St. Lucia, Queensland: University of Queensland, 1986.

Kerr, E. Bartlett. *Surrender and Survival: The Experience of American POWs in the Pacific, 1941–1945.* New York: Morrow, 1985.

Kivig, Clifford. *River Kwai Railway: The Story of the Burma–Siam Railroad.* London: Brassey's, 1992.

Knox, Donald. *Death March: Survivors of Bataan.* New York: Harcourt Brace Jovanovich, 1981, 1983.

Krammer, Arnold. "Japanese Prisoners of War in America." *Pacific Historical Review* 52 (1982): 67–91.

Lael, Richard L. *The Yamashita Precedent: War Crimes and Command Responsibility.* Wilmington, DE: Scholarly Resources, 1982.

Lewis, C.G.S., and J. Mewha. *History of Prisoner of War Utilization by the United States Army, 1776–1945.* Washington, DC: Department of the Army, 1955.

MacKenzie, S. P. "The Treatment of Prisoners of War in World War II." *Journal of Modern History* 66 (1994): 487–520.

Mason, W. Wynne. *Official History of New Zealand in the Second World War: Prisoners of War.* Wellington, NZ: War History Branch, Department of Internal Affairs, 1954.

Minear, Richard H. *Victors' Justice: The Tokyo War Crimes Trial.* Princeton: Princeton UP, 1971.

Murata, Kiyoaki. *An Enemy among Friends.* Tokyo: Kondansha International, 1991.

Myer, Dillon S. *Uprooted Americans: The Japanese Americans and the War Relocation Authority during World War II.* Tuscon: University of Arizona, 1971.

Nagata, Donna K. *Legacy of Injustice: Exploring the Cross-Generational Impact of the Japanese American Internment.* New York: Plenum, 1993.

Nelson, Hank. *Prisoners of War: Australians under Nippon.* Canberra: Australian Broadcasting Corporation, 1985.

Onorato, Michael Paul. *Forgotten Heroes: Japan's Imprisonment of American Civilians in the Philippines, 1942–1945: An Oral History.* Westport, CT: Meckler, 1990.

Piccigallo, Philip R. *The Japanese on Trial: Allied War Crimes Operations in the East, 1945–1951.* Austin: University of Texas, 1979.

Roland, Charles. "Allied POWs, Japanese Captors, and the Geneva Convention." *War and Society* 9 (1991): 83–101.

————. "Stripping Away the Veneer: P.O.W. Survival in the Far East as an Index of Cultural Atavism." *Journal of Military History* 53 (1989): 79–84.

Röling, Bernard Victor Aloysius. *The Tokyo Trial and Beyond: Reflections of a Peacemonger.* Edited by Antonio Cassese. Cambridge: Polity, 1993.

Roy, Pat E., J. L. Granatstein, Masako Iino, and Hiroko Takamara. *Mutual Hostages: Canadians and Japanese during the Second World War.* Toronto: University of Toronto, 1990.

Spicer, Edward H., et al. *Impounded People: Japanese-Americans in the Relocation Centers.* Tuscon: University of Arizona, 1946, 1969.

Tateishi, John. *And Justice for All: An Oral History of the Japanese American Detention Camps.* New York: Random House, 1984.

Taylor, Lawrence. *A Trial of Generals: Homma, Yamashita, MacArthur.* South Bend, IN: Icarus, 1981.

Taylor, Sandra C. *Jewel of the Desert: Japanese American Internment at Topaz.* Berkeley: University of California, 1993.

TenBroek, Jacobus, Edward N. Barnhart, and Floyd W. Matson. *Japanese American Evacuation and Resettlement.* Vol. 3: *Prejudice, War and the Constitution.* Berkeley: University of California, 1954.

Thomas, Dorothy Swaine. *Japanese American Evacuation and Resettlement.* Vol. 2: *The Salvage.* Berkeley: University of California, 1952, 1974.

Thomas, Dorothy Swaine, and Richard S. Nishimoto. *Japanese American Evacuation and Resettlement.* Vol. 1: *The Spoilage.* Berkeley: University of California, 1946.

Vance, Jonathan M. *Objects of Concern: Canadian Prisoners of War through the Twentieth Century.* Vancouver: University of British Columbia, 1994.

Vaughan, Elizabeth Head. *Community under Stress: An Internment Camp Culture.* Princeton: Princeton UP, 1949.

Waterford, Van. *Prisoners of the Japanese in World War II: Statistical History, Personal Narratives and Memorials concerning POWs in Camps and on Hellships, Civilian Internees, Asian Slave Laborers and Others Captured in the Pacific Theatre.* Jefferson, NC: McFarland, 1994.

Weglyn, Michi. *Years of Infamy: The Untold Story of America's Concentration Camps.* New York: Morrow, 1976.

Weisbord, Merrily, and Merilyn Simonds Mohr. *The Valour and the Horror: The Untold Story of Canadians in the Second World War.* Toronto: HarperCollins, 1991.

Williams, Peter, and David Wallace. *Unit 731: Japan's Secret Biological Warfare in World War II.* New York: Free, 1989.

Yatsushiro, Toshio. *Politics and Cultural Values: The World War II Japanese Relocation Centers.* New York: Arno, 1978.

Yoshiko, Uchida. *Desert Exile: The Uprooting of a Japanese American Family.* Seattle: University of Washington, 1982.

GENERAL THEMES

PART IV

The War in Science, Technology, Propaganda, and Unit Histories

12 Science, Technology, and Weapons Development

Benjamin H. Kristy

The Second World War marked the close of one era of military technology and the start of a new one. Both the Allies and the Axis entered the war with numerous weapons that had been designed and developed based on the lessons and traditions of World War I. Yet, by the end of World War II, these forces had deployed new military technologies that dramatically altered the nature of armed conflict and whose descendants continue to serve with front-line units today.

Such transitional episodes make the construction and upkeep of large fighting forces all the more difficult and expensive. New military technologies have the lure of offering a qualitative edge over one's opponent. This edge can come in many forms—range, firepower, performance, accuracy, and so on. However, new technology is a double-edged sword for those armed forces that embrace it. Most new military technologies come only at a huge price in funds, materials, training, and personnel. Witness the massive capital investment that the United States made to build only three atomic weapons. Second, new technologies can lead to a false sense of security or superiority. Note, for example, the blind faith of the German Luftwaffe in the effectiveness of dive-bombing, while the Allies placed more value on the heavy bomber. While the German JU-87 proved to be a highly effective bomber in tactical situations, neither it nor any of the other German light or medium bombers could swing the larger strategic situation to Germany's favor.

With hindsight it is clear to see that during World War II the Allies proved to be far more effective at wielding the double-edged sword of technology than the Axis powers were. Partially, this was due to the massive industrial and financial power of the United States (and the fact that America was not subjected to heavy bombardment). Another factor was the cyclical nature of technology. When the war started (in Europe anyway) in 1939, the Germans and the Japanese were just reaching the end of a cycle of modernization and rearmament. This provided both powers with a qualitative technological edge over their opponents, as well as a quantitative edge in some areas (such as number of fighters and naval auxiliary vessels).

Yet, for the United States and Britain, 1939 marked a point midway through a period of modernization. This meant that for the Allies, older weapons, like the Hawker Hurricane or the *Lexington*-class aircraft carriers, would square off against more advanced and more numerous enemy opponents. The Allies' indifference to advances in military technology during the 1920s and 1930s proved to be a huge disadvantage for the first few years of the war before the massive industrial power of the Allies could be brought on-line to produce newer weapons systems that could replace or augment the older weapons. However, the fact that the Allies had not completed their technological cycle when the war began did give them the added bonus of being able to quickly meet the need for improved designs based on the experience of the first few months and years of the war. Throughout 1939 and 1940, Allied factories and research labs turned out new weapons of all types, which rapidly moved through the prototype stage and into the production stage.

By and large, the Allies had a better understanding that science and new technologies could help win the war, but only if they were applied in the right areas and directions. Hence, the Allies developed new technologies that would directly apply to situations along the front lines— long-range strategic bombers and escort fighters, naval surface radar and sonar systems, and improved amphibious landing craft and vessels. For their part, the Axis powers expended their resources in scientific efforts to develop new military technologies that did not bring a large return on the battlefield (the Japanese *Okha* bomb and German V weapons are good examples) or that were "catch-up" responses to newer Allied weapons (although, to their credit, the Germans did field the most advanced fighter of the war in the Me 262 and arguably the best medium and heavy tanks in the Panther and Tiger and the technologically superb Type XXI submarine). The Japanese efforts to build the world's two largest battleships to fight a naval war that was dominated not by naval guns, but rather by naval aircraft, are an indication of Japanese lack of vision in terms of weapons development.

World War II saw the deployment of certain new technologies that played a major role in the outcome of the war and that have largely defined how wars have been fought since its end. These technologies, radar, jets, missiles, and the atomic bomb, represent a leap forward in military technology and receive extensive coverage in this chapter. The wide variety of sources discussed later represents only the proverbial "tip of the iceberg." The role of technology and science in the development of weapons during the Second World War can be found in many different forms.

GENERAL WORKS

The interaction between warfare and technology is a subject that continues to intrigue historians and spark many to write general works that explore how the introduction of new technologies has affected military performance throughout the ages. The scope of these works is almost incalculable, and each author chooses to emphasize different developments and areas of scientific advancement. Four key works deal extensively with the technological landscape of World War II, as well as provide the reader with a larger understanding of the interaction of warfare and technological advance. The earliest is J. F. C. Fuller's *Armament and History*, written in 1945. This book is one of his better efforts and continues to serve as the model for similar, more recent works. Although published before Fuller could fully assess the impact of the atomic bomb and its perceived role on the "modern" battlefield, he concluded that military victory can be virtually assured if the right weapons are available at the right moment.

Bernard and Fawn M. Brodie's *From Crossbow to H-Bomb* examined the same ground as Fuller, but with the experience of both the Cold War and Vietnam. The Brodies saw the atomic bomb as a major break with linear progression of weapons development, and a large portion of their work deals with the various effects that the atomic bomb has had on development of both nuclear and conventional weapons. Similar and more recent, Van Creveld's *Technology and War* is broken into clearly defined sections (land warfare, sea warfare, etc.), and while this construction is useful for the earlier periods, the section lines tend to interrupt the flow of the work during the discussion on the twentieth century. Additionally, Van Creveld gives far more weight to the importance of "automation" in modern warfare than did the Brodies, dividing the twentieth century between World War II (a "systems" war) and more recent wars ("automated" wars). He concludes with a highly useful bibliographic essay.

One of the more unique works on the importance of technology and warfare is Pokrovsky's *Science and Technology in Contemporary War*. Written during the height of the Cold War, it is therefore not surprising that Pokrovsky pays the most attention to the development and role of atomic weapons and to the technologies that best served the Soviet Union during World War II—armored forces and heavy artillery. Additionally, Pokrovsky's work is interesting simply because it represents the "other side of the coin" from that of the Brodies and Fuller.

THE ATOMIC BOMB

The creation of the atomic bomb altered the nature of warfare like no other weapon. Its use during the waning days of the Pacific War helped to dictate how every major armed conflict has been fought since. Without a doubt, the atomic bomb has been one of the most written about examples of how science and technology can have a critical effect upon the field of battle. Thankfully, researchers can utilize Graetzer's *The Atomic Bomb: An Annotated Bibliography* to aid them through the dense forest of works on the bomb. This slim work is broken down into clearly defined areas and is fairly complete, and the annotations give the reader a clear and concise picture of the works described—a wonderful resource.

Within the massive collection of works on the development of the atomic bomb, a number share common goals, themes, and frameworks. The largest group of these is made up of sources that detail the lengthy and costly process of producing the first bomb. The best of these is David Hawkins, Edith Truslow, and Ralph Smith, *Project Y: The Los Alamos Story*, a reprint (and slight rewrite) of the original report of the Los Alamos Laboratory. The work is, at times, highly technical but overall is easy to understand. Smyth's *Atomic Energy for Military Purposes* is a reprint of the 182-page pamphlet that was released by the U.S. government only days after the use of the bomb. While some information was still secret at the time, this pamphlet is informative and is historical in its own right. Cave Brown and MacDonald's *The Secret History of the Atomic Bomb* includes the original text of Smyth's pamphlet with an additional 250 pages of selections from the history of the Los Alamos Laboratory. Unfortunately, the authors do not include an index or bibliographic information on any of the materials from the National Archives. Jones' *Manhattan, the Army, and the Atomic Bomb* is a well-constructed blend of technical and administrative history. Lansing, a journalist, details the first test firing of an atomic weapon in his *Day of Trinity*, a work most useful for its extensive bibliography. Lastly, Rhodes' award-winning *The Making of the Atomic Bomb* is arguably the best-written and most commercially successful general history of the construction of the bomb.

Due to the importance and size of the Manhattan project, it is not surprising to find that members of the large, yet fragmented, design team penned works exploring their own efforts. Groves' *Now It Can Be Told: The Story of the Manhattan Project* and Nichols' more recent *The Road to Trinity* are the most commonly recognized works of this type. Groves was the U.S. Army general in charge of the Manhattan project and offers some unique insights on his duties as head of the atomic bomb project but is not immune from emotional biases. Nichols, the project's district engineer, presents a more balanced view of the inner workings of the bomb design team, as well as his role in the administrative workings of the bomb project. Nichols also touches upon how the Manhattan project affected the U.S. atomic energy program into the early 1950s. However, by far the best insider account of the Manhattan project is found in Compton's *Atomic Quest: A Personal Narrative*. Compton was responsible for coordinating the efforts of the geographically separated research labs and thousands of scientists, and his work is a masterpiece of nontechnical history.

The United States was not the only nation frantically working on atomic weapons during the war. One of the driving forces behind the rapid development of the American bomb was the fear that the Axis, in particular Nazi Germany, would complete an atomic weapon first. The German program is the focus of Goudsmit's *Alsos*, Irving's *The German Atomic Bomb*, and Powers' *Heisenberg's War: The Secret History of the German Bomb*. Individually, none of these three sources provide a complete history, but together they provide a very vivid and comprehensive picture of German efforts. Powers' effort is the best written of the three; Goudsmit's book is a part of "The History of Modern Physics, 1800–1950" series and is as much a spy story as it is a historical examination; and Irving's work is particularly useful for its examination of the major scientists and army officers involved with the German bomb project. Wilcox's *Japan's Secret War* is a controversial look at the efforts of Japan to build and use atomic weapons during its waning days. Though Wilcox's arguments are not fully supported at times, his work effectively describes the relationship that Japan and Germany established for sharing technical information and new equipment.

Finally, one source deserves special mention. *The Manhattan Project—A Documentary Introduction to the Atomic Age*, edited by Staff, Fanton, and Williams, is a collection of primary documents on the development, use, and fallout of the atomic bomb. Entries range from Einstein's famous letter to Roosevelt to the U.S. Strategic Bombing Survey's report on "The Effect of the Atomic Bombs." This work is a highly creative look at the bomb and is most useful to teachers and researchers alike.

RADAR

The development of radar and its naval counterpart, sonar, has been one of the twentieth century's most important advances in military technology. Almost from the first shots fired, the outcomes of aerial, naval, and subsurface engagements fought during World War II were determined, in part, by the ability of one side to pinpoint electronically the enemy forces. It is not surprising, therefore, that the development of radar prior to, and during, World War II has been the focus of many works.

Fisher's *A Race on the Edge of Time: Radar—The Decisive Weapon of World War II* is the most passionately written examination of the wartime uses of radar. Fisher states that radar was "the most important scientific/political/military invention of them all, bar none" (p. xi). Perhaps Fisher has overstated radar's importance, but his work is an excellent, nontechnical introduction to the development and uses of military radar (mostly Allied) systems during the war.

For more technical information on the wartime radar systems, students should consult Guerlac's massive, two-volume *Radar in World War II*. Based on primary research and the files of the Radar Program of the National

Defense Research Committee, these volumes document the pre-1939 radar research conducted by the British, the U.S. Army Signal Corps, and the U.S. Navy, as well as the technical developments made during the war. Howse's *Radar at Sea: The Royal Navy in World War II* is also an exceptional source and has highly useful appendixes. *Radar Development to 1945*, edited by Burns, is a worthwhile overview of the technological advances made in radar technology through the end of the war, as is Page's older *The Origins of Radar*. Researchers interested in American wartime developments in aerial and early-warning radar technologies should hunt out Price's *The History of U.S. Electronic Warfare*, vol. 1: *The Years of Innovation—Beginnings to 1946*, as it continues to be the best and most detailed source on the subject.

SCIENTISTS AND RESEARCH LABS

The degree to which the combatants of World War II were able to organize, regulate, and supply their respective scientific communities played a critical role in the ability of each country to introduce new technologies. Following the close of the war, historians, scientific agencies, and individual scientists found a common interest in detailing the efforts of the various research and development organizations. Since 1945, countless works exploring the various scientific agencies and programs undertaken during the war by both the Allies and Axis have been published.

Clark's *The Rise of the Boffins* is probably the best-known example from a larger group of works that examine the effort of scientists to adapt or invent new technologies to counter those of their enemies. *The Rise of the Boffins* details the efforts of British civil and military technicians working within the RAF to develop means of countering German radar bombing systems, the V weapons, and the German radar air defense system. Just as science was used to counter the German air defense network, so, too, did Allied researchers seek to use advanced technologies to defeat the Axis from beneath the waves.

Clark is not the only author to look at the wartime effort of Britain's scientific community. Macrae's *Winston Churchill's Toyshop* is the story of the Ministry of Defense 1 (MD1) department. Penned by the head of MD, it is an easy-to-read blend of administrative and nontechnical history and describes the effort of the author's staff to develop weapons ranging from booby traps to large bridge-laying equipment. Pawle's *The Secret War, 1939–45* is also a particularly well written account of the workings of the British Department of Miscellaneous Weapon Development and is a good companion volume to Stuart's work. Terrell's *Admiralty Brief: The Story of Inventions That Contributed to Victory in the Battle of the Atlantic* explores the work of British scientists to counter the Axis submarine threat as well as try to improve the performance of their own submarines and antisubmarine warfare (ASW) systems. *Scientists at War* by Eggleston covers the effort by the Canadian National Research Council to contribute to the Allied weapons developmental programs. This work is neatly laid out into major topic and subject areas and touches on such topics as minesweeping, proximity fuzes, surface radars, and smoke screens. Lastly, certain English scientists involved in research during the war have not been immune from the temptation of self-congratulation while writing valuable accounts of their wartime service, as illustrated by Watson-Watt's *The Pulse of Radar: The Autobiography of Sir Robert Watson-Watt* and *Three Steps to Victory: A Personal Account of Radar's Greatest Pioneer.*

On the American side of the Atlantic, scientific research was also being conducted at a fever pitch. Two works are particularly useful when looking at the subject of American research and development (R&D) effort. The first is Thiesmeyer and Waterman's *Combat Scientists*, a classic work from the Office of Scientific Research and Development's "Science in World War II" series. The two authors explore the field exploits of American scientists during the war as well as provide a very interesting and detailed study of the technological difficulties of amphibious landings. The other work is Baxter's *Scientists against Time*. Written just after the war's end, this one-volume history of the U.S. Office of Scientific Research and Development explores the role of science and strategy during the war as well as details American research in such areas as radar, loran, fire control systems, incendiaries, insecticides, and new scientific training methods. Due to security restrictions in place at the time at which it was published, *Scientists against Time* is not completely forthcoming with information about certain projects, such as the bomb, and the work is valued more for its discussion of scientific research than for its discussion of the events of the war found in the book's first section. Finally, Meigs' *Slide Rules and Submarines: American Scientists and Subsurface Warfare in World War II* is an entertaining and informative, nontechnical look at American submarine and ASW research during the war. This work is best used in conjunction with Terrell's work on British research in the same area.

As for Axis research labs, there are few good sources in English. Simon's two-part study of German wartime research, *German Scientific Establishments* and *German Research in World War II: An Analysis of the Conduct of Research*, is, despite the study's age, the best source on the German research labs of World War II, from which came some of the most effective and horrific weapons of the twentieth century. Japanese research labs are completely ignored, and this is a subject that demands more scholarship. One notable exception is Horikoshi's *Eagles of Mitsubishi*, which details the development of the famed Type 0 fighter.

Four particular works deal with the use and organization of scientific research during the war that, because of their merit, warrant special mention. First is *Applied Physics* by Jones et al. This massive volume, also from the "Science in World War II" series, is a highly technical and detailed discussion on the development of "window," microwave communications, optics, and metallurgy, as well as the organizational effort required to make such developments possible. The organizational history found in *Applied Physics* is expanded and fleshed out in Stewart's *Organizing Scientific Research for War*. This work is the official administrative history of the Office of Scientific Research and Development and is a must for any student interested in American weapon development programs during the war. Zimmerman's recent examination of Canada's attempts to develop radar systems in *The Great Naval Battle of Ottawa* illuminates the difficulties with command and political backing that all military research centers faced. Finally, Richards' *Scientific Information in Wartime: The Allied-German Rivalry, 1939–1945* is a very interesting study of how the Axis and Allies attempted to keep abreast of each other's advances and failures. This work has an excellent bibliography and appendix; however, there is little or no discussion of Japan's role in the transfer of scientific information during the war.

One of the longest-lasting effects of the interaction of science and technology during World War II was the rapid growth of research laboratories in the United States. Many of the research establishments created during the war continue to be thriving centers of scientific and military technology research. Christman's *Sailors, Scientists, and Rockets* details the earliest tests of U.S. rockets at the China Lake facility, which continues to be an important test range today. The interaction between American civilian research labs and the military during World War II is further explored in Koppes' "The Sky Is the Limit," a two-part study of the California Institute of Technology's Guggenheim Aeronautical Laboratory and Jet Propulsion Laboratory (JPL). The Guggenheim Laboratory developed the first American composite solid propellant motor, and the JPL worked on jet-assisted takeoff methods for American military aircraft. Both labs flourished after the war, thanks, in part, to their ability to link civilian research with military needs. Similarly, Williams' article "From the Hill to the Hilltop" explores how the cyclotron (which was built for medical research) at Washington University allowed that institution to become part of the Manhattan Project. At the close of the war, the university was able to take the facilities and funds it received as part of its participation and improve the school's basic research programs.

AIR, LAND, and NAVAL WEAPONS DEVELOPMENT

Given the massive number of works published each year dealing with the weapons used during the Second World War, it is virtually impossible to keep track of, and examine, each of the sources on the development of aerial, land, and naval weapons from 1939 to 1945. It is important to keep in mind that with the exception of the specific technologies mentioned in the introduction of this chapter, the vast majority of weapons fielded during the Second World War did not represent major advances in technology. The aircraft, ships, guns, tanks, support vehicles, and electronic communication devices used in combat were merely improvements (sometimes drastic improvements) over systems that had been developed earlier in the century. For this reason, the sources listed here are heavily weighted toward the more general works dealing with the development and use of weapons in combat, rather than toward those on specific hardware.

Air

The case can be made that airpower, particularly in the Pacific theater, was the dominating factor of the Second World War. Historians who support this view continue to produce works on airpower and specific aircraft types at a breakneck pace. Despite the number of its competitors, one work, Overy's *The Air War 1939–1945*, continues to be the single best work on the role of airpower during the Second World War. In his masterpiece, Overy includes a detailed breakdown of the strengths and weaknesses of each major combatant's air forces, as well as provides the reader with sections that explore how the aeronautical economies and scientific research communities in each country either helped or hindered the efforts of that country's air forces. A newer work that reaches for the same lofty goals, Boyne's *Clash of Wings—World War II in the Air* enjoys more spirited writing but does not succeed, as Overy does, in creating a balanced, all-encompassing picture of the air war.

Higham's *Air Power—A Concise History* is at its finest when it describes the "wave theory" of technological advancement. Using this theory, Higham clearly illustrates why the Axis powers were slow to catch up with the newly introduced Allied designs after 1942 and why the Allies streamlined their own aeronautical research programs after the war's outcome became apparent in 1944. For Germany, both Murray's *Strategy for Defeat: The Luftwaffe 1933–1945* and Bekker's *The Luftwaffe War Diaries* (published in German in 1964), while not dedicated to a technical history of the German air force, include discussions and examples of where the Luftwaffe's insistence on accuracy via dive-bombing led to ultimate disaster through neglect of the heavy, four-engined bomber. The standard work on the Japanese naval and army air forces continues to be Francillon's older *Japanese Aircraft of the Pacific War*. Francillon includes not only an explanation of the Japanese designation system (which has continued to confuse historians to this day) but also a wonderfully detailed analysis of the Japanese aeronautical industry and R&D efforts during the war. For the U.S. Army Air Force (USAAF), Bodie's *Republic P-47 Thunderbolt* and

The Lockheed P-38 Lightning are examples of a much larger body of high-quality, but limited-scope, works on individual aircraft designs. Meanwhile, Tillman's *Avenger at War* is one example of this ever-growing collection of works on U.S. (and British) World War II naval aircraft.

One of the issues concerning World War II that continue to interest historians today is the Allied "precision" bombing campaigns against both Germany and Japan. A recent work, McFarland's *America's Pursuit of Precision Bombing, 1910–1945* examines the role of the Sperry and Norden Companies to develop bombsights that would allow American bombers to hit targets with "unnerving accuracy." Some of the same ground is covered in Schaffer's *Wings of Judgment* and Sherry's *The Rise of American Air Power*, although both works are more useful for their examination of the moral implications of the use of such advanced technologies on civilian targets.

The development of aircraft engines is a subject that has not escaped the attention of historians. Taylor's "Aircraft Propulsion: A Review of the Evolution of Aircraft Piston Engines" is a difficult work to find but is well worth the effort. This source includes a lengthy discussion on the differences between various engine manufacturers as well as engine-related topics such as propellers and superchargers. As a bonus, Taylor includes an excellent bibliography and appendixes. In the same vein is Smith's *A History of Aircraft Piston Engines*. Smith's work is not as detailed or inclusive as Taylor's but is much more available and is an adequate single-volume treatment of aircraft engines.

The birth of the first militarily viable rockets and intertheater missiles is a subject that has not escaped the notice of military historians. Klee and Merk's *The Birth of the Missile—The Secrets of Peenemünde* remains the best single source on the German rocket and missile development program. This work, which includes an introduction by Wernher von Braun, is based on rare primary documents and explores the development of the V-2 from the earliest test flights to the most advanced versions, which were designed to strike New York City. Other works on the German rocket program and its military effectiveness include De La Ferte's *Rocket*, Garlinski's *Hitler's Last Weapons*, Johnson's *V-1, V-2: Hitler's Vengeance on London*, and Longmate's *Hitler's Rockets: The Story of the V-2s*. These works share much in common but take different angles and reach different conclusions. Longmate's work looks at the V-2's development program and blends in a great deal of bibliographic work on various German rocket scientists. Johnson's effort is a highly passionate look at the use of the V-1s and V-2s against Britain and at the varied British defensive measures. De La Ferte's book is noteworthy mostly for its interesting discussion of how the V-2 affected North Atlantic Treaty Organization (NATO) during the early days of the Cold War. A fresh examination of the V-2 program is provided by Neufeld's *The Rocket and the Reich: Peenemünde and the Coming of the Ballistic Missile Era*, and the author details the direct links between this revolutionary weapon system and the current generation of intercontinental ballistic missiles (ICBMs). Lastly, Piszkiewicz's *The Nazi Rocketeers— Dreams of Space and Crimes of War* delves into the more personal aspects of the Nazi rocket program. This work details the use of concentration camp labor to build various rocket-testing sites as well as the influence of the Nazi Party on the development of the V-1 and V-2.

While the new technologies embodied in the atomic bomb, radar, and the V-1 and V-2 missiles have all received extensive attention from historians, the development of the jet engine and jet-powered fighters during the war is a subject that, by and large, continues to be sorely neglected. Nichelson's dissertation, "Early Jet Engines," is a detailed look at the development of both centrifugal and axial engines but is hardly suitable for the general reader. Ethell and Price's *World War II Fighting Jets* is a valued photographic record but also falls short of being complete. One very intriguing source on the development of early jets is Heiman's *Jet Pioneers*. This work is a collection of short biographies of various jet engineers and designers such as Ernst Heinkel, Frank Whittle, Don Keirn, and Kelly Johnson. Boyne's *Messerschmitt Me-262: Arrow to the Future*, which describes the production of the best jet fighter of the war, is a step in the right direction, but more work needs to be done on the development and use of jet technology during the war.

Sea

Beyond the development of sonar and search radar systems, advances in naval technologies during World War II were characterized by the evolution of earlier designs. The aircraft carriers, submarines, battleships, and naval auxiliaries built during the war were basically larger, more complex, and (in most cases) more capable descendants of interwar vessels. Much of the scientific effort put forth by the Allies during the war went toward better antisubmarine warfare (ASW) equipment. The Axis, particularly the Germans, spent vast resources trying to counter the new Allied ASW technologies. This back-and-forth technological battle has been well represented in World War II historiography. Bagnasco's *Submarines of World War Two* is a good general introduction to the various submarine classes employed during the war. Lipscomb's older *The British Submarine* examines the history of the British underwater force from its beginnings through the mid-1950s and includes some remarkable information on British developments during the interwar years. Carpenter and Polmar's *Submarines of the Imperial Japanese Navy* examines the technically advanced, yet poorly utilized, Japanese submarine force. Boyd and Yoshida's newer *The Japanese Submarine Force and World War II* covers much of the same ground as Carpenter and Polmar's effort but takes a wider view of the Japanese effort to develop a creditable submarine force and includes an extensive and very useful set of appendixes. Finally, Rössler's *The U-Boat: The Evolution and Technical History of German Submarines* is the best single guide to the massive German submarine corps. This work is complete with technical drawings and photographs as well as design and combat histories for each class of German submarine—a must-have for any naval historian.

World War II saw the reemergence of large-scale amphibious assaults. The American island-hopping campaign in the Pacific has been the subject of countless works. Three works in particular, however, touch upon the technical developments that allowed such large-scale amphibious landings to occur at all. Baily's *Alligators, Buffaloes, and Bushmasters* details the development of American landing craft and vehicles. Equally important is Strahan's *Andrew Jackson Higgins and the Boats That Won World War II*, an examination of the development and production of the personnel and vehicle landing craft that were critically important to the Allied victory. Lastly, Clifford's *Amphibious Warfare Development in Britain and America from 1920–1940* examines the advances made by the Allies in the area of amphibious operations during the interwar period.

Norman Friedman's collection of works published by the Naval Institute Press have become the standard guides to the development of American (and many Allied) combat vessels of the war; especially noteworthy are *U.S. Cruisers* and *U.S. Aircraft Carriers*. All of Friedman's works are highly detailed and include technical drawings and a general account of how the various ship types fared under combat conditions. Despite the lack of a large-scale "climactic" battleship versus battleship engagement during World War II, the development of such ships during the war has also been well documented. *Build the Musashi!* by Yoshimura examines the efforts of the Japanese to build the world's largest battleships. Garzke and Dulin's *Battleships* is an excellent source on the battleships of Axis (particularly German) and neutral powers. Stillwell's *Battleship Arizona* is a well-researched and illustrated history of the famous ship sunk at Pearl Harbor and is one of a series of similar works by this author. Jurens' article "The Evolution of Battleship Gunnery in the U.S. Navy, 1920–1945" is an analysis of internal U.S. Navy reports on gunnery exercises and illustrates how new technologies increased the accuracy of the battleship's big guns. Finally, *Sacred Vessels: The Cult of the Battleship and the Rise of the U.S. Navy* by O'Connell illustrates how an ill-founded attachment to outdated technology can have costly outcomes on the high seas. Further examples of the dangers of turning a blind eye to advances in naval technology are laid out in Milner's article "The Implications of Technological Backwardness: The Royal Canadian Navy 1939–1945." Milner argues that the Canadian navy was seriously handicapped during the Battle for the Atlantic because its ships were not as advanced as those found in either the British or American navies.

Land

The collection of sources on land weapons used in World War II is similar in nature to that on naval vessels or aircraft. Many works are highly detailed examinations of a single weapon or type of weapon, and others explore wider technical issues. Not surprisingly, the extensive use of armored and mechanized forces during the war has been a center of a great deal of writing since 1945. Macksey and Batchelor's *Tank: A History of the Armoured Fighting Vehicle* is a general guide to the development of main battle tanks from 1914 to 1970. This source is especially good at highlighting and describing the major trends in tank development over the years and is well illustrated. Forty's *World War Two Tanks* is a well-illustrated (including some color plates) and thoughtfully laid-out introduction to the heavy, medium, and light tanks developed and employed by all the major ground forces during the war. While Forty does not explore all of the subtypes of each design, this work is highly recommended as a basic guide to tanks of the Second World War. *A New Excalibur: The Development of the Tank 1909–1939* by Smithers examines how the British army used the experiences of World War I to develop new tank technologies and tactics during the interwar period. Baily's *Faint Praise* is a critical look at how the American army built, designed, and used tanks and tank destroyers during the war and is a particularly well written book. Edwards' *Panzer: A Revolution in Warfare, 1939–1945* is a wartime chronology as well as a technical history and is an excellent introduction to the complexities and innovations in mechanized warfare created by the German land and air forces.

Hunnicutt's *Sherman: A History of the American Medium Tank* and Hoffschmidt and Tantum's *German Tank and Anti-tank in World War II* are two examples taken from a much larger collection of works that examine the technical histories of particular weapons or families of weapons, often in exhaustive detail. Hunnicutt's work is well known for its meticulous attention to detail and is the best single source on the Allies' most famous medium tank. Ogorkiewicz's *Armoured Forces: A History of Armoured Forces and Their Vehicles* is useful because it illustrates how the technological advances made in armored warfare during World War II have affected armored vehicle design since. Finally, although the use of chemical weapons was not as widespread in World War II as it was in the Great War, the development and use of such weapons have been the focus of several works. Brophy and Fisher's *The Chemical Warfare Service* is an official history and examines how the chemical warfare branch of the U.S. Army organized itself for war. *The Chemical Warfare Service in World War II, a Report of Accomplishments*, written by the Chemical Corps Association, is a precursor to the volumes of the "Green Series," which deal with the Chemical Warfare Service, and details the combat use of such weapons as the 4.2-inch chemical mortar, smoke generators, and flamethrowers.

AREAS FOR FURTHER RESEARCH IN THE FIELD

The first works discussed earlier dealt with the interaction of science, technology, and warfare in the most general of terms and with the widest of scopes. It is unfortunate that no military historian has yet produced a work dedicated to the examination of this relationship solely in terms of the Second World War. Authors have tackled the role of technology as it applied to the development of a specific weapon system or how new weapons allowed one side or another to win a specific encounter or campaign (although jet technology continues to be largely ignored). However, a satisfactory work that discusses how science and technology affected the whole of the war has yet to be produced.

This gap in World War II historiography is made all the more damaging by the fact that the First World War has already received the treatment that the Second World War so desperately needs. Hartcup's *The War of Invention: Scientific Developments, 1914–18* devotes a chapter-length discussion to the development of each of the "new" military technologies introduced during the First World War: the tank, the airplane, chemical weapons, and so on. Additionally, Hartcup discusses how the various warring parties organized their respective scientific communities and (more importantly) how the various technologies developed for combat affected postwar society.

Corum's *The Roots of Blitzkrieg* is another work that, while not explicitly dealing with the Second World War, should serve as a guide for historians wishing to explore the effects that weapons development had on the war's outcome. *The Roots of Blitzkrieg* is an exquisitely written and well-researched look at how Germany, largely under the guidance of Hans von Seeckt, rebuilt its military establishment during the 1920s and 1930s. While Corum includes several arguments that directly touch upon the war in Europe, for the purpose of this chapter, this work is more useful for how it deals with the interaction between technology and the development of new battlefield tactics. Corum convincingly concluded that Germany's ability to match new weapon systems (such as tanks, ground support aircraft, and light infantry guns) to a new way of tactical thinking, the blitzkrieg, allowed it to dominate the European battlefield during the early and middle stages of the Second World War. Corum's ability to combine the role of tacticians and scientists is to be applauded.

The work that comes the closest to filling this gap in World War II historiography is Crowther and Whiddington's *Science at War*. Using mostly British examples, the two authors explain how the scientific breakthroughs in such forms as the atomic bomb, sonar, and search radars directly affected the outcome of the Second World War. Most of all, the work accomplishes this without the use of confusing scientific explanations or terminology. However, *Science at War* is in dire need of updating and does not provide adequate discussion of Japanese or Soviet weapons development programs.

A more recent example of the kind of research needed in this field can be found in Roland's article "Technology, Ground Warfare, and Strategy." This short piece is an excellent example of scholarship that explores how the Second World War altered the relationship between technology and strategy. Roland argues that prior to 1940, the American military did not view technology as having a large role in the development of strategy. However, after the war, this situation had completely reversed; technology now played such a primary role in military planning that often it overshadowed strategy. Roland's article is a must-read for students interested in the relationship between technology and strategy.

As seen in the preceding, historians and authors have devoted page after page to the development of specific weapons during the Second World War and the role that scientific advancement played in creating those new systems. While Roland's article is an important step in the right direction, there remains a definite lack of scholarship on the ways in which science, technology, and weapons development were interlinked and *in general* affected the outcome of the war. Whichever military historian is able to successfully combine Hartcup's scope and framework, Corum's ability to explain how technology and tactics affect each other, Crowther and Whiddington's skill at explaining highly confusing scientific processes in laymen's terms, and Roland's clarity is sure to produce one of the most important, influential, and commercially viable works on the Second World War ever printed.

BIBLIOGRAPHY

Bagnasco, Erminio. *Submarines of World War Two.* Annapolis, MD: NIP, 1973.

Baily, Alfred Dunlop. *Alligators, Buffaloes, and Bushmasters: The History of the Development of the LVT through World War II.* Washington, DC: Marine Corps Historical Center, 1986.

Baily, Charles M. *Faint Praise: American Tanks and Tank Destroyers during World War II.* Hamden, CT: Archon, 1983.

Baxter, James Phinney, III. *Scientists against Time.* Boston: Little, Brown, 1946.

Bekker, Cajus. *The Luftwaffe War Diaries: The German Air Force in World War II.* New York: Da Capo, 1964.

Bodie, Warren M. *The Lockheed P-38 Lightning.* Hiawassee, GA: Widewing, 1991.

———. *Republic's P-47 Thunderbolt: From Seversky to Victory.* Hiawassee, GA: Widewing, 1994.

Boyd, Carl, and Akihiko Yoshida. *The Japanese Submarine Force and World War II.* Annapolis, MD: NIP, 1995.

Boyne, Walter. *Clash of Wings—World War II in the Air.* New York: Simon and Schuster, 1994.

———. *Messerschmitt Me 262: Arrow to the Future.* Atglen, PA: Schiffer Military/Aviation History, 1994.

Brodie, Bernard, and Fawn M. Brodie. *From Crossbow to H-Bomb—The Evolution of the Weapons and Tactics of Warfare.* Bloomington: Indiana UP, 1973.

Brophy, Leo P., and George J. B. Fisher. *The Chemical Warfare Service: Organizing for War.* Washington, DC: GPO, 1958.

Burns, Russell, ed. *Radar Development to 1945.* Piscataway, NJ: Peregrinus/I.E.E.E., 1988.

Carpenter, Dorr, and Norman Polmar. *Submarines of the Imperial Japanese Navy.* Annapolis, MD: NIP, 1986.

Cave Brown, Anthony, and Charles B. MacDonald. *The Secret History of the Atomic Bomb.* New York: Dial, 1977.

Chemical Corps Association. *The Chemical Warfare Service in World War II, a Report of Accomplishments.* New York: Reinhold, 1948.

Christman, Albert B. *Sailors, Scientists, and Rockets: Origins of the Navy Rocket Program and of the Naval Weapons Center, China Lake, California.* Vol. 1. Washington, DC: Naval History Division, 1971.

Clark, Ronald William. *The Rise of the Boffins.* London: Phoenix House, 1962.

Clifford, Kenneth. *Amphibious Warfare Development in Britain and America from 1920–1940.* Laurens, NY: Edgewood, 1983.

Compton, Arthur H. *Atomic Quest: A Personal Narrative.* New York: Oxford UP, 1956.

Corum, James S. *The Roots of Blitzkrieg—Hans von Seeckt and German Military Reform.* Lawrence: University of Kansas, 1992.

Crowther, J. G., and R. Whiddington. *Science at War.* New York: Philosophical Library, 1948.

Edwards, Roger. *Panzer: A Revolution in Warfare, 1939–1945.* London: Arms and Armour, 1989.

Eggleston, Wilfrid. *Scientists at War.* London: Oxford UP, 1950.

Ethell, Jeffrey, and Alfred Price. *World War II Fighting Jets.* Annapolis, MD: NIP, 1994.

Ferte, Philip Joubert De La. *Rocket.* London: Hutchinson; New York: Philosophical Library, 1957.

Fisher, David E. *A Race on the Edge of Time: Radar—The Decisive Weapon of World War II.* New York: McGraw-Hill, 1988.

Forty, George. *World War Two Tanks.* London: Osprey, 1995.

Francillon, René J. *Japanese Aircraft of the Pacific War.* Annapolis, MD: NIP, 1970, 1979; London: Putnam, 1970.

Friedman, Norman. *U.S. Aircraft Carriers: An Illustrated Design History.* Annapolis, MD: NIP, 1983.

———. *U.S. Cruisers: An Illustrated Design History.* Annapolis, MD: NIP, 1984.

Fuller, J. F .C. *Armament and History.* New York: Charles Scribner's Sons, 1945.

Garlinski, Jozef. *Hitler's Last Weapons: The Underground War against the V-1 and V-2.* London: J. Friedmann, 1978.

Garzke, William H., Jr., and Robert O. Dulin, Jr. *Battleships—Axis and Neutral Battleships in World War II*. Annapolis, MD: NIP, 1985.

Goudsmit, Samuel Abraham. *Alsos*. Los Angeles: Tomash, 1983.

Graetzer, Hans G. *The Atomic Bomb: An Annotated Bibliography*. Pasadena, CA: Salem, 1992.

Groves, Leslie R. *Now It Can Be Told: The Story of the Manhattan Project*. New York: Harper and Brothers, 1962.

Guerlac, Henry. *Radar in World War II*. 2 vols. New York: American Institute of Physics; Los Angeles: Tomash, 1987.

Hartcup, Guy. *The War of Invention: Scientific Developments, 1914–18*. London: Brassey's Defense, 1988.

Hawkins, David, Edith C. Truslow, and Ralph Carlisle Smith. *Project Y: The Los Alamos Story*. Los Angeles: Tomash, 1983.

Heiman, Grover. *Jet Pioneers*. New York: Duell, Sloan, and Pearce, 1963.

Higham, Robin. *Air Power—A Concise History*. New York: St. Martin's, 1972.

Hoffschmidt, E. J. H., and W. H. Tantum. *German Tank and Anti-tank in World War II*. Greenwich, CT: W. E., 1968.

Horikoshi, Jiro. *Eagles of Mitsubishi: The Story of the Zero Fighter*. Seattle: University of Washington, 1981.

Howse, Derek. *Radar at Sea: The Royal Navy in World War II*. Annapolis, MD: NIP, 1993.

Hunnicutt, R. P. *Sherman: A History of the American Medium Tank*. Belmont, CA: Taurus Enterprises, 1978.

Irving, David. *The German Atomic Bomb: The History of Nuclear Research in Nazi Germany*. New York: Simon and Schuster, 1967.

Johnson, David. *V-1, V-2: Hitler's Vengeance on London*. New York: Stein and Day, 1982.

Jones, Edgar L., Louis Jordan, H. Kirk Stephenson, and C. G. Suits. *Applied Physics*. Boston: Little, Brown, 1948.

Jones, Vincent C. *Manhattan, the Army, and the Atomic Bomb*. Washington, DC: Center for Military History, U.S. Army, 1985.

Jurens, W. J. "The Evolution of Battleship Gunnery in the U.S. Navy, 1920–1945." *Warship International* 28 (1991): 240–271.

Klee, Ernst, and Otto Merk. *The Birth of the Missile—The Secrets of Peenemünde*. London: George G. Harrap, 1965.

Koppes, Clayton R. "The Sky Is the Limit: JPL and the Origins of American Rocketry." *American History Illustrated* 18:9, 10 (1984): 10–19, 18–25.

Lansing, Lamont. *Day of Trinity*. New York: Atheneum, 1965.

Lipscomb, Frank W. *The British Submarine*. London: Adam and Charles Black, 1954.

Longmate, Norman. *Hitler's Rockets: The Story of the V-2s*. London: Hutchinson, 1985.

Macksey, Kenneth, and John H. Batchelor. *Tank: A History of the Armoured Fighting Vehicle*. New York: Ballantine, 1971.

Macrae, R. Stuart. *Winston Churchill's Toyshop*. New York: Walker, 1971.

McFarland Stephen L. *America's Pursuit of Precision Bombing, 1910–1945*. Washington, DC: Smithsonian Institution, 1995.

Meigs, Montgomery C. *Slide Rules and Submarines: American Scientists and Subsurface Warfare in World War II*. Washington, DC: National Defense UP, 1990.

Milner, Marc. "The Implications of Technological Backwardness: The Royal Canadian Navy 1939–1945." *Canadian Defense Quarterly* 19 (1989): 46–53.

Murray, Williamson. *Strategy for Defeat: The Luftwaffe 1933–1945*. Maxwell Air Force Base, AL: Air UP, 1983.

Neufeld, Michael. *The Rocket and the Reich: Peenemünde and the Coming of the Ballistic Missile Era*. New York: Free, 1994.

Nichelson, Brian J. "Early Jet Engines and the Transition from Centrifugal to Axial Compressors: A Case Study in Technological Change." Ph.D. diss., University of Minnesota, 1988.

Nichols, K. D. *The Road to Trinity*. New York: William Morrow, 1987.

O'Connell, Robert L. *Sacred Vessels: The Cult of the Battleship and the Rise of the U.S. Navy*. New York: Oxford UP, 1991.

Ogorkiewicz, Richard M. *Armoured Forces: A History of Armoured Forces and Their Vehicles*. London: Arms and Armour, 1970.

Overy, Richard J. *The Air War 1939–1945*. New York: Stein and Day, 1980.

Page, Robert Morris. *The Origins of Radar*. New York: Doubleday Anchor, 1962.

Pawle, Gerald. *The Secret War, 1939–45*. New York: W. Sloane Associates, 1957.

Piszkiewicz, Dennis. *The Nazi Rocketeers—Dreams of Space and Crimes of War*. Westport, CT: Praeger, 1995.

Pokrovsky, G. I. *Science and Technology in Contemporary War*. New York: Praeger, 1959.

Powers, Thomas. *Heisenberg's War: The Secret History of the German Bomb*. New York: Knopf, 1993.

Price, Alfred. *The History of U.S. Electronic Warfare*. Vol. 1: *The Years of Innovation— Beginnings to 1946*. Westford, MA: Association of Old Crows, 1984.

Rhodes, Richard. *The Making of the Atomic Bomb*. New York: Simon and Schuster, 1986.

Richards, Pamela Spence. *Scientific Information in Wartime: The Allied–German Rivalry, 1939–1945*. Westport, CT: Greenwood, 1994.

Roland, Alex. "Technology, Ground Warfare, and Strategy: The Paradox of American Experience." *Journal of Military History* 55 (1991): 447–467.

Rössler, Eberhard. *The U-Boat: The Evolution and Technical History of German Submarines*. London: Arms and Armour, 1981.

Schaffer, Ronald. *Wings of Judgment—American Bombing in World War II*. New York and Oxford: Oxford UP, 1985.

Sherry, Michael S. *The Rise of American Air Power: The Creation of Armageddon*. London: Yale UP, 1987.

Simon, Leslie Earl. *German Research in World War II: An Analysis of the Conduct of Research*. New York: Wiley, 1947.

———. *German Scientific Establishments*. Brooklyn, NY: Reproduced by Mapleton House, 1947.

Smith, Herschel. *A History of Aircraft Piston Engines*. Manhattan, KS: Sunflower UP, 1981.

Smithers, A. J. *A New Excalibur: The Development of the Tank 1909–1939*. London: Leo Cooper in association with Secker and Warburg, 1986.

Smyth, Henry DeWolf. *Atomic Energy for Military Purposes: The Official Report on the Development of the Atomic Bomb under the Auspices of the United States Government, 1940–1945*. Stanford, CA: Stanford UP, 1989.

Staff, Michael B., Johnathan F. Fanton, and R. Hal Williams, eds. *The Manhattan*

Project—A Documentary Introduction to the Atomic Age. New York: McGraw-Hill, 1991.

Stewart, Irvin. *Organizing Scientific Research for War—The Administrative History of the Office of Scientific Research and Development.* Boston: Little, Brown, 1948.

Stillwell, Paul. *Battleship Arizona:—An Illustrated History.* Annapolis, MD: NIP, 1991.

Strahan, Jerry E. *Andrew Jackson Higgins and the Boats That Won World War II.* Baton Rouge: Louisiana State UP, 1994.

Syrett, David. *The Defeat of the German U-Boats: The Battle of the Atlantic.* Columbia: University of South Carolina, 1994.

Taylor, C. Fayette. "Aircraft Propulsion: A Review of the Evolution of Aircraft Piston Engines." *Smithsonian Annals of Flight,* vol 1:4. Washington, DC: Smithsonian Institution, 1971.

Terrell, Edward. *Admiralty Brief: The Story of Inventions That Contributed to Victory in the Battle of the Atlantic.* London: Harrap, 1958.

Thiesmeyer, Lincoln Reuber, and John E. Waterman. *Combat Scientists.* Boston: Little, Brown, 1947.

Tillman, Barrett. *Avenger at War.* London: Ian Allan, 1979.

Van Creveld, Martin. *Technology and War: From 2000 B.C. to the Present.* London: Brassey's; New York: Free; Toronto: Maxwell Macmillan Canada, 1991.

Watson-Watt, Robert. *The Pulse of Radar: The Autobiography of Sir Robert Watson-Watt.* New York: Dial, 1959.

———. *Three Steps to Victory: A Personal Account of Radar's Greatest Pioneer.* London: Odhams, 1957.

Wilcox, Robert K. *Japan's Secret War.* New York: William Morrow, 1985.

Williams, Robert Chadwell. "From the Hill to the Hilltop: Washington University and the Manhattan Project, 1940–1946." *Gateway Heritage* 9 (1988–1989): 14–27.

Yoshimura, Akira. *Build the Musashi!: The Birth and Death of the World's Greatest Battleship.* New York: Kodansha International, 1991.

Zimmerman, David. *The Great Naval Battle of Ottawa: How Admirals, Scientists, and Politicians Impeded the Development of High Technology in Canada's Wartime Navy.* Toronto: University of Toronto, 1989.

13 Propaganda, Public Opinion, and Censorship during the Second World War

Loyd E. Lee

While propaganda has undoubtedly played some role in all armed conflicts, in the twentieth century it became a central concern of all governments and increasingly so in World War II. Unlike in other languages, the English use of the word "propaganda" has had a negative connotation since the First World War. In the 1930s, the British studiously avoided the word, while the Americans devised the neologism "psychological warfare" in the 1940s to use in place of "propaganda," though that term is often used with a broader meaning.

The political extremes of both Left and Right had no such reservations. Believing in the efficacy of British propaganda in undermining German morale during World War I, Hitler rejected Goebbels' suggestion to establish a "Ministry of Information" in favor of a "Ministry of Popular Enlightenment and Propaganda," while making its practice a core part of Nazi policy. In the Soviet Union the Bolsheviks had their "Agitprop," a department in the Central Committee of the Communist Party dedicated to agitation and propaganda. Nonetheless, propaganda was no one's monopoly. All belligerents in the Second World War created agencies and ministries to promote their ideas and to spread information, whether true or not, favorable to their cause. They also censored or suppressed ideas and information they considered harmful. They did this in an effort to positively affect domestic public attitudes or to damage popular opinion within enemy countries.

In this chapter the term "propaganda" is used in a broad sense to describe official, governmental efforts to influence public opinion through media, especially in print and radio forms. Broader themes and other aspects of mass communications can be found in Chapters 15 through 17, which include discussions of the historiography of wartime film, Chapter 7 on Japanese occupation in Asia, Chapter 8 on Japanese society at war, and in Chapters 22, 23, and 25 of the companion volume *World War II in Europe, Africa, and the Americas* on the domestic histories of the major belligerents.

The academic study of propaganda was well under way in the 1930s, especially in response to the greatly expanded quantity of fascist propaganda, notably in Germany, where Goebbels' activities represented the most thorough attempt to shape opinion and society through the dissemination and control of ideas and culture. Especially prominent was the growing importance of radio broadcasting. Its low cost and increased reliability brought this new medium to mass audiences who need not be literate and who could listen while working or at leisure. While film and print media remained important, radio achieved predominance domestically on lower frequencies and internationally by shortwave broadcasting. It could carry the same messages as the other media but deliver them more widely and cheaply, and it could not be so easily banned and censored.

THEORETICAL WORKS

Among prominent prewar students of propaganda were Harwood Childs, Daniel Lerner, Hans Speier, Robert Lasswell, Leonard Doob, and others whose writings can be sampled in Lerner's *Propaganda in War and Crisis* or Lasswell, Casey, and Smith's *Propaganda, Communication, and Public Opinion.* Two American students of propaganda, Lavine and Wechsler, in *War Propaganda and the United States*, published in May 1940, explained the limits of propaganda—it could influence, not shape, public opinion— yet they also thought German, British, and French propaganda in the United States could help prevent an informed and rational debate on foreign policy, especially during a presidential election. Eduard Lindeman, president of the Institute for Propaganda Analysis, mused in his introduction to their volume whether or not "a new profession of propaganda analysis has arisen" (viii). How effective would propaganda be in winning the coming struggle?

A partial answer came in *Propaganda by Short Wave*, edited by Childs and Whitton; it details the 1939–1941 Princeton Listening Center's monitoring of shortwave broadcasts from Europe and the center's attempt to determine their impact on American public opinion (the original transcriptions are in the Princeton University Library). The anthology includes various analyses of the broadcasts by participating researchers. Childs concluded that "European short-wave broadcasts to this country have had little effect." Most Americans were simply not interested. "All the evidence now available clearly indicates that propaganda by short wave is a potential rather than an actual danger" (305).

Such inconclusive findings led to renewed interest in the problem of the impact of propaganda, which the German refugee social scientists Ernst Kris and Hans Speier carefully investigated. Their 1944 study, *German Radio Propaganda,* based on BBC-supplied transcripts of German broadcasts from April 1941 through 1943, concluded that prewar fears of popular gullibility were unfounded. "The experience of the Second World War is gradually destroying the myth of propaganda that arose as an aftermath of the first [world war]. Belief in the dark powers of propaganda is being replaced by a better understanding of its limitations and functions, which vary with the social order and the situation" (477). Nonetheless, neither Kris and Speier nor anyone else has been able to demonstrate the exact effectiveness or ineffectiveness of propaganda. What can be shown, however, is that governments considered it worth the expense and effort.

Other important works from the war years include Doob's *Public Opinion and Propaganda* and Lerner's *Propaganda in War and Crisis* or his earlier *Psychological Warfare against Nazi Germany* (originally titled *The Sykewar Campaign*). The most complete general study of propaganda is Qualter's *Opinion Control in the Democracies,* a thorough history and analysis that expands on his earlier important study, *Propaganda and Psychological Warfare.* He later focused more specifically on the experiences of World War II. Qualter argued that propaganda or public information, as he thought it should be called, is an essential ingredient of all modern societies, especially democratic ones. In a classic formulation he concluded: "Any act of promotion can be propaganda only if and when it becomes part of a deliberate campaign to induce action through influencing attitudes. . . . This is not to suggest that all propagandists are the same, or that no moral judgements can be made" (122). It is "the deliberate attempt by the few to influence the attitudes and behaviour of the many by the manipulation of symbolic communication" (124). He distinguished propaganda from intimidation, force, or bribery.

Except for bibliographies included in studies cited later, the only general bibliography of works in English on World War II propaganda is Smith's *The Secret Wars* with 190 citations. What is lacking is an annotated bibliography of works in all major languages, a prerequisite for the comparative study of wartime propaganda.

GENERAL WORKS

Few general histories of propaganda bring together theory and praxis from several belligerents. The best of these are limited to film studies, for which see Chapters 15 through 17. A partial exception is Balfour's *Propaganda in War.* Balfour served in the British Ministry of Information and the Political Warfare Executive (later the Psychological Warfare Division of Supreme Headquarters, Allied Expeditionary Force—SHAEF) and wrote what still stands as the most important comparative history of propaganda, detailing in sixty chapters the organization of British and German propaganda, with specific examples of propaganda activities. It is a sober, objective, and comprehensive study that not only sets forth the main history but also develops nuanced, complex conclusions on the importance and role of propaganda within each country and abroad. Taylor in "Propaganda in International Politics, 1919–1939" provides a sweeping, though brief, comparative commentary on the press, radio, and film within and among the major powers during the interwar period. For radio propaganda, still in its early stages of development in the 1930s, see a short comparison of the Nazi, Soviet, American, and British efforts in Hale's *Radio Power*. The early portions of Fraser's *Propaganda* combine a comparison of broadcast propaganda before and during the war with an analysis of its content and impact. He granted it had limited effectiveness among the young in reinforcing attitudes already held but had little impact on mature adults.

BRITAIN

Britain lacked a unified system of propaganda during the war, in part reflecting conservative ambivalence regarding the new media technologies and the ways they might strengthen the role of the labor movement in politics. Pronay's "Introduction" and his chapter on "The News Media at War" provide broad surveys of all the communications media, even though the collection in which they appear, *Propaganda, Politics and Film*, has a different focus.

The British Ministry of Information originally had broad responsibility for official news, censorship, and propaganda at home and abroad. Soon after the war began, however, it lost responsibility for censorship and later yielded control of propaganda abroad to the Political Warfare Executive (PWE). McLaine's *Ministry of Morale* credits its early failures to its class-rooted distrust of the people and bureaucratic infighting, though in time it came to appreciate the value of truthful news. For the Political Warfare Executive see Balfour's *Propaganda* noted before. Cruickshank's older *Fourth Arm: Psychological Warfare* covers much the same ground; it is based on extensive interviews of participants and archival material.

Radio broadcasting by the British Broadcasting Corporation (BBC) is the best-known British source of wartime information. The BBC stuck to "white" broadcasting, leaving the "black" (that is, broadcasting pretending to come from behind enemy lines) to the PWE. The BBC gained an enviable reputation of accuracy, consistency, and truthfulness and established itself as a truly world service, broadcasting in forty-five languages by war's end. For its history, based on a thorough investigation of the BBC's archives, see the classic, authoritative *War of Words* by Briggs, the third volume of his *History of Broadcasting in the United Kingdom.* His lengthy introductory "Perspectives" gives an overview. Nicholas' more recent *The Echo of War* goes beyond Briggs' work by focusing more directly on the BBC's importance to British public opinion and wartime mobilization. He wanted "to restore the BBC to centre stage in its role as propagandist for the Home Front" (2). Though its impact is hard to quantify, the service itself was transformed at home as well as abroad: the hours of broadcasting expanded from morning until late at night, it became more popular, and its "style" was "revolutionized." Several BBC propagandists gained notoriety, most notably George Orwell. See Fleay's "Looking into the Abyss" for his war years with the BBC, and, of course, read Orwell's novels *Animal Farm* and *1984* and West's editions of his *War Broadcasts* and *War Commentaries.*

The impact of BBC broadcasting has not been comprehensively studied. Using published and unpublished British and Danish sources, Bennett's *British Broadcasting and the Danish Resistance Movement* fully documents both senders and listeners of the broadcasts and the world impact of news regarding the Danish struggle. Haestrup, the leading authority on the Danish resistance, sums up the conclusion: "It is hardly possible to overestimate the importance the B. B. C. broadcasts had for occupied Denmark" (Preface, xi). The BBC's reputation suggests that the same was true elsewhere, but studies in support of that conclusion are still lacking.

Ellic Howe, who worked for the Political Warfare Executive, a secret service engaged in propaganda and subversive warfare, used Public Records Office material for *The Black Game: British Subversive Operations against the Germans during the Second World War.* Black propaganda was only part of its work. Also see Sefton Delmer's *Black Boomerang: An Autobiography.* Delmer, an Australian who grew up in Berlin, directed subversive broadcasts to Germany. "Boomerang" refers to British propaganda alleging that the Wehrmacht resisted Hitler, a myth postwar German officers used in denying their support of national socialism. Young edited and reduced the estimated 3 million words of the gossipy *Diaries of Sir Robert Bruce Lockhart,* head of PWE from March 1942 to the war's end, to two volumes. A prewar socialite, Lockhart knew many wartime leaders.

Domestic propaganda was often closely linked to foreign policy. Bell in *John Bull and the Bear* (i.e, the Soviet Union) suggested, "It should cause no surprise that publicity and propaganda policy, and on occasion censorship, were directed primarily to the end of ensuring that public revulsion against Soviet ideology, or tyranny, or brutality, however appalling, should not interfere with the creation or the working of that alliance" (185). He still concluded, however, that public opinion had a life of its own and that the conduct of foreign policy continued to rest with a small number of men in the government. Active British propaganda in the United States was also directed to favorable foreign policy goals.

Brewer's dissertation, "Creating the 'Special Relationship,'" demonstrates how Britain, through the Foreign Office, the Ministry of Information, and the BBC, analyzed American political culture with the aim of creating a climate of opinion favorable to Britain. She concentrated on two issues, the empire (especially India) and lend-lease. *Selling War: The British Propaganda Campaign against American "Neutrality" in World War II* by Cull also shows deliberate British efforts, obfuscated after the war, to influence American opinion. "The full effort . . . stands as one of the most diverse, extensive, and yet subtle propaganda campaigns ever directed by one sovereign state at another" (4). Cole's *Britain and the War of Words in Neutral Europe* concentrates on the neutral wartime European countries, Spain, Portugal, Switzerland, and Sweden, but includes other countries as well. In spite of bureaucratic disarray, the British succeeded in keeping the neutral states neutral, though their attempt to emerge as Europe's leader ran against the realities of postwar Soviet and American military power.

Numerous studies examine other aspects of British propaganda overseas. Due largely to the public reaction against official propaganda, Britain relinquished its World War I lead in this field to the Germans. Nonetheless, as Taylor in *The Projection of Britain* shows, the Foreign Office mounted a modest, but increasingly important, News Department in the interwar period to counter foreign anti-British propaganda. A trailbreaker, Taylor offered tentative arguments on the importance, in fact, necessity, of official efforts to influence leaders and opinion makers around the world.

GERMANY

It is appropriate that Germany, the first and foremost belligerent practitioner of propaganda, has received the most scholarly attention. Zeman's *Nazi Propaganda* is a brief, classic introduction, including chapters on internal propaganda and foreign propaganda as well as a history of changes in German propaganda efforts, which declined after 1943 in the face of military setbacks. He argued that the Nazis' electoral success was due to their propaganda. Baird's thorough 1974 *Mythical World of Nazi War Propaganda* distinguishes itself by its concentration on the "mythical" elements in Nazi propaganda, the merging of traditional German themes such as anti-Semitic *völkish* racism, the virtues of war, sacrificial death, anti-Bolshevism, British plutocracy, and the führer cult. Individual chapters take up key wartime events from the Battle of Poland to the increasingly chimerical elements surrounding the collapse of the Reich. Little new has been written on these themes.

Using Security Service (*Sicherheitsdienst,* SD) surveys, Steinert in *Hitler's War and the Germans* effectively tackled propaganda within Germany from the recipients' viewpoint, arguing that a sphere of public opinion resistant to official propaganda persisted. Welch's *Nazi Propaganda* includes his own introduction and nine brief essays by various experts on diverse topics, from the Nazis' chief propagandist Goebbels to architecture, film, workers' morale, housewives, and propaganda in the Netherlands. Based on his detailed study of *Popular Opinion and Political Dissent* in Bavaria, Kershaw's concluding essay in that volume, "How Effective Was Nazi Propaganda?" considered domestic German propaganda after 1933 to challenge the common view that propaganda was *The War That Hitler Won*, the title of a study by Herzstein. More recently, in *The Third Reich: Politics and Propaganda*, Welch confirmed Zeman and Baird's conclusions that Nazi propaganda became less effective as it deviated from reality. Otherwise, he argues a middle ground between those who discount the effectiveness of propaganda and those who see it as formative of German public opinion. His useful survey of the literature and summary analysis of issues relating to "Propaganda and Indoctrination in the Third Reich" conclude that "Nazi propaganda was in tune with the real aspirations of large sections of the German people" (419). *The Third Reich* is to be recommended for its straightforward discussion of the issues of German public opinion during the Hitlerian period within the context of the *Historikerstreit* (the debate over whether or not Nazi crimes are comparable to, or even of a lesser magnitude than, those of the Stalinist Soviet Union) and the question of a unique or "peculiar" German path toward a modern industrial society. Bennet's dissertation on "Public Opinion and Propaganda in National Socialist Germany during the War against the Soviet Union" gives further proof that the failure of the German war against the Soviet Union undermined official propaganda; ingrained attitudes could be reinforced by propaganda, but opinion could not be changed in the face of military setbacks.

There is a large literature in German and in English on Goebbels, head of the newly established Nazi Ministry of Popular Enlightenment and Propaganda from 1933. Boelcke's *Secret Conferences of Dr. Goebbels* includes excerpts from his briefings with the German-controlled press and radio after 1939. The appendix lists those who attended (about twenty in 1939, rising to fifty later) and notes his sources. There are several partial translations of Goebbels' diaries in English: *The Goebbels Diaries*, edited by Lochner; *The Goebbels Diaries: The Last Days*, edited by Trevor-Roper; and *The Goebbels Diaries*, edited and translated by Taylor. All extant portions of the diaries, *Tagebücher*, are being published in Germany under the editorship of Fröhlich.

Though Bramsted's *Goebbels and National Socialist Propaganda* appeared before more recently discovered sources were available, it is based on extensive primary material. A very readable account, it is less a biography than a study of the organization of propaganda and the Nazi Party from before 1933 through the war. Heiber's scholarly biography *Joseph Goebbels* lacks footnotes even in the original German edition. It is superseded by Reuth's *Goebbels*, which uses new sources from the former East German Stasi (State Secret Police) files and the private papers of a Swiss attorney. He also takes into account the changing historiography of the Third Reich of the past twenty years.

Of interest because of his role as prosecutor in the Nuremberg trials is the American Hardy's *Hitler's Secret Weapon: The "Managed" Press and Propaganda Machine of Nazi Germany*. He used Nuremberg documents from the trials and included photos and eight appendixes of organizational charts and documents.

Several citizens of Allied countries were propagandists for the Third Reich. Since their impact on British and American public opinion was overwhelmingly negative, interest in their activities arises largely from their personalities and a fascination with the fringes of political extremism. Edwards' fine *Berlin Calling: American Broadcasters in Service to the Third Reich* will remain the definitive study of five American journalists. Most famous is the American *Lord Haw-Haw and William Joyce* (Joyce was his name), for which Cole used BBC and Foreign Office as well as unnamed German sources. Selwyn's more recent *Hitler's Englishman: The Crime of "Lord Haw-Haw"* added little to Cole's study; he was intrigued by Joyce the man and questioned whether his execution was justifiable.

UNITED STATES

American propaganda during the war was not as centrally administered as that of Britain or Germany, though it was still pervasive—and very much needed to keep the civilian population aware of foreign dangers and of the facts of war. Dyer's 1959 *Weapon on the Wall* surveys "political communication," as he preferred to call propaganda or psychological warfare. An experienced news correspondent, Dyer worked for the Office of War Information during the war. He examined the learning experiences of World War II with the purpose of drawing lessons for the "present conflict." Though the third volume of Culbert's *Film and Propaganda in America* is on films, it has an excellent introduction to the literature and general themes of all wartime propaganda in the United States.

An early history of American efforts is Linebarger's *Psychological Warfare*. It distilled the author's experiences and those of his colleagues in the U.S. Army Psychological Warfare Branch. He included a history of propaganda and examples of propaganda analysis and intelligence as well as planning and operations. The last section of the 1947 edition on "Psychological Warfare and Disarmament" was replaced in the 1954 edition with a section on Cold War developments. Numerous illustrations and charts add to its value. For a rare inquiry on how *Propaganda Analysis* might be used to determine the enemy's intentions behind the content of its propaganda, see George's *Propaganda Analysis*, which concluded that the Foreign Broadcast Intelligence Service of the Federal Communications Commission made correct inferences about 80 percent of the time. According to George, only the United States and Great Britain undertook such analysis during the war.

Instrumental in American propaganda were the famous *FDR's Fireside Chats*, reproduced and edited with commentary by Buhite and Levy; it includes eighteen foreign policy talks from September 1939 to January 1945. Braverman's anecdotal *To Hasten the Homecoming: How Americans Fought World War II through the Media* comprehensively covers a wide variety of themes. Though a good introduction, it is not based on original research and does not engage the key issues of interest to students of propaganda and public opinion.

Winkler's *The Politics of Propaganda: The Office of War Information* (OWI) is a carefully researched history of the agency created by Roosevelt in 1942. His theme was to reveal "what the nation considered important as it strove to reconcile its basic values and the requirements of war" (7). Under the direction of former CBS news analyst Elmer Davis, the OWI coordinated, rather than directed, American film, print, and broadcast propaganda, especially in domestic media. Congressional Republicans charged the OWI with fostering pro-New Deal viewpoints and managed to curtail its budget. Overseas, the OWI's Voice of America began in 1942 to propagate official policies on shortwave radio, a history covered by Shulman's *The Voice of America* (VOA). She dissented from Winkler's views, finding that the war changed American bureaucratic and cultural approach to propaganda as it became more pragmatic and less idealistic. Shulman's useful study suffers from its focus on only one country, France, and the absence of any analysis of French political culture in relation to VOA's message.

Neither Winkler nor Shulman was able to document the specific impact of official efforts on public opinion or the course of the war. In *The Propaganda Warriors* Laurie states he was less interested in evaluating the quality and effectiveness of propaganda than in analyzing the various approaches to propaganda and their institutionalization within the Office of Strategic Services Morale Operations Branch, the OWI's overseas branch, and the U.S. Army. Nonetheless, he commented that propaganda played an important role and noted campaigns that succeeded and those that failed. As in the case of the studies of the BBC, we still need careful investigations of the impact of American propaganda on the targeted societies.

Soley's *Radio Warfare: OSS and CIA Subversive Propaganda* is a first study of that topic, but it lacks analysis among its mass of details. Early chapters are on British propaganda efforts, with the final chapters explaining the

American imitation of their methods. The important U.S. Armed Forces Radio Service (AFRS) has received little attention, though by war's end it was worldwide. DeLay's dissertation, "An Historical Study of the Armed Forces Radio Service to 1946," describes the development of the AFRS and its postwar contributions to the development of the radio industry's standards and practices.

Of particular interest is Roeder's *The Censored War: American Visual Experience during World War II* for its combination of propaganda, censorship, and photography. The government initially shielded Americans from the reality of war but then rationed it out to overcome complacency, though only after the war were images of dead Americans released for publication. Four chapters are accompanied by four visual essays with eighty-nine photos, many of which were among those censored. Washburn's *Question of Sedition* shows that while the government investigated the Afro-American press, and many leaders urged stiffer censorship of the more critical black journalists and publishers, Attorney General Francis Biddle refused to charge them with sedition. The story does not entirely exonerate American freedom of the press, as black publishers moderated their criticism as the war went on, with one eye on the government and the other on their advertisers.

Americans had their alleged propaganda traitors as well. Seven of twelve Americans indicted for treason in World War II were radio announcers. The most famous was "Tokyo Rose." Iva Toguri was indicted and convicted for the crime, though "Tokyo Rose" never existed; and no one ever called herself that name. The full story of the legend and the judicial travesty is told by Howe in *Hunt for "Tokyo Rose."* Toguri served six years in prison and received a presidential pardon in 1977.

OTHER COUNTRIES

English-language studies of propaganda in non-English-speaking countries, other than Germany, are rare. Though in French, the exemplary *La Propagande sous Vichy 1940–1944* by Gervereau and Peschanski is accessible to anyone because of its several hundred reproductions of cartoons, posters, and photographs, many in color. Written to accompany a 1990 Paris exposition organized by Musée d'histoire contemporaine de la bibliothèque de documentation internationale contemporaine, it also includes commentary by leading French historians.

The most thorough study in English of Soviet domestic propaganda during the war is Brody's *Ideology and Political Mobilization.* Soviet propaganda may have never been very effective. In any case, Brody concluded that official ideology was ineffective even among party members and undoubtedly less so among the general population. Brody also wrote a 1994 dissertation, "All for the Front?" concentrating less on propaganda and more on the power of the party in relation to popular wartime life and culture. Barber's brief "Image of Stalin" authoritatively asks important questions about how Soviet society endured the catastrophe of invasion and how it related to the government, but its brevity makes it only an introduction.

For casual references on fascist Italy, see Arnold's dissertation, "Fascist War Propaganda." In Italy the state did not control mass media, perhaps a factor in the regime's inability to sustain support for the war. Arnold's net is cast wide, concentrating on the Ministry of Popular Culture, and studies the organization of propaganda and the timing of propaganda campaigns as well as Mussolini's role and the impact of propaganda.

For Australia see Hilvert's *Blue Pencil Warriors*, a useful chronological and administrative history, rooted in bureaucratic theory, of the Department of Information. Hilvert argued that the department and the media worked well together. Japan's pathetic efforts to influence Australian opinion, especially after the tides of war turned toward Allied victory, are examined in detail in Meo's *Japan's Radio War on Australia*. She includes the organization of propaganda, its contents (based on broadcast transcripts), and official views on Australia's role in Asia.

Group Psychology of the Japanese during Wartime by Iritani is an expanded version of his Japanese-language book. While it seeks to establish responsibility for the war, it is also a rare study of propaganda, what he calls "fascist indoctrination."

Japanese "cultural propaganda" is the theme of five essays by Southeast Asian experts in Goodman's *Japanese Cultural Policies in Southeast Asia during World War 2*. Each is based on a different region or country. Goodman summarizes their common features in a short introduction. Goto wrote on "Indonesian Studies in Japan," while Kurasawa contributed a lengthy essay on "Films in Java." Reynolds contributed a general essay on "Japan's Cultural Program in Thailand," and Akashi wrote on the same theme for Malaya and Singapore. The concluding essay is Terami-Wada's "Japanese Propaganda Corps in the Philippines." Generally, Japan was unprepared for a well-developed propaganda effort because of its historical orientation toward Chinese civilization and its fear of Russia (reinforced under the communists) as well as its recent decision to conquer the region. Under military rule, the intellectuals (*bunkajin*) sent into Southeast Asia shared the militarists' ultranationalist goals. Nonetheless, they recruited students for education in Japan, many of whom had lasting, positive experiences.

CONCLUSION

The importance of propaganda in World War II may never be determined. Sources tend to limit what can be done to studies of official agencies and the leaders of their organizations. The effect of propaganda on the public and its activities is hard to measure. Ironically, it was in the totalitarian societies with extensive police surveillance that most can be learned. On the other hand, careful analyses of public opinion polls, diaries, letters, and other material generated by the public could add to our understanding. Cross-cultural and transnational studies, though difficult to carry out, should prove to show the truer dimensions of the impact of propaganda.

BIBLIOGRAPHY

Akasi, Yoji. "Japanese Cultural Policy in Malaya and Singapore, 1942–1945." In Grant K. Goodman, ed., *Japan*, 117–172. New York: St. Martin's, 1991.

Arnold, W. Vincent. "Fascist War Propaganda, 1939–1943." Ph.D. diss., Miami University, 1990.

Baird, Jay W. *The Mythical World of Nazi War Propaganda, 1939–1945*, 38–49. Minneapolis: University of Minnesota, 1974.

Balfour, Michael. *Propaganda in War. 1939–1945.* London: Kegan Paul; Boston: Routledge, 1979.

Barber, John. "Image of Stalin in Soviet Propaganda during World War 2." In John G. Garrard and Carol Garrard, eds., *World War 2 and the Soviet People: Selected Papers from the Fourth World Congress for Soviet and East European Studies, Harrogate, 1990*, 38–49. New York: St. Martin's; London: Macmillan, 1993.

Bell, P. M. H. *John Bull and the Bear: British Public Opinion, Foreign Policy and the Soviet Union 1941–1945.* London: Edward Arnold, 1990.

Bennet, Victor Kenneth. "Public Opinion and Propaganda in National Socialist Germany during the War against the Soviet Union." Ph.D. diss., University of Washington, 1990.

Bennett, Jeremy. *British Broadcasting and the Danish Resistance Movement 1940–1945: A Study of the Wartime Broadcasts of the B.B.C. Danish Service.* Cambridge: Cambridge UP, 1966.

Boelcke, Willi A., ed. *The Secret Conferences of Dr. Goebbels: The Nazi Propaganda War, 1939–43.* Translated by Edward Osers. New York: E. P. Dutton, 1970.

Bramsted, Ernest Kohn. *Goebbels and National Socialist Propaganda, 1925–1945.* East Lansing: Michigan State UP, 1965.

Braverman, Jordan. *To Hasten the Homecoming: How Americans Fought World War II through the Media.* Lanham, MD, New York, and London: Madison, 1996.

Brewer, Susan Ann. "Creating the 'Special Relationship': British Propaganda in the United States during the Second World War." Ph.D. diss., Cornell University, 1991.

Briggs, Asa. *History of Broadcasting in the United Kingdom.* Vol. 3: *The War of Words.* Oxford: Oxford UP, 1970.

Brody, Richard Joseph. "All for the Front? Party Authority, Popular Values and the Soviet Civilian Experience of World War II." Ph.D. diss., University of Michigan, 1994.

Brody, Richard J. *Ideology and Political Mobilization: The Soviet Home Front during World War II.* Pittsburgh: Center for Russian and East European Studies, University of Pittsburgh, 1994.

Buhite, Russell D., and David W. Levy, eds. *FDR's Fireside Chats.* Norman: University of Oklahoma, 1992.

Childs, Harwood Lawrence, and John B. Whitton, eds. *Propaganda by Short Wave.* Princeton: Princeton UP; London: Oxford UP, 1942.

Coers, Donald V. *John Steinbeck as Propagandist: The Moon Is Down Goes to War.* Tuscaloosa: University of Alabama, 1991.

Cole, J. A. *Lord Haw-Haw and William Joyce: The Full Story.* New York: Farrar, Straus, and Giroux, 1964.

Cole, Robert. *Britain and the War of Words in Neutral Europe, 1939–1945: The Art of the Possible.* New York: St. Martin's; London: Macmillan, 1990.

Cruickshank, Charles. *The Fourth Arm: Psychological Warfare 1938–1945.* London: Davis-Poynter, 1977; Oxford: Oxford UP, 1977, 1981.

Culbert, David, ed. *Film and Propaganda in America: A Documentary History.* Vol. 2, part 1. Westport, CT: Greenwood, 1990.

Cull, Nicholas John. *Selling War: The British Propaganda Campaign against American "Neutrality" in World War II.* Oxford: Oxford UP, 1994.

DeLay, Theodore Stuart. "An Historical Study of the Armed Forces Radio Service to 1946." Ph.D. diss., University of Southern California, 1951.

Delmer, Sefton. *Black Boomerang: An Autobiography.* London: Secker and Warburg; New York: Viking, 1962.

Doob, Leonard W. *Public Opinion and Propaganda.* New York: Henry Holt, 1948.

Dyer, Murray. *The Weapon on the Wall: Rethinking Psychological Warfare.* Baltimore: Johns Hopkins, 1959; New York: Arno, 1979.

Edwards, John Carver. *Berlin Calling: American Broadcasters in Service to the Third Reich.* New York: Praeger, 1991.

Fishman, Sarah. "Grand Delusions: The Unintended Consequences of Vichy France's Prisoner of War Propaganda." *Journal of Contemporary History* 26 (1991): 229–254.

Fleay, C. Sanders. "Looking into the Abyss: George Orwell at the BBC." *Journal of Contemporary History* 24 (1989): 503–518.

Fraser, Lindley Macnaghten. *Propaganda.* London and New York: Oxford UP, 1957, 1962, 1986.

George, Alexander. *Propaganda Analysis.* Westport, CT: Greenwood, 1959, 1973.

Gervereau, de Laurent, and Denis Peschanski. *La Propagande sous Vichy 1940–1944/ Ouvrage Publié sous la Direction de Laurent Gervereau et Denis Peschanski.* Paris: Diffusion, Editions La Decouverte, 1990.

Goebbels, Joseph. *Die Tagebücher von Joseph Goebbels: Samtliche Fragmente, Teil I, Aufzeichnungen 1924–1941.* Edited by Elke Frölich. Munich: K. G. Saur, 1987.

———. *Die Tagebücher von Joseph Goebbels, Teil II, Diktate 1941–1945.* Edited by Elke Frölich. 15 vols. Munich: K. G. Saur, 1995–1996.

———. *The Goebbels Diaries, 1939–1941.* Edited and translated by Fred Taylor. New York: G. P. Putnam's Sons, 1983.

———. *The Goebbels Diaries: The Last Days.* Edited by Hugh Trevor-Roper and translated by Richard Barry. London: Book Club Associates, 1978.

———. *The Goebbels Diaries, 1942–1943.* Edited and translated by Louis Lochner. Garden City, NY: Doubleday; Washington, DC: Infantry Journal, 1948.

Goodman, Grant K., ed. *Japan: Japanese Cultural Policies in Southeast Asia during World War 2.* New York: St. Martin's, 1991.

Goto, Kenichi. " 'Bright Legacy' or 'Abortive Flower': Indonesian Students in Japan during World War 2." In Grant K. Goodman, ed., *Japan*, 7–35. New York: St. Martin's, 1991.

Hale, Julian Anthony Stuard. *Radio Power: Propaganda and International Broadcasting.* Philadelphia: Temple UP, 1975.

Hardy, Alexander G. *Hitler's Secret Weapon: The "Managed" Press and Propaganda Machine of Nazi Germany.* New York: Vantage, 1967.

Heiber, Helmut. *Joseph Goebbels.* Translated by John K. Dickinson. New York: Hawthorn, 1972.

Herzstein, Robert E. *The War That Hitler Won: Goebbels and the Nazi Media Campaign.* New York: Paragon House; London: Hamilton, 1987. Also subtitled *The Most Infamous Propaganda Campaign in History.* London: Hamish Hamilton, 1979.

Hilvert, John. *Blue Pencil Warriors: Censorhip and Propaganda in World War II.* St. Lucia: University of Queensland, 1984.

Howe, Ellic. *The Black Game: British Subversive Operations against the Germans during the Second World War.* London: Michael Joseph, 1982.

Howe, Russell Warren. *The Hunt for "Tokyo Rose."* Lanham, MD: Madison, 1990.

Iritani, Toshio. *Group Psychology of the Japanese during Wartime.* London and New York: Kegan Paul International, 1991.

Jeffreys-Jones, Rhodri. "The Perils of Propaganda in War and Peace." *Diplomatic History* 16 (1992): 605–618.

Kershaw, Ian. "How Effective Was Nazi Propaganda?" In David Welch, ed., *Nazi Propaganda: The Power and the Limitations*, 180–205. Totowa, NJ: Barnes and Noble, 1983.

———. *Popular Opinion and Political Dissent in the Third Reich.* Oxford: Clarendon; New York: Oxford UP, 1983.

Kris, Ernst, and Hans Speier. *German Radio Propaganda: Report on Home Broadcasts during the War.* London, New York, and Toronto: Oxford UP, 1944.

Kurasawa, Aiko. "Films as Propaganda Media on Japan under the Japanese, 1942–45." In Grant K. Goodman, ed., *Japan*, 36–92. New York: St. Martin's, 1991.

Lasswell, Harold D., Ralph D. Casey, and Bruce Lannes Smith, eds. *Propaganda, Communication, and Public Opinion: An Annotated Bibliography.* Chicago: University of Chicago, 1969.

Laurie, Clayton D. *The Propaganda Warriors: America's Crusade against Nazi Germany.* Lawrence: University of Kansas, 1996.

Lavine, Harold, and James Wechsler. *War Propaganda and the United States.* New Haven, CT: Yale University, 1940; New York: Arno, 1972.

Lerner, Daniel. *Psychological Warfare against Nazi Germany: The Sykewar Campaign, D-Day to VE-Day.* Cambridge: MIT, 1971. Originally published as *Sykewar: Psychological Warfare against Germany, D-Day to VE-Day.* Cambridge: MIT, 1949.

———, ed. *Propaganda in War and Crisis: Materials for American Policy.* New York: G. W. Steward, 1951.

Linebarger, Paul Myron Anthony. *Psychological Warfare.* Washington, DC: Infantry Journal, 1954; New York: Arno, 1972.

McLaine, Ian. *Ministry of Morale: Home Front Morale and the Ministry of Information in World War II.* London: George Allen and Unwin, 1979.

Meo, Lucy D. *Japan's Radio War on Australia, 1941–1945.* Carlton, Victoria, London, and New York: Melbourne UP, 1968.

Nicholas, Siân. *The Echo of War: Home Front Propaganda and the Wartime BBC, 1939–45.* Manchester and New York: Manchester UP, 1996.

Orwell, George. *Animal Farm.* London: Secker and Warburg; New York: Harcourt, Brace, 1945.

———. *1984: A Novel.* London: Secker and Warburg; New York: New American Library, 1949.

———. *Orwell, the War Broadcasts.* Edited by W. J. West. London: Duckworth; New York: Pantheon, 1985.

———. *Orwell, the War Commentaries.* Edited by W. J. West. London: Duckworth; New York: Pantheon, 1985.

Padover, Saul Kussie. *Experiment in Germany: The Story of an American Intelligence Officer.* New York: Duell, Sloan, and Pearce, 1946.

Pool, Ithiel de Sola, ed. *Handbook of Communication.* Chicago: Rand McNally College, 1973.

Pronay, Nicholas, and D. W. Spring, eds. *Propaganda, Politics and Film, 1918–1945.* London and Basingstoke: Macmillan, 1982.

Qualter, Terence H. *Opinion Control in the Democracies.* New York: St. Martin's, 1985.

———. *Propaganda and Psychological Warfare.* New York: Random House, 1962.

Reuth, Ralf Georg. *Goebbels.* Translated by Krishna Winston. New York: Harcourt, Brace, 1993.

Reynolds, E. Bruce. "Imperial Japan's Cultural Program in Thailand." In Grant K. Goodman, ed., *Japan,* 93–115. New York: St. Martin's, 1991.

Roeder, George H., Jr. *The Censored War: American Visual Experience during World War II.* New Haven, CT: Yale UP, 1993.

Selwyn, Francis. *Hitler's Englishman: The Crime of "Lord Haw-Haw."* London: Routledge and Kegan Paul, 1987.

Short, Kenneth R. M., ed. *Film and Radio Propaganda in World War II.* Knoxville: University of Kentucky, 1983.

Shulman, Holly Coward. *The Voice of America: Propaganda and Democracy, 1941–1945.* Madison: University of Wisconsin, 1990.

Simmonds, Roy S. *John Steinbeck: The War Years, 1939–1945.* Cranbury, NJ, London, and Mississauga, Ontario: Associated UP, 1996.

Smith, Myron J., Jr. *The Secret Wars: A Guide to Sources in English.* Vol. 1: *Intelligence, Propaganda and Psychological Warfare, Resistance Movements, and Secret Operations, 1939–1945.* Santa Barbara, CA: ABC-Clio, 1980.

Soley, Lawrence C. *Radio Warfare: OSS and CIA Subversive Propaganda.* New York and London: Praeger, 1989.

Steinert, Marlis G. *Hitler's War and the Germans: Public Mood and Attitude during the Second World War.* Edited and translated by Thomas E. J. de Witt. Athens: Ohio UP, 1977.

Taylor, Philip M. *The Projection of Britain: British Overseas Publicity and Propaganda, 1919–1939.* Cambridge and New York: Cambridge UP, 1981.

———. "Propaganda in International Politics, 1919–1939." In Kenneth R. M. Short, ed., *Film and Propaganda,* 17–47. Knoxville: University of Kentucky, 1983.

Taylor, Richard. *Film Propaganda: Soviet Russia and Nazi Germany.* London: Croom Helm; New York: Barnes and Noble, 1979.

Terami-Wada, Motoe. "The Japanese Propaganda Corps in the Philippines: Laying the Foundation." In Grant K. Goodman, ed., *Japan*, 173–211. New York: St. Martin's, 1991.

Thompson, Eric. "Canadian Warcos in World War II: Professionalism, Patriotism and Propaganda." *Mosaic* (Winnipeg, Manitoba) 23 (1990): 55–72.

Thomson, Oliver. *Mass Persuasion in History: An Historical Analysis of the Development of Propaganda Techniques.* Edinburgh: Paul Harris; New York: Crane, Russak, 1977.

Washburn, Patrick S. *A Question of Sedition: The Federal Government's Investigation of the Black Press during World War II.* New York and Oxford: Oxford UP, 1986.

Welch, David. *Nazi Propaganda: The Power and the Limitations.* Totowa, NJ: Barnes and Noble, 1983.

———. "Propaganda and Indoctrination in the Third Reich: Success or Failure?" *European History Quarterly* 17 (1987): 403–422.

———. *The Third Reich: Politics and Propaganda.* London and New York: Routledge, 1993.

Winkler, Allan M. *The Politics of Propaganda: The Office of War Information, 1942–1945.* New Haven, CT: Yale UP, 1978.

Young, Kenneth, ed. *The Diaries of Sir Robert Bruce Lockhart.* London: Macmillan, 1973–1980.

Zeman, Z. A. B. *Nazi Propaganda.* London: Oxford UP, 1964.

14   Unit Histories and the Experience of Combat

Loyd E. Lee

The term "unit history" here refers to a history of an organized military formation regardless of the size of the unit. As a genre such histories vary greatly in quality and have generally not been studied as a separate topic. They have, however, been used as the basis for analyzing the experience of combat, the study of combat motivation, and leadership effectiveness, a topic taken up toward the end of this chapter.

Official unit histories were compiled after the war to keep a record of a unit's activities and to provide a basis for later analysis, with little regard to their possible general interest. They often did not appear in print, though they were used in the preparation of official histories. For a guide to those, see Higham's *Official Histories* and other guides to military history in Rasor and Lee's "Reference Works." Many veterans and their associations published their own histories for commemorative purposes; they continue to appear, though many such volumes resemble commemorative annuals rather than analytical or narrative studies. A few units have attracted professional military historians who sometimes write to celebrate a unit's exploits, but also with an eye to recounting soldiers' experiences and explaining their role in the war. Unit histories of all sorts have also been a source for answering questions regarding the nature of combat and, especially, its effectiveness.

What follows is necessarily limited to some of the more important or interesting of the several thousand published unit histories in English from the United States, Britain and the Commonwealth, and Germany. The bibliography provides further guidance. Many unit histories were printed in limited or subscription editions or by obscure presses, a further restriction on their availability.

AMERICAN

Dornbusch's *Unit Histories of World War II: United States Army, Air Force, Marines, Navy* includes all histories, whether published or not. He defined "unit history" as "any record of unit activities produced by or for a military unit regardless of the size of the unit or the finished documents" (Preface). Though now out-of-date, it includes 1,223 entries.

Army

Basic for the U.S. Army is Controvich's *United States Army Unit Histories: A Reference and Bibliography*, with two supplements. It is without commentary, but it is current and includes unit chronologies, order of battles, ground participation credits, commanding generals, and much else. Pappas' *United States Army Unit Histories* is a guide to the collection in the U.S. Army Military History Institute's research collection at Carlisle Barracks, Pennsylvania. Also see Sommers' "World War II Holdings of the U.S. Army Military History Institute." Kahn and McLemore's *Fighting Divisions* originally appeared in 1946; each division was allotted two pages. They included organizational charts, the campaigns and battles each division participated in, a chronology, maps, and color reprints of shoulder patches.

The greatest number of unit histories covers elements of the U.S. Army. Several were published soon after the war and have often been reprinted. Among infantry divisions, the following are noteworthy. Draper's *The 84th Infantry Division in the Battle of Germany*, first published in 1946, is a frequently reprinted classic. It covers the division's 171 days on the line, attempting to integrate the events of the entire division as well as the view from the average soldier. Ewing's *29, Let's Go! A History of the 29th Infantry Division* is a fine history based on after-action reports and other contemporary materials as well as interviews, taking the division's history from boot camp to the end of the war. Frankel's *The 37th Infantry Division in World War II* is a similar, excellent account, also published soon after the war.

In the 1970s a renewed interest in publishing unit histories developed, as veterans reached middle age and grew more interested in making their wartime service known to a younger generation. Many had also retired and had the time to write such histories.

For example, Scott's *The Blue and White Devils* combines an account of the Third Infantry Division's combat operations in North Africa and Western Europe with his personal recollections and the daily news summaries he prepared for distribution among the division's units. Astor followed up his *Blood-Dimmed Tide: The Battle of the Bulge by the Men Who Fought It* with *"Battling Buzzards" The Odyssey of the 517th Parachute Regimental Combat Team*

1943–1945. His intent was to analyze factors making for an effective combat unit; his sources were interviews of veterans, plus his own memory.

Stannard, a rifleman in the 193d Division and professional journalist who later turned oral historian, wrote the frank and thorough *Infantry: An Oral History of a World War II American Infantry Battalion.* Companies are described in detail, with each interviewee clearly identified, followed by a series of topical chapters.

Hofmann's *The Super Sixth: History of the 6th Armored Division,* written by an academician and participant, is an interesting mix of scholarly history and affection for the division's postwar association. Another armored division history, Houston's *Hell on Wheels: The 2nd Armored Division* is based on archival materials, interviews, and correspondence. Activated in 1940, it fought in North Africa and across Western Europe and to the Elbe. *First across the Rhine: The 291st Engineer Combat Battalion in France, Belgium, and Germany* by Pergrin is something of a unit autobiography. Writing in the first person, Pergrin used the recollections of other veterans and other unpublished sources to amplify his own experiences.

Ambrose, *Band of Brothers: E Company, 506th Regiment, 101st Airborne from Normandy to Hitler's Eagle's Nest,* is based on taped oral histories collected after 1988 as well as other sources. It includes photos and a postwar account of the unit's members' careers. A companion piece is *Rendezvous with Destiny: A History of the 101st Airborne Division,* a lengthy account by Rapport and Northwood begun in France under S. L. A. Marshall, chief historian for the European theater, and continued privately after the 101st was deactivated. They used the many unit studies compiled during the war. Fry's *Combat Soldier* on the 350th Infantry Regiment of the eighty-eighth "Blue Devil" Infantry Division was begun in 1944 and covers two months of combat near the Gustav line in southern Italy. Major General Fry, the unit's commander, wanted to answer the question, "How are men best led?" and to "unmask" the glamour of war. Finally, Leinbaugh and Campbell, *The Men of Company K: The Autobiography of a World War II Rifle Company,* is an engrossing narrative, without notes or bibliography but based on interviews (including some with Germans), after-action reports, letters home, and Draper's history of the eighty-fourth Division. Cave's *Beyond Courage: One Regiment against Japan* treats the oldest continuous military unit in the United States, one recruited from New Mexico and captured at Bataan. It is based on a wide range of interviews, diaries, memoirs, and correspondence.

There are several histories of racially segregated American military units. Neither Hargrove's *Buffalo Soldiers in Italy: Black Americans in World War II* nor the fragmentary memoirs in Arnold's *Buffalo Soldiers: The 92nd Infantry Division and Reinforcements in World War II* have settled controversy about the performance of the division whose officers down to battalion levels were all whites. Sandler, *Segregated Skies: All-Black Combat Squadrons of World War II,* based on interviews and official records, is a history of the

332d Fighter Group made up of all black pilots of the ninety-ninth Fighter Squadron (Colored)(Separate) and the 477th Bombardment Group (Medium). Murphy's *Ambassadors in Arms: The Story of Hawaii's 100th Battalion* records the story of the first U.S. Army combat unit composed of Americans of Japanese ancestry; it was recruited before December 1941. A professional historian, Murphy primarily used manuscript sources in Hawaii. It should be supplemented by Shirey's somewhat anecdotal *Americans, the Story of the 442d Combat Team* and Duus' more recent *Unlikely Liberators*; Duus used declassified sources and a large number of interviews.

Army Air Force

Dornbusch's guide to *Unit Histories of the United States Air Forces* is comprehensive and also includes privately printed personal narratives and documentary sources. Maurer's *Air Force Combat Units* lists all combat groups with details regarding their assignments, stations, campaigns, emblems, and so forth; his *Combat Squadrons* is a complement.

Werrell's *Eighth Air Force Bibliography* lists published and unpublished materials, including personal accounts, with commentary on each. *The Mighty Eighth: A History of the Units, Men, and Machines of the U.S. 8th Air Force* by Freeman is an oversized work with many photos and drawings of planes and references to unit histories. Caine, *Eagles of the RAF: American Pilots in the RAF*, is based on interviews with 35 pilots (of approximately 80 of the 244 pilots known to be alive at the time); he consulted original source material to describe their experiences and contributions to the air war. Sturzebecker's *The Roarin' 20's* is a good example of an encyclopedic commemoration of a bombardment group in the USAAF, with extensive information, photos, and memorabilia from the author's own collection. An account from the Pacific is *Lightning Strikes: The 475th Fighter Group in the Pacific War* by Yoshino, constructed from a survey of unit survivors, interviews, journals, and the group's official history. Britt's *The Long Rangers* covers one unit, the 307th Bombardment Group (H) of the thirteenth U.S. Army Air Force in the Southwest Pacific from December 1942. He conducted interviews and used diaries and air force archives. Molesworth's *Sharks over China: The 23rd Fighter Group in WWII* is a detailed story of the unit that replaced the American Volunteer Group, the "Flying Tigers," in 1942. Though less analytic and more like a novel than other works, it is grounded in interviews, unpublished unit histories, and other sources and is well written.

Navy

Unit histories in the navies include individual ships of all classes and their crews as well as units not associated with any particular vessel. An indispensable guide is Mawdsley's *Cruise Books of the United States Navy in*

World War II, which lists and, in some cases, describes the contents of some 800 volumes, most published between 1945 and 1947 in limited editions. It includes not only ships but naval aviation units, construction brigades, and other units. Motley and Kelly's *Now Hear This!* has brief ship histories with an appendix of citations, a list of vessels, operations, and photographs.

Cressman's *That Gallant Ship: USS Yorktown* details the original carrier by that name, sunk at Midway, with many photographs, while Reynolds' *The Fighting Lady* is a longer history of the second *Yorktown*, now to be seen in its postwar refitting at Charleston, South Carolina. Bryan's 1945 diary aboard the *Yorktown* is in *Aircraft Carrier.*

The Ghost That Died at Sunda Strait by Winslow recounts the feats of the flagship of the U.S. Asiatic Fleet, USS *Houston*, sunk in February 1942 off Java. Crew member Helm's *Ordeal by Sea* carefully narrates the actions of the heavy cruiser USS *Indianapolis*, commissioned in 1932, and its doubly tragic end two weeks before Japan's surrender. Sailing without escort, the USS *Indianapolis* was torpedoed, sinking within minutes. Three-fourths of the crew escaped, but most of them perished when a communication failure led to a delay in searching for survivors. Hoehling's *The Lexington Goes Down* used extensive interviews, correspondence, and official reports and includes many photographs.

Of particular note is Muir's expert introduction to the *Iowa Class Battleships*, of which four were commissioned, the *Iowa*, the *New Jersey*, the *Missouri*, and the *Wisconsin*. *Lucky Lady and the Navy Mystique* by Hindle is a history of the escort carrier USS *Chenango* in the North Atlantic. Mason's *"We Will Stand by You" Serving in the Pawnee* is a well-written account of a fleet tug in the Solomons and the Western Pacific by and for its crew members.

Kelly's *Proudly We Served* used interviews to relate the story of the predominantly black crew aboard the USS *Mason*, a destroyer escort in the Atlantic. The other all-black commissioned American ship during the war was subchaser USS *PC 1264*. Purdon used interviews, diaries, and naval records to tell its story in *Black Company*. Gugliotta's *Pigboat 39: An American Sub Goes to War* is a well-written account by the wife of the submarine's captain of the Pacific War. She based it on many interviews, personal communications, and navy documents with good photos.

Marines

For U.S. Marine Corps unit histories, see Moran's bibliography *Creating a Legend*, the official histories, and personal accounts. McMillan's 1949 *The Old Breed; A History of the First Marine Division in World War II* is a well-crafted, gripping story of young men in war—one of the best ever written. McMillan was a writer for various national publications, an alumnus of the Federal Writers Project, and a marine combat correspondent to the division. A very different book, pathbreaking for its method and cultural approach to war and combat, is Cameron's *American Samurai*. Though also focused on the First Marine Division, it is not a narrative and operational history but a study of "myth and imagination" within the Marine Corps and the corps' transformation from pre–Pearl Harbor days through Guadalcanal and Okinawa. Some readers may think it unbalanced as, for example, in its comparisons of the Marines with the Nazi SS.

GREAT BRITAIN AND THE BRITISH COMMONWEALTH

For a bibliography of Britain and the British empire, the last version of Perkins' *Regiments* covers all modern periods, with a paragraph description and evaluation of each history. Hallows' *Regiments and Corps of the British Army* lists without annotation all British units (i.e., those from the United Kingdom) with a brief history, honors, and awards, as well as journals, museums, and regimental or corps histories, if any. Dornbusch covered the *Canadian Army*, the *Australian Military*, and the *New Zealand Army* units in other volumes.

Army

Major E. G. Godfrey's *The Duke of Cornwall's Light Infantry*, a historically sensitive and detailed account, narrates its progress from 1940 in France through India, Iraq, the Western Desert, Italy, France, and Germany. He linked regimental documents with veterans' personal accounts. Another thorough, well-written unit history covering the entire war years is Hallam's *History of the Lancashire Fusiliers*, based on a rediscovered postwar draft manuscript, as well as the Fusiliers' publications, personal diaries, and official accounts. Lionel Ellis, author of several war-related books, wrote a good campaign history of the *Welsh Guards at War*, though he did not specify his sources. There are good maps and photographs. British novelist and author of other World War II books Patrick Howarth wrote the absorbing history of the Eighth Army, *"My God, Soldiers,"* with its international cast of soldiers in North Africa, Italy, and Austria, treating the story as a journey rather than as a series of battles.

Originally written for the veterans of *The 43rd Wessex Division at War*, Essame presented a detailed portrayal of its fight from 1944 to victory in 1945. In a factual, interesting account Forbes' *6th Guards Tank Brigade* took this unit from its first action in Normandy to the Baltic Sea, stressing the process of learning how to do the job and the importance of tanks and infantry working together.

A model regimental history, uniting the interests of its Canadian veterans with sound research, is Tooley's *Invicta: The Carleton and York Regi-*

ment. Based on war diaries, post-action reports, and other documents, it both narrates a history and attempts to evaluate the regiment's combat effectiveness. Similar in approach, with half of the book devoted to World War II, Greenhous' *Semper Paratus* gives a professional treatment of one Canadian regiment's history from the disastrous Dieppe raid of 1942 through the rest of the war. Also see the early unit history by McAvity, *Lord Strathcona's Horse (Royal Canadians)* for a tank history. Finally, Morrison and Slaney's *The Breed of Manly Men: The History of the Cape Breton Highlanders* details, but with little analysis, the second Battalion of the Nova Scotia Highlanders from their calling up in 1939 to combat in Europe.

The Australian government sponsored many published unit histories immediately after the war, which can be found among the official histories. Hay's *Nothing over Us* and Austin's *To Kokoda and Beyond* are recent important contributions, with Austin's noteworthy in its thoroughness of sources and attempt to relate the battalion's history to general topics of military history.

Air Force

Kent's *First In! Parachute Pathfinder Company. A History of the 21st Independent Parachute Company* recounts the unique story of a British unit. Based on ex-members' recollections, it includes a chronology, maps, and photos, though the sources are not identified. Poolman's *Night Strike from Malta: 830 Squadron RN and Rommel's Convoys* relates the squadron's training, preparation, and battles with the enemy. He relied on interviews, museum records, and journal articles.

Navy

The Royal Navy in World War Two by Law is a model guide to the literature not only of the Royal Navy but of some Allied units as well. He included autobiographies, unit histories, anthologies, art, poetry, and fiction arranged by service branch with specific comments on contents and extensive cross-referencing. Middlebrook and Mahoney's *Battleship: The Sinking of the Prince of Wales and the Repulse* is a thorough account based on archives and extensive interviews of the double disaster for the Royal Navy immediately upon entry into the Pacific War. Pattinson's *Mountbatten and the Men of the "Kelly"* is an affectionate accounting of the destroyer (sunk in the battle for Crete), its captain Mountbatten, and crew.

GERMANY

Many unit histories of the German army in English are uncritical, being anecdotal in character. They often overlook issues of their association with the crimes of the regime and generally ignore matters of recruitment, training, and doctrine. There are some recent anecdotes, though still insufficient compared to the best American works. Luther's *Blood and Honor: The History of the 12th SS Panzer Division "Hitler Youth," 1943–1945* is important on questions of organization, training, tactics, and the context of combat for a key division in 1944 in France. Sydnor takes up similar topics in his history of an SS division in *Soldiers of Destruction*, including matters of ideology, personality, and the division's role in the regime's crimes. Also see the various works by Lucas, including *Das Reich: The Military Role of the 2nd SS Division; Germany's Elite Panzer Force: Grossdeutschland*; and, with Matthew Cooper, *Hitler's Elite: Leibstandarte SS, 1933–45*. Bergot's *The Afrika Korps* is a brief campaign history but includes appendixes on organization, order of battle, and biographical notes.

Three other studies deserve special note, though none are, strictly speaking, unit histories. *Hitler's Army: Soldiers, Nazis, and War in the Third Reich*, the most recent of several studies by Bartov, questions almost every received opinion about the effectiveness of the German army and its relationship to Nazi racism. Fritz's goal in *Frontsoldaten* was "to allow average German [combat] soldiers to speak, with a minimum of external interference" (vii). He used 240 collections of letters and diaries and, like Bartov, found soldiers both ideologically motivated to support Nazi policies and willing participants in committing atrocities. Only after the war did they develop an ambiguous attitude to the whole experience. *Ordinary Men* by Browning examined extensive postwar trial records, concluding that peer pressure overrode moral factors and ideology in leading the men to murder on a mass scale.

Navy

Garrett's *Scharnhorst and Gneisenau* is a well-researched, sound history based on official records and personal accounts of the twin German battle cruisers that threatened British merchant shipping until they fled the coast of France for Germany before being neutralized. The larger *Tirpitz*, sister ship of the *Bismarck*, is the subject of Kennedy, who used ULTRA records in writing his *Menace: The Life and Death of the Tirpitz*. The *Tirpitz* threatened Allied shipping from its position off the coast of Norway before finally being sunk in November 1944.

THE EXPERIENCE OF COMBAT AND COMBAT EFFECTIVENESS

Combat effectiveness and morale have always been of great military concern, but the Second World War produced an extensive literature and controversy on the topic. Lord Moran, Churchill's physician, began an interest in the topic during the First World War and during the Second published *The Anatomy of Courage* and lectured on the topic. This includes his diary from 1914 to 1917 and his analysis of how to manage fear and cultivate courage among soldiers. Fear, he argued, is not overcome by experience, and courage cannot be preserved; it is spent by combat and has to be restored.

Another classic from the war is S.L.A. Marshall's popular account *Men against Fire.* He concluded that only a small proportion of soldiers in situations where they should do so, actually fired their weapons. He was, of course, interested in finding a cure, which he generally located in numbers (small group cohesion), leadership, and keeping up the rate of fire. Smoler charged in "The Secret of the Soldiers Who Didn't Shoot" that Marshall fudged his data, a claim doubted by Williams in *SLAM;* at least the accusations have not been proven.

For other early basic investigations on related themes see Stouffer, *Studies in Social Psychology in World War II,* especially volume 2, *The American Soldier: Combat and Its Aftermath,* and the three volumes by Ginzberg, Herma, and Ginsburg, *The Ineffective Soldier.* This latter study was commissioned by Eisenhower. Kellett's *Combat Motivation* expertly summarized the literature in 1982; he applied its findings to two case studies from World War II and two from the postwar period. Steckel's dissertation, "Morale and Men: A Study of the American Soldier in World War II," is a thorough investigation of the literature and the "state of the question" when it was written. The third volume of Millett and Murray's *Military Effectiveness, The Second World War,* is less concerned with tactical combat effectiveness than with overall military performance at its strategic and operational level. It has seven chapters on the major belligerents and three general chapters, all by leading authorities. The issues taken up there are included in other chapters in this handbook and its companion handbook, *World War II in Europe, Africa, and the Americas,* edited by Lee.

Three years before Kellett's study, Dupuy in *Numbers, Prediction, and War* tried to give a quantitative basis for devaluing American men in combat in comparison to the German soldier. This is a view reflected in Van Creveld's frequently cited *Fighting Power,* though Van Creveld's sources generally reiterated official views and secondary literature on both sides, rather than a fresh analysis. Ellis' *The Sharp End: The Fighting Man of World War II,* published in the United States as *On the Front Lines,* is a general survey that includes chapters on the induction process, training, combat, various service branches, discipline, and morale as well as tables on casualties. Critical of Allied military leaders, he attributes Allied victory more to production of matériel rather than soldierly superiority. Though not primarily addressing these questions, Hastings' widely read *Overlord* reinforced this image of the "ineffective" American, as did Weigley's highly praised *Eisenhower's Lieutenants.*

Brown produced in *Draftee Division: The 88th Infantry Division in World*

War II a splendid unit history of the longest serving conscript division in the war serving in Italy. It is also a spirited, well-researched defense of the division's combat performance, a performance he favorably applied to the thirty-seven other draftee divisions. Brown specifically took Dupuy to task in an appendix and in the journal *Military Affairs.*

Indispensable for anyone interested in these questions is Doubler's *Closing with the Enemy: How GIs Fought the War in Europe.* Making extensive use of after-action reports, unit histories, and other sources close to individual soldiers in combat, Doubler showed that the U.S. soldiers learned on the job. He credits their achievements to an American entrepreneurial spirit and their society's democratic practices. He concluded that Americans were superior to the German soldiers.

Another important study is Wells' *Courage and Air Warfare: The Aircrew Experience in World War II,* a study of aircrew stress (extraordinarily high), morale, and combat effectiveness among both day and night bomber crews. Wells also took into account American fighter pilots and crews of the British Bomber Command. His sources included medical and psychiatric records, disability statistics, questionnaires to veterans, correspondence, and many diaries and memoirs. "The principal reason most airmen stuck things out in combat was because of the spirit of cohesion and teamwork that permeated units and individual aircrews," while the "major mental conflict arose from attempts to reconcile or overcome one's fundamental need for self-preservation and the relentless, and often hopeless, demands for duty" (211).

There are other excellent books on the American soldier in the war. *G.I.: The American Soldier in World War Two* by Kennett draws primarily on many personal accounts. MacDonald's *Company Commander* is a classic, something of a cross between a personal account by a captain of two units, Companies I and G, twenty-third Infantry, and a history of those units in Western Europe.

While not a unit history and not citing any, Fraser's *And We Shall Shock Them* covers much the same ground as Doubler, but without the latter's exquisite detail: how a small professional army turns a mass of conscripts, after a long learning period, into an effective army.

Reading unit histories can be a pleasure as well as an excellent way to learn about the nature of Second World War warfare. The best ones are more than just narratives, with stories of courage, adventure, disaster, death, and ultimate victory or defeat.

BIBLIOGRAPHY

Also see the subject index for unit histories in other chapters and Lee, "Personal Narratives of Sailors, Soldiers, and Civilians," for additional material relating to unit histories.

Ambrose, Stephen. *Band of Brothers: E Company, 506th Regiment, 101st Airborne from Normandy to Hitler's Eagle's Nest.* New York: Simon and Schuster, 1992.

Arnold, Thomas St. John. *Buffalo Soldiers: The 92nd Infantry Division and Reinforcements in World War II, 1942–1945.* Manhattan, KS: Sunflower UP, 1990.

Astor, Gerald. *"Battling Buzzards": The Odyssey of the 517th Parachute Regimental Combat Team 1943–1945.* New York: D. I. Fine, 1983.

———. *A Blood-Dimmed Tide: The Battle of the Bulge by the Men Who Fought It.* New York: D. I. Fine, 1992.

Austin, Victor, comp. *To Kokoda and Beyond: The Story of the 39th Battalion 1941–1943.* Carleton, Victoria: Melbourne UP, 1988.

Bartov, Omer. *Hitler's Army: Soldiers, Nazis, and War in the Third Reich.* New York: Oxford UP, 1991.

Bergot, Erwan. *Afrika Korps.* Barcelona, Spain: A.T.E., 1977; New York: Charter; London: Wingate, 1976.

Britt, Sam S., Jr. *The Long Rangers: A Diary of the 307th Bombardment Group (H).* Baton Rouge, LA: Reprint, 1990.

Brown, John Sloan. "Colonel Trevor N. Dupuy and the Mythos of Wehrmacht Superiority: A Reconsideration." *Military Affairs* 50: 1 (1986): 16–20; response 1987, 51, 146–147.

———. *Draftee Division: The 88th Infantry Division in World War II.* Lexington: University of Kentucky, 1986.

Browning, Christopher R. *Ordinary Men: Reserve Police Battalion 101 and the Final Solution in Poland.* New York: HarperCollins, 1992.

Bryan, Joseph, III. *Aircraft Carrier.* New York: Ballantine, 1954, 1984.

Caine, Philip D. *Eagles of the RAF: American Pilots in the RAF: The WWII Eagle Squadrons.* London and Washington, DC: Brassey's, 1993.

Cameron, Craig M. *American Samurai: Myth, Imagination, and the Conduct of Battle in the First Marine Division, 1941–1951.* Cambridge and New York: Cambridge UP, 1994.

Cave, Dorothy. *Beyond Courage: One Regiment against Japan, 1941–1945.* Las Cruces, NM: Yucca Tree, 1992.

Controvich, James T., ed. *United States Army Unit Histories: A Reference and Bibliography.* Manhattan, KS: Sunflower UP, 1983, 1992.

Cressman, Robert. *That Gallant Ship: U.S.S. Yorktown CV-5.* Missoula, MT: Pictorial Histories, 1985.

Dornbusch, Charles E. *Australian Military Bibliography.* Cornwallville, NY: Hope Farm, 1963.

———. *The Canadian Army, 1855–1965: Lineages; Regimental Histories.* Cornwallville, NY: Hope Farm, 1966.

———. *The New Zealand Army: A Bibliography.* Cornwallville, NY: Hope Farm, 1963.

———. *Unit Histories of World War II: United States Army, Air Force, Marines, Navy.* Washington, DC: Office of the Chief of Military History, n.d.

Dornbusch, Charles E., Lawrence J. Paszek, and James B. Gilbert, eds. *Unit Histories of the United States Air Forces: Including Privately Printed Personal Narratives and United States Air Force History: A Guide to Documentary Sources.* Salem, NH: Ayer, 1979.

Doubler, Michael D. *Closing with the Enemy: How GIs Fought the War in Europe, 1944–1945*. Lawrence: UP of Kansas, 1994.

Draper, Theodore. *The 84th Infantry Division in the Battle of Germany, November 1944–May 1945*. New York: Viking, 1975.

Dupuy, Tervor N. "Mythos or Verity? The Quantified Judgment Model and German Combat Effectiveness." *Military Affairs* 50: 4 (1986): 204–210.

———. *Numbers, Prediction, and War*. London: MacDonald and James, 1979.

Duus, Masayo Umezawa. *Unlikely Liberators: The Men of the 100th and 442nd*. Honolulu: University of Hawaii, 1987.

Ellis, John. *The Sharp End: The Fighting Man of World War II*. London: Winthrow and Greene, 1991. Also published as *On the Front Lines: The Experience of War through the Eyes of the Allied Soldiers in World War II*. Newton Abbot: David and Charles; New York: Scribner, 1980; New York: Wiley, 1991.

Ellis, Lionel F. *Welsh Guards at War*. London: Stamp Exchange, 1989.

Essame, Hubert. *The 43rd Wessex Division at War, 1944–1945*. London: William Clowes, 1952.

Ewing, Joseph H. *29, Let's Go! A History of the 29th Infantry Division in World War Two*. Washington, DC: Infantry Journal, 1948; Paducah, KY: Turner, 1992.

Forbes, Patrick. *6th Guards Tank Brigade: The Story of Guardsmen in Churchill Tanks*. London: Sampson Low, 1946.

Frankel, Stanley A. *The 37th Infantry Division in World War II*. Washington, DC: Infantry Journal, 1949.

Fraser, David. *And We Shall Shock Them: The British Army in the Second World War*. London: Hodder and Stoughton, 1983.

Freeman, Roger Anthony. *The Mighty Eighth: A History of the Units, Men, and Machines of the U.S. 8th Air Force*. New York: Orion, 1970.

Fritz, Stephen G. *Frontsoldaten: The German Soldier in World War II*. Lexington: University of Kentucky, 1995.

Fry, James C. *Combat Soldier*. Washington, DC: National, 1968.

Garrett, Richard. *Scharnhorst and Gneisenau: The Elusive Sisters*. Newton Abbott: David and Charles, 1978.

Ginzberg, Eli, John L. Herma, and Sol W. Ginsburg. *The Ineffective Soldier*. Vol. 1: *The Lost Divisions*; Vol. 2: *Breakdown and Recovery*; Vol. 3: *Patterns of Performance*. New York and London: Columbia UP, 1959.

Godfrey, E. G., in collaboration with R. F. K. Goldsmith. *The Duke of Cornwall's Light Infantry, 1939–45*. Upton-upon-Severn, U.K.: Images (Malvern), 1994.

Greenhous, Brereton. *Semper Paratus, the History of the Royal Hamilton Light Infantry (Wentworth Regiment) 1862–1977*. Rev. ed. Hamilton, Canada: R.H.L.I. Historical Association, 1977.

Gugliotta, Bobette. *Pigboat 39: An American Sub Goes to War*. Lexington: University of Kentucky, 1984.

Hallam, John. *The History of the Lancashire Fusiliers 1939–45*. Stroud, Glouchestershire, and New York: Alan Sutton, 1993.

Hallows, Ian S. *Regiments and Corps of the British Army*. London: Arms and Armour, 1991.

Hargrove, Hondon B. *Buffalo Soldiers in Italy: Black Americans in World War II*. Jefferson, NC, and London: McFarland, 1985.

Hastings, Max. *Overlord: D-Day and the Battle for Normandy.* New York: Simon and Schuster, 1984.

Hay, David. *Nothing over Us: The Story of the 2/6th Australian Infantry Battalion.* Canberra: Australian War Memorial, 1984.

Helm, Thomas. *Ordeal by Sea: The Tragedy of the USS Indianapolis.* New York: Dodd, Mead, 1963.

Higham, Robin D. S., ed. *Official Histories; Essays and Bibliographies from around the World.* Manhattan: Kansas State University, 1970.

Hindle, Brooke. *Lucky Lady and the Navy Mystique: The Chenango in WWII.* New York: Vantage, 1991.

Hoehling, Adolph A. *The Lexington Goes Down.* Englewood Cliffs, NJ: Prentice-Hall, 1971.

Hofmann, George F. *The Super Sixth: History of the 6th Armored Division in World War II and Its Post-War Association.* Louisville, KY: Sixth Armored Division Association, 1975.

Houston, Donald E. *Hell on Wheels: The 2nd Armored Division.* San Rafael, CA: Presidio, 1977.

Howarth, Patrick. *"My God, Soldiers": From Alamein to Vienna.* London: Hutchinson, 1989.

Kahn, Ely Jacques, and Henry McLemore. *Fighting Divisions: Histories of Each U.S. Army Combat Division in World War II.* Washington, DC: Zenger, 1980.

Kellett, Anthony. *Combat Motivation: The Behavior of Soldiers in Battle.* Boston: Kluwer-Nijhoff, 1982.

Kelly, Mary Pat. *Proudly We Served: The Men of the USS Mason.* Annapolis, MD: NIP, 1995.

Kennedy, Ludovic. *Menace: The Life and Death of the Tirpitz.* London: Sidgwick and Jackson; Boston: Little, Brown, 1979.

Kennett, Lee. *G.I.: The American Soldier in World War Two.* New York: Scribner, 1987; Warner, 1989.

Kent, Ron. *First In! Parachute Pathfinder Company. A History of the 21st Independent Parachute Company.* London: B. T. Batsford; New York: Hippocrene, 1979.

Law, Derek G. *The Royal Navy in World War Two.* London: Greenhill, 1988.

Lee, Loyd E. "Personal Narratives of Sailors, Soldiers, and Civilians." In Loyd E. Lee, ed., *World War II in Europe, Africa, and the Americas, with General Sources: A Handbook of Literature and Research.* Westport, CT: Greenwood, 1997.

Leinbaugh, Harold P., and John D. Campbell. *The Men of Company K: The Autobiography of a World War II Rifle Company.* New York: William Morrow, 1985.

Lucas, James. *Das Reich: The Military Role of the 2nd SS Division.* London, New York: Arms and Armour, 1991.

———. *Germany's Elite Panzer Force; Grossdeutschland.* London: Macdonald and Jane's, 1978.

———. *Panzer Army Africa.* San Rafael, CA: Presidio, 1978.

———. *War on the Eastern Front, 1941–1945: The German Soldier in Russia.* New York: Bonanza, 1979.

Lucas, James, and Matthew Cooper. *Hitler's Elite: Leibstandarte SS, 1933–45.* London: Macdonald and Jane's, 1990.

Luther, Craig W. H. *Blood and Honor: The History of the 12th SS Panzer Division "Hitler Youth", 1943–1945.* San Jose, CA: Bender, 1987.

MacDonald, Charles B. *Company Commander.* New York: Bantam, 1982; Washington, DC: Infantry Journal, 1947.

Marshall, Samuel Lyman Atwood. *Men against Fire: The Problem of Battle Command in Future Wars.* Gloucester, MA: Peter Smith, 1978.

Mason, Theodore C. *"We Will Stand by You": Serving in the Pawnee, 1942–1945.* Columbia: University of South Carolina, 1990.

Maurer, Maurer, ed. *Air Force Combat Units of World War II.* Washington, DC: GPO, 1961, 1963, 1983.

———. *Combat Squadrons of the Air Force, World War II.* Washington, DC: GPO, 1969.

Mawdsley, Dean L. *Cruise Books of the United States Navy in World War II: A Bibliography.* Washington, DC: Naval Historical Center, Department of the Navy, 1993.

McAvity, J. M. *Lord Strathcona's Horse (Royal Canadians): A Record of Achievement.* Toronto: Brigdens, 1947.

McMillan, George. *The Old Breed; A History of the First Marine Division in World War II.* Washington, DC: Infantry Journal, 1949.

Middlebrook, Martin, and Patrick Mahoney. *Battleship: The Sinking of the Prince of Wales and the Repulse.* London: Allen Lane, 1977.

Millett, Allan R., and Williamson Murray, eds. *Military Effectiveness.* Vol. 3: *The Second World War.* Boston: Allen and Unwin, 1988.

Molesworth, Carl. *Sharks over China: The 23rd Fighter Group in WWII.* Washington, DC, and London: Brassey's, 1994.

Moran, John B. *Creating a Legend: The Complete Record of Writing about the U.S. Marine Corps.* Chicago: Moran/Andrews, 1973.

Moran, Charles. *The Anatomy of Courage.* London: Constable, 1945.

Morrison, Alex, and Ted Slaney. *The Breed of Manly Men: The History of the Cape Breton Highlanders.* Toronto: Canadian Institute of Strategic Studies, 1994.

Motley, John J., and Philip R. Kelly. *Now Hear This! Histories of U.S. Ships in World War II.* Washington, DC: Zenger, 1947, 1979.

Muir, Malcolm. *The Iowa Class Battleships: Iowa, New Jersey, Missouri and Wisconsin.* New York: Dorset, 1987.

Murphy, Thomas D. *Ambassadors in Arms: The Story of Hawaii's 100th Battalion.* Honolulu: University of Hawaii, 1954.

Pappas, George S. *United States Army Unit Histories.* Carlisle Barracks, PA: U.S. Army Military History Research Collection, 1971.

Pattinson, William. *Mountbatten and the Men of the "Kelly."* Wellinborough, Northants, U.K.: Patrick Stephens, 1986.

Pergrin, David E., with Eric Hammel. *First across the Rhine: The 291st Engineer Combat Battalion in France, Belgium, and Germany.* New York: Atheneum, Ballantine, 1989.

Perkins, Roger. *Regiments—Regiments and Corps of the British Empire and Commonwealth 1758–1993: A Critical Bibliography of Their Published Histories.* Newton Abbot, Devon, U.K.: Roger Perkins, 1994.

Poolman, Kenneth. *Night Strike from Malta: 830 Squadron R. N. and Rommel's Convoys.* London: Jane's, 1980.

Purdon, Eric. *Black Company: The Story of Subchaser PC 1264.* New York: McKay, 1971.

Rapport, Leonard, and Arthur Northwood, Jr. *Rendezvous with Destiny: A History of* the 101st Airborne Division. Washington, DC: Infantry Journal, 1948, 101st Airborne Division, Greenville, TX, 1965.

Rasor, Eugene L., and Loyd E. Lee. "Reference Works: Bibliographies, Encyclopedias, Dictionaries, Atlases, and Chronologies." In Loyd E. Lee, ed., *World War II in Europe, Africa, and the Americas, with General Sources: A Handbook of Literature and Research*, 45–57. Westport, CT: Greenwood, 1997.

Reynolds, Clark G. *The Fighting Lady: The New Yorktown in the Pacific War*. Missoula, MT: Pictorial Histories, 1986.

Sandler, Stanley. *Segregated Skies: All-Black Combat Squadrons of World War II*. Washington, DC: Smithsonian Institution, 1992.

Scott, Hugh A. *The Blue and White Devils: A Personal Memoir and History of the Third Infantry Division in World War II*. Nashville, TN: Battery, 1984.

Shirey, Orville Cresap. *Americans, the Story of the 442d Combat Team*. Washington, DC: Infantry Journal, 1947.

Smoler, Fredric. "The Secret of the Soldiers Who Didn't Shoot." *American Heritage* 40: 2 (1989): 36–46.

Sommers, Richard J. "World War II Holdings of the U.S. Army Military History Institute." *World War Two Studies Association Newsletter* 47 (Spring 1992): 30–35.

Stannard, Richard M. *Infantry: An Oral History of a World War II American Infantry Battalion*. Boston: Twayne, 1992.

Steckel, Francis C. "Morale and Men: A Study of the American Soldier in World War II." Ph.D. diss., Temple University, 1990.

Stouffer, Samuel. *Studies in Social Psychology in World War II*. Vol. 2: *The American Soldier: Combat and Its Aftermath*. Princeton: Princeton UP, 1949.

Sturzebecker, Russell L. *The Roarin' 20's: A History of the 312th Bombardment Group, U.S. Army Air Force, World War II*. West Chester, PA: Sturzebecker, 1976.

Sydnor, Charles W., Jr. *Soldiers of Destruction: The SS Death's Head Division, 1933–1945*. Princeton: Princeton UP, 1977.

Tooley, Robert. *Invicta: The Carleton and York Regiment in the Second World War*. Fredricton, NB, Canada: New Ireland, 1989.

Van Creveld, Martin. *Fighting Power: German and United States Army Performance, 1939–1945*. Westport, CT: Greenwood, 1982; London: Arms and Armour, 1983.

Weigley, Russell F. *Eisenhower's Lieutenants: The Campaign of France and Germany, 1944–1945*. Bloomington: Indiana UP, 1990.

Wells, Mark. *Courage and Air Warfare: The Aircrew Experience in World War II*. Ilford, Essex, U.K. and Portland, OR: Frank Cass, 1995.

Werrell, Kenneth P. *Blankets of Fire: U.S. Bombers over Japan during World War II*. Washington, DC: Smithsonian Institution, 1996.

———. *Eighth Air Force Bibliography: An Extended Essay and Listing of Published and Unpublished Materials*. Strasburg, PA: 8th Air Force Memorial Museum Foundation, 1997.

Williams, F. D. G. *SLAM: The Influence of S.L.A. Marshall on the United States Army*. Fort Monroe, VA: Office of the Command Historian, U.S. Army Training and Doctrine Command, 1990.

Winslow, Walter G. *The Ghost That Died at Sunda Strait.* Annapolis, MD: NIP, 1994, 1984.

Yoshino, Ronald W. *Lightning Strikes: The 475th Fighter Group in the Pacific War, 1943–1945.* Manhattan, KS: Sunflower UP, 1988.

PART V

War, the Arts, and the Life of the Spirit

15   The War and Film in the United States and Britain

Stephen Curley

The Second World War was fought not only on the European and Pacific fronts but also on movie screens. The history of the war can be relived through movies. *Blood on the Sun* (1945) deals with Japan's seizing of Manchuria in the 1930s. The Spanish civil war is the subject of *For Whom the Bell Tolls* (1943). *A Yank in the RAF* (1941) tells us the story of the British army forced into the sea at Dunkirk. Before America enters the war, *Action in the North Atlantic* (1943) shows the American merchant marine making the Murmansk run; *Flying Tigers* (1942) shows us so-called commercial American pilots fighting in China.

The battles are fought in *Thirty Seconds over Tokyo* (1944), *Midway* (1976), *Guadalcanal Diary* (1943), *Twelve O'Clock High* (1949), *A Walk in the Sun* (1945). *The Longest Day* (1962) depicts the Allies invading Normandy. *Battleground* (1949) shows us the last major German counterattack. *Sands of Iwo Jima* (1949) recounts American victories in the Pacific. Germany surrenders in *The Victors* (1963). The atom bomb is dropped on Japan in *Above and Beyond* (1952). Nazi leaders are tried for war crimes in *Judgment at Nuremberg* (1961).

Most people know about the experience of war only through its screen images. When a boyish-looking GI, worried just before the big battle, shows a picture of his girlfriend to Sarge, the experienced moviegoer knows that the boy won't make it back alive. When a soldier's best buddy is killed, we know that the soldier will overcome his fright to lead the successful charge against the enemy machine-gun nest. War films are loaded with standard iconography. Certain actors—Gary Cooper, John Wayne, Audie Murphy, Van Johnson, William Bendix—lent their standard characterization to many different war stories, regardless of the front or the battle depicted. American audiences respond predictably to the doughboy helmets that signify America's unpreparedness at the start of

World War II; uniforms decorated excessively with the medals of pomposity; the evil look of Nazi accoutrements of the luger, the earflap helmet, the SS death's head insignia; the theaters of war—the deserts of North Africa, the snow-covered hills of Northern Europe, the steamy jungles of the Pacific islands.

Movies about the Second World War have had a profound emotional effect. In his brilliant and influential study *The Face of Battle,* John Keegan confessed, "I have not been in a battle, not near one, nor heard one from afar, nor seen the aftermath." But he said he has seen a great deal of battle in "dramatized feature film" (13). In *Goodbye Darkness* William Manchester observed that few of his fellow marines had read about war but almost all had seen "B movies about bloodshed," and if a platoon leader had watched Douglas Fairbanks, Jr., Errol Flynn, Victor McLaglen, John Wayne, or Gary Cooper, "he was likely to follow his role model" (83). During the filming of *The Outsider* (1961), the story of Ira Hayes (the Native American who helped raise the flag atop Mount Suribachi), director Delbert Mann asked some young marine recruits at Camp Pendleton why they had enlisted. Half of them said that they had been inspired by John Wayne movies. William Calley testified at his court-martial for war crimes in Vietnam, "I was John Wayne" (Holmes, *Acts of War,* 68). Ron Kovic, in his bitterly antiwar memoir *Born on the Fourth of July* (later turned into a movie), stated that he and his playmates watched *Sands of Iwo Jima* "The Marine Corps hymn was playing in the background as we sat glued to our seat, humming the hymn together and watching Sergeant Stryker, played by John Wayne, charge up the hill and get killed just before he reached the top. And then they showed the men raising the flag on Iwo Jima with the marine's hymn still playing, and . . . [we] cried in our seats" (54–55).

The war film, although less studied than the western or the gangster film, has received its share of attention. Both popular and scholarly studies have taken into account various aspects of the war film: artistic merit, historical accuracy, political influence, behind-the-scenes filmmaking, anecdotes about actors and directors, and so on. Four trends in these studies are worth noting. First, more films and studies of films focus on World War II than on any other war: it was the object of a vast cinematic effort by a film industry still in its golden age and especially in Hollywood under the strong influence of the studio system. Second, the combat-action film is the most often studied subgenre of the war film; indeed, movies about the home front are frequently ignored. Third, a great deal of what is written is gossip-with-photos for fans (both of war and war movies). Fourth, serious study of the war film has increased since the mid-1970s.

The following bibliographical essay, primarily about American war films, surveys books, essays, or chapters in books and articles that comment about World War II films; it omits narrower studies that focus on only one film or one filmmaker. After defining the genre of war films, it discusses their use as propaganda and their cultural implications both during wartime and afterward. It also contains information about studies that identify certain kinds of combat movies, viewers' guides, and the influence of national film studios.

GENRE

A number of studies try to define the war film as a genre, or a kind of film with its own conventions. The most prevalent definition says that war films depict combat, which gradually welds self-interested individuals into a selfless fighting team. For example, *A Walk in the Sun* (1945) follows the old formula of the melting-pot platoon (one Texan, one Jew, one farm boy, etc.), in which ordinarily isolated men become as one in the great communal action of fighting. War films often focus on the tiny details of the community of the killing zone that allows the uninitiated moviegoer to begin, in a small way, to understand the comradeship that bonds men together in battle and to see the experience, despite its horror, as appealing.

The genre may be expanded, however, beyond the combat film. A perceptive wartime reviewer, Farber called the war film a "slight" genre with four subjects: praising one branch of service, dramatizing actual battles, recounting the resistance of occupied nations, and showing life on the home front; "the first and second produced the best pictures, the fourth the worst and the third the most" ("Movies in Wartime," 18). His influential study shows that war films borrowed images from westerns and avoided controversial issues. Jacobson, "Cowboy, Pioneer and American Soldier," also saw the western influences and claimed that the screen cowboy's heroic image influenced the expectations and behavior of American soldiers in two world wars. In *Visions of War*, Kane saw both westerns and gangster films in the conventions of the World War II combat film: she identified recurring motifs and formulas of theme, character, setting, and plot. She later argued persuasively for the "World War II Combat Film" as the central genre of war films. Yacowar's "Bug in the Rug" treated carnage-and-destruction war films as part of the genre of disaster films. Ray argued in *A Certain Tendency* that wartime Hollywood combat films merely recast old melodramas in new settings, adhering to the morale-boosting, good-teamwork formula established by Howard Hawks' *Only Angels Have Wings* (1939). Woll, in a scholarly treatment, showed that the most successful *Hollywood Musical*, "the dominant genre of wartime Hollywood" (ix), deals with serious war and economic issues; such films were not pure escapism.

Other studies look at the genre from different perspectives. Basinger presented "a history of *World War Two Combat Films*, tracing their origin and evolution and indicating important information about the system that produced them, the individuals that created them, and the technological developments that changed them'' (ii). She claimed that the war's combat movie established the pattern for all combat movies and influenced the entire concept of the war film. This influential work is especially valuable for its fully annotated, fifty-four-page, chronological filmography of American World War II combat films from 1942 through 1980. War films show us moral degradation, said Belmans in "Cinema and Man at War," but reflect society's view that war is a necessary "consequence of our state of civilization" (23). Dirty-faced cinematic heroes, as if in a trance, engage in the sensuality of bloodshed. Belmans' discussion is turgid but challenging. Manchel used the Beograd [Belgrade] Film Institute's definition that a war film "treats war events either on the front or behind enemy lines" ("A Representative Genre of the Film," 58). He showed that the treatment and the emphasis of war films, 1914–1970, responded to prevailing public attitudes at the time of the film's making: for instance, *Catch-22* satirized the stupidity of World War II for the Vietnam-era moviegoer. Solomon, in the chapter "Wars: Hot and Cold" in *Beyond Formula* claimed the war movie is a relatively formless genre. He discussed topics like propaganda, war in the air, war as background, victims of war, exiles, and isolated heroes. Christensen's chronological survey, *Reel Politics*, of politically motivated message-movies included substantial commentary on films of World War II. Wetta and Curley's *Celluloid Wars* surveyed published material to construct a brief, comprehensive view of the genre.

PROPAGANDA

War film and propaganda go hand in hand, even when government control and censorship are not involved. For instance, *Bataan*, aside from its obvious entertainment value, clearly identifies Americans as being on the right side and applauds their endurance in the face of overwhelming odds. American movie propaganda has received much attention. An essay by McClure, "Hollywood at War," reprinted as the introduction in Jones and McClure's *Hollywood at War*, showed that American wartime films tried to give unity of purpose to the war effort and strength of purpose to the home front. Shain in *An Analysis of Motion Pictures about War* said that screen image was more influenced by the era of production than it was by the war depicted; for instance, the friendly Russian ally of wartime films was replaced by the Soviet spy of postwar films. In a suggestive filmography of 815 films, he noted which American films received assistance from the Department of Defense. Their scripts were submitted for government approval of the way they depicted the American action.

Bohn analyzed characteristic elements and qualities in Frank Capra's series of documentaries *Why We Fight* (1942–1945), which he saw as some of the best military propaganda films ever produced. Suid's *Guts and Glory*, a reliable and scholarly book, focused on the creation of the American military image in seventy-two Hollywood feature films since 1915. His detailed analysis of the relationship between Hollywood and the American defense establishment is based on more than 300 interviews with people in the film industry (actors, producers, directors), the media, and the military. He devoted an entire chapter to the mutually influential relationship of marines and John Wayne. Fyne's "Unsung Heroes" offered a nostalgic, superficial overview of B-production propaganda films that contains a useful list of neglected actors and film titles. Fyne later focused a broader study on American propaganda in World War II movies, *The Hollywood Propaganda*. Polan, in a study of American films, *Power and Paranoia*, included chapters on representations of wartime unity and fictions about war. Shull and Wilt in *Doing Their Bit* analyzed propaganda in wartime American cartoons, with bibliography and filmography.

Allied propaganda has also had considerable attention. In *The War Film* Butler surveyed chronologically by production date the main trends in the treatment of war by fictional cinema shown in Britain and America from 1910 to 1977. His solid, reliable study showed that film follows, rather than leads, pro- or antiwar propaganda. Krome's *A Weapon of War* focused on British and American World War II propaganda movies as a weapon of war; he includes a useful bibliographic essay. Evans' controversial *John Grierson* looked at the role played by Canadian wartime film propaganda as education in democracy. Johnston's *Memo on the Movies*, the first book-length treatment of war propaganda published by a university press, is lamentably undocumented. It argues that pro-war propaganda in film is controlled by financial and political interests. Furhammer and Isaksson's *Politics and Film* discusses propaganda, images of heroes, allies, and enemies in their analysis of the political content of war films. Thorpe's *British Official Films* annotated about 2,000 British government-sponsored World War II propaganda films, indexed by titles and credits.

Propaganda film of the Axis powers also receives attention. Baskett studied colonial propaganda in Japanese movies made from 1937 to 1945 in his "Japanese Colonial Film Enterprise." Nornes and Yukio in *The Japan/America Film Wars: WWII* studied the cultural contrast in World War II propaganda films by the United States and Japan. In *From Caligari to Hitler* Kracauer analyzed the "deep psychological dispositions" of German films, 1918–1933. See his interesting supplement "Propaganda and the Nazi War Film." Deutschmann analyzed German propaganda as seen in the film *Triumph of the Will*. Taylor's *Film Propaganda* analyzed eight propaganda films, four each from Soviet Russia and Nazi Germany, and included a good bibliography.

Culbert collected documents important for understanding the role of *Film and Propaganda* during wartime (volumes 2 and 3 cover World War

II). Short's *Film and Radio Propaganda*, an anthology of essays from a 1982 conference about World War II film and radio, took a global view of Allied, fascist Europe, and Japanese propaganda.

PSYCHOLOGICAL AND PHILOSOPHICAL STUDIES

Some of the most interesting studies make use of psychological and philosophical interpretations of war films. Tyler's *Magic and Myth in the Movies*, a fascinating and original study by a major critic, gives a Freudian interpretation of war films as "waxworks" that unintentionally emphasized America's neuroses and psychopathic traits. Hughes' impressive *Film*, with a pacifist bent, included shooting scripts of censored documentaries: John Huston's *Let There Be Light* (1945) and Jean Resnais' *Night and Fog* (1956) and a roundtable discussion of eminent film professionals on the problems of making effective films about war.

Deming interpreted the content of such films as *Mr. Lucky* (1943) and *To Have and Have Not* (1944) psychologically as wishful dreams and said that 1940s films unconsciously portray the condition from which we want to escape as more real than any hope we have of escaping from it. This original, if somewhat perverse, study is worth a look. Jacobs' "World War II" discussed American World War II films that go beyond propaganda and entertainment in their examination of the horrors of fascism and war. In "Bloody Popcorn" Grossman offered an insightful interpretation of *Patton* and *Catch 22* as attempts to satisfy unconscious guilt feelings by letting civilians experience the horrors of war. Virilio's *War and Cinema*, a challenging, but often turgid, philosophical analysis, is concerned with "the osmosis between industrialized warfare and cinema" (58). He said war is life-size cinema; cinema is war.

CULTURAL IMPLICATIONS

Some studies focus on the screen images of distinct groups. For instance, just as the war changed the roles traditionally played by women, war movies such as *Mrs. Miniver* (1942), *Since You Went Away* (1944), and *From Here to Eternity* (1953) depicted a new woman. In *Images of Women* Baker said that women were especially esteemed in wartime films for the patriotic, self-sacrificing spirit that led them to fill jobs vacated by men who went off to combat; however, images in postwar films showed that they were expected to leave the labor force for home and family. Renov's *Hollywood's Wartime Woman* found negative images: job stealer, glamour girl, and excess labor. Lant's *Blackout* traced the changed roles played by women in British movies released during the war. Other groups have also been studied. In *Images of Children*, Jackson found that children in post–

World War II films are portrayed as less innocent. Rollins' cultural an-thology, *Hollywood as Historian*, included a scholarly essay on Capra's *The Negro Soldier* (1944).

Some studies look at the relation of movies to their social and cultural milieu. Zinsser in his essay "She Made Him Forget He Was a Soldier" took a witty and lighthearted look at Hollywood's exaggerated image of the wartime soldier. King gave a nostalgic and witty account of teenaged moviegoers during World War II in "The Battle of Popcorn Bay." He depicted the audience's total emotional involvement with admittedly sim-plistic renderings of combat and noted recurrent film themes and the change from blood-and-thunder to fluff films as the war was ending.

A fascinating aspect of film study focuses on the relation of war movies to the moviegoing public. Lingeman's *Don't You Know* showed the social and cultural effect of World War II movies on the American home front. Jowett's *Film* treated the social history of World War II films thoroughly: politics, propaganda, and entertainment. He argued that film has helped replace small-town values with a national consciousness. In *Hollywood Goes to War* Shindler, from the practitioner's perspective of a British television producer, described postwar American films that responded to, and in-tensified, social, political, and ideological stimuli. He said that studios made what the public wanted. Doherty wrote a scholarly *Projections of War* from the American perspective. Aldgate and Richards' *Britain Can Take It* analyzed "good, popular" films that shed light on issues at stake in the war. They focused on British issues but also discussed American ones as well, with a substantial filmography. Sklar's *Film* discussed film and the war from an international perspective.

Some writers have been primarily concerned with the historical impli-cations of war films. Taylor collected essays, *Britain and the Cinema*, from a 1985 conference of historians interested in the same topic as Aldgate and Richards. Rubin, in an informative and readable study, *Combat Films*, presents behind-the-scenes information about eight realistically detailed World War II films that focus on history rather than heroics, among them *Battleground, The Longest Day, Twelve O'Clock High, Hell Is for Heroes*, and *Patton*. He emphasized the filmmakers' painstaking attempts at accurate renderings. Pitts' *Hollywood and American History* has a generously anno-tated filmography of feature films (plus some shorts and series) on Amer-ican history. The index contains cross-references to specific wars. Eiserman's *War on Film*, intended as a guide for teachers of American military history, contains a useful list of documentaries, arranged by sub-jects like general military history, commanders, unit histories, and specific wars. O'Connor and Jackson in *American History/American Film* antholo-gized six scholarly essays, introduced by Arthur M. Schlesinger, Jr., about World War II, American history, and the movies.

WARTIME AND POSTWAR PERSPECTIVES

As this chapter has already noted, perspectives changed as the war progressed and then receded into the past. Wartime movies evolved from glamorous recruiting vehicles to more realistic, gritty films as the war went on. Isaacs' "Shadows of War," a chatty, wartime perspective of films released and under production, commented on training films of the Signal Corps, information shorts of the Office of War Information, and seized Nazi propaganda films. Mast collected important early essays on war films in "The War Abroad."

Postwar movies are a different matter. Not long after the Second World War ended, and the Cold War began, war films, freed from patriotic restraints of the war years, became more searching or complex in their messages. Motivation and behavior were subjected to deeper critical investigation. As the Cold War reshuffled alliances, the movie image of former enemies and former friends reflected changed perceptions. Gillett, contrasting British and American postwar films in "Westfront," found that Americans focus on neurotic soldiers in a conflagration whereas British stress the stiff upper lip of ordinary heroes doing their job. Dworkin examined the trend in some American and British World War II films like *The Desert Fox* and *The Young Lions* to distinguish between bad Nazis and good, civilized Germans ("Clean Germans and Dirty Politics"). Lewis and Sherman showed the cycle of post–World War II "War Movies."

In commenting on violent films in general, Alloway, in a slick book about a New York Museum of Modern Art exhibit, *Violent America*, had some interesting things to say about how war films made during the Cold War era reflect a cynical pragmatism about killing. Manvell, in an impressively detailed study, discussed a cross-section of international films, both fictional and factual, to show the popular image of World War II and its motivation. Allies and enemies became psychologically more complex in later films. Mariani, in a revealing survey, showed that the screen image of Nazis evolved from heavily accented spies in prewar movies, to despicable madmen in wartime movies, to either war criminals or admirably apolitical Germans in postwar movies. Reimer and Reimer, part of Twayne's filmmakers series, showed how postwar German films depict Nazis and included a thirty-page bibliography.

KINDS OF COMBAT

A number of writers focus on a certain aspect or type of combat. Thomas in his chapter "War on Water" (96–123) surveyed sea-warfare films, 1940–1980, with a brief commentary and plot summary. Beigel offered an illustrated overview of World War II movies about the U.S. Navy, including a filmography. Skogsberg in a technically knowledgeable and readable *Wings on the Screen* (mostly plot summaries) offered a generously illustrated study about flying in both peace and war movies. He included a profile of William Wellman and indexed movies by film title, country of origin, filmmaker, and aircraft type. Farmer discussed the impact of movies and television from 1908 to 1950 on aviation in *Celluloid Wings*. He annotated 300 "air film" titles, indexed by screen appearances of specific aircraft types. Pendo's *Aviation in the Cinema* annotated feature and television films that highlight some aspect of aviation, indexed by particular wars. It includes a fifty-eight-page bibliography of film reviews and articles. In *From the Wright Brothers to Top Gun* Paris surveyed flight in motion pictures.

World War II films also introduced the threat of nuclear weaponry to the screen. Shaheen collected essays on twelve feature films about *Nuclear War*, including *The Beginning of the End*. He also dealt with documentaries and educational shorts about nuclear threats. Dowling annotated 300 films, primarily documentaries, on the nuclear theme in "Nuclear War and Disarmament." He made detailed suggestions for using films in study groups and public programs. Broderick's *Nuclear Movies* briefly annotates 500 international feature films about nuclear materials or warfare.

VIEWER'S GUIDES AND PICTURE BOOKS

A great many popular studies that are written for casual viewers also contain valuable insight into the war film. Pickard in *A Companion to the Movies* identified production facts, commented briefly about ten "milestone" films, and included a useful who's who of filmmakers, with emphasis on the British. Landrum and Eynon listed fifty-eight annotated sources for the study of "World War II in the Movies." Kagan's *The War Film* is a sketchy, illustrated treatment of fifty-nine key films from 1915 to 1970 that indicated major trends. It is useful for a quick overview.

Jacoby and Fulfer's *Reel Wars* offers a pleasant collection of 325 trivia questions for fans of war films; the categories of the questions suggest trends and themes. Garland's annotated *War Movies* of some 450 films is indexed by war and type (e.g., useful overlapping subdivisions like "World War II, combat," "World War II, air action," and "World War II, biography"). Langman and Borg's *Encyclopedia* gives brief entries on 2,000 American-made war films (fiction and documentary) and American military history. They included mostly plot summaries plus overviews of filmed wars, battles, famous soldiers, and odd topics (e.g., spy films, sea warfare, doctors in war, service comedies), but no entries on key film topics such as filmmakers, studios, and actors. See their Appendix C for a list of wars and their related films; it is an excellent companion for scholars and history buffs. Parish discussed key twentieth-century combat films in *The Great Combat Pictures* and included a filmography. In *When the Stars Went to War* Hoopes recounted anecdotes about World War II actors and actresses.

Jones and McClure's *Hollywood at War* is a photo book with film credits; they identified actors and their roles, the distributors, and directors for some 450 influential World War II films but without discussion or analysis. For a more selective and informative treatment, see Morella, Epstein, and Griggs, *The Films of World War II*, one of the better coffee-table books, which lists details for the most significant 100 World War II films, with excerpts from contemporary reviews (Judith Crist wrote its eloquent introduction). Perlmutter's *War Movies*, a lavishly illustrated book of stills, frame enlargements, posters, and double-page foldouts, discussed the history and criticism of war films. Jeavons' rambling *Pictorial History* of films depicted armed conflict in the twentieth century. *Look Magazine* gave a generously illustrated study by a popular wartime magazine. Dolan's coffee-table *Hollywood Goes to War* has text focused specifically on the two world wars; it contains a list of major awards and nominations for war films. CineBooks' *War Movies* offered a generously annotated viewer's guide, based on the general film encyclopedia of Nash and Ross, *The Motion Picture Guide*, to 500 war films on videocassette.

NATIONAL STUDIOS

Sklar produced a well-written and carefully documented discussion of Hollywood's activities in war service and under suspicion by the House Un-American Activities Committee (HUAC) in *Movie-Made America*. Dick's *Star-Spangled Screen* also examined the American studio system and culture that created the war film; his bibliographical essay included archival material and dissertations. Koppes and Black in their worthwhile *Hollywood Goes to War* showed that the Office of War Information and box office receipts influenced the content of Hollywood movies; he claimed that war films distort as they reflect society. Simon in *Hollywood at War* explored the role of Hollywood studios in making World War II movies and includes bibliographical references and index.

Coultass covered British feature and documentary movies during the war years in *Images for Battle*. In *Stranded Objects* Santner saw postwar German movies as part of national guilt and mourning. Thompson et al. in their *Red Screen*, an anthology of Soviet cinema, included an essay on World War II films with bibliography and index.

BIBLIOGRAPHY

Aldgate, Anthony, and Jeffrey Richards. *Britain Can Take It: The British Cinema in the Second World War*. 2d ed. Edinburgh: Edinburgh UP, 1994.

Alloway, Lawrence. *Violent America: The Movies 1946–1964.* New York: Museum of Modern Art, 1971.

Baker, M. Joyce. *Images of Women in Film: The War Years, 1941–45.* Ann Arbor: University of Michigan, 1980.

Basinger, Jeanine. *The World War Two Combat Film: Anatomy of a Genre.* New York: Columbia UP, 1988.

Baskett, Michael Dennis. "The Japanese Colonial Film Enterprise 1937–1945: Imagining the Imperial Japanese Subject." Master's thesis, UCLA, 1993.

Beigel, Harvey M. *The Fleet's In: Hollywood Presents the U.S. Navy in World War II.* Missoula, MT: Pictorial Histories, 1994.

Belmans, Jacques. "Cinema and Man at War." *Film Society Review* 7 (1972): 22–37.

Bohn, Thomas William. *An Historical and Descriptive Analysis of the "Why We Fight" Series.* New York: Arno, 1977.

Broderick, Mick. *Nuclear Movies: A Filmography.* Northcote, Australia: Post-Modern, 1988.

Butler, Ivan. *The War Film.* New York: Barnes, 1974.

Christensen, Terry. *Reel Politics: American Political Movies from Birth of a Nation to Platoon.* New York: Blackwell, 1987.

CineBooks. *War Movies.* Evanston, IL: CineBooks, 1989.

Coultass, Clive. *Images for Battle: British Film and the Second World War, 1939–1945.* Newark: University of Delaware, 1989.

Culbert, David, ed. *Film and Propaganda in America: A Documentary History.* 5 vols. New York: Greenwood, 1990– .

Deming, Barbara. *Running Away from Myself: A Dream Portrait of America Drawn from the Films of the Forties.* New York: Grossman, 1969.

Deutschmann, Linda. *Triumph of the Will: The Image of the Third Reich.* Wakefield, NH: Longwood Academic, 1991.

Dick, Bernard. *The Star-Spangled Screen: The American World War II Film.* Lexington: UP of Kentucky, 1985.

Doherty, Thomas Patrick. *Projections of War: Hollywood, American Culture, and World War II.* New York: Columbia UP, 1993.

Dolan, Edward F., Jr. *Hollywood Goes to War.* New York: Smith, 1985.

Dowling, John. "Nuclear War and Disarmament." *Sightlines* 15:3 (1982): 19–21.

———. *War-Peace Film Guide.* 3d ed. Chicago: World without War Council, 1980.

Dworkin, Martin S. "Clean Germans and Dirty Politics." *Film Comment* 3:1 (Winter 1965): 36–41.

Eiserman, Frederick A. *War on Film: Military History Education.* Historical Bibliography No. 6. Fort Leavenworth, KS: U.S. Army Command and General Staff College, 1987.

Evans, Gary. *John Grierson and the National Film Board: The Politics of Wartime Propaganda.* Toronto: University of Toronto, 1984.

Farber, Manny. "Movies in Wartime." *New Republic* 3 (January 1944): 16–20.

Farmer, James H. *Celluloid Wings: The Impact of the Movies on Aviation.* Blue Ridge Summit, PA: Tab, 1984.

Furhammer, Leif, and Folke Isaksson. *Politics and Film.* New York: Praeger, 1971.

Fyne, Robert. *The Hollywood Propaganda of World War II.* Metuchen, NJ: Scarecrow, 1994.

————. "The Unsung Heroes of World War II." *Literature/Film Quarterly* 7:2 (1979): 148–154.

Garland, Brock. *War Movies: The Complete Viewer's Guide.* New York: Facts on File, 1987.

Gillett, John. "Westfront 1957." *Sight and Sound* 27:3 (Winter 1957–1958): 122–127.

Grossman, Edward. "Bloody Popcorn." *Harper's* (December 1970): 32–40.

Harwood Academic. *The Japan/American Film Wars: World War II Propaganda and Its Cultural Contexts.* Philadelphia: Harwood, 1994.

Holmes, Richard. *Acts of War: The Behavior of Men in Battle.* New York: Free, 1985.

Hoopes, Roy. *When the Stars Went to War: Hollywood and World War II.* New York: Random, 1994.

Hughes, Robert, ed. *Film, Book 2: Films of Peace and War.* New York: Grove, 1962.

Isaacs, Hermine Rich. "Shadows of War on the Silver Screen." *Theatre Arts* 26:11 (November 1942): 689–696.

Jackson, Kathy Merlock. *Images of Children in American Film.* Metuchen, NJ: Scarecrow, 1986.

Jacobs, Lewis. "World War II and the American Film." *Cinema Journal* 7 (Winter 1967–1968): 1–21.

Jacobson, Herbert L. "Cowboy, Pioneer and American Soldier." *Sight and Sound* 22 (1953): 189–190.

Jacoby, Monica E., and Frederick C. Fulfer. *Reel Wars: A Facts Quiz Book about War Films.* Middletown, CT: Southfarm, 1986.

Jeavons, Clyde. *A Pictorial History of War Films.* Secaucus, NJ: Citadel, 1974.

Johnston, Winifred. *Memo on the Movies: War Propaganda, 1914–1939.* Norman: University of Oklahoma, 1939.

Jones, Ken D., and Arthur F. McClure. *Hollywood at War: The American Motion Picture and World War II.* New York: A. S. Barnes, 1973.

Jowett, Garth. *Film: The Democratic Art.* Boston: Little, Brown, 1976.

Kagan, Norman. *The War Film: A Pyramid Illustrated History of the Movies.* New York: Pyramid, 1974.

Kane, Kathryn. *Visions of War: Hollywood Combat Films of World War II.* Ann Arbor: University of Michigan, 1982.

————. "The World War II Combat Film." In Wes D. Gehring, ed., *Handbook of American Film Genres,* 85–102. Westport, CT: Greenwood, 1985.

Keegan, John. *The Face of Battle.* Middlesex: Penguin, 1976, 1983.

King, Larry. "The Battle of Popcorn Bay." *Harper's* (May 1967): 50–54.

Koppes, Clayton R., and Gregory D. Black. *Hollywood Goes to War: How Politics, Profits and Propaganda Shaped World War II Movies.* New York: Free, 1987.

Kracauer, Siegfried. *From Caligari to Hitler: A Psychological History of the German Film.* Princeton: Princeton UP, 1947.

Krome, Frederic James. *A Weapon of War Second to None: Anglo-American Film Propaganda during World War II.* Ann Arbor: UMI, 1992.

Landrum, Larry M., and Christine Eynon. "World War II in the Movies: A Selected Bibliography of Sources." *Journal of Popular Film* 1 (1972): 147–153.

Langman, Larry, and Ed Borg. *Encyclopedia of American War Films.* New York: Garland, 1989.

Lant, Antonia. *Blackout: Reinventing Women for Wartime British Cinema.* Princeton: Princeton UP, 1991.

Lewis, Leon, and William David Sherman. "War Movies." In *The Landscape of Contemporary Cinema,* 49–55. Buffalo: Buffalo Spectrum, 1967.

Lingeman, Richard R. *Don't You Know There's a War On? The American Home Front, 1941–1945.* New York: Putnam, 1970.

Look Magazine. Movie Lot to Beachhead: The Motion Picture Goes to War and Prepares for the Future. Salem, NH: Ayer, 1945, 1980.

Manchel, Frank. "A Representative Genre of the Film." In Frank Manchel, *Film Study: A Resource Guide,* 55–83. Rutherford, NJ: Fairleigh Dickinson UP, 1973.

Manchester, William. *Goodbye Darkness: A Memoir of the Pacific War.* New York: Dell, 1980.

Manvell, Roger. *Films and the Second World War.* New York: A. S. Barnes, 1974.

Mariani, John. "Let's Not Be Beastly to the Nazis." *Film Comment* 15:1 (January–February 1979): 49–53.

Mast, Gerald. "The War Abroad, a War at Home (1941–1952)." Part 6 in *The Movies in Our Midst: Documents in the Cultural History of Film in America.* Chicago: University of Chicago, 1982.

McClure, Arthur F. "Hollywood at War: The American Motion Picture and World War II, 1939–1945." *Journal of Popular Film* 1:2 (Spring 1972): 123–135.

Morella, Joe, Edward Z. Epstein, and John Griggs. *The Films of World War II.* Secaucus, NJ: Citadel, 1973.

Nash, Jay Robert, and Stanley Ralph Ross. *The Motion Picture Guide, 1927–1983.* 12 vols. Chicago: CineBooks, 1985.

Nornes, Abé Mark, and Fukushima Yukio. *The Japan/America Film Wars: WWII. Propaganda and Its Cultural Contexts.* Switzerland: Harwood Academic, 1994.

O'Connor, John E., and Martin A. Jackson, eds. *American History/American Film: Interpreting the Hollywood Image.* New York: Ungar, 1988.

Paris, Michael. *From the Wright Brothers to Top Gun: Aviation and Popular Cinema.* Manchester, U.K.: Manchester UP, 1995.

Parish, James Robert. *The Great Combat Pictures: Twentieth-Century Warfare on the Screen.* Metuchen, NJ: Scarecrow, 1990.

Pendo, Stephen. *Aviation in the Cinema.* Metuchen, NJ: Scarecrow, 1985.

Perlmutter, Tom. *War Movies.* Secaucus, NJ: Castle, 1974.

Pickard, Roy. *A Companion to the Movies: From 1903 to the Present Day.* London: Lutterworth, 1972.

Pitts, Michael R. *Hollywood and American History: A Filmography of Over 250 Motion Pictures Depicting U.S. History.* Jefferson, NC: McFarland, 1984.

Polan, Dana. *Power and Paranoia: History, Narrative, and the American Cinema, 1940–1950.* New York: Columbia UP, 1986.

Ray, Robert B. *A Certain Tendency of the Hollywood Cinema, 1930–1980.* Princeton: Princeton UP, 1985.

Reimer, Robert C., and Carol J. Reimer. *Nazi-Retro Film: How German Narrative Cinema Remembers the Past.* New York: Twayne, 1992.

Renov, Michael. *Hollywood's Wartime Woman: Representation and Ideology.* Ann Arbor, MI: UMI, 1988.

Rollins, Peter C., ed. *Hollywood as Historian: American Film in a Cultural Context.* Lexington: UP of Kentucky, 1983.

Rubin, Steven Jay. *Combat Films: American Realism, 1945–1970.* Jefferson, NC: McFarland, 1981.

Santner, Eric L. *Stranded Objects: Mourning, Memory, and Film in Postwar Germany.* Ithaca, NY: Cornell UP, 1990.

Shaheen, Jack G., ed. *Nuclear War Films.* Carbondale: Southern Illinois UP, 1978.

Shain, Russell Earl. *An Analysis of Motion Pictures about War Released by the American Film Industry, 1930–1970.* New York: Arno, 1976.

Shindler, Colin. *Hollywood Goes to War: Films and American Society, 1939–1952.* Boston: Routledge, 1979.

Short, Kenneth R. M., ed. *Film and Radio Propaganda in World War II.* Knoxville: University of Tennessee, 1983.

Shull, Michael S., and David E. Wilt. *Doing Their Bit: Wartime American Animated Short Films, 1939–1945.* Jefferson, NC: McFarland, 1987.

Simon, Charnan. *Hollywood at War: The Motion Picture Industry and World War II.* New York: Franklin Watts, 1995.

Sklar, Robert. *Film: An International History of the Medium.* New York: Abrams, 1993.

———. *Movie-Made America: A Cultural History of American Movies.* New York: Random, 1975.

Skogsberg, Bertil. *Wings on the Screen: A Pictorial History of Air Movies.* Translated by George Bisset. San Diego: A. S. Barnes, 1981.

Solomon, Stanley J. *Beyond Formula: American Film Genres.* New York: Harcourt, 1976.

Suid, Lawrence H. *Guts and Glory: Great American War Movies.* Reading, MA: Addison, 1978.

Taylor, Philip M., ed. *Britain and the Cinema in the Second World War.* New York: St. Martin's, 1988.

Taylor, Richard. *Film Propaganda: Nazi Germany and Soviet Russia.* New York: Barnes, 1979.

Thomas, Tony. *The Cinema of the Sea: A Critical Survey and Filmography, 1925–1986.* Jefferson, NC: McFarland, 1988.

Thompson, Kristin, et al. *The Red Screen: Politics, Society, Art in Soviet Cinema.* London: Routledge, 1992.

Thorpe, Frances, and Nicholas Pronay, with Clive Coultass. *British Official Films in the Second World War: A Descriptive Catalogue.* Oxford: Clio, 1980.

Tyler, Parker. *Magic and Myth in the Movies.* New York: Simon, 1947.

Valleau, Marjorie A. *The Spanish Civil War in American and European Films: Studies in Cinema.* Ann Arbor, MI: UMI, 1982.

Virilio, Paul. *War and Cinema: The Logics of Perception.* Translated by Patrick Camiller. New York: Routledge, 1988.

Wetta, Frank, and Stephen Curley. *Celluloid Wars: A Guide to Film and the American Experience of War.* Westport, CT: Greenwood, 1992.

Woll, Allen L. *The Hollywood Musical Goes to War.* Chicago: Nelson, 1982.

Yacowar, Maurice. "The Bug in the Rug." In Barry Keith Grant, ed., *Film Genre Reader.* Austin: University of Texas, 1986.

Zinsser, William. "She Made Him Forget He Was a Soldier." In William Zinsser, *Seen Any Good Movies Lately?*, 183–95. New York: Doubleday, 1958.

16 Japanese War Films

William B. Hauser

Japanese war films vary in thematic content, quality, and perspective. Those produced during the war attempted to rally the Japanese public, the combatants, and the residents of Japanese colonies and occupied areas to support the war effort. In general, they support Japan's wartime goals and actions. Those produced after the war tended to assess blame, champion the new democratic values of postwar Japan, or reinterpret the war to an audience with largely negative memories or no memories at all.

WARTIME FILMS

Japan was a major film producer prior to World War II but had little experience in war films prior to the 1930s. The focus of most war films was on service to the nation, on the need to set aside personal goals, and on sacrifice to support Japanese state interests. Themes of major importance include (1) training young men and women for war service; (2) war production; (3) home front support; (4) the war front and military service; (5) Japanese war aims or national policy; and (6) the nature of the Western, imperialist enemy.

Training

Wartime training is a common element of many war films. This includes the training of combatants—the soldiers, sailors, and airmen required to conduct the war in China and the Pacific region. Several films reflect the attraction of aerial warfare and stress pilot training. Examples are *Sora no shonenhei* [*Young Pilots in the Sky*], 1942, *Aiki minami e tobu* [*Flying South in His Plane*], 1943, *Kessen no ozora e* [*Toward the Decisive Battle in the Sky*], 1943, directed by Kunio Watanabe, and *Kaigun* [*Navy*], 1943, directed by

Tasaka Tomotaka. Each championed the importance of army or navy pilot training. Combatants were not the only focus of training films. *Ane no shuppei* [*Sister Goes to War*], 1943 focused on nurses training, while *Shidō monogatari* [*A Story of leadership*], 1941 was about training railway engineers. These films focused on support staff, not just warriors. Pilots were important, but nurses and railway engineers were also essential for Japan's war effort.

War Production

War matériel production was necessary. *Hachijūhachi nenme no taiyō* [*The Sun after 88 Years*], 1941 is set in a naval shipyard; in *Aiki minami e tobu* [*Flying South in his plane*], the pilot's mother works in an aircraft factory; *Watakushi tachi wa hatarite iru* [*We Are Working*], 1942 deals with women workers in a uniform factory; and *Uma* [*Horse*], 1941, directed by Yamamoto Kajirō, treats raising horses for the army. Each film emphasizes the importance of war production and dedication to providing state needs.

The Home Front

Home front pictures emphasize community support for the war effort despite individual hardships. *Shōshūrei* [*The Induction Order*], 1934 encourages support for military families; *Bakuon* [*Airplane Drone*], 1939, Tasaka Tomotaka, director, calls for public contributions to purchase aircraft; *Hokushi no sora o tsuku* [*Thrust into the Skies of* North China], 1937 is about war reporters; *Rikugun* [*Army*] champions patriotism and support for men in the army; *Chokorē-to to heitai* [*Chocolate and Soldiers*], 1941, Take Sado, director, blends infantry combat in China with family and community support at home. Other films in this category include *Atatakai kaze* [*Warm wind*], 1943, *Aikoku no hana* [*Flower of Patriotism*], 1942, and the films on war production. These films are realistic and emphasize the need to persevere, despite difficulties. Not all the combatants will return. Those who survive must support the war effort.

The War Front

Combat films depict conflict and comradeship. The horror of warfare is minimized, and fighting spirit is lionized to encourage sacrifice for the nation. Army films include *Shingun no uta* [*Song of the Advancing Army*], 1937 and two films directed by Tasaka Tomotaka, *Gonin no sekkōhei* [*Five Scouts*], 1939 and *Tsuchi to heitai* [*Mud and Soldiers*], 1939. *Nishizumi senshachō den* [*Story of Tank Commander Nishizumi*], 1940, directed by Yoshimura Kimisaburo, honors a war hero, as does *Marei no tora* [*Tiger of*

Malaya], 1943. Naval combat is celebrated in *Shanghai no rikusentai* [*The Naval Landing at Shanghai*], 1939 by Tōhō, and *Hawaii-Marei oki kaisen* [*The War at Sea from Hawaii to Malaya*], 1942. Some of these films include documentary combat footage for additional realism. Combat animation includes *Mabo no kokuhei* [*Mabo the Pilot*], *Mabo no tekketsu rikusentai* [*Mabo's Strong Marine*], and *Mabo no rakkasen butai* [*Mabo's Parachute Unit*] by Sato Gonjirō and Chiba Hiromichi; and *Momotarō no umiwashi* [*Momotarō's Sea Eagle*], 1943 and *Momotarō—umi no shinpei* [*Momotarō—Divine Troops of the Ocean*], 1945 by Seo Mitsuyo (Nornes and Fukushima, 191–195). In contrast to American films, the images of fighting and individual heroism are minimized, and group solidarity is glorified in Japanese wartime films.

National Policy

These films address Japanese objectives in occupied areas and the goals of the Greater East Asian Co-Prosperity Sphere. Many were coproduced with Chinese or Manchurian film companies. *Byakuran no uta* [*Song of the White Orchid*], 1939; *Shina no yoru* [*China Night*], 1940, with three endings for Japanese, Chinese, and Southeast Asian audiences; and *Nessa no chikai* [*Vow in the Desert*], 1941 are representative. Other films include *Ajiya no musume* [*Daughter of Asia*], 1938 and *Sakura no kuni* [*Land of Cherry Blossoms*], 1941. A more violent film is *Bōrō no kesshitai* [*Suicide Troops of the Watch Tower*], 1943, about the need to fight for the rights of Japanese colonial settlers in Korea.

The Enemy

In contrast to the negative and racist stereotyping of the Japanese enemy in American war films, Japanese films tend to minimize images of the enemy and portray those resisting Japanese objectives as misguided nationalists, communists, or criminals. The national policy pictures use these images repeatedly. Several films directly depict Western imperialists and illustrate the ways they exploit Asians. *Ahen sensō* [*The Opium War*], 1943 shows British merchants and diplomats forcing Chinese to accept opium imports and undermining the integrity of the Chinese government. *Susume dokuritsu ki* [*Progress toward Independence*], 1943 portrays Japanese efforts to help Indian nationalists work for independence from British colonial rule. Both films paint the British diplomats and businessmen in highly unfavorable terms. The second directly contrasts Japanese support for Asian independence movements with British colonial suppression of Indian nationalists. While many of the combat films suggest that enemy forces are devious and untrustworthy, most combat is abstracted or shot at a distance, minimizing the need to portray the enemy in any detail.

Summary

Japanese war films encouraged self-sacrifice by Japanese civilians and combatants, urged the suppression of personal interests in favor of supporting state goals, and glorified serving the emperor. The war was presented as a conflict between Asian and Western cultures. Japan's war aims were to free the peoples of Asia from Western domination. Japanese culture was presented as pure and unselfish; Western cultures are stereotyped as individualistic and exploitative.

The quality of films varied dramatically. Some, like *Chocolate and Soldiers, Five Scouts,* and *The Story of Tank Commander Nishizumi,* are highly effective and moving films that provide a solid narrative treatment of their primary themes. Others are less successful, incorporating multiple themes or offering a pseudodocumentary approach to feature films. Some of the later films, like *Tiger of Malaya* (1943), *Navy* (1943), and *Heading South in His Plane* (1943), are disjointed and fail to sustain a consistent narrative. By the time of their production Japan was no longer winning the war, casualties were mounting, and enthusiasm for the conflict was diminishing. Japan's capacity to confidently overcome all odds was no longer apparent. The theme of death in combat became increasingly evident in Japanese wartime films. Military service was less romanticized by 1940 as casualties in China increased. *Tank Commander Nishizumi* (1940) dies in combat. While lionized for his efforts to serve Japan and protect innocent Chinese civilians, his death is poignant. In *Chocolate and Soldiers* (1938), the father dies, but the emphasis is on community support for his wife and children back home. Stoicism, not sacrifice, is stressed. Later films are more candid about the costs of the war, not just the need to endure. Assuring national survival required the ultimate sacrifice.

POSTWAR FILMS

Postwar films include many of the same themes, but from a different perspective. After the war, censorship by the Allied Occupation limited the content of films and required an emphasis on the democratic values of the new Japan. Blame and the struggle for survival are prominent film subjects. After 1952, wartime suffering and social dislocation are joined by explicit antiwar and antimilitary themes. Both the home front and the war front are included, and the family-style army and navy are replaced by images of brutalization and dehumanization in training and combat. The noble fight to the death is replaced by the humanistic ideal of survival. Japan must rebuild and reject the values of the war period. Democracy and individualism supplanted militarism and ultranationalism as the underlying ideological message in most postwar films.

Blame and Victimization

The Occupation era saw films about wartime victimization of the Japanese. *Minshū no teki* [*Enemy of the People*], 1946 treats war profiteers and military and business corruption. *Osone-ke no asa* [*A New Morning for the Osone*], 1946 illustrates wartime victimization of cosmopolitan, peace-loving Japanese by militarists and ultranationalists and hopes for a democratic future. *Waga seishun ni kui nashi* [*No Regrets for Our Youth*], 1946, directed by Kurosawa Akira, depicts the suffering of those who protested the war and calls for egalitarian values and democracy. This controversial film illustrates peasant brutality against those who refused to conform with nationalist values. *Hachinosu no kodomotachi* [*Children of the Beehive*], 1948 treats the need to resettle war orphans and veterans and the dislocation of postwar society.

Antiwar and Antimilitary Films

Nijūshi no hitomi [*Twenty-four Eyes*], 1954, directed by Kinoshita Keisuke, shows the impact of militarism and war on an isolated village teacher and her students. *Biruma no tategoto* [*Harp of Burma*], 1956, directed by Ichikawa Kon, shows the plight of Japanese soldiers at the end of the war and calls for respect and proper burial for the war dead. *Nōbi* [*Fires on the Plain*], 1959 by Ichikawa Kon illustrates the brutality and dehumanization of war. See Hauser's "*Fires on the Plain.*" *Ningen no jōken* [*The Human Condition*], 1958–1961, directed by Kobayashi Masaki, is a ten-hour, three-part film on the war in China and its brutal impact on a well-meaning Japanese intellectual. This is one of the most virulently antimilitary films of the postwar era and champions individualism. *Heitai yakuza* [*Hoodlum Soldier*], 1965, directed by Masumura Yasuzō, in a humorous and chilling manner shows the morals of a gangster as superior to those of Japanese military leaders. *Mikan no taikyaku* [*The Go Master*], 1982 is a joint Sino-Japanese production on the China War with multiple directors and viewpoints. Japanese military brutality against both Chinese and Japanese is depicted in brutal detail in a beautiful, but disturbing, film.

Revisionism

Since the 1970s there have been many films placing a positive spin on the Japanese war effort. Few of these films were released in the United States, but *Dai Nippon Teikoku* [*The Imperial Japanese Empire*], 1982, directed by Masuda Toshio, is representative. Representing Tōjō Hideki as a heroic family man and patriot, the film blends period documentary footage and stereotyped images of the British and American enemies into a celebration of the war effort. This is a bad film and makes a poor case for the Ministry of Education-sanctioned perspective on the Pacific War. It is but one example of films that champion the lost cause of the war and that reflect, in part, the enmity between Japan and the United States over economic issues. The 15 August 1995 apology by Prime Minister Murayama Tomiichi for wartime suffering caused by Japan suggests that many Japanese are now prepared for a more objective reexamination of the Pacific War. See Bailey's "War Films."

Summary

Since the end of the Pacific War Japan has produced many films dealing with the conflict. The image of combat, the justification for the war, and the depiction of the plight of both civilians and combatants differ radically. The immediate postwar films focus on bitterness and blame, on the suffering of the Japanese during the war. Some films include images of war protesters and the humiliation and repression they experienced from their countrymen. The brutality and dehumanization of military training and military service are also important themes. The brutalization of the citizens of Japanese-occupied areas, as well as of Western POWs, is also candidly treated. Revisionist views of the war have appeared since the 1970s as Japanese heroism and efforts to assert and protect national interests became cinematic subjects. Few of these films have circulated, as their viewpoints are unpopular outside Japan. While some Japanese accept the idea that Japan attempted to protect Asia from Western imperialism and free Asia for the Asians, this perspective is not shared by the majority of Japanese and is rejected by the peoples of areas conquered by Japan during the war. T. R. Reid, in a 17 August 1995 National Public Radio interview, reported that 70 percent of Japanese accept Japan's responsibility for the Pacific War. The reluctance of the Japanese government to formally admit to war guilt and the repression of other Asian peoples is no longer supported by public opinion.

SUGGESTIONS FOR FURTHER RESEARCH

Videotapes of wartime and postwar films have enhanced access to many titles previously unavailable outside museum or library collections. The films mentioned earlier represent only a small portion of the material now available for analysis. Individual films, film genres within the category of war films, the use of Japanese films for supporting national policy at home and abroad, and government control of the film industry could all benefit from further study. Wartime censorship makes analysis of popular responses to wartime films difficult. The increased availability of diaries and personal accounts of the war offers important avenues for exploring the importance of war films to Japanese wartime and postwar cultural history.

The bibliography offers a selection of materials in English and a small segment of the Japanese-language materials of interest. These works discuss individual films, the nature of wartime and postwar film production, important film directors, the role of censorship, and the objectives of government policy on control of the film medium.

NOTE

Many of the wartime films were viewed at the Japan Film Center of the Tokyo National Museum of Modern Art, the Motion Picture Division of the Library of Congress, and a traveling film series circulated by the Japan Society of New York. Postwar films were viewed in Japan or in the United States and are more readily available. Videotapes of war films are widely available in Japan.

BIBLIOGRAPHY

Anderson, Joseph L., and Donald Richie. *The Japanese Film: Art and Industry.* Expanded ed. Princeton: Princeton UP, 1982.

Bailey, James. "War Films Depict Japan as a Misunderstood Victim." *New York Times,* November 10, 1985, Section II, 17.

Basinger, Jeanine. *The World War II Combat Film: Anatomy of a Genre.* New York: Columbia UP, 1986.

Baskett, Michael Dennis. "The Japanese Colonial Film Enterprise 1937–1945: Imagining the Imperial Japanese Subject." M.A. thesis, University of California at Los Angeles, 1993.

Benedict, Ruth Fulton. *Japanese Films: A Phase of Psychological Warfare.* Washington, DC: Foreign Morale Analysis Division, Office of War, 30 March 1944.

Bock, Audie. *Japanese Film Directors.* Tokyo: Kodansha International, 1978.

Burch, Noël. *To the Distant Observer: Form and Meaning in the Japanese Cinema.* Berkeley and Los Angeles: University of California, 1979.

Dower, John W. "Japanese Cinema Goes to War." In John W. Dower, *Japan in War and Peace, Selected Essays,* 33–54. New York: W. W. Norton, 1993.

———. *War without Mercy: Race and Power in the Pacific War.* New York: Pantheon, 1986.

Hauser, William B. "*Fires on the Plain*: The Human Cost of the Pacific War." In Arthur Nolletti, Jr., and David Desser, eds., *Reframing Japanese Cinema: Authorship, Genre, History,* 193–209. Bloomington: Indiana UP, 1992.

———. "Women and War: The Japanese Film Image." In Gail Lee Bernstein, ed., *Recreating Japanese Women, 1600–1945,* 296–313. Berkeley: University of California, 1991.

Kasza, Gregory J. *The State and the Mass Media in Japan, 1918–1945.* Berkeley: University of California, 1988.

Loader, Ned. "Listen to the Voices from the Sea: The Art and Politics of a Japanese Anti-War Film." Ph.D. diss., Emory University, 1993.

Mellen, Joan. *The Waves at Genji's Door: Japan through Its Cinema.* New York: Pantheon, 1976.

Nornes, Abé Mark, and Fukushima Yukio. *The Japan/America Film Wars: WWII Propaganda and Its Cultural Contexts.* Switzerland: Harwood Academic, 1994.

Richie, Donald. *Japanese Cinema: Film Style and National Character.* Garden City, NY: Anchor, 1971.

Sakuramoto, Tomio. *Daitōa sensō to Nihon eiga: Tachimi no senchū eigaron* [*The Greater East Asian War and Japanese Films: A Theory for Viewing Wartime Films*]. Tokyo: Aoki Shobo, 1993.

Sato, Tadao. *Currents in Japanese Cinema: Essays by Tadao Sato.* New York: Kodansha International/USA, 1982.

———. "Sensō Eiga no sensōkan" ["War Imagery from War Films"]. In *Nihon Eiga to Nihon bunka [Japanese Films and Japanese Culture]*, 110–139. Tokyo: Miraisha, 1987.

———. "War as a Spiritual Exercise: Japan's National Policy Films." *Wide Angle* 2: 1 (1977): 22–24.

Sensō to Nihon Eiga, Kōza Nihon Eiga. Vol. 4 [*War and Japanese Film,* vol. 4 of *Lectures on Japanese Film*]. Tokyo: Iwanami shōten, 1986.

Uriu, Tadao. *Sengo Nihon Eiga shoshi* [*A Short History of Postwar Japanese Films*]. Tokyo: Hosei UP, 1981.

17   The Holocaust and Film

Judith E. Doneson

The cinema has played a consequential role both in the history of the Holocaust and in the retelling of the event, particularly with attempts to shape memory. The Nazis, for instance, utilized anti-Semitic films as a means of influencing public perceptions as they moved toward the Final Solution. The Soviet Union and the United States made feature films in the 1930s confronting Nazi persecution of the Jews. American newsreels, a common event preceding the main feature in movie theaters, played their role in parlaying information on German anti-Semitism.

The post-Holocaust cinematic response began almost immediately upon completion of the war and continues into the present, with Steven Spielberg's *Schindler's List* (1993) exemplifying the extraordinary impact of film both on the public and on the historical discourse. Indeed, the most recent contribution to the literature of film and the Holocaust is found in a volume of academic essays edited by Loshitsky entitled *Spielberg's Holocaust*.

Three early fiction films seemed almost prescient in their willingness to confront the dangers of Nazi anti-Semitism. The first two come from the United States: *The House of Rothschild* (1934), on the surface, a fictional narration of the rise of the Rothschild banking family but, on the latent level, a warning about the dangers confronting the Jews of Germany, and Charlie Chaplin's *The Great Dictator* (1940), a contemporary tale of the battle of the German against the Jew. In Doneson's *The Holocaust in American Film*, one finds a contextual study of these and other American feature films confronting the Holocaust. The third film, *Professor Mamlock* (1938) appeared in the Soviet Union prior to the German-Soviet pact and clearly states the nasty conditions of German Jewry up until *Kristallnacht*. For further discussion on the Soviet and Eastern European cinema see Stoil, *Cinema beyond the Danube*.

Several segments of *The March of Time*, one of the more prominent newsreels appearing in cinemas, were important in introducing American audiences to events occurring in Europe in the 1930s and 1940s. Of interest with regard to the Jewish predicament were *Inside Nazi Germany*, *Poland and the War*, *Nazi Conquest*, and *The Refugee*. Fielding's *The March of Time, 1935–1951* is a standard study of this series.

Of course, there was the Nazi perspective of the Jewish issue in film. Prior to the actual destruction of European Jewry, Goebbels' Ministry of Propaganda requested a series of anti-Semitic films, some say to prepare the public for what was to come. One, *The Rothschilds' Shares in Waterloo* (1940), was both anti-British and anti-Jewish. Two of these films, anti-Semitic in focus, are particularly remembered for the extreme nature of their content: *Jud Suss* (1940) was a historical fiction with a message for the present—Germany must rid itself of its Jews—and *The Eternal Jew* (1940), a "documentary" filmed in a pseudoscientific, overly virulent manner, embodied the most extreme Nazi ideology regarding the Jews. Several studies and articles have appeared dealing with this subject. Among them are Culbert and Hornshoj-Moller, "*Der Ewige Jude*: Joseph Goebbels Unequaled Monument to Anti-Semitism"; Doneson, "Nazi Anti-Semitic Film"; Hull, *Film in the Third Reich*; Leiser, *Nazi Cinema*; Taylor, *Film Propaganda: Soviet Russia and Nazi Germany*; and Welch, *Propaganda and the German Cinema, 1933–1945*.

The growing body of films dealing with the subject of the Holocaust since the end of the war is not limited by geographical boundaries. One finds both fiction and nonfiction films that, in some manner, depict what historian Raul Hilberg termed the step-by-step process begun in 1933 that climaxed in the Final Solution.

The earliest examples are nonfiction newsreels. These include footage such as *Nazi Concentration Camps* (1945), compiled from film shots of the camps by the liberating armies. Later examples of similar footage discovered in the archives of the former Soviet Union include *The Liberation of Auschwitz* (1986), *Majdanek 1944—Victims and Criminals* (1986), and *Memory of the Camps* (1985), comprising Bergen-Belsen material located in the Imperial War Museum in London. Incidentally, it is relevant to point out that one must be vigilant regarding the use of nonfiction footage, because the only authentic films of the period either were shot by the liberating armies, and this, indeed, is more the result of the Holocaust, or are Nazi anti-Semitic footage, oftentimes elicited by force in the newly created Jewish ghettos in Eastern Europe. There seems to be no existing film of the death camps from the period of the war.

Because of this absence of verified footage, fiction films have played a major role in interpreting the Holocaust. Among the first representations of the destruction of European Jewry is a group of films from Eastern Europe.

From Poland, *Border Street* (1948), a film about the Warsaw ghetto, and *The Last Stop* (1948) were actually filmed at the site of Auschwitz. *Distant Journey* (1949) was made in Czechoslovakia, and its story takes place in the Terezin ghetto.

Both Avisar's *Screening the Holocaust* and Insdorf's *Indelible Shadows* cover a broad vista in their studies on films and the Holocaust. Langer's "The Americanization of the Holocaust on Stage and Screen" deals with specific American films, and Doneson's "The Feminization of the Jew in Holocaust Film" spotlights an ongoing image that feminizes the Jew in nonfiction Holocaust films. Liehm's *Closely Watched Films* gives us a panorama of Czech films. In addition, Doneson's "Films on the Holocaust" offers an overview of films dealing with the Final Solution.

Returning to Poland, we find a number of films from renowned filmmaker Andrej Wajda. His postwar trilogy, *Generation* (1954), *Kanal* (1956) and *Ashes and Diamonds* (1958), is remembered here for its absence of content on the Final Solution. Wajda, however, did make several films that focus more on the Holocaust. These include *Samson* (1961), whose action is located in the Warsaw ghetto, *Landscape after Battle* (1970), whose story revolves around survivors in a displaced person's camp, and *Korczak* (1990), the story of a Jewish doctor who chooses death with his "children" from the orphanage he runs. Wajda's colleague, Agnieska Holland, scriptwriter for *Korczak*, also made two films about the Holocaust, though they were produced in West Germany: *Angry Harvest* (1985), about a Polish man who hides a Jewish woman, and *Europa, Europa* (1990), the adventures of a Jewish boy hiding his identity in order to survive the war. The Polish film *The Passenger* (1962) tells of a woman on a train in 1960 who, in recognizing her former guard from Auschwitz, attempts to come to terms with her concentration camp experience.

Czechoslovakia has contributed its share of Holocaust films, the result of the country's suffering during World War II. Here we find *Sweet Light in a Dark Room* (1960), about a Czech boy hiding a Jewish girl from the Nazis; *Diamonds of the Night* (1964), depicting two boys escaping a transport as they are chased by hunters; *The Shop on Main Street* (1965), about an elderly Jewish woman and her fascist "protector"; and *The Fifth Horseman Is Fear* (1964), a tale of frightened informers.

From Hungary come two particularly poignant films. *The Revolt of Job* (1983) deals with parents' attempts to secure the safety of their adopted son. *Elysium* (1986) tells of a Jewish boy taken to a children's camp in which medical experiments are performed.

Italy has turned out a number of relevant films. We have *Kapo* (1960), the story of a Jewish overseer in a concentration camp; *The Gold of Rome* (1961) about a fine imposed on the Jewish community of Rome by the Nazis; and the remarkable *The Garden of the Finzi-Continis* (1970), which tells of the Jewish community's deportation from the town of Ferrara. Italy has also produced several controversial films confronting the Holocaust, including *The Night Porter* (1974), in which a survivor carries on a relationship with her former persecutor, and *Seven Beauties* (1975), a tale of survival at any cost.

France has also created some very engrossing films about the destruction of European Jewry. An early example is *The Two of Us* (1966) about a young Jewish boy being hidden by an anti-Semite. *The Sorrow and the Pity* (1970), a French nonfiction film that exposed France as a collaborator with the Germans under the Occupation, elicited a strong cinematic response by way of feature films such as *Les Violons du Bal* (1973), the tale of a Jewish family's escape into Switzerland; *Lacombe, Lucien* (1974), which tells of a young French fascist who "protects" a Jewish tailor and his daughter; *Black Thursday* (1974), about the July 1942 roundup of Jews in Paris by the French police; *Mr. Klein* (1976), a case of exploitation and mistaken identity during a time of crisis for the Jews of Paris; and *The Last Metro* (1980), the story of a drama troupe that continues performing under the guidance of its Jewish director, who is hidden in the cellar. Somewhat later, *Au Revoir les Enfants* (1987) appeared as a remembrance of a Jewish boy deported from his French school during the war. Of interest here is a study by Friedman entitled "Exorcising the Past: Jewish Figures in Contemporary Films."

Both East and West Germany have contributed, in their own peculiar manner, to the effort to retell history on the screen. Of interest from East Germany is *Jacob, the Liar* (1978), the tale of a Jew who tries to instill hope into the hearts of his ghetto inmates. A former East German citizen who worked in West Germany, Hans-Jürgen Syberberg, is responsible for *The Confessions of Winifred Wagner* (1975), who claimed she would be happy to see Hitler walk through the door. But more important, Syberberg created *Our Hitler* (1978), a seven-hour cinematic spectacle, his work of "mourning" as he confronts the "Hitler in all of us" while attempting to come to terms with the German past. Also from West Germany are films like *David* (1979), about a young Jewish boy trying to escape Nazi Germany, and *The Nasty Girl* (1990), which portrays a real-life, young student's efforts to force her town to confront its role in the Final Solution. For the most part, however, the West German cinema is more comfortable with films like Karl Reitz's sixteen-hour saga *Heimat* (1984), which all but ignores the Holocaust. The thrust of these films is more to work out postwar German trauma rather than to confront the Holocaust. Kaes, *From Heimat to Hitler*, Santner, *Stranded Objects*, and issue number 72 of the journal *October*, coedited by Liebman, examine this perspective. It remains to be seen what a united Germany will create.

Interestingly, the American cinema has played a pivotal role in disseminating memory of the Holocaust. Films like *The Diary of Anne Frank* (1959), *Judgment at Nuremberg* (1961), and especially the NBC/TV telefilm

Holocaust (1978) and *Schindler's List* (1993) have managed to imprint this event into the American imagination, while they propelled confrontation with the past in Germany and the rest of Europe as well. Additionally, the American cinema has produced *Sophie's Choice* (1982), a controversial film due to the portrayal of a Polish Catholic survivor of the Holocaust as symbolic of the event. Other American films of interest include *The Pawnbroker* (1965), a study of a Holocaust survivor haunted by the past; *Ship of Fools* (1965), a shipboard plot that reveals a cross-section of characters about to be immersed in the tragedy of Nazi Germany; *Cabaret* (1972), an engrossing account of the last days of Weimar Germany, that is, on the eve of the Nazi rise to power; *Voyage of the Damned* (1976), about the tragic sailing from Hamburg of the ship *St. Louis*, whose doomed Jewish passengers were refused entry into Cuba and the United States and forced to return to Nazi Germany; and *Julia* (1977), a tale of intrigue and resistance in occupied Europe. Several dramas made for television need to be recognized: *Wallenberg: A Hero's Story* (1985), which tells of the valiant efforts of a Swedish diplomat to save Hungarian Jewry; *Escape from Sobibor* (1987), about the Jewish uprising in the death camp; and *War and Remembrance* (1988–1989), an epic drama that includes an impressive attempt to confront the Holocaust.

Also worth mentioning are two fictional films, both jointly produced. Switzerland, West Germany, and Austria joined together in bringing us *The Boat Is Full* (1980), a tale of Jewish refugees denied asylum in Switzerland. *Charlotte* (1981), made mutually by the Netherlands and West Germany, recounts the story of Charlotte Salomon, a young Jewish artist who dies in Auschwitz.

In the arena of nonfiction film, we find an interesting mixture of films coming from various countries. *The Illegals* (1947), filmed by American author Meyer Levin, follows the illicit crossing of Europe by a group of Holocaust survivors attempting to reach Palestine. *Night and Fog* (1955) from France is a startling juxtaposition of present and past in its depiction of the concentration camp universe. Noticeable to many, however, is the absence of any reference to Jews in its text. Both visually and narratively informative are *Mein Kampf* (1960) from Sweden and *The Life of Adolf Hitler* (1961) from Great Britain, each dealing with the rise of the Nazi Party and the Holocaust. Britain's BBC compiled *The Warsaw Ghetto* (1968), utilizing controversial footage shot by the Nazis. Also from Great Britain comes the segment "Genocide" (1973) from *The World at War* series. An American film entitled *Genocide* (1981) won an Academy Award for Best Documentary Film. *Who Shall Live and Who Shall Die* (1981) explores America's lack of response to the Jewish persecutions, while *Hotel Terminus* (1988) is an excellent study of the Final Solution through the prism of the trial of war criminal Klaus Barbie.

We conclude with French filmmaker Claude Lanzmann's nine-and-one-half-hour nonfiction film *Shoah* (1985). Using the Hebrew word for Holocaust as its title, *Shoah* has an urgency and insistence in its text that compel us to confront an event that seems impenetrable. It is a film of voices, of memories, of disbelief, and of truth. Lanzmann's complete text, entitled *Shoah: An Oral History of the Holocaust*, is available in English.

When considering the destruction of European Jewry in film, the problems in representing and popularizing such a subject are inherent to the topic. Several studies delve into these matters: Friedlander's *Probing the Limits of Representation*; Doneson's "*Holocaust* Revisited: A Catalyst for Memory or Trivialization?"; Jick's "The Holocaust: Its Use and Abuse within the American Public"; and Marrus, "The Use and Misuse of the Holocaust."

The utilization of film offers a unique perspective in the study of history and should be of value in guiding us visually through the history of the Final Solution.

FILMOGRAPHY

Angry Harvest. West Germany, 1985. Director: Agnieska Holland.

Ashes and Diamonds. Poland, 1958. Director: Andrej Wajda.

Au Revoir Les Enfants. France, 1987. Director: Louis Malle.

Black Thursday. France, 1974. Director: Michel Mitrani.

The Boat Is Full. Switzerland/West Germany/Austria, 1980. Director: Markus Imhoof.

Border Street. Poland, 1948. Director: Alexander Ford.

Cabaret. United States, 1972. Director: Bob Fosse.

Charlotte. Holland/West Germany, 1981. Director: Franz Weisz.

The Confessions of Winifred Wagner. West Germany, 1975. Director: Hans-Jurgen Syberberg.

David. West Germany, 1979. Director: Peter Lilienthal.

Diamonds of the Night. Czechoslovakia, 1964. Director: Jan Nemec.

The Diary of Anne Frank. United States, 1959. Director: George Stevens.

The Distant Journey. Czechoslovakia, 1949. Director: Alfred Radok.

Elysium. Hungary, 1986. Director: Erika Szanto.

Escape from Sobibor. United States, 1987 (CBS/TV). Director: Jack Gold.

The Eternal Jew. Germany, 1940. Director: Fritz Hippler.

Europa, Europa. West Germany, 1990. Director: Agnieska Holland.

The Fifth Horseman Is Fear. Czechoslovakia, 1964. Director: Zbynek Brynuch.

The Garden of the Finzi-Continis. Italy, 1970. Director: Vittorio De Sica.

Generation. Poland, 1954. Director: Andrej Wajda.

"*Genocide.*" Great Britain, 1973 (Thames TV for *World at War Series*). Director: Michael Darlow.

Genocide. United States, 1981. Director: Arnold Schwartzman.

The Gold of Rome. Italy, 1961. Director: Carlo Lizzani.

The Great Dictator. United States, 1940. Director: Charles Chaplin.

Heimat. West Germany, 1984. Director: Karl Reitz.

Holocaust. United States, 1978 (NBC/TV). Director: Marvin Chomsky.

Hotel Terminus. United States, 1988. Director: Marcel Ophuls.

The House of Rothschild. United States, 1934. Director: Alfred Werker.

The Illegals. United States, 1947. Director: Meyer Levin.

Jacob, the Liar. East Germany, 1978. Director: Frank Beyer.

Jud Suss. Germany, 1940. Director: Veit Harlan.

Judgment at Nuremberg. United States, 1961. Director: Stanley Kramer.

Julia. United States, 1977. Director: Fred Zinnemann.

Kanal. Poland, 1956. Director: Andrej Wajda.

Kapo. Italy, 1960. Director: Gillo Pontecorvo.

Korczak. Poland, 1990. Director: Andrej Wajda.

Lacombe, Lucien. France, 1974. Director: Louis Malle.

Landscape after Battle. Poland, 1970. Director: Andrej Wajda.

The Last Metro. France, 1980. Director: François Truffaut.

The Last Stop. Poland, 1948. Director: Wanda Jakubowska.

The Liberation of Auschwitz. West Germany, 1986. Directors: Bengt and Irmgard von Zur Muehlen.

The Life of Adolf Hitler. Great Britain, 1961. Director: Paul Rotha.

Majdanek 1944—Victims and Criminals. West Germany, 1986. Directors: Bengt and Irmgard von Zur Muehlen.

The March of Time. United States, 1935–1951.

    "Inside Nazi Germany," 1938.

    "Nazi Conquest," n.d.

    "Poland and the War," n.d.

    "The Refugee," 1935.

Mein Kampf. Sweden, 1960. Director: Erwin Leiser.

Memory of the Camps. Great Britain, 1985.

Mr. Klein. France, 1976. Director: Joseph Losey.

The Nasty Girl. West Germany, 1990. Director: Michael Verhoeven.

Nazi Concentration Camps. United States, 1945. Filmed by liberating armies.

Night and Fog. France, 1955. Director: Alain Resnais.

The Night Porter. Italy, 1974. Director: Liliani Cavani.

Our Hitler, a Film from Germany. West Germany, 1978. Director: Hans-Jürgen Syberberg.

The Passenger. Poland, 1962. Director: Andrej Munk (Completed by Witold Lesiewicz).

The Pawnbroker. United States, 1965. Director: Sidney Lumet.

Professor Mamlock. USSR, 1938. Directors: Adolf Minkin and Herbert Rappaport.

The Revolt of Job. Hungary, 1983. Directors: Imre Gyongyossi and Barna Kabay.

The Rothschilds' Shares in Waterloo. Germany, 1940. Director: Erich Waschneck.

Samson. Poland, 1961. Director: Andrej Wajda.

Schindler's List. United States, 1993. Director: Steven Spielberg.

Seven Beauties. Italy, 1975. Director: Lina Wertmuller.

Ship of Fools. United States, 1965. Director: Stanley Kramer.

Shoah. France, 1985. Director: Claude Lanzmann.

The Shop on Main Street. Czechoslovakia, 1965. Directors: Jan Kadar and Elmar Klos.

Sophie's Choice. United States, 1982. Director: Alan Pakula.

The Sorrow and the Pity. France, 1970. Director: Marcel Ophuls.

Sweet Light in a Dark Room. Czechoslovakia, 1960. Director: Jiri Weiss.

The Two of Us. France, 1966. Director: Claude Berri.

Les Violons du Bal. France, 1973. Director: Michel Drach.

Voyage of the Damned. United States/Great Britain, 1976. Director: Stuart Rosenberg.

Wallenberg: A Hero's Story. United States, 1985 (NBC/TV). Director: Lamont Johnson.

War and Remembrance. United States, 1988–1989 (ABC/TV). Director: Dan Curtis.

Warsaw Ghetto. Great Britain, 1968 (BBC/TV).

Who Shall Live and Who Shall Die. United States, 1981. Director: Laurence Jarvik.

BIBLIOGRAPHY

Avisar, Ilan. *Screening the Holocaust.* Bloomington: Indiana UP, 1989.

Culbert, David, and Stig Hornshoj-Moller. "*Der ewige Jude*: Joseph Goebbels' Unequaled Monument to Anti-Semitism." *Historical Journal of Film, Radio and Television* 12:1 (1992): 41–67.

Doneson, Judith E. "The Feminization of the Jew in Holocaust Film." *Shoah: A Review of Holocaust Studies and Commemorations* 1:1 (1978): 11–13, 18.

———. "Films on the Holocaust." In Israel Gutman, ed., *Encyclopedia of the Holocaust*, vol. 2, 485–488. New York: Maxwell Macmillan International, 1990.

———. *The Holocaust in American Film.* Philadelphia: Jewish Publication Society, 1987.

———. "*Holocaust* Revisited: A Catalyst for Memory or Trivialization?" *The Annals of the American Academy of Political and Social Science* 548 (1996): 70–77.

———. "Nazi Anti-Semitic Film." In Israel Gutman, ed., *Encyclopedia of the Holocaust*, vol. 2, 484–485. New York: Maxwell Macmillan International, 1990.

Fielding, Raymond. *The March of Time, 1935–1951.* New York: Oxford UP, 1978.

Friedlander, Saul, ed. *Probing the Limits of Representation: Nazism and the Final Solution.* Cambridge: Harvard UP, 1992.

Friedman, R. M. "Exorcising the Past: Jewish Figures in Contemporary Films." *Journal of Contemporary History* 19 (1984): 511–527.

Hull, David Stewart. *Film in the Third Reich: A Study of the German Cinema, 1933–1945.* Berkeley: University of California, 1969.

Insdorf, Annette. *Indelible Shadows: Film and the Holocaust.* Cambridge: Cambridge UP, 1990.

Jick, Leon A. "The Holocaust: Its Use and Abuse within the American Public." *Yad Vashem Studies* 14 (1981): 303–318.

Kaes, Anton. *From Heimat to Hitler: The Return of History as Film.* Cambridge: Harvard UP, 1989.

Langer, Lawrence. "The Americanization of the Holocaust on Stage and Screen." In Sarah Blacher Cohen, ed., *From Hester Street to Hollywood*, 213–230. Bloomington: Indiana UP, 1983.

Lanzmann, Claude. *Shoah: An Oral History of the Holocaust.* New York: Pantheon, 1985.

Leiser, Erwin. *Nazi Cinema.* New York: Collier, 1975.

Liebman, Stuart, guest coed. *October* 72 (1995).

Liehm, Antonin J. *Closely Watched Films: The Czechoslovak Film Experience.* New York: International Arts and Sciences, 1974.

Loshitsky, Yosefa, ed. *Spielberg's Holocaust.* Bloomington: Indiana UP, 1997.

Marrus, Michael R. "The Use and Misuse of the Holocaust." In Peter Hayes, ed., *Lessons and Legacies,* 106–119. Evanston, IL: Northwestern UP, 1991.

Santner, Eric L. *Stranded Objects: Mourning, Memory and Film in Postwar Germany.* Ithaca, NY: Cornell UP, 1990.

Stoil, Michael Jon. *Cinema beyond the Danube: The Camera and Politics.* Metuchen, NJ: Scarecrow, 1974.

Taylor, Richard. *Film Propaganda: Soviet Russia and Nazi Germany.* New York: Barnes and Noble, 1979.

Welch, David. *Propaganda and the German Cinema, 1933–1945.* London: Oxford UP, 1983.

18   The "Western" Fiction of World War II

M. Paul Holsinger

"War" fiction is, by its very nature, hard to define to everyone's satisfaction. Certainly, no one would deny that stories with actual combat settings, whether on land, sea, or air, qualify for such a designation. But what about fictive literature that focuses exclusively on a particular home front in the midst of war? Are works about civilians, affected by the conflict that swirls around them, war stories? What about books that deal with spies and espionage behind enemy lines? Do those concerned with prisoners of war and their confinement or, in some cases, their escape fit into the genre? What about accounts of the "ethnic cleansing" of "undesirable" peoples in conquered countries?

Though each specialist has his or her own definition of what constitutes war fiction, this chapter, of necessity, looks only at those works that, in novel format, tell a tale whose major feature is combat and action on some battlefront. No dramas, even those with a military focus, no poems, no short stories appear. Life on the various home fronts, as important as it was to the war effort, has been ignored unless it serves as a coherent part of a book dealing predominantly with the military side of the war. So, too, have the literally hundreds of often exceptional novels dealing with the Holocaust, whether against Jews, Gypsies, homosexuals, or others. Even stories centered around military men held in captivity such as Boule's often cited *The Bridge on the River Kwai* or Clavell's *King Rat*, both later made into fine motion pictures, are not included. Only novels from five major Western nations: Great Britain; France; Russia and the other parts of what was, during the war, the USSR; the United States; and Germany are noted. Though there are also many fine works from less important, but clearly not insignificant, countries such as Canada, Australia, New Zealand, the Netherlands, the Scandinavian countries (especially Denmark and Norway), Switzerland, Greece, Italy, Czechoslovakia, Poland, and Yugoslavia, they are not discussed because of the limitation of space.

Since September 1939, no fewer than 6,000 and perhaps as many as 7,000 novels on some aspect of the war have been published in the five nations under consideration. Though some of the best still have not been translated into English and made readily available for a wider audience, probably at least 3,000 deal primarily with events surrounding one or more military action sequences. No comprehensive bibliography of fictional works about World War II exists—perhaps it never will—but Taylor, *The Novels of World War II: An Annotated Bibliography*, provides a good start. Listing more than 3,700 novels that were published in English between 1939 and 1990, Taylor provides generally thoughtful, brief discussions of the merits of nearly all of them. Smith's *War Story Guide* or Paris' *The Novels of World War Two*, neither as complete or so well done, also can be very useful to the student of Western war studies. Holsinger in *The Ways of War: The Era of World War II in Children's and Young Adult Fiction* catalogs and annotates more than a thousand full-length books written for younger readers that deal with many aspects of the war. Most of these are not discussed in any of the bibliographies listed earlier. A brief, but perceptive, interpretive study of some of the best available fiction is Klein's *The Second World War in Fiction*.

The books noted later are representative of the very best of the thousands of novels annotated by Taylor and his contemporaries. They are not necessarily those of the highest quality or influence or even those that sold more than any others, though in some cases they are both. They are, instead, works that shed light on one or more aspects of the military side of the war, novels that are representative of both the breadth and the depth of the overwhelming number that any devotee of fiction can read and, for the most part, truly appreciate.

In Great Britain, interest in fiction about the Second World War has remained as strong as it was more than fifty years ago. This has been particularly so in regard to the Royal Navy's pivotal role in the British war effort. Books that focus on that time, whether skillfully or not, seem to be guaranteed best-sellers. There are some authors, indeed, whose livelihood has revolved almost exclusively around tales dealing with the naval side of the war. J. E. MacDonnell, for instance, has produced more than 150 popular novels about the war at sea. None of these are more than formulaic in style, but this has not disturbed the author's huge number of admirers. Douglas Reeman and Philip McCutchan, if not so prolific, also have authored dozens of similar works. Reeman, who fought with the Royal Navy throughout the war, brings to all his novels an intense knowledge of what it was like to be a part of that thin line that stood between Great Britain's life and death. His *A Prayer for the Ship*, *Rendezvous South Atlantic*, and *A*

Ship Must Die are all excellently told accounts. McCutchan's two separate series of naval adventures, thirteen volumes featuring a young reserve officer, Donald Cameron, and the more recent five-volume "Convoy" books also make for exciting and often tense reading. The American Library Association's *Booklist* noted some years ago that McCutchan's "Cameron" stories were "rousing World War II adventure." They remain so today.

It is probably true, as some scholars in the British Isles have insisted, that none of these publications are memorable or of a quality to be called "literature" in the best sense of that term, but such works are intensely popular not only in Great Britain but also in the United States, Canada, Australia, and any number of European countries. Millions of copies of these adventures, often printed only in paper editions, have been sold, and there appears no reason to assume that the reading public will tire of them anytime in the near future.

Certainly, the most famous and perhaps the best novel dealing with the Royal Navy during the years of World War II is Monsarrat's 1951 bestseller, *The Cruel Sea*. The story of the officers and crew of one of the many escort corvettes assigned to protect the North Atlantic convoy routes that were literally keeping England alive during the early days of the war, the novel sweeps through almost the entire war, from November 1939 to May 1945. Monsarrat, who served on such ships during the war and whose earlier series of excellent, short autobiographical sketches established him as a deft re-creator of the war at sea, focuses on two officers, the ship's captain and first lieutenant, but he never allows his reader to forget that it was the average man who suffered and, ultimately, was victorious. The author's later novella, *H.M.S. Marlborough Will Enter Harbour*, though not so detailed, also emphasizes a similar theme. Almost as strong is MacLean's first and perhaps best novel, *H.M.S. Ulysses*, which imaginatively re-creates the events of the doomed convoy PQ-17 to Murmansk in June and July 1942. Callison's *A Flock of Ships* is a gripping story of the British in the South Atlantic. During the war Nevil Shute, far better known today for his Japanese prisoner-of-war saga *A Town like Alice* or the non–World War II classic *On the Beach*, wrote two fine novels centered around the war at sea. *Landfall. A Channel Story* and *Most Secret* tell of the constant battles that took place during the war years between German and British forces in the English Channel. Trevor's *The Big Pickup, a Novel of Dunkirk* is an account of that famous rescue mission by the Royal Navy, well worthy of any reader's attention. Though the plot of *Kleber's Convoy* by Trew is rather run-of-the-mill, its scenes of naval engagement are carefully done. Readers also should not overlook Rayner's *The Enemy Below* and Fullerton's *The Waiting Game* or his more recent *All the Drowning Seas*.

The war in the air, especially the bravery of those few airmen who fought and won the Battle of Britain in late 1940 and early 1941, remains one of the most idealized themes in British war fiction. Here, the Royal

Air Force literally soars. Among the earliest are Adams' two novels about fighter pilots: *Readiness at Dawn* and *We Rendezvous at Ten*. Deighton's more recent *Bomber* brings the war in the air down to intimately personal terms in one attack over occupied Europe, as does Dunmore's *Bomb Run*, published the following year. Robinson's *Piece of Cake*, a work that has already become something of a miniclassic since its publication in 1983, vividly re-creates the earliest days of the war, both in France and then during the Battle of Britain, as RAF airmen come to realize how different modern air combat is from the heady days of 1918. Shute's *Pastoral* also does a fine job of looking at the role that the RAF played in the days up to D-Day. Smith's *633 Squadron* and its subsequent eight sequels, though designed for a popular audience, are carefully researched and historically sound.

British fiction regarding the war on land, whether in the Mediterranean, in the North African desert, in the jungles of Burma or Malaya, or on the European continent after June 1944, is plentiful and often does an excellent job of drawing readers into the action of battle or campaign. Particularly strong are such works as Aldridge's *Signed with Their Honour*, a thoughtful novel about the British Expeditionary Force's losing battle on Crete in the spring of 1941; Majdalany's *Patrol*; Fuller's *Desert Glory*; Andrews' three excellent examinations of the army in Asia: *The Patrol*, set in Burma, *Tattered Battalion*, and *Of Lesser Renown*; Keneally's *Season in Purgatory*; and Baron's *From the City, from the Plough*. Baron's *The Human Kind: A Sequence*, from which the popular Hollywood movie *The Victors* was made, is also well worth reading, as is Bell's *Side-Show*, a thoughtful and, at times, harrowing account of the last days of the war in Burma. White has written nine different adventures focusing on the British soldier during the war, including *The Long Day's Dying*, an intense study of a handful of British soldiers trapped behind German lines. Some reviewers have found fault with the literary quality of White's books, but no one has challenged their authenticity in capturing the feel of battle.

If Waugh's *Sword of Honor* trilogy—*Men at Arms*, *Officers and Gentlemen*, and *Unconditional Surrender*—does not provide as much direct action as do some of the other volumes, it paints, in its own way, almost a grotesque, interrelated landscape of the war in the Middle East and the Balkans. Its antihero, Guy Crouchback, comes to see that neither courage nor a just cause is particularly relevant in a war as bloody as World War II. Perhaps the best of all English novels to come out of the war is Towry's *Trial by Battle*, a study of a young officer who moves inexorably from his garrison in India to his death in the Malayan jungle. Clifford's *A Battle Is Fought to Be Won* is almost as strong with its intense emphasis on life and death on the field of battle. Trevor's *The Killing Ground* is almost documentary in its many pictures of the life of a British tank troop fighting in Normandy in the summer of 1944. Culminating with the virtual annihilation of the

German defenders in the Falaise Pocket in August of that year, it is often brilliant in its ability to catch the real horror of the war. Both Shapiro's *The Sixth of June* and Mason's *The Wind Cannot Read* include overbearing romantic love triangles in the hope of appealing to a wider audience, but each also offers a solid account of combat from a British perspective.

France's overwhelming defeat and humiliation at the hands of seemingly invincible German armies condition nearly every French work of war fiction written since the spring of 1940. Some authors have tried to explain what happened by showing not inept, weak men of the line but treachery and collusion from on high. One of the first to make such an assertion in fictional form was Pozner, less than two years after the occupation of his country by German forces. His *The Edge of the Sword* condemns those authorities in power as incompetent and anxious to save themselves at all costs. What little hope there is for the future lies, he maintains, only in those brave fighting men who are free to rise up again against their oppressors. At the same time, Druon's *The Last Detachment* takes a close look at, and then glorifies, a young group of cadets from the French Cavalry School at Saumer who are ordered into the line on the Loire in May 1940. Only partially trained and unquestionably doomed from the beginning, the youth fight a valiant, but losing, battle in this thoughtfully created, obviously autobiographical work.

The best action-oriented French novels, however, do not deal with that nation's defeat. One of the strongest is Gary's *A European Education*, a work originally issued in its native land as *Forest of Anger*. Set in the forests near Wilno, Poland, at the time of the Battle of Stalingrad on the Eastern front, it is a story of bravery, sudden death, and moral conflict, not of Frenchmen but of partisans fighting destructive battles against overwhelming odds. Perhaps even more unique is Sajer's *The Forgotten Soldier*. Students of the volume debate whether it is fiction or autobiography, and, since Sajer—if that is, indeed, his real name—has chosen not to come forth publicly, we may never know. If it is fiction, as many reviewers believe, it is one of the most detailed and brilliant descriptions of military defeat in contemporary literature. Ironically, however, it is not a soldier in the French army but one in the forces of Nazi Germany who is the "hero" of the account. Sajer (or his fictional hero), the son of a French mother and a German father, joins the German army as a teenager in the summer of 1942 and is almost immediately sent to Russia just after the Stalingrad debacle. There, he experiences the horror of the constant Soviet advances all along the line as he and his comrades are overwhelmed again and again. In the end, he is a survivor, returning to his native France at war's end to vanish from sight. Few books coming out of World War II offer a more evocative view of total defeat than Sajer's large, perceptive study. Certainly, there is no fictional study of the French defeat in 1940 that approaches it in power or in drama.

For the French, there was, with the exception of those men under the leadership of Charles de Gaulle, little participation in the military side of the war until just before the fall of Paris in August 1944. Two for whom this was not true, Roy and Clostermann, flew with the British Royal Air Force, and, at war's end, both powerfully re-created the war they knew. Roy's *The Happy Valley* and his as yet untranslated *Return from Hell* recount bombing missions over Germany. In *The Big Show* and *Flames in the Sky*, Clostermann's "reportage," as he calls it, captures the drama and excitement of aerial combat in much the same way Saint-Exupéry does in his highly praised *Flight to Arras*. The most decorated French flier of World War II and the eventual winner of that nation's *Légion d'Honneur*, he offers his readers an almost "you are there" feeling as he brings them inside the cockpit of his Spitfire on attacks against the German forces then occupying France.

For the most part, however, French novelists desiring to record heroism under fire were forced to turn to those men and women of the Resistance who, far too often, gave their lives in an effort to overthrow their German overlords. One of the best is Kessel's *Army of Shadows*. Though he was emphatic in claiming that what he wrote was neither fiction nor propaganda, it can quickly be seen as both. Deeply involved in the Resistance himself, Kessel creates a series of episodes that allow him to tell the story of the freedom fighters who led the battle to free France after 1940. Some die; others survive to fight another day. While hardly a great novel, it, like the work of authors such as Gary or Druon, paints a clear picture of both time and place and how the fear of being caught, tortured, or killed was omnipresent.

Probably the best novel dealing with life in France during the Occupation, however, is Curtis' *The Forests of the Night*. Looking closely at the Occupation by inventing an imaginary town, Saint-Clar, and peopling it with collaborators and resisters alike, Curtis captures his nation and a people denied the opportunity to fight openly for freedom. Unlike so many other books that praise the forces of the Resistance out of hand, Curtis' fighting men and women are, at times, as prone to be antiheroic as they are demigods of patriotic action. A second volume, *The Side of the Angels*, explores these themes further.

German war fiction, unlike that of either the British or the French, has had to come to grips with that nation's total defeat, a defeat made that much harder by the revelations of the evil of the Nazi regime before May 1945. Every work since the end of hostilities has tried to deal with that agony of loss. Just as other writers did a generation earlier, however, German authors refuse to ascribe their nation's downfall to the German soldier, sailor, or Luftwaffe pilot. Nearly all were brave men who fought to the best of their ability, only to be crushed because of the incompetence and venality of their national leaders. One of the most powerful works to make such a claim, perhaps *the* most powerful, is Plievier's *Stalingrad*, written while that author was in exile in Moscow. Central to the novel is Plievier's description of the horror of war and the appalling and senseless loss of life. Able to interview some of the survivors of the routed Sixth Army in their prisoner-of-war camps and to apply their perceptions to his polished, thoughtful novel, Plievier sees the area around Stalingrad as a vast apocalyptic graveyard, a place worthy of the most hellish scenes in Dante's *Inferno*. Two other books, *Moscow* and *Berlin*, carry the story both backward and forward. In all three volumes, Plievier sees the cause of the average soldier's enormous suffering as Adolf Hitler and his minions. No matter how hard they fight, no matter how brave they may be, the soldiers have, even at the beginning, little hope and then, finally, none at all. It is no accident that the first pages of *Stalingrad* depict a group of German soldiers engaged in a mass burial detail of their comrades because, to Plievier, in the end, war on the Eastern front brings only death and endless rows of frozen or rotting corpses.

Other writers also emphasize the hopelessness of the war, at least after late 1941. Gerlach's *The Forsaken Army, a Novel*, a work about the defeat of the German Sixth Army at Stalingrad, rivals, though perhaps does not surpass, Plievier's brilliant re-creations. Two of Böll's brilliant early novels, *Adam, Where Art Thou?* and *The Train Was on Time*, are also strong. In the latter, a young soldier traveling toward the Eastern front realizes that almost certain death awaits him, and the fatalism with which he accepts his future epitomizes the pathos as well as the irony that most young German writers felt in the postwar years. Similar works abound. Gaiser's *The Last Squadron* vividly presents a group of elite Luftwaffe fighter pilots at the end of the war who, even while having pride in their personal ability as military men, realize the war is lost, and there is nothing that they can do to prevent it. Heinrich's *The Willing Flesh* dramatically makes the same point. Corporal Rolf Steiner, Heinrich's antiheroic central character, and the rifle squad that he leads throughout southern Russia are brave, resourceful, and dedicated. They are also clearly doomed to defeat and death, thanks to the stupidity of their officers, too many of whom, like the egomaniacal Captain Stransky, care more for personal honors than victory. *The Cross of Iron*, as this volume was renamed when it was later published in the United States, is one of the very best military-oriented novels to appear during the past fifty years. All fourteen of Hassel's often powerful volumes about the German army in battle, such as *The Legion of the Damned*, are also, to use his words, "strictly antimilitary." Hassel, a Danish volunteer in the Wehrmacht from 1936 to the end of the war and the winner of the Iron Cross for bravery, once noted about all his novels that he wrote to warn youth against war.

Buchheim's controversial *The Boat* expresses a similar theme. There are glamour, bravery, and honor in the U-boat service, but, ultimately, fear, horror, death, and defeat prove to be the most salient characteristics. Buchheim's captain, no Nazi, fights bravely for his country, yet, in the end, he dies at a moment of seeming triumph, along with many of his men. A final example is Gregor's excellent *The Bridge*. In May 1945 seven young high school boys, all members of their local Hitler Youth Corps, are symbolically sent to guard the bridge that protects their small town from the advancing American army. None of their officers expect them to stay once the enemy gets close. Though all the older men desert rather than fight in the face of the overwhelming odds, the seven teenagers, with blind obedience, stubborn pigheadedness, or both, decide to hold "their" bridge no matter the cost. In doing so, they inflict a bloody toll on the first American GIs whom they encounter. Inexorably, however, all but one of the boys are killed, and the Americans move onward to ultimate victory.

Cynicism and disillusionment run through nearly all German fiction about the war. As they look for some meaning amid the senselessness of the war, German authors such as Kirst in *The Revolt of Gunner Asch, Gunner Asch Goes to War,* and *The Return of Gunner Asch* or Grass in *The Tin Drum* and *Cat and Mouse* find only emptiness. There is no glory in the war, as nearly every character soon discovers.

A fine example can be found in Grund's *Never to Be Free*, which stresses the futility seen by nearly all German authors. In the novel, sixteen-year-old Gustav Briel heads off to man an antiaircraft piece early in 1945. He dreams, as he has since he was a small child, that he will be able to shoot down at least one of the Allied bombers that, day after day, pour death and destruction down from the sky. What he finds, to his dismay, is that war is nothing like what he imagined. Many of his friends die indiscriminately, yet the Nazi leaders appear far more concerned with killing their personal opponents than the Allied enemies. By the time that a bomb splinter permanently disables him six months after his induction, Gustav's father, who is an officer in the Wehrmacht, has been killed, his home has been destroyed, and his only feeling is one of abject failure. Hans Peter Richter, the author of a trilogy of well-received novels dealing with the disintegration of German idealism among its youth, stresses that same theme of despair. In *I Was There*, a volume that spans the first ten years of Nazi rule in Germany only to end in a wave of Russian artillery fire on the Eastern front, he writes: "I am reporting how I lived through that time and what I saw no more. I was there. I was not merely an eyewitness. I believed and I will never believe again" (vii).

Though most German authors of World War II-focused fiction are angry at that conflict's outcome, they rarely do anything to destroy the image of the fighting man in battle. If a good many works do look with disdain on the officer class, the average soldier in the field is praised and, not infrequently, honored. Kluge's *The Battle*, a taut account based on the attack on Stalingrad, repeatedly lauds, directly and indirectly, the traditional men in the lower ranks, as do Hans Werner Richter's *The Odds against Us*, with its setting on the bloody Monte Cassino battlefield, and Meichsner's *Vain Glory*, focusing on a small unit of German soldiers in the Bavarian Alps. In *The Torrents of War*, Sentjurc examines the fate of the German army from the summer of 1943 to its ultimate defeat in the spring of 1945, and his view of the average German soldier is no less praiseworthy.

Interest in the German soldier has not waned as years have passed. Stachow's *If This Be Glory*, for instance, offers powerful descriptions of the Wehrmacht on the Eastern front. Three intensely honest explorations of war from the average German soldier's point of view, Weitzer's *Panzergrenadier*, *Genocide at St-Honor*, and *Sonderkommando*, can be read as almost documentary accounts of the last days before the German army's defeat at the hands of the Allies. Ironically, the two most prolific writers of fiction dealing with German army themes in recent years have been non-Germans. Charles Whiting, writing as Leo Kessel, has produced more than sixty different, carefully crafted, popular novels featuring the exploits of heroic German soldiers. None will disappoint readers who thrive on exciting, realistic accounts. The same can be said about the nine books of Gunther Lutz, the pseudonymous name used by the popular British writer of military fiction, David Williams, which all feature the Wehrmacht in true-to-life stories.

Russian fictive literature about the war years is voluminous, though much of it is little more than badly written, clumsy, communist propaganda. Thankfully, most of the latter has gone untranslated into English. Perhaps more than any other group of writers, Soviet novelists, poets, and dramatists from 1941 to the beginning of the 1990s emphasize the overwhelming costs of the conflict, with its attendant pain and death. If Germany was unquestionably the enemy, the average Russian citizen appears as the true hero, fighting for Mother Russia against overwhelming odds.

Baklanov, one of the best of modern authors, offers an excellent example of such writing in his finely crafted autobiographical novel *Forever Nineteen*. Of the twenty young boys in his high school graduating class, the author notes, he alone survived the war. It is youth like nineteen-year-old Volodya Tretyakov, Baklanov's fictional army lieutenant who is blown to bits at the end of this novel, who must be remembered. "Only in memory are people who no longer exist still alive and still young. I wanted them to come alive when I wrote this book. I wanted people living now to care about them as friends, as family, as brothers," he wrote (viii). Such thoughts underlie not only Baklanov's two other translated World War II related novels, *The Foothold* and *South of the Main Offensive*, but also the works of nearly every other Russian interpreter past and present.

World War II was quickly designated "the Great Patriotic War" in the Soviet Union, and all fiction dealing with that period in history emphasizes an intense patriotism coupled with an even greater hatred for every-thing German. Many novels appear to be almost religious in their delineation of Soviet "good" versus Nazi "evil." Hatred of the nation's common foe soon became endemic as author after author was forced to describe terrible atrocities, more often than not based on actual events from the front lines. In so doing, however, each expressed a demand for unremitting vengeance against an enemy that seemingly was making bar-barism into an art form. In *One Desire*, a shocking tale by Sobolev, an orphaned boy is forced to watch his father, a local commissar, tied to two German tanks and torn apart for the sport of it. In Wasilewska's *Rainbow, a Novel*, a pregnant partisan is forced to run naked through the snow and then, after giving birth in a barn under the watchful eyes of the jeering enemy, is bayoneted and thrown into a hole along with her dead child. The peasant heroes and heroines of Tolstoy's *The Stories of Ivan Sudarev* often suffer at the hands of the Germans, dying at times in equally terrible ways. Nearly forty years after the war's end, similar accounts such as that of the slaughter of a young, pregnant female soldier in Bykov's *Pack of Wolves*, were still being published.

Many Russian, combat-focused novels show effectively the horror of the bitter fighting, in the Soviet army itself and also in its civilian, partisan counterparts behind the lines. Fadeyev's *The Young Guard*, Kazakevich's *Star, a Story*, and his *Two Men on the Steppe* are all solid examples. *Star*, an account of Russian scouts behind German lines, is particularly powerful in capturing life on the Eastern front. Even stronger is Bogomolov's *Ivan*, the story of a twelve-year-old who, after the death of his family at the hands of the Germans, is "adopted" by a unit of regular army soldiers, serving as a spy for them behind enemy lines before he is eventually caught and executed by the Germans. Acclaimed throughout the USSR, *Ivan* was sub-sequently transformed into one of the most highly praised films of Soviet cinema, 1962's *My Name Is Ivan*, directed by Andrei Tarkovsky.

Soviet fictional writing about the days of World War II is overwhelmingly fatalistic. Day to day, death is omnipresent, and most authors make no attempt to blunt the truthfulness of such a fact. Simonov's *Days and Nights*, considered by many in the Soviet Union during the war to be the best book about the battle of Stalingrad, is a gloomy, combat-filled account that stresses the massive bloodletting and death that marked the nation's eventual victory. In Grossman's novel *Life and Fate*, a work that has often been compared, if only because of its mammoth 900 pages, with Leo Tol-stoy's *War and Peace*, the constant defeats of the Soviet military in the months before its great victory at Stalingrad also play a prominent role. Grossman's well-received *The People Are Immortal* and Vassilyev's often mov-ing *The Dawns Are Quiet Here* offer equally morose views.

Sadly, however, most Soviet literature, even the majority of those works that have been tabbed as "best," is authored by men who, in nearly every other country, would be termed simply hack writers. The insistence of the government, in all cases before the end of the Stalinist era and in some others long afterward, that all fiction ought to show Stalin, the Communist Party, and its supporters in only a positive manner resulted in many fictional heroes becoming comic-book types who never lose faith, no matter how great the adversity they face. Bubennov's *The White Birch, a Novel*, for instance, while at times a thoughtful study of the disastrous Russian retreat from Moscow in 1941, spends more time stressing the unique strength of the army's will than its often incompetent leadership. Bubennov was awarded the Stalin Prize for Literature for this novel after its original appearance in the Soviet Union. Polevoy's *A Story about a Real Man* provides another excellent example of propagandized fiction. Based loosely on the real-life biography of Aleksey Mares'ev, a fighter pilot who lost both legs as a result of the war but nonetheless continued his career, the novel almost matter-of-factly recounts any number of air engagements as well as the downing of the hero's plane and his bravery under fire as if they were everyday occurrences.

Most Russian novelists do understand that if bravery is encountered in any war, so, too, are incompetence and failure. Such fine novels as Simonov's *People Are Not Born Soldiers*, which focuses on the slaughter that occurred during the Kharkov counteroffensive of 1942, and Sholokhov's unfinished novel *They Fought for Their Country* offer good examples. If the latter work is nowhere nearly as famous as the author's great *And Quiet Flows the Don*, which pictured the last years of World War I and the days of the Russian civil war, it is still an often vivid picture of life at the front. Perhaps even stronger are Kazakevich's *Spring on the Oder* and Bykov's *The Third Flare* and *The Ordeal*, all of which point out forcibly that dedication and the desire to do the right thing often end only in utter defeat. One reason for this, some Soviet authors stress, was the stupidity of official government leadership. Nekrasov's *Front-line Stalingrad*, written during the war but unpublished for many years because of its criticism of Communist Party blunders, offers one powerful example. It ends not with a celebration of the victory that occurred but with the death of most of one small battalion ordered to capture a nonstrategic location simply to cover up the stupidity of the leaders who planned the unnecessary attack. Another equally insightful view is seen in Simonov's *Victims and Heroes*, an account of blundering so great on the part of party officials that it results not only in the deaths of almost an entire company of men but also in the government's subsequent refusal to allow the survivors to be active participants in future military engagements.

From the moment that the United States joined the Second World War after the Japanese attack on Hawaii in December 1941, American writers of fiction have produced, almost on a regular and unceasing basis, a voluminous number of novels dealing with various aspects of the conflict in both major theaters of war. Though the huge majority of such works are easily ignored and preferably forgotten, the hundreds of sex-saturated, mass-market paperbacks that have appeared regularly continue to fascinate readers who, year after year, buy millions of such volumes. On the other hand, many of the most world-renowned fictional re-creations of the military side of the conflict—Mailer's *The Naked and the Dead,* Jones' *The Thin Red Line,* Wouk's *The Caine Mutiny,* and Shaw's *The Young Lions,* to mention only a handful of the very best—are products of American authors. A wealth of other novels originally published in the United States offer a strong evocation of what the long days of training and the even more bloody days of combat were like.

Though many volumes have little or nothing to do with the fighting side of the conflict, Cozzens' Pulitzer Prize-winning *Guard of Honor,* set at an air base in northern Florida, comes instantly to mind as the best known of the genre written by American authors who deal with the action on the battlefield itself. Harry Brown's finely crafted *A Walk in the Sun,* for example, follows the fate of one veteran infantry platoon in the Italian campaign at Salerno. Assigned to move inland and capture a strategic farmhouse, the soldiers do their job but not without their share of losses from combat fatigue and death. The story is told in a matter-of-fact way; there are no heroes in the novel nor any exciting campaign tactics. More than fifty years after its first printing, Brown's work still remains one of the best studies of young American GIs at war.

Kahn's less well known *Able One Four* is equally successful in revealing an everyday picture of battle. Told from the point of view of a five-member tank crew advancing with the infantry into Germany, it lets the reader get to know the five men, their dreams and desires, but the focus of the story is clearly the action that constantly confronts them. When they encounter two enemy Tiger tanks during their advance, there is no melodramatic, last-minute reprieve from the inevitable death that follows. Jones' *The Thin Red Line* is as intense. The officers and men of Charlie Company struggle to capture a mythical hill on Guadalcanal. Vivid and brutal, the novel is, as Mailer graciously noted, "so broad and true a portrait of combat that it could be used as a textbook at the Infantry school if the Army is any less chicken than it used to be" (in *Cannibals and Christians,* 112). The war in the Pacific as Jones depicts it is anything but melodramatic. Many men die, some live, but all go through the cauldron of combat with its unyielding terror.

Horror is never underplayed in American war fiction. Few novels do a better job of this than Mailer's seminal *The Naked and the Dead.* From the moment that the U.S. Army lands on the mythical Pacific island of Anopopei, Mailer's account offers an overwhelming picture of the sustained fear and physical exhaustion that always accompany combat. It is a brutal view but one so accurately honest that nearly all other subsequent works dealing with American troops at war have been compared to it ever since its first publication. Bowman, in *Beach Red*, his unique blank verse account of another attack on yet another Japanese stronghold in the Pacific, probably comes as close to stating the truth the most simply when he has his narrator comment at the very end of the novel: "You cannot see the war because of all the fighting and you cannot see its ugliness because of the stinking horror and you cannot see humanity because of the people" (121). The Americans win, but not before the narrator and hundreds of others on both sides die horrible, wasted deaths.

If there is an occasional flag-waving speech in a novel or two, Doug Roberts' statement while serving on a supply ship behind the lines in Heggen's excellent *Mr. Roberts* that "the war seems to me . . . immensely worthwhile and I feel a hell of a compulsion to be in it" (163) comes instantly to mind. It is not the United States or even the freedom of the downtrodden peoples of the world for which most GIs in the line appear to fight.

Jones zeroes in on this theme directly in *Whistle*, the unfinished third volume in his war trilogy, which also includes his more famous *From Here to Eternity*. When a young, badly wounded winner of the Bronze Star for gallantry in the Pacific is asked by his Indiana hometown Elks Club to talk about the war to a group of soon-to-depart draftees, he says candidly: "You don't think much about God, or the Four Freedoms, or loving your country, when you're in a fight. . . . Mostly you think about getting your ass out of there, and about killing those other people so they won't kill you. . . . I can safely assure you that the soldier's first responsibility is to stay alive" (168). The fliers in Heller's *Catch 22* are no different. Far from longing to fly to ultimate victory over their German foes, men like the central character, the antiheroic Yossarian, try only to find some way to escape the war with its overwhelming promise of death and destruction. Indeed, if there is one villain, it is not the enemy at all but rather the corrupt or stupid men in command of the American base from which the men fly.

Most novelists were appalled at the animal-like living, killing, and dying faced by the American GI. In novel after novel, death and destruction are portrayed along with the sheer capriciousness of the terror. Brave men too frequently die; cowards often live to fight another day. Sergeant Bing, one of the truly "good" leaders in Heym's *The Crusaders*, is doomed from the start. So, too, is Alan Newcombe in Myrer's classic of the marines in the Pacific, *The Big War*. Even those who survive often suffer catastrophic wounds. In his excellent *Raspberry One*, Ferry, for instance, recounts the fates of the surviving two officers from a three-man navy torpedo bomber's crew after their friend, the plane's pilot, dies trying to land on the deck of their aircraft carrier. They barely manage to escape the wrecked plane before both men are mortally wounded minutes later when a Japanese kamikaze plane crashes into the ship. One's hand is literally torn off his arm; the other suffers a leg wound that leaves him crippled for life.

It is hard not to be cynical in such circumstances. Many novelists repeatedly reflect on the war's wastefulness. Was there really any reason worth fighting or dying for? Probably not, is the usual response. "Fighting a war to fix something works about as good as going to a whorehouse to get rid of the clap" (578), says a minor figure in *The Naked and the Dead.*

In a chapter as short as this, it is impossible to do more than indicate some of the very best American novels that deal with the war. Dodson's *Away All Boats,* Beach's *Run Silent, Run Deep,* Forester's intense *The Good Shepherd,* and, of course, Wouk's *The Caine Mutiny* are all excellent accounts of the war at sea from an American perspective. So, too, are Claggett's two companion volumes, *Surprise Attack* and *Typhoon 1944,* about the naval Battle of Leyte Gulf and its aftermath. Though both are written predominantly with a young adult audience in mind, any reader will find them tensely drawn and exciting.

There are a number of finely crafted stories about the U.S. Army in Europe. Among the best are Calmer's *The Strange Land,* centering on the American attack on the Siegfried Line in the late fall of 1944; Matheson's *The Beardless Warriors,* a study of the Battle of the Bulge; and Wharton's *A Midnight Clear.* In his *Soldiers of '44,* McGivern also looks at the Battle of the Bulge not only through the eyes of its GI participants but also from the perspective of a group of German infantrymen who are attempting to destroy their American foes. Olson's *The Iron Foxhole* closely follows a tank crew, most of whom are destined to die, during a three-day period in late 1944, as they and their fellows try to break through German lines in eastern France. Woodruff's little-known *Vessel of Sadness* is a powerful account of the Anzio campaign, and Gaffney's *A World of Good* takes readers into battle with a small group of paratroopers. Though Joe David Brown's *Kings Go Forth* gets sidetracked with several minor subplots involving a romantic triangle laced with racial bigotry, his scenes of combat between attacking American GIs and the German defenders in Italy and southern France are among the best available.

The view from the Pacific theater is equally strong, whether depicted in writings about U.S. Marines island-hopping their way across that ocean or about army troops fighting in such places as China or Burma. Besides Mailer's perceptive *The Naked and the Dead* or Jones' several volumes dealing with the war against the Japanese, not to be missed are such other solid tales as Chamales' *Never So Few,* Cochrell's *Barren Beaches of Hell,* written by a former marine officer in the Pacific and offering a vivid picture of the Tarawa campaign, and Uris' overly praised *Battle Cry.*

American authors of military fiction have always been fascinated by the brave men who, day after day, flew in the air over Occupied Europe with the famous Eighth Air Force or other less well known groups. Falstein's *Face of a Hero*, which zeroes in on the life of one such B-24 crew, is particularly powerful. Falstein allows the tension to mount as he follows the fate of the men as, day after day, they return to the sky over German targets. Desmond Taylor, one of the most astute observers of American war fiction, has noted that it is not only one of the best works about the combat over Europe but, in many ways, also one of the singularly best about any aspect of World War II. Hersey's *The War Lover*, Killens' *And Then We Heard the Thunder* (a unique look at the many African-American airmen often ignored in most conventional novels), and Shepard's *Paper Doll* also deal in thoughtful ways with the American side of the conflict. So, too, does Harkins' long-forgotten juvenile tale *Bomber Pilot*, one of the few studies written for young adults before 1945 that picture with any honesty the war in the air. Few works of quality focus readers' attentions to the Pacific theater of operations. One that does, Skidmore's *Valley of the Sky*, is a tensely exciting account of one bomber crew's flights to attack the Japanese. When it first appeared in 1944, it was widely praised by many critics. Today, though it is rarely read, it should be.

Mazer's *The Last Mission*, a novel in which the central character, fifteen-year-old Jack Raab, lies about his age so that he can enlist in the U.S. Army Air Corps and participate in the fight against Nazi tyranny, is also worthy of examination. Shot down in the last weeks of April 1945, the only survivor of his B-17, the young boy is captured by German soldiers and sent for the duration of the war to a prison camp in Czechoslovakia. Some months later, back in the Bronx but still unable to forget how his best friend's blood and brains had splattered over his flight jacket, Jack tells his former high school classmates simply: "War is one stupid thing after another. [It's] not like the movies. It's not fun and songs. It's not about heroes. It's about awful, sad things" (188). Few authors, irrespective of their nationality, have summed up the main theme of the majority of western World War II–related combat fiction more succinctly.

BIBLIOGRAPHY

Adam, Ronald. *Readiness at Dawn*. London: Tandem, 1970, 1941.

———. *We Rendezvous at Ten*. London: Tandem, 1970, 1942.

Aldridge, James. *Signed with Their Honour*. London: Michael Joseph, 1942; Boston: Little, Brown, 1942.

Andrews, Laurie. *Of Lesser Renown*. London: Cassell, 1958.

———. *The Patrol*. London: Cassell, 1956. Published in the United States as *Deadly Patrol*. New York: David McKay, 1956.

———. *Tattered Battalion*. London: Cassell, 1957.

Baklanov, Grigory. *The Foothold*. Translated by R. Ainsztein. London: Chapman and Hall, 1962; Philadelphia: Dufour Editions, 1964.

————. *Forever Nineteen.* Translated by Antonina W. Bouis. New York: Lippincott, 1989.

————. *South of the Main Offensive.* Translated by R. Ainsztein. London: Chapman and Hall, 1963; Philadelphia: Dufour Editions, 1963.

Baron, Alexander [Joseph Alec Bernstein]. *From the City, from the Plough.* London: Cape, 1948; New York: I. Washburn, 1949.

————. *The Human Kind: A Sequence.* London: Cape, 1953; New York: I. Washburn, 1953.

Beach, Edward. *Run Silent, Run Deep.* New York: Holt, 1955; London: Allan Wingate, 1955.

Bell, Gerald. *Side-Show.* London: F. Muller, 1953.

Blake [Ronald Adams]. *Readiness at Dawn.* London: Gollancz, 1941.

————. *We Rendezvous at Ten.* London: Gollancz, 1942.

Bogomolov, Vladimir. *Ivan.* Translated by Bernard Isaacs. In *Three War Stories.* Moscow: Foreign Languages Publishing House, 1963.

Böll, Heinrich. *Adam, Where Art Thou?* Translated by Mervyn Savill. London: Arco, 1955; New York: Criterion, 1955.

————. *The Train Was on Time.* Translated by Richard Graves. London: Arco, 1956; New York: Criterion, 1956.

Boule, Pierre. *The Bridge on the River Kwai.* Translated by Xan Fielding. London: Secker and Warburg, 1954; New York: Grosset and Dunlap, 1954.

Bowman, Peter. *Beach Red.* New York: Random House, 1945.

Brown, Harry [Peter M'Nab]. *A Walk in the Sun.* New York: Alfred A. Knopf, 1944; London: Secker and Warburg, 1944.

Brown, Joe David. *Kings Go Forth.* New York: William Morrow, 1956.

Bubennov, Mikhail. *The White Birch, a Novel.* Translated by Leonard Stoklitsky. Moscow: Foreign Languages Publishing House, 1949.

Buchheim, Lothar-Günther. *U-Boat.* Translated by Maxwell Brownjohn. London: Collins, 1975. Published in the United States as *The Boat.* Translated by Denver Lindley and Helen Lindley. New York: Alfred A. Knopf, 1975.

Bykov, Vasil. *The Ordeal.* Translated by Gordon Clough. London: Bodley Head, 1972, New York: Dutton, 1972.

————. *Pack of Wolves.* Translated by Lynn Solotaroff. New York: Thomas Y. Crowell, 1981.

————. *The Third Flare.* Translated by Robert Daglish. In *Three War Stories.* Moscow: Foreign Languages Publishing House, 1963.

Callison, Brian. *A Flock of Ships.* London: Collins, 1970; New York: Putnam's, 1970.

Calmer, Ned. *The Strange Land.* New York: Scribner's, 1950.

Chamales, Tom. *Never So Few.* New York: Scribner's, 1957.

Claggett, John. *Surprise Attack.* New York: Julian Messner, 1968.

————. *Typhoon 1944.* New York: Julian Messner, 1970.

Clavell, James. *King Rat.* Boston: Little, Brown, 1962; London: M. Joseph, 1963.

Clifford, Francis [Arthur Leonard Bell Thompson]. *A Battle Is Fought to Be Won.* London: Hamish Hamilton, 1960; New York: Coward-McCann, 1961.

Clostermann, Pierre. *The Big Show: Some Experiences of a French Fighter Pilot in the R.A.F.* Translated by Oliver Berthoud. London: Chatto and Windus, 1951; New York: Random House, 1961.

———. *Flames in the Sky*. Translated by Oliver Berthoud. London: Chatto and Windus, 1954.

Cochrell, Boyd. *The Barren Beaches of Hell*. New York: Holt, 1959. Published in Great Britain as *Beaches of Hell*. London: Deutsch, 1960.

Cozzens, James Gould. *Guard of Honor*. New York: Harcourt, Brace, and World, 1948.

Curtis, Jean Louis. *The Forests of the Night*. Translated by Nora Wydenbruck. London: John Lehmann, 1950; New York: G. P. Putnam's Sons, 1951.

———. *The Side of the Angels*. Translated by Humphrey Hare. London: Seeker and Warburg, 1956; New York: Putnam's, 1956.

Deighton, Len. *Bomber: Events Relating to the Last Flight of an R.A.F. Bomber over Germany on the Night of June 31, 1943*. London: Jonathan Cape, 1970; New York: Random House, 1970.

Dodson, Kenneth. *Away All Boats, a Novel*. Boston: Little, Brown, 1954.

Druon, Maurice [Maurice Kessel]. *The Last Detachment: The Cadets of Saumur, 1940; A Novel*. Translated by Humphrey Wire. London: Hart-Davis, 1946.

Dunmore, Spencer. *Bomb Run*. London: Peter Davies, 1971; New York: Morrow, 1971.

Fadeyev, Alekandr. *The Young Guard, a Novel*. Translated by Violett Dutt. Moscow: Foreign Languages Publishing House, 1958.

Falstein, Louis. *Face of a Hero*. New York: Harcourt, Brace, 1950. Published in Great Britain as *The Sky Is a Lonely Place, a Novel*. London: Rupert Hart Davis, 1951.

Ferry, Charles. *Raspberry One*. Boston: Houghton Mifflin, 1983.

Forester, C. S. *The Good Shepherd*. Boston: Little, Brown, 1955; London: Michael Joseph, 1955.

Fuller, John. *Desert Glory*. London: John Spencer, 1960.

Fullerton, Alexander. *All the Drowning Seas*. London: M. Joseph, 1981.

———. *The Waiting Game, a Novel*. London: Peter Davies, 1961; New York: I. Washburn, 1962.

Gaffney, Robert. *A World of Good*. New York: Dial, 1970.

Gaiser, Gerd. *The Last Squadron*. Translated by Paul Findlay. New York: Pantheon, 1956. Published in Great Britain as *The Falling Leaf*. London: Collins, 1956.

Gary, Romain [Romain Kassef]. *A European Education*. New York: Simon and Schuster, 1960. Published in Great Britain as *Nothing Important Ever Dies*. London: Cresset, 1960.

Gerlach, Heinrich. *The Forsaken Army, a Novel*. Translated by Richard Graves. London: Weidenfeld and Nicolson, 1958; New York: Harper and Brothers, 1958.

Grass, Günter. *Cat and Mouse*. Translated by Ralph Manheim. New York: Harcourt, Brace, and World, 1963.

———. *The Tin Drum*. Translated by Ralph Mannheim. New York: Pantheon, 1963.

Gregor, Manfred. *The Bridge*. Translated by Robert S. Rosen. New York: Random House, 1960.

Grossman, Vasilii. *Life and Fate*. Translated by Robert Chandler. London: Collins, Harvill, 1985; New York: Harper and Row, 1986.

———. *The People Are Immortal*. Translated by Elizabeth Donnelly. Moscow: Foreign Languages Publishing House, 1943; London: Hutchinson, 1943. Published in the United States as *No Beautiful Nights*. Adapted by Leo Lerrman. New York: J. Messner, 1944.

Grund, Joseph. *Never to Be Free.* Translated by Lucile Harrington. Boston: Little, Brown, 1970.

Harkins, Philip. *Bomber Pilot.* New York: Harcourt, Brace, 1944.

Hassel, Sven [Børge Willie Arbing]. *The Legion of the Damned.* Translated by Maurice Michael. London: Allen and Unwin, 1957; New York: Farrar, Straus, and Giroux, 1957.

Heggen, Thomas. *Mr. Roberts.* Boston: Houghton Mifflin, 1946.

Heinrich, Willi. *The Willing Flesh.* Translated by R. C. Winston. London: Weidenfeld and Nicolson, 1956. Published in the United States as *The Cross of Iron.* Indianapolis: Bobbs-Merrill, 1956.

Heller, Joseph. *Catch 22, a Novel.* New York: Simon and Schuster, 1961; London: Jonathan Cape, 1962.

Hersey, John. *The War Lover.* New York: Knopf, 1959; London: Hamish Hamilton, 1959.

Heym, Stefan. *The Crusaders.* Boston: Little, Brown, 1948.

Holsinger, M. Paul. *The Ways of War: The Era of World War II in Children's and Young Adult Fiction.* Metuchen, NJ: Scarecrow, 1995.

Jones, James. *From Here to Eternity.* New York: Charles Scribner's Sons, 1951.

———. *The Thin Red Line.* New York: Charles Scribner's Sons, 1962.

———. *Whistle.* New York: Delacorte, 1978.

Kahn, Lawrence. *Able One Four.* Denver: Alan Swallow, 1952.

Kazakevich, Emanuil. *Spring on the Oder, a Novel in Three Parts.* Moscow: Foreign Languages Publishing House, 1953.

———. *Star, a Story.* Translated by Leonard Stoklitsky. Moscow: Foreign Languages Publishing House, 1950. Also in *Soviet War Stories: A Selection of the Best.* Moscow: Raduga, 1990.

———. *Two Men in the Steppe.* Moscow: Progress, 1978.

Keneally, Thomas. *Season in Purgatory.* London: Collins, 1976; New York: Harcourt Brace Jovanovich, 1977.

Kessel, Joseph. *Army of Shadows.* Translated by Haakon Chevalier. London: Cresset, 1944; New York: Alfred A. Knopf, 1944.

Killens, John Oliver. *And Then We Heard the Thunder.* New York: Alfred A. Knopf, 1962.

Kirst, Hans Helmut. *Gunner Asch Goes to War: Zero Eight Fifteen, II, a Novel.* Translated by Robert Kee. London: Weidenfeld and Nicolson, 1956. Published in the United States as *Forward, Gunner Asch!* Boston: Little, Brown, 1956.

———. *The Return of Gunner Asch.* Translated by Robert Kee. London: Weidenfeld and Nicolson, 1957; Boston: Little, Brown, 1957.

———. *The Revolt of Gunner Asch.* Translated by Robert Kee. London: Weidenfeld and Nicolson, 1955; Boston: Little, Brown, 1955.

Klein, Holger, John Flowers, and Eric Herberger, eds. *The Second World War in Fiction.* London: Macmillan, 1984.

Kluge, Alexander. *The Battle.* Translated by Leila Vennewitz. New York: McGraw-Hill, 1967.

MacLean, Alistair. *H.M.S. Ulysses.* London: Collins, 1955; Garden City, NY: Doubleday, 1956.

Mailer, Norman. *Cannibals and Christians.* New York: Dial, 1966.

———. *The Naked and the Dead.* New York: Rinehart, 1948.

Majdalany, Fred. *Patrol.* London: Longmans Green, 1953; Boston: Houghton Mifflin, 1953.

Mason, Richard. *The Wind Cannot Read, a Novel.* London: Hodder and Stoughton, 1947.

Matheson, Richard. *The Beardless Warriors.* Boston: Little, Brown, 1960.

Mazer, Harry. *The Last Mission.* New York: Delacorte, 1979.

McGivern, William. *Soldiers of '44.* New York: Arbor House, 1979.

Meichsner, Dieter. *Vain Glory.* Translated by Charlotte Lloyd and Albert Lloyd. London: Putnam, 1953; New York: Funk and Wagnalls, 1953.

Monsarrat, Nicholas. *The Cruel Sea.* London: Cassell, 1951; New York: Alfred A. Knopf, 1952.

———. *H.M.S. Marlborough Will Enter Harbour.* London: Cassell, 1947; New York: Ballantine, 1947.

Myrer, Anton. *The Big War.* New York: Appleton-Century-Crofts, 1957; London: Hamish Hamilton, 1957.

Nekrasov, Viktor. *Front-Line Stalingrad.* Translated by David Floyd. London: Collins and Harvill, 1962.

Olson, Gene. *The Iron Foxhole.* Philadelphia: Westminster, 1968.

Paris, Michael. *The Novels of World War Two: An Annotated Bibliography of World War Two Fiction.* London: Library Association, 1990.

Plievier, Theodor. *Berlin.* Translated by Louis Hagen and Vivian Milroy. London: Hammond, Hammond, 1956; Garden City, NY: Doubleday, 1957.

———. *Moscow.* Translated by Stuart Hood. London: F. Muller, 1953; Garden City, NY: Doubleday, 1954.

———. *Stalingrad.* Translated by H. Langmead Robinson. London: Athenaeum, 1948; New York: Appleton, 1948.

Polevoy, Boris [Boris Kampov]. *A Story about a Real Man.* Translated by J. Fineberg. Moscow: Foreign Languages Publishing House, 1949.

Pozner, Vladimir. *The Edge of the Sword.* Translated by Haakon Chevalier. New York: Modern Age, 1942.

Rayner, D. A. *The Enemy Below.* London: Collins, 1956; New York: Holt, 1957.

Reeman, Douglas. *A Prayer for the Ship.* London: Jarrolds, 1958.

———. *Rendezvous South Atlantic.* London: Huthinson, 1972; New York: Putnam's, 1972.

———. *A Ship Must Die.* London: Hutchinson, 1979; New York: William Morrow, 1979.

Richter, Hans Peter. *I Was There.* Translated by Edite Kroll. New York: Holt, Rinehart, and Winston, 1972.

Richter, Hans Werner. *The Odds against Us.* Translated by Robert Kee. London: MacGibbon and Kee, 1950. Published in the United States as *Beyond Defeat.* New York: G. P. Putnam's Sons, 1950.

Robinson, Derek. *Piece of Cake.* London: Hamish Hamilton, 1983.

Roy, Jules. *The Happy Valley.* Translated by Edward Owen Marsh. London: Gollancz, 1952.

Saint-Exupery, Antoine de. *Flight to Arras.* Translated by Lewis Galantiere. New York: Reynal and Hitchcock, 1942; New York: Harcourt, Brace, and World, 1942.

Sajer, Guy. *The Forgotten Soldier.* Translated by Lily Emmet. New York: Harper and Row, 1971.

Sentjurc, Igor. *The Torrents of War.* Translated by Eric Mosbacher. New York: David McKay, 1962. Published in Great Britain as *Thou Shall Not Kill.* London: Constable, 1963.

Shapiro, Lionel [Sebastian Berk]. *The Sixth of June.* Garden City, NY: Doubleday, 1955.

Shaw, Irwin. *The Young Lions.* New York: Random House, 1948; London: Jonathan Cape, 1949.

Shepard, Jim. *Paper Doll.* New York: Alfred A. Knopf, 1986.

Sholokhov, Mikhail. *They Fought for Their Country.* Moscow: Raduga, 1984.

Shute, Nevil [Nevil Shute Norway]. *Landfall. A Channel Story.* London: Heinemann, 1940; New York: William Morrow, 1940.

———. *Most Secret.* London: Heinemann, 1945; New York: William Morrow, 1945.

———. *On the Beach.* New York: William Morrow, 1957.

———. *Pastoral.* London: Heinemann, 1944; New York: William Morrow, 1944.

———. *A Town like Alice.* London: Heinemann, 1950. Published in the United States as *The Legacy.* New York: William Morrow, 1950.

Simonov, Konstantin. *Days and Nights.* Translated by Joseph Barnes. London: Hutchinson International Authors, 1945; New York: Simon and Schuster, 1945.

———. *People Are Not Born Soldiers.* In *Soviet War Stories.* London: Hutchinson, 1944.

———. *Victims and Heroes.* Translated by R. Ainsztein. London: Hutchinson, 1962. Published in the United States as *The Living and the Dead.* Garden City, NY: Doubleday, 1962.

Skidmore, Hobert Douglas. *Valley of the Sky.* Boston: Houghton Mifflin, 1944.

Smith, Frederick E. *633 Squadron.* London: Hutchinson, 1956.

Smith, Myron J. *War Story Guide: An Annotated Bibliography of Military Fiction.* Metuchen, NJ: Scarecrow, 1980.

Sobolev, Leonid. *One Desire.* Moscow: Foreign Languages Publishing House, 1942.

Stachow, Hasso. *If This Be Glory.* Translated by J. Maxwell Brownjohn. Garden City, NY: Doubleday, 1982.

Taylor, Desmond. *The Novels of World War II: An Annotated Bibliography.* New York: Garland, 1993.

Tolstoy, Alekesy. *The Stories of Ivan Sudarev.* In *My Country: Articles and Stories of the Great Patriotic War of the Soviet Union.* London: Hutchinson, 1943; Moscow: Foreign Languages Publishing House, 1983.

Towry, Peter [David Piper]. *Trial by Battle.* London: Hutchinson, 1959; New York: Chilmark, 1959.

Trevor, Elleston [Trevor Dudley-Smith]. *The Big Pickup, a Novel of Dunkirk.* London: Heinemann, 1955; New York: Macmillan, 1955.

———. *The Killing Ground.* London: Heinemann, 1956; New York: Macmillan, 1957.

Trew, Anthony. *Kleber's Convoy.* New York: St. Martin's, 1973; London: Collins, 1974.

Uris, Leon. *Battle Cry.* New York: Putnam's, 1953; London: Alan Wingate, 1953.

Vassilyev, Boris. *The Dawns Are Quiet Here.* Translated by Hilda Perham and Natasha Johnston. In *Soviet War Stories: A Selection of the Best.* Moscow: Raduga, 1990.

Wasilewska, Wanda. *Rainbow, a Novel.* Translated by George Hanna and Elizabeth Donnelly. Moscow: Foreign Languages Publishing House, 1943. Translated by Edith Bone. London: Hutchinson, 1943; New York: Simon and Schuster, 1944.

Waugh, Evelyn. *Men at Arms, a Novel.* London: Chapman and Hall, 1952; Boston: Little, Brown, 1952.

———. *Officers and Gentlemen.* London: Chapman and Hall, 1955; Boston: Little, Brown, 1955.

———. *Unconditional Surrender.* London: Chapman and Hall, 1961. Published in the United States as *The End of the Battle.* Boston: Little, Brown, 1962.

Weitzer, Horst. *Genocide at St-Honor.* Translated by George Hirst. London: New English Library, 1981.

———. *Panzergrenadier.* Translated by George Hirst. London: New English Library, 1981.

———. *Sonderkommando.* Translated by George Hirst. London: New English Library, 1982.

Wharton, William. *A Midnight Clear.* New York: Alfred A. Knopf, 1982.

White, Alan. *The Long Day's Dying.* London: Barrie and Jenkins, 1965. Published in the United States as *Death Finds the Day.* New York: Harcourt, Brace, and World, 1965.

Woodruff, William. *Vessel of Sadness.* Gainesville, FL: Kallman, 1969.

Wouk, Herman. *The Caine Mutiny, a Novel of World War II.* Garden City, NY: Doubleday, 1951; London: Jonathan Cape, 1952.

19   Lines (In)Formation: Anglophone Poetry in the Second World War

Jonathan W. Bolton

"War is the enemy of creative activity," wrote Cyril Connolly in May 1940, "because the military virtues are in conflict with the creative, and because it is impossible in wartime for most people to concentrate on the values of literature and art" ("Comment," 5). Time would prove Connolly wrong.

The Second World War was certainly a catalyst for literary activity, but it has taken considerable time for the poetry written about the war to be integrated into the literary canon. Consequently, most of the scholarly work in this field has been engaged primarily in acts of recovery, sifting through a mass of negligible verse in order to uncover works of value.

Such efforts characterize most of the major studies of the poetry in the war, such as Shires' *British Poetry of the Second World War* and Scannell's *Not without Glory: Poets of the Second World War*, which contain chapters on individual poets and groups of poets, and historical surveys such as Tolley's *The Poetry of the Forties*, Hewison's *Under Siege: Literary Life in London, 1939–1945*, and most recently, Bergonzi's *Wartime and Aftermath: English Literature and Its Background 1939–1960*. Though there is a slight disagreement among these critics concerning what is of lasting value, they do agree that the reason for the neglect of the poetry of the Second World War stems from two historical factors: first, the poetry written during the war has been viewed through what Shires calls "the distorted lenses of the 1950s poets and critics," who were bent on establishing the importance of their own work (xiii); second, the poetry of World War II has been unfairly judged to be second-rate according to standards of war poetry established in the Great War. Therefore, nearly all of the aforementioned scholars have tended to highlight the different historical and aesthetic contexts between the two wars in order to judge the poetry of the Second World War according to its own imperatives.

Unlike for the Great War, the experience of the Second World War was not confined to the fighting man in the trenches; rather, its reverberations were felt by soldier and civilian alike, and conflict extended to all corners of the globe. As Linda Shires has noted, "In the Second World War, there were various kinds of war poetry: poetry of battles, poetry of exile, anti-war poetry, and much verse written against the background of war, but not necessarily about the war" (56). Due to the nature of the war, most scholars agreed to broaden genre distinctions relating to war poetry, thereby admitting poetry written by civilian poets as well as those in uniform.

In the United States, the literary climate was very different. Less encumbered than British poets by a legacy of Great War poetry, American writers such as Randall Jarrell and Karl Shapiro were able to break new ground and to situate war poetry firmly in the American idiom. As poet and critic Vernon Scannell put it in *Not without Glory*, "[T]he first World War had not become for them a powerful tragic myth but was, rather, a national triumph, one episode in a saga of success" (173).

This cursory account of the poetry of the Second World War and the growing body of scholarly work devoted to it no doubt omits some work that is valuable and noteworthy. But the aim is to give a general impression of the poetry that was written, identify the major figures behind this work, and highlight some of the prevailing themes, images, and concerns that have been noted by scholars.

BRITISH POETRY

The Battle of Britain, which began in July 1940, officially brought the devastation of war home to Britain. Poets tended to respond to these events in one of two ways: either they disengaged themselves from political affairs and withdrew into the private realm of self and imagination, or they explored the religious and psychological implications of humanity at war with itself. In *Thirties and After*, Stephen Spender recalled the "religious mood" of the period and his sense of the "phoenix-like rebirth of the English spirit" (72–73). In many ways, this religious feeling originated with W. B. Yeats and his notion of "tragic joy." In "Lapis Lazuli" (1938), Yeats had written, "All things fall and are built again/ And those who build them are gay" (160), and many poets held a similar faith in regeneration. In "East Coker," T. S. Eliot wrote that "to be restored, our sickness must grow worse" (188). A similar feeling of hope amid despair is expressed in David Gascoyne's "A Wartime Dawn," particularly his image of peeling back a blackout cloth to reveal "crack-of-dawn's first glimmer" (128), and Edith Sitwell's "Still Falls the Rain" concludes with a promise of redemption.

For other poets, particularly the leftist poets of the 1930s who were disillusioned by the defeat of the Republican Army in Spain, W. H. Auden, Louis MacNeice, Stephen Spender, and C. Day Lewis, the future was less hopeful. Despite the outcome in Spain, these poets continued to write about the poet's function in society, particularly during wartime. W. H. Auden published three volumes of verse and composed two of his most famous poems, "In Memory of W. B. Yeats" and "September 1, 1939," in which he urged fellow poets to "show an affirming flame" (89). Stephen Spender wrote a number of fine war poems, such as "To Poets and Airmen" and "Rejoice in the Abyss." One of the most quoted poems of the war, "Where Are the War Poets?" which advises poets "to defend the bad against the worse" (335), came from the pen of C. Day Lewis. Louis MacNeice also made a considerable contribution to the body of war poetry, including *Autumn Journal* (1939), a personal account of his mood and feelings at the outset of the war, "Brother Fire," a powerful statement on humanity's self-destructive impulse, and "Epitaph for Liberal Poets," in which he hopes that poets may "Leave behind certain frozen words/ Which someday, though not certainly, may melt" (97). Most of the scholarly work on the Auden generation focuses on their poetry of political engagement in the 1930s, and very little attention has been paid to their collective response to the war.

Following Auden's departure for America in 1939, a door was opened for a new movement of poets, known as the New Apocalypse, led by J. F. Hendry and Henry Treece, who felt that the poetry of Auden and company had neglected the private life of the individual. Through a series of anthologies, *The New Apocalypse* (1939), *The White Horseman* (1941), and *The Crown and the Sickle* (1943), the Apocalyptics became prominent in Britain during the war, though most scholars now agree that they produced little work of lasting value. However, the Apocalyptics' icon, Dylan Thomas, though not officially a member of the group, wrote some fine poems on victims of the London Blitz, such as "Ceremony after a Fire Raid," "Among Those Killed in the Dawn Raid Was a Man Aged a Hundred," and "A Refusal to Mourn the Death, by Fire, of a Child in London," in which he concludes that "After the first death, there is no other" (192). Thomas' elegy to end all elegies, however, did not divert other poets from the expression of grief, and some of the most memorable war poetry was written to memorialize the dead, such as Auden's "In Memory of Sigmund Freud," Louis MacNeice's "The Casualty," which eulogizes his boyhood friend, Graham Shephard, whose ship was torpedoed in the North Atlantic, G. S. Fraser's "S.S. City of Benares," written in memory of the drowned passengers, and Sidney Keyes' eloquent "Elegy (In Memorium SKK)."

During the first years of the war, when a poet in the mold of Wilfred Owen or Rupert Brooke failed to materialize, the English public began to wonder, Where are the war poets? The answer, as scholarship has now revealed, is that they were in Burma, East Africa, Australia, the Balkans, and Cairo. That is, the poets who experienced the war firsthand, such archetypal "soldier-poets" as Keith Douglas, Alun Lewis, Charles Causley, Roy Fuller, and Henry Reed, were far removed from the literary establishment in London. In addition, most of these poets' work was not published until after the war, and public recognition was slow in coming. Initially, for these poets, the problem was not so much obscurity as a sense of belatedness. As Keith Douglas saw it, "The hardships, pain and boredom; the behavior of the living and the appearance of the dead, were so accurately described by the poets of the Great War that everyday on the battlefields . . . their poems are illustrated" (*The Complete Poems*, 119–120). In *Poets of the 1939–1945 War*, Currey argues, "Nearly all the good poetry of the Second War sprang from the Siegfried Sassoon-Wilfred Owen line of succession"(7). Consequently, one often encounters allusions to the work of their predecessors, as in Alun Lewis' homage to his Welsh countryman, Edward Thomas, in "All Day It Has Rained," and Keith Douglas' reference in "Desert Flowers" to the blood-red poppies of Isaac Rosenberg's "Break of Day in the Trenches."

Despite the influence of the Great War antecedents, however, both Lewis and Douglas broke new ground and have emerged as the two dominant and most widely anthologized poets of the war generation. Alun Lewis served in the Royal Corps of Engineers in Bombay and at the Burmese front, where he accidentally shot and killed himself in 1944. His first book of poetry, *Raiders' Dawn* (1942), achieved some notoriety in England, with poems such as "Infantry" sating the public's desire for descriptions of life on the front, but Lewis never saw any real action, and much of his poetry concerns life among the Indian peasantry. Pikoulis' *Alun Lewis: A Life* and an edition of his writings have revived interest in Lewis' work. Unlike Lewis, Douglas saw extensive action as a tank commander in the Eighth Army and participated in major battles at El Alamein and Enfidaville. Hence, his poetry and war memoir, *Alamein to Zem Zem*, contain some of the most vivid descriptions of war casualties and of the landscape of the desert war. Douglas' reputation has grown steadily since the publication of his *Selected Poems* (1964), and his poems "How to Kill," "Vergissmeinicht," "Simplify Me When I'm Dead," and "Cairo Jag" are now recognized as major war poems. The earlier collection of his work was expanded and republished in 1978 as *Keith Douglas: The Complete Poems*, edited by Graham, who is also the author of *Keith Douglas: A Biography*. *Keith Douglas: A Study* by Scammell appeared in 1988. After surviving the North African campaign, Douglas was killed during a reconnaissance mission near St. Pierre, France, on 9 June 1944, making him the closest thing the Second World War had to a "poet-martyr" in the mold of Owen and Brooke.

Douglas was one of many poets who were either stationed in, or exiled to, Egypt during the war, and a number of his poems appeared in the verse periodical *Personal Landscape*, which also published work by Lawrence Durrell, Bernard Spencer, and the Greek Nobelist George Seferis. The proximity of the desert war and the threat of Rommel's Afrika Korps, the mobilization of troops in and out of Cairo, and the exotic flavor of Levantine life are captured in a collection of poetry from their magazine, *Personal Landscape: An Anthology of Exile* (1945), edited by Durrell, Fedden, and Spencer, one of the best anthologies to come out of the war. A fascinating account of the artistic and personal relations among these Cairo poets and an evaluation of their work can be found in Bowen's *Many Histories Deep*.

Whereas Keith Douglas complained in his letters that he had little time in which to write during the North African campaign, for poets in the navy, such as Roy Fuller, Charles Causley, and Henry Reed, the problem was more one of relieving the boredom of long hours at sea. Causley's "Chief Petty Officer" deals with the monotony of life and scenery at sea, which contrasts sharply with the excitement of disembarking at exotic ports. In "Demobilisation Leave" he compares the dreariness of his native Cornwall to the creative stimuli of foreign settings: "I have seen the white tiger/ Imagination, / In the Douanier Rousseau forest" (29), and in "H.M.S. Eclipse Approaches Freetown," he writes of "The hills rich and bursting with the brown and orange of Gaugin" (23). Causley's war poems were gathered together in *Farewell, Aggie Weston* (1951) and have subsequently received much critical acclaim.

Roy Fuller spent much of the war in Kenya working as a radar technician. Before shipping out to Africa, Fuller published some of the finest poems about life in London during the Blitz in *The Middle of a War* (1942), many of which concern the dilemma of being a pacifist compelled to write about the war. In "Autumn 1941," he wrote that "the only truth is the truth of graves and mirrors" (48), and in "Battersea: After Dunkirk," he senses that "there is nothing to say/Or do, except to watch disintegration" (35). In Fuller, one encounters a poet torn between action and commitment, on one hand, and ironic detachment on the other, as in "Soliloquy during an Air-Raid." Though Fuller produced a number of quality poems about the war and garnered a considerable postwar reputation, his poetry has received little scholarly attention.

Unlike Fuller, Henry Reed is chiefly known as a war poet and as the author of a single poem, "Lessons of War." Reed served in the Royal Army Ordnance Corp and later with Naval Intelligence, where he would occasionally entertain comrades by imitating senior officers. In one instance, he recited passages from an instruction manual for new recruits in the manner of a drill sergeant known for his flights of fancy. From this idle pantomime came perhaps *the* most widely anthologized poem of the Second World War, "Naming of Parts," from his *Map of Verona*, in which the actions of the bumbling recruits and the beauty of spring are commingled:

> The early bees are assaulting and fumbling the flowers;
> They call it easing the Spring. (49)

After his debut in *Map of Verona* (1947), little of his work was published until his *Collected Poems*, edited and with an introduction by Jon Stallworthy, appeared posthumously in 1991.

AMERICAN POETRY

American poetry of the Second World War emerges from a very different tradition from that of the British. Though most American war poets were familiar with the work of British poets of the Great War, they were not pressured to live up to an established precedent. Surprisingly, American poetry of World War II has received very little scholarly attention compared to that of English poets, not so much because it constitutes a lesser achievement but because most who produced the important war poetry were either peacetime poets commenting on the war, such as Marianne Moore, Wallace Stevens, and Robert Frost, or servicemen who survived the war and went on to achieve recognition for their work on other themes. In addition, if the British poetry of the Second World War was overshadowed by that of its Great War precursors, American war poetry has been subsequently eclipsed by that of the Vietnam War era, which has received a great deal more critical attention. Clearly, the subject of American poetry of the Second World War remains a rich and relatively untouched field of inquiry. Of the studies mentioned at the outset of this chapter, only Vernon Scannell, in *Not without Glory*, discusses the American contribution to the canon of war poetry.

A brief survey of the noteworthy poetry written by American servicemen and civilians, however, can be found in Walsh's *American War Literature: 1914 to Vietnam*, which focuses on poets' responses to the machinery of the war in light of religious, political, and moral issues, but his discussion is limited to Chapter 8: "The Machine and God."

More recently, Schweik's important study *A Gulf So Deeply Cut: American Women Poets and the Second World War* (1991) introduced race and gender issues into discourse on war poetry and helped to recover important writing by women authors. Schweik devotes chapters to the concerns of major women poets, such as Marianne Moore, Edna St. Vincent Millay, Muriel Rukeyser, Gwendolyn Brooks, Elizabeth Bishop, and H. D., with additional chapters on Japanese-American women poets and women's epistolary verse. Overall, the critical neglect of American poetry of the Second World War is unfortunate, especially when one considers the illustrious careers of those who wrote about the war, namely, Randall Jarrell, Karl Shapiro, Howard Nemerov, Louis Simpson, Richard Eberhart, and John Ciardi.

Although Walsh notes that "[t]he diversity of war poetry, written by civilians and combatants alike, resists facile survey or definition," there are marked similarities and recurring themes to be found in the work of these poets. For instance, there is a shared concern for eulogizing fallen comrades (images of burning planes and shot-down pilots abound), in protesting the failure of government to avert war, and a preoccupation with the destructive potential of military machinery. With the exception of Karl Shapiro, who worked as a medical clerk in the South Pacific, all of the aforementioned poets were involved in some capacity with aerial warfare. Randall Jarrell, although he failed to make the grade as a pilot, served as a control tower operator at an air base in Tucson, Arizona. Howard Nemerov was a flying officer, first in the Royal Canadian Air Force and later in the U.S. Army Air Force. Richard Eberhart enlisted in the navy and taught aerial gunnery, and both John Ciardi and Louis Simpson were bombardiers, the latter winning two Purple Hearts and a Bronze Star flying missions over Europe. Of this group, Randall Jarrell has secured a preeminent position in the canon of American war poetry. His best war poems explore the thoughts and moods of bombardiers as they count or pass time between missions ("Losses"), ponder the moral consequences of being an agent of destruction ("Siegfried"), and, in his famous "The Death of the Ball Turret Gunner," speak of death from beyond the grave: "I woke to black flak and the nightmare fighters. / When I died they washed me out of the turret with a hose" (144).

Both Karl Shapiro and Richard Eberhart had long and productive careers, though they are largely remembered for their early war poems. Karl Shapiro wrote in 1945 that "I have tried to be on guard against becoming a 'war poet' " in *V-Letter* (26–27). He never was able to shake this label, however, and the success of his second volume, *V-Letter and Other Poems* (1945), which brought him a Pulitzer Prize, and an appointment as poetry consultant to the Library of Congress have overshadowed his later achievements. The title poem, "V-Letter," which pledges eternal love to his fiancée, "Whether I live or fail" (155), is arguably the best epistolary love poem of the war, and "Poet," about a soldier-poet who drowns and is subsequently forgotten, is also noteworthy.

Richard Eberhart's war poetry, *Collected Poems*, on the other hand, adopts a more religious tone, as in "Dam Neck, Virginia," where he speaks of the "beautiful disrelation of the spiritual" (90), and in his most famous poem, "The Fury of Aerial Bombardment," he asks, "Is God by nature indifferent, beyond us all?" (90). Like Jarrell, Eberhart's poems exhibit a strong sympathy for pilots and gunners, whom he refers to in "Dam Neck, Virginia" as those "scientists of the skill to kill" (90). One of his more neglected pieces, "The Preacher Sought to Find Out Acceptable Words," is noteworthy for the manner in which Eberhart juxtaposes the ideals of courage and patriotism and the celestial beauty of flight to the Icarus-like descent of a shot-down airman. An excellent analysis of Eberhart's war poetry can be found in Fein's "The Cultivation of Paradox," and a statement by Eberhart on war poetry opens his anthology, *War and the Poet: An Anthology of Poetry Expressing Man's Attitude to War from Ancient Times to the Present.*

If Henry Reed's "Lessons of War" was the embodiment of English soldierly humor, then the work of John Ciardi and Louis Simpson constitutes the best of American poetry in that vein. Though both Ciardi and Simpson wrote somber war poems as well, the black humor of Ciardi's "Elegy, Just in Case," "Song," and "Goodmorning with Light" and Simpson's "Arm in Arm," "A Witty War," and the more solemn "Carentan O Carentan" constitute their major contribution to the poetry of World War II. When asked why he wrote about the war long after it was over, Simpson cited a need to recover his identity and, simply, to remember the war, and poems about his war experience appear in several volumes, *The Arrivistes* (1949), *Good News of Death and Other Poems* (1954), and *A Dream of Governors* (1959). In his autobiography, *Air with Armed Men* (1972), Simpson gives a fascinating account of his war experience.

Howard Nemerov's first book of poetry, *The Image and the Law* (1947), contains a number of accomplished meditations on the war, such as the elegiac "Who Did Not Die in Vain," "The Situation Does Not Change," and "For W_____, Who Commanded Well," and a superb study of the psychological effects of war on identity, "Glass Dialectic." Perhaps Nemerov's most lasting contribution to the poetry of the war, however, is the manner in which he addressed issues of survival, return, and memory in poems such as "The Soldier Who Lived through the War" and "For the Squadron." Despite Nemerov's considerable accomplishments as a poet, including a Pulitzer Prize and National Book Award for his *Collected Poems* (1977) and a poet laureateship, his success has been followed by little critical attention, but his war poetry is extensive enough and of sufficient quality to merit critical inquiry.

American civilian poets were more isolated from the war than their British counterparts, which is perhaps why they produced fewer memorable war poems. Marianne Moore's "In Distrust of Merits," which views the war as a projection of an internal struggle, or, as she put it, "There never was a war that was not inward" (138), remains one of the most highly regarded poems about the psychological causes of war, though Randall Jarrell later criticized the poem for defining the war in "blindly moral terms" (129). A number of interesting poems about the war came from older, established poets, including Robert Frost's "The Gift Outright" and "The Soldier," Wallace Steven's more oblique commentaries in "Estèthique du Mal" and "A Woman Sings a Song for a Soldier Come Home," and H. D.'s (Hilda Doolittle) epic poem *The Walls Do Not Fall.* Having already lived through a world war, these venerable poets evoke a sense that, though there have been wars before and will be again, civilization and culture endure. These and other civilian poets, as well as a number of eminent poets of the postwar period, including James Dickey, Alan Dugan, Anthony Hecht, Richard Hugo, Stanley Kunitz, Muriel Rukheyser, and Richard Wilbur, are well represented in Stokesbury's excellent anthology *Articles of War: A Collection of American Poetry about World War II* (1990), which opens with an "Introduction" by Paul Fussell. The publication of this anthology, however, has not led to the sort of critical interest that one might have expected.

OTHER ANGLOPHONE POETRY

The cursory nature of this chapter prevents me from devoting more attention to the body of war poetry produced by English-speaking poets from other nations. Any survey of the poetry of the Second World War, however, would be incomplete without mention of the South African poet F. T. Prince's "Soldier's Bathing." Other poets of note include the Australians David Campbell and Kenneth Slessor, whose "Men in Green" and "Beach Burial," respectively, are noteworthy. In addition, important poems were produced by Canadian poets E. J. Pratt, particularly his verse documentary *Behind the Log* (1947), about a North Atlantic convoy escorted by the Royal Canadian Navy, and Earle Birney, whose "D-Day" represents one of the most profound reactions to the war.

In many ways, as I have suggested, the poetry of the Second World War cannot be defined simply as what was written, either by soldier or civilian, during the war years. As Hamburger notes in *The Truth of Poetry,* "In the era of total politics . . . war poetry has become continuous, unbiquitous, and hardly distinguishable from any other kind of poetry" (175). Hamburger's observation raises some urgent questions about genre distinctions relating to the poetry of the Second World War, the vast range of war experience recorded in verse, and the far-reaching influence of that experience in the poetry of the postwar period. As it stands, scholars have been at work identifying and evaluating the most significant poets and poems of the war, while critical studies, such as Schweik's, and anthologies, such as Reilly's *Chaos of the Night: Women's Poetry and Verse of the Second World War,* have opened up exciting new areas of investigation. Now that critics have recovered a major body of war poetry, there is a need to consolidate this work, through either analyses of individual poets or, particularly in the case of the American war poetry, more comprehensive studies.

BIBLIOGRAPHY

Poetry

Auden, W. H. "September 1, 1939," "In Memory of W. B. Yeats," "In Memory of Sigmund Freud," and "At the Grave of Henry James." In Edward Mendelson, ed., *Selected Poems*. New York: Viking, 1979.

Birney, Earle. "D-Day." In *Collected Poems*. Toronto: McClelland and Stewart, 1975.

Campbell, David. "Men in Green." In *Selected Poems: 1942–1968*. Sydney: Angus and Robertson, 1973.

Causley, Charles. "Demobilisation Leave" and "H.M.S. Eclipse Approaches Freetown." In *Union Street*. Boston: Houghton Mifflin, 1960.

———. *Farewell, Aggie Weston*. Aldington, Kent: Hand and Flower, 1951.

Ciardi, John. "Elegy, Just in Case," "Goodmorning with Light," and "Song." In *Selected Poems*. Fayetteville: University of Arkansas, 1989.

Douglas, Keith. *Alamein to Zem Zem*. London: Poetry Editions, 1946.

———. *A Prose Miscellany*. Edited by Desmond Graham. Manchester: Carcanet, 1985.

———. *Selected Poems*. New York: Chilmark, 1964.

———. "Simplify Me When I'm Dead," "Desert Flowers," "How to Kill," "Vergissmeinicht," "Cairo Jag," "On a Return from Egypt." In Desmond Graham, ed., *The Complete Poems*. New York: Oxford UP, 1987.

Eberhart, Richard. "The Fury of Aerial Bombardment," "Dam Neck, Virginia," and "The Preacher Sought to Find Out Acceptable Words." In *Collected Poems 1930–1970*. New York: Oxford UP, 1960.

Eliot, T. S. "East Coker." In *Collected Poems 1909–1962*. New York: Harcourt Brace Jovanovich, 1963.

Fraser, G. S. "S. S. City of Benares." In *Poems of G. S. Fraser*. Leicester, U.K.: Leicester UP, 1981.

Frost, Robert. *The Gift Outright*. New York: Spiral Press, 1942.

Fuller, Roy. "Autumn 1941," "Battersea: After Dunkirk," and "Soliloquy during an Air-Raid." In *New and Collected Poems*. London: Secker and Warburg, 1985.

———. *The Middle of a War*. London: Hogarth, 1942.

Gascoyne, David. "A Wartime Dawn." In *Collected Poems*. London: Oxford UP, 1985.

H. D. *The Walls Do Not Fall*. Oxford and New York: Oxford UP, 1944; Manchester, U.K.: Carcanet, 1973, 1988.

Jarrell, Randall. "The Death of the Ball Turret Gunner," "Eighth Air Force," "Losses," and "Siegfried." In *The Complete Poems*. New York: Noonday, 1990.

Keyes, Sidney. "Elegy (In Memoriam SKK)." In *Collected Poems*. London: Routledge, 1988.

Lewis, Alun. "All Day It Has Rained" and "Infantry." In *Selected Poems*. London: Allen and Unwin, 1982.

———. *Raiders' Dawn and Other Poems*. New York: Macmillan, 1942; London: G. Allen and Unwin, 1962, 1946.

Lewis, C. Day. "Where Are the War Poets?" In *The Complete Poems*. Stanford, CA: Stanford UP, 1992.

MacNeice, Louis. *Autumn Journal.* London: Faber and Faber, 1939, 1996.

―――. "Brother Fire" and "The Casualty." In *The Collected Poems.* Cambridge: Cambridge UP, 1967.

Moore, Marianne. "In Distrust of Merits." In *The Complete Poems of Marianne Moore.* New York: Penguin, 1986.

Nemerov, Howard. *The Image and the Law.* New York: H. Holt, 1947.

―――. "Who Did Not Die in Vain," "The Situation Does Not Change," "For W_____, Who Commanded Well," "Glass Dialectic," "The Soldier Who Lived through the War," and "For the Squadron." In *The Collected Poems of Howard Nemerov.* Chicago: Chicago UP, 1977.

Pratt, E. J. *Behind the Log.* Toronto: Macmillan, 1947.

Prince, F. T. "Soldier's Bathing." In *Collected Poems.* London: Menard, 1978.

Reed, Henry. *A Map of Verona.* London; Jonathan Cape, 1946, 1970. "Lessons of War." In Jon Stallworthy, ed., *Collected Poems.* Cambridge: Cambridge UP, 1991.

Shapiro, Karl. "V-Letter" and "Poet." In *Poems: 1940–53.* New York: Random House, 1953.

―――. *V-Letter and Other Poems.* New York: Reynal and Hitchcock, 1944; London: Secker and Warburg, 1945.

Simpson, Louis. "Arm in Arm," "A Witty War," and "Carentan O Carentan." In *Collected Poems.* New York: Paragon House, 1988.

―――. *The Arrivistes: Poems, 1940–1949.* New York: Fine Editions, 1949.

―――. *A Dream of Governors: Poems.* Middletown, CT: Wesleyan UP, 1959, 1967.

―――. *Good News of Death and Other Poems.* Vol. 2 of *Poets of Today.* New York: Scribner, 1954, 1961.

Sitwell, Edith. *The Collected Poems.* London: Vanguard, 1968.

Slessor, Kenneth. "Beach Burial." In *Poems.* Sydney: Angus and Robertson, 1957.

Spender, Stephen. *Collected Poems, 1928–1953.* New York: Random House, 1953.

Stevens, Wallace. "Esthètique du Mal" and "A Woman Sings a Song for a Soldier Come Home." In Samuel French Morse, ed., *Poems by Wallace Stevens.* New York: Vintage, 1959.

Thomas, Dylan. "A Refusal to Mourn the Death, by Fire, of a Child in London," "Ceremony after a Fire Raid," and "Among Those Killed in the Dawn Raid Was a Man Aged a Hundred." In *The Poems of Dylan Thomas.* New York: New Directions, 1974.

Yeats, William Butler. "Lapis Lazuli." In M. L. Rosenthal, ed., *Selected Poems and Two Plays of William Butler Yeats.* New York: Collier, 1962.

―――. "Letter to Dorothy Wellesley, July 6, 1935." In Allan Wade, ed., *The Letters of W. B. Yeats.* New York: Octagon, 1980.

Criticism and Anthologies

Bergonzi, Bernard. *Wartime and Aftermath: English Literature and Its Background 1939–1960.* New York: Oxford UP, 1993.

Bowen, Roger. *Many Histories Deep.* Madison, NJ: Fairleigh Dickinson UP, 1995.

Connolly, Cyril. "Comment." *Horizon* 1:7 (July 1940): 532–535.

Currey, R. N. *Poets of the 1939–1945 War.* London: Longmans, Green, 1960.

Durrell, Lawrence, Robin Fedden, and Bernard Spencer, eds. *Personal Landscape: An Anthology of Exile.* London: Editions Poetry, 1945.

Eberhart, Richard, and Selden Rodman, eds. *War and the Poet: An Anthology of Poetry Expressing Man's Attitude to War from Ancient Times to the Present.* Westport, CT: Greenwood, 1974.

Fein, Richard J. "The Cultivation of Paradox: The War Poetry of Richard Eberhart." *Forum* (Spring 1969): 56–64.

Fussell, Paul. *Wartime: Behavior and Understanding in the Second World War.* New York: Oxford UP, 1989.

Gardner, B., ed. *The Terrible Rain: The War Poets, 1939–45.* London: Methuen, 1988.

Graham, Desmond. *Keith Douglas: A Biography.* London: Oxford UP, 1974.

Hamburger, Michael. *The Truth of Poetry: Tensions in Modernist Poetry since Baudelaire.* London: Weidenfeld and Nicolson, 1968; Anvil Press Poetry, 1996.

Hendry, J. F., and H. Treece, eds. *The Crown and the Sickle.* London: Routledge, 1943.

———. *The New Apocalypse.* London: Fortune, 1939.

———. *The White Horsemen.* London: Routledge, 1941.

Hewison, Robert. *Under Siege: Literary Life in London 1939–1945.* New York: Oxford UP, 1977.

Pikoulis, John. *Alun Lewis: A Life.* Brigend, Wales: Seren, 1984.

Reilly, Catherine, ed. *Chaos of the Night: Women's Poetry and Verse of the Second World War.* London: Virago, 1984.

Scammell, William. *Keith Douglas: A Study.* London: Faber and Faber, 1988.

Scannell, Vernon. *Not without Glory: Poets of the Second World War.* London: Woburn, 1976.

Schweik, Susan M. *A Gulf So Deeply Cut: American Women Poets and the Second World War.* Madison: University of Wisconsin, 1991.

Shapiro, Karl. "Statement on War Poetry." In Oscar Williams, ed., *The War Poets: An Anthology of the War Poetry of the 20th Century.* 26–27. New York: John Day, 1945.

Shires, Linda M. *British Poetry of the Second World War.* London: Macmillan, 1985.

Simpson, Louis. *Air with Armed Men.* London: London Magazine Editions, 1972.

Spender, Stephen. *Thirties and After: Poetry, Politics, and People 1933–1970.* New York: Vintage, 1979.

Stokesbury, Leon, ed. *Articles of War: A Collection of American Poetry about World War II.* Fayetteville: University of Arkansas, 1990.

Tolley, A. T. *The Poetry of the Forties.* Manchester, U.K.: Manchester UP, 1985.

Walsh, Jeffrey. *American War Literature: 1914 to Vietnam.* New York: St. Martin's, 1982.

20   The War and the Visual Arts

Brian Foss

There has yet to be a Second World War equivalent of Richard Cork's large-scale survey of international trends in the visual culture of the First World War, *A Bitter Truth: Avant-Garde Art and the Great War.* As the subtitle of Cork's book implies, one reason for this discrepancy derives from the remarkable correspondence between the formal attributes of European avant-garde art movements—futurism, vorticism, and expressionism, for example—and the technology, speed, and apocalyptic nihilism of the war. Such correlations between the war and the avant-garde also reinforced the perception of 1914–1918 as a radical rupture between past and future.

In contrast, the 1939–1945 conflict seemed less a traumatic break than the tragic, inevitable playing out of problems rooted at least as far back as 1918. Certainly, the war had a strong impact on the visual arts; for example, it virtually crippled the social viability of certain branches of surrealism by demonstrating the apparent impracticability of its utopian objectives. Yet much of the art with which the war came to be associated was—like the war itself—hardly shocking or unexpected in 1939. British neo-Romanticism, for example, found a great deal in the war that was congenial to its development, but it had already built a solid history during the 1930s and was, in any case, strongly oriented not to the future but to the past. Similarly, the bland, naturalist genre painting that is most frequently identified with state art in Germany had already gained considerable international attention (and condemnation) by the time war was finally declared.

GERMANY

It is thus not surprising that historians and critics who have dealt with German art in particular have almost never concentrated their inquiries specifically on the years 1939–1945. Instead, they have preferred to avoid differentiating the war years from the 1930s. The exception to this tendency is what little literature exists on those artists who sketched and painted military portraits and battle scenes. Artist-correspondents had supplied sketches to the periodical press since the beginning of the war. In 1941 the *Oberkommandowehrmacht* instituted the *Kriegsmaler und Pressezeichner* [War Painters and Press Artists] program, in which artists were given commissions to produce fine-art records of their experiences with the military. This work—still largely neglected by historians despite a 1975 exhibition in the United States—is the subject of *The German War Artists* by Weber. This book is noteworthy not only because it features reproductions of portrait and battle drawings and paintings by *Kriegsmaler* artists but also because it reprints Gordon W. Gilkey's informative 1947 report on the history of the *Kriegsmaler* and *Pressezeichner* program and documents the policies and procedures by which Nazi artworks were confiscated by American authorities after the German surrender.

Aside from Weber's book, however, German art in wartime is almost always discussed within a larger temporal framework: German art under national socialism. This approach also tends to be employed in discussions of the art of other dictatorships, such as Italy and the USSR. But the historiography of German art of this period is particularly interesting. In large part this is because national socialist regulation of the visual arts was so extreme and was an essential constituent element of such an appalling larger reality that the process of dealing with it tends to force writers to situate themselves on specific issues of ideology and method. Though these issues also characterize, to varying degrees, the historiography of the art of other dictatorships, they have been particularly pressing for historians of the visual culture of the Third Reich.

One such issue grows out of the thoroughness with which Nazi culture politicized aesthetics and aestheticized politics. These twin phenomena were exemplified in Hitler's fondness for politics as theatrical spectacle and in his claim that he could have become a modern-day Michelangelo had he not been destined to serve as architect of the Third Reich. The same intermingling of aesthetics and politics has been identified in the construction of gargantuan ceremonial buildings and complexes that were more symbolic than practical. The very materials out of which these structures were made—marble and granite especially—also contributed to Albert Speer's "theory of ruin value," the aesthetics-derived ideal of having official Nazi state architecture ultimately decay into sublime ruins visually akin to those of classical antiquity.

The implications of these types of mutually sustaining interaction between politics and aesthetics have been explored in a number of sources, including Cohen's film *The Architecture of Doom*, with its chillingly detailed demonstration that national socialism was based at least as much on aesthetics as on politics and that aesthetic—not political—need formed the basis for the policies of racial extermination. The Nazi fascination with aesthetics, beauty, and the symbolic potential of art is also assessed in several published studies of national socialist architecture. Scobie, for example, in *Hitler's State Architecture*, considers, among other things, the give-and-take between politics and architectural aesthetics in the articulation of a "pagan" totalitarian state.

Perhaps the most comprehensive treatment of the degree to which an obsession with aesthetics permeated the personal as well as the professional lives of many members of the party's upper echelons is Petropoulos' "Art as Politics." Petropoulos first considers the governmental machinery for controlling and confiscating art, in Germany and later the occupied territories, between 1933 and 1945. He then examines the art collections and the art-collecting practices of the party leaders. These groundbreaking chapters include analysis of the ways in which the collecting of art reflected worldviews, facilitated interpersonal relations, and established social status. They thus build an overwhelming case for the thoroughness with which concern for art and aesthetics saturated the ideological organization of the upper reaches of the national socialist hierarchy.

"Degenerate Art"

Along with the conflation of politics and aesthetics, a second subject favored by writers on German art at the time of Hitler is the war on the "degenerate" modernism associated with the Weimar Republic, Jews and foreigners. The popularity of this subject is hardly a surprise; the scale and audacity of the regime's attack on contemporary modernist art beggar belief. The list of artists who were persecuted, forbidden to practice their art, driven into exile, or murdered includes such luminaries of twentieth-century art as Max Beckmann, Otto Dix, George Grosz, Ernst Ludwig Kirchner, Paul Klee, Käthe Kollwitz, Oskar Schlemmer, and Karl Schmidt-Rotluff. In 1937, in what has become the single most notorious manifestation of the Nazi antimodernism vendetta, some 650 examples of "degenerate" art were shown in the *Entartete Kunst* exhibition. These works—selected to demonstrate a supposed link between racial "impurity," mental degeneracy, and modernist distortions of "beauty"—were but a fraction of the estimated 16,000 items expropriated from German public collections in the mid-1930s. Small wonder, then, that many historians have been fascinated by the fate of contemporary art under the national socialist regime.

Aside from a wealth of monographs on artists who found themselves the objects of unwelcome Nazi attention, there are also important studies of general persecution of artists and their patrons. These include Rave's invaluable *Kunstdiktatur im Dritten Reich*. Based largely on his experiences while a curator at Berlin's *Nationalgalerie* in the 1930s, Rave provides a detailed history of events at German museums during the time works were being confiscated. He also includes a nearly complete list of items shown in *Entartete Kunst* and describes the layout of the exhibition. More recently, *Entartete Kunst* has been thoroughly examined in the Los Angeles County Museum of Art's *"Degenerate Art"*. This catalog, edited by Barron, gives detailed plans of the design of the 1937 exhibition, identifies and illustrates the exhibits, and features ten essays on subjects ranging from the relationship between modern art and politics in prewar Germany (Barron), to earlier displays of "degenerate" art and the tour of the 1937 exhibition (Zuschlag), to the dispersal of the thousands of works impounded from German galleries (Huneke; Barron).

National Socialism and Modernism

There is, however, a danger that studies of modernist artists persecuted by the Nazis may generalize the relationship between artist and state as always being one of victim and persecutor. In reality the association between artists and the *Reichskulturkammer* (RKK, the regulatory body created in 1933 by Joseph Goebbels) was somewhat more complex. The need for an appropriately detailed analysis was emphasized in Dahm's "Die Reichskulturkammer als Instrument kulturpolitischer Steuerung und sozialer Reglementierung" and is answered, in part, in Steinweis' *Art, Ideology, and Economics in Nazi Germany*.

Steinweis presents a thoughtful analysis of the RKK and arguably the most important appraisal in English of the Nazi bureaucratic apparatus for controlling the arts. He reminds us that the artists and movements that dominate art-historical publications today made up only part of the German art scene in the 1930s. He questions the credibility, therefore, of neatly distinguishing between government officials and the cultural elite, examines closely the professional/economic goals of the cultural establishment from the Weimar Republic onward, and concludes that the RKK co-opted and transformed the Republic's embryonic professional "estate" system for artists into a tool for cultural regulation. Artists whose life in the Weimar Republic had given them a healthy concern about high unemployment, for example, found that the RKK offered a measure of social security for which the sacrifice of autonomy and artistic freedom, especially after 1935, was not necessarily considered too high a price. Steinweis' book thus blurs the distinction between the modernist years of the Republic and the retrograde years of national socialism. In so doing, it demonstrates the shortcomings of histories that generalize the Nazis' attacks on modernist art into attacks on German artists as a whole.

As Steinweis examines the relations between the state and the cultural elite, so Heskett probed the equally misunderstood relationship between national socialist art and modernism itself. In an important essay, "Art and Design in Nazi Germany," Heskett evaluated a selection of recent publications, exhibitions, and conference papers and concluded that "there was a strong element of continuity in art and design between the Weimar Republic and the Third Reich, but the nature of this continuity is complex, [and] riddled with paradoxes and ambivalences" (151).

The approach outlined in this 1978 article has been more recently used to good effect in his "Modernism and Archaism in Design in the Third Reich," one of thirteen essays in Taylor and Will's collection entitled *The Nazification of Art*. A similar tactic is adopted in Taylor's "Post-Modernism in the Third Reich" in the same collection. Taylor stresses that, while Hitler caricatured and pilloried a simplified definition of cultural modernism, formal and aesthetic aspects of a more broadly defined modernism made their presence felt in official Nazi art and culture.

The preceding discussions indicate that the literature on the Nazi regime's relation to the art community in general and to modernism in particular, as well as the literature on the cross-pollination of politics and aesthetics, is large and varied. However, a comparable voluminousness does not distinguish the study of a third aspect of the historiography of art under national socialism: state-approved art.

The sweeping away of "degenerate" modern art left the field clear for the airlessly academicized naturalist paintings and histrionic sculptures so favored by Hitler and others. The paucity of writing on this art is due partly to the fact that much Nazi art was impounded immediately after the war and that access to a substantial amount of it—including a large collection in government storage in Carson, Colorado—is still restricted. In addition, as was demonstrated by public reaction to a 1974 exhibition of Nazi state-approved images (*Kunst im Dritten Reich: Dokumente der Unterwerfung*, edited by Bussman for the Frankfurt *Kunstverein*), much suspicion and hostility exist regarding the motives of those who wish to exhibit or view Nazi art. A third and particularly important reason for the lack of literature on this subject is the fact that the very concept of Nazi *art* has proved deeply problematic for many historians. Nowhere is this more evident than in the weighty catalog (more than 500 pages long) published for the Royal Academy of Arts (London) exhibition *German Art in the 20th Century*. In the catalog's detailed, year-by-year, schematic, chronological breakdown of events in politics, art, and culture, there are no entries whatsoever under "Art" for any of the years from 1940 to 1945, inclusive. Nor, among the 299 exhibits, are there any examples of Nazi-approved art. The war years are represented by works by seven artists, all of them—including Max Beckmann and Kurt Schwitters—victims of Nazi persecution.

Yet interest in Nazi paintings and sculptures, aesthetically insignificant though most of them are, has been growing since the early 1970s. This is undoubtedly related to the eclipse of modernism by postmodernism in a number of fields and the consequent weakening of the aesthetic certainties that had banished Nazi art as thoroughly as the Nazis had exiled "degenerate" modernism. The time was thus ripe in 1994 for the publication of *Kunst und Diktatur: Architektur, Bildhauerei und Malerei in Österreich, Deutschland, Italien und der Sowjetunion 1922–1956.* Edited by Tabor, this two-volume (almost 1,000-page) catalog, accompanying an extremely ambitious exhibition at the *Kunstlerhaus* in Vienna, consists of 126 texts, most of them very brief but many covering topics relating directly to the Second World War. Even a cursory sampling gives an indication of the breadth of subjects addressed. The essays on Germany alone include—among much else—studies of Europa as a theme in Nazi art (Pulle), the operation and output of the SS porcelain factory located at Dachau (Landauer), and the mass production of portraits of Hitler (Waldstein). Thus, by any reckoning this catalog is an absolutely essential addition to the study of totalitarian art not only in Germany but also (as the substantial collections of essays on each of these countries attest) in Austria, Italy, and the USSR.

More easily accessible to readers of English is Hinz's *Art in the Third Reich.* In this much-needed work, first published in German in 1974, Hinz proposes a methodological approach that situates the particularly controversial "official" art of national socialism squarely within a rigorously defined sociopolitical context. This approach has the outstanding advantage of relating national socialist art to the static genre and figure painting that had been displaced by "degenerate" modern art under the Weimar Republic. Hinz's approach thus recalls Alan Steinweis' insistence upon the importance of linking Goebbels' bureaucratic regulation of German art to structures and concerns that predated the rise to power of the Nazi Party.

Hinz's achievement in viewing Nazi art as something other than an atypical blip without any grounding in German political, social, or aesthetic history is an important and enduring one. However, in emphasizing sociopolitical context in his approach to national socialist art he tends to concentrate on subject matter almost to the exclusion of any formal or stylistic discussion of the individual works. This minimizes art's specific properties as a mode of expression, largely reducing it to something resembling a mirror in which viewers could see reflected concrete themes and ideas.

In contrast, writers on the types of art attacked by the Nazi state rely very heavily on formal/stylistic analysis in their discussions. Willett in "Art of a Nasty Time" has argued that Hinz's concentration on the tangible (the content of the paintings and sculptures) at the expense of the less tangible (style, spirit) hampers the fullest potential development of Hinz's argument. He further suggests that this type of problem is not unique to *Art in the Third Reich* and that it also permeated the assumptions of the organizers of the aforementioned 1974 exhibition at the Frankfurt *Kunst-verein.*

Hinz's book also takes a stand on yet another (fourth) problem that besets historians who deal with German art between 1933 and 1945: the degree to which Nazi art may be seen as exemplifying tendencies in art in other, contemporaneous dictatorships. On this point Hinz is very clear: he rejects the "widely held view that similar governmental systems will produce similar art" (vii). He therefore restricts his inquiry to national socialism, rather than treating it in tandem with other manifestations of fascism. In this regard his book marks a significant departure from the strategy of discussing the art produced during the war under different dictatorships as a more or less unified totality—a tendency fairly well represented in the literature.

Lehmann-Haupt's earlier *Art under a Dictatorship* was the first book in English to have adopted the latter approach. The argument laid out by Lehmann-Haupt has subsequently been explored in Golomstock, *Totalitarian Art in the Soviet Union, the Third Reich, Fascist Italy and the People's Republic of China.* In contrast, the two-volume study edited by Tabor noted before, though it also groups together art produced under selected totalitarian governments, discusses the regimes separately rather than conceiving of them as ideologically and artistically more or less interchangeable.

Although Lehmann-Haupt claims that "certain characteristics of the Nazi program" (e.g., extreme nationalism) are "typically German," he also asserts that "there are important, indeed very important, elements of the Nazi art program that not only closely resemble, but are virtually identical with the art programs of other totalitarian states" (216–217). This he attempts to prove by following some 150 pages of text on national socialist art with less than a single page of commentary on Italian art and some twenty pages on art from the USSR.

There is much to recommend Lehmann-Haupt's basic argument; national socialist art and Soviet socialist art have a great deal in common, in terms both of technique and of their conceptual bases. As Taylor and van der Will have pointed out in "Aesthetics and National Socialism," Goebbels' 1936 interdiction of art criticism, as well as the institution of the *Reichskulturkammer* in 1933 and the purge of recalcitrant artists, all had their closely contemporary counterparts in the Soviet Union. One is nonetheless made uneasy by Lehmann-Haupt's sweeping conflation of national socialism and Soviet socialism as ideological systems, as well as by his definition of totalitarian governments as those governments that invariably attempt to thwart the individuality and autonomy of the artist.

Certainly, Lane found these assumptions superficial. In *Architecture and Politics in Germany, 1918–1945* she criticizes historians such as Lehmann-Haupt for overly insisting upon totalitarianism's rejection of the modernist ideal of self-expression and for thus neglecting the more difficult question of why national socialism repudiated Bauhaus modernism *in particular*. Plunging into the history of German architecture under the Weimar Republic and German intellectual history from before 1918, she demonstrates that the Nazi regime—far from inventing the idea that architectural styles could be interpreted in political terms—actually inherited a strong tradition of conflating politics and architecture. Outlining reasons that the Bauhaus had been associated with left-wing thought well before Hitler became chancellor, she effectively grounds Nazi architectural theory and practice not in the broad notion of totalitarian ideology but in the specific historical situation of Germany between 1933 and 1945.

The work of Lane and historians like her is thus in opposition both to Lehmann-Haupt's 1954 study and—for the same reasons—to Golomstock's more closely argued book. Golomstock devotes most of his book to a detailed comparison of the art and architecture of Nazi Germany and of the Soviet Union, suggesting that all twentieth-century totalitarian systems share a "specific ideology, aesthetics, organization and style" (xv). He concludes his study with seventy-seven reproductions of "the most important and typical works of totalitarian art" (307). But by what criteria have these images been selected as the most important and typical, and does this not imply the preestablished existence of a universal category—"totalitarian art"—deriving from the equally universal category "totalitarian state"? It is unclear how Golomstock reconciles his argument with the fact that, for example, only a small proportion of the art commissioned and purchased in Italy during the late 1930s and the first half of the 1940s can be accommodated within a notion of Nazi-style painting and sculpture.

ITALY

The artistic policy of Mussolini's regime was remarkably tolerant, albeit decreasingly so after the outbreak of the war. *Secondo Futurismo* artists like Enrico Prampolini could be openly hostile to the very idea of classifying any art as "degenerate," while at the same time the often nonfigurative *Secondo Futurismo* artists made occasional claims about futurism as the official fascist style in art. Given that futurists were included in an official exhibition of Italian art that was sent to Berlin in 1937—the year of *Entartete Kunst*—this was not such an outlandish claim. Indeed, only on the eve of the war did abstract art fall into general official disfavor in Italy. Yet as late as 1939 the minister of national education, Giuseppe Bottai, instituted the liberal Premio Bergamo art competition in reaction against the establishment by Roberto Farinacci, earlier that year, of the highly reactionary Premio Cremona. In 1940 the Bergamo Prize was awarded to Renato Guttuso—a choice unthinkable in Germany.

Predictably, then, most of the literature on Italian art under fascism has devoted attention to artists and groups that contributed to fascist culture but whose work rarely seems classifiable according to the narrow definitions of fascist style favored by Lehmann-Haupt and Golomstock. For example, the Royal Academy of Art's catalog *Italian Art in the 20th Century*, edited by Braun, features relevant essays by Cannistraro, "Fascism and Culture in Italy, 1919–1945"; Crispolti, "Second Futurism"; Braun, "Mario Sironi and a Fascist Art"; Vivarelli, "Personalities and Styles in Figurative Art in the Thirties"; and Caramel, "Abstract Art of the Thirties." Each of these essays stresses the heterogeneous mixture of styles practiced by artists, many of whom—until after the start of the war—were not only tolerated by the government but often the recipients of state patronage. Similarly, the Italian section of Tabor's *Kunst und Diktatur* includes essays on fascism and futurism, fascism and the Novecento movement, and fascism and rationalist architecture. Plurality and debate are also highlighted in Bossaglia's text, also in *Kunst und Diktatur*, on art criticism and art magazines and in Rodeschini-Galati's study of the Bergamo and Cremona art competitions in 1939–1942.

Among other sources that adopt a comparable approach to Italian art during the war years, Silva's *Ideologia e Arte del Fascismo* is particularly important. Silva provides a detailed analysis of the roots and nature of fascist ideology and a summary of the ways in which artists circulated fascist iconography through their work without being identified as official artists of the regime. Tempesti (in *Arte dell'Italia Fascista*) accomplishes much the same thing by constructing a detailed, chronological review of the multifaceted relationship of negotiation, accommodation, and manipulation between the Italian state and the arts. These and similar studies—such as, for the USSR, James' *Soviet Socialist Realism*—demonstrate the need for historians of wartime art in totalitarian states to give due consideration to the specificity of the aesthetic and to the uniqueness of sociopolitical conditions in different societies.

It is nonetheless true that Second World War art in all totalitarian countries was expected to function not only as documentary (see Weber's *The German War Artists*) but also as propaganda. In democratic countries, however, art related to the war was most often documentary rather than propagandist in intent, although the latter concern was also present among individual artists and in the publicity and propaganda branches of governments. As a result, historians dealing with these countries have not been so pressed to come to terms with the large-scale problems and issues with which historians of wartime art in Germany in particular have grappled: the conflation of aesthetics and politics, the demonization of key aspects of aesthetic modernism, the analysis of state-approved art, and the question of whether twentieth-century totalitarian art may be seen as a generally homogeneous international phenomenon.

NORTH AMERICA, AUSTRALIA, AND SOUTH AFRICA

Historians of wartime art in North America, Australia, and South Africa have therefore tended to concentrate upon documentary war art: art purchased or commissioned by the nation to record its war efforts both at home and abroad. These war art projects varied greatly in scope. Britain's War Artists' Advisory Committee, for example, acquired some 6,000 works from more than 400 artists, including thirty-seven official war artists. Canada, less ambitious, had thirty-two official war artists and gave short-term contracts to just a few others, while only seven official war artists and a small group of contract artists contributed to the South African project.

Literature on the smaller examples of these projects tends to be both modest and scarce. For example, Canada's war art program is covered in two comparatively brief exhibition catalogs: Murray's *Canadian Artists of the Second World War* and Tippett's *Lest We Forget.* These two sources discuss the steps taken to implement the Canadian war art program, comment on the experiences of the artists involved, and note the types of subjects drawn or painted. Two books have also been published on Australian war art of the twentieth century: Reid's *Australian Artists at War* and *Masterpieces of the Australian War Memorial* by Fry and Gray. Both are more useful for the biographical information they supply than for discussion of the organization and operation of Australia's war art project. Biographies of South Africa's artists, along with a very brief survey of the Second World War project in that country, are given in *South African Images of War*, compiled by Kruger, which as a publication has the merit of situating the 1940–1945 project within the much larger context of South African war art from 1652 to the 1980s. Biographies of the seven official war artists, along with small, briefly annotated reproductions of their work and that of three other South African artists, also appear in Huntingford's *A Selection of South African Military Art.*

However, despite the availability of these sources, as well as the existence of monographs on several official war artists, much remains to be done in terms of analyzing the operation and results of the war art projects in such countries as Canada, Australia, and South Africa. Commentary on subjects, iconography, and style, in particular, is quite rudimentary (indeed, often nonexistent), as is research into contracts issued by industrial manufacturers to have artists document war production subjects.

This assessment also applies to literature on war art from the United States, where the researcher must resort, for the most part, to monographs published during the war itself. Among these are Crane's *Art in the Armed Forces* and *Marines at War* and Baldwin's *The Navy at War.* These are well-illustrated publications (e.g., *Art in the Armed Forces* has more than 200 pages) and are thus very useful overviews of the scope of American military art of the Second World War. The texts, though, were intended as undetailed and laudatory introductions to their subjects and consequently tend to lack critical analysis. Researchers may also benefit from such books as Hjerter's *The Art of Tom Lea*, in which reproductions of fifty drawings and paintings by the most prolific of the nine war artists commissioned by *Life* magazine are accompanied by a summary biographical essay. Lea was a particularly well traveled artist, logging some 100,000 miles around the world during the five years (1941–1946) that he was on contract to *Life*. Also useful as sources of information on official war art are journals and autobiographies by war artists; see especially John Browning's *An Artist at War*, Edward Reep's *A Combat Artist in World War II*, and Harry Townsend's *War Diary of a Combat Artist*.

Two other useful sources on the American experience deal with the relation of American art to the war years and the war effort in general, rather than with the depiction of military subjects in particular. Landau's *Artists for Victory* is a brief, but illuminating, history of Artists for Victory, the umbrella group that had a membership of more than 10,000 in 1943 and that effectively promoted the use of artists' talents in the waging of the war. Chapters 8 and 9 of Contreras' "The New Deal Treasury Department Art Programs and the American Artist" survey the projects, some directly correlated to the war, undertaken by the Treasury Department's Section of Fine Arts before public objections and government hesitancy regarding arts funding in wartime resulted in its liquidation in June 1943. A more summary treatment of this subject is given in McKinzie's *The New Deal for Artists*.

GREAT BRITAIN

British war art has, since the early 1980s, been subjected to somewhat more scrutiny than that of the other Allied countries. Meirion and Susie Harries' *The War Artists: British Official War Art of the Twentieth Century* provides a useful introductory summary of the organization of the Ministry of Information committee charged with documenting the war in art. It also presents a geographically and thematically organized overview of the work of the more prolific artists. A comparable, though more anecdotal and less detailed, approach is adopted in Ross' *Colours of War*, which, unlike the Harries' book, does not provide the reader with any potentially helpful background information on the British First World War art project. There also exist, as in the literature for other countries, a substantial number of studies of the work of the better-known war artists, including Henry Moore, Paul Nash, John Piper, and Graham Sutherland.

The most detailed treatments of official war art in the United Kingdom are Foss' "British Artists and the Second World War, with Particular Reference to the War Artists' Advisory Committee of the Ministry of Information" and a subsequent article, "Message and Medium: Government

Patronage, National Identity and National Culture in Britain 1939–45."
Both sources examine how the organization and operation of the war art
project may be seen to have articulated a British national identity based
on freedom, tolerance, individuality, and a perceived unwillingness to con-
flate fine art and visual propaganda. Analyses both of the subjects and of
the formal/stylistic aspects of the war art further suggest that the collection itself reinforced the notion of a national identity that was implicitly
juxtaposed to the characterization of Nazi Germany as a state where art
was denied its role as a free expression of individual sensibility. State support of war art in Britain thus came to symbolize the very ideals of freedom
from governmental interference and control that the war was ostensibly
being waged to defend.

However, although histories of official war art projects constitute the
bulk of the literature on art and the Second World War, accounts of other
points of contact between art and the war are also available. For example,
Leventhal in " 'The Best for the Most': CEMA and State Sponsorship of
the Arts in Wartime, 1939–1945" examines the Council for the Encouragement of Music and the Arts (CEMA) as the crucial body for the dissemination and popularization of art in wartime Britain. Founded in 1939,
CEMA was so outstandingly successful over the next six years that at the
end of the war it was reconstituted as the Arts Council of Great Britain.
Although there is a fast-growing literature on the growth of British state
patronage of art, Leventhal's rigorous archival study is the only detailed
investigation into the important subject of CEMA's creation, structure,
and activities.

A second, particularly noteworthy study of wartime art not centered on
the war art projects of the Allied states is Sillars' *British Romantic Art and
the Second World War.* Though not a product of the war and though certainly not classifiable as a "national style," neo-Romanticism struck a deep
chord during the reflective, apocalyptic years 1939–1945. Sillars conducts
a detailed examination of the complexity of neo-Romanticism as a style,
demonstrating its permeation of much contemporaneous visual art and
poetry. This he accomplishes by approaching the movement from a variety
of angles ("Romantic Realism," "Blitz Sublime," "The Nurturing Earth,"
and so on), studiously combining social contextualization with formal
analyses of several works of art. His extended relation of this specific aesthetic to the emotional and social contexts occasioned by the war is a rare
example, outside the framework of totalitarian political systems, of a close
affinity between the war years and a specific visual sensibility.

HOLOCAUST AND CONCENTRATION CAMP ART

Sillars' book is somewhat unusual in the present chapter because, unlike
most of the other entries, it deals with art that did not have significant

indebtedness, in either ideological or patronage-related terms, to a national state. The same may be said of Holocaust art, of which an estimated 30,000 examples survive in North American, European, and Israeli collections. Selections from these collections have been included in many exhibitions and publications over the past half century.

Three books on art from Nazi camps may be singled out for their comprehensiveness and general accessibility: *The Living Witness* by Costanza and Levin, *Art of the Holocaust* by Blatter and Milton, and *Spiritual Resistance* by Novitch, Dawidowicz, and Freudenheim. All three of these publications are as valuable for their biographical information on the individual artists as for their extensive illustrations of rarely seen works. The essays in *Art of the Holocaust* are particularly informative on such subjects as the media and materials employed by concentration camp artists, the variety of subjects and styles in the artworks, and the circumstances under which the art was made. The book's value is further enhanced by its organization into a series of chapters that divide the many illustrations according to when and where they were produced: "The First Response," "Ghettos," "Transit Camps," "Prisons and POW Camps," "The Illegals: In Hiding and as Partisans," "Concentration Camps," "The First Observers," and "[Postwar] Memory."

In addition to these three books on Nazi camps, Gesensway and Roseman's *Beyond Words* surveys artwork produced in American detention camps by men, women, and children of Japanese ancestry. Here, context is provided by three chapters detailing the political and social history of the camps, while the remainder of the book reproduces images and narratives by twenty-five individuals to evoke the experience of being interned in the country of one's birth.

Nazi camp inmates were not the only prisoners of war to make art in desperate circumstances; the same was done by some of the Allied soldiers captured in Asia, for example. One of the most extensive and moving of these visual records was compiled by Ronald Searle, a British soldier who spent the last four years of the war in Japanese camps in Singapore and Burma. His written account of his experiences, published in his book *To the Kwai and Back*, is accompanied by reproductions of more than 300 of the resulting drawings.

In addition to documentary images, concentration camp prisoners drew cartoons. Examples of these, along with cartoons from such sources as newspapers, leaflets, and posters, are reproduced and discussed in Bryant's *World War Two in Cartoons*. The latter is structured principally as a series of reproductions of, and commentaries on, specific cartoons (both from Axis and from Allied countries) rather than being based on a more general historical narrative. A slightly different approach is adopted in Darracott's *A Cartoon War*, which features somewhat more extensive historical background on cartooning during the period and generally shorter texts on the individual images. Like Bryant, Darracott adopted an international perspective featuring the work of cartoonists from various countries. More specifically, his book is organized on the basis of nine generally chronological chapters—ranging from "Britain Alone" to "Towards Nagasaki"—each of which presents the various reactions of a range of artists to a specific theme.

Broad surveys such as those by Bryant and Darracott are supplemented by published collections of the work of individual cartoonists. For example, David Low's *Years of Wrath* covers the artist's work from 1931 to 1945, with approximately two-thirds of the almost 300 images (most of them originally published in the *London Evening Standard*) dealing directly with the war and many of the others with the deteriorating political situation in Europe during the 1930s. However, because the text is limited to one-paragraph summaries of the contemporary events represented in each image, it neither places the cartoons within the larger context of cartooning as an art in wartime nor deals with formal aspects of Low's work.

PHOTOGRAPHY

Although the emphasis in this chapter has been on painting and sculpture in particular, it must be noted that photography was an important medium of wartime documentation and record making. Although war art projects often justified themselves with the shaky assertion that the camera was incapable of interpretation and therefore could not capture the "feel" of the war, photographers were naturally in heavy demand by newspapers, magazines, propaganda offices, intelligence organizations, and the services themselves.

There exist large numbers of publications by and about photographers known for their interest in wars in general and in the Second World War in particular; among those best served by such sources are Cecil Beaton, Margaret Bourke-White, Robert Capa, Lee Miller, Joe Rosenthal, and W. Eugene Smith. Most such studies have been devoted to photographers who were members of the military or who, like Bourke-White and Miller, acted as foreign correspondent-photographers. Also noteworthy are monographs on a smaller number of professional civilian photographers who, like Bill Brandt, recorded such subjects as life in London during the Blitz.

However important these artists' photographs are, they are vastly outnumbered by those taken by anonymous artists. The work of the latter photographers, while obviously not susceptible to treatment in biographical studies, is represented in the increasingly plentiful supply of large-scale surveys of war photography. Two examples, by Lewinski and by Fabian and Adam, are typical. Lewinski's *The Camera at War* includes a substantial section on the Second World War, provides cursory information on arrangements made in various countries for the establishment of networks of military photographers, and comments briefly on the work of selected photographers working in Europe, North Africa, and Asia and the Pacific. Fabian and Adam's text, in *Images of War*, also features a chapter on the Second World War and employs an approach very similar to that used by Lewinski.

In general, though, there is a lack of detailed studies of the organization and practice of military photography during the war. Moeller's *Shooting War*, though it deals with a total of five wars, differs from the two publications just cited by being both more narrowly defined (American combat photographs published in mass-market periodicals) and more detailed. She discusses such topics as censorship, arrangements for publication, subjects, and aesthetics. Even more focused is Maslowski's *Armed with Cameras: The American Military Photographers of World War II*, which, unusually, not only deals at length with only one type of photographer but also is concerned exclusively with the Second World War. Maslowski discusses individual photographers and units, technical aspects of military photography as a genre, the bureaucratic operations involved in coordinating and equipping the photographers, and the propaganda, training, and tactical uses to which the resulting images were put.

The recent trend in the literature on war photography toward a greater proliferation of sources and a growing interest in more focused and detailed studies is paradigmatic of the literature on art in the Second World War in general. The last fifteen years have seen a marked increase in interest in many aspects of wartime visual art and a correspondingly large number of articles, exhibition catalogs, and monographs. However, as is evident from this bibliographic essay as a whole, there remains substantial room for research on virtually every aspect of the relationship of the visual arts to the war. For example—to identify only two topics out of many— little of note has been published on either the impact of the war on the professional practice and livelihood of artists or the iconography of war art as a genre. On these and many other subjects, much work remains to be done.

BIBLIOGRAPHY

Baldwin, Hanson Weightman. *The Navy at War: Paintings and Drawings by Combat Artists.* New York: W. Morrow, 1943.

Barron, Stephanie, ed. *"Degenerate Art": The Fate of the Avant-Garde in Nazi Germany.* Los Angeles: Los Angeles County Museum of Art, 1991.

Blatter, Janet, and Sybil Milton. *Art of the Holocaust.* New York: Rutledge, 1981.

Braun, Emily, ed. *Italian Art in the 20th Century: Painting and Sculpture, 1900–1988.* London: Royal Academy of Arts; Munich: Prestel-Verlag, 1989.

Browning, John Gaitha. *An Artist at War: The Journal of John Gaith Browning.* Edited by Oleta Stewart Toliver. Denton: University of North Texas, 1994.

Bryant, Mark. *World War Two in Cartoons.* London: W. H. Smith/Bison, 1989.

Bussman, Georg, ed. *Kunst im Dritten Reich: Dokumente der Unterwerfung.* Frankfurt: Der Verein, 1974.

Contreras, Belisario Ramon. "The New Deal Treasury Department Art Programs and the American Artist: 1933 to 1943." Ph.D. diss., American University, Washington, DC, 1967.

Cork, Richard. *A Bitter Truth: Avant-Garde Art and the Great War.* New Haven, CT: Yale University, in association with the Barbican Art Gallery, 1994.

Costanza, Mary, and Nora Levin, eds. *The Living Witness: Art in the Concentration Camps.* Philadelphia: Museum of American Jewish History, 1978.

Crane, Aimée, ed. *Art in the Armed Forces, Pictured by Men in Action.* New York: Garland, 1972.

———, ed. *Marines at War.* New York: Hyperion, 1943.

Dahm, Volker. "Die Reichskulturkammer als Instrument kulturpolitischer Steuerung und sozialer Reglementierung." *Vierteljahreshefte für Zeitgeschichte* 34 (January 1986): 53–84.

Darracott, Joseph. *A Cartoon War.* London: Leo Cooper, 1989.

Fabian, Rainer, and Hans Christian Adam. *Images of War.* Translated by Fred Taylor. London: New English Library, 1983.

Foss, Brian. "British Artists and the Second World War, with Particular Reference to the War Artists' Advisory Committee of the Ministry of Information." Ph.D. diss., University of London, 1991.

———. "Message and Medium: Government Patronage, National Identity and National Culture in Britain 1939–45." *Oxford Art Journal* 14 (1991): 52–72.

Fry, Gavin, and Anne Gray. *Masterpieces of the Australian War Memorial.* Adelaide, Australia: Rigby, 1982.

Gesensway, Deborah, and Mindy Roseman. *Beyond Words: Images from America's Concentration Camps.* Ithaca, NY: Cornell University, 1987.

Golomstock, Igor. *Totalitarian Art in the Soviet Union, the Third Reich, Fascist Italy and the People's Republic of China.* Translated by Robert Chandler. New York: HarperCollins, 1990.

Harries, Meirion, and Susie Harries. *The War Artists: British Official War Art of the Twentieth Century.* London: Michael Joseph, in association with the Imperial War Museum and the Tate Gallery, 1983.

Heskett, John. "Art and Design in Nazi Germany." *History Workshop Journal,* no. 6 (Autumn 1978): 139–153.

———. "Modernism and Archaism in Design in the Third Reich." In Brandon Taylor and Wilfried van der Will, eds., *The Nazification of Art,* 110–127. Winchester, U.K.: Winchester, 1990.

Hinz, Berthold. *Art in the Third Reich.* Translated by Robert and Rita Kimber. New York: Pantheon, 1979.

Hjerter, Kathleen G., comp. *The Art of Tom Lea.* College Station: Texas A&M University, 1989.

Huntingford, N. P. C., comp. *A Selection of South African Military Art/'N Versameling van Suid-Afrikaanse Militere Kuns, 1939–1945, 1975–1985.* Pretoria, South Africa: Military Art Advisory Board Defence Headquarters, 1986.

James, Caradog Vaughan. *Soviet Socialist Realism: Origins and Theory.* London: Macmillan, 1973.

Kruger, C., comp. *Suid-Afrikaanse Oorlogskuns in Beeld/South African Images of War.* Johannesburg: South African National Museum of Military History, 1990.

Landau, Ellen G. *Artists for Victory: An Exhibition Catalog*. Washington, DC: Library of Congress, 1983.

Lane, Barbara Miller. *Architecture and Politics in Germany, 1918–1945*. Cambridge: Harvard University, 1968.

Lehmann-Haupt, Hellmut. *Art under a Dictatorship*. New York: Oxford University, 1954.

Leventhal, Fred M. " 'The Best for the Most': CEMA and State Sponsorship of the Arts in Wartime, 1939–1945." *Twentieth Century British History* 1 (1990): 289–317.

Lewinski, Jorge. *The Camera at War: A History of War Photography from 1848 to the Present Day*. New York: Simon and Schuster, 1978.

Low, David. *Years of Wrath: A Cartoon History, 1931–45*. New York: Simon and Schuster, 1946.

Maslowski, Peter. *Armed with Cameras: The American Military Photographers of World War II*. New York: Free, 1993.

McKinzie, Richard D. *The New Deal for Artists*. Princeton: Princeton UP, 1973.

Moeller, Susan D. *Shooting War: Photography and the American Experience of Combat*. New York: Basic, 1989.

Murray, Joan. *Canadian Artists of the Second World War*. Oshawa, Ontario: Robert McLaughlin Gallery, 1981.

Novitch, Miriam, Lucy Dawidowicz, and Tom L. Freudenheim. *Spiritual Resistance: Art from Concentration Camps, 1940–1945; A Selection of Drawings and Paintings from the Collection of Kibbutz Lohamei Haghetaot, Israel*. Philadelphia: Jewish Publication Society of America, 1981.

Petropoulos, Jonathan George. "Art as Politics: The Nazi Elite's Quest for the Political and Material Control of Art." Ph.D. diss., Harvard University, 1990.

Rave, Paul Ortwin. *Kunstdiktatur im Dritten Reich*. Edited by Uwe M. Schneede. Berlin: Argon, 1987.

Reep, Edward. *A Combat Artist in World War II*. Lexington: UP of Kentucky, 1987.

Reid, John. *Australian Artists at War, Compiled from the Australian War Memorial Collection*. 2 vols. South Melbourne, Australia: Sun, 1977.

Ross, Alan. *Colours of War: War Art 1939–45*. London: Jonathan Cape, 1983.

Scobie, Alex. *Hitler's State Architecture: The Impact of Classical Antiquity*. Pennsylvania and London: Pennsylvania State UP, for the College Art Association, 1990.

Searle, Ronald. *To the Kwai and Back*. London: Collins, in association with the Imperial War Museum, 1986.

Sillars, Stuart. *British Romantic Art and the Second World War*. New York: St. Martin's, 1991.

Silva, Umberto. *Ideologia e Arte del Fascismo*. Milan: G. Mazotta, 1973.

Steinweis, Alan E. *Art, Ideology, and Economics in Nazi Germany: The Reich Chambers of Music, Theatre, and the Visual Arts*. Chapel Hill: University of North Carolina, 1993.

Tabor, Jan. *Kunst und Diktatur: Architektur, Bildhauerei und Malerei in Österreich, Deutschland, Italien und der Sowjetunion 1922–1956*. 2 vols. Baden, Germany: Grasi, 1994.

Taylor, Brandon. "Post-Modernism in the Third Reich." In Brandon Taylor and Wilfried van der Will, eds., *The Nazification of Art*, 128–143. Winchester, U.K.: Winchester, 1990.

Taylor, Brandon, and Wilfried van der Will. "Aesthetics and National Socialism." In Brandon Taylor and Wilfried van der Will, eds., *The Nazification of Art*, 1–13. Winchester, U.K.: Winchester, 1990.

——, eds. *The Nazification of Art: Art, Design, Music, Architecture and Film in the Third Reich*. Winchester, U.K.: Winchester, 1990.

Tempesti, Fernando. *Arte dell'Italia Fascista*. Milan: Feltrinelli, 1976.

Tippett, Maria. *Lest We Forget/Souvenons-Nous*. London, Ontario: London Regional Art and Historical Museums, 1989.

Townsend, Harry Everett. *War Diary of a Combat Artist*. Edited by Alfred E. Cornebise. Niwot, CO: UP of Colorado, 1991.

Weber, John Paul. *The German War Artists*. Columbia, SC: Cerberus, 1979.

Willett, John. "Art of a Nasty Time." *The New York Review of Books* 27 (26 June 1980): 9–12.

21 Art Music and World War II

Ben Arnold

Between 1939 and 1945 composers of art music (as opposed to popular or folk music) wrote over 200 compositions influenced directly by the events of the Second World War. Since 1945, composers from twenty-five countries have added more than 200 additional works about World War II to the repertory. In the decade between 1980 and 1990, for example, composers wrote nearly thirty works that dealt with the atomic bomb, the Holocaust, or some other aspect of World War II, clearly indicating the enduring interest in the war. Art compositions dealing with World War II include all classical genres (i.e., symphony, opera, and oratorio). Compositions written during the early years of the war primarily displayed a heroic, patriotic side to war. Some of them were optimistic, even defiant.

Dmitri Shostakovich's patriotic Seventh Symphony, first performed in Kuibyshev, 5 March 1942, was the most celebrated war-related work written during the war. It became an influential propaganda work, depicting the dauntless Soviet stand against the Nazi aggressor. In Shostakovich's *Testimony*, Solomon Volkov argued that this was probably the first time in musical history that a symphony played so political a role (136).

While not as consequential politically during the war, several works written during the war years have become musically important. Oliver Messiaen composed his *Quartet for the End of Time* while a prisoner of war. The idea for Michael Tippett's *A Child of Our Time* grew out of the general situation of the world before World War II, and he composed the work as the war progressed. Roy Harris originally dedicated his Symphony No. 5 to the heroic and freedom-loving people of our great ally, the Union of Soviet Socialist Republics, before he later removed the dedication. Arnold Schoenberg composed his *Ode to Napoleon* at the height of World War II to illustrate the similarities between Hitler and Napoleon. Aaron Copland concluded his *A Lincoln Portrait* with a section from Lincoln's

Gettysburg Address to honor the war dead of World War II. In two parts Paul Creston's *Chant of 1942* dealt with the despair as well as the hope exhibited during the year 1942.

Bohuslav Martinù wrote his *Memorial to Lidice* quickly upon his learning of the Nazi massacre there, and George Antheil conceived the second and third movements of his Symphony No. 4 (1942) in response to this tragedy in Czechoslovakia. Shostakovich's Eighth Symphony sounds much darker and more explosive than his Seventh, with a frenzied scherzo movement, which repeats a rhythmic pattern continuously until it reaches its harrowing climax in the next movement. Influenced by the newsreels during the war years, Igor Stravinsky parodied the goose step of the Nazi soldiers in the third movement of his *Symphony in Three Movements.* Richard Strauss' *Metamorphosen,* written as Germany lay in the chaos of defeat, illustrates the despair associated with war and ends with a reference to the funeral march from Beethoven's *Eroica Symphony.*

Sergei Prokofiev's *Ode to the End of the War* was the most notable of the victory celebrations at war's end. In England, Ralph Vaughan Williams composed and recorded his *Thanksgiving for Victory* before the end of the war so that it could be broadcast the day the Allies defeated the Germans. Bernard Stevens dedicated his *Symphony of Liberation* to Clive Branson, who was killed in battle in 1944. Composed during the German Blitz of London, the symphony is in three movements, "Enslavement," "Resistance," and "Liberation."

After 1945, music related to the war was rarely patriotic or victorious; rather, the music was more frequently horrific, experimental, or mournful. Paul Hindemith's *When Lilacs Last in the Door-yard Bloom'd: A Requiem for Those We Love,* along with Britten's *War Requiem,* is one of the most significant choral compositions influenced by war in this century. In eleven numbered parts, this intense setting of Whitman's poem captures the elegiac atmosphere of the suffering of war directly and simply. Hindemith dedicated his requiem to the memory of President Roosevelt and to the American soldiers killed during World War II. Gian Francesco Malipiero included a funeral march in his Symphony No. 4 "In Memoriam" written as a memorial to those who died in the war. Arthur Honegger wrote his Symphony No. 3 "Liturgique" in response to war and ended with a call for peace. This brilliant composition is in three movements: "Dies irae," "De profundis clamavi," and "Dona nobis pacem."

In his *Canticle No. 3,* Op. 55, Benjamin Britten set "Still Falls the Rain," a World War II poem by Edith Sitwell, in two parts: "The Raids, 1940" and "Night and Dawn." The music is mournful, using repetitive melodic phrases. Britten composed his *War Requiem,* based on the World War I poetry of Wilfred Owen in addition to the traditional Latin requiem text, for the reopening of Coventry Cathedral, which had been bombed during World War II. Arguably the best-known war-related work of the century, this requiem is a poignant combination of texts and musical styles, ranging from its haunting tritone relationships in the beginning to its asymmetrical rhythmic outbursts in the "Dies irae."

Luigi Nono based his *Il canto sospeso* on letters from resistance leaders who were killed in the war. The second movement of Shostakovich's *Eighth String Quartet*, written against fascism, is similar to the scherzo of the Eighth Symphony with its intense rhythmic drive. Gordon Mumma presents a highly individualistic account of the firebombing of Dresden in his electronic *Dresden Interleaf 13 February 1945*. Boris Schifrin's *Cantata from the Rise and Fall of the Third Reich* is in fifteen sections, including "Following the First World War," "The Creation of Hitler," "Bonfires Were Built," "The War," and "The Fall." Several fragments from Hitler's speeches appear in between sections of the chorus screaming "Heil. Heil. Siegheil." Built upon a three-note cell, Andrzej Panufnik's *Katyń Epitaph* expresses his outrage that the Katyn atrocity was largely forgotten. He dedicated the work to the memory of the 15,000 Poles who died in this massacre. Georg Katzer based his *Aide Memoire*, subtitled "Seven Nightmares from the Thousand Year Night" and written for the fiftieth anniversary of Hitler's rise to power in 1933, on acoustic fragments of music and text from original recordings dating from Hitler's rise of power in 1933 to his demise in 1945. Katzer considered the war years as a great and terrible nightmare. In his composition he made a collage of items from Nazi documents of the time and created seven scenes in which the dreamer tosses restlessly among these nightmares. Siegfried Matthus based his opera *Die Weise von Liebe und Tod des Cornets Christoph Rilke* on poems of Rilke that soldiers carried to the front in both world wars and deals with the destruction of Dresden. Dedicated to the victims of the Katyn forest massacre, Nancy Van de Vate's *Kracow Concerto "Katyń"* uses quotations from Polish folk songs and Renaissance composers coupled with dissonances and gunshots.

Music dealing with the bombing of Japan and with the massacre of the Jews emerged as the two most salient World War II themes in the 1950s, however. In the early 1950s, Masao Ohki composed two symphonic works dealing with the atomic bomb, Symphony No. 5 "Atomic Bomb" and *Hiroshima*. The latter work, inspired by the paintings *Pictures of the Atom Bomb* of Iri Maruki and Thshiko Akamatsu, is a graphic portrayal of, and a polemic about, the event. Years after Ohki's pioneering efforts, Japanese composers contributed highly sensitive and imaginative works on these tragedies. Most important are Toshiya Sukegawa's *the eternal morning 1945.8.6* and Masaaki Hayakawa's *Inori for Hiroshima* for soprano, contrabass, and percussion. Sukegawa's twenty-minute work uses electronic sounds of roaring engines, sirens, and knocking sounds combined with an out-of-tune piano damaged during the bombing. He adds these devices to screeching, high-pitched sonorities in the string orchestra to provide a realistic portrayal and reenactment of the bombing of Hiroshima. Hayakawa's work, based on the poem *Lamentation* by Kazuko Yamada, depicts a mother looking for her lost sons separated after the atomic blast. Most moving is the eleventh part of the poem in which she repeatedly calls for her children: "Hey Shoji! Hey Yasushi! Hey Shoji! Hey Yasushi!" Written in graphic notation, Mayako Kubo's *Iterum meditemur for Hiroshima* for trombone and tape is an angry work, including sounds of Oriental wind chimes and a voice reading clips from an American newspaper in the 1940s. Yori-Aki Matsudaira's *Dark Mirror: Young Orpheus on a Theme of the Atomic Bomb*, first performed in Osaka in 1962, is virtually unknown in the West. Tomiko Kojiba's *Hiroshima Requiem* for string orchestra and antique cymbals is a melancholy composition in the tradition of Strauss' *Metamorphosen*.

Composers from other countries have been quite prolific in writing about the bombing of Japan as well. Krzysztof Penderecki's *Threnody to the Victims of Hiroshima*, the most celebrated composition on the effects of the atom bomb and one of the most famous works of the century, was first performed on 31 May 1961. This work for strings has received hundreds of performances and has been anthologized in numerous twentieth-century texts and anthologies. It is extraordinary and innovative, using strings in experimental ways to make the sounds of bombs dropping, the roar of airplane engines, and a rugged, horrific atmosphere of dissonance through the use of sound-mass, glissandi, and piercing high notes. Penderecki's composition highly influenced R. Murray Schafer's *Threnody*, written for five young narrators, youth chorus, voices, orchestra, and tape in 1966. Schafer parodies the scientific thought behind the dropping of the bomb on Nagasaki. Men speak on a tape about the success of the bombing and how delighted the politicians were, after which children recite gory texts taken from eyewitnesses of the event.

Siegfried Behrend composed his *Requiem auf Hiroshima* for voice, mandolin, guitar, percussion, and plucked string instruments and also includes vocal groans, shrieks, and instrumental cacophony. After counting down from ten to zero, Paul Dessau's *Einstein* includes a boys' chorus frantically singing "Hiroshima" and "Nagasaki" and leads to Einstein's descriptions of the cities destroyed. Gaetano Giuffrè's *Hiroshima* employs speaking and frequent changes in tempo and meter in a precisely notated lament. Luigi Nono's *Sul Ponte di Hiroshima* for soprano, tenor, and orchestra premiered in 1963, and Carmen Petra-Basacopol's *Pro pace* is a cycle of three songs dealing with the dropping of the bomb on Hiroshima: "Meeting Hiroshima," "Choir of the Killed Children," and "The Voices of the Birds of Hiroshima." William Mathias wrote his *Ceremony after a Fire Raid* with graphic texts and a chorus that yells, whispers, and speaks in addition to singing in its depiction of the bombing of Hiroshima. Gérard Condé's *Memorial* for narrator and string quintet is an experimental portrayal of the bombing of Nagasaki. Michael Berkeley's *Or Shall We Die?* includes a section depicting a survivor from Hiroshima looking for her lost daughter. The Soviet composer Yury Levitin uses clusters, glissandi, *Sprechstimme*, and other dramatic effects in his *Hiroshima Must Not Be Repeated* to produce a protest against dropping this bomb on innocent people. In these six movements, Levitin makes particular use of a children's chorus in the fourth and sixth movements. Titles of movements include "Children of Hiroshima Are Drawing," "The Girl Sakaya Is Dying," and the last, "Hiroshima Must Not Be Repeated." The only American composition specifically about Hiroshima or Nagasaki is Jackson Hill's *Tōrō Nagashi*, which deals with the ceremonial lighting of candles each year in memory of those who died in the blast at Nagasaki.

A number of composers lost their lives in the concentration camps, but music continued to be composed and, in some cases, performed. Viktor Ullmann's opera *The Emperor of Atlantis* was composed in the Terezín concentration camp; however, it was so anti-Hitler and antiwar that it was never performed during the war years. Karel Berman began his *Suite for Piano Solo (1939–1945)* in the Terezín concentration camp and originally entitled it *Suite Terezín*. Starting with "Youth" and "Family Home," the movements outline Berman's life and also include "15 March 1939 Occupation," "Auschwitz Corpse Factory" (originally named "Horror"), "Typhus in the Kauffering Concentration Camp," "Alone Alone," and "New Life."

Arnold Schoenberg's *A Survivor from Warsaw*, scored for narrator, chorus, and orchestra, is a highly structured composition strictly employing twelve-tone technique. Schoenberg takes his text from a true story of a survivor from the Warsaw ghetto and presents it virtually verbatim in his composition. A speaker narrates the story using *Sprechstimme*, which enables every word to be clearly discernible. Benjamin Frankel dedicated his Violin Concerto to the memory of the 6 million Jews who lost their lives during World War II. Shostakovich set Yevgeny Yevtushenko's poem *Babi Yar* in the first movement of his Thirteenth Symphony. The Nazis slaughtered over 70,000 Jews and buried them in the deep ravine outside Kiev known as Babi Yar. Shostakovich's music in this movement is dark and foreboding, consisting of men's choir and bass soloists in addition to five-string double basses and tolling bells. In memorial to Jews slain by the Nazis, Wilfred Josephs based his ten-movement *Requiem* on Kaddish, the Hebrew Prayer for the Dead. All of the movements are in slow tempos, and the unusual format includes a string quintet performing without any text in several movements.

The first work to incorporate electronic techniques into a Holocaust composition was Luigi Nono's *Ricorda cosa ti hanno fatto in Auschwitz*. Nono uses a soprano and a children's chorus with electronic manipulations of sound to create a haunting and oppressive atmosphere of sorrow. Ellwood Derr dedicated his *I Never Saw Another Butterfly* to the everlasting memory of the children who suffered and made these poems. The work contains five movements based on selected poems from the publication of the title: "Terezín," "The Butterfly," "The Old Man," "Fear," and "The Garden."

Penderecki's *Dies irae*, dedicated to the memory of those murdered at Auschwitz, was first performed on the grounds of Auschwitz in 1967. In the first movement, "Lamentation," Penderecki creates an artistic world of anguish and despair through his use of glissandi, high tessituras, and indeterminate chanting. Sholom Secunda composed his large-scale *Yiskor in Memory of the Six Million* as an attack on humankind and a plea not to forget the Holocaust. Srul Irving Glick's *I Never Saw Another Butterfly*, written for Maureen Forrester and commissioned by the Canadian Broadcasting Corporation, is a subtle, evocative setting of *To Olga; Yes, That's the Way Things Are; The Little Mouse; On a Sunny Evening; The Narrative;* and *The Butterfly*. Shulamit Ran set to music five poems by Nelly Sachs in her *O, the Chimneys: A Dead Child Speaks, Already Embraced by the Arm of Heavenly Solace, Fleeing, Someone Comes,* and *Hell Is Naked*. The first poems deal with the death of a child, but the last one broadens the horror to the end of the world. In this last song, the composer adds a pretaped excerpt containing metallic sirens and tolling bells to assist in depicting the death of all.

Oskar Morawetz's *From the Diary of Anne Frank* is a dramatic narrative about the horror and despair of the concentration camps displayed in this large-scale, tonal composition. Morawetz also created an excerpt from this work called *Who Has Allowed Us to Suffer*. Francis Schwartz's *Caligula* is noted for its ugliness of sound in attempting to portray the devastation of those who lived and died during unbelievable wartime conditions. He dedicated his composition to the victims of Auschwitz, Mylai, and other places.

Henryk Górecki's Symphony No. 3 "Symphony of Sorrowful Songs" has become the best-known work composed in the last two decades on the subject of the Holocaust, chiefly because of the best-selling compact disc with Dawn Upshaw and the London Sinfonietta. This work is not a traditional orchestral symphony but includes a soprano solo in each of its three movements. Górecki based the second movement on a brief, four-line text scribbled by an eighteen-year-old girl on the wall of her cell in a prison at Zakopane. The eight-and-a-half-minute movement uses only a few bare chords, but this sparsity of texture establishes a rare and ethereal atmosphere.

Tera de Marez Oyens' *Charon's Gift* for piano and strings begins with an otherworldly, glasslike opening, which sets the stage for this haunting, often hypnotic, and pointillistic work. Mikis Theodorakis' *Liturgie. Den Kindern, getötet in Kriegen* contains fourteen unaccompanied songs ranging from *Abendgebet* and *Die heilige Mutter*, to *Anne Frank Ibrahim Emilano, Der*

Tag der Apokalypse, Der heilige Che [Gueverra], and *Totem Sohne.* Penderecki's *Polish Requiem* represents his more romantic, conservative style, which he adopted in the 1970s. The "Dies irae" of this enormous work commemorates the Warsaw uprising against the Nazis in 1944, and the "Recordare, Jesu pie" was written in response to a victim of Auschwitz. Steve Martland's *Babi Yar* is a highly angular and disjointed work with metallic and repetitive patterns based on the massacre at Babi Yar.

In his *Anne Frank Cantata: A Child of Light*, Hans Kox has a bass representing evil (and singing passages based on sayings of the SS and Hitler) and a soprano representing Anne Frank. Benjamin Lees wrote his Symphony No. 4 "Memorial Candles" as an hour-long work to commemorate the fortieth anniversary of the Holocaust's end. Arnold Rosner based his *From the Diaries of Adam Czerniakow* on the graphic diaries that discuss the hunger, the killing, the suicides, and the epidemics of the concentration camps. Part II "Eleni" of Morton Subotnick's *Jacob's Room* is a setting in which a young boy discovers the death of his mother at the end of World War II, and Part III "Night" tragically depicts a train journey to the concentration camps. The soprano speaks dramatically and sings with a wide range, using falsetto, extended trills, glissandi, and other unusual special vocal techniques.

Steve Reich composed his autobiographical *Different Trains* for string quartet and tape, using fragments from taped interviews of Holocaust survivors to provide the pitched, musical motives for some of the themes in the work. The three movements in Reich's typical, minimalistic style represent various train rides but three highly different journeys: Reich's boyhood journey between New York and Los Angeles before World War II; the journey to the death camps that he as a Jew would have likely taken had he lived in Central Europe during the war; and the journey back in the states after the war.

Lukas Foss wrote his *Elegy for Anne Frank* for the sixtieth anniversary of the birth of Anne Frank and for a memorial service at the Cathedral of St. John the Divine in New York City. This brief elegy uses a childlike melody to represent Anne's innocence and interrupts it with a militant, Nazi hymn. Foss later incorporated this independent work into his Symphony No. 3 "Symphony of Sorrows" in 1991.

The literature in English written about art music and World War II is small but growing. Ben Arnold's *Music and War: A Research and Information Guide* provides the most comprehensive survey, supplying bibliographic and discographic information of over 400 art compositions dealing with World War II. Of the more specialized studies of the Holocaust, Joža Karas' *Music in Terezín: 1941–1945* is particularly noteworthy. Karas examines the opera and orchestral productions in Terezín as well as the important composers imprisoned there: Gideon Klein, Pavel Haas, Hans Krása, and Viktor Ullmann. Three autobiographical accounts of the music making in the camps are stirring re-creations of that eerie world: Josef Bors' *The Terezín Requiem*, Fania Fénelon's *Playing for Time*, and Szymon Laks' *Music of Another World*. Gila Flam's *Singing for Survival: Songs of the Lodz Ghetto, 1940–45* is an account of a camp in which his father was imprisoned.

Several studies have also appeared on music in Germany during the Third Reich, but these studies do not specifically discuss compositions related to the war. Michael Meyer's *The Politics of Music in the Third Reich* looks at the roles of musicians, publishers, and promoters of music in a totalitarian state. Erik Levi's *Music in the Third Reich* examines art music during that era, concentrating chiefly on the social history, seeking to illustrate how German music progressed during the Hitler years.

NOTE

Much of the information in this chapter is based on research published earlier in *Music and War: A Research and Information Guide* (New York: Garland, 1993). Used with permission of Garland.

COMPOSITIONS CITED

Works are selected because of their importance and the availability of scores or recordings. Recordings given are only samples of available recordings. An asterisk (*) indicates recording information.

Antheil, George. Symphony No. 4 ("1942") [1942]. London: Boosey and Hawkes, 1947. *Everest KOBR 6013.

Behrend, Siegfried. *Requiem auf Hiroshima* [1973]. Cologne: Musikverlag H. Gerig, 1976. *Capella Thorofon CTH 2026.

Berkeley, Michael. *Or Shall We Die?* [1982]. London: Oxford UP, 1982. *EMI ASD 2700581.

Berman, Karel. *Suite for Piano Solo (1939–1945)*. Piano [1944, revised 1984]. *Channel Classics CCS 3191.

Britten, Benjamin. *Canticle No. 3*, Op. 55 [1954]. London: Boosey and Hawkes, 1956. *Argo ZRG 946.

———. *War Requiem*, Op. 66 [1961]. London: Boosey and Hawkes, 1962. *Angel CDC-47033.

Condé, Gérard. *Memorial* [c. 1980]. Paris: Éditions musicales transatlantiques, 1980.

Copland, Aaron. *A Lincoln Portrait* [1942]. New York: Boosey and Hawkes, 1943. *CBS MK-42431.

Creston, Paul. *Chant of 1942*, Op. 33 [1943]. New York: G. Schirmer. *Crystal Records CD 508.

Derr, Ellwood. *I Never Saw Another Butterfly* [1966]. Islington, MA: Dorn Production, 1977.

Dessau, Paul. *Einstein* [1971–1973]. Berlin: Henschelverlag Kunst and Gesellschaft, 1973.

Foss, Lukas. *Elegy for Anne Frank* [1989]. New York: Carl Fischer, 1989.

Frankel, Benjamin. Violin Concerto, Op. 24 [1951]. London: Augener, 1952. *Rococo (RR) 2101.

Giuffrè, Gaetano. *Hiroshima* [1964–1965]. New York: Seesaw Music, 1979.

Glick, Srul Irving. *I Never Saw Another Butterfly* [1968]. Willowdale, Ontario: Leeds Music (Canada), 1972. *Canadian Broadcasting CSC 122.

Górecki, Henryk. Symphony No. 3 "Symphony of Sorrowful Songs," Op. 36 [1977]. Kracow: Polskie wydawnictwo muzyczne, 1977. *Elektra Nonesuch 79282–2.

Harris, Roy. Symphony No. 5 [1942]. New York: Mills Music, 1961. *Albany AR 012–2.

Hayakawa, Masaaki. *Inori for Hiroshima* [after 1945]. *Fontec RFO-1043.

Hill, Jackson. *Tōrō Nagashi (Lanterns of Hiroshima)* [1977]. Wolverhampton, PA: Faircloth House, 1977.

Hindemith, Paul. *When Lilacs Last in the Door-yard Bloom'd: A Requiem for Those We Love* [1946]. New York: Associated Music, 1948. *Telarc CD-80132.

Honegger, Arthur. Symphony No. 3 "Liturgique" [1946]. Paris: Salabert, 1946. *DG 423242–2 GC.

Josephs, Wilfred. *Requiem* [1963]. London: Josef Weinberger, 1965. *Unicorn-Kanchana DKP 9032.

Katzer, Georg. *Aide Memoire* [1983]. *Recommended Records RRP22.

Kojiba, Tomiko. *Hiroshima Requiem* [1979].

Kox, Hans. *Anne Frank Cantata: A Child of Light* [1985]. Amsterdam: Donemus, 1985. *Composers Voice Special 1987/4.

Kubo, Mayako. *Iterum meditemur for Hiroshima* [1978]. Vienna: Ariadne, 1979.

Lees, Benjamin. Symphony No. 4 "Memorial Candles" [1985]. New York: Boosey and Hawkes, 1986.

Levitin, Yury. *Hiroshima Must Not Be Repeated* [1967]. Moscow: Soviet Kompositor, 1972.

Malipiero, Gian Francesco. Symphony No. 4 "In Memoriam" [1946]. Milan: G. Ricordi, 1948.

Marez Oyens, Tera de. *Charon's Gift* [1982]. *Composers Voice 8702.

Martinù, Bohuslav. *Memorial to Lidice* [1943]. Moscow: State Music, 1966. *Unicorn RHS 309.

Martland, Steve. *Babi Yar* [1983]. London and New York: Schott, 1989. *Factory Classical Record FACT 266.

Mathias, William. *Ceremony after a Fire Raid*, Op. 63 [1973]. London: Oxford UP, 1975.

Matsudaira, Yori-Aki. *Dark Mirror: Young Orpheus on a Theme of the Atomic Bomb* [c. 1962].

Matthus, Siegfried. *Die Weise von Liebe und Tod des Cornets Christoph Rilke* [1986]. Leipzig: Deutscher Verlag für Musik, 1986.

Messiaen, Oliver. *Quartet for the End of Time* [1941]. Paris: Durand, 1988. *DG 423247–2 GC.

Morawetz, Oskar. *From the Diary of Anne Frank* [1970]. *Radio Canada International RCI 601.

———. *Who Has Allowed Us to Suffer?* CMC 0281; Centrediscs.

Mumma, Gordon. *Dresden Interleaf 13 February 1945* [1965]. *Lovely Music/Vital Records VR 1091.

Nono, Luigi. *Il canto sospeso* [1956]. Mainz: Ars Viva, 1956. *Sony Classical SK 53360.

————. *Ricorda cosa ti hanno fatto in Auschwitz* [1965]. *Wergo WER 60038.

————. *Sul Ponte di Hiroshima* (from *Canti di vita e d' amore*) [1962]. Mainz: Ars Viva, 1963. *Wergo 6229–2.

Ohki, Masao. *Hiroshima* [1953]. Tokyo: Zen-On Music, 1956.

————. Symphony No. 5 "Atomic Bomb" [c. 1953].

Panufnik, Andrzej. *Katyń Epitaph.* [1967, rev. 1969]. London: Boosey and Hawkes, 1972. *Unicorn-Kanchana DKP 9016.

Penderecki, Krzysztof. *Dies irae* [1967]. Celle: Moeck, 1967. *Philips 839701.

————. *Polish Requiem* [1983]. Mainz: B. Schott's Söhne, 1984.

————. *Threnody to the Victims of Hiroshima* [1959–1960]. Warsaw: Polskie wydawnictwo muzyczene, 1961. *Philips 412 0301.

Petra-Basacopol, Carmen. *Pro pace* [c. 1973]. s.l.: Editura muzicala a uniunii compozitoriler, 1973.

Prokofiev, Sergei. *Ode to the End of the War,* Op. 105 [1945]. New York: Belwin Mills, 1979. *Melodiya A10 00083005.

Ran, Shulamit. *O, The Chimneys* [1969]. New York: Carl Fischer, 1975. *Turnabout TV-S 34492.

Reich, Steve. *Different Trains* [1988]. *Elektra/Nonesuch 79176.

Rosner, Arnold. *From the Diaries of Adam Czerniakow.* [1985–1986].

Schafer, R. Murray. *Threnody* [1966]. Toronto: Berandol Music, 1970. *Melbourne SMLP 4017.

Schifrin, Lalo (Boris). *Cantata from the Rise and Fall of the Third Reich* [1967]. New York: Hastings Music, 1967. *MGM1SE 12ST.

Schoenberg, Arnold. *Ode to Napoleon,* Op. 41 [1942]. New York: G. Schirmer, 1945. *DG 415982–2 GH.

————. *A Survivor from Warsaw,* Op. 46 [1947]. New York: Bomart Music, 1949. *DG 431774–2 GH.

Schwartz, Francis. *Caligula* [1975]. New York: Peer-Southern International. *Serie Musica Contemporanea ICPC17.

Secunda, Sholom. *Yiskor in Memory of the Six Million* [c. 1967]. Carlstadt, NJ: Ethnic Music, 1967.

Shostakovich, Dmitri. String Quartet No. 8, Op. 110 [1960]. New York: Kalmus, 1960. *Angel CDC-47507.

————. Symphony No. 7, Op. 60 [1941]. New York: Leeds Music, 1945. *London 417392–2.

————. Symphony No. 8, Op. 65 [1943]. Leipzig: Breitkopf & Härtel, 1947. *London 411616–2 LH.

————. Symphony No. 13 ("Babi Yar"), Op. 113 [1962]. New York: Leeds Music, 1970. *London 417261–2 LH2.

Stevens, Bernard. *Symphony of Liberation,* Op. 7 [1940–45]. *Meridian CDE 84124.

Strauss, Richard. *Metamorphosen* [1945]. New York: Boosey and Hawkes, 1946. *DG 423888–2 GGA.

Stravinsky, Igor. *Symphony in Three Movements* [1942–1945]. New York: Associated Music, 1946. *Columbia MS 6331.

Subotnick, Morton. *Jacob's Room* [1985–1986]. *Wergo WER 2014–50 (includes first and last sections).

Sukegawa, Toshiya. *the eternal morning 1945.8.6* [1983]. *Vienna Modern Masters VMM 3006.

Theodorakis, Mikis. *Liturgie. Den Kindern, getötet in Kriegen* [1982]. Leipzig: Deutscher Verlag für Musik, 1983.

Tippett, Michael. *A Child of Our Time* [1939–1941]. London: Schott, 1944. *Philips 6500985.

Ullmann, Viktor. *The Emperor of Atlantis* [1944]. London: British Broadcasting, 1974.

Van de Vate, Nancy. *Kracow Concerto "Katyń"* [1989]. *Conifer CDCF185.

Vaughan Williams, Ralph. *Thanksgiving for Victory* (later renamed *A Song of Thanksgiving*) [1944]. London: Oxford UP, 1945. *HMV ED 2902581.

BIBLIOGRAPHY

Arnold, Ben. *Music and War: A Research and Information Guide.* New York: Garland, 1993.

Bors, Josef. *The Terezín Requiem.* New York: Knopf, 1963.

Fénelon, Fania. *Playing for Time.* New York: Atheneum, 1977.

Flam, Gila. *Singing for Survival: Songs of the Lodz Ghetto, 1940–1945.* Urbana: University of Illinois, 1991.

Karas, Joža. *Music in Terezín 1941–1945.* New York: Beaufort in association with Pendragon, 1985.

Laks, Szymon. *Music of Another World.* Evanston, IL: Northwestern UP, 1989.

Levi, Erik. *Music in the Third Reich.* New York: St. Martin's, 1994.

Meyer, Michael. *The Politics of Music in the Third Reich.* American University Studies Series IX, History, vol. 49. New York: Peter Lang, 1991.

Shostakovich, Dmitri. *Testimony: The Memoirs of Dmitri Shostakovich.* Edited by Solomon Volkov. New York: Harper and Row, 1979.

22 Popular Culture and World War II

Ruth Elwell

Popular culture is difficult to define without being too limiting or too inclusive. Authors use the term in a variety of interconnected, but not necessarily synonymous, ways to refer to a wide range of elements of mass experience, often in contradistinction to high culture, though it can also mean the culture of the common people and includes those aspects of daily life that go beyond work and subsistence. With the exception of film, the study of popular culture in World War II has been spotty. There are a wealth of accessible original source materials and a relative dearth, with some notable exceptions, of important analytic work. Much of what has been written is aimed at a general, rather than an academic, audience, so many components of popular culture remain wide open for serious scholarship.

Three books serve as models for research that explores or incorporates popular culture. *Visions of War*, edited by Holsinger and Schofield, is a collection of essays that look at literature and popular culture to investigate the impact of the war on people's lives, both on the war front and at home. Hung's study of the use of drama, cartoons, and newspapers in the resistance against the Japanese occupation of China, *War and Popular Culture*, uses a literary-cultural approach to establish cultural artifacts within specific contexts and look at how they interacted in different milieus and how urban cultural forms were politicized and spread to rural areas, analyzing the differences between their use by the Nationalists as patriotic tools and by the communists to fashion a new people's culture. Fussell's unique and lucid *Wartime* examines the psychology of the war in the United States and Britain through poetry, novels, and films, as well as advertising, popular songs, folklore, and humor. Especially noteworthy is his discussion of the customs, beliefs, and rituals of the war itself. Chapters on blunders, rumors, and idiom are of exceptional interest.

HOME FRONT

The home front is the focus of the majority of relevant books and articles. Graebner's excellent, scholarly analysis of the American experience, *The Age of Doubt*, deals with both popular and high culture as reflections of American attitudes and ideology. Besides material on the war years, the postwar sections deal with the cultural changes brought about by the war. *The Best War Ever* by Adams looks at how the war is remembered in American popular culture, citing Bush and Reagan's presentation of their war background, and includes a discussion of the birth of teen culture.

Lingeman's *Don't You Know There's a War On?* provides an overview of such diverse topics as the publishing industry, advertising, Broadway, popular music and dancing, nightclubs, teenagers, newspapers and magazines, sports, eating habits, consumer behavior, women's fashion and the beauty industry, and housing conditions. *Days of Sadness, Years of Triumph* by Perrett deals briefly with vacations, liquor consumption, Frank Sinatra's hysterical fans, fads and crazes, and burlesque and strip shows, along with more commonly discussed elements of popular culture. Blum's *V Was for Victory* has a section on consumer behavior and consumer-oriented businesses, including the marketing of soft drinks and chewing gum. In *Home Front, USA* Hoehling discusses some of the more obscure items affected by wartime production and rationing—diapers, toys, hearing-aid batteries, and liquor—and mentions children's participation in salvage drives and victory gardens. He also deals with the United Service Organizations (USO) and the entertainment of troops. *Virtue under Fire* by Costello, about the changing roles of, and attitudes toward, women, includes material on popular music, radio, troop entertainment, pinups, and GIs in England.

Since popular culture is frequently a feature of participants' most vivid memories of the war years, oral histories often contain some relevant material. Hoopes' *Americans Remember the Home Front*, arranged by topic, includes interviews with show business and sports figures, and Satterfield's *The Home Front* has chapters on childhood and youth culture and rationing and one on entertainers featuring musicians, comedians, singers, movie and radio personalities, and magicians.

For Britain, *The Home Front* by Briggs features photos, cartoons, ads, magazine illustrations, movie posters, comic strips, and sheet music, offering a wide range of popular culture materials intelligently organized and presented to give a picture of daily life in Britain during the war. *The Forties* by Jenkins is another well-illustrated, large-format book on the home front. Longmate's *The Home Front* is a rather eccentric, but readable, anthology. Extracts of reminiscences and printed materials create a chronological narrative of England during the war years, with popular culture material scattered throughout. Grant and Maddren's evocative *The Coun-*

tryside at War contains excellent photos on almost every page, providing a good sense of rural life during the war.

A Lovely Day Tomorrow by Hamish, about popular culture in New Zealand in the 1940s, is illustrated with ads, photos, posters, and magazine covers and includes sections on home and garden, transportation, entertainment, and fashion and beauty.

FOOD AND COOKING

Though most of the books on Britain include some material on food, it is the main focus of Raynes' entertaining and informative *Bombers and Mash*. Illustrated with photographs and ads, it discusses rationing, the Dig for Victory campaign, and cooking, including a generous selection of recipes. Food is also the focus of *The Bread of Affliction* by Moskoff, about the impact of the German invasion of the Soviet Union on agriculture, the necessity of feeding the army, and the resulting shortages. Recipes from women's magazines are indicators of the contents of diet. Examining Canada in "Changing Traditional Foodways in Wartime," Rickey looks beyond issues of nutrition to disruptions of culture-based aspects: morale implications of particular foods for military personnel, the impact of civilian rationing on dietary habits, and government propaganda aimed at women to encourage a sense of patriotism and participation in the war effort.

SERVICEMEN'S CULTURE

Longmate's *The G.I.'s* examines the impact of American servicemen on life in England, including material on food, music, recreation, entertainment, and romance. Potts' *Yanks Down Under 1941–45* is a similar study of Australia, while "When They Send the Last Yank Home" by Cleveland looks at GIs stationed in New Zealand. Blum's "The G.I. in the Culture of the Second World War" details the role of the Office of War Information and war correspondents in creating the American media image of humble, ordinary, usually rural hero soldiers and explores how nostalgia for an idealized notion of home was an important motivator for soldiers. Westbrook focuses on the popularity of pinups with servicemen in "I Want a Girl, Just Like the Girl That Married Harry James." Insight into the culture of servicemen is available in Anglo, *Service Newspapers of the Second World War*, covering both British and American publications and including illustrations and reprinted material plus well-written historical information. On popular culture among captured GIs, Paterson's "Artist in Stalag III-B" uses sketches done in a prisoner of war (POW) camp outside Berlin to illustrate a description of living conditions and the recreational activities the Young Men's Christian Association (YMCA) organized for POWs.

NAZISM AND FASCISM

Mosse's *Nazi Culture,* a collection of translated original documents, contains a prescient introduction on the function of popular culture in Nazism and provocative materials on radio programming, theater, and popular fiction. Grunberger's comprehensive and well-illustrated *The 12-Year Reich* provides an overview of consumer behavior, youth culture, family life, education, humor, the theater, radio programs, and popular music. *Inside Nazi Germany* by Peukert analyzes how ordinary people lived under Hitler, deals extensively with pro- and anti-Nazi youth subcultures, and explores the blurring of the political and the nonpolitical in Nazi cultural policy. Frogacs' *Italian Culture in the Industrial Era 1880–1980* discusses cultural industries under fascism: book and magazine publishing and radio, film, and foreign influences through imported (largely American) entertainment, with bibliographic citations of secondary source materials in Italian.

ADVERTISING

Advertising during World War II has received significant scholarly attention. A chapter in Wood's *The Story of Advertising* mentions Germany and Britain but focuses on the United States, discussing the affordability of advertising due to the excess profits tax, war themes in ads for products ranging from nuts and bolts to soft drinks, the organization and activities of the War Advertising Council to put the advertising industry at the disposal of the government, and organized labor's antagonism to such advertising. Fox in *Madison Avenue Goes to War* investigates what the war did to the advertising business and what advertising did for the war by looking at the form and content of ads and considering how they influenced public perception of the war, with illustrations demonstrating the use of war imagery in ads aimed at civilian consumption. Begley's *Keep Mum! Advertising Goes to War* about the British advertising industry describes patriotic messages used to sell unlikely products (laundry soap that helps clothing wear longer) and the use of guilt-inducing messages to encourage public participation in the war effort.

Tansey and Hyman have written several articles on advocacy advertisements, examining how advertisers violated the Advertising Federation of America's ethical code in their patriotic zeal in ads about absenteeism and carelessness, Rickenbacker's campaign as an unofficial spokesman for business leaders, and labor unions' response. Sentman and Washburn in "How Excess Profits Tax Brought Ads to Black Newspapers in World War II" suggest that this federal tax, which allowed advertising deductions, made advertising in black newspapers more attractive for white-owned companies and was the source of its dramatic increase.

Honey in "The 'Womanpower' Campaign" examines the way advertisers created an ideological framework for the employment of women in male-identified blue-collar jobs, emphasizing the temporary nature of their employment, aspiration to be full-time housewives, and continuing domestic activities even when dressed in factory overalls, as well as how advertisers used the home as a symbol of American values. Ohmer's "Female Spectatorship and Women's Magazines" looks at how ads and articles in *Good Housekeeping* conveyed ideology on women's role, focusing on Hollywood-related images—ads for films, product ads featuring film personalities, and articles about film stars.

CLOTHING

Fashion has only recently received scholarly attention, even though the war influenced what people wore in a variety of ways: fabric shortages in Britain and the United States, the constraints imposed on haute couture by the German occupation of Paris, the participation of women in industrial production, and the use of military motifs in design. Chapters in such general histories as Bond's *The Guinness Guide to 20th Century Fashion* and Baker's *Fashions of a Decade: The Forties* provide some information but serve primarily to indicate possible directions for research. For example, the utility schemes of the British Board of Trade to cope with fabric shortages and the response of manufacturers, retailers, and customers are studied by Sladen in *The Conscription of Fashion*, while the imagery of knitting by women in fiction and film is explored in Macheski's essay in *Visions of War*. The most extensive, serious, analytic work has been done on one specific aspect of men's fashion, the zoot suit. Cosgrove, "The Zoot Suit and Style Warfare," looks at its origins as a subculture fashion, its implication as a rebellion against wartime rationing, and the patriotism symbolized by military uniforms, as well as the racial implications of the so-called zoot-suit riots. Mazón's *The Zoot Suit Riots*, though more about crowd behavior than fashion, discusses the zoot suit's symbolic meaning as an assertion of adolescent identity and rebellion against adult authority. Chibnall in "Whistle and Zoot" roots it in American black urban culture and the jazz scene and discusses its transference to Britain, where it was adopted by urban working-class youth toward the end of the war.

CHILDHOOD AND YOUTH

Westall in *Children of the Blitz* and Wicks in *No Time to Wave Goodbye* use excerpts from reminiscences and photographs to describe the wartime experiences of English children. Wicks concentrates on the evacuation from London during the Blitz, while Westall also includes children's responses to major events, examples of the influence of the war on play and school experience, and an excellent chapter on food. *Daddy's Gone to War* by Tuttle discusses the influences of the war in American classrooms in the Schools at War Program; gender differences in playing war with improvised and commercial toy weapons, dress-up uniforms, and Boy and Girl Scout activities; war themes in the wide variety of popular media aimed at children; and the continuing impact of the experience of growing up in a war-dominated society.

Halls, *The Youth of Vichy France*, provides a detailed discussion of education and government-sponsored youth organizations under the Vichy regime and their programs to regiment and indoctrinate children and adolescents and includes a chapter on physical education and sports and the impact of food shortages on health. Simons begins with an exploration of Dutch children's books in the between-war years and considers the impact of Nazi censorship and controls in "Juvenile Books in the Netherlands during the German Occupation," while Skjonsberg in "Snorre the Seal" describes the encoding by the Norwegian resistance of hidden meanings into words and pictures in a children's book that could slip by the censors but be intelligible to the public.

Eisen in his extraordinary book *Children and Play in the Holocaust* seeks to understand everyday life in the Holocaust through the role that play, sports, concerts, and theatrical performances served in heightening morale and self-esteem and fostering a will to survive. He explores childhood in the ghettos and camps, with play as a means for social and psychological adaptation in times of duress and the paradox of mass murder and play coexisting, asserting that children's play, rather than being divorced from reality, reflected it and articulated skills for survival.

COMICS, CARTOONS, AND HUMOR

Comics, aimed primarily at children, served a powerful propaganda function. Couperie in *A History of the Comic Strip* points out that many American comics, pro-Allied and pro-intervention from the outset of hostilities, were already potent propaganda weapons by Pearl Harbor. Besides action-adventure war strips, he covers humor strips aimed specifically at GIs, as well as Italian and French comics, including their use by the Nazis to indoctrinate youth in occupied France.

"Little Orphan Annie" is readily accessible and, because of its blatant political message, has received noteworthy attention. *Arf! The Life and Hard Times of Little Orphan Annie 1935–1945* reprints all the strips from these years, with a biographical sketch of Annie's creator, Harold Gray. Smith's *The History of Little Orphan Annie* discusses its influence on kids' participation in the war effort through the "Junior Commando" movement and war themes expressing Gray's political views, especially his anti-Roosevelt stance. Kehl in "Defender of the Faith" focuses on Gray's politics, his abhorrence of the New Deal, and his criticism of government regulation of the economy during the war. Young covers similar ground in "That Indomitable Redhead."

The Office of War Information, interested in the propaganda potential of comic strips, began by studying the war-related content of newspaper strips and eventually supplied its own comics to newspapers and magazines. Other departments, especially treasury, used comics to promote their programs to the public. Barkin in "Fighting the Cartoon War" provides an overview and terse, but thoughtful, critique of this subject. Brief introductory material and reprints of war and superhero comics can be found in Uslan's *America at War: The Best of DC War Comics* and Feiffer's *The Great Comic Book Heroes*, which contains a discussion of Oriental villains and reprints of a "Wonder Woman" featuring references to Mussolini and the first "Captain America" adventure. *The Comic-Book Book* by Thompson and Lupoff includes aviation-adventure pulps and comics, providing descriptions of some of the stories and such nonfiction features as biographies of military aviation heroes and flying and aircraft maintenance tips.

An unusual and important example of analysis, Chang's "Superman Is About to Visit the Relocation Centers and the Limits of Wartime Liberalism" discusses a planned story line in the highly popular "Superman" newspaper strip in which the hero would uncover and defeat a nefarious plot at a Japanese relocation center. Chang focuses on the government's response to this comic and on public attitudes in general toward relocation to exemplify the bankruptcy of wartime liberalism.

Comics continue to appear as a means of conveying the experience of the war. Besides Spiegelman's depiction of the Holocaust in *Maus*—discussed by Joseph Witek in *Comic Books as History*—Keiji Nakazawa's *Barefoot Gen* has been translated into English. This comic book presents the last days of the war and the bombing of Hiroshima from a child's point of view.

Editorial cartoons were a related medium for expressing and shaping wartime attitudes. Douglas in *The World War 1939–1945* uses cartoons to study the course of the war from different national standpoints and from different standpoints within a particular nation. The fiftieth-anniversary reprint of Mauldin's *Up Front* contains a narrative and cartoons of his experiences in the forty-fifth Division in Italy. Mauldin's cartoons are among the examples discussed in "What's Funny about That?" by Waldmeir, an examination of humor aimed at servicepeople. Stokker's "Heil Hitler—God Save the King," on the Norwegian Resistance, compares jokes to other forms of resistance communication, relating their nature and content to folk traditions and analyzing the functions humor served: to communicate resistance spirit, educate and inculcate messages, encourage a sense of solidarity, and raise morale.

POPULAR FICTION

Popular fiction served a number of different wartime functions, not least as entertainment for soldiers. Cole, *Books in Action,* includes several short essays about the Armed Services Editions (ASE), pocket-size paperbacks distributed to GIs, a bibliography of articles on the ASE, and a list of the titles published. "Books, Soldiers and Censorship during the Second World War" by Leary provides background on the publishing industry's Council on Books in Wartime and the selection, publication, and distribution of the ASE, dealing with censorship issues and the Soldier Voting Act's restrictions on government-sponsored distribution of books and other popular media to servicemen.

Honey provides a model of how cultural values were shaped by embedding ideological goals into entertainment in "New Roles for Women and the Feminine Mystique," a case study of the Office of War Information program to organize magazine formula fiction writers and funnel requests for the inclusion of specific messages in stories through the War Writer's Board. "History with Frills" by Harper considers how the ideology of class relations was expressed in art, specifically popular historical fiction. She looks at the reasons for the popularity of historical fiction among women during the war and what this meant to the study of popular taste and cultural resources.

RADIO

The Golden Web by Barnouw and *Don't Touch That Dial* by MacDonald both contain chapters on radio during the war years. Barnouw discusses the role of government censorship and propaganda programming, advertising, the "monopoly" probe of broadcasting, the Dies (un-American Activities) Committee investigation of "subversives" in radio, and Armed Forces Radio, including the participation of Hollywood stars. MacDonald shows how radio presented the war to the public and how war themes were incorporated in entertainment programs, especially adventure serials. Thematic chapters on black programming and soap operas also include extensive discussions of the war years. Wertheim, *Radio Comedy,* and Stedman, *The Serials,* are also of interest. Stedman discusses how war themes were incorporated into soap operas, thrillers, westerns, and juvenile programs. *Radio: The Great Years* by Parker, a history of the BBC, provides information on the difficulties of broadcasting under wartime conditions, propaganda and war news, and programming: variety shows, comedy, dramas with military settings, and information programs aimed at women.

Two articles analyzing the propaganda use of entertainment programming are Ferguson's "Americanism in Late Afternoon Radio Adventure

Serials" and MacDonald's "Government Propaganda in Commercial Radio." Ferguson assesses the meaning and implications of the term "Americanism" as an unquestioning support for an idealized "American way of life" and how the war served as a catalyst for this kind of feeling, discussing specific programs targeted at adolescents and often based on comic book heroes. MacDonald looks at techniques for molding entertainment programming featuring big-name talent in dramas and musical selections into a successful propaganda effort by the Treasury Department to sell . war bonds.

POPULAR MUSIC

Country music enjoyed a surge of popularity, thanks to demographic and social changes, the breakdown of regionalism and rise of commercialization, and the frequency of the war and patriotism as subjects for country songs. Grand Ole Opry produced a traveling unit to entertain at army bases and hospitals, "barn dance" programs proliferated on radio, and country performers began appearing in movies. Malone's *Country Music U.S.A.* includes an informative chapter on the war years, while Chinn in "There's a Star Spangled Banner Waving Somewhere" looks at two types of country songs: war songs, strongly patriotic and with a morale-building aim; and sentimental songs reflecting personal and emotional experiences, parting, and loss. Braun uses popular music and dance as his focus in *Toward a Theory of Popular Culture*, his discussion of the war years noting the nationalistic spirit implicit in the lindy and the square dance revival and songs that reflected the tide of the war.

On wartime African-American music, *Scandalize My Name* by Denison contains a much too brief, but interesting, discussion. More detail is provided in Reagon, "World War II Reflected in Black Music," a study of songs created by the black community and an examination of their potential as historical documents. Songs she collected on the war period, soldiers, the national defense industry, disruption of family, heroes and villains, and hopes and fears of the black community are discussed with reference to historical context.

The Army Music Program gave structure to music in the lives of soldiers. Helbig, *A History of Music in the U.S. Armed Forces during World War II*, provides a detailed description of how this program was organized, utilized, recorded, and broadcast, along with reprints of original documents. Soldiers also created their own lyrics to well-known tunes, collected and discussed in *Fighting Songs and Warring Words* by Murdoch and *Kiss Me Goodnight, Sergeant-Major* by Page.

Popular music served as a focus for several books on the British home front. Huggett's *Goodnight Sweetheart* provides a history of the music industry while also using popular music as a framework for a general discussion of daily life and popular culture. *Great Songs of World War II, with the Home Front in Pictures* by Leitch includes sheet music for thirty-one songs, with illustrations covering the Blitz, entertainment, fashion, victory gardens, food, and GIs. A short introduction for each section and picture captions provide general background and place the songs in context.

In a more analytic vein, Raskin, " 'Le Chant des partisans,' " outlines the background and dissemination of the major song of the French Resistance, then analyzes the psychosocial functions it served: strengthening social cohesion, counteracting anxieties, unburdening with regard to hardships incurred, promoting confidence, and legitimating violence.

THEATER AND ENTERTAINMENT

The chapter on the war and postwar years in *Musical Comedy in America* by Smith mentions military themes in several musicals, while the chapter on the 1940s in Bordman's *American Musical Revue* talks about the loss of young talent and the presentation of war-related and patriotic themes. One such revue was a spectacular pageant of the history of the air force; it enjoyed a successful Broadway run, followed by a national tour, and is the subject of "Moss Hart and *Winged Victory*" by Farmer. Musicals lacking in explicitly war-related content were also products of their time. Hasbany's "Bromidic Parables" covers the role of commercial theater as an institution in wartime culture, government attitudes and policies, and economic considerations, before discussing the indirect influence of the wartime environment on the development of unity and integration of plot, music, and dance in shows such as *Oklahoma!*, compared to standard Broadway revues during the early days of the war. Donovan's "Oh, What a Beautiful Morning" analyzes the success of *Oklahoma!*, looking at its themes in the context of the general mood of optimism about improving economic conditions, the course of the war, and the security of the postwar world.

In Britain, the Entertainments National Service Association (ENSA) was involved in troop entertainment, public performances for civilians to boost morale, and radio broadcasts. *The Theatre at War* by Dean is a well-illustrated personal account of ENSA's activities by one of its organizers, a successful theater producer. *Fighting for a Laugh* by Fawkes, an extensively illustrated popular history of British troop entertainment activities, includes material on American performers and shows in the Middle East and the Far East and during the occupation of Germany, demonstrating the incredible range of entertainment provided to servicemen, from classical concerts, to comedy and popular music, to gang shows and musical revues featuring female impersonators performed by RAF units. Britain is also the subject of *The Greasepaint War* by Hughes, who, as a young actor, was involved in entertaining troops and based this book on his own and other performers' reminiscences. American soldiers received their own dose of culture thanks to Maurice Evans, who began his career as a popularizer of Shakespeare in Broadway productions during the 1930s. Shulimson in "Maurice Evans, Shakespeare and the U.S. Army" emphasizes Evans' approach to Shakespeare as good entertainment accessible to the masses and chronicles how he recruited GIs into his production company and produced a series of plays, including a GI *Hamlet*. Soldiers were not the only participants in the war effort to take part in theatrical productions. Almaráz, "The Little Theatre in the Atomic Age," tells the story of an amateur theater group organized in Los Alamos in 1943 as a response to the cultural isolation, boredom, and tension of the personnel gathered to develop the atomic bomb.

SPORTS

An overview of baseball, college and pro football, basketball, boxing, golf, and tennis is available in *The Games They Played* by Noverr and Ziewacz. They cover the scarcity of players, the importance of sports for morale, civilian sports programs, and even the impact of shortages on equipment—the rubber shortage and golf and tennis balls. "A Call to Arms" by Fimrite profiles five athletes, a baseball player, a basketball player, an Olympic runner, a pole-vaulter, and a football player. Based on present-day interviews, this article examines the impact (either pro or con) of their years in the service on their athletic careers. Furlong's "How the War in France Changed Football Forever" is an unusual and provocative article on how coach Shaughnessy adapted the blitzkrieg strategy, used by Germany to defeat France, to develop the modern T formation.

Baseball during the war is the subject of numerous books, few of any interest. *They Also Served* by Gilbert, one of the better examples, mentions the importance of baseball for morale, the difficulty in finding adequate players to fill rosters, and the inconvenience of gas rationing. Goldstein's *Spartan Seasons* is much more informative, stressing the patriotic fervor of baseball and its role in morale building, the participation of pro ball in blood drives, scrap drives, and the War Bond League, as well as the impact of personnel problems due to the war on the quality of play. Briley's "Where Have You Gone William Bendix?" exemplifies the sort of scholarship that is all too rare in this field. Based largely on wartime feature articles from mass-circulation magazines, Briley begins with how soldier fans were presented in Hollywood war movies and discusses the symbolic significance of baseball as exemplary of the American (as opposed to Japanese and German) way of life and as representation of democratic values.

DIARIES AND LETTERS

Bloom analyzes the value of diaries as subjective, popular history sources in "The Diary as Popular Culture," based on the diary kept by Natalie

Crouter, an American missionary in the Philippines, during her years in an internment camp. Litoff and Smith have published a number of works on letter writing during the war. "Writing Is Fighting, Too" detailed how they set up their archive, the World War II Letters of American Women. "Will He Get My Letter?" emphasized the morale issue and discussed mail as a theme in Rockwell's magazine covers, Mauldin's cartoons, magazine articles, radio programs, popular songs, and advertising. Their source material is available in *Since You Went Away*, a collection of letters arranged by subjects such as courtship and war work, and Somerville's *Dear Boys*, excerpts from a newspaper column in the form of letters, a common device during the war.

REMEMBERING THE WAR AND THE HOLOCAUST

An example of the work done on the continuing role of the war in popular culture is "The Holocaust in American Popular Culture" by Rosenfeld. His concern is with public understanding and perceptions, based on such materials as the television miniseries *Holocaust*, which he assumes served as the major education source for most viewers on the history of the Holocaust. He discusses adventure and romantic pulp fiction that exploited Nazism and the Holocaust, the fascination with Nazi and World War II memorabilia among fans of punk and hard rock music, and Nazi and anti-Semitic imagery in humor, cartoons, and popular expression, suggesting that these trivializations and vulgarizations were the negative side of the growing popular consciousness of the Holocaust. Doneson in "American History of Anne Frank's Diary" analyzes the evolution of the diary from a European document to an Americanized representation of the Holocaust. Its transformation into a play and film, which reflected the sociopolitical milieu of the United States in the 1940s and 1950s, universalized the Holocaust for American audiences.

With the fiftieth anniversaries of major World War II events, representations and memorializations of the wartime experience have proliferated in the popular media. Serious scholarship on this reification of the war into an artifact of popular culture should prove fruitful.

BIBLIOGRAPHY

Adams, Michael C. C. *The Best War Ever*. Baltimore: Johns Hopkins, 1994.

Almaráz, Felix Díaz, Jr. "The Little Theatre in the Atomic Age." *Journal of the West* 17 (1978): 72–82.

Anglo, Michael. *Service Newspapers of the Second World War*. London: Jupiter, 1977.

Baker, Patrica. *Fashions of a Decade: The Forties*. New York: Facts on File, 1992.

Barkin, Steve M. "Fighting the Cartoon War." *Journal of American Culture* 7 (1984): 113–117

Barnouw, Erik. *The Golden Web*. New York: Oxford, 1968.

Begley, George. *Keep Mum! Advertising Goes to War.* London: Lemon Tree, 1975.

Bloom, Lynn Z. "The Diary as Popular Culture." *Journal of Popular Culture* 9 (1976): 784–807.

Blum, John M. "The G.I. in the Culture of the Second World War." *Ventures* 8 (1968): 51–56.

———. *V Was for Victory.* New York: Harcourt Brace Jovanovich, 1976.

Bond, David H. *The Guinness Guide to 20th Century Fashion.* London: Guinness, 1988.

Bordman, Gerald. *American Musical Revue.* New York: Oxford, 1985.

Braun, Duane D. *Toward a Theory of Popular Culture.* Ann Arbor, MI: Ann Arbor, 1969.

Briggs, Susan. *The Home Front.* London: Weidenfeld and Nicolson, 1975; New York: American Heritage, 1975.

Briley, Ronald F. "Where Have You Gone William Bendix?" *Studies in Popular Culture* 8 (1985): 18–32.

Chang, Gordon H. "Superman Is About to Visit the Relocation Centers and the Limits of Wartime Liberalism." *Amerasia Journal* 19 (1993): 37–59.

Chibnall, Steve. "Whistle and Zoot." *History Workshop Journal* 20 (1985): 56–81.

Chinn, Jennie A. "There's a Star Spangled Banner Waving Somewhere." *JEMF Quarterly* 16 (1980): 74–80.

Cleveland, Les. "When They Send the Last Yank Home." *Journal of Popular Culture* 18 (1984): 31–36.

Cole, John Y. *Books in Action.* Washington, DC: Library of Congress, 1984.

Cosgrove, Stuart. "The Zoot Suit and Style Warfare." In Angela McRobbie, ed., *Zoot Suits and Second-Hand Dresses,* 3–22. Boston: Unwin Hyman, 1988.

Costello, John. *Virtue under Fire.* Boston: Little, Brown, 1985.

Couperie, Pierre. *A History of the Comic Strip.* New York: Crown, 1968.

Dean, Basil. *The Theatre at War.* London: George G. Harrap, 1956.

Denison, Sam. *Scandalize My Name.* New York: Garland, 1982.

Doneson, Judith E. "American History of Anne Frank's Diary." *Holocaust and Genocide Studies* 2 (1987): 149–160.

Donovan, Timothy P. "Oh, What a Beautiful Morning." *Journal of Popular Culture* 8 (1973): 477–488.

Douglas, Roy. *The World War 1939–1945.* London and New York: Routledge, 1990.

Eisen, George. *Children and Play in the Holocaust.* Amherst: University of Massachusetts, 1988.

Farmer, Patrick A. "Moss Hart and *Winged Victory.*" *Southern Speech and Communications Journal* 49 (1984): 187–197.

Fawkes, Richard. *Fighting for a Laugh.* London: Macdonald and Jane's, 1978.

Feiffer, Jules. *The Great Comic Book Heroes.* New York: Dial, 1965.

Ferguson, Robert C. "Americanism in Late Afternoon Radio Adventure Serials." *North Dakota Quarterly* 40 (1972): 20–29.

Fimrite, Ron. "A Call to Arms." *Sports Illustrated* 75 (1991): 98–109.

Fox, Frank W. *Madison Avenue Goes to War.* Provo, UT: Brigham Young, 1975.

Frogacs, David. *Italian Culture in the Industrial Era 1880–1980.* Manchester and New York: Manchester, 1990.

Furlong, William Barry. "How the War in France Changed Football Forever." *Smithsonian* 16 (1986): 125–138.

Fussell, Paul. *Wartime.* New York: Oxford, 1989.

Gilbert, Bill. *They Also Served.* New York: Crown, 1992.

Goldstein, Richard. *Spartan Seasons.* New York: Macmillan, 1980.

Graebner, William S. *The Age of Doubt.* Boston: Twayne, 1991.

Grant, Ian, and Nicholas Maddren. *The Countryside at War.* London: Jupiter, 1975.

Gray, Harold. *Arf! The Life and Hard Times of Little Orphan Annie 1935–1945.* New Rochelle, NY: Arlington House, 1970.

Grunberger, Richard. *The 12-Year Reich: A Social History of Nazi Germany.* New York: Holt, Rinehart, and Winston, 1971, 1979.

Halls, W. D. *The Youth of Vichy France.* New York: Oxford, 1981.

Hamish, Keith. *A Lovely Day Tomorrow.* Aukland: Random Century, 1991.

Harper, Sue. "History with Frills." *Red Letters: A Journal of Culture* 14 (1982–1983): 14–23.

Hasbany, Richard. "Bromidic Parables." *Journal of Popular Culture* 6 (1973): 642–665.

Helbig, Otto H. *A History of Music in the U.S. Armed Forces during World War II.* Philadelphia: M. W. Lads, 1966.

Hoehling, A. A. *Home Front, USA.* New York: Crowell, 1966.

Holsinger, M. Paul, and Anne Schofield, eds. *Visions of War.* Bowling Green, OH: Popular, 1992.

Honey, Maureen. "New Roles for Women and the Feminine Mystique." *American Studies* 24 (1983): 37–51.

———. "The 'Womanpower' Campaign." *Frontiers: A Journal of Women Studies* 6 (1981): 50–56.

Hoopes, Roy. *Americans Remember the Home Front.* New York: Hawthorn, 1977.

Huggett, Frank E. *Goodnight Sweetheart.* London: W. H. Allen, 1979.

Hughes, John G. *The Greasepaint War.* London: New English Library, 1976.

Hung, Chang-tai. *War and Popular Culture.* Berkeley: University of California, 1994.

Jenkins, Alan. *The Forties.* London: Heineman, 1977.

Kehl, James A. "Defender of the Faith." *South Atlantic Quarterly* 76 (1977): 454–465.

Leary, William M., Jr. "Books, Soldiers and Censorship during the Second World War." *American Quarterly* 20 (1968): 237–245.

Leitch, Michael. *Great Songs of World War II, with the Home Front in Pictures.* London: Wise, 1975.

Lingeman, Richard R. *Don't You Know There's a War On?* New York: Putnam's, 1970.

Litoff, Judy Barrett, and David C. Smith. *Since You Went Away.* New York: Oxford, 1991.

———. "Will He Get My Letter?" *Journal of Popular Culture* 23 (1990): 21–43.

———. "Writing Is Fighting, Too." *Georgia Historical Quarterly* 76 (1992): 436–457.

Longmate, Norman. *The G.I.'s.* New York: Scribner's, 1975.

———. *The Home Front.* London: Catto and Windus, 1981.

MacDonald, J. Fred. *Don't Touch That Dial.* Chicago: Nelson-Hall, 1979.

———. "Government Propaganda in Commercial Radio." *Journal of Popular Culture* 12 (1978): 285–304.

Macheski, Cecilia. "'Some Classic Pattern.'" In M. Paul Holsinger and Anne Schofield, eds., *Visions of War,* 170–180. Bowling Green, OH: Popular, 1992.

Malone, Bill C. *Country Music U.S.A.* Austin: University of Texas, 1968.

Mauldin, Bill. *Up Front.* New York: Norton, 1991.

Mazón, Mauricio. *The Zoot Suit Riots*. Austin: University of Texas, 1984.

Moskoff, William. *The Bread of Affliction*. New York: Cambridge, 1990.

Mosse, George L. *Nazi Culture*. New York: Grosset and Dunlap, 1966.

Murdoch, Brian. *Fighting Songs and Warring Words*. London and New York: Routledge, 1990.

Nakazawa, Keiji. *Barefoot Gen*. Philadelphia: New Society, 1987.

Noverr, Douglas A., and Lawrence E. Ziewacz. *The Games They Played*. Chicago: Nelson-Hall, 1983.

Ohmer, Susan. "Female Spectatorship and Women's Magazines." *The Velvet Light Trap Review of Literature* 25 (1990): 53–68.

Page, Martin. *Kiss Me Goodnight, Sergeant-Major*. London: Hart-Davis, 1973.

Parker, Derek. *Radio*. London: David and Charles, 1977.

Paterson, Thomas. "Artist in Stalag III-B." *American History Illustrated* 18 (1983): 48–53.

Perrett, Geoffrey. *Days of Sadness, Years of Triumph*. Madison: University of Wisconsin, 1985.

Peukert, Detlev J. K. *Inside Nazi Germany*. New Haven, CT: Yale, 1987.

Potts, E. Daniel, and Annette Potts. *Yanks Down Under 1941–45*. Melbourne: Oxford, 1985.

Raskin, Richard. " 'Le Chant des partisans.' " *Folklore* 102 (1991): 62–77.

Raynes, Minass. *Bombers and Mash*. London: Virago, 1980.

Reagon, Bernice. "World War II Reflected in Black Music." *Southern Exposure* 1 (1974): 169–184.

Rickey, Cathy. "Changing Traditional Foodways in Wartime." *Canadian Folklore Canadien* 12 (1990): 99–109.

Rosenfeld, Alvin H. "The Holocaust in American Popular Culture." *Midstream* 29 (1983): 53–59.

Satterfield, Archie. *The Home Front*. New York: Playboy, 1981.

Sentman, Mary Alice, and Patrick S. Washburn. "How Excess Profits Tax Brought Ads to Black Newspapers in World War II." *Journalism Quarterly* 64 (1987): 769–774.

Shulimson, Jack. "Maurice Evans, Shakespeare and the U.S. Army." *Journal of Popular Culture* 10 (1976): 255–266.

Simons, William J. "Juvenile Books in the Netherlands during the German Occupation." *Phaedrus* (1981): 13–17.

Skjonsberg, Kari. "Snorre the Seal." *Phaedrus* (1981): 18–19.

Sladen, Christopher. *The Conscription of Fashion*. Aldershot, U.K.: Scholar, 1995.

Smith, Bruce. *The History of Little Orphan Annie*. New York: Ballantine, 1982.

Smith, Cecil M. *Musical Comedy in America*. New York: Theatre Arts, 1978.

Somerville, Mrs. Keith Frazier. *Dear Boys*. Jackson: University of Mississippi, 1991.

Spiegelman, Art. *Maus*. New York: Pantheon, 1986.

Stedman, Raymond William. *The Serials*. Norman: University of Oklahoma, 1971.

Stokker, Kathleen. "Heil Hitler—God Save the King." *Western Folklore* 50 (1991): 171–190.

Tansey, Richard, and Michael R. Hyman. "Ethical Codes and the Advocacy Advertisements of World War II." *International Journal of Advertising* 12 (1993): 351–366.

———. "Public Relations, Advocacy Ads, and the Campaign against Absenteeism during World War II." *Business and Professional Ethics Journal* 11 (1992): 129–163.

Thompson, Don, and Dick Lupoff. *The Comic-Book Book.* New Rochelle, NY: Arlington House, 1973.

Tuttle, William M., Jr. *Daddy's Gone to War.* New York: Oxford, 1993.

Uslan, Michael. *America at War.* New York: Simon and Schuster, 1979.

Waldmeir, Joseph J. "What's Funny about That? Humor in the Literature of the Second World War." *Journal of American Culture* 12 (1989): 11–18.

Wertheim, Arthur Frank. *Radio Comedy.* New York: Oxford, 1979.

Westall, Robert. *Children of the Blitz.* New York: Viking-Penguin, 1985.

Westbrook, Robert B. "I Want a Girl, Just like the Girl That Married Harry James." *American Quarterly* 42 (1990): 587–614.

Wicks, Ben. *No Time to Wave Goodbye.* New York: St. Martin's, 1988.

Witek, Joseph. *Comic Books as History.* Jackson: University of Mississippi, 1989.

Wood, James P. *The Story of Advertising.* New York: Ronald, 1958.

Young, William H. "That Indomitable Redhead." *Journal of Popular Culture* 8 (1974): 309–319.

23 American Christianity on the Home Front during the Second World War

Gerald L. Sittser

INTRODUCTION

The Christian religion and war have been on friendly terms throughout most of Western history. In the name of God, armies have ruined rival cities, invaded rival nations, and fought rival empires. While a small stream of pacifism has fed itself into the Christian church since the apostolic age, the major currents of Christianity have rejected pacifism in favor of a more militarist approach. In America, for example, religion played a decisive role in inspiring colonists to start the Revolutionary War. It contributed to the nation's division during the Civil War. It resisted and later cheered participation in the Great War.

Historians have studied the involvement of religion in every one of America's wars, with the one exception of World War II. For some reason scholars have overlooked how the American churches participated in the war and how the war affected the churches. Some excellent work has been done on specific topics, such as the military chaplaincy and conscientious objectors. Still, on a wide range of fronts much work still needs to be done.

The critical question concerning American religion and the Second World War is as simple as the historical literature is sparse: what kind of contribution did American religion make to the nation's involvement in the Second World War? Generally speaking, what meager literature there is shows that the churches in America supported the Allied effort to win the war, but they did so with sobriety and caution. The churches lacked enthusiasm, recoiled from fanaticism and hatred, and pursued other causes that were much less popular. These other causes reminded the American people that issues like civil liberties were as important to America's future as winning the war. The two books that deal extensively with

American religion and the Second World War, Sittser's *A Cautious Patriotism* and Marty's *Under God, Indivisible,* argue this general thesis, as do such shorter works as Abrams' "The Churches and the Clergy," Bainton's *Christian Attitudes toward War and Peace,* and Pierard's "World War II."

This tension of patriotic support and sober caution was the product of two opposing forces. On one hand, many Christian leaders looked back on World War I as a bitter reminder of the failure of war, diplomacy, and religion. The debacle of Versailles only added to their regret and shame. As a result of the war's vain effort to "make the world safe for democracy," many clergy turned in the 1930s to pacifism, ecumenism, and the social gospel to spare the world from another disaster. They hated war and would have nothing to do with it.

On the other hand, events taking place in Europe in the 1930s forced Christians to question their commitment to pacifism and diplomacy. The rise of totalitarianism, especially in Nazi Germany, awakened Americans to the threat of an evil ideology. The outbreak of war in Europe compelled Americans to admit that Western civilization itself was imperiled. The tension between these contradictory impulses—commitment to peace and fear of totalitarianism—tells the story of American religion and the Second World War. One finds ambivalence everywhere in the primary sources. This ambivalence often led to a strange combination of commitments: recruitment of military chaplains *and* support of conscientious objectors, exhortations to cooperate in patriotic programs *and* alarm about the loss of civil liberties, longing for victory *and* pressure to win a just and durable peace.

This general thesis of "a cautious patriotism" begs for more historical support or refutation. Most of the scholarly work has yet to be done.

THE GREAT DEBATE

Historians have documented the significant impact that World War I and Versailles had on American clergy, as well as the popularity of pacifism, disarmament, and internationalism in the 1920s and 1930s. They have also studied the emergence of "Christian realism," which challenged the churches to oppose totalitarianism, even if such opposition would lead to war. The tension between religious pacifism and political realism in the 1930s and early 1940s erupted into the "great debate" over American entry into the war.

Meyer's *The Protestant Search* outlines the struggle that many Christian leaders faced as they tried to remain true to pacifist convictions in light of totalitarian threat. It also explores the dynamic relationship between Protestant idealism and political realism, as epitomized by Reinhold Niebuhr. Miller's *American Protestantism* provides extensive documentation on mainline Protestantism and social issues during the war, such as race relations and economic policy. Both books provide excellent background studies for religion and World War II. They show that the Protestant churches developed a sophisticated political agenda before World War II that shaped debate and ministry during the war.

McNeal's *The American Catholic Peace Movement* analyzes the relatively small, but influential, group of pacifists within American Catholicism, such as Dorothy Day's Catholic Worker movement, that lobbied to keep America out of the war. O'Brien's *Public Catholicism* shows, however, that though the vast majority of Catholics were neutralists before Pearl Harbor, their opinion changed quickly after Poland, a Catholic stronghold, fell to Germany.

Several books explore the pacifist movement as it emerged before the war and then responded to the war. These books include Nelson's *The Peace Prophets*, Moellering's *Modern War and the American Churches*, Wittner's *Rebels against War*, and Muelder's *Methodism and Society in the Twentieth Century*. Moellering's book is useful because it documents the struggle within several denominations over America's involvement in the war and mentions other issues, such as lax moral standards and the breakdown of the family, that alarmed religious groups during the war. Muelder analyzes the pronouncements of the Methodist Church on a wide range of social issues. Nelson presents the pacifist perspective on a number of issues, such as social justice, economic problems, and international conflict. Wittner takes a historical approach, explaining pacifism as a dynamic movement that had to respond to historical forces outside its control.

Two dissertations address the great debate from the perspective of response to the emergence of the Nazi Party. Murphy shows that religious groups in America were slow to condemn Hitler because they were so conscious of the abuse Germany suffered after the First World War and viewed the church situation in Germany in light of their own denominational loyalties. Though anti-Semitism was denounced, it appeared to be pro forma until *Kristallnacht*. After the war began, however, religious groups identified Nazism as a major threat to Christianity and Western civilization. Wentz's "Reaction of the Religious Press" outlines four basic religious responses to Nazism. Liberal groups in America expressed opposition because the ideology of national socialism ran contrary to social justice. Mainline Protestant groups were wary of all forms of collectivism, whether Nazi or communist. Millennial groups reacted to Nazism as simply another atheistic force leading to Armageddon. Finally, Catholics opposed any movement that undercut the power of Catholicism in Europe.

Ribuffo's *The Old Christian Right* explores the role that three far-right leaders played in resisting America's entry into the war because of their attraction to fascism and their hatred of Jews. Both William Pelley and Gerald Winrod had legal problems during the war and lost considerable support. The more moderate Gerald L. K. Smith, however, found an audience, published *The Cross and the Flag,* opposed intervention, and organized the American First Party, as McEnaney points out in "He-Men." The American First Party stood for such "traditional" American values as home and family.

Hudnut-Beumler's "The American Churches" on interventionism uses World War II as one of several examples to make three basic points about the relationship between religion and intervention in American history. First, though the American churches have opposed intervention in their official pronouncements, they have supported intervention de facto whenever it appeared to advance their own interests. Second, the churches in public gatherings have gravitated toward pacifism but have rarely lived consistently with the implications of that conviction. Third, the American churches have oscillated between utopianism and realism in American foreign policy, often with tragic consequences. The article concludes by advocating what Reinhold Niebuhr believed was the best approach: to intervene for a just peace, to restrain from intervention when it is based on self-interest, and to gain wisdom to discern the difference between the two.

The religious dimension of the great debate has not received the scholarly attention it deserves. Several primary sources present the opinions of the major players in the debate. Charles Clayton Morrison, editor of the *Christian Century,* opposed American entry into the war for political as well as religious reasons. He wrote *The Christian and the War* to argue that belligerency was wrong because it would involve the United States in an imperialistic war, roll back civil liberties, and keep America from playing a key role in negotiating peace. His ally Muste, secretary of the Fellowship of Reconciliation, presented a pacifist Quaker perspective on American involvement in his *Non-Violence in an Aggressive World.* Catholics such as John LaFarge and Francis Talbot of the Jesuit weekly *America* disavowed pacifism but still advocated neutrality. Reinhold Niebuhr and his colleagues from *Christianity and Crisis* challenged all of these neutralists. Niebuhr's *Christianity and Power Politics,* a collection of essays published in 1940, aimed sharp criticism against Morrison and Muste's pacifism, calling it bad politics, bad ethics, and bad religion. Fox's biography of Niebuhr tells the story of this debate.

WARTIME THEODICY

Theodicy addresses how believers make sense of the existence of evil in light of their confidence in the sovereignty and goodness of God. The problem of theodicy received a great deal of attention during the war.

In most cases these wartime theodicies reflected a tension. They abhorred World War II because war itself was repugnant for religious reasons. But they justified World War II because the war itself was popular for political reasons. Morrison pushed hard to keep the United States out of the war. When the United States entered the war, he believed that such involvement violated Christian principles. Ironside's *The Lamp of Prophecy* and Rice's *World-Wide War* reflected the perspective of millions of fundamentalists in America, showing how someone like a Hitler could gain so much power, why he would eventually fail, and what America had to do to spare itself from decline and conquest.

Many theodicies asserted the special role that America was supposed to play in world affairs. These theodicies interpreted the war as a judgment of evil and as a warning to America. These theodicies urged Americans to recover their Christian heritage. One of many who presented such an "American theodicy" was Mackay, president of Princeton Seminary, in his *Heritage and Destiny*. As most of the sources on theodicy are primary, a solid secondary work still needs to be written.

CHRISTIANITY AND DEMOCRACY

The rhetoric used during World War I found similar expression in World War II. It was a war being fought to defend democracy and to preserve Western civilization, except, in the case of World War II, the enemy appeared to be genuinely pagan and evil. National socialism and Japanese imperialism were identified as totalitarian, unjust, and evil, while Western civilization was assumed to be democratic, just, and good. Books written during the war aimed to prove that democracy was a superior political system and that Christianity was essential for democracy's survival. Especially influential were Brown, Finkelstein, and Ross' *The Religions of Democracy*, Holt's *Christian Roots of Democracy*, Landis' *Religion and the Good Society*, and Sheen's *Philosophies at War*. No secondary work has been written yet on religion and democracy or church and state during the war.

Still, there were disagreements over which tradition of Christianity was the most suitable foundation for democracy. Conflicts among various Christian groups simmered throughout the war because they were competing for the right to shape America's democratic future. Morrison wondered, *Can Protestantism Win America?* Catholics countered with their own arguments about the role Catholicism could play in the nation, as in Boland and Ryan's *Catholic Principles of Politics*.

Though Protestants assumed that Christianity was foundational for democracy, they were wary of any kind of church establishment, which is why they reacted with particular alarm to Roosevelt's intention to send Myron C. Taylor as an ambassador to the Vatican, as Conway in "Taylor's Mission" points out. Protestants argued that the appointment violated the First Amendment and unmasked the danger of Catholic ambition. Church leaders were equally wary of state interference in church affairs.

Christians in America believed that the world desperately needed the

Christian faith. Many denominations began programs of evangelism during the war to increase their influence in American society. This forward thrust in church programming has been largely overlooked by scholars, with the one exception of Carpenter's "The Renewal of American Fundamentalism," which tells the story of the growth of fundamentalism before and during the war.

The American people appeared to respond with enthusiasm after America entered the war. Some 10 million American men and women joined the military, and many millions more contributed to the war on the home front. Still, at least two religious groups refused to support the military effort—the historic peace churches (the Friends, the Brethren, and the Mennonites) and organizations like the Fellowship of Reconciliation (FOR). Their stories are told in Keim and Stoltzfus' *The Politics of Conscience* and Brock's *Twentieth-Century Pacifism.* As these books point out, the peace churches and FOR encouraged their followers to resist the draft or register to become conscientious objectors.

Most religious groups supported conscientious objectors (COs), even though the majority of their members enlisted in one of the branches of the armed services. Church leaders opposed any conscription bill that, in their minds, established criteria that were too narrow for classifying COs. COs came from virtually every denomination and were allowed to work in Civilian Public Service (CPS) camps, which were founded and administered by the historic peace churches. Other Protestant groups helped to defray the costs. Still, several thousand COs were sent to prison for refusing to register or to work in CPS camps, the largest being the Jehovah's Witnesses.

A number of studies have been written on COs and CPS camps. Eller's *Conscientious Objectors* and Grimsrud's "Conscientious Objectors to World War II" analyze the ethics of COs. Eller's book explores the ideological breadth found among COs, although it shows that all COs were united in opposition to war as a means of settling international disputes. Jacobs and Sibley's *Conscription of Conscience* provides a historical overview of the experience of COs during the war. McNeal's *The American Catholic Peace Movement* contains one chapter on Catholic pacifism and COs during World War II. It explores the interplay between official Catholic policy, which supported the war effort, and such protest groups as PAX and the Catholic Worker. Mitchell's *We Would Not Kill* gives an account of CO work from a Friends perspective. Four works provide valuable information about Civilian Public Services camps. Zahn's "Descriptive Study" focuses on the background of the people who ended up in CPS camps, while his *Camp Simon Story* explores the protest launched at one CPS camp. French's *Civilian Public Service* explains how CPS camps were organized and run, while Gingerich's *Service for Peace* gives the history of Mennonite CPS camps.

MOBILIZATION, MILITARY SERVICE, AND MINISTRY

Americans of all stripes helped to mobilize for war. Millions participated in rationing programs, bought war bonds, and moved from familiar homes and communities to work in war industries. The story of religious support of mobilization has yet to be told. The same could be said of the religious concern about the impact of mobilization on the growth of big business and the loss of power in organized labor, two trends that liberal Protestants and Roman Catholics observed with alarm.

The churches organized for mobilization within weeks of Pearl Harbor. The Federal Council of Churches (FCC) started the Coordinating Committee for War Services, which served as an umbrella organization for a number of wartime ministries. Many denominations formed their own organizations to help with mobilization, such as the National Lutheran Council and the National Catholic Community Service. The Service Men's Christian League and Service Women's Christian League were begun during the war as cooperative ventures among mainline Protestant groups. The two leagues published *The Link* to reach men and women in uniform. The United Service Organizations included Protestant, Catholic, and Jewish agencies to serve men and women in industry and the military. Thousands of local synagogues, parishes, and churches started ministries of their own to address the needs of Americans whose lives were disrupted by the war.

A few books give valuable information about these mobilization ministries. Historians of particular denominations devote one or several chapters to World War II. Among the best is a book telling the story of Lutherans, Nelson's *Lutheranism in North America*. Hershberger gives an account of Mennonite ministries during the war. Lynn provides important information about the National Catholic Community Service organization.

The ministry of military chaplains has been well documented, although almost exclusively from the perspective of the military. Drury's *History of the Chaplain Corps* tells the story of navy chaplains, Jorgensen's *The Service of Chaplains* tells the story of those in the air force, while Gushwa's *The Best and Worst of Times* and Honeywell's *Chaplains* discuss army chaplains. These histories give statistics about numbers of chaplains, provide information about protocol, methods, and services, and tell moving stories about how individual chaplains performed in the line of duty against great odds. Nance's *Faith of Our Fighters* tells the story of the religious convictions held by the troops. Several autobiographical accounts describe the religious experience of military personnel during the war, such as Whittacker's *We Thought We Heard the Angels Sing*, Rickenbacker's *Seven Came Through*, and Scott's *God Is My Co-Pilot*. Donald Crosby's book, *Battlefield Chaplains*, gives a Catholic accounting of priests during the war. Still, more research could be done to study the struggle within denominational groups over the very *idea* of clergy's serving in, and answering to, the military and to investigate such controversial issues as "open" as opposed to "closed" Communion, proselytizing in the pluralistic setting of the military, and ecumenism among the chaplains. Scholars could also explore the impact of military service on postwar religious commitment, organization, and ministry.

CIVIL LIBERTIES

Wartime creates circumstances that allow people to vent hostilities, to persecute marginal people, and to deprive cultural outsiders of their civil liberties. World War II displays a mixed record on civil liberties. Over 110,000 Japanese Americans were forced to live in internment camps during the war. The story of the Christian response to the internment has been largely ignored by scholars. Matsumoto's *Beyond Prejudice* and Suzuki's *Ministry* give valuable accounts of Christian work in the internment camps, but their scope is limited. Okihiro's "Religion and Resistance" presents another side to the complex story, that of protest in the camps.

It is no surprise that many Christians joined the ranks of the persecutor. Bennett's *Party of Fear* contains a chapter on the antialien sentiments of the religious Right. Still, some Christian leaders protested the government's policy and tried to assist Japanese Americans during the evacuation. They stored furniture, donated food, and offered a range of services to people in the camps. They also supported Japanese Americans when they started to reenter civilian life after the war. The full story of the Christian response to the internment has yet to be told.

Religion played a minor role in the wartime civil rights movement, too. At the beginning of the war African Americans were almost completely segregated from wartime industry and military service, which led African-American leaders to protest, beginning with the March on Washington movement. They argued that fighting for democracy abroad was hypocritical if democracy failed at home. Scholars such as Garfinkel have given an excellent account of *The March on Washington Movement*, and Finkle's *Forum for Protest* has chronicled the reaction of the African-American press to the war. Unfortunately, scholars have largely overlooked the role that the churches played in the civil rights movement during the war. Many mainline leaders protested, as Orser pointed out in "Social Attitudes" and in his article "Racial Attitudes in War." No historian has explored the reaction of the African-American churches and religious press to the issue of civil rights during the war.

THE COST OF WAR

War exacts a terrible cost. Ordinary life is disrupted, families separated, moral standards lowered. The churches in America were aware of these costs during World War II and took steps to mitigate them. Special attention was given to the problem of social disruption, family breakdown, juvenile delinquency, and moral compromise, like the abuse of alcohol. These concerns have been addressed in books like Costello's *Virtue under Fire*. But research still needs to be done on the *religious* response to social disruption and moral erosion engendered by the war, as well as on the religious reaction to the changing role of women.

The plight of refugees during the war has received a great deal of scholarly attention. Two historians have investigated the Christian response to the refugee crisis, both arguing that Christian groups knew much about the crisis but did little to help. Wyman's *Paper Walls* and Genizi's *American Apathy* provide accounts of this story.

Americans did form a number of organizations to assist in war relief efforts. Two books explore this organizational activity. Morton's *War Relief Agencies* provides a general account of war relief agencies, while Seymour's *Design for Giving* tells the story of one such agency, the National War Fund. Christian groups started fund drives and organized their own agencies to assist in relief efforts. Catholics, for example, started the Bishop's War Emergency and Relief Committee, and the National Association of Evangelicals founded the War Relief Commission. Unruh's *In the Name of Christ* tells the story of the Mennonite Central Committee's work during the war, as does Hershberger's *The Mennonite Church*. *The Story of Christian Science Wartime Activities* does the same for Christian Science. The work of other such agencies still needs to be studied.

The plight of the Jews deserves special attention. The question of how much was known, when it was known, and what was done or not done as a result of what was known has been addressed in Ross' *So It Was True*. It proves that the American Protestant press knew early on what was being done to Jews but failed to marshal enough support to launch a significant protest. Camp's "Religion and Horror" gives an account of how the religious press reported the discovery of the death camps. Snoek's *The Grey Book* demonstrates that religious groups in America did condemn the Nazi persecution of the Jews, although they fell short in their efforts to mold public opinion and change public policy. Tragically, the indifference of Christian groups far surpassed their willingness to act.

The problem of obliteration or saturation bombing is explored in Hopkins' excellent article "Bombing and the American Conscience." The article shows that this brutal form of bombing was tolerated and even applauded by most Americans, with a few notable exceptions. Two of those exceptions came in the form of influential articles written during the war. Brittain's "Massacre by Bombing" and Ford's "The Morality of Obliteration Bombing" condemned the Allied strategy of bombing civilian targets. A few Protestant leaders objected, too, but with little success. The use of the atomic bomb brought relief but also caused alarm, as *Atomic Warfare*, written in 1946 by the leaders of the Federal Council of

Churches, illustrates. A secondary source on the initial response of the churches to the use of the atomic bomb still needs to be written.

POSTWAR PLANNING

The cessation of hostilities affected thousands of communities and millions of families that suddenly had to return home and adjust to peacetime life. Little research has been done on Christian plans and ministries at the end of the war. Conflicting visions of the world—for example, the degree to which religion should involve itself in political as opposed to spiritual concerns—contributed to tensions among conservative and liberal religious groups after the war.

Postwar plans for peace are more thoroughly documented. Burroway's "Christian Witness" and Whyatt's "Planning for the Postwar World" give accounts of Protestant plans for peace. Ludlow's article on "The International Protestant Community" during the war and Neill and Rouse's *A History of the Ecumenical Movement* show the important role that ecumenism played during and after the war. Roy's *Communism and the Churches* explores the response of religious groups to communism. He argues that religious groups tolerated Russia as an American ally but, with only a few exceptions, despised communism.

John Foster Dulles became a major presence among Protestants involved in postwar planning for peace and in the formation of the United Nations organization. Keim's "Dulles and the Protestant World Order" on Dulles' activities before the war and Toulouse's *The Transformation of John Foster Dulles: From Prophet of Realism to Priest of Nationalism* provide useful details not only about Dulles but also about Protestant involvement in the peace settlement. Denominational groups were active in postwar planning, too. The Methodists initiated the Crusade for a New World Order, one of many such movements started by Christian groups to inform and mobilize church members to lobby for a just peace. The Federal Council initiated the Crusade for Christ to spread the Christian message and attract Americans back to the church. Two books touch on the war's impact on postwar American religion and life. Wuthnow's *The Restructuring* gives a sociological account of significant changes in American religion after the war, and Silk's *Spiritual Politics* explores the dynamic relationship between religion and politics after the war. The dramatic impact that the war itself had on American religion in the decades following the war has still not been investigated in depth.

BIBLIOGRAPHY

Abrams, Ray H. "The Churches and the Clergy in World War II." *The Annals of the American Academy of Political and Social Science* 256 (March 1948): 110–119.

Atomic Warfare and the Christian Faith. New York: Federal Council of Churches, 1946.

Bainton, Roland H. *Christian Attitudes toward War and Peace: A Historical Survey and Critical Re-evaluation.* New York: Abingdon, 1960.

Bennett, David H. *The Party of Fear: From Nativist Movements to the New Right in American History.* Chapel Hill: University of North Carolina, 1988.

Boland, Francis J., and John A. Ryan. *Catholic Principles of Politics.* New York: Macmillan, 1940.

Brittain, Vera. "Massacre by Bombing." *Fellowship* 10 (March 1944): Part II, 50–63.

Brock, Peter. *Twentieth-Century Pacifism.* New York: Van Nostrand Reinhold, 1970.

Brown, William Adams, Louis Finkelstein, and J. Elliot Ross. *The Religions of Democracy: Judaism, Catholicism, and Protestantism in Creed and Life.* New York: Devin-Adair, 1943.

Burroway, Jessie J. "Christian Witness concerning World Order: The Federal Council of Churches and Postwar Planning, 1941–1947." Ph.D. diss., University of Wisconsin, 1954.

Camp, William D. "Religion and Horror: The American Religious Press Views Nazi Death Camps and Holocaust Survivors." Ph.D. diss., Carnegie-Mellon University, 1981.

Carpenter, Joel A. "The Renewal of American Fundamentalism, 1930–1945." Ph.D. diss., Johns Hopkins University, 1984.

Conway, John S. "Myron C. Taylor's Mission to the Vatican, 1940–1950." *Church History* 44 (1975): 85–99.

Costello, John. *Virtue under Fire: How World War II Changed Our Social and Sexual Attitudes.* Boston: Little, Brown, 1985.

Crosby, Donald F. *Battlefield Chaplains: Catholic Priests in World War II.* Lawrence: UP of Kansas, 1994.

Drury, Clifford Merrill. *The History of the Chaplain Corps, United States Navy.* Vol. 2: *1939–1949.* Washington, DC: GPO, n.d.

Eller, Cynthia. *Conscientious Objectors and the Second World War: Moral and Religious Arguments in Support of Pacifism.* New York: Praeger, 1991.

Finkle, Lee. *Forum for Protest: The Black Press during World War II.* Cranbury, NJ: Associated UP, 1975.

Ford, John C. "The Morality of Obliteration Bombing." *Theological Studies* 5 (1944): 261–309.

Fox, Richard Wightman. *Reinhold Niebuhr: A Biography.* San Francisco: Harper and Row, 1985.

French, Paul Comly. *Civilian Public Service.* Washington, DC: National Service Board for Religious Objectors, 1944.

Garfinkel, Herbert. *When Negroes March: The March on Washington Movement in the Organizational Politics for FEPC.* Glencoe, IL: Free, 1959.

Genizi, Haim. *American Apathy: The Plight of Christian Refugees from Nazism.* Jerusalem: Bar-Ilan UP, 1983.

Gingerich, Melvin. *Service for Peace: A History of the Mennonite Civilian Public Service.* Akron, PA: Mennonite Central Committee, 1949.

Grimsrud, Theodore G. "An Ethical Analysis of Conscientious Objectors to World War II." Ph.D. diss., Graduate Theological Union, 1988.

Gushwa, Robert L. *The Best and Worst of Times: The U.S. Army Chaplaincy, 1920–1945.* Washington, DC: GPO, 1977.

Hershberger, Guy Franklin. *The Mennonite Church in the Second World War.* Scottdale, PA: Mennonite Publishing House, 1951.

Holt, Arthur E. *Christian Roots of Democracy in America.* New York: Friendship, 1941.

Honeywell, Roy J. *Chaplains of the U.S. Army.* Washington, DC: GPO, 1958.

Hopkins, George E. "Bombing and the American Conscience during World War II." *The Historian* 28 (1966): 451–473.

Hudnut-Beumler, James. "The American Churches and U.S. Interventionism." In Dieter T. Hessel, ed., *The Church's Public Role.* Grand Rapids, MI: William B. Eerdmans, 1993.

Ironside, H. A. *The Lamp of Prophecy, or Signs of the Times.* Grand Rapids, MI: Zondervan Publishing House, 1940.

Jacobs, Philip E., and Mulford Q. Sibley. *Conscription of Conscience: The American State and the Conscientious Objector, 1940–1947.* Ithaca, NY: Cornell UP, 1952.

Jorgensen, Daniel B. *The Service of Chaplains to Army Air Units, 1917–1946.* Washington, DC: GPO, n.d.

Keim, Albert N. "John Foster Dulles and the Protestant World Order Movement on the Eve of World War II." *Journal of Church and State* 21 (1979): 73–89.

Keim, Albert N., and Grant M. Stoltzfus. *The Politics of Conscience: The Historic Peace Churches and America at War, 1917–1955.* Scottdale, PA: Herald, 1988.

Landis, Benson Y., ed. *Religion and the Good Society: An Introduction to the Social Teachings of Judaism, Catholicism and Protestantism.* New York: National Conference of Christians and Jews, 1942.

Ludlow, Peter W. "The International Protestant Community in the Second World War." *Journal of Ecclesiastical History* 29 (1978): 311–362.

Lynn, Rita LeBille. *The National Catholic Community Service in World War II.* Washington, DC: Catholic University of America, 1952.

Mackay, John. *Heritage and Destiny.* New York: Macmillan, 1943.

Marty, Martin E. *Modern American Religion.* Vol. 3: *Under God, Indivisible, 1940–1960.* Chicago: University of Chicago, 1996.

Matsumoto, Toru. *Beyond Prejudice: A Story of the Church and Japanese-Americans.* New York: Friendship, 1946.

McEnaney, Laura. "He-Men and Christian Mothers: The America First Movement and the Gendered Meanings of Patriotism." *Diplomatic History* 18 (1994): 47–57.

McNeal, Patricia F. *The American Catholic Peace Movement, 1928–1972.* New York: Arno, 1978.

Meyer, Donald B. *The Protestant Search for Political Realism, 1919–1941.* Berkeley: University of California, 1960.

Miller, Robert Moats. *American Protestantism and Social Issues, 1919–1939.* Chapel Hill: University of North Carolina, 1958.

Mitchell, Hobart. *We Would Not Kill.* Richmond, IN: Friends United, 1983.

Moellering, Ralph Luther. *Modern War and the American Churches: A Factual Study of the Christian Conscience on Trial from 1939 to the Cold War Crisis of Today.* New York: American, 1956.

Morrison, Charles Clayton. *Can Protestantism Win America?* New York: Harper and Brothers, 1948.

————. *The Christian and the War.* New York: Willett, Clark, 1942.

Morton, Malvin. *The Development and Structure of the War Relief Agencies.* Pittsburgh: Bureau of Social Research, 1945.

Muelder, Walter G. *Methodism and Society in the Twentieth Century.* New York: Abingdon, 1961.

Murphy, Frederick. "The American Christian and Pre-War Hitler's Germany, 1933–1939." Ph.D. diss., University of Florida, 1971.

Muste, A. J. *Non-Violence in an Aggressive World.* New York: Harper and Brothers, 1940.

Nance, Ellwood C., ed. *Faith of Our Fighters.* St. Louis, MO: Bethany, 1944.

Neill, Stephen Charles, and Ruth Rouse, eds. *A History of the Ecumenical Movement, 1517–1948.* Philadelphia: Westminster, 1993.

Nelson, Clifford E. *Lutheranism in North America, 1914–1970.* Minneapolis, MN: Augsburg Publishing House, 1972.

Nelson, John K. *The Peace Prophets: American Pacifist Thought, 1919–1941.* Chapel Hill: University of North Carolina, 1967.

Niebuhr, Reinhold. *Christianity and Power Politics.* New York: Charles Scribner's Sons, 1940.

O'Brien, David J. *Public Catholicism.* New York: Macmillan, 1989.

Okihiro, Gary Y. "Religion and Resistance in America's Concentration Camps." *Phylon* 45 (1984): 220–233.

Orser, William Edward. "Racial Attitudes in War: The Protestant Churches during the Second World War." *Church History* 41 (Summer 1972): 337–353.

————. "The Social Attitudes of the Protestant Churches during the Second World War." Ph.D. diss., University of New Mexico, 1969.

Pierard, Richard V. "World War II." In Ronald A. Wells, ed., *The Wars of America: Christian Views,* 180–214. Grand Rapids, MI: William B. Eerdmans, 1981.

Ribuffo, Leo P. *The Old Christian Right: The Protestant Far Right from the Great Depression to the Cold War.* Philadelphia: Temple UP, 1983.

Rice, John R. *World-Wide War and the Bible.* Wheaton, IL: Sword of the Lord, 1940.

Rickenbacker, Edward V. *Seven Came Through.* Garden City, NY: Doubleday, Doran, 1943.

Ross, Robert W. *So It Was True: The American Protestant Press and the Nazi Persecution of the Jews.* Minneapolis: University of Minnesota, 1980.

Roy, Ralph Lord. *Communism and the Churches.* New York: Harcourt, Brace, 1960.

Scott, Robert L., Jr. *God Is My Co-Pilot.* New York: Charles Scribner's Sons, 1943.

Seymour, Harold J. *Design for Giving: The Story of the National War Fund, Inc., 1943–47.* New York: Harper and Brothers, 1947.

Sheen, Fulton J. *Philosophies at War.* New York: Charles Scribner's Sons, 1943.

Silk, Mark. *Spiritual Politics: Religion and America since World War II.* New York: Simon and Schuster, 1988.

Sittser, Gerald L. *A Cautious Patriotism: The American Churches and the Second World War.* Chapel Hill: University of North Carolina, 1997.

Snoek, Johan M. *The Grey Book: A Collection of Protests against Anti-Semitism and the Persecution of Jews Issued by Non-Roman Catholic Churches and Church Leaders during Hitler's Rule.* Assen, Netherlands: Koninklijke Van Gorcum and Comp. N.V., 1968.

The Story of Christian Science Wartime Activities, 1939–1946. Boston: Christian Science Publishing Society, 1947.

Suzuki, Lester E. *Ministry in the Assembly and Relocation Centers of World War II.* Berkeley: Yardbird, 1979.

Toulouse, Mark G. *The Transformation of John Foster Dulles: From Prophet of Realism to Priest of Nationalism.* Atlanta: Mercer UP, 1985.

Unruh, John D. *In the Name of Christ: A History of the Mennonite Central Committee and Its Services, 1920–1951.* Scottdale, PA: Herald, 1952.

Wentz, Frederick K. "The Reaction of the Religious Press in America to the Emergence of Nazism." Ph.D. diss., Yale University, 1954.

Whittacker, James C. *We Thought We Heard the Angels Sing.* New York: E. P. Dutton, 1943.

Whyatt, Nelson Thomas. "Planning for the Postwar World: Liberal Journalism during World War II." Ph.D. diss., University of Minnesota, 1971.

Wittner, Lawrence S. *Rebels against War: The American Peace Movement, 1933–1983.* Philadelphia: Temple UP, 1984.

Wuthnow, Robert. *The Restructuring of American Religion: Society and Faith since World War II.* Princeton: Princeton UP, 1988.

Wyman, David S. *Paper Walls: America and the Refugee Crisis, 1938–1941.* Amherst: University of Massachusetts, 1968.

Zahn, Gordon C. *Another Part of the War: The Camp Simon Story.* Amherst: University of Massachusetts, 1979.

———. "A Descriptive Study of the Sociological Background of Conscientious Objectors in Civilian Service Camps during World War II." Ph.D. diss., Catholic University of America, 1953.

24 Christianity Outside North America

Richard V. Pierard

The role of religion in World War II has not been explored in a comprehensive manner, although an extensive, albeit fragmentary, body of literature exists. Much work has been done on Judaism, but unfortunately very little material exists on the non-Western religious traditions because the war had little effect upon them, and spiritual leaders of these faiths rarely were directly involved in the war effort. As for Christianity, many aspects of the buildup to, and the conduct of, the war did impact upon it, but the scholarly attention that this has attracted is uneven. Not only are several important questions now just beginning to be examined, but also some of the most relevant works have been published in languages other than English. Further, there are no comprehensive treatments of the churches and the war in the various European countries like the ones Gerald Sittser provides for the United States and Charles Faulkner for Canada.

Even though religion clearly impinged on many facets of the war effort, the following discussion is restricted to subjects not covered at all or lightly touched upon elsewhere in this volume. Since other chapters deal with the war against the Jews, the concentration camps, refugee matters, and Christianity on the American home front, these topics are mentioned only tangentially to avoid unnecessary duplication or repetition. This chapter examines the relevant literature on a variety of topics rather than country by country, and with a few exceptions it treats only English-language materials. Coverage of the literature is selective rather than exhaustive.

NAZISM AND THE CHURCHES

Perhaps nothing on the religious front in Europe during the 1930s attracted more attention than the *Kirchenkampf* (church struggle), the contest between the national socialist state and the Evangelical or Protestant churches, although the conflict was hardly restricted to that one segment of German Christianity. The international press covered the events in great detail, and books and articles about them abounded. After the war the church struggle and the closely related topic of the Holocaust became the focal point of enormous scholarly attention, and the quantity of literature has reached mind-boggling proportions. Most of the source documents, first-person accounts, and monographs are in German, including the multivolume series *Arbeiten zur Geschichte des Kirchenkampfes*, but enough translated primary material and relevant secondary literature in English are available to enable an adequate comprehension of the problems. A brief compilation of documents that provides some insights is Matheson, *The Third Reich and the Christian Churches.*

Conway, *The Nazi Persecution of the Churches*, and Helmreich, *The German Churches under Hitler*, are the best one-volume surveys of the topic. Although a great deal of scholarly material appeared subsequently that refined details and extended knowledge into hitherto dark corners, they still remain eminently readable and reliable accounts. The magisterial work is by the Tübingen church historian Klaus Scholder, *The Churches and the Third Reich*, which, because of the author's premature death in 1985, carries the story only through the crucial year of 1934. Many of Scholder's insights, which would have found their way into subsequent volumes, are contained in *A Requiem for Hitler and Other New Perspectives on the German Church Struggle*, a posthumously published collection of essays.

A number of studies deal with major questions in the church struggle. The basic issue in 1933 was whether or not the Protestant Church would be Nazified. The 600,000-strong faction of "German Christians" wanted to bring the church into line with the new order, and their efforts were countered by a group organized by Pastor Martin Niemöller known as the Confessing Church. The defining moment was the synod of the Confessing Church in Wuppertal-Barmen on 29–31, May 1934. The Barmen Declaration, largely drafted by Karl Barth, called the German church back to the central tenets of Christianity and rejected the totalitarian claims of the state in religious and political matters. This theological document, directed against the heretical distortions of the German Christians, was not intended as a political protest. The Confessing Church did not plan to spearhead resistance to Nazism; its leaders repeatedly affirmed their loyalty to the state and the führer. The relationship was, as Wall shows, a cooperative one, and only after the outbreak of war did some of its leaders become involved in the anti-Hitler resistance. Baranowski makes clear in her book on the Confessing Church that it had been organized by conservative elites who, for the most part, were resisting Nazi intrusion into their traditional ecclesiastical control. This conservatism is also noted in Barnes' study of Protestant social thought in the interwar years.

The most important treatment of the German Christians is Bergen, *Twisted Cross*, which is based on the latest scholarship and traces the movement even into the postwar era. It replaces the more limited study by Zabel, *Nazism and the Pastors*. The Barmen Declaration itself is examined in Arthur Cochrane, *The Church's Confession under Hitler*, an analysis that was influential in North American church circles and elsewhere in the 1960s. The fiftieth anniversary of the event occasioned a torrent of literature on both sides of the Atlantic, and the two volumes edited by Locke, the background essays for the North American symposium, *The Church Confronts the Nazis: Barmen Then and Now*, and the follow-up *Barmen Confession: Papers from the Seattle Assembly*, are particularly noteworthy.

The theological responses to Nazism are traced out in several works. The most significant is by Ericksen, who homes in on the conservative Lutherans Gerhard Kittel, Paul Althaus, and Emanuel Hirsch in *Theologians under Hitler*. It is an insightful and disturbing book for those Christians who think that such a fatal compromise could never happen again. Feige, *The Varieties of Protestantism in Nazi Germany*, treats the problem by examining five theopolitical positions, ranging from Barth, Althaus, and Hirsch, to the liberals Martin Rade and Paul Tillich. Forstman, *Christian Faith in Dark Times*, covers much of the same ground, while adding Rudolf Bultmann and Friedrich Gogarten to the mix and focusing on what prompted the various theologians either to resist or to support the Nazi movement. In a *Covenant Quarterly* essay Pierard draws some lessons from the church struggle for people today. Zehrer, *Evangelische Freikirchen und das Dritte Reich*, examines how the Nazi state treated the various free churches, those marginal Protestant bodies not linked to the regional churches such as the Lutheran Free Churches, Baptists, Methodists, Mennonites, and Moravians. King, *The Nazi State and the New Religions*, deals with the vicissitudes of five dissenting groups—the Christian Scientists, Latter-Day Saints (Mormons), Seventh-Day Adventists, New Apostolic Church, and Jehovah's Witnesses. The personal reminiscences of Stewart Herman, who served as pastor of the American Church in Berlin, is a poignant and insightful, contemporary, firsthand account of the life and trials of German Christians in the Nazi era and the first two years of the war.

More recent scholarship has broadened the discussion to include the Nazi war against the Jews, that is, the Holocaust. The pioneering work in this development is the symposium edited by Littell and Locke, *The German Church Struggle and the Holocaust*, the published papers of a meeting held in Detroit in 1970, the first major conference in the United States that examined both phenomena simultaneously. The essays, which ranged widely over the topics of Nazi oppression of Protestant and Catholic churches, resistance by people in the two religious communities, and Jewish suffering and destruction at the hands of the Nazis, broke much new ground. Since then annual Scholars Conferences on the Holocaust and the Churches have taken place at various venues in the United States, as well as two major international *Remembering for the Future* congresses (Oxford, 1988, and Berlin, 1994). The published papers of the latter reveal clearly how closely linked the Holocaust and church struggle are.

In the West the best-known figure of the Confessing Church was Martin Niemöller (1892–1984). Although essentially a conservative who even admitted to having once voted for the Nazi Party, the former U-boat commander who entered the ministry after World War I showed remarkable courage in countering the aberrations of the German Christians and even confronting Hitler face-to-face. The Berlin pastor was continually harassed by the Gestapo and finally in July 1937 was arrested. After spending eight months in prison, he was tried and virtually acquitted with a sentence of time served. Hitler was furious and ordered him detained as his personal prisoner. Niemöller was placed in the Sachsenhausen concentration camp and three years later moved to Dachau, where he remained until his release at the end of the war. His treatment was constantly mentioned in the foreign press and was a deep embarrassment to the Nazi regime. Many of his sermons were translated into English and were widely read in Britain and the United States before and during the war. The letters he wrote while being held for trial were later edited by Locke as *Exile in the Fatherland.* Schmidt's popular biography has been superseded by Bentley's more scholarly one. Zerner disclosed the origins of Niemöller's famous "first they came for the Communists" quotation in an essay in the Perry and Schweitzer symposium.

THE AMBIGUOUS STANCE OF THE ROMAN CATHOLIC CHURCH TOWARD FASCISM AND NAZISM

The Roman Catholic Church in Germany was quite ambiguous toward the new order. Hitler, an admitted Catholic, allowed the church tax to be deducted from his salary all the way to the end. He respected the church's organization as such but was contemptuous of all religion, Catholic and Protestant alike. In fact, several studies, most notably Angebert, *The Occult and the Third Reich,* and Goodrick-Clarke, *The Occult Roots of Nazism,* as well as Carr's sensationalist *The Twisted Cross,* show convincingly that Hitler's thinking was shaped far more by occultic and neopagan sectarianism than by any expression of Christianity.

Regardless of what Catholic leaders may have known about the führer's outlook, the church's political arm, the Center Party, meekly assented in March 1933 to the Enabling Act, giving Hitler the authority to rule by decree, and four months later voluntarily dissolved itself. In return, the Nazi state in July 1933 signed a concordat with the Holy See that guaranteed Catholics freedom to profess and practice their religion, protected the Catholic educational system, continued public funding for the church, allowed it to provide pastoral care in the army, prisons, and hospitals, and forbade all political activities by the clergy. That the document was little more than a scrap of paper was borne out by the Nazi actions in the Warthegau, the model district carved out of conquered Polish territory around Poznan in early 1940, which provided for a church strictly controlled by the state and marked for eventual extinction. It wiped out the Polish Catholic Church entirely and placed German Catholics there under severe restrictions.

Dietrich in *Catholic Citizens in the Third Reich* traces out the dilemmas that devout, but patriotic, Catholics faced in Nazi Germany. He shows that their spiritual leaders failed to understand the malevolent nature of Hitler's totalitarian rule and did not seek to control Hitler and his minions politically because the church's traditional mission was religious in nature. Because of a deep-seated, religiously based (not racial) anti-Semitism that regarded Jews as outsiders, Catholics did little to oppose Jewish persecution. In the euthanasia controversy they were moved to action only when they realized that those close to them were being killed. In short, the church tried to combine essentially incompatible loyalties to God and to the legal Nazi government and thus was never able to utilize the spiritual and moral resources at its disposal.

In fact, as the Nazis gradually destroyed the network of Catholic organizations in Germany proper and clamped down on the Catholic press and schools, some churchmen began to express alarm over the spread of a new heathenism. They turned to the Vatican for help, and Pope Pius XI on 14 March 1937 drafted a carefully worded encyclical *Mit brennender Sorge*, which criticized the excesses of Nazi doctrines without denouncing the regime's totalitarianism, thus keeping the door open for reconciliation. Some historians feel he was about to be more forthright in his criticisms of the Nazi state, but he died in March 1939 and was succeeded by the accomplished diplomat Cardinal Eugenio Pacelli. The new pope, Pius XII, was deeply committed to bringing peace to the world, but he harbored no illusions about either communism or Nazism, both of which he detested. He had spent thirteen years in Germany as a papal nuncio, first in Bavaria and then in Berlin, before becoming papal secretary of state in 1930, and he negotiated the 1933 concordat. He also succeeded in establishing better relations with Mussolini's fascist regime in Italy, which in spite of tensions over its treatment of the Catholic Action organization enjoyed the support of churchmen for its overseas ventures, especially the intervention on Franco's side in the Spanish civil war. Thus, as Delzell demonstrates in "Pius XII," his cautious diplomatic behavior prevented him from becoming a first-rate moral leader during this time of unprecedented violence and destruction. In fact, the Vatican followed an appeasement policy that tried to keep Italy out of the European War but backed away from this once Mussolini decided to enter the conflict. Only gradually would the pope become disillusioned with the duce.

As archival materials became increasingly available, criticism of the Catholic Church's behavior in Germany intensified. Zahn shows in *German Catholics and Hitler's Wars* and Lewy in *The Catholic Church and Nazi Germany* that Catholics gave in to Hitler's demands from the very beginning and with a few exceptions did nothing to resist his policies and military aggression. Zahn, in fact, argues that the German church operated as an agency of social control inspiring and strengthening Catholic support for the Nazi war effort. Looking elsewhere, the frightening documentation of the Utashi terror compiled by Paris, *Genocide in Satellite Croatia*, reveals how the Croatian Catholic hierarchy, with the full knowledge of the Vatican, supported the local fascist effort to exterminate Serbian Orthodox Christians. Steinberg's "The Roman Catholic Church and Genocide in Croatia" fully corroborates Paris' findings. British relations with the Holy See from 1935 to 1945 are detailed in Chadwick, *Britain and the Vatican during the Second World War*. Catholic connections with other European fascist movements in the interwar and early World War II years are mentioned in Payne, *A History of Fascism 1914–1945*. A documents book compiled by Delzell, *The Papacy and Totalitarianism between the Two World Wars*, provides a comprehensive view of the Vatican's policies through this period.

The polemics over Pope Pius XII's actions (or lack thereof) escalated with the opening of Hochhuth's play *Der Stellvertreter* (*The Deputy*) in Berlin in February 1963. The text was published in English the following year as well as Bentley's collection of criticial assessments. Hochhuth accused Pius of tacit complicity in the destruction of the Jews because he did not speak out against Hitler's actions. The reason for his silence was that he saw Nazi Germany as a bulwark against Soviet communism, an even worse evil. In 1964 Friedländer unleashed a stinging attack in a document collection that revealed that Pius had a predilection for Germany that did not appear to have been diminished by the nature of the Nazi regime and that he feared a Bolshevization of Europe more than anything else. The pontiff hoped that if Hitler's Germany eventually reconciled with the Western Allies, it would then become the essential rampart against the Soviet Union. This explains why he said nothing about the extermination of the Jews. In *The Silence of Pius XII*, a book based heavily on archival sources in Poland and Yugoslavia and published in Italy in 1965, Falconi condemned the pope's indifference toward the German destruction of Poland and the atrocities of the Catholic Utashi regime as well.

From this point, most works either condemned the Vatican for its failure to speak out against the Nazi destruction of the Jews or tried to defend the pope. In *Vatican Diplomacy during the Holocaust*, Morley faulted Pius XII for a single-minded reliance on diplomacy that was marked by reserve and prudence and that could not coexist with humanitarian concern. Because Vatican diplomacy failed both the Jews and members of the Catholic Church who suffered at the hands of Nazis, it betrayed its own ideas. The nuncios, papal secretary of state, and, above all, the pope himself must share responsibility for the failure to confront the evils besetting Europe and the Jewish people. Zuccotti went further to charge that Pius was supremely frightened of two things—Bolshevism and Hitler's establishing a separate Catholic Church—and this explains his inaction in the Jewish question. Although various Catholic writers defended the pope, perhaps the most eloquent was the Irish priest Michael O'Carroll. In *Pius XII: Greatness Dishonoured*, O'Carroll made extensive use of published Vatican materials to rebut the charges made against the pontiff. Papal actions are treated positively in a semiofficial document collection *Pius XII and the Holocaust.*

To summarize the debate, most historians now agree that (1) Pius XII never promulgated an explicit, direct condemnation of the Nazi war of aggression or of the acts of violence against innocent peoples carried out by the Germans and their accomplices under cover of the war; (2) he had full knowledge of the gravity and extent of the events taking place and probably was better informed than any other head of state in the world about what was happening; and (3) he remained silent, even though victims and governments urged him to speak out. The debate centers around whether or not the events per se and the circumstances in which they occurred were of a kind to demand the "witness to the truth" required by his office, and if they were, whether or not the reasons given by Pius to justify his reserve are really sufficient to gain one's approval of his choice.

Defenders of the pope argue that speaking out would be dangerous for the church and other victims and in any case was useless. They also cite the many things the Holy See did to help the victims of Nazism, such as Gallagher's biography of Monsignor Hugh O'Flaherty, who hid escaped British war prisoners in the Vatican. To strengthen its case, the Vatican authorized archivist Blet and others to publish the relevant official documents, beginning with Cardinal Pacelli's elevation to the papacy in March 1939. Critics maintain that Pius (1) regarded Soviet communism as a worse evil than Nazism, (2) possessed a strong Germanophilia that was a result of his years as papal nuncio there, (3) was preoccupied with ensuring the Catholic Church's survival in Europe and guaranteeing it sufficient energy to exercise decisive influence in the postwar world, and (4) had a blind faith in the efficacy of diplomacy as opposed to noisy gestures. As long as the Concordat of 1933 was intact, he thought he could exercise influence over the German leaders.

CHRISTIAN ATTITUDES IN THE WEST

The outbreak of war was a traumatic experience for Christians in the West, particularly Britain. Still, their reaction was more sober and measured than it had been during the First World War, even though the Religious Division of the Ministry of Information began issuing a weekly *Home Bulletin on the Spiritual Issues of the War,* whose intent was to elucidate the spiritual issues at stake in the war and to provide information concerning the British churches in wartime, as well as their contribution to postwar reconstruction. Between late 1939 and June 1945 some 294 numbers of the bulletin appeared. Robbins points out that when Britain faced the onslaught of Nazism in the summer of 1940, many churchmen and political figures alike saw themselves as the defenders of Christian civilization, but this tended to recede (but not disappear) as the immediate threat to British survival eased. Such distinguished personalities as Anglican theologian Alec Vidler, Archbishop of Canterbury, William Temple, and International Missionary Council secretary William Paton published books explaining the meaning of the war, talking of the distinctive message the church can give in a war-torn world, calling for a just peace, and looking for a new and better world after the defeat of Nazism. Even Catholic Hilaire Belloc joined his Protestant counterparts in expounding the religious aspects of the war. Chandler shows in his 1990 Cambridge dissertation, "The Church of England," that the Church of England uniformly and firmly supported the war against Nazi Germany. Without exception, church figures regarded it as a righteous one, and, considering the wickedness of the enemy, many unhesitatingly pronounced it a crusade.

Thus, the issue of pacifism was quite troubling to British churchmen, since many of them had been actively involved in peace movements during the preceding decade. London pastor Albert Belden gave a stirring defense of Christian pacifism right in the midst of the war (1942). He argued that war in itself is sin, the church should have nothing to do with it, and Christians should launch a new missionary movement to bring an end to war and introduce ultimate pacifism. Two years earlier J. Middleton Murry accused churches in all of the warring countries of having betrayed Christ because they failed to prevent the war and now supported their countries' positions. The more moderate pacifist Cecil John Cadoux saw a practical role for peace advocates. They should become involved in public life to work for ultimate peace even as the war was going on. On the other hand, Anglican layman F. A. Walker denounced the pacifists for being shortsighted and misrepresenting the teachings of Christ. These were the same sort of war and peace issues that contemporary American theologians were debating. Wilkinson's *Dissent or Conform?* is an important book on the tensions in the churches over pacifist attitudes during this period.

The policy of obliteration bombing presented churchmen with a peculiar dilemma, as Chandler points out in "The Church of England," because this sort of violence against civilians contradicted their fundamental moral principles. Although Archbishop Temple waffled on the bombing issue, George Bell, bishop of Chichester, was forthright in his opposition to it. As both Chandler and Hein make clear, Bell was unwavering in his attacks on British government policy and military strategy, even in wartime. His published speeches and essays, *The Church Calling* and *The Church and Humanity*, and the Chandler document collection *Brethren in Adversity* bear this out. Through his ecumenical ties Bell knew about the German resistance and learned that the bombing policy was undermining their efforts to overthrow Hitler. He also argued that it undercut the moral justness of the Allied cause. His biographers Jasper and Rupp show that his opposition to bombing cost him advancement in the church.

In neutral Switzerland two commentators were particularly influential. Adolf Keller, secretary of the European Central Bureau of Inter-Church Aid, was a prominent figure in the ecumenical movement and before the war authored numerous books on developments within the churches. One of these, *Church and State on the European Continent*, contains much useful information on the status of Christianity under the dictatorships. Being the citizen of a neutral country, he could travel widely, and in 1942 he produced an informative, insightful, firsthand account of affairs in the churches in areas under Nazi rule. Theologian Karl Barth, who was expelled in 1935 from his post at the University of Bonn, returned to his hometown of Basel and assumed an appointment at the university there. He continued to be critical of Hitler, and in letters to French and British Protestants during 1939–1941 he urged resistance to Nazism. In a 1944 work, *The Church and the War*, he insisted that it is right to work for the defeat of national socialism because it is inherently evil, a wholly destructive, antispiritual nihilism. Articles by Okholm and Aboagye-Mensah analyzing Barth's position on World War II point out that he was highly critical of the churches' prewar stance. He held to a just war position and rejected conscientious objection as an absolute principle. He said that all share in the guilt of war, although one side could be more righteous than the other. Although every war is a judgment of God on human society, it was the clear will of God for Christians to support this one because of the totalitarian nature of Hitlerism, which threatened the integrity of the church and the proclamation of the Word of God. Ludlow analyzes the problems and ambiguities of the European War with which Barth and others in the international Protestant community wrestled.

The war did have a deep impact on the foreign missionary endeavors that the Protestant churches in Europe and North America sponsored. The topic needs considerable research, since the best treatment is still the chapter "World Christianity and World Conflict, 1938–48" in Hogg's classic study *Ecumenical Foundations.* In a description of the "orphaned missions" program of the International Missionary Council Hogg argues that its conception and achievement were unique in the history of the church and that it linked together Christians across the warring lines in the task of the evangelization of humankind. Unlike the deep bitterness that hindered ecumenical relations after World War I, this enabled an immediate resumption of planning and cooperation with German mission societies once the war had ended.

In contrast to the earlier conflict, where the optimistic findings of the U.S. Committee on the War and the Religious Outlook study in 1920 were largely ignored, missionary leaders seized the opportunity to move ahead with their ecumenical vision of Christian extension in the new era. The theoretical basis for this was laid in two important wartime books, Edmund Soper, *The Philosophy of the Christian World Mission,* and Walter Van Kirk, *A Christian Global Strategy.* However, the predominant feature of the renewed missionary movement was a shift from the ecumenical churches of Europe and North America to the so-called evangelicals, whose numbers were greatest in the United States. As Henry Van Dusen suggests, American servicemen discovered missions and indigenous churches in the various parts of the world where they were serving. When they returned home, many of them were energized to return to the places where they had fought or were stationed and carry the gospel message to the people they had come to know. Pierard maintains in *"Pax Americana* and the Evangelical Missionary Advance" that war imagery inspired people to volunteer and prepare for service and that in sheer numbers U.S. evangelical missionaries surpassed those from mainline denominations and European mission societies.

CHRISTIANS AND THE RESISTANCE TO NAZISM

During the war years it was known in the West that Christians in Germany and throughout occupied Europe were rendering considerable opposition to the Nazis. Hugh Martin's *Christian Counter-Attack* (1944) documented religious resistance in Germany, its uneasy allies, and all the countries under German occupation. Other contemporary accounts of religious resistance were those of J. H. Boas and W. A. Visser 't Hooft about the Netherlands. A decade after the war Gollwitzer edited *Dying We Live,* inspiring excerpts from letters and diaries of Christians who engaged in various sorts of oppositional efforts. Gallin focuses on the spiritual backgrounds of those involved in the ill-fated conspiracy of 20 July, 1944 in *German Resistance to Hitler.*

The literature on the anti-Nazi resistance has reached massive proportions, and in both the religious as well as the secular opposition it concentrates largely on the main figures. By far the most widely discussed
individual has been Dietrich Bonhoeffer (1906–1945). From a distinguished academic family, he earned a doctorate in theology at Berlin and
gained extensive foreign experience through pastorates in Spain and England, studies in the United States, and participation in ecumenical organizations. He headed a Confessing Church underground seminary that
the Gestapo shut down, then engaged in a pastoral circuit, and in 1940
found employment (through his brother-in-law) as a courier in the army
counterintelligence agency. Now deeply involved in the resistance, Bonhoeffer used his ecumenical ties to make contact with people in the West,
especially his friend Bishop Bell, but could not gain any support. Arrested
in April 1943 on suspicion of oppositional activities, the authorities could
pin nothing on him until some documents exposing the military plotters
were discovered in October 1944, and he was executed just before the
war's end.

Bonhoeffer was not well known in the West until the publication of
Prisoner for God in 1953 (later titled as *Letters and Papers from Prison*). This
went through numerous editions and gave the martyred pastor and theologian a reputation he had not had in life; they can be found in his *Works*.
Most of his other books and sermons were quickly published in German
and then translated into English, and in 1958 the first volume of his *Ges-
ammelte Schriften* (Collected Works) appeared. By 1996 this had reached
thirteen volumes, and the first installment of the English translation (volume 5, *Life Together* and *Prayerbook of the Bible*) had been released. A convenient, useful, one-volume collection of Bonhoeffer's most important
writings is *A Testament to Freedom*, edited by Kelly and Nelson. The authoritative biography, *Dietrich Bonhoeffer*, is by Bethge, his pupil and general
editor of the German collected works. Among other noteworthy recent
biographies are those by Bosanquet, Robertson, Wind, and Huntemann.
Of particular interest is the attention that Bonhoeffer attracted in South
Africa, as his theology and experience spoke directly to the crisis situation
of apartheid. The series of essays and lectures Bethge compiled for a
South African tour in 1973, *Bonhoeffer: Exile and Martyr*, and the insightful
study by University of Cape Town scholar John de Gruchy, *Bonhoeffer and
South Africa*, reveal his significance for the struggle there.

More recently, Barnett, *For the Soul of the People*, and Thomas, *Women
against Hitler*, have examined the life and witness of relatively inconspic-
uous figures in the Confessing Church. By interviewing survivors, they
discovered models of faithful living in extreme times, but they also warned
against any comfortable equation of doctrinal integrity and political virtue.
Pejsa's *Matriarch of Conspiracy* focuses on Ruth von Kleist, a noblewoman
in Pomerania who was a devout Christian and closely involved with the

Bonhoeffer family and the conspiracy against Hitler. An early martyr of the Nazis was Pastor Paul Schneider, who was executed in Buchenwald in 1939 and whose autobiography was published after the war. Another noteworthy personality was Edith Stein, a Carmelite nun who had converted from Judaism but still was murdered at Auschwitz as a Jew. The biography by Graef does not detail the controversy that has swirled around her in recent years. Alfred Delp, a Jesuit who was implicated in the conspiracy against Hitler, wrote a series of *Prison Meditations* between the time of his arrest and execution that is a respected work of Catholic piety.

An interesting personality is the only saint to emerge from the ranks of the wartime martyrs, Maximilian Kolbe (1894–1941). A Polish Franciscan priest known for his Marian devotion who had spent some years as a missionary in Japan, Kolbe was arrested by the Nazis for carrying on forbidden educational activities and incarcerated in Auschwitz. When a prisoner escaped, and the Nazi guards retaliated by selecting ten people to die in a starvation bunker, Kolbe volunteered to take the place of a man who had a family. He died on 14 August 1941. The archbishop of Krakow, Cardinal Karol Wojtyla, obtained his beatification in 1971, and then Pope John Paul II personally declared him a martyr for the faith, thus enabling his elevation to sainthood in 1982. Dewar provides the fullest account of his life, but as Cunningham points out in "The Politics of Canonization," this was very much a political action. However, church officials looked the other way when it came to the fate of another Catholic martyr, a simple Austrian peasant named Franz Jägerstätter, who refused induction into the German army. He insisted that Hitler's government was pagan, and military service was against the gospel. His life and execution are poignantly detailed in Zahn, *In Solitary Witness*. The church ignored his witness against nationalist sentiment because it feared this would demoralize the many Catholics who had served in the army.

The religious dimensions of the French resistance are not as well known in the English-speaking West because several major studies are in German or French. However, Perrin, *Priest-Workman in Germany*, is an interesting diary of a priest who volunteered to work in the factories with French conscript laborers in Germany and minister to them. Hellman, *The Knight-Monks of Vichy France*, tells about a charismatic and aristocratic group that founded a kind of training school at Uriage and endeavored to utilize France's national humiliation as an opportunity to bring the people back to the Catholic faith. Zaretsky, *Nîmes at War*, explains how traditional confessional tensions between Catholics and Protestants colored the wartime experiences of the population in the Gard. Hall, *Politics, Society and Christianity in Vichy France*, is the most comprehensive treatment of clerical conformity and resistance in these years and reveals the ambiguities of the church leader's positions.

The symbolic figure of resistance in Norway was the chief bishop of the

Norwegian church, Eivind Berggrav. He led the religious opposition to the collaborationist puppet government of Vidkun Quisling, and he and all the other bishops resigned in February 1941 rather than give in to Nazi demands. He was arrested a few weeks later and put under house arrest for the remainder of the war. His ideas are spelled in his essay collection _With God in the Darkness_ and an article by Hassing. The Church of Norway's resistance activities are detailed in Godal's biography of Berggrav and an article by Torleiv in the journal _Mid-Stream_. Hannu analyzes the English reactions to the situation throughout Scandinavia in a symposium essay.

Much less has been written about the churches in the East during the war, although the contemporary accounts by Keller, _Christian Europe Today_, and Martin, _Christian Counter-Attack_, do give some information. Montclos, _Les Chrétiens Face au Nazisme et au Stalinisme_, is an important comparative study of totalistic policies toward the churches in the areas under Nazi and Soviet rule. Jerabek shows that Nazi military and civil administrators in the Ukraine encouraged religious tolerance to counter Soviet sympathies but would not allow nationalistic activities to become part of religious celebrations.

An important kind of Christian witness was that of rescuing Jews. Rittner and Myers edited _The Courage to Care_, a heartwarming collection of stories about Christians in various parts of Europe who rescued or hid Jews. Gushee, _The Righteous Gentiles of the Holocaust_, is an incisive analysis of the behavior of those who were motivated by Christian ethics to act on behalf of the victims. Tec, _When Light Pierced the Darkness_, is a moving account of Christians in Poland who saved Jews. Corrie ten Boom and Diet Eman were Dutch Christians who hid Jews in their homes and engaged in resistance. Hallie, _Lest Innocent Blood Be Shed_, tells how French Protestant pastor André Trocmé and the members of his congregation in Le Chambon carried out a remarkable rescue operation. Lubac, _Christian Resistance to Anti-Semitism_, is an important, first-person account of the oppositional activities of a prominent French Catholic churchman and later cardinal.

RELIGION AND THE WAR IN THE PACIFIC

In contrast to the European theater very little has appeared on the religious dimensions of the war in Asia and the Pacific. Oe details the tensions between the Protestant churches and the Japanese state, where around thirty denominations joined in the merger on 25 June 1941 to create the United Church of Japan (_Nihon Kiristo Kyodan_). Although this was the result of government pressure, many Protestant ecumenists had long favored the move, but the Holiness churches and the Jehovah's Witnesses refused to unite, and the Anglican Church in Japan was divided over the matter. Mikizo shows in "Recollection of Christian Suffering" that Catholic and Protestant Christians alike suffered in wartime Japan, but the Kyodan attempted to uphold the faith and represent the interests of Christians who endured persecution. In "Ideology and Utopianism" Mullins examines the courageous resistance of several smaller evangelical sects to the demands of state Shinto. The memoir of the veteran Baptist missionary to Japan William Axling, who lived there during the early years of the Pacific War and was interned after Pearl Harbor, is valuable for its commentary on Japanese life.

The best-known Japanese Christian in the West was Toyohiko Kagawa (1888–1960). A socialist and pacifist as well as a luminary on the ecumenical scene, he was the object of considerable government hostility. He was a member of the eight-man delegation of Japanese Christian leaders who came to the United States in April 1941 at the joint invitation of the Federal Council of Churches and Foreign Missions Conference. They met with representatives from these groups in Riverside, California, to pray and work for peace, in this the last major ecumenical effort to head off the impending conflict. A Kyodan supporter, during the war he was kept under constant surveillance and on occasions imprisoned. He was critical of both Japanese and American behavior in the war effort. Davey's biography, *Kagawa of Japan*, is a recent treatment.

There are numerous autobiographical accounts by missionaries who were interned, of which the distinguished American theologian Langdon Gilkey's *Shantung Compound* is probably best known. Judy Hyland, *In the Shadow of the Rising Sun*, is the story of a Lutheran missionary who was held in a prison camp for women and children in the Philippines. In *Guerrilla Padre* James Haggerty recounts the activities of a Christian pastor working with a guerrilla band in Mindanao, while Go Paun-seng, the publisher of the main Chinese-language newspaper in the Philippines and an aggressive opponent of Japanese expansion in Asia, tells how he hid out in the mountains for three years and how his Christian faith kept him going even when all seemed lost. A different type of book entirely is Benda, *The Crescent and the Rising Sun*, a scholarly account of the tensions between the Japanese occupation authorities and Islamic elites on the Indonesian island of Java.

MILITARY CHAPLAINS

The literature on military chaplains is quite sketchy. Zahn's *The Military Chaplaincy*, an empirical study of British Royal Air Force chaplains made in the mid-1960s, does give some indication of their wartime experiences and tensions, as does Clifford's more popular collection of British chaplains' stories, *Thank You, Padre*. The activities of Canadian chaplains are traced out in an article by Hamilton. Arthur Glasser, *And Some Believed*, is the autobiographical account of a former missionary who worked as a U.S.

Marine chaplain in the South Pacific. Hourihan briefly describes the work of the German army chaplains, who, in fact, were in very short supply, while German Catholic priest and theologian Bernard Häring tells in his memoir *Embattled Witness* how, although he was just a conscript soldier, he was able to conduct religious services and provide spiritual counseling. Bergen shows that nearly a third of the chaplains were pro-Nazi German Christians, but their influence was in ironic tension with Nazi ideology, which was resolutely anti-Christian. By their commitment to Hitler's war, they promoted atrocities and genocide and undermined what little moral authority they had. Schabel, *Herr, in Deine Hände*, is a compilation of reports by chaplains in the armed forces of the various warring powers, particularly the German army, about their pastoral ministries. Rozen, *Cry in the Wilderness*, is the account of a Jewish chaplain in Soviet Russia. It is clear that the topic of the wartime military chaplaincy sorely needs further investigation.

Although several aspects of Christianity during the war are well treated, some areas are much in need of further exploration. These include its role in the Asian theater and the colonies of the Allied powers, the religious life of the fighting men on both sides, and Christian resistance in the areas under Axis rule.

BIBLIOGRAPHY

Aboagye-Mensah, Robert. "Karl Barth's Attitude to War in the Context of World War II." *Evangelical Quarterly* 60 (1988): 43–59.

Angebert, Jean-Michel. *The Occult and the Third Reich: The Mystical Origins of Nazism and the Search for the Holy Grail.* New York: Macmillan, 1974.

Axling, William. *Japan at the Midcentury: Leaves from Life.* Philadelphia: Judson, 1957.

Baranowski, Shelley. *The Confessing Church, Conservative Elites, and the Nazi State.* Lewiston, NY: Edwin Mellen, 1986.

Barnes, Kenneth C. *Nazism, Liberalism, and Christianity: Protestant Social Thought in Germany and Great Britain 1925–1937.* Lexington: UP of Kentucky, 1991.

Barnett, Victoria. *For the Soul of the People: Protestant Protest against Hitler.* New York: Oxford UP, 1992.

Barth, Karl. *The Church and the War.* New York: Macmillan, 1944.

———. *This Christian Cause.* New York: Macmillan, 1941; British ed., *A Letter to Great Britain from Switzerland.* London: Sheldon, 1941.

Belden, Albert D. *Pax Christi, the Peace of Christ: A New Policy for Christendom Today.* London: George Allen and Unwin, 1942.

Bell, G. K. A. *The Church and Humanity (1939–1946).* London: Longmans, Green, 1946.

———. *The Church Calling: Six Talks on the Church and World Order.* London: Edinburgh House, 1942.

Belloc, Hilaire. *The Catholic and the War.* London: Burns, Oates, 1940.

Benda, Harry J. *The Crescent and the Rising Sun: Indonesian Islam under the Japanese Occupation 1942–1945.* The Hague: W. van Hoeve, 1958.

Bentley, Eric, ed. *The Storm over The Deputy.* New York: Grove, 1964.

Bentley, James. *Martin Niemöller.* New York: Free, 1984.

Bergen, Doris L. " 'Germany Is Our Mission—Christ Is Our Strength!' The Wehrmacht Chaplaincy and the 'German Christian' Movement." *Church History* 66 (1997): 522–536.

———. *Twisted Cross: The German Christian Movement in the Third Reich.* Chapel Hill: University of North Carolina, 1966.

Berggrav, Eivind. *With God in the Darkness.* London: Hodder and Stoughton, 1943.

Bethge, Eberhard. *Bonhoeffer: Exile and Martyr.* New York: Seabury, 1975.

———. *Dietrich Bonhoeffer: Man of Vision, Man of Courage.* New York: Harper and Row, 1970.

Blet, Pierre, et al., eds. *Records and Documents of the Holy See Relating to the Second World War.* 9 vols. Washington, DC: Corpus, 1965–75.

Boas, J. H. *Resistance of the Churches in the Netherlands.* New York: Netherlands Information Bureau, 1944.

Bonhoeffer, Dietrich. *Werke.* Edited by Eberhard Bethge et al. 13 vols. München: Chr. Kaiser, 1958– .

———. *Works.* Edited by Wayne Whitson Floyd. Minneapolis: Fortress, 1996– .

Bosanquet, Mary. *The Life and Death of Dietrich Bonhoeffer.* New York: Harper and Row, 1968.

Cadoux, Cecil John. *Christian Pacifism Re-examined.* Oxford: Basil Blackwell, 1940.

Carr, Joseph J. *The Twisted Cross: The Occultic Religion of Hitler and the New Age Nazism of the Third Reich.* Shreveport, LA: Huntington House, 1985.

Chadwick, Owen. *Britain and the Vatican during the Second World War.* Cambridge: Cambridge UP, 1986.

Chandler, Andrew. *Brethren in Adversity: Bishop George Bell, the Church of England and the Crisis of German Protestantism, 1933–1939.* London: Church of England Record Society, 1996.

———. "The Church of England and Nazi Germany." Ph.D. diss., Cambridge University, 1990.

———. "The Church of England and the Obliteration Bombing of Germany in the Second World War." *English Historical Review* 108 (1993): 920–946.

Clifford, Joan. *Thank You Padre: Memories of World War II.* London: Collins, 1989.

Cochrane, Arthur C. *The Church's Confession under Hitler.* Philadelphia: Westminster, 1962.

Conway, John S. *The Nazi Persecution of the Churches, 1933–45.* New York: Basic, 1968.

Cunningham, Lawrence S. "The Politics of Canonization." *Christian Century* 100 (11 May 1983): 454–455.

Davey, Cyril J. *Kagawa of Japan.* Nashville, TN: Abingdon, 1960.

De Gruchy, John W. *Bonhoeffer and South Africa.* Grand Rapids, MI: Eerdmans, 1984.

Delp, Alfred. *Prison Meditations.* Montreal: Palm, 1963.

Delzell, Charles F. *The Papacy and Totalitarianism between the Two World Wars.* New York: Wiley, 1974.

———. "Pius XII, Italy, and the Outbreak of War." *Journal of Contemporary History* 2 (1967): 137–161.

Dewar, Diana. *Saint of Auschwitz: The Story of Maximilian Kolbe.* San Francisco: Harper and Row, 1982.

Dietrich, Donald J. *Catholic Citizens in the Third Reich: Psycho-Social Principles and Moral Reasoning.* New Brunswick, NJ: Transaction, 1988.

Eman, Diet, with James Schaap. *Things We Couldn't Say.* Grand Rapids, MI: Eerdmans, 1994.

Ericksen, Robert P. *Theologians under Hitler: Gerhard Kittel, Paul Althaus, and Emanuel Hirsch.* New Haven, CT: Yale UP, 1985.

Evangelische Kirche in Deutschland. *Arbeiten zur Geschichte des Kirchenkampfes.* Göttingen: Vandenhoeck and Ruprecht, 1958–1975.

Falconi, Carlo. *The Silence of Pius XII.* Boston: Little, Brown, 1970.

Faulkner, Charles. "For Christian Civilization: The Churches and Canada's War Effort, 1939–1942." Ph.D. diss., University of Chicago, 1975.

Feige, Franz G. M. *The Varieties of Protestantism in Nazi Germany: Five Theopolitical Positions.* Lewiston, NY: Edwin Mellen, 1990.

Forstman, Jack. *Christian Faith in Dark Times: Theological Conflicts in the Shadow of Hitler.* Louisville, KY: Westminster/John Knox, 1992.

Friedländer, Saul. *Pius XII and the Third Reich: A Documentation.* New York: Alfred A. Knopf, 1966.

Gallagher, J. P. *Scarlet Pimpernel of the Vatican.* New York: Coward-McCann, 1968.

Gallin, Mary Alice. *German Resistance to Hitler: Ethical and Religious Factors.* Washington, DC: Catholic University of America, 1961.

Gilkey, Langdon B. *Shantung Compound: The Story of Men and Women under Pressure.* New York: Harper and Row, 1966.

Glasser, Arthur F. *And Some Believed: A Chaplain's Experiences with the Marines in the South Pacific.* Chicago: Moody, 1946.

Go, Paun-seng. *Refuge and Strength.* Englewood Cliffs, NJ: Prentice-Hall, 1970.

Godal, Odd. *Eivind Berggrav: Leader of Christian Resistance.* London: SCM, 1949.

Gollwitzer, Helmut, et al. *Dying We Live: The Final Messages and Records of the Resistance.* New York: Pantheon, 1956.

Goodrick-Clarke, Nicholas. *The Occult Roots of Nazism: Secret Aryan Cults and Their Influence on Nazi Ideology.* New York: New York UP, 1992.

Graef, Hilda C. *The Scholar and the Cross: The Life and Work of Edith Stein.* Westminster, MD: Newman, 1955.

Gushee, David P. *The Righteous Gentiles of the Holocaust: A Christian Interpretation.* Minneapolis: Fortress, 1994.

Haggerty, James E. *Guerrilla Padre in Mindanao.* New York: Longmans, Green, 1946.

Hall, W. D. *Politics, Society and Christianity in Vichy France.* Providence, RI: Berg, 1995.

Hallie, Philip. *Lest Innocent Blood Be Shed.* New York: Harper and Row, 1979.

Hamilton, Thomas James. " 'The Delicate Equilibrium': Canada's Protestant Chaplains during the Second World War." *Journal of the Canadian Church History Society* 35 (1993): 105–120.

Hannu, Heikkila. "English Reactions on the Situations of the Churches in Finland and Scandinavia 1940–1941." In Carsten Nicolaisen, ed., *Nordische und deutsche Kirchen im 20. Jarhundert: Referate auf der Internationlen Arbeitstagung in Sandbjerg, Dänemark,* 212–217. Göttingen: Vandenhoeck and Ruprecht, 1982.

Häring, Bernard. *Embattled Witness: Memories of a Time of War.* New York: Seabury, 1976.

Hassing, Arne. "The Core Ideas of the 'Nazi Church' in Occupied Norway 1940–45." *Studia Theologica: Scandinavian Journal of Theology* 42:1 (1988): 1–20.

Hein, David. "George Bell, Bishop of Chichester, on the Morality of War." *Anglican Episcopal History* 58 (1989): 498–509.

Hellman, John. *The Knight-Monks of Vichy France: Uriage 1940–1945.* Montreal: McGill-Queens UP, 1993.

Helmreich, Ernst C. *The German Churches under Hitler.* Detroit: Wayne State UP, 1979.

Herman, Stewart W., Jr. *It's Your Souls We Want.* New York: Harper and Brothers, 1943.

Hochhuth, Rolf. *The Deputy.* New York: Grove, 1964.

Hogg, William Richey. *Ecumenical Foundations: A History of the International Missionary Council and Its Nineteenth Century Background.* New York: Harper and Brothers, 1952.

Hourihan, William J. "Wehrmacht Chaplains in World War II." *Army Chaplain* (1993): 62–64.

Huntemann, Georg. *The Other Bonhoeffer: An Evangelical Reassessment of Dietrich Bonhoeffer.* Grand Rapids, MI: Baker, 1993.

Hyland, Judy. *In the Shadow of the Rising Sun.* Minneapolis: Augsburg, 1984.

Jasper, Ronald C. D. *George Bell: Bishop of Chichester.* London: Oxford UP, 1967.

Jerabek, Blanca. "National Socialist Religious Policy in Ukraine, 1941–1944." *Ukrainean Review* 35:3 (1987): 3–11.

Keller, Adolf. *Christian Europe Today.* New York: Harper and Brothers, 1942.

———. *Church and State on the European Continent.* London: Epworth, 1936.

Kelly, Geffrey B., and F. Burton Nelson, eds. *A Testament to Freedom: The Essential Writings of Dietrich Bonhoeffer.* San Francisco: HarperSan Francisco, 1990; Morganville, NJ: Present Truth, 1995.

King, Christine E. *The Nazi State and the New Religions: Five Case Studies in Non-Conformity.* Lewiston, NY: Edwin Mellen, 1982.

Lewy, Guenter. *The Catholic Church and Nazi Germany.* New York: McGraw-Hill, 1964.

Littell, Franklin H., and Hubert G. Locke. *The German Church Struggle and the Holocaust.* Detroit: Wayne State UP, 1974.

Locke, Hubert G., ed. *The Barmen Confession: Papers from the Seattle Assembly.* Lewiston, NY: Edwin Mellen, 1986.

———. *The Church Confronts the Nazis: Barmen Then and Now.* Lewiston, NY: Edwin Mellen, 1984.

———. *Exile in the Fatherland: Martin Niemöller's Letters from Moabit Prison.* Grand Rapids, MI: Eerdmans, 1986.

Lubac, Henri de. *Christian Resistance to Anti-Semitism: Memories from 1940–1944.* San Francisco: Ignatius, 1990.

Ludlow, Peter W. "The International Protestant Community in the Second World War." *Journal of Ecclesiastical History* 29 (1978): 311–362.

Matheson, Peter. *The Third Reich and the Christian Churches.* Grand Rapids, MI: Eerdmans, 1985.

Martin, Hugh, et al. *Christian Counter-Attack: Europe's Churches against Nazism.* New York: Charles Scribner's, 1944.

Mikizo, Matsuo. "Recollection of Christian Suffering during the National Crisis." *Japan Christian Quarterly* 49 (1983): 134–137.

Montclos, Xavier de. *Les Chrétiens Face au Nazisme et au Stalinisme. L'épreuve totalitaire 1939–1945*. Paris: Plon, 1983.

Morley, John F. *Vatican Diplomacy and the Jews during the Holocaust 1933–1945*. New York: KTAV Publishing House, 1980.

Mullins, Mark R. "Ideology and Utopianism in Wartime Japan." *Japanese Journal of Religious Studies*. 21 (1994): 261–280.

Murry, J. Middleton. *The Betrayal of Christ by the Churches*. London: Andrew Dakers, 1940.

Niemöller, Martin. *First Commandment*. London: W. Hodge, 1937.

———. *From U-Boat to Pulpit*. London: W. Hodge, 1936; Chicago: Willett, Clark, 1937; reissued in 1939 as *From U-Boat to Concentration Camp*.

———. *The Gestapo Defied, Being the Last Twenty-eight Sermons*. London: W. Hodge, 1942.

———. *Here Stand I*. Chicago: Willett, Clark, 1937.

O'Carroll, Michael. *Pius XII: Greatness Dishonoured*. Chicago: Franciscan Herald, 1980.

Oe, John Mitsuru. "Church and State in Japan during World War II." *Anglican Episcopal History* 59 (1990): 202–223.

Okholm, Dennis. "Defending the Cause of the Christian Church: Karl Barth's Justification of War." *Christian Scholar's Review* 16:2 (1987): 144–162.

Paris, Edmond. *Genocide in Satellite Croatia, 1941–1945: A Record of Racial and Religious Persecutions and Massacres*. Chicago: American Institute for Balkan Affairs, 1961.

Paton, William. *The Church and the New Order*. London: SCM, 1941.

———. *The Church Calling: Six Talks on the Church and World Order*. London: Edinburgh House, 1942.

———. *The Message of the World-Wide Church*. London: Sheldon, 1940.

Paul Schneider, the Pastor of Buchenwald: A Free Translation of the Story Told by His Widow, with Many Quotations from His Diary and Letters. London: SCM, 1956.

Payne, Stanley G. *A History of Fascism, 1914–1945*. Madison: University of Wisconsin, 1995.

Pejsa, Jane. *Matriarch of Conspiracy: Ruth von Kleist 1867–1945*. Cleveland: Pilgrim, 1992.

Perrin, Henri. *Priest-Workman in Germany*. London: Sheed and Ward, 1947.

Perry, Marvin, and Frederick Schweitzer. *Jewish-Christian Encounters over the Centuries*. New York: Peter Lang, 1994.

Pierard, Richard V. "Implications of the German Church Struggle for Christians Today." *Covenant Quarterly* 33 (1981): 3–16.

———. "*Pax Americana* and the Evangelical Missionary Advance." In Josef Carpenter and Wilbert Shenk, eds., *Earthen Vessels*, 155–179. Grand Rapids, MI: Eerdmans, 1990.

Pius XII and the Holocaust: A Reader. Milwaukee: Catholic League for Religious and Civil Rights, 1988.

Religious Division of the Ministry of Information. *Home Bulletin on the Spiritual Issues of the War*. London, The Division, 1939–1945.

Remembering for the Future: The Impact of the Holocaust and Genocide on Jews and Christians. Oxford: Pergamon, 1988.

Remembering for the Future II: The Holocaust. Stamford, CT: Vista InterMedia, 1995.

Rittner, Carol, and Sandra Myers, eds. *The Courage to Care: Rescuers of Jews during the Holocaust.* New York: New York UP, 1986.

Robbins, Keith G. "Britain, 1940, and 'Christian Civilization.' " In Derek Beales and Geoffrey Best, eds., *History, Society, and the Churches: Essays in Honour of Owen Chadwick,* 279–199. Cambridge: Cambridge UP, 1985.

Robertson, Edwin H. *The Shame and the Sacrifice: The Life and Teaching of Dietrich Bonhoeffer.* London: Hodder and Stoughton, 1987.

Rozen, Leon S. *Cry in the Wilderness, a Short History of a Chaplain: Activities and Struggles in Soviet Russia during World War II.* New York: N.p., 1966.

Rupp, George. *I See My Brethren : Bishop George Bell and the German Churches.* London: Epworth, 1965.

Schabel, Wilhelm, ed. *Herr, in Deine Hände. Seelsorge im Kriege, Dokumente der Menschlichkeit aus der ganzen Welt.* Bern and Stuttgart: Alfred Scherz Verlag, 1963.

Schmidt, Dietmar. *Pastor Niemöller.* Garden City, NY: Doubleday, 1959.

Scholder, Klaus. *The Churches and the Third Reich.* Vol. 1: *Preliminary History and the Time of Illusions, 1918–1934;* Vol. 2: *The Year of Disillusionment, 1934.* Philadelphia: Fortress, 1988–1989.

———. *A Requiem for Hitler and Other New Perspectives on the German Church Struggle.* Philadelphia: Trinity International, 1989.

Sittser, Gerald L. *A Cautious Patriotism: The American Churches and the Second World War.* Chapel Hill: University of North Carolina, 1997.

Soper, Edmund Davison. *The Philosophy of the Christian World Mission.* Nashville, TN: Abingdon-Cokesbury, 1943.

Steinberg, Jonathan. "The Roman Catholic Church and Genocide in Croatia, 1941–45." In Diana Wood, ed., *Christianity and Judaism: Studies in Church History,* 463–480. Oxford: Blackwell, 1992.

Tec, Nechama. *When Light Pierced the Darkness: Christian Rescue of Jews in Nazi-Occupied Poland.* New York: Oxford UP, 1986.

Temple, William. *The Hope of a New World.* New York: Macmillan, 1942.

———. *Thoughts in War-Time.* London: Macmillan, 1940.

ten Boom, Corrie. *The Hiding Place.* Carmel, NY: Guideposts, 1971.

———. *Corrie ten Boom's Prison Letters.* Fort Washington, PA: Fleming H. Revell, 1975; London: Hodder and Stoughton, 1976; New York: Bantam, 1978.

Thomas, Theodore N. *Women against Hitler: Christian Resistance in the Third Reich.* Westport, CT: Praeger, 1995.

Torleiv, Austad. "Eivind Berggrav and the Church of Norway's Resistance against Nazism 1940–45." *Mid-Stream* 26 (1987): 51–61.

Van Dusen, Henry P. *They Found the Church There: The Armed Forces Discover Christian Missions.* New York: Charles Scribner's, 1945.

Van Kirk, Walter W. *A Christian Global Strategy.* Chicago: Willett, Clarke, 1945.

Vidler, Alec R. *God's Judgment on Europe.* London: Longmans, Green, 1940.

Visser't Hooft, W. A. *The Struggle of the Dutch Church for the Maintenance of the Commandments of God in the Life of the State.* New York: American Committee for the World Council of Churches, 1945.

Walker, F. A. *The Blunder of Pacifism.* London: Hodder and Stoughton, 1940.

Wall, Donald D. "The Confessing Church and the Second World War." *Journal of Church and State* 23 (1981): 15–34.

Wilkinson, Alan. *Dissent or Conform?: War Peace and the English Churches, 1900–1945.* London: SCM, 1986.

Wind, Renate. *Dietrich Bonhoeffer: A Spoke in the Wheel.* Grand Rapids, MI: Eerdmans, 1992.

Zabel, James A. *Nazism and the Pastors: A Study of the Ideas of Three Deutsche Christen Groups.* Missoula, MT: Scholars, 1976.

Zahn, Gordon C. *German Catholics and Hitler's Wars: A Study in Social Control.* New York: Sheed and Ward, 1962.

———. *In Solitary Witness: The Life and Death of Franz Jägerstätter.* New York: Holt, Rinehart, and Winston, 1964.

———. *The Military Chaplaincy: A Study of Role Tension in the Royal Air Force.* Manchester, U.K.: University of Manchester, 1969.

Zaretsky, Robert. *Nîmes at War: Religion, Politics and Public Opinion in the Gard, 1938–1944.* University Park: Pennsylvania State UP, 1995.

Zehrer, Karl. *Evangelische Freikirchen und das Dritte Reich.* Berlin: Evangelische Verlagsanstalt, 1986.

Zuccotti, Suzan. *The Italians and the Holocaust: Persecution, Rescue, and Survival.* New York: Basic, 1987.

25   Cultural Background to the War

Donald J. Mrozek

War is among the most dramatic and consequential expressions of culture, and the power of culture in causing and facilitating war, as well as in shaping its dimensions and characteristics, can scarcely be exaggerated. Its force is as great when unconscious as when conscious, and it is pervasive.

An understanding of key cultural forces in the 1930s assists greatly in appreciating the structure, dynamics, and intensity of World War II. The 1930s were a time when suspicion of democracy emerged alongside celebration of the masses. It was a time when patriotic renewal drew to the brink of national chauvinism. It was a time when a taste for authoritarian governance coexisted with presentation of the "folk" as the underlying heroic force in the nation-state. It was a time when the experience of cultural and societal disarray brought forth images of community and cultural uniformity—a time when radio, glossy magazines, and movies intensified images. It was a time, compromised by economic depression and the experience of powerlessness, when a yearning for control over one's destiny grew strong.

CULTURE AND NATIONAL COMMITMENT

During the 1930s, culture was the vehicle through which individuals could regain and articulate their commitment to respective national traditions and, in some places, to a reconceived nation-state. The intention to recommit to past principles and to restore traditional elements in the life of common citizens actually did much to facilitate change. Susman in *Culture and Commitment, 1929–1945* argued how the central government and other institutional authority was reaffirmed, even while populist themes were celebrated. When assuming the American presidency in 1933 during a time of great crisis in national confidence, Franklin Roosevelt invited a solution through attitude as much as through action, describing "nameless, unreasoning fear" as the people's real enemy. In fact, recognizing that the anxieties of Americans were rooted in real material conditions, Roosevelt set in motion a myriad of measures whose value rested in the image of activism as much as in the practical consequences of the actions themselves. As suggested in Brinkley, *Voices of Protest,* an image of dynamic personal leadership helped to counter the likes of Huey Long and Father Charles Coughlin. Roosevelt's willingness to change policy, whether termed "pragmatism" or "lack of principle," bore kinship to the supremacy of action over thought that went far toward explaining the ruling habits of Adolf Hitler and Joseph Stalin. Roosevelt used the plans of the technocratic elite that served him, notably, his "brain trust," but did so apparently without ever committing to their philosophical bases. Image and impressions constituted as powerful a force in the real world as ever before.

Expressed benignly, an especially powerful impulse in the 1930s took shape in America as "the power of positive thinking." Seen less favorably, it was a rush away from fixed normative values and toward cultural relativism. In *How to Win Friends and Influence People,* Dale Carnegie argued that success depended on adapting oneself to the preferences of others and on avoiding giving offense. The individual could regain a sense of power but only by sharing it with others following the same rules. Oliver and Dudley claimed as much for America's Civilian Conservation Corps in *This New America,* also later described in Salmond's *The Civilian Conservation Corps,* while Mosse traced a yet more destructive German version of the experience in *Nazi Culture.*

Reassessment of the relationship of the individual to the masses occurred widely around the world, often including fervid argument over the role of the leader relative to the group. Into this global debate were injected cultural proclivities that went far beyond rational calculation of political benefit, making politics itself one element among many in a complex cultural psychodynamic. To a substantial degree, the poet William Butler Yeats was right to say of the age: "The best lack all ambition, while the worst are full of passionate intensity." The best included principled, but enfeebled, democrats, often thinking their way into inactivity. The worst included nihilistic fascists, for whom action was its own justification and in whom quasi-romantic vitalism played the role of ideology.

Ambivalence toward the masses pervaded European culture, with opinion running the extremes from denunciation to celebration. In works such as *The Revolt of the Masses,* (1929) Jose Ortega y Gasset derided man in the mass as incapable of thought, motivated only by feeling, sentiments contributing to his hostility to fascism during the Spanish civil war. Communist and fascist elements meanwhile glorified an anti-intellectual vitalism, leading toward the destruction of class distinctions by the imposition of a uniform cultural experience. Jelagin in *Taming the Arts* suggests this for the Soviet Union, as do Leyda, *Kino*, and Tucker, *Stalin in Power*. Socialists and others looked uncomfortably for a fusion of the "hand" and the "head," as Fritz Lang did in the film *Metropolis* (1926), warning that only the "heart" could unite the two otherwise hostile forces. It was an aspiration meaningful to intellectuals such as Oswald Spengler in *Preussentum und Sozialismus* [*Prussianism and Socialism*] and Friedrich Meinecke in *The German Catastrophe*. The quest for a sense of popular community, or *Volksgemeinschaft*, then, carried both the appeal of national restoration and the threat of authoritarian rule at the hands of a manipulated mob.

In France, the defeatism evident in the dilatory response to the German invasion of Poland in 1939 came only as the climax of a long process of self-doubt and discouragement. There, as for proponents of the anti-interventionist America First Committee such as Charles Lindbergh, Germany seemed to have a new vitality, an animating force of spirit and will, and thus acquired an air of invincibility. *British Appeasement in the 1930s* by Rock follows this cultural force into politics, as does Gilbert and Gott's *The Appeasers*.

The amalgamation of popular force and aggressive leadership into a triumphant and seemingly organic vitalism was celebrated in Leni Riefenstahl's *The Triumph of the Will* (1935), her documentary of the Nazi Party rally at Nuremberg in 1934. Even more revealing as a demonstration of the bond between the masses and their champion was *Olympia* (1936), her film of the 1936 Berlin Olympic Games, in which the overt political propagandizing of *Triumph of the Will* was virtually absent. In its place was the glorification of the human body and will, inseparably connected, with strength seen as the source of joy and joyous devotion portrayed as the means to strength. Mosse's *Nazi Culture* also illuminates this dynamic. The evocative power of *Kraft durch Freude*—strength through joy—affected those who felt the lack of it, such as the French, as much as those who reveled in its presence, such as the Germans. It, too, contributed to levels of passivity and aggressiveness at the end of the 1920s.

The peace movement in France owed as much to a widespread culture of despair as to anything else, as maintained by Ingram in *The Politics of Dissent*. Peace became necessary the more war—or, more precisely, victory at war—became unimaginable. A declining birthrate, too, no matter its cause, cast a shadow of decline over the country, especially when contrasted with governmentally fostered increases in birthrates in Germany and Italy. The appeal of emotionally charged, vitalistic fascist ideology in Germany led to a highly popular indigenous fascist movement within France that appealed to recurrent cultural themes such as renaissance, racism, and anti-Semitism, as Nolte in the *Three Faces of Fascism* showed.

The increasingly tense international politics of the 1930s arose from the fracturing of underlying systems of cultural valuation. The emergence of cultural relativism in the anthropological work of the 1920s and 1930s, for example, took away from imperialism and colonialism all pretense of justification based on the inherent superiority of white Europeans and their ways. The anthropologist Franz Boas had led the way toward this vision of a multifarious world in works such as *General Anthropology* or studies of the Inuit, and Margaret Mead defended specific alternatives to American and other Western models in social structure, as in her *Cooperation and Competition among Primitive Peoples.*

In the 1930s, fascination with folk culture—with potentially anti-intellectual implications—appeared in Chase's *Mexico: A Study of Two Americas,* even though Chase just as dangerously saw a culturally neutered economic modernism overtaking the older folkways. Also, in *Patterns of Culture,* Ruth Benedict succinctly summarized a range of folkways that might have been called "alternative lifestyles" in a later day. Even though anthropologists, like others, were well aware of the drive toward scientific management, planning, and order, they nonetheless brought forth much evidence for a seemingly instinctual apprehension of social and political truths. Like Adlerian psychologists, they were describing spontaneous acceptance of conformity to the natural demands of community.

In retrospect, their descriptions sounded much like later commentaries on Japan, including Benedict's own *The Chrysanthemum and the Sword.* The assumption of conformity united with a revered tradition of racial unity and superiority. Reischauer and Craig in *Japan* studied both more recent transformation and underlying tradition, as Fairbank and Reischauer did in *China* for Japan's East Asian wartime rival. Similarly pertinent is Coox and Conroy's *China and Japan.*

There was widespread preoccupation with physical expression of inner political and social order, such as in the political pageantry of Germany, Italy, and Japan, including their mass calisthenic demonstrations, as well as the somewhat different, yet related, pageantry in the United States and the Soviet Union. These countries, of course, were scarcely all the same. Yet the celebration of the "folk" or of the "common man," who was in some ways just the authoritarian instinct of the "folk" with a smile on its face, became increasingly a worldwide phenomenon.

In the 1930s, American culture was swept by many strange enthusiasms as the means and substance of a mass culture keyed to popular taste emerged, and the ambivalent character of mass culture revealed itself in the artifacts of the era. The highly popular and critically acclaimed films of Frank Capra extolled the "common man," as *Mr. Deeds Goes to Town* (1936) and *Mr. Smith Goes to Washington* (1939). Yet the celluloid "everyman," elevated to heroism in fulfilling the demands of common decency, was often subjected even to humiliation at the hand of the masses, shown as fickle and easily misled by conspiratorial elites. A member of the elite, Franklin Roosevelt nonetheless grasped how to communicate with the mass public as well as anyone in the era identified by his name, even feeding the popular taste for conspiracy with denunciation of "economic royalists." Roosevelt nudged, coaxed, inspired, and led the mass public, yet he was also limited in advancing his own policies by the pace of change in popular temperament.

The volatility of the American masses and the need to focus their potency became clear with the meteoric rise of politician Huey Long, as well as with the vogue of popular movements from radio evangelist Father Charles Coughlin to the German-American Bund. The line between an inspired democratic public and a fascist mass sometimes blurred. It was not without reason, then, that Franklin Roosevelt saw a need to mobilize the American people for the war and to teach them a "right thinking" democratic perspective. Frank Capra, a U.S. Army colonel during World War II, transformed his prewar "common man" into a democratically motivated, freedom-loving, generous "GI Joe." Not the least significant fact about Capra's series of films *Why We Fight* was their vigorous definition of the "American way of life" and the perceived need for the series at all.

PATRIOTIC REVIVAL AND THE MASSES

A spirit of "patriotic revival" affected many countries—the United States, Germany, and Japan among them—and it served as a means of reasserting group identity and overcoming the sense of powerlessness that had been fostered by the global economic depression of the 1930s. In Germany, the effect was heightened by the desire to break free of the limits of the Treaty of Versailles, whose compromise of German autonomy such as in the Rhineland had rankled from the first. In *Mutual Images*, Iriye offers examples of a decline in the will toward international cooperation and a rise of nationalism toward supremacy. In all instances, patriotic rededication eventually contributed to readiness to defend the homeland against enemies understood to embody principles and practices diametrically at odds with one's own.

In America, there were many signs of "patriotic revival," as Warren Susman has noted, suggesting the sense of conservative restoration underlying the era. One was the rebuilding of Williamsburg—new structures, for the most part, whose shells bore the image of the old, yet whose purpose was the shaping and celebration of a new patriotic self-consciousness. Even more striking as an exercise in civil religion was the dedication of Mount Rushmore, upon whose cliffs the faces of four symbolically evocative American presidents were carved. Officially designated a "National

Shrine of Democracy,'' Mount Rushmore epitomized the appropriation of ritual and a quasi-religious air for political purposes that extended widely around the world.

The American Legion, formed after World War I, grew in strength, and the commemoration of the seventy-fifth anniversary of the Battle of Gettysburg suggested a romantic fascination for conflict that reached its theatrical height with the film *Gone with the Wind* (1939). In the 1930s, too, the term "American way of life" came into currency, as if cloaking contemporary developments in the mantle of traditionalist uniformity. Perceptions of disorder and fears of class divisions, as well as worry over the destiny of American youth, fostered federal intervention to cultivate in young people a sense of loyalty to the state.

In the Soviet Union, Stalin brought about what historian Robert C. Tucker has called a "cultural revolution from above," leaving leftist socialism behind and creating a "statist and Russian nationalist Bolshevism of the radical right." The keynotes were not faithfulness to Marx and Lenin but submissiveness to state power and loyalty to Stalin himself. Stalin forced the dissolution of the Russian Association of Proletarian Writers, which had governed literary life in 1928–1931, a development chronicled in Brown, *The Proletarian Episode in Russian Literature, 1928–1932.* Stalin's dislike of the association's spirit of autonomy as well as its instinct for ideological purity led to the exclusion of politically suspect writers from membership and compromised comprehensive state control of all writers. In its place, Stalin created the new Soviet Writers' Union, which substituted top-down control for proletarian collective governance and constituted one of several steps toward imposing "socialist realism."

"Socialist realism" presented all life experiences in black-and-white terms, inculcating a habit of oversimplification of state affairs among the Soviet people. This would repay itself with high dividends during the "Great Patriotic War" against the Germans and their allies in World War II. As a "least common denominator" cultural force, "socialist realism" narrowed the range of the permissible, emphasizing in music, for example, the patriotic nationalism of older works, such as Glinka's *Ruslan and Ludmilla,* and deriding the most innovative works of talented composers such as Shostakovich as the "formalism" of decadent aesthetes. Accessibility to ordinary people became the cultural norm, and the unity of the state rested on an expansive Russian nationalism rather than on proletarian internationalism.

Portrayal of life's struggles in simplistic binary terms, celebration of the "great man" as savior of the people, and an anticipatory suspicion of Germany ran through Soviet film in the 1930s. Notable in expressing all these themes was Sergei Eisenstein's *Alexander Nevsky* (1938), one of many works specifically assigned and reviewed by Stalin, as well as altered at his command. It was a far cry from Eisenstein's *Potemkin* (1925), in which the masses, rather than their master, make history.

All politically right-thinking Soviet citizens became heroes, even the most banal activity qualifying for the accolade, all under the aegis of the supreme hero, Stalin. In this way, "socialist realism" created a cultural subtext of submissiveness to authority, a cult of subordination to the great man at the top, and an internalized self-deception concerning the dynamics of state affairs as well as personal ones—all qualities peculiarly suited to the demands of the state at war.

The cult of Stalin in the Soviet Union was surely matched, if not surpassed, by the cult of Adolf Hitler in Germany. Here, too, cultural ferment fed the overt political phenomena. If the Soviet Union had a terroristic regime in which popular approval was scarcely an issue, Germany was marked by a terroristic regime that a large majority appears to have approved. The modern German experience had focused largely on the definition of "Germany" itself and correspondingly on the clarification of German identity. The nineteenth-century movement toward German nationalism had worked largely, though by no means exclusively, through cultural expression, as suggested in the work of the brothers Grimm and of *turnverein* advocate Friedrich Jahn. To regard culture as "spiritual," as transcending mere social logic and political compromise, and as inextricably tied to race was an easy step to take. That the German war effort included elements that looked a great deal like "irrational" transcendent commitment and an equally "irrational" racism thus cannot be surprising. The racism and anti-Semitism behind the wartime death camps, for example, stretched back not only into the 1930s but into previous centuries.

Elsewhere as well, ritualized inculcation of devotion to the state, usually through a tribal rhetoric of "folk" and "leader," appeared. Yet in Germany the stagecraft became impeccable with practice. The appeal to the masses exceeded logical calculation, as technically sophisticated means were exploited to achieve the aims of psychological persuasion and of a conviction rooted in emotion. The Nazi Party rallies, such as the 1934 assembly at Nuremberg glorified in Riefenstahl's *Triumph of the Will*, made each member of the mass in attendance a celebrant in a quasi-religious ritual. Firelight and torchlight evoked primeval feelings, SS officers taught the meaning of ancient Nordic runes, and ritual swearing of oaths to Adolf Hitler contributed to a liturgy that made loyalty virtually a sacramental confirmation rather than a simple political act. Sentimentalized echoes of Wagnerian drama were often intended and unmistakable. The Great War was reinterpreted into the sacrificial act of heroes betrayed by conniving elites, and the value of war as a character-enhancing, intense experience increasingly displaced disillusionment born of defeat. George Mosse explored the intertwining of ideology and imagery in *Fallen Soldiers* and *Masses and Man*.

In Great Britain, such ritualized celebration of the "folk" tended to be conspicuous by its absence, and labor unrest added to other domestic uncertainties that made unswerving commitment of the British government to international security commitments highly doubtful. To some in the British elite, Germany posed an appealing model of revitalization. To others, it stood as a force too strong to resist with safety and hope of success. Prime Minister Neville Chamberlain, as suggested in Rock, *British Appeasement in the 1930s,* followed a policy later decisively denounced as "appeasement" and as a cause for losing the peace, yet one that in its own day expressed the lingering British sense of distance from the affairs of the continent as well as growing fears that Britain could not survive German bombing.

Chamberlain, amid a major war scare at the time of the Munich conference of 1938, referred to the very parts of Europe whose violation the next year would begin World War II as a faraway place "about which we know nothing." This was not an act of deception so much as an expression of history. Hope to limit the growth of German power was genuine, but so was the disdain for the sacrificial victims of the appeasement policy. Those who found Germany's successes appealing as well as threatening, such as the members of the Cliveden set, may not best be accused of betraying their beliefs so much as giving vent to many of them. The evolution of British views is covered sharply in Charmley, *Chamberlain and the Lost Peace.*

Throughout the era, national revival ran perilously close to the cultivation of myths of racial superiority. Anti-Japanese sentiment in the West epitomized it, but so did Japanese belief in their own superiority over the Chinese and Koreans and, eventually, over the Western democracies as well. Racism does not suffice to explain the coming of World War II, but it helps to explain the texture and intensity of the war when it came.

IMPLICATIONS OF THE SPANISH CIVIL WAR

The ambivalence and equivocation of official British policy and conduct showed themselves during the Spanish civil war. Adhering to a policy of neutrality with remarkable faithfulness, the British government risked compromising the substance of its own international political integrity while diligently meeting its form. Crown authorities brought prosecution against some British subjects who, in violation of Britain's neutrality, went to Spain to fight in defense of the elected government of the Republic. Some of these individuals, whom Winston Churchill wryly defended as "armed tourists," were in the dock in autumn 1939, when the failure of Chamberlain's policy was patent. Forced to decide whether to drop charges in light of events in Poland, the prosecutors proceeded as if, as

Hugh Thomas put it in *The Spanish Civil War*, the defendants were guilty of the crime of "premature antifascism."

The Spanish civil war (1936–1939) was as much a clash of cultures as a battle among armed forces. The war's resonance throughout Europe and in the Americas depended on the international currency of these cultural issues and on their correlation to political ideology and militaristic authoritarianism. As historian Gabriel Jackson has observed in *The Spanish Republic and the Civil War, 1931–1939*, the descent of Spanish politics to virtual chaos could be marked by ever more fierce anticlerical rhetoric, the degeneration of discourse in the Spanish parliament, the Cortes, crudity of manners among elected officials—visible signs of a lack of political grace. As Thomas noted in *The Spanish Civil War*, the alignment of forces during the Spanish civil war depended only in part on political ideology as such and far more on more subjective and emotionally freighted personal experiences and even on the accident of one's whereabouts at the outset of the war.

Compatibility of political ideology was no requirement for fighting on the same side. Among the Republicans, resisting a military takeover, the Basques and the Catalonians were united by little but their desire to strengthen their own distinct cultures through the constitutional device of limited autonomy. Among the Nationalists, aiming to crush a debilitated democracy, royalists vied with fascists and with a largely opportunistic military dictatorship. Republican Spanish intellectuals such as Jose Ortega y Gasset and Miguel de Unamuno called for an integrated state that transcended partisan bickering and narrow local interest, but they had not bargained on a military dictatorship as the means of achieving it.

The combination of personal viciousness and technical proficiency to be found in the Spanish civil war anticipated much in the conduct of World War II. That political outcomes were at stake was no less true in Spain than, later, in the rest of Europe and in the Pacific. Yet the passions in Spain transcended simple politics, as Thomas' *The Spanish Civil War* amply illustrates. The manner of some deaths inflicted, such as the crucifixion of especially unpopular priests, speaks to motive as well as intensity. The manner of other deaths, such as the many hundreds killed by strafing and incendiary bombing at Guernica in 1937, anticipated the "way of war" increasingly common in World War II. The siege of Madrid, also including aerial bombing, added regularity to what had seemed unique in the case of Guernica and risked making it seem commonplace and tolerable. The boundaries between civilian and military targets blurred, whether from the air or on the ground. Old culture and new technological potential merged, as seen in Fussell's *Wartime*. Events in East Asia and the Pacific came to the same end, as advanced in Iriye's *Power and Culture*, a study of the nature of the Japanese-American war. As American political commentator Dwight Macdonald claimed, perhaps people were now oblivious to horror, much as in Greek myth King Midas took ever greater doses of arsenic in hope of developing immunity. By the end of the Spanish civil war in 1939, the poison could be swallowed without gagging.

ISOLATIONISM AND INTERNATIONALISM

The cultural tension between isolationist sentiment and an internationalist vision cannot be overstated. It transcended specific political problems and military threats, going to the heart of the individual's and the nation's sense of identity, and was not confined to any one nation. In the United States and in other countries, political isolationism commonly betrayed an underlying cultural insularity, seeking the preservation of a "way of life" by the avoidance of contaminating contact. These tensions form part of the story in Iriye's *Across the Pacific.* War could allow for some continuation of this cultural insularity, even in a somewhat strengthened variation.

For some people in the industrialized countries, it seemed possible to fight a hostile force without actually contacting them. Notable among advocates of airpower in the United States was a disproportionately high representation of persons identified as isolationists. As a spokesman for the America First Committee, seeking to avoid involvement in a European war, Charles Lindbergh represented the simultaneous appreciation of technology and disparagement of a morally corrupted Europe.

References to such persons as part of a "peace movement" overlook their often benign view of technology, including military technology, and their more discrete condemnation of European politics as a hopeless morass. At times their motive may have been less a love of peace than contempt for Europe. In Britain, Alexander Korda's film *Things to Come* (1936), based on a futuristic novel by H. G. Wells, put forward the vision of a peace created by the "airmen," a technocratic elite imposing its version of a perfected society after subduing a world hopelessly mired in conflict with a "peace gas" delivered from airplanes. Less fanciful in some ways but no less ambitious, Alexander DeSeversky's *Victory through Air Power* (1942), quickly made into a feature cartoon by Walt Disney, proposed winning the war against Germany and Japan from the air and thus avoiding contaminating contact with the people of either country.

The distaste for European "entanglements" that dated at least from George Washington's Farewell Address at the end of his presidency lingered in theories of war in which machines precluded person-to-person contact. For the American example, see Weigley's revealing *The American Way of War.* But there could be no mistaking the "progressive" and "modern" elements in such schemes, either. In *Arms and Men* Millis viewed

America as passing from an industrial into a scientific revolution, and so were forms of conflict. In America, preoccupation with machines and systems reflected a larger interest in centralized planning, also suggested in big federal projects such as the Tennessee Valley Authority and showcased in the New York World's Fair of 1939–1940 as "the World of Tomorrow." If science transcended local cultural characteristics, perhaps some kind of global network—"one world," in the phrase of Republican presidential candidate Wendell Willkie and others—was ultimately unavoidable.

The vogue of geopolitics hinted at much the same. An illusively scientific theory, geopolitics was based in the material circumstances of the earth itself, seeing political conditions as the evolving outcome of geographical conditions. There was a telic quality in such thinking that matched the sense of destiny espoused by Hitler and Mussolini. In the work of Karl Haushofer, a pro-Nazi geopolitics suggested a fundamental validity to racist and opportunistic claims such as those of Hitler and Mussolini. But even in the less provocative work of Sir Halford Mackinder, as is evident in Blouet's *Sir Halford Mackinder*, there was a tendency toward the concentration of power on a binary basis, leading toward the prospect of an eventual "showdown" in global conflict.

Against such a backdrop, the world peace movement cast a thin shadow. In America, the peace movement in a fuller sense—that is, a movement rooted in a fundamentally pacifist impulse—drew upon a religious tradition of separatism and autonomy. Cutting loose from this base, to which even a secretary of state, William Jennings Bryan, had remained firm in the earlier world war, suggested a great departure from a deeply rooted cultural, social, and religious tradition. So the literary vogue concerning the once-pacifist Sergeant Alvin York, capped by the telling of his life in the film *Sergeant York* (1941), was especially evocative in the cultural sense, even if it was not directly important in political terms. For the moral lesson of Sergeant York, who became a military hero in the Great War, was that one could escape one's own beliefs and adopt those of the larger society. It was a lesson learned widely around the world.

The meaning of Sergeant York's experience was that all the world was interconnected and that no place was safe until all were safe. In one way, this was an idealistic vision. Yet, structurally, it was compatible with wideranging forces heavily laden with disparaging and often racist sentiments—ones that contributed to a binary confrontational mentality, which not only helped the war to occur but invited its expansiveness and highly elevated level of violence.

FOR FURTHER RESEARCH

The study of war as a cultural phenomenon has been among the leastpracticed branches of either military or cultural history. Although the combat operations, campaigns, and planning of World War II have been extensively studied, works on the war's direct cultural impact are relatively few. Those touching on the culture of the 1930s as its source are even fewer, making the field virtually an open one.

More work would be welcome on the effect that culture, as distinct from politics and diplomacy, had in establishing patterns of identification and alienation, which contributed to military alignments during World War II. Comparative studies, taken on without the pejorative presumption that totalitarian regimes and democracies lack points of similarity and intersection, could explore whether wartime alliances were just brief "marriages of convenience" or, instead, were affairs in which the passions were genuine, if brief.

Asymmetries invite study, too. For example, Japan developed both a continental and a maritime strategy, while Britain had much more the latter than the former. What differences in cultural development and in means of dealing with new challenges account for this? Also, in what other ways did each country's cultural tradition contribute to a distinctive manner of involvement in World War II? In *The American Way of War*, Russell Weigley opened this issue boldly for the American case. Further study comparing different national experiences would be useful, such as the Chinese, American, British, and Japanese with regard to East Asia. Also, World War I did not have the same meaning for all countries, the Americans even symbolically linking the doughboys with Native American warriors in ceremonies at the Tomb of the Unknown Soldier. Did this contribute to different visions of "the next war"?

It would also be useful to know what impact advancements in electronic communications of the 1920s and 1930s played in sharpening international awareness of political and military crises and in contributing toward a sense of connection and interdependency. The role of the military as a transforming cultural force within a nation is suggested in China's Red Army but could be explored profitably in other countries, counterbalanced by occasional recognition and suppression, such as with Stalin, of this transforming potential.

BIBLIOGRAPHY

Benedict, Ruth. *The Chrysanthemum and the Sword: Patterns of Japanese Culture.* Boston: Houghton Mifflin, 1946.
———. *Patterns of Culture.* Boston: Houghton Mifflin, 1934.
Blouet, Brian W. *Sir Halford Mackinder, 1861–1947: Some New Perspectives.* Oxford: School of Geography, University of Oxford, 1975.
Boas, Franz, ed. *General Anthropology.* Boston: D. C. Heath, 1938.
Brinkley, Alan. *Voices of Protest: Huey Long, Father Coughlin, and the Great Depression.* New York: Knopf, 1982.

Brown, Edward J. *The Proletarian Episode in Russian Literature, 1928–1932.* New York: Columbia University, 1971.

Carnegie, Dale. *How to Win Friends and Influence People.* New York: Simon and Schuster, 1937.

Charmley, John. *Chamberlain and the Lost Peace.* London: Hodder and Stoughton, 1989.

Chase, Stuart. *Mexico: A Study of Two Americas.* New York: Macmillan, 1931, 1946.

Coox, Alvin D., and Hilary Conroy, eds. *China and Japan: Search for Balance since World War II.* Santa Barbara, CA: ABC-Clio, 1978.

DeSeversky, Alexander. *Victory through Air Power.* New York: Simon and Schuster, 1942.

Fairbank, John K., and Edwin O. Reischauer. *China: Tradition and Transformation.* Boston: Houghton Mifflin, 1978.

Fussell, Paul. *Wartime: Understanding and Behavior in the Second World War.* New York: Oxford UP, 1989.

Gilbert, Martin. *Britain and Germany between the Wars.* London: Longmans, 1964.

Gilbert, Martin, and Richard Gott. *The Appeasers.* 2d ed. London: Weidenfeld and Nicolson, 1967; Boston: Houghton Mifflin, 1963.

Ingram, Norman. *The Politics of Dissent: Pacifism in France, 1919–1939.* Oxford: Clarendon, 1991.

Iriye, Akira. *Across the Pacific: An Inner History of American-East Asian Relations.* New York: Harcourt, Brace, and World, 1967.

———. *Mutual Images: Essays in Japanese-American Relations.* Cambridge: Harvard UP, 1975.

———. *Power and Culture: The Japanese-American War, 1941–1945.* Cambridge: Harvard UP, 1981.

Jackson, Gabriel. *The Spanish Republic and the Civil War, 1931–1939.* Princeton: Princeton UP, 1965.

Jelagin, Juri [Elagin, Iurii]. *Taming the Arts.* Translated by Nicholas Wreden. New York: Dutton, 1951.

Leyda, Jay. *Kino: A History of Russian and Soviet Film.* Princeton: Princeton UP, 1973, 1983.

Macdonald, Dwight. *Memoirs of a Revolutionist.* New York: Farrar, Straus, and Cudahy, 1957.

Mead, Margaret. *Cooperation and Competition among Primitive Peoples.* New York: McGraw-Hill, 1937.

Meinecke, Friedrich. *The German Catastrophe.* Boston: Beacon, 1963.

Millis, Walter. *Arms and Men: A Study in American Military History.* New York: Putnam, 1956.

Mosse, George L. *Fallen Soldiers: Reshaping the Memory of the World Wars.* New York: Oxford UP, 1990.

———. *Masses and Man: Nationalist and Fascist Perceptions of Reality.* New York: H. Fertig, 1980.

———. *Nazi Culture: Intellectual, Cultural, and Social Life in the Third Reich.* New York: Grosset and Dunlap, 1966.

Nolte, Ernst. *Three Faces of Fascism: Action Francaise, Italian Fascism, National Socialism.* New York: Holt, Rinehart, and Winston, 1966.

Oliver, Alfred C., Jr., and Harold M. Dudley. *This New America: The Spirit of the Civilian Conservation Corps.* London: Longmans, Green, 1937.

Ortega y Gasset, Jose. *The Revolt of the Masses.* New York: Norton, 1929, 1957.

Reischauer, Edwin O., and Albert M. Craig. *Japan: Tradition and Transformation.* Boston: Houghton Mifflin, 1978.

Rock, William R. *British Appeasement in the 1930s.* New York: Norton, 1977.

Salmond, John A. *The Civilian Conservation Corps, 1933–1942.* Durham, NC: Duke UP, 1967.

Spengler, Oswald. *Preussentum und Sozialismus.* Munich: Beck, 1934.

Susman, Warren I. *Culture and Commitment, 1929–1945.* New York: George Braziller, 1973.

Terkel, Studs. *"The Good War": An Oral History of World War II.* New York: Pantheon, 1984.

Thomas, Hugh. *The Spanish Civil War.* 3d ed. London: Hamish Hamilton, 1961, 1977.

Tucker, Robert C. *Stalin in Power: The Revolution from Above, 1928–1941.* New York: W. W. Norton, 1992.

Weigley, Russell F. *The American Way of War: A History of United States Military Strategy and Policy.* New York: Macmillan, 1973.

PART VI

World War II and Postwar International Relations

26 Allied Summit Diplomacy

Mark A. Stoler

One of the most notable features of World War II diplomacy was the extensive use Allied leaders made of summit meetings to strengthen their coalition, as well as plan for the postwar world, via personal contact and reconciliation of their numerous political and military differences. A total of sixteen such meetings took place between 1941 and 1945: eleven between Churchill and Roosevelt (one including Jiang); two between Churchill and Stalin in Moscow; two between all three at Teheran and Yalta; and a third Big Three meeting, after Roosevelt's death, with Truman at Potsdam. While by no means the totality of Allied wartime diplomacy, these meetings clearly constituted the focal points of that diplomacy and cannot be separated from it.

Historical analysis of these conferences and of Allied diplomacy in general constitutes an area of intense historiographical dispute, primarily because of the enormous influence of the ensuing Cold War on the interpreters. Indeed, from the earliest interpretations to the present, most historians have treated Allied diplomacy more as the first round of the postwar conflict than as part of World War II, and their interpretations thus have not followed standard historiographical patterns. Within the Soviet Union, virtually all works for four decades defended Soviet behavior while condemning British and American behavior as aggressive, duplicitous, and responsible for the postwar conflict. Early British and American works condemned Stalin and the Soviet Union in a parallel fashion, but most of them were also highly critical of Anglo-American, especially U.S., policies for naively appeasing Stalin and allowing him to become a postwar menace. Indeed, such criticisms surfaced before any defense of American policies and virtually became the official version in the United States, albeit in modified form, for twenty years.

Early proponents of this interpretation included anti-New Deal and anti-interventionist opponents of Roosevelt's prewar policies, former advisers who had disagreed with his cooperative approach to the Soviets, Polish-Americans and East European émigrés who felt betrayed by his wartime policies, British officials, and journalists such as Chester Wilmot in *The Struggle for Europe* and the American Hanson Baldwin in *Great Mistakes of the War*, who saw in Churchill's rejected wartime strategies and policies the ones the United States should have followed vis-à-vis the Soviets. Although Churchill himself consciously downplayed many Anglo-American wartime differences in his memoirs so as not to damage postwar relations between the two countries, those memoirs nevertheless provided substantial ammunition for such attacks on U.S. policies and exercised an extraordinary influence over historians because of their high quality and early publication before the release of many documents.

International and domestic events in the decade following World War II made this assault on American wartime diplomacy not only popular but, as Theoharis in *The Yalta Myths* makes clear, also an extremely powerful and emotional issue in U.S. domestic politics. Indeed, the frustrations of perceived Cold War defeats in China and Korea in 1949–1950, combined with loss of the U.S. nuclear monopoly and revelations regarding wartime Soviet spies, led U.S. politicians such as Joseph McCarthy to accuse Roosevelt and his associates of treason rather than mere naïveté, appeasement, and blundering. By the early 1950s the Yalta conference had become virtually synonymous with both sets of charges and had led to demands, met in 1955 by the State Department, for release of the conference documents. Those documents did not provide evidence for any of the extreme charges, but their early publication clearly helped to make Yalta the most studied as well as condemned summit conference of the war.

Roosevelt's supporters and numerous historians within the realist school of international relations criticized the ahistorical framework upon which the Yalta and related attacks were based by emphasizing that the key issue from 1941–1945 had not been the Cold War but military necessity and the need to maintain the Grand Alliance in order to defeat the Axis. Defeat and military realities, most notably those created by the advancing Red Army, rather than blunders, naïveté, appeasement, or treason, had led inevitably to an enormous increase in Soviet power. Stalin's supposed territorial gains at Yalta, as Snell and three colleagues emphasized in this regard in their 1956 *The Meaning of Yalta*, preceded and resulted from these realities rather than Roosevelt's policies.

Other defenses of U.S. wartime diplomacy published from 1945 to 1965 exhibited a fascinating duality, however, for most of the writers agreed with the charges of naïveté being leveled against Roosevelt, if not with the more extreme partisan charges of treason by the anticommunist McCarthyites. Naïveté was one of the basic characteristics of all U.S. foreign policy, according to the realist critique then being expounded, as well as a key component of traditional American self-perception and British view of the United States. Furthermore, most of Roosevelt's defenders had by this time become Cold Warriors themselves and were thus neither willing nor able to defend the cooperative approach he had attempted with the Soviets. In the process of defending U.S. wartime diplomacy against its extreme critics, most of these individuals thus wound up attacking it on grounds similar to those the critics had used.

This duality was clearly visible in two comprehensive and excellent "first-generation" histories of the wartime alliance, *America, Britain and Russia* by McNeill and *Churchill, Roosevelt, Stalin* by former official Feis, who was given special access to government files and private papers, as well as in numerous interpretive assessments of U.S. foreign and military policies written between 1945 and 1965. These works clearly recognized Allied differences and the likelihood, if not inevitability, of conflict, and they praised Roosevelt and his associates for an exceptional ability to compromise those differences so that Nazi Germany could be defeated. Yet they also criticized the president for his separation of military from political issues, his single-minded devotion to military victory, his naive Wilsonianism regarding the postwar world, and his placing too much faith in Stalin's goodwill and his own powers of persuasion. All of these criticisms had originally been made by Roosevelt's detractors, and by the early 1960s this view thus constituted the dominant consensus. Indeed, by that time scholars such as Armstrong and Smith appeared to be agreeing with Roosevelt's severest critics in the process of supposedly attacking them.

This historical consensus was clearly related to the Cold War consensus that had come to dominate American politics. Just as that latter consensus was shattered by the events of the 1960s, most importantly the Vietnam War, so was the historical one as new schools of interpretation emerged in that decade to challenge the prevailing wisdom.

The first of these, which included historians preparing the massive official U.S. histories of the war as well as others who made use of these volumes and/or the enormous documentary record then becoming available (most notably in the annual and special wartime summit conference volumes of the State Department's *Foreign Relations* series and the Soviet publication of the complete Big Three correspondence), argued that Roosevelt's policies and strategies had been highly realistic rather than naive and that he had clearly controlled his military advisers rather than vice versa, as critics had charged. Emerson in "Roosevelt as Commander-in-Chief" and army chief historian Greenfield in *American Strategy* were particularly notable in this regard.

So was Snell, who in his 1963 *Illusion and Necessity*, a brief, comparative history of wartime diplomacy, argued that Axis leaders rather than Roosevelt had based their policies on illusions and thereby lost the war. Allied policies, on the other hand, had been highly realistic and resulted in total military victory. Since cooperation was essential to that victory, and expanded postwar Soviet power an inevitable outcome of it, Roosevelt's cooperative approach was unavoidable. Snell further defended the much-maligned unconditional surrender policy that the president had enunciated at the January 1943 Casablanca Summit and his postponement of all territorial settlements as highly realistic and pragmatic attempts to promote U.S. interests while simultaneously reconciling Allied differences and maintaining domestic support. In pursuing these policies, the president had established the key prerequisites for both wartime victory and postwar cooperation with the Soviets while simultaneously placing limits on their expansion should cooperation not occur—limits clearly illustrated by the fact that Stalin's territorial gains did not exceed those Czar Nicholas II would have obtained at the end of World War I had he remained in power.

This thesis received reinforcement in the late 1960s from two directions. In major reassessments Divine's *Roosevelt and World War II* and Burns' *Roosevelt: The Soldier of Freedom* argued that Roosevelt (FDR) had been very practical and realistic. Rather than FDR's being duped by Stalin, Divine argued, the public and historians had been duped by the president's Wilsonian public statements delivered to protect his domestic flank and contradicted by his pragmatic private comments and actions. Such pragmatism had helped the alliance maintain itself during the war, both historians argued, but ironically doomed Roosevelt's hopes for postwar cooperation—because it led him to misunderstand Stalin, according to Divine, and/or because it increased Soviet suspicions, according to Burns. Simultaneously, numerous British and U.S. historians, most notably Howard, *The Mediterranean Strategy*; Ambrose, *Eisenhower and Berlin*; O'Connor, *Diplomacy for Victory*; and Higgins, *Soft Underbelly*, began to reexamine the supposedly realistic alternative strategies and policies Churchill had provided. They concluded that fear of postwar Soviet power was a much less important motivation than the British leader had led his readers to believe and that irrational as well as narrowly nationalistic motivations lay behind his proposals.

The so-called New Left school of interpretation also made extensive use of the massive documentation then becoming available to attack the notion of American blunders and naïveté during the war, but it did so in such a way as to sharply condemn, rather than defend, U.S. policy and to assert that aggressive U.S. behavior during the war had been one, if not the primary, cause of the ensuing Cold War. This assault was far from monolithic, however. Basing their work on the "Open Door" thesis, which William Appleman Williams had developed to critique U.S. foreign policy in general, historians produced several broad and highly critical interpretations of all Roosevelt's foreign policies, such as Gardner's *Economic As-*

pects of New Deal Diplomacy, Architects of Illusion, and *Spheres of Influence.*
Kolko's *Politics of War* provided the most extensive and extreme socioeconomic criticism of U.S. wartime policies, asserting that Washington had
realistically and aggressively attempted to promote its own postwar capitalist expansion at the expense of the British empire as well as the Soviet
Union and the indigenous Left (he also argued that Roosevelt was not as
central to U.S. policy as previous writers had maintained).

In more specialized revisionist works, however, others, such as Alperovitz in *Atomic Diplomacy* and Clemens in *Yalta,* harked back to D. F. Fleming's earlier and more specific Cold War revisionism, rather than Williams'
general economic approach, to defend Roosevelt's cooperative policy with
the Soviet Union and to blame Truman for reversing it in 1945. Alperovitz
saw such a reversal in the decision to drop the atomic bomb, a decision
motivated primarily by a desire to blackmail the Soviets rather than end
the war quickly, as Feis had earlier claimed in *Japan Subdued.* Clemens
concluded her detailed revisionist analysis of Yalta by maintaining that
Truman, rather than Stalin, had broken the accords, even though Stalin,
rather than Roosevelt, had made the bulk of the concessions at the conference.

Consensus historians sharply attacked this New Left assault on prevailing interpretations of World War II diplomacy and the origins of the Cold
War, with the debate often as heated as the larger political one over the
Vietnam War. By the end of that conflict in the mid-1970s, however, new
works on U.S. World War II as well as Cold War diplomacy were moving
far beyond such polarized confrontations and into an era of detailed
monographs, attempted synthesis, and entirely new approaches. Numerous factors accounted for this shift. The early debate had clearly reached
a stalemate by the mid-1970s, while some historians realized that the di-
vergent schools did share some important conclusions and attempted the
first syntheses. Gardner's 1970 *Architects of Illusion* and Gaddis' 1972 *The
United States and the Origins of the Cold War* were two of the earliest such
attempts from the revisionist and traditionalist perspectives, respectively.
Mee's 1975 popular history *Meeting at Potsdam* challenged the standard
version of that conference offered by Feis in his 1960 *Between War and
Peace* by using both revisionist and traditionalist findings to condemn all
three leaders. As the years passed, the shared conclusions became more
visible as a result of the calmer international environment of the detente
era, the calmer domestic political environment that followed Watergate
and the end of the Vietnam War, and the emergence of a new generation
of historians not personally linked to the older battles—or to the personal
experience of World War II, for that matter.

This new generation, in turn, possessed new evidence not available to
its predecessors. The works of the 1960s had been based primarily on
documentary information in the *Foreign Relations* series, the Big Three

published correspondence, the multivolume British and American official histories, memoirs, and recently opened manuscript collections. Some of the most important official histories were not available in their entirety until the 1970s, however, when the final volume in the six-volume British *Grand Strategy* series edited by J. R. M. Butler and the unabridged, five-volume *British Foreign Policy in the Second World War* by Sir Llewellyn Woodward were published. Simultaneously, the bulk of the official World War II record in both Britain and the United States was declassified and made available to researchers. This declassification was staggering both quantitatively and qualitatively. U.S. Army files alone weighed 17,120 tons, enough to fill 188 miles of filing cases end-to-end. Within those files lay not only enormously detailed evidence to revise previous analyses but also revelations that opened entirely new areas of inquiry. Most notable in this regard was the "ULTRA Secret" and other critical intelligence data, which one British diplomat labeled the missing dimension of most diplomatic history.

Two additional and related factors also deserve mention, though their full impact would not be felt until the 1980s. Historical study in general was being altered by the use of new social science models and the computer as well as a new emphasis on social, cultural, and comparative history. Furthermore, U.S. diplomatic historians came under sharp attack for not participating in these changes and for limiting both their research and their focus to their own country. Although this criticism was overstated and ignored numerous pioneering efforts in the new areas and methods of inquiry, it clearly affected numerous scholars who attempted to incorporate such approaches into their work.

The resultant outpouring of scholarship on Allied diplomacy during the 1970s cut in many directions. The new availability of military as well as diplomatic British and U.S. documents led to numerous reexaminations of Anglo-American and Soviet-American wartime relations in general and such highly controversial alliance issues as *Aid to Russia* (see Herring), the second front dispute, the Darlan affair, postwar decolonization and economic organization, Middle East oil, and the atomic bomb decision. Two of the earliest of these works focused on previously neglected summit conferences: Wilson's 1969 *The First Summit* on the first Churchill–Roosevelt meeting in August 1941, and Beitzell's 1972 *The Uneasy Alliance* on the summit conferences of 1941–1943. Most of the others offered detailed analyses of the portions of specific summit conferences relevant to their particular topics.

Contradicting the image Churchill had sought to project in his memoirs, many of these studies emphasized intense Anglo-American as well as Soviet-American differences and tensions throughout the war. In 1978 Louis took such analyses a step further in *Imperialism at Bay* by using multiarchival research to examine intragovernmental as well as Anglo-

American conflicts during the war over postwar decolonization and trusteeships. Simultaneously, other scholars used the newly available material to shift the focus away from Anglo-American and Soviet-American relations and onto U.S. and British wartime policies vis-à-vis other nations during the war, as well as colonial areas.

On some issues the result was the creation of a new consensus. Most notable in this regard were works on the atomic bomb by Bernstein (most notably in "Roosevelt, Truman and the Atomic Bomb" and "The Uneasy Alliance") and Sherwin, *A World Destroyed*, each of whom concluded independently that the United States had, indeed, practiced "atomic diplomacy" against the Soviets, as Alperovitz had argued, but that this had been a secondary motive to ending the war quickly, as Feis had earlier maintained. They also emphasized in a major revision to the standard approach that such atomic diplomacy had been a key component of Roosevelt's as well as Churchill's policies and that Truman had thus not reversed his predecessor's attitudes on the weapon vis-à-vis the Soviets.

A new consensus also began to emerge on U.S. wartime policy toward China, though here the result was more a reversal than a synthesis of previous interpretations. Those interpretations, written at the height of Sino-American conflict in the 1950s and 1960s, had criticized Roosevelt and his advisers for insufficient support of Jiang and nonrecognition of the menace posed by the communist Mao. Writing in the 1970s, a decade of intense Sino-Soviet conflict and tremendously improved U.S.–Chinese relations, numerous scholars criticized the president for not having dropped the hopeless Jiang in favor of Mao during the war.

The decade ended with two major works by a U.S. and a British scholar that attempted both to synthesize the numerous recent monographs into a new consensus and to point the way for new lines of inquiry. In a detailed and exhaustive analysis of *Roosevelt and American Foreign Policy*, Dallek sided with a decade of FDR defenders by dismissing all the supposed "blunders" listed by previous critics and by emphasizing both his realism and the severe domestic as well as international constraints under which he had operated. Dallek's assessment was not uniformly positive, however; echoing a series of recent studies, he criticized the president sharply for his sanctioning of illegal wiretaps and mail openings as well as the internment of Japanese Americans and his overly cautious response (or lack of response) to the Nazi destruction of European Jewry. Simultaneously, Thorne in *Allies of a Kind* broke new ground by publishing the first diplomatic history of the Pacific War and by emphasizing, within that pathbreaking work of multiarchival research, Anglo-American friction, anticolonialism, relations with other Pacific nations, and racism as key themes.

Additional studies soon appeared that both supported and filled in gaps within these two key works. Gaddis in his 1982 *Strategies of Containment* credited Roosevelt with a highly realistic, though flawed, wartime strategy of "containment by integration" of the Soviet Union and argued, as had Dallek and a few others, that had Roosevelt lived longer, he would have probably shifted to a tougher strategy after obtaining victory over the Axis. Simultaneously, Gilbert in *Auschwitz and the Allies*, Wyman in *Abandonment of the Jews*, and numerous other scholars expanded upon previous criticisms of Allied refugee policy during the Holocaust in comprehensive, multiarchival works, while Anderson in *The United States, Great Britain and the Cold War*; Dobson in *U.S. Wartime Aid to Britain*; Harbutt, *The Iron Curtain*; Hathaway, *Ambiguous Partnership*; Reynolds, *The Creation of the Anglo-American Alliance*; and Sbrega, *Anglo-American Relations and Colonialism in East Asia*, explored Anglo-American wartime conflicts within their multiarchival analyses of U.S.-British relations during and immediately after World War II. In doing so they completed the demolition of Churchill's one-sided interpretation and exposed a relationship that, although, indeed, remarkable, had been marked by severe disagreements and became "special" only gradually, fitfully, and incompletely. In the words of Thorne and Reynolds (*A Study in Competitive Co-operation*), respectively, the two were "allies of a kind" engaged throughout the war in "competitive cooperation." Their famous wartime friendship and numerous summit meetings notwithstanding, neither Churchill nor Roosevelt ever forgot this fact.

In 1985 Thorne produced a comparative follow-up work, *The Issue of War*, a thematic analysis that attempted to remove the boundaries between Western and non-Western history and to fuse diplomatic with economic and intellectual history as well as sociology and social psychology into a new "international history." Many of these themes and approaches were also evident in the continuing flood of studies on Anglo-American wartime relations with other nations and parts of the world. As in the 1970s such studies continued to focus (though not exclusively) on areas of recent and contemporary concern, most notably Indochina and the Middle East. With the opening of Korean War documentation came an additional focus on the wartime origins of that conflict. Many of these new bilateral studies extended into the late 1940s or early 1950s rather than stopping in 1945, thereby continuing the tendency to focus on the World War II years as a prelude to Cold War-era policies.

The tremendous impact of all these studies, from the late 1960s through the mid-1980s, and the differences between the old consensus and the newly emerging one could be most clearly seen in a comparison of the first and second editions of one of the major syntheses and undergraduate texts in the field, Smith's *American Diplomacy during the Second World War*. When first published in 1965, that volume had clearly illustrated the extent to which Roosevelt's supposed defenders had accepted the critics' assault on his diplomacy in their attacks on him for placing military before political factors, having too much faith in a Wilsonian postwar collective security organization, and naively trying to charm Stalin. In the preface to the 1985 edition, however, Smith admitted that he had been overly harsh in 1965 and not appreciative of the limits under which FDR worked. Although he still considered Roosevelt's postwar policies a failure, he now concluded that the president had been less naive than he originally thought, and he questioned whether or not American interests, which focused first and foremost on Axis defeat, would have been better served by the open arguments within the tenuous alliance that would have flowed from different policies. Equally noteworthy was Smith's much greater emphasis in the second edition on decolonization as a major wartime issue and on U.S. policies regarding Latin America, the Middle East, and the Far East—especially Korea, China, and Indochina.

Smith's work and others notwithstanding, the promising new synthesis did not continue far into the 1980s. Instead, the second half of that decade witnessed both extensive fragmentation and another massive interpretive debate over Allied diplomacy, one that, in many ways, repeated with equal intensity and heat those that had taken place in the early 1950s and late 1960s.

The focus of the renewed debate was, once again, Roosevelt's policies toward the Soviet Union. Dallek's 1979 synthesis, *Roosevelt and American Foreign Policy*, was essentially the capstone of the defense of Roosevelt-as-realist that had become more and more pronounced throughout the 1960s and 1970s. As such it was able to subsume the earlier interpretations within this school and, to an extent, those of the New Left critics. The schools that had combined in the 1950s and early 1960s to form the original, negative assessment of Roosevelt remained only partially convinced at best, however, and in the mid-1980s they replied. So did some New Left historians from the late 1960s such as Alperovitz, who in a second, 1985 edition to his 1965 *Atomic Diplomacy* essentially reiterated and defended an updated version of his original interpretation against his numerous critics.

For the most part, however, the 1980s critique of U.S. wartime diplomacy echoed earlier criticisms from the Right rather than the Left and focused on Roosevelt's supposed blunders, naïveté, and failures vis-à-vis the Soviet Union. Smith, as previously noted, retained his 1965 critique of Roosevelt in this regard, albeit in milder form. Attacks also emerged in two major 1985 studies of the previously neglected 1943 Cairo-Teheran conferences, Eubank's *Summit at Teheran* and Sainsbury's *The Turning Point*. Both saw Teheran as the pivotal tripartite conference, one that had, in many ways, determined the agenda for, and the results of, the later Yalta meeting, and both, in effect, projected the old criticism of American and Rooseveltian naïveté at Yalta back to this earlier meeting—though for the British Sainsbury, as for Smith, with clear recognition of the numerous limits within which FDR had to work and the dangers posed by an alternative policy of confrontation. Buhite revealed a similar depth of understanding in his 1986 *Decisions at Yalta*, while echoing similar criticisms of the president for poor diplomacy. He also criticized FDR for being too concerned with the domestic consequences of failure at Yalta and for even desiring the conference in the first place; summit conferences in general, Buhite concluded in a sweeping critique, were counterproductive and invited the sorts of misunderstandings and defeats that had taken place in the Crimea.

The year 1988 also witnessed the publication of two works more critical of Roosevelt's diplomacy than any published since the 1950s: Nisbet's *Roosevelt and Stalin* and Marks' *Wind over Sand*. Nisbet's brief volume essentially updated and reiterated the old assault on Roosevelt for extraordinary naïveté regarding Stalin, with Teheran replacing Yalta as the epitome of Roosevelt's appeasement of Stalin and where the Cold War had begun. Marks went even further, arguing that all Roosevelt's diplomacy from 1933 to 1945 had been marked by ambivalence, indecisiveness, narrow domestic motivation, parochialism, and failure.

This renewed assault on Roosevelt was clearly linked to the domestic and international environments of the 1980s, which differed substantially from those of the 1970s. Most important in this regard were the rise of the neoconservative movement and revival of the Cold War, which accompanied Reagan's election to the presidency, and the ensuing revival of a Manichean worldview that labeled the Soviet Union the "evil empire." Along with this came a revival of the view that cooperation with the Soviet Union was and always had been impossible, given its ideology, and that Roosevelt had thus been a fool to try it. In 1985, the neoconservative journal *Commentary* published a series of articles from Roosevelt's British and American critics, including Nisbet, that hammered away at these points in terms that seemed to repeat verbatim the criticisms uttered more than three decades earlier.

Such assaults did not go unchallenged. Clearly influenced by them as well as recent Soviet-American tensions and charges, Leffler in "Adherence to Agreements" concluded in 1986 that each power had complied with some components of the Yalta accords while disregarding others and that the United States had used supposed Soviet violations to excuse its own. In that same year Draper angrily responded to the *Commentary* attacks in the *New York Review of Books*, making extensive use of the previous decade's defenses of Roosevelt and attacks on Churchill to emphasize the fact that Roosevelt had given away nothing and labeling the neoconservative assault a perversion of history by political extremists determined to discredit liberal internationalism. The ensuing rejoinders made such language appear mild in comparison. They were far from the final words in the debate, as Nisbet followed with a lengthy article that he expanded into his previously mentioned 1988 book, and Draper with a three-part review of David Eisenhower's wartime biography of his grandfather, which emphasized his politicomilitary realism and the centrality of the Soviet war effort to all U.S. strategy and diplomacy; in 1988 he republished all these essays in *A Present of Things Past.*

Draper was, of course, far from the only defender of Roosevelt during the 1980s. Most of the previously cited works published during the decade provided at least partial defenses. They tended to echo Draper and Dallek in emphasizing the domestic and international constraints under which the president had to work, however, and thus his lack of viable alternatives regarding the Soviet Union. Kimball, who had previously published both a detailed 1969 analysis of *The Most Unsordid Act: Lend-Lease* and in 1984 *Churchill and Roosevelt: The Complete Correspondence* with detailed commentary, challenged this conclusion in his 1991 *The Juggler,* a series of essays seeking to comprehend Roosevelt's assumptions and worldview as well as his specific actions. Such an analysis was more an exploration and explanation than a defense of Roosevelt's ideas and policies, but in the environment of the 1980s simply to argue that FDR possessed an overall vision and made logical choices was to defend him from severe critics like Marks. Similarly, Kimball's use of "liberal" as a key descriptive term for the president's vision rather than as an epithet and his equation of liberalism with "Americanism" constituted a powerful, if indirect, defense of Roosevelt against the neoconservative assault.

Reinforcement for both sides in this renewed debate came from scholars such as Mastny in *Russia's Road,* McCagg in *Stalin Embattled,* McCauley in *The Origins of the Cold War,* Resis in "The Churchill-Stalin Secret 'Percentages' Agreement,'' and Taubman, working with the thin, but growing, trickle of available Soviet sources. Many of them emphasized Stalin's caution, pragmatism, and lack of any overall "master plan" during the war years, as well as his desire to obtain limited gains within a framework of continued collaboration with his wartime allies. They disagreed, however, as to how extensive his aims actually were and whether or not a clear definition of acceptable limits by FDR and Churchill during the war would have made any difference. Mastny in *Russia's Road to the Cold War* and Taubman in *Stalin's American Policy* saw those aims as quite extensive and were highly critical of Roosevelt's refusal to provide such a definition, though they held that postwar Soviet suspicion, hostility, and aggression would have resulted from any U.S. policy. Similar criticisms and conclusions appeared in Bennett's 1990 *Roosevelt and the Search for Victory,* but alongside them was a strong defense of FDR's pragmatic approach and achievement of his primary objectives.

Debate during the 1980s was by no means limited to assessments of U.S.-Soviet diplomacy. The decade also witnessed an outpouring of scholarship on major British figures, most notably Gilbert's completion of the multivolume official biography of Churchill, and on Anglo-Soviet as well as Anglo-American relations during the conflict. These also provided ammunition for both sides in the debate over U.S. policies. While the biographical studies tended to defend the British position in Anglo-American wartime disputes, the studies of Anglo-Soviet relations by scholars, such as Gorodetsky, *Stafford Cripps' Mission to Moscow*, Kitchen, *British Policy towards the Soviet Union*; Miner, *Between Churchill and Stalin*; Ross, *The Foreign Office and the Kremlin*; and Rothwell, *Britain and the Cold War*, were marked by detailed analyses of disagreements within the British government over Soviet policy and by conclusions just as polarized as those to be found in the decade's studies of U.S.-Soviet diplomacy. Examining those Anglo-Soviet relations during the early years of the war, for example, Gorodetsky criticized Churchill and some of his advisers for a virtual nonpolicy (if not an anti-Soviet one) and implied that Cripps' more cooperative approach might have avoided the Cold War if implemented, while Miner criticized the British for trying to appease Stalin and pointed to the hard-line American opposition to territorial settlements in 1942 as the policy London should have followed. Ironically, the pro-cooperation Gorodetsky thereby indirectly provided Roosevelt's anticooperation critics with additional ammunition, while the anticooperation Miner did the same for Roosevelt's defenders.

As this irony clearly reveals, the earlier conflicting schools of interpretation had by the late 1980s developed into an extremely complex and confusing historiography, with one's position dependent on not only a reading of the documents but also political and ideological beliefs—particularly whether one viewed Stalin's Soviet Union as simply a traditional Great Power with which compromise was possible or a monstrosity incapable of cooperation or normal diplomatic behavior because of its ideology and/or its dictator's personality. Reinforcing the importance of these nondocumentary factors in assessing the U.S. component of Allied diplomacy were Roosevelt's notorious secrecy and deviousness, which resulted in a paucity of meaningful and clear statements of what he truly believed despite the enormous volume of his papers. Even when FDR did break down and say something meaningful for the record, one was often unsure if it was what he really thought or even what it really meant. In their 1986 debate, for example, Nisbet and Draper both used the same 1942 Roosevelt comment to reach diametrically opposed conclusions about the president's policies.

While Grand Alliance scholars continued to argue throughout the 1980s, other diplomatic historians proceeded during this time to explore the new areas and approaches being illuminated by social scientists and social/cultural historians as they applied to World War II. In doing so they began to alter the terms of the debate over Allied diplomacy by redefining the major issues, questions, and themes to be addressed and in the process to remove some of the focus from summit diplomacy. The works of Thorne and others in the realms of multiarchival research and the comparative cultural approach of the new international history have already been noted in this regard.

Equally notable was an increasing emphasis on bureaucratic politics by Woods, *A Changing of the Guard*; Martel, *Lend-Lease, Loans and the Coming of the Cold War*; Stoler, *The Politics of the Second Front*; and Wilson, *The First Summit*. They used that idea as one of their major tools to analyze Anglo-American wartime policies and disputes regarding decolonization, the Middle East, global strategy, and postwar Allied relations. In one sense this was nothing new; analysis of disagreements within the Anglo-American bureaucracies had always been part of World War II diplomatic histories, and the archival openings of the 1970s enabled historians to trace in detail internal disagreements and their resolution within the policy-making process.

Some scholars began to argue, however, that social science theories of bureaucratic behavior were central to understanding why as well as how specific policies had been initiated and implemented and implicitly to reject FDR's centrality to the debate by denying his ability, or that of any other single individual, to dictate or implement policy. Rather, policy often emerged from a welter of bureaucratic desires and conflicts that bore little, if any, relationship to national interests or to what national leaders had desired—or ordered. Sigal's 1988 *Fighting to a Finish* boldly illustrated the revolutionary consequences of such an analysis by arguing that neither the United States nor Japan had followed any rational plan for ending the war; rather, different segments of the bureaucracy in each country had proposed policies geared to their own worldviews and self-aggrandizement.

Culture and bureaucratic politics were by no means the only new areas to be explored in the 1970s and 1980s. Major analyses focusing on public opinion, gender, national security, international organization, corporatism, psychology, balance of power, world systems, ideology, and "mental maps" also emerged during the two decades, both for international relations in general and for World War II in particular, as seen in Hogan and Paterson's *Explaining the History of American Foreign Relations*. In his fascinating "The Map as an 'Idea,' " Henrickson explored the dramatic shift that had occurred in the American mental map of the globe during the war and its impact on the origins of the Cold War. Paterson in *Soviet-American Confrontation* similarly analyzed the impact of the war on American ideological perceptions of Stalin and the Soviet Union, while Bell, *John Bull and the Bear*; Levering in *American Opinion and the Russian Alliance*; and others focused on wartime British and American public opinion of the Soviet Union. Scholars also examined numerous other aspects of public opinion, with Widenor in "American Planning" and others asking if this might not be the key motivating factor in FDR's postwar planning.

Campbell's *Masquerade Peace* and, more recently, Hilderbrand's *Dumbarton Oaks* explored the triumph of purely national over truly international definitions of security in the wartime formulation of the postwar international security organization, and Leffler carefully noted in *A Preponderance of Power* the importance of the World War II experience in the new, global definition of American national security, which he viewed as central to the origins and development of the Cold War. Of related interest and focus were "American Policy" by Mark and, more recently, Gardner in *Spheres of Influence*, which reassessed U.S. wartime attitudes toward such spheres. Many of these works focused far beyond the confines of summit diplomacy and expanded the very definition of wartime international relations.

The increasing volume of these new approaches in the late 1980s and early 1990s coincided, to an extent, with the dramatic changes taking place within Eastern Europe, capped in the years 1989–1991 by the end not only of the Soviet empire but also of the Cold War and even the Soviet Union itself. These extraordinary events, it appeared, were helping to break the virtual stranglehold the Cold War had held over interpretations of Allied diplomacy for the preceding forty to forty-five years. Highly illustrative of this shift, as well as the neoconservative one that had marked British as well as U.S. politics in the 1980s, was Charmley's highly provocative revisionist assault in *Churchill's Grand Alliance* on Churchill's anti-German and pro-U.S. policies for resulting in the loss of the British empire.

While the end of the Cold War was obviously important to the development of alternative ways of viewing Allied wartime diplomacy, most of these new approaches had first appeared while the Cold War was still in progress and in many ways reflected changes within Britain and America more than changes within international relations. Furthermore, numerous scholars made use of many of the new approaches to reassess and reargue traditional questions about summit diplomacy and the origins of the Cold War rather than explore different themes. Although the dramatic events in Eastern Europe may have indirectly added to the popularity within the profession of different themes, those events were simultaneously laying the groundwork for another generation of Anglo-Soviet-American studies by accelerating both scholarly contact between the three countries and the long-desired opening of Soviet archives, without which all histories of Allied diplomacy had been woefully incomplete. Consequently, the late 1980s and early 1990s witnessed a continued deluge of scholarship on the Grand Alliance.

It is too soon to ascertain the results. The past decade has witnessed the publication and translation of numerous Soviet documents and reminiscences and important revelations regarding both Stalin and specific wartime episodes. It has also witnessed the publication of the first book-length study of Soviet foreign policy under Stalin and Khrushchev based on the new Soviet sources, Zubok and Pleshakov's *Inside the Kremlin's Cold War*, as well as two edited collections—*Soviet-U.S. Relations* (cited under this title) and *Allies at War* (edited by Reynolds, Kimball, and Chubarian)—by Russian, American, and British World War II scholars who met on a regular basis from 1986 to 1992 in all three countries to reanalyze the Grand Alliance. Release of Soviet documents remains highly erratic, incomplete, and unpredictable, however. Furthermore, neither the documents released to date nor the post–Cold War international environment has resulted in any resolution of the existing disputes over wartime summit diplomacy. Indeed, studies of that diplomacy written by Nadeau, *Stalin, Churchill, and Roosevelt Divide Europe*, Edmonds, *Big Three*, and others in the early 1990s clearly illustrate that, far from resolving the debate, recent events and new Russian documents are merely providing additional ammunition to continue it. While Nadeau concluded that these show the validity of the old charge that Roosevelt won the war but lost the peace because his innocence and misplaced idealism allowed Europe to be divided in the first place, Edmonds concluded that they actually illustrate the reverse.

Recent interpretations of Allied diplomacy can thus be divided into two major and separate, if overlapping, categories: those that make use of the new documentation, approaches, and international environment to reargue the original debate over Rooseveltian naïveté; and those that use the new documentation, approaches, and environment to redefine the questions being asked and shift the focus away from the Big Three and their summit meetings. Both approaches will probably continue throughout the remainder of the 1990s and beyond and will be visible within a continuing flood of specialized studies that fill in the remaining gaps in the literature.

Despite the deluge of studies in the 1970s and 1980s, gaps in the secondary literature of summit diplomacy remain. Numerous volumes now exist on the interaction between Churchill, Roosevelt, and Stalin, on each of the Big Three meetings at Teheran, Yalta, and Potsdam, and on the complex Roosevelt–Churchill relationship—most recently Kimball's *Forged in War* and Sainsbury's *Churchill and Roosevelt at War*. Book-length analyses of the individual Anglo-American summit conferences, however, are surprisingly rare. Only the first one at Placentia Bay in August 1941 has received such treatment, though their two Cairo meetings (the first with Jiang) before and after Teheran are discussed in books on the latter, as their Malta/Great Bitter Lake meetings before and after Yalta are discussed in books on that conference. No volumes based on archival research have yet been written, however, on any of their three meetings in Washington, the one in Casablanca, or the two in Quebec; nor do any exist on either of the Churchill–Stalin meetings in Moscow. An analysis of some of these based on published documents can be found in Beitzell, while articles and books on specific issues associated with individual conferences (i.e., the atomic bomb and Potsdam; unconditional surrender and Casablanca; the Morgenthau plan and the second Quebec conference) often provide important, if incomplete, material on those meetings. Similar gaps exist in the study of Allied wartime relations with individual countries and parts of the world—especially within Africa—and in biographies of key advisers to the Big Three.

Within future works, one should expect continued debates over both Roosevelt's importance vis-à-vis the bureaucracy and his responsibility for the Cold War—despite the demise of that conflict and the Soviet Union. Indeed, while the opening of Soviet archives will enable scholars finally to analyze the alliance from a trilateral perspective, it will probably continue to reinforce, rather than resolve, the old debate. The present direction of Russian scholarship is toward sharper and sharper condemnation of Stalin's policies, which has already provided additional ammunition to Roosevelt's critics. As previously noted, however, it has also provided ammunition for Roosevelt's defenders. Furthermore, to assume that this anti-Stalin trend will continue indefinitely or that all the Soviet documents will support this approach would be extraordinarily naive. As Russian scholarship develops, and additional archives are opened, sharp disagreements should be expected to take place. Since Stalin was at least as secretive and confusing as Roosevelt, those documents will also, in all likelihood, be inconclusive. Thus, no final and definitive conclusions may be possible on numerous issues, and the debate over Soviet-American relations during World War II is far from over. A new synthesis does appear to be emerging on Anglo-American wartime relations, as Reynolds has noted in "Roosevelt, Churchill," but debates continue on Anglo-Soviet relations and Anglo-American wartime conflicts regarding the Soviets.

Along with these continuing debates one should expect to see new studies addressing areas of contemporary international concern. These would include, but by no means be limited to, Allied wartime policies toward the different groups within the former Yugoslavia, Italy's African colonies, Palestine, the Islamic world, Japan, Germany, and international organization. Within these studies a myriad of the new approaches will be used, often in combination. These will tend to further blur the distinctions between diplomatic and other histories in terms of topics and research.

The limits of the new approaches for Allied diplomacy are as unclear as the results of the end of the Cold War. They raise important new questions and provide fresh perspectives, but presently they are not sufficiently numerous or complete to reach substantial conclusions as to their overall impact. Yet it is already clear that for most of them, as for the traditional studies, World War II seems to constitute merely a precursor or "seed time" to the really important years that followed. Such a tendency is completely understandable—and perhaps inevitable. It also has positive consequences in that it links ideas and events in the war years to their full development and results after the achievement of victory in 1945. It is regrettable, however, in that it fails to deal with World War II on its own terms. Indeed, it often distorts Allied policies during the war by ignoring wartime, as opposed to postwar priorities and by sharply separating British, Soviet, and U.S. diplomacy into pre-and post-1941 eras, which seem to bear little, if any, relationship to each other. It also risks a continuation of the Cold War-era tendency to project later conflicts, issues, and perspectives onto an earlier time period. Rather than more studies that try to cover Allied summit diplomacy as a precursor to what followed, one would hope to see more studies analyzing that diplomacy on its own—and/or as the result of what preceded it.

NOTE

This chapter is a shortened and revised version of "A Half-Century of Conflict: Interpretations of U.S. World War II Diplomacy," which appeared in *Diplomatic History* 18(1994): 375–404 and in Michael J. Hogan, ed., *America in the World: The Historiography of American Foreign Relations since 1941*, pp. 166–305 (Cambridge: Cambridge UP, 1996). The author gratefully acknowledges the permission of Michael J. Hogan to reprint it here.

BIBLIOGRAPHY

Alperovitz, Gar. *Atomic Diplomacy: Hiroshima and Potsdam.* New York: Simon and Schuster, 1965, 1985.

Ambrose, Stephen. *Eisenhower and Berlin: The Decision to Halt at the Elbe, 1945.* New York: W. W. Norton, 1967.

Anderson, Terry. *The United States, Great Britain and the Cold War, 1944–1947.* Columbia: University of Missouri, 1981.

Armstrong, Anne. *Unconditional Surrender: The Impact of the Casablanca Policy in World War II.* New Brunswick, NJ: Rutgers UP, 1961.

Baldwin, Hanson W. *Great Mistakes of the War.* New York: Harper and Brothers, 1949.

Beitzell, Robert. *The Uneasy Alliance: America, Britain and Russia, 1941–1943.* New York: Alfred A. Knopf, 1972.

Bell, P. M. H. *John Bull and the Bear: British Public Opinion, Foreign Policy and the Soviet Union, 1941–1945.* London: E. Arnold, 1990.

Bennett, Edward M. *Franklin D. Roosevelt and the Search for Victory: American-Soviet Relations, 1939–1945.* Wilmington, DE: Scholarly Resources, 1990.

Bernstein, Barton J. "Roosevelt, Truman and the Atomic Bomb, 1941–1945: A Reinterpretation." *Political Science Quarterly* 90 (1975): 23–69.

———. "The Uneasy Alliance: Roosevelt, Churchill, and the Atomic Bomb, 1940–1945." *Western Political Quarterly* 29 (1976): 202–230.

Buhite, Russell D. *Decisions at Yalta: An Appraisal of Summit Diplomacy.* Wilmington, DE: Scholarly Resources, 1986.

Burns, James M. *Roosevelt: The Soldier of Freedom, 1940–1945.* New York: Harcourt Brace Jovanovich, 1970.

Butler, James R. M. *Grand Strategy.* 5 vols. London: HMSO, 1952–1972.

Campbell, Thomas. *Masquerade Peace: America's UN Policy, 1944–1945.* Tallahassee: Florida State UP, 1973.

Charmley, John. *Churchill's Grand Alliance: The Anglo-American Special Relationship, 1940–1957.* New York: Harcourt, Brace, 1995.

Clemens, Diane Shaver. *Yalta.* New York: Oxford UP, 1970.

Commentary. 80 (September 1985):41–47; (November 1985): 25–28, 50–52, 56–60, 73–76.

Dallek, Robert. *Franklin D. Roosevelt and American Foreign Policy, 1932–1945.* New York: Oxford UP, 1979.

Divine, Robert A. *Roosevelt and World War II.* Baltimore: Johns Hopkins, 1969.

Dobson, Alan P. *U.S. Wartime Aid to Britain, 1940–1946.* New York: St. Martin's, 1986.

Draper, Theodore. "Neoconservative History" and "Eisenhower's War." *New York Review of Books,* 16 January, 24 April, 25 September, 9 and 23 October 1986, reproduced in Theodore Draper, *A Present of Things Past.* New York: Hill and Wang, 1990.

Edmonds, Robin. *The Big Three: Churchill, Roosevelt, and Stalin in Peace and War.* New York: W. W. Norton, 1991.

Emerson, William. "Franklin D. Roosevelt as Commander-in-Chief in World War II." *Military Affairs* 22 (1958–1959): 181–207.

Eubank, Keith. *Summit at Teheran.* New York: William Morrow, 1985.

Feis, Herbert. *Between War and Peace: The Potsdam Conference.* Princeton: Princeton UP, 1960.

———. *Churchill, Roosevelt, Stalin: The War They Waged and the Peace They Sought.* Princeton: Princeton UP, 1957, 1967.

———. *Japan Subdued: The Atomic Bomb and the End of the War in the Far East.* Princeton: Princeton UP, 1961, 1966 (2d ed. retitled *The Atomic Bomb and the End of World War II*).

Fleming, D. F. *The Cold War and Its Origins, 1917–1960.* 2 vols. Garden City, NY: Doubleday; London: Allen and Unwin, 1961, 1969.

Gaddis, John Lewis. *Strategies of Containment: A Critical Appraisal of Postwar American National Security Policy.* New York: Oxford UP, 1982.

———. *The United States and the Origins of the Cold War, 1941–1947.* New York: Columbia UP, 1972.

Gardner, Lloyd C. *Architects of Illusion: Men and Ideas in American Foreign Policy, 1941–1949.* Chicago: Quadrangle, 1970.

———. *Economic Aspects of New Deal Diplomacy.* Madison: University of Wisconsin, 1964.

———. *Spheres of Influence: The Great Powers Partition Europe, from Munich to Yalta.* Chicago: Ivan R. Dee, 1993.

Gilbert, Martin. *Auschwitz and the Allies.* New York: Holt, Rinehart, and Winston, 1981.

———. *Churchill: A Life.* London: Heineman, Minerva; New York: Holt, 1992.

Gorodetsky, Gabriel. *Stafford Cripps' Mission to Moscow, 1940–1942.* Cambridge: Cambridge UP, 1984.

Greenfield, Kent R. *American Strategy in World War II: A Reconsideration.* Baltimore: Johns Hopkins UP, 1963.

Harbutt, Fraser J. *The Iron Curtain: Churchill, America and the Origins of the Cold War.* New York: Oxford UP, 1986.

Hathaway, Robert M. *Ambiguous Partnership: Britain and America, 1944–1947.* New York: Columbia UP, 1981.

Henrickson, Alan. "The Map as an 'Idea': The Role of Cartographic Imagery during the Second World War." *The American Cartographer* 2 (April 1975): 19–53.

Herring, George C. *Aid to Russia, 1941–1946: Strategy, Diplomacy, and the Origins of the Cold War.* New York: Columbia UP, 1973.

Higgins, Trumbull. *Soft Underbelly: The Anglo-American Controversy over the Italian Campaign, 1943–1945.* New York: Macmillan, 1968.

Hilderbrand, Robert C. *Dumbarton Oaks: The Origins of the United Nations and the Search for Postwar Security.* Chapel Hill: University of North Carolina, 1990.

Hogan, Michael, and Thomas Paterson, eds. *Explaining the History of American Foreign Relations.* New York: Cambridge UP, 1991.

Howard, Michael. *The Mediterranean Strategy in the Second World War.* London: Weidenfeld and Nicolson, 1968.

Kimball, Warren F., ed. *Churchill and Roosevelt: The Complete Correspondence.* 3 vols. Princeton: Princeton UP, 1984.

———. *Forged in War: Roosevelt, Churchill and the Second World War.* New York: Morrow, 1997.

———. *The Juggler: Franklin Roosevelt as Wartime Statesman.* Princeton: Princeton UP, 1991.

———. *The Most Unsordid Act: Lend-Lease, 1939–1941.* Baltimore: Johns Hopkins UP, 1969.

Kitchen, Martin. *British Policy towards the Soviet Union during the Second World War.* New York: St. Martin's, 1986.

Kolko, Gabriel. *The Politics of War: The World and United States Foreign Policy, 1943–1945.* New York: Random House, 1968.

Leffler, Melvyn P. "Adherence to Agreements: Yalta and the Experiences of the Early Cold War." *International Security* 11 (1986): 88–123.

———. *A Preponderance of Power: National Security, the Truman Administration, and the Cold War.* Stanford, CA: Stanford UP, 1992.

Levering, Ralph B. *American Opinion and the Russian Alliance, 1939–1945.* Chapel Hill: University of North Carolina, 1976.

Louis, William Roger. *Imperialism at Bay: The United States and the Decolonization of the British Empire.* New York: Oxford UP, 1978.

Mark, Eduard. "American Policy towards Eastern Europe and the Origins of the Cold War, 1941–1946: An Alternative Interpretation." *Journal of American History* 68 (1981): 313–336.

Marks, Frederick W., III. *Wind over Sand: The Diplomacy of Franklin Roosevelt.* Athens: University of Georgia, 1988.

Martel, Leon. *Lend-Lease, Loans and the Coming of the Cold War: A Study of the Implementation of Foreign Policy.* Boulder, CO: Westview, 1979.

Mastny, Vojtech. *Russia's Road to the Cold War: Diplomacy, Warfare, and the Politics of Communism, 1941–1945.* New York: Columbia UP, 1979.

McCagg, William O. *Stalin Embattled, 1943–1948.* Detroit: Wayne State UP, 1978.

McCauley, Martin. *The Origins of the Cold War.* London: Longman, 1983, 1995.

McNeill, William Hardy. *America, Britain and Russia: Their Cooperation and Conflict, 1941–1946.* London: Oxford UP, 1953.

Mee, Charles L., Jr. *Meeting at Potsdam.* New York: M. Evans, 1975.

Miner, Steven Merritt. *Between Churchill and Stalin: The Soviet Union, Great Britain, and the Origins of the Grand Alliance.* Chapel Hill: University of North Carolina, 1988.

Nadeau, Remi. *Stalin, Churchill, and Roosevelt Divide Europe.* New York: Praeger, 1990.

Nisbet, Robert. *Roosevelt and Stalin: The Failed Courtship.* Washington, DC: Regnery Gateway, 1988.

O'Connor, Raymond G. *Diplomacy for Victory: FDR and Unconditional Surrender.* New York: W. W. Norton, 1971.

Paterson, Thomas G. *Soviet-American Confrontation: Postwar Reconstruction and the Origins of the Cold War.* Baltimore: Johns Hopkins UP, 1973.

Resis, Albert. "The Churchill–Stalin Secret 'Percentages' Agreement on the Balkans, Moscow, October, 1944." *American Historical Review* 83 (1978): 368–387.

———. "Spheres of Influence in Soviet Wartime Diplomacy." *Journal of Modern History* 53 (1981): 417–439.

Reynolds, David. "The 'Big Three' and the Division of Europe, 1945–1948: An Overview." *Diplomacy and Statecraft* 1 (1990): 111–136.

———. *The Creation of the Anglo-American Alliance, 1937–1941: A Study in Competitive Co-operation.* Chapel Hill: University of North Carolina, 1981.

———. "Roosevelt, Churchill, and the Wartime Anglo-American Alliance: Towards a New Synthesis." In William Roger Louis and Hedley Bull, eds. *The Special Relationship: Anglo-American Relations since 1945.* New York: Oxford UP, 1986.

Reynolds, David, Warren F. Kimball, and A. O. Chubarian, eds. *Allies at War: The Soviet, American and British Experience.* New York: St. Martin's, 1994.

Ross, Graham, ed. *The Foreign Office and the Kremlin: British Documents on Anglo-Soviet Relations, 1941–1945.* Cambridge: Cambridge UP, 1984.

Rothwell, Victor. *Britain and the Cold War, 1941–1947.* London: Jonathan Cape, 1982.

Sainsbury, Keith. *Churchill and Roosevelt at War: The War They Fought and the Peace They Hoped to Make.* New York: New York UP, 1994.

———. *The Turning Point: Roosevelt, Stalin, Churchill, and Chiang-Kai-Shek, 1943, The Moscow, Cairo, and Teheran Conferences.* New York: Oxford UP, 1985.

Sbrega, John J. *Anglo-American Relations and Colonialism in East Asia, 1941–1945.* New York: Garland, 1983.

Sherwin, Martin J. *A World Destroyed: The Atomic Bomb and the Grand Alliance.* New York: Random House, 1975.

Sigal, Leon V. *Fighting to a Finish: The Politics of War Termination in the United States and Japan, 1945.* Ithaca, NY: Cornell UP, 1988.

Smith, Gaddis. *American Diplomacy during the Second World War.* New York: John Wiley and Sons, 1965, 1985.

Snell, John L. *Illusion and Necessity: The Diplomacy of Global War, 1939–1945.* Boston: Houghton Mifflin, 1963.

————, ed. *The Meaning of Yalta: Big Three Diplomacy and the New Balance of Power.* Baton Rouge: Louisiana State UP, 1956.

Soviet–U.S. Relations, 1933–1942. Moscow: Progress, 1989.

Stoler, Mark A. *The Politics of the Second Front: American Military Planning and Diplomacy in Coalition Warfare, 1941–1943.* Westport, CT: Greenwood, 1977.

Taubman, William. *Stalin's American Policy: From Entente to Detente to Cold War.* New York: W. W. Norton, 1982.

Theoharis, Athan G. *The Yalta Myths: An Issue in U.S. Politics, 1945–1955.* Columbia: University of Missouri, 1970.

Thorne, Christopher. *Allies of a Kind: The United States, Britain, and the War against Japan.* New York: Oxford UP, 1978.

————. *The Issue of War: States, Societies, and the Far Eastern Conflict of 1941–1945.* New York: Oxford UP, 1985. Also published as *The Far Eastern War: States and Societies, 1941–45.* London: Unwin, 1986.

Widenor, William C. "American Planning for the United Nations: Have We Been Asking the Right Questions?" *Diplomatic History* 6 (1982) : 245–265.

Wilmot, Chester. *The Struggle for Europe.* New York: Harper and Brothers, 1952.

Wilson, Theodore A. *The First Summit: Roosevelt and Churchill and Placentia Bay, 1941.* 1st ed. New York: Houghton Mifflin, 1969. 2d ed. Lawrence: UP of Kansas, 1991.

Woods, Randall. *A Changing of the Guard: Anglo-American Relations, 1941–1946.* Chapel Hill: University of North Carolina, 1990.

Woodward, Llewellyn. *British Foreign Policy in the Second World War.* London: HMSO, 1962, 1971–1976.

Wyman, David. *The Abandonment of the Jews: America and the Holocaust, 1941–1945.* New York: Pantheon, 1984.

Zubok, Vladislav, and Konstantin Pleshakov. *Inside the Kremlin's Cold War: From Stalin to Khrushchev.* Cambridge: Harvard UP, 1996.

27 Planning for the Postwar World Economy and the United Nations

Georg Schild

Leo Pasvolsky, special assistant to the secretary of state in charge of American postwar planning, wrote in 1942 in McConnell's *A Basis for the Peace to Come* that after the current war, the central problems confronting humankind would be the same as those that challenged the world after World War I. Those problems were

First, to create a system of international political relationships . . . for the preservation of a just peace among nations; and second, to create economic conditions which would make possible a progressive movement toward an efficient utilization of the human and material resources of the world . . . to insure . . . full and stable employment accompanied by rising standards of living everywhere. (84)

The view that wartime planning efforts had to ensure economic recovery and international security was at the heart of American and Allied postwar planning during World War II. This planning culminated in the Allied conferences of Bretton Woods, Dumbarton Oaks, and San Francisco in 1944 and 1945. At Bretton Woods, delegations from forty-four countries agreed upon the creation of two new financial institutions, the International Monetary Fund (IMF) and the International Bank for Reconstruction and Development (IBRD). Those institutions were expected to be the cornerstones of a new global economic order ensuring reconstruction of war-devastated nations and guaranteeing economic prosperity without recurring depressions. At Dumbarton Oaks, four countries, the United States, Great Britain, the Soviet Union, and China, agreed upon a draft charter for the United Nations organization (UN) to provide effective collective security against future breaches of the peace. At the San

Francisco conference in June 1945, fifty governments signed the United Nations Charter.

Allied planning for the United Nations and the International Monetary Fund was based on continued postwar cooperation among the three Allies that bore the brunt of World War II fighting, the United States, Great Britain, and the Soviet Union. With the onset of the Cold War in the second half of the 1940s, the basis for American and Allied postwar planning had vanished. The institutions that had been created at the end of the war continued to exist throughout the Cold War years but played far less important roles than their creators had assumed.

In his essay "American Planning for the United Nations: Have We Been Asking the Right Questions?" Widenor presented a survey of the conflicting assessments about the planning for postwar reconstruction and international security that historians have reached in recent years. Due to the limited role that the UN and the IMF played in postwar international politics and economics, few studies have focused on the planning processes for those institutions. Instead, analyses have concentrated on the relationship between postwar planning and the Cold War, asking whether or not it was futile for the United States and Great Britain to attempt creating a postwar political system based on cooperation with the Soviet Union. So-called traditionalist historians such as Perlmutter in *FDR and Stalin* have criticized American efforts to base postwar security on the creation of an international organization. The planning for the United Nations was proof to them that President Franklin D. Roosevelt could not stand up to Soviet dictator Joseph Stalin. They pointed out not only that the United States granted the Soviets a free hand in areas occupied by the Red Army but that Washington also accepted the Soviet Union as a Great Power in the United Nations. Revisionists such as Kolko, *The Politics of War*, on the other hand, argued that the American goal of creating a new economic order at the Bretton Woods conference was mainly designed to achieve economic hegemony and that it contributed to the deterioration of Allied postwar relations. Revisionist historians maintained that the global multilateral economic structure that the Treasury Department had proposed since 1942 primarily served the needs of American businesses.

Only in recent years have analyses of postwar preparations stepped out of the shadow of the Cold War. Historians have begun casting new light on the intricacies of American and British—and, to a much more limited extent, Soviet—economic and political postwar goals and plans. The end of the Cold War has created a political and economic environment similar to the one postwar planners expected to encounter after the Second World War. That has permitted historians to take a new look at postwar planning.

PLANNING FOR POSTWAR INTERNATIONAL SECURITY

In the United States, planning for a postwar political and security structure went on simultaneously in the White House and in the State Department. President Roosevelt's approach to postwar planning, however, differed from that of Secretary of State Cordell Hull and most departmental officials. Throughout 1942 and 1943, Roosevelt proposed a plan under which the United States, Great Britain, the Soviet Union, and China should guarantee international security in the postwar period. In case of a breach of peace, those "four policemen," as Roosevelt called them, would jointly blockade the disturber of the peace and confront him militarily if he would not abandon his aggressive stand. While all other countries would have to disarm, Bennett noted in *Franklin D. Roosevelt and the Search for Victory* that the policemen would "retain sufficient armed forces to impose peace and would arrange adequate inspection agreements to prevent secret rearmament such as Hitler had managed" (53–54).

Most historians consider the policemen proposal the result of Roosevelt's realist assessment of postwar security options. Kimball has argued in *The Juggler* that Roosevelt did not believe that Great Britain or any other Western democracy could alone guarantee peace in Europe and that the president realized that the Soviet Union would play an important role in postwar politics. A victorious USSR, Kimball noted, "would be a postwar power of major geographical strength, putting it in the same arena with the United States" (90). Since he considered quarrels among smaller states a prime source for future conflicts, Great Power cooperation appeared to him as the logical way to maintain peace.

There is disagreement among historians, however, about how Roosevelt expected the policemen to work together and whether or not he considered Great Power domination a suitable basis for long-term security. The president's biographer Burns concluded in *Roosevelt: Soldier of Freedom* that the president may have hoped that "Big Four policing might work so well that it could go on indefinitely" (359). Other historians differ from that opinion. In his *Roosevelt and World War II*, Divine found that U.S.–Soviet cooperation was only the basis for creating a universal international security organization. Divine noted that Roosevelt "was under no illusions about the difficulty of securing Russian co-operation, but he told [Undersecretary of State Sumner] Welles he would do all he could to achieve it, since he was convinced that the future of international organization depended upon 'the way by which the Soviet Union and the United States can work together' " (62–63). American cooperation with the Soviet Union would be the nucleus for a universal security organization. This aspect of Roosevelt's postwar planning has met criticism from traditionalist historians. They believed that the president unnecessarily accommodated the Soviet Union. In *FDR and Stalin*, Perlmutter maintained that

Roosevelt's vision of a postwar world "was idealistic, Wilsonian, totally at odds with reality." The president's wartime diplomacy was fueled by "what could almost be called a desperate desire to fulfill the dream that the Soviets would be America's postwar partner. This required an amazing ignorance, a willingness to ignore past and present facts, and a complete misunderstanding of the Soviet system and of Stalin" (215).

In contrast to those opinions that stressed Roosevelt's goal of achieving American–Soviet cooperation, Sherry pointed out in *Preparing for the Next War: American Plans for Postwar Defense* that the president spoke of four policemen but that he envisioned two marshals and two deputies. The four policemen would not share equal power: "At least during the first years of peace, Roosevelt and Churchill agreed, the United States and Britain alone would carry nuclear bombs, with the United States as the dominant partner in the atomic alliance" (43). Sherry believed that Roosevelt wanted to dominate international security affairs after the war.

While there is no agreement among historians today about Roosevelt's exact postwar goals, three aspects appear beyond dispute: first, through 1943, the president advocated a postwar security structure that granted the leading Allied countries political prerogatives in a postwar security structure. Second, Roosevelt's policemen proposal was only one of several different plans designed to provide the Great Powers with significant rights and responsibilities. Both British Prime Minister Winston Churchill and Stalin thought along similar lines. Churchill proposed a postwar peace structure based on several regional organizations that were dominated by the Great Powers. Though less is known about Stalin's postwar plans, his position at the Teheran and Yalta conferences and his secret "percentages deal" with Churchill in November 1944 demonstrate that he, too, according to Campbell's *Masquerade Peace: America's UN Policy, 1944–1945*, thought in terms of dominating smaller states. Third, in early 1944, Roosevelt gave up his policemen concept in favor of an alternative plan drafted by the State Department.

In contrast to Roosevelt's policemen proposal and Churchill's advocacy of regional security blocs, State Department postwar plans were based on the creation of a single universal security organization in which the Great Powers would share peacekeeping responsibilities with other states and would enjoy much more limited prerogatives than under the policemen proposal. The creation of a new world organization as successor to the League of Nations appeared to the State Department, as Russell argued in her book *A History of the United Nations Charter*, as the solution to a whole range of anticipated postwar political problems. The existence of such an organization would facilitate the peace settlements because countries would emphasize a "broader community of interests" (953) instead of particular concerns, and it would allow the United States to withdraw its troops from Europe soon after the end of the hostilities.

A number of studies on postwar planning have been devoted to the State Department's preparations. One of the earliest accounts was the 1949 study *Postwar Foreign Policy Preparation, 1939–1945* written and compiled by Harley Notter, the State Department's chief of the division of international security and organization. Notter described the complex interconnections among countless State Department committees and subcommittees working simultaneously on different aspects of postwar planning. Their suggestions concerning postwar security initially included a wide range of options but soon narrowed down to creating an international organization as a powerful successor to the League of Nations. It should consist of two chambers, a universal General Assembly representing all member states and a smaller Security Council composed of less than a dozen nations and charged with maintaining international peace.

Notter's work, however, was not a comprehensive history of American postwar planning. Such a study appeared a decade after the end of the war with Russell's already mentioned *History of the United Nations Charter*. The book presents a detailed analysis of postwar planning at the executive branch level from the Atlantic conference of 1941 to the Yalta and San Francisco conferences of 1945. Russell, like Notter a member of the wartime State Department, saw U.S. postwar planning developing in a number of steps that corresponded with international events. The central aspect of U.S. postwar preparations after entering the war was to ensure continued cooperation of all major anti-Axis countries. Russell considered the November 1943 Moscow Foreign Ministers' conference a milestone in the cooperation with the Soviet Union and in the development of a universal security organization. There, a "formal Soviet commitment was obtained to follow a policy of postwar collaboration and, specifically, to support an international organization." The United States, Great Britain, and the Soviet Union signed a declaration recognizing the "necessity of establishing at the earliest practicable date a general international organization, based on the principle of the sovereign equality of all nations, and open to membership by all nations, large and small, for the maintenance of international peace and security" (3).

Since early 1944, the United States, Great Britain, and the Soviet Union officially cooperated in the planning for a universal security organization. Roosevelt's turning away from the policemen proposal and adopting the State Department's planning appear to be based on domestic political considerations. He believed the policemen proposal was ideally suited to maintain Allied unity, but he expected that it would meet a hostile reception in smaller states and in the American public. In August 1944, Republican presidential candidate Thomas E. Dewey attacked the administration for allegedly advocating a Great Power dictatorship. Cordell Hull denied that the United States or any of the Great Powers had any intentions to "coerce the rest of the world."

The problem that was at the heart of Allied postwar preparations in

1944 and 1945 was how to balance Great Power prerogatives that were considered necessary to maintain effective collective security with upholding the rights of other sovereign states. That question was debated within the American and British governments, dominated the proceedings of the conference of Dumbarton Oaks, and played an important role at the Yalta conference in February 1945.

The Soviet delegation at the Dumbarton Oaks conference wanted to grant the United Nations the most far-reaching responsibilities, including the establishment of an international air corps as a deterrent to aggressors. The UN could fulfill its policing task, the Soviets argued, only if all Great Powers agreed to each military operation. Each Great Power should therefore be able to veto UN resolutions, including those that related to disputes to which one of the powers was a party. The British Dumbarton Oaks proposal provided the UN with much more limited responsibilities and rejected the idea of a Great Power veto. Initially undecided about its own policy, the Roosevelt administration came to side with the British proposal during the course of the conference, thereby limiting the scope of the United Nations and turning away from Great Power domination of postwar security. The issue of Great Power prerogatives dominated the Dumbarton Oaks conference. Despite intensive debates, the delegates were unable to reach a solution to the Great Power veto issue. A compromise was reached at the Yalta conference when Roosevelt, Churchill, and Stalin agreed upon a veto power for decisions of Security Council enforcement measures, even if a Great Power was involved in that conflict.

In the most detailed study about the Dumbarton Oaks conference to date, *Dumbarton Oaks: The Origins of the United Nations and the Search for Postwar Security*, Hilderbrand concluded that the course of the Dumbarton Oaks conference indicated a deterioration in Allied relations toward the end of the war. Dumbarton Oaks came at the time of the transition from Allied wartime internationalism to increased concerns about the protection of their own national interests and sovereignty. The conference was ultimately unsuccessful, in his view, because it failed in its efforts at creating a powerful United Nations organization. A strong UN was the first victim of the emerging Cold War. By the time of the conference, the American delegates viewed the Soviet Union less as a fellow policeman and more as a threat to peace. That change of attitude grew even more pronounced during the conference and had an effect on the American negotiators' "hardening attitude toward the veto question." Hilderbrand believed that the American negotiating behavior regarding the Security Council voting issue was difficult to explain "except in terms of their more general attitude toward the Soviet Union." In "less than a month's time, the American group had moved from almost unanimous support of the USSR's position regarding the Great Power veto to a vigorous rejection of that view" (212).

Not all historians share this critical assessment. Wheeler-Bennett and

Nicholls concluded in their *Semblance of Power: The Political Settlement after the Second World War* that the Great Power veto formula reached at Yalta was "far from ideal but it represented a basis of realistic compromise" (545). They considered it necessary that the Great Powers that were ultimately responsible for enforcing Security Council decisions could not be pushed into collective action they did not approve. The authors also doubted that either the U.S. Senate or Stalin would have approved membership in a universal security organization without those protections of their country's Great Power status.

American political postwar planning started with the goal of advocating Great Power domination in the postwar world. Since early 1944, the United States turned away from that goal to creating a more democratic organization. At the same time, the Soviet Union increasingly sought security outside the United Nations by creating spheres of influence in Eastern Europe. From the Cold War perspective, American and Allied political postwar planning appeared as a failure. Despite all appeals to the Kremlin by the United States, Ruth Russell wrote, "the Soviet Union continued creating exactly the kind of world that the United States opposed." This was the mold for most Cold War analyses of postwar planning and its failure to provide Great Power cooperation following World War II. Feis' *Churchill, Roosevelt, Stalin: The War They Waged and the Peace They Sought* describes Western postwar planning as an honest effort toward creating international peace that met with Soviet ambivalence: the Kremlin kept itself in a position "to impose its own will in matters deemed vital to the Soviet security or prestige, even while wanting and seeking continued cooperation" (433).

Postwar planning did not develop the way American and Allied planners had intended. Instead of creating "one world," they produced a bipolar world in which two armed camps faced each other. The resulting political stalemate allowed Western and—to a lesser degree—Eastern Europe to recover. Gardner argued in *Spheres of Influence: The Great Powers Partition Europe, from Munich to Yalta* that the peace process even "required a temporarily divided Europe in order to provide a time of healing for the nearly fatal wounds Hitler had inflicted on the Continent" (265). Only the division of Europe and the extension of Soviet influence into Central Europe made continuous American intervention in Europe possible. It was difficult to imagine, he wrote,

how the United States could have managed economic recovery without the Soviet sphere of influence in Eastern Europe. What incentives would Congress have had to support Truman's major initiatives without the Cold War? . . . Without an "enemy" to focus on, how could the bedeviling European rivalries of the interwar years have been overcome? (263)

The Cold War, in his interpretation, is an unwritten agreement between the United States and Great Britain, on one hand, and the Soviet Union, on the other. Gardner quoted Soviet Foreign Minister Vyacheslav Molotov defining in later years what the term "Cold War" meant: "They [Western countries] certainly hardened against us, but we had to consolidate our conquests. We had our own socialist Germany out of our part of Germany" (264–265).

The Cold War made it impossible for the United Nations—the organization on which Roosevelt and the State Department had set their hopes—to guarantee international security for almost forty years. The North Atlantic Treaty Organization (NATO) and the Warsaw pact, the regional military and defense alliances, took over that task. Only now in the post–Cold War period does the United Nations face increasing responsibilities.

PLANNING FOR INTERNATIONAL ECONOMIC RECONSTRUCTION

The second pillar of postwar planning was the preparation for postwar economic reconstruction. Due to different anticipated problems, American economic plans differed from the political and security planning efforts. While there was hope that the Great Powers might be able to avert wars in the future, widespread economic problems reminiscent of the post–World War I period or even the Great Depression appeared all but unavoidable after the war. The fighting in Europe and Asia had destroyed industries and infrastructures and had depleted the financial assets of countless countries. Postwar planners believed that economic reconstruction depended on making financial resources available to European states.

Wartime economists also foresaw economic problems for the United States. The American economy might not be able to absorb the millions of demobilized soldiers returning to civilian jobs after the war without creating a huge unemployment problem. Economic conditions, however, developed differently from the mostly gloomy predictions during the war. After the end of World War II, the Western European economies recovered quickly, and the United States developed the most prosperous economy in history.

There was general agreement in the Roosevelt administration about seeking international cooperation for solving postwar economic problems. The American goal was to increase international trade through a mutual, simultaneous reduction of trade barriers among the principal trading nations of the world. Such a policy, Woods determined in his *A Changing of the Guard: Anglo-American Relations, 1941–1946*, "promised to banish unemployment from America in a generation while leaving the free enterprise system relatively intact" (2).

The main postwar economic planners during World War II were Harry Dexter White of the U.S. Treasury Department, a close confidant of Secretary of the Treasury Henry Morgenthau, and British economist John

Maynard Keynes. In contrast to the elaborate postwar planning structure set up by the State Department, White laid the groundwork for American postwar economic recovery plans almost single-handedly. A number of books, among them Richard Gardner's *Sterling-Dollar Diplomacy*, Moggridge's *Maynard Keynes*, Eckes' *A Search for Solvency: Bretton Woods and the International Monetary System*, Rees' *Harry Dexter White: A Study in Paradox*, and Woods' *Changing of the Guard*, provide general overviews of White's and Keynes' planning efforts as well as the Bretton Woods conference.

White's postwar economic reconstruction plan was based on the creation of two international financial institutions, the IMF and the IBRD, which would provide governments with short- or long-term loans. White considered $8 billion for the IMF and $10 billion for the IBRD as sufficient to provide all necessary credits. In return for having access to this source of liquidity, governments had to subscribe to certain economic principles, among them not to devalue their currencies. The Treasury Department regarded this provision as a central aspect of its postwar plan because it believed that the Great Depression had been prolonged by European inflationary policies during the 1930s that had devalued their currencies and had made exports—including American—more difficult.

Economist John Maynard Keynes, in addition to negotiating the lend-lease conditions, drafted the official British plan for postwar economic recovery. Economic historians Moggridge in *Maynard Keynes*, Williams in *Postwar Monetary Plans and Other Essays*, and Imre de Vegh in "The International Clearing Union" emphasize Great Britain's serious financial problems after the beginning of the Second World War that influenced Keynes' postwar planning. Correcting Britain's anticipated postwar economic problems would require changes in the pattern of international trade. In particular, the problem of maintaining equilibrium in the balance of payments between countries had to be solved. Keynes turned away from the gold standard because it was deflationary. Instead, Keynes proposed that the creditor nations should assume a larger role in maintaining balanced trade and that the movement of capital funds be regulated by central banks. Keynes called for an "International Clearing Union" to provide the necessary capital for economic reconstruction. Unlike the White plan, the Clearing Union would possess no assets of its own. Instead, it would balance member states' trade surpluses with their deficits. A state with a trading surplus against another state could use that credit to buy merchandise from the creditor. No money would flow. Keynes believed that $26 billion in overdraft authorizations would be necessary to stimulate the postwar economies.

While the White and Keynes plans were similar in their goal of increasing international trade, they differed in terms of implementing them. Under the White plan, the United States would assume only a limited financial responsibility that would not exceed the contribution to the fund and the bank, about $2 billion to $3 billion for each institution. Under the Clearing Union concept, the American financial commitment could theoretically reach $26 billion if all other states would use their overdraft rights to purchase goods in the United States.

White made it clear to Keynes in 1943 and 1944 that the U.S. Congress would never agree to the Clearing Union concept because it would violate the constitutional authority of Congress to authorize federal spending. Keynes had no choice but to agree to the White plan. At the Bretton Woods conference of July 1944, forty-four countries—among them the Soviet Union—accepted the American proposal and agreed to the creation of the International Monetary Fund and the International Bank for Reconstruction and Development.

The British journal *The Economist* commented in "The American Challenge" as early as 1942 that the American approach to political and military problems was "vague." In the economic sphere, in contrast, "there is evidence of an entirely new and dynamic concept of post-war world relations." The key, the journal continued, was "expanding markets," in other words, a "global mass consumption" great enough to use mass production. "Let there be no mistake about it. The policy put forward by the American Administration is revolutionary. It is a genuinely new conception of world order." Arthur Krock added in the *New York Times* that "economic freedom for all" was the basic American foreign policy for the prevention of war. " 'Political Freedom' can be read whenever 'economic freedom' is used in an American State paper."

The impact of the Bretton Woods institutions on postwar economics, however, remained limited. Due to the inflationary economic climate of the postwar years, the $18 billion credit ceiling soon proved to be too low for effective reconstruction. During the early Cold War years, the United States provided Western European states with additional financial aid to rebuild them as strong democratic and anticommunist nations. Some historians have nevertheless come to positive assessments about the Bretton Woods agreement. Dormael wrote in his *Bretton Woods* that the agreement "would stand during a quarter of a century as the foundation upon which world trade, production, employment and investment were gradually built" (307). Oliver remarked in his study about the International Bank for Reconstruction, *International Economic Co-operation and the World Bank*, that the "practical people who made the Bank work have been . . . important to the advancement of mankind, but Keynes, White, and the other founding fathers of the International Bank for Reconstruction and Development, would also have reason to be proud of the creative vision without which the Bank's contribution to civilization would not have been possible" (278).

Historians who have come to more critical conclusions about the economic postwar planning have blamed the United States for the small impact of the fund and the bank on postwar recovery. The American postwar economic proposal, Rose noted in *Dubious Victory: The United States and the End of World War II,* was "ably suited to deal with the kind of breakdown in international trade and finance that would accompany a great international depression such as that of 1929–1939." It was of little value, however, to the "materially shattered world of 1944." The fund could not deal adequately with the postwar dollar gap between debtor and creditor nations, and "it had no authority to use its resources for relief or reconstruction; it made no provision for large and/or *sustained* outflows of capital suffered by one or a group of member nations" (73).

The resistance to establishing a postwar economic structure that went beyond the Bretton Woods proposal centered around conservative and isolationist members of the U.S. Senate. In his *Changing of the Guard,* Woods emphasized the relationship between conservative domestic forces and the international postwar economic structure: "Thanks in part to the efforts of congressional conservatives, neither Bretton Woods nor the Anglo-American Financial Agreement of 1946 was liberal enough to ensure a smoothly functioning system of international payments." That had a particularly devastating effect on Great Britain, diminishing its ability to maintain a balance of power on the continent. Woods concludes by comparing the American political and financial reactions to World War II and the Cold War: "America's strategic and economic policies converged in 1941 and diverged in 1946 because those leading the charge against Germany were pragmatic liberals and those comprising the cutting edge of interventionism in 1946 were fiscal conservatives and isolationists" (399, 401, 406).

In *Sterling-Dollar Diplomacy* Gardner demonstrated that American decisions prior to, and at, Bretton Woods—most importantly, the decision not to accept Keynes' Clearing Union concept—were based on the belief that the United States would never need assistance from the fund. Based on the assumption that it would be a perpetually surplus country, the United States attempted to limit the money available to other countries through the fund. "Only much later," Gardner wrote in the introduction to the revised edition to his book in 1969, "did the United States come to realize that today's surplus country may be in deficit tomorrow—and that a liberal multilateral solution to the liquidity problem can therefore serve the interests of all" (1).

Liberal historians have not been the only critics of the American position at Bretton Woods. Revisionist and New Left Cold War historians have contended that American foreign economic policy was an effort to increase international trade to benefit primarily American industries. Williams argued in *The Tragedy of American Diplomacy* that the main foreign economic concern of the administration was fear that America's economic system would suffer a serious depression if it did not continue to expand overseas. Kolko contended in *The Politics of War* that American postwar economic policy was designed to find profitable markets for its exports and investments. In principle, the United States wished to see the markets of the world open to all nations, but primarily for the benefit of the United States.

Specialized studies on postwar planning have mainly focused either on political or on economic postwar preparations. Schild's *Bretton Woods and Dumbarton Oaks: American Economic and Political Postwar Planning in the Summer of 1944* addresses the question whether or not there was one overarching interest in American postwar planning linking the economic and political sectors. He compared State and Treasury Department postwar planning efforts and analyzed the proceedings at Bretton Woods and Dumbarton Oaks. Schild concluded that while the ultimate goal—international postwar cooperation—was similar in both conferences, the two departments followed distinctly different strategies. At Bretton Woods, the U.S. goal was to establish a postwar economic organization that would fulfill certain predetermined designs, such as ensuring exchange rate stability. Only governments that agreed to those specific goals would be accepted as members in the IMF. At Dumbarton Oaks and San Francisco the goal was different. The State Department tried to create an organization that would have to consist of as many countries as possible to be successful. While traditionalist historians are right in pointing out that at Dumbarton Oaks and San Francisco the United States accepted the Soviet Union as a Great Power, revisionists are equally right pointing out that at Bretton Woods the United States established an economic order that served primarily American interests.

When viewed in retrospect, the Bretton Woods and Dumbarton Oaks agreements appear extraordinarily optimistic. Against the background of the failed peace efforts at Versailles, the magnitude of destruction in Europe and Asia, and the different postwar political opinions in Washington, London, and Moscow, it appears almost unbelievable that postwar planners could have assumed that they had paved the way for general postwar economic recovery and political stability by creating the International Monetary Fund, the International Bank for Reconstruction and Development, and the United Nations. President Roosevelt himself at times voiced doubts about the American plans. After his return from Yalta, he told Congress that no postwar plan was perfect and that whatever proposal would be adopted would have to be amended time and again over the years: "No one can say exactly how long any plan will last. Peace can endure only so long as humanity really insists upon it, and is willing to work for it—and sacrifice for it" (Burns, *Roosevelt*, 581–582).

BIBLIOGRAPHY

"The American Challenge." *The Economist.* 18 (July 1942): 66–67.

Bennett, Edward M. *Franklin D. Roosevelt and the Search for Victory: American-Soviet Relations 1939–1945.* Wilmington, DE: Scholarly Resources, 1990.

Burns, James MacGregor. *Roosevelt: The Soldier of Freedom, 1940–1945.* New York: Harcourt Brace Jovanovich, 1970.

Campbell, Thomas M. *Masquerade Peace: America's UN Policy, 1944–1945.* Tallahassee: Florida State UP, 1973.

de Vegh, Imre. "The International Clearing Union." *American Economic Review* 33 (1943): 534–556.

Divine, Robert A. *Roosevelt and World War II.* Baltimore: Johns Hopkins UP, 1969.

Dormael, Armand Van. *Bretton Woods: Birth of a Monetary System.* New York: Holmes and Meier, 1978.

Eckes, Alfred E., Jr. *A Search for Solvency: Bretton Woods and the International Monetary System, 1941–1971.* Austin: University of Texas, 1975.

Feis, Herbert. *Churchill, Roosevelt, Stalin: The War They Waged and the Peace They Sought.* Princeton: Princeton UP, 1957.

Gardner, Lloyd C. *Spheres of Influence: The Great Powers Partition Europe, from Munich to Yalta.* Chicago: Ivan R. Dee, 1993.

Gardner, Richard N. *Sterling-Dollar Diplomacy: The Origins and the Prospects of Our International Economic Order.* 2d ed. New York: McGraw-Hill, 1969.

Hilderbrand, Robert C. *Dumbarton Oaks: The Origins of the United Nations and the Search for Postwar Security.* Chapel Hill: University of North Carolina, 1990.

Kimball, Warren F. *The Juggler: Franklin Roosevelt as Wartime Statesman.* Princeton: Princeton UP, 1991.

Knorr, Klaus. "The Bretton Woods Institutions in Transition." *International Organization* 2 (1948) :19–38.

Kolko, Gabriel. *The Politics of War: The World and United States Foreign Policy, 1943–1945.* New York: Pantheon, 1990.

Krock, Arthur. *New York Times,* 27 May 1942, 4.

McConnell, Francis J., ed. *A Basis for the Peace to Come.* New York: Abingdon-Cokesbury, 1942.

Moggridge, Donald E. *Maynard Keynes: An Economist's Biography.* London: Routledge, 1992.

Notter, Harley. *Postwar Foreign Policy Preparation, 1939–1945.* Department of State Publication 3580. Washington, DC: GPO, 1949.

Oliver, Robert W. *International Economic Co-operation and the World Bank.* London: Macmillan, 1975.

Perlmutter, Amos. *FDR and Stalin: A Not So Grand Alliance, 1943–1945.* Columbia: University of Missouri, 1993.

Rees, David. *Harry Dexter White: A Study in Paradox.* New York: Coward, McCann, and Geoghegan, 1973.

Reynolds, David. *Britannia Overruled: British Policy and World Power in the 20th Century.* London: Longman, 1991.

Rose, Lisle A. *Dubious Victory: The United States and the End of World War II.* Kent, OH: Kent State UP, 1973.

Rosenman, Samuel I., ed. *The Public Papers and Addresses of Franklin D. Roosevelt.* 13 vols. New York: Harper and Brothers, 1938–1950.

Russell, Ruth B. *A History of the United Nations Charter: The Role of the United States 1940–1945.* Washington, DC: Brookings, 1958.

Schild, Georg. *Bretton Woods and Dumbarton Oaks: American Economic and Political Postwar Planning in the Summer of 1944.* New York: St. Martin's, 1995.

Sherry, Michael S. *Preparing for the Next War: American Plans for Postwar Defense, 1941–1945.* New Haven, CT: Yale UP, 1976.

Stromberg, Roland. *Collective Security and American Foreign Policy: From the League of Nations to NATO.* New York: Praeger, 1963.

Wheeler-Bennett, John, and Anthony Nicholls. *The Semblance of Power: The Political Settlement after the Second World War.* New York: St. Martin's, 1972.

Widenor, William C. "American Planning for the United Nations: Have We Been Asking the Right Questions?" *Diplomatic History* 6 (1982): 245–265.

Williams, John. *Postwar Monetary Plans and Other Essays.* New York: Knopf, 1947.

Williams, William A. *The Tragedy of American Diplomacy.* New York: Dell, 1962.

Woods, Randall Bennett. *A Changing of the Guard: Anglo-American Relations, 1941–1946.* Chapel Hill: University of North Carolina, 1990.

Woodward, Llewellyn. *History of the Second World War: British Foreign Policy in the Second World War.* 5 vols. London: HMSO, 1970–1976.

28 The Breakdown of the Grand Alliance and the Origins of the Cold War, 1945–1947

Lawrence Aronsen

INTERPRETATIONS OF THE ORIGINS OF THE COLD WAR

The Cold War was the focal point and defining characteristic of international relations from the end of the Second World War to the dismantling of the Berlin Wall in 1989 and the final collapse of the Soviet empire in 1991. The term was first coined in the autumn of 1946 by Herbert Bayard Swope, a member of the American delegation to the Atomic Energy Commission. Swope's immediate superior on the commission, Bernard Baruch, later publicized the idea of a Cold War in a widely quoted speech to the Industrial College of the U.S. Armed Forces in June 1947. Baruch observed that a new kind of struggle, characterized by neither all-out war nor peaceful coexistence, had replaced the wartime alliance.

The hundreds of Cold War historians listed in Black's *Annotated Bibliography* are in general agreement that the major protagonists were the capitalist Allies led by the United States versus the communist bloc countries directed by the Soviet Union. There is a basic consensus that the key period for an understanding of the breakdown in relations between the two sides was 1945 to 1947, but some historians have preferred to cast a broader historical net.

The essential character of the Cold War is not in question; it was a limited conflict in which both sides relied on the use of propaganda, espionage, subversion, economic embargoes, diplomatic coercion, and threats. Occasionally, as in the case of the wars in Korea, Vietnam, and Angola, states employed military force via proxy countries in order to gain strategic advantage over an adversary. In determining the cause of, and, specifically, apportioning blame for, the international polarization that arose during the early postwar period, historians continue to divide.

Four basic schools of interpretation—anticommunist conservatives, orthodox nationalists, left-revisionists, and realist/postrevisionists—have appeared to explain how and why the wartime alliance so quickly disintegrated between 1945 and 1947. Historians from Europe and Canada have contributed their own unique perspective that combines elements of these schools. For a complete understanding of the origins of the Cold War, Fleming's *The Cold War and Its Origins* and Williams' *Tragedy of American Diplomacy* began with Allied efforts to contain the Bolshevik Revolution from 1918 to 1920. Most historians, however, have concentrated on specific regional conflicts after the war: the implementation of the Yalta accords, particularly in the case of Poland; the Iranian issue in early 1946; and the disagreements over Greece and Turkey in 1947. Attention has also been paid to what effect the atomic bombing of Japan, the Chinese civil war, and American efforts to reconstruct the world economy had on the breakdown of the wartime alliance. Questions about the causes of the Cold War relate to the personalities of Soviet and American leaders, the structure and function of domestic political economics, and the nature of the international system itself.

The orthodox-nationalist school occupied the center stage of debate from the 1940s to the 1960s. Several well-known diplomatic historians of an earlier generation were identified with this school, notably, Schlesinger in "Origins of the Cold War," Feis in *From Trust to Terror*, and Ferrell in "Truman Foreign Policy." Their perspective assumed that the Soviet Union was inherently aggressive and that American policy was simply a reaction to communist expansion in Eastern Europe and the Middle East. Orthodox-nationalists did not offer a precise analysis of the motivations of Soviet policy except to say that a combination of ideology, opportunism, and Stalin's paranoia led to a confrontation. Most of their attention is paid to an examination of American foreign policy in the face of the communist threat, described by Schlesinger as "the brave and essential response of free men to communist aggression." The Truman administration acted decisively but in an evenhanded manner designed to contain communism but not provoke Soviet military action. The best assessment was that it balanced realism and idealism. American foreign policy makers understood the Soviet threat to the balance of power and adopted an appropriate mix of diplomatic and economic measures to contain further Soviet expansion. Their motives were idealistic in that they formulated policies within a clear legal-moral framework toward the end of promoting peace and prosperity in Europe and elsewhere.

Throughout the 1950s the most vituperative and politically charged critique of the orthodox-nationalist interpretation came from anticommunist conservative writers such as Chamberlain in *Beyond Containment*, Burnham in *Containment or Liberation?*, and the European émigré political scientists Strausz-Hupé and Possony in their *International Relations*. Criticism centered on the Truman administration's viewing of international affairs through the lenses of New Deal liberalism and its failure to appreciate the messianic nature of communism, the military threat posed by the Soviet army, and the uncompromising fanaticism of Joseph Stalin.

Consequently, in their view, the Truman administration did not recognize early enough the communist threat to Europe and the Far East, which by 1949 had come under the direct control of the Soviet Union. Instead of using diplomatic pressure and, if necessary, the threat of military force to reverse the communist advances, the Truman administration, in Burnham's opinion, offered only "a cautious, relativistic, Machiavellian liberalism" that settled for containment and "the enslavement of captive peoples."

Traditional realists such as Morgenthau, *In Defense of the National Interest*, and Graebner, *Cold War Diplomacy*, offered a different analysis of the underlying causes of the Cold War, focusing on the condition of anarchy in an international system insufficiently tempered by international law, morality, and organization. The twentieth century in particular can be characterized as a Hobbesian struggle of "each against all" that contains within it the possibility for instability, conflict, and the potential for total war and annihilation of nation-states. The shift from a multipolar international system in the 1930s to a bipolar one by the end of the 1940s, owing primarily to the decline of German and Japanese power, opened significant and unprecedented power vacuums in Europe and Asia. Inevitably, the Soviet Union and the United States clashed in their efforts to establish separate spheres of influence; each bears some of the responsibility for the breakdown of the wartime alliance. While anarchic international conditions and the rapidly shifting balance of power set the stage for a Soviet-American confrontation, the Soviet Union under Stalin exacerbated this situation by the suddenness of its communization of Eastern Europe and the brutal methods used to achieve this end. The United States misinterpreted the Soviets' legitimate, if calloused, search for security, overreacted through the use of rhetoric rather than diplomacy, and escalated the confrontation to the larger global stage.

Ideas about the inhospitable nature of the international system and nation-states' consequent search for security have been incorporated into the writing of a more recent generation, described as neorealist or post-revisionist, led by Gaddis. See his *The United States and the Origins of the Cold War*. These historians borrowed from Mastny's *Russia's Road to the Cold War*, a study of Stalin's foreign policy emphasizing the dictator's pragmatic ruthlessness in extending Soviet domination over Eastern Europe. They also agree on the virtual indifference as to how Western Europe and the United States might view this dramatic shift in the balance of power. It is important to note, however, that while the Soviet leader was opportunistic and calculating, he nonetheless had limited objectives and was not driven by an expansionist communist ideology. On the American side of the ledger, postrevisionists often point out that President Truman did not have the same flexibility to maneuver as did Stalin and was always subjected to pressures from domestic partisan politics, ethnic and religious voting blocs, and legislative-executive rivalries.

Left-revisionist critics have mounted the most vociferous critique of American Cold War policy. Early on, Fleming in *The Cold War and Its Origins* and then Gardner in *Architects of Illusion* and LaFeber in *America, Russia, and the Cold War* drew attention to the negative qualities of Harry Truman's personality. The president was irascible, uncompromising, and brusque, as demonstrated by his sharp comments to Soviet Foreign Minister Molotov in June 1945 for not respecting the Yalta agreements on Poland. Although Truman was frequently decisive, he was not particularly well informed of the complexity of the issues compared to his predecessor, Franklin Roosevelt. Other critics, especially Williams in *The Tragedy of American Diplomacy*, focused on the retrograde expansionist ideology that produced conflicts with the British and Spanish in the nineteenth century and the Soviet Union in the twentieth. The most radical of the left-revisionists suggest that capitalism, in its drive to secure foreign markets and outlets for investment, made conflict with the progressive and centrally planned economies of the communist bloc inevitable. From the Soviet viewpoint, expansion into Eastern Europe and other areas was incremental, justified by long-standing concerns about national security, and always in response to some provocation by Western capitalist nations.

Contemporary radical critics, while still assigning responsibility for the onset of the Cold War to the United States, have tempered their writing style and incorporated new approaches. The insights of world systems theory with its emphasis on the requirements of a global capitalist system, rather than merely those of the American economy, have been adopted by a former student of Williams, McCormick, in his *America's Half-Century*. Hogan, "Corporatism," and others have borrowed from the work of organizational historians and focused on the structure and function of the decision-making process with particular reference to the role of private-sector groups from business, labor, and agriculture in foreign policy making. The implication is that elites acting in the pursuit of economic self-interest, not necessarily the overall interests of American capitalism and its ruling class, control the political process, albeit in a somewhat antidemocratic manner. The most recent criticism has been developed by Leffler and Painter, who argue in *Origins of the Cold War* that an ideology of national security became institutionalized into large bureaucracies: State Department, Defense, and the National Security Council. From the perspective of these departments the long-term threat—one in which a potential adversary would gain the economic resources necessary for a sustained military attack—posed the greatest danger to American security. The United States did not define its national security simply, however, as the defense of its territory and sovereignty to immediate threats posed by the Soviet Union. An expanded vision of what constituted security included the continued survival of core values and ideological predilections such as individual liberty, private property, and due process, ideas associated with Lockean liberalism. Policymakers sought to create an international environment conducive to the survival of these ideas as well as a balance of power that would ensure security from a direct military attack.

Historians in Canada and Europe who have written extensively on the Cold War selectively borrow from the work of the Americans but add insights based on work in their respective national archives. Aronsen and Kitchen's *Origins of the Cold War* and Smith's *The Diplomacy of Fear* explain the emergence of an anti-Soviet perspective in Canada within the context of North Atlantic triangle relations as well as a function of Canada's unique strategic-geographic position between the two major Cold War protagonists. European historians have examined the origins of a Cold War mind-set within their region based on perceptions of how the Soviets were changing the continental balance of power. Bullock's biography of *Ernest Bevin: Foreign Secretary* develops this theme particularly well. Lundestad's *The American Non-Policy towards Eastern Europe* discussed how European countries generally extended an "invitation" for American economic and military support during the crisis years 1945 to 1950.

THE ATOMIC BOMB, THE WAR IN ASIA, AND ITS AFTERMATH

The dropping of the atomic bombs on Hiroshima and Nagasaki has been described by left-revisionists as the first political act in the growing conflict with the Soviet Union rather than the final execution of the military strategy to end the Second World War. In his *Atomic Diplomacy* Alperovitz, the leading critic of the atomic bombing policy, maintained that the Japanese in August 1945 were on the verge of surrender, and the Truman administration was fully aware that an invasion would, in all probability, be unnecessary.

Under the Yalta agreement the Soviet Union promised to enter the war against Japan as soon as possible following the German surrender. After the successful testing of the bomb in July 1945 President Truman and his advisers, notably Secretary of State Byrnes, recognized that Soviet assistance was now unnecessary and, in fact, presented a disadvantage to postwar American plans for Asia. Although the Truman administration was aware that the Japanese were defeated, the bomb presented an opportunity to end the war immediately before the anticipated Soviet attack on Japanese troops in Manchuria, which would set the stage for future Soviet involvement in the Far East. Thus, the dropping of the bomb would assure the maintenance of the "open door" for American trade and investment in China, encourage the Russians to be more accommodating in their occupation of Poland and other Eastern European countries, and improve the American position in postwar peace negotiations.

Several points have been made in response to the questions raised by Alperovitz. Sherwin in *A World Destroyed* noted that the exclusion of the Soviets from the Manhattan project was originally Churchill's, rather than Roosevelt's, idea. Moreover, it was difficult for Roosevelt to cooperate, given Stalin's unwillingness in 1942 to share research and development information regarding various weapons systems such as tanks, heavy artillery, and rocket technology. Bernstein's writings, especially "Understanding the Atomic Bomb and the Japanese Surrender," and Walker in "The Decision to Use the Bomb" developed several other analytical threads. The dropping of the atomic bombs ended the war on American terms, punished the Japanese for Pearl Harbor and the Bataan "Death March," and avoided what could perhaps be a costly invasion. They also stress bureaucratic momentum generated by the fact that the atomic bomb project was the largest weapons development program during the war. In the end there was little serious criticism offered by key administration officials within the Manhattan project.

In *Marching Orders* Lee used deciphered Japanese codes to conclude that the Truman administration fully understood that although Japan was defeated, the military elite remained intransigent and unwilling to surrender. McCullough in his *Truman* adds that the president would have been impeached were it found out later he sent troops to their death if the bomb could have been dropped instead.

Other aspects of American policy in Asia from 1945 to 1947 have come under criticism as contributing factors in the onset of the Cold War. The Truman administration excluded the Soviet Union from any discussion or participation in the occupation of Japan. The Department of Defense as early as 1945 began establishing air and naval bases in Japan, described by Dower in "Occupied Japan and the American Lake" as "ominous and provocative." The United States further signaled its counterrevolutionary designs in East Asia through the policies of the Occupation government under General MacArthur, which restricted communist influence on political and labor movements.

In the case of China, the United States pursued what Moscow officials perceived to be unnecessarily provocative policies backing the Chiang Kai-shek government on the basis of its anticommunist policies. At the Potsdam Conference in July 1945 the president pressed the Soviet leader to play a lesser role in Manchuria and North China than had been previously agreed to at Yalta. Later that year the United States deployed troops to Manchuria, fueling Stalin's concerns about capitalist expansion. The underlying purpose of securing the East Asian sphere of influence, from the perspective of radical critics like the Kolkos in their *Limits of Power*, was to stabilize the Pacific Rim trading system and "to get businessmen back into China for their sake and for China's sake."

Recent studies indicate that American Far Eastern policy was more complicated than left-revisionists have suggested. It is correct to emphasize that Presidents Roosevelt and Truman pursued a serious role for the United States in East Asia, viewing China as the major regional stabilizing power while limiting the expansion of Soviet power in that area. Toward this end, the basic objective in 1945/1946 was to avert a civil war between the Nationalist government and the communist rebels, a situation that, if it were to arise, would present an opportunity for further Soviet meddling in Asia. According to President Roosevelt, the situation was similar to the Spanish civil war, "only on a far greater scale, and with graver dangers inherent in it." Larger geopolitical considerations prevailed, and there is little evidence that policy was determined on the basis of the possibility of economic expansion in the postwar China market. If domestic factors played a role in policy making, they were anticommunist ideology and partisan politics, specifically the influence of the China lobby and of conservative Republicans in Congress.

Anticommunist historians believe that the Maoist communists were simply agents of the Soviet Union, while contemporary postrevisionists believe the ties were always tenuous. There is a consensus however, that although the Truman administration extended $3 billion in military and economic aid to the Nationalist government between 1945 and 1948, little was done to "save China." Instead, the highest priority was given to the application of the containment policy in Europe. There were limits, moreover, in applying such a policy to China because by 1947 President Truman recognized that such a policy was not practicable, given the corruption and general incompetence of the Chiang Kai-shek regime. Consequently, American policy from 1947 to 1949 remained unfocused and not especially provocative toward the Soviet Union until the final triumph of the communists led by Mao Tse-tung.

In *Patterns in the Dust,* Tucker makes a case that Truman and his secretary of state, Dean Acheson, had reconsidered earlier views about the monolithic nature of Asian communism and by 1949 viewed Mao as a potential Chinese Tito. Some documentation exists indicating that the United States was considering diplomatic recognition prior to the outbreak of the Korean War in June 1950. Other evidence provided by Heinrichs, "American China Policy," suggests that two ways of thinking prevailed from 1947 to 1950. One view popular in the State Department continued to hold out hope for a new Tito; the other, held by the Department of Defense, believed that China under the Maoist communists would be "a satellite of the Soviet Union and a springboard for Soviet expansion." In "United States, the Chinese Communist Party, and the Soviet Union" Sheng drew on declassified communist Chinese sources and interviews, as did Kuisong in "The Soviet Factor." The picture that is now beginning to emerge is that Mao was much closer to Stalin than previously believed, and his suspicions of the United States were deeply rooted. These authors concluded that a policy of accommodation based on the idea of Mao as a potential "Asian Tito" would have encountered little success.

THE COMMUNIZATION OF EASTERN EUROPE

A decline in criticism of the United States and a shift in emphasis toward the aggressive behavior of the Soviet Union are most notable in the writing on Eastern Europe. The left-revisionist interpretation acknowledges that the Soviet Union may have been politically intemperate in the consolidation of its control over Poland, Hungary, Czechoslovakia, Rumania, and Bulgaria. Stalin was, however, a generally cautious and pragmatic politician and acted only in response to what he perceived as aggressive behavior on the part of the United States. Given the history of invasions throughout Poland and other countries, the Soviets had legitimate security concerns that justified the creation of a defensive zone along their western borders.

The tightening of Soviet control over Eastern Europe correlated with several provocative acts carried out by the United States, including the abrupt termination of lend-lease, stalling on a proposed $10 billion reconstruction loan, and the limiting of trade in 1945–1946. The Soviets were understandably annoyed by the American double standard of maintaining a sphere of influence in the Western Hemisphere while arguing for liberal democracies and an open door for trade and investment in Eastern Europe. Furthermore, it was their understanding that the United States supported the British idea of spheres of influence incorporated in the 1944 agreement between Churchill and Stalin. Left-revisionists have identified a series of specific provocative acts committed by the United States between 1945 and 1947: public criticism of the absence of democracy in Poland, the decision to fuse the British and American zones in Germany, and the imposition of restrictions on exports to the Soviet-occupied zone in 1946. By 1947 the Soviets viewed everything in terms of a zero-sum game and were not receptive to Marshall plan overtures to provide aid to Eastern Europe in 1947. They became suspicious of the intentions of the Truman doctrine and therefore did not feel compelled to live up to the Yalta accords or the sovereignty provisions in the United Nations Charter.

Realist historians have also criticized American policy in Eastern Europe. The Roosevelt and Truman administrations, influenced by domestic political considerations and the universalist aspirations of Wilsonian ideology, unnecessarily antagonized the Soviets in 1944–1945 by not accepting a spheres of influence arrangement. Moreover, Washington officials did not appreciate the Soviet contribution to winning the war and did not understand the implications of the Red Army's occupation of Eastern Europe. Given these realities, it was impossible to bring about a neutralized Eastern Europe through the use of diplomatic pressure or economic instruments of policy. Consolidation of Soviet power was inevitable, and any pressure that the West exerted on Stalin only exacerbated and tightened Soviet control of the area.

Anticommunist historians and specialists on Soviet foreign policy have been prolific in their research and publication on issues connected with the Cold War in Eastern Europe. In contrast to most American diplomatic historians, Mastny (*Russia's Road*) and Taubman (*Stalin's American Policy*) have shifted the discussion to an examination of Stalin's motivations and intentions, disputing claims that the Sovietization of the region was a defensive response to the West. The decision to establish a sphere of total control regardless of what the United States and its allies did was made during the Second World War, before problematic questions could be raised about Poland and the Balkans. In April 1945 Stalin ominously reminded his wartime Allies that social systems are imposed by occupying armies and not necessarily through the use of free and open elections. Bulgaria became a memorable example of how the Stalinist formula was going to be applied. Despite that country's long-standing friendly relationship with the Soviet Union, the occupying Red Army provided the surreptitious cover for the effective dismemberment of the Sofia government by the end of 1945. Sovietization was imposed on other parts of the Balkans before the Marshall plan and the promulgation of the Truman doctrine, two factors that have been cited by left-revisionists as the provocation that led Stalin to order the integration of Hungary and Czechoslovakia into the communist bloc.

Mastny pointed out that the Western Allies missed an opportunity to stand up to the Soviets before the German surrender because, as important as the Red Army was to the outcome of the war, it was less crucial after the June 1944 Normandy invasion. Stalin was not ready to risk a total diplomatic break with his wartime Allies, and he vacillated between cautiousness and opportunism, depending on the circumstances. Consequently, it is likely that the Soviet dictator would have responded favorably at Yalta if the West had insisted on ironclad guarantees to maintain a democratic government in Poland. Given the brutality of the communization of Eastern Europe, the West was right to denounce, at least publicly, Moscow's predatory behavior.

The motivations and basic objectives of American East European policy have also come under close examination by historians who do not share the realist or left-revisionist point of view. Mark, in taking to task the realist interpretation, argued in "American Policy toward Eastern Europe" that

Washington's opposition to spheres of influence was conditional and not absolute in that Soviet control over the foreign policies of its eastern satellites would be tolerated, but not the imposition of totalitarian regimes domestically. Realists also overlooked documentary evidence indicating that State Department officials did, indeed, recognize the limits of American power in affecting the course of events in the region, the implications of the Red Army's 1944 offensive for future political developments, and the futility of consistently challenging the Soviets in their own sphere of influence.

As for the underlying causes of policy, left-revisionists have been unable to establish a connection between the pursuit of capitalist interests and the containment of communism in Eastern Europe. Although the United States paid some attention to loosening Polish and Yugoslavian ties to the Soviet Union, it did not, according to Lundestad in *The American Non-Policy Towards Eastern Europe*, have a clear and consistent policy overall. The United States had negligible trade and investment ties historically, and there is little documentation to suggest that policy was based on economic considerations about securing an "open door." American investments in Eastern Europe before the war constituted only 4 percent of worldwide investments, and trade amounted to 2.1 percent of the total. Businessmen's complaints about communist nationalization after 1945 were generally ignored by the State Department. In short, American policy toward Eastern Europe from 1945 to 1947 was erratic, characterized by diplomatic efforts to secure liberal democracies while, at other times, overlooking the excesses of Sovietization. These inconsistencies reflected the changing influence of the Polish-American community and the media on decision making in Washington, competing views among State Department officials, strategic considerations, legal-moral concerns among White House advisers, and the idiosyncratic impulses of the president.

THE MIDDLE EAST

After the consolidation of Soviet power in 1945 throughout the inner-sphere countries, Poland, Rumania, and Bulgaria, the growing Soviet-American confrontation shifted into the Mediterranean region and the Middle East. The sequence of events in 1946–1947 followed a pattern of American reaction to perceived Soviet expansion beyond its recognized sphere of influence in Eastern Europe. At the end of 1945 Radio Moscow announced the creation of an autonomous Republic of Azerbaijan in the northwestern part of Iran, where Red Army troops were stationed. Under the 1942 occupation agreement, the Allies were to withdraw all their troops from Iran within six months of the end of the war. But it was only after the British first confronted the Soviets to withdraw and Whitehall's efforts to persuade Washington to take a more activist role, that President

Truman in March 1946 imposed an ultimatum calling for the withdrawal of the Red Army. Later in August of that year Stalin exerted pressure on Turkey to get access to the Dardenelles as well as territorial concessions along its eastern borders. Reports reached the State Department, at the same time, indicating that communist guerrillas in Greece were being trained and equipped in Yugoslavia, Albania, and Bulgaria.

Interpretation of these events has essentially been polarized between left-revisionists and those historians critical of the Soviet Union but generally supportive of the Truman administration. In the case of Turkey, left-revisionists have emphasized Moscow's legitimate security interests in the context of Turkey's long-standing hostility to communism. Stalin in particular hated everything Turkish except their cigarettes. The demand for joint control of the Dardenelles was a reasonable security consideration, given the fact that the Soviet Black Sea fleet had no other access to the Mediterranean. The eastern border controversy in 1946, a minor issue exaggerated by the Turks, was simply an effort on the part of the Soviets to regain former territories lost in 1921 that had belonged to Armenia and Georgia. The civil war in Greece, at least from the perspective of the Kolkos, *The Limits of Power*, and Kofas, *Intervention and Underdevelopment*, was a legitimate uprising against a reactionary regime partial to the Nazi occupation during the war. Even though some aid came from Yugoslavia, Tito acted independently of Moscow in supporting the Greek guerrillas. The announcement of the Truman doctrine in 1947, which called for military assistance to Greece and Turkey, was simply a pretext to undermine all left-wing movements around the world regardless of their ties with the Soviet Union. American meddling in Iran reflected a predatory design to carve out a sphere of influence in order to gain access to oil, at the expense of the Soviet Union and its unsuspecting ally Great Britain.

Other scholars have offered a significantly different interpretation. Kuniholm's "U.S. Policy in the Near East" argues that the Turkish incident was not an isolated regional development but was correctly viewed by Washington as a part of larger Soviet strategy to expand its influence in the Middle East at the expense of Britain's. In recognition of the decline of British power, the United States acted not to compromise its steadfast ally but to maintain the empire's traditional sphere of interest in the region. Similarly, in the case of Greece, White House officials viewed the communist uprising as linked to Soviet efforts to expand into the Mediterranean. Stavrakis' *Moscow and Greek Communism*, based on access to Greek Communist Party documents, suggests that between mid-1945 and late 1946 the Soviet Union supported the Greek uprising indirectly through surrogate countries. The Labor government, according to Bullock in his *Ernest Bevin*, first became alarmed over Soviet influence in the Middle East, and, despite presumed ideological conflict, Prime Minister

Attlee and his foreign secretary, Bevin, made every effort possible to secure further involvement from the capitalist Americans.

The 1945–1946 crisis in Iran provides still another example of how other countries attempted to manipulate the United States in the pursuit of their own national interests. Having a long history of Great Power intervention in their domestic affairs, the Tehran government under the shah attached the highest priority to removing Soviet troops stationed in the northern province of Azerbaijan. To this end, the Iranian ambassador in Washington, Hossein 'Ala, complained to the media, State Department officials, and the White House about the Soviet efforts at propaganda and subversion through the Tudeh Party to establish a separate communist state in the northern part of the country. These accounts exaggerated Soviet meddling, as did later reports about units of the Red Army marching toward Tehran. McFarland's "A Peripheral View of the Origins of the Cold War" concludes that Iranian efforts contributed significantly to the direct involvement of the United States by March 1946. The larger point highlighted by this incident is that under the right circumstances even smaller Third World countries can give direction to events, often playing off one Great Power against another.

Other historians have suggested that Iranian efforts to manipulate American opinion unfolded within the larger context of bureaucratic politics in Washington. Some State Department officials, disposed toward democratic ideals, believed the liberal intentions of the shah to reform his country. Department of Defense officials, taking a more pragmatic view, emphasized the importance of Iranian oil in strategic military planning. Most influential was the effect of captured German wartime documents indicating that Soviet designs on the Middle East were continuous with those of the czarist government of the nineteenth century. Secretary of State Byrnes therefore recommended by March 1946 that a traditional balance of power approach be adopted, the central assumption being the need to support British interests in the region to contain further Soviet expansion. The German documents and other evidence convinced President Truman that the Iranian incident was part of a larger initiative to dominate the Middle East and that it was now time to stop "babying" the Soviets.

CONCLUSION

Some commentators on the writing of Cold War history have observed a tempering in the hitherto acrimonious debates about American responsibility for the breakdown of the wartime alliance. Historians of the early postwar period had become, by the 1990s, more sophisticated in their methodology, more internationalist in their research, and less ideologically driven in their assessments about capitalism. The tone of this writing, however, is one of lament over the decline of left-revisionism coupled with a self-congratulatory view that only those on the Left have offered an alternative to the official pronouncements of the Truman administration. In "Commentary: Ideology and Neorealist Mirrors" Stephanson, for example, believes that traditionalists and even some realists/postrevisionists have simply styled themselves as "ersatz policymakers" or "straightforward apologists" for the power structure. No mention is made of the 1950s conservative anticommunist critics of the containment doctrine. Those like Stephanson who are informed by a leftist critical perspective should not be too alarmed because the recent outpouring of books by Cumings, *The Origins of the Korean War*; Hogan, "Corporatism"; Leffler, "New Approaches"; and McCormick, *America's Half-Century* suggests there is still a strong undercurrent of opinion that the United States holds most of the blame for the cause of the Cold War.

While the debate that began in the 1960s about the extent of American responsibility for the Cold War continues, the work of Gaddis, *United States and the Origins of the Cold War*; Kuniholm, *Origins of the Cold War*; Pollard, *Economic Security and the Origins of the Cold War*; and Woods and Jones, *Dawning of the Cold War*, together with the perspective of Aronsen's *Origins* and Lundestad's *American Non-Policy*, has restored the academic balance of power through an updated nationalist and postrevisionist analysis. These historians do not dwell on the hegemonic implications of American efforts to expand the world capitalist system.

Questions can now be raised about why the United States acted with such restraint to impose market economies on Eastern Europe, Asia, and some of the Western Allies. Why, for example, was a $3.6 billion loan extended to the British in 1946 after that government stated its commitment to socialist policies such as nationalizing major industries and redistributing income, not to mention its restrictive trade practices imposed by the imperial preference system? Why did the Truman administration and Congress settle for the creation of an imperfect world trading system under the General Agreement on Tariffs and Trade (GATT), which provided for modest tariff reductions and the continuation of nontariff barriers? In the pursuit of national security objectives to unify the Western bloc, to what extent did the United States extend favorable loan conditions, implement international pricing levels conducive to the success of foreign raw materials producers, and encourage defense-related technological transfers through the expansion of the multinational corporations? If communist countries viewed American foreign economic policy from 1944 to 1947 as aggressively uncompromising, why did they by the 1970s seek out assistance from the World Bank and membership in the GATT?

Another reason for the shift away from a radical critique relates to the appearances of dozens of new Cold War scholars over the past decade

who, in the never-ending pursuit of publication, have led to the uncov-
ering of a multiplicity of factors underlying policy making. In several instances policy making cannot be directly connected to the dictates of
capitalism, the influence of the military-industrial complex, or the shortcomings of Truman's personality. For example, legislative-executive conflicts are important considerations when looking at Eastern Europe, the
Marshall Plan, and the creation of the North Atlantic Treaty Organization
(NATO). Foreign economic policy has been the product of interactions
among the State Department, the Treasury, and the White House staff.
For an understanding of military strategy one must first come to know the
nature of bureaucratic rivalries within the Defense Department and between it and other government agencies.

Recent research on the relationship between the state of American strategic capability from 1945 to 1947 and foreign policy objectives suggests
that the United States wished to maintain at least a modus vivendi with
the Soviet Union. Borowski in *Hollow Threat* and Williamson and Rearden
in *The Origins of U.S. Nuclear Strategy* emphasize the inattention to building
up the atomic arsenal—as late as the spring of 1947 President Truman
did not know how many bombs were in the stockpile. By the summer of
that year the Atomic Energy Commission reported that there were thirteen bombs available and seventeen atomic-modified B-29 bombers. The
first strategic atomic plan, code-named BROILER, was not approved by
the Joint Chiefs of Staff until the fall of 1947. This suggests that little
thought was given to atomic diplomacy as a means of seriously confronting
the Soviet Union in the immediate postwar period. For the most part,
President Truman was primarily concerned with balancing the budget and
less about preparing for a major confrontation with the Soviet Union,
which could escalate into World War III.

Whatever responsibility may be assigned to the United States for the
breakdown in relations between the superpowers begins to pale in the
light of recently declassified Soviet documents, memoirs, and publications
of Russian revisionist historians. The availability of these new materials has
prompted some diplomatic historians such as Gaddis (see his "Tragedy
of Cold War History") to turn their attention to Stalin: his paranoid personality, Machiavellian political style, and relentless probing for weaknesses in the Western position. Historians formerly attached to Soviet
academic apparatus such as Vladislav Zubok and Konstantin Pleshakov
have produced essays showing how Stalin created a "culture of confrontation" with the West in order to blame his own nation's failings on an
external threat. These studies, in some respects, have turned the clock
back to the questions raised by nationalist and anticommunist historians
in the 1950s.

If less blame can rightfully be attached to the United States, one should
not overlook some of the major shortcomings of the Truman administra-

tion's policy from 1945 to 1947 that later set the stage for major miscalculations. Communism came to be viewed as a global, monolithic, and relentlessly expansionistic force. Thus, in the words of the State Department's China Paper, Maoist revolutionaries had not created an independent state but a "Soviet Manchukuo." Tito's pressure on Trieste in 1945, the shooting down of American transport planes the following year, and military aid to the Greek communists were viewed as actions controlled totally by Moscow, not an independent Yugoslavia. While the United States recognized the nationalistic aspect of Tito's government by 1948, it did not recognize the difference between the Vietnamese and Chinese communists in the 1960s. Similarly, the United States consistently misperceived Soviet military capabilities, an example being the overreaction to the 1947 flyby in Moscow leading to fears about the long-range threat posed by Soviet bombers. A final problem was that in its efforts to stop further communist expansion, the United States ended up supporting questionable regimes, ones not particularly informed by the values of Lockean liberalism.

Acknowledging these weaknesses, especially in the aftermath of the Cold War, may prevent historians from falling into the abyss of what Leffler describes as "moral triumphalism" in "New Approaches." Leffler drew attention to the curious amorality and indifference on the part of President Truman to Stalin's contempt for human rights at home but an excessive preoccupation with the projection of Soviet power abroad. Although the aims and objectives of Soviet expansion remain vague, Gaddis concluded in "Tragedy" that it meant "complete insecurity for everyone else." This expansion from 1945 to 1947 was undertaken so completely and with an efficiency comparable to Hitler's absorption of Czechoslovakia and Poland that nobody among the Western Allies knew where it would end. Former secretary of state, Dean Acheson, reminded us in *Present at the Creation* that in a world not restrained by international law or morality, a natural order will prevail. But, he warned, "the price that nature extracts upon error is death." In the inhospitable world of 1947 this was a not unreasonable assumption to make, given the challenges facing American leaders.

BIBLIOGRAPHY

Acheson, Dean. *Present at the Creation: My Years in the State Department.* New York: Norton, 1969, 1983.

Alperovitz, Gar. *Atomic Diplomacy: Hiroshima and Potsdam.* New York: Random House, 1965.

Aronsen, Lawrence, and Martin Kitchen. *The Origins of the Cold War in Comparative Perspective: American, British and Canadian Relations with the Soviet Union, 1941–48.* London: Macmillan, 1988.

Bernstein, Barton J. "Roosevelt, Truman and the Atomic Bomb, 1941–1945: A Reinterpretation." *Political Science Quarterly* 90 (1975): 23–69.

———. "Understanding the Atomic Bomb and the Japanese Surrender: Missed Opportunities, Little-Known Near Disasters, and Modern Memory." *Diplomatic History* 19 (Spring 1995): 227–273.

Black, J. L. *Origins, Evolution, and the Nature of the Cold War. An Annotated Bibliography.* Santa Barbara, CA: ABC-CLIO, 1985.

Borowski, Harry. *Hollow Threat: Strategic Air Power and Containment before Korea.* Westport, CT: Greenwood, 1982.

Bullock, Allan. *Ernest Bevin: Foreign Secretary, 1945–1951.* New York: Heinemann, 1983.

Burnham, James. *Containment or Liberation? An Inquiry into the Aims of United States Foreign Policy.* New York: Day, 1952.

Chamberlain, William H. *Beyond Containment.* Chicago: Henry Regnery, 1953.

Cumings, Bruce. *The Origins of the Korean War.* 2 vols. Princeton: Princeton UP, 1981, 1990.

Dower, John W. "Occupied Japan and the American Lake, 1945–1950." In Edward Friedman and Mark Selden, eds., *America's Asia: Dissenting Essays of Asian-American Relations*, 186–206. New York: Vintage, 1971.

Feis, Herbert. *From Trust to Terror: The Onset of the Cold War, 1945–1950.* New York: Norton, 1970.

Ferrell, Robert. "Truman Foreign Policy: A Traditionalist View." In Richard S. Kirkendall, ed., *The Truman Period as a Research Field: A Reappraisal, 1972*, 11–45. Columbia: University of Missouri, 1974.

Fleming, D. F. *The Cold War and Its Origins, 1917–1960.* 2 vols. Garden City, NY: Doubleday, 1961.

Gaddis, John Lewis. "The Tragedy of Cold War History." *Diplomatic History* 17 (1993): 1–16.

———. *The United States and the Origins of the Cold War, 1941–1947.* New York: Columbia UP, 1972.

Gardner, Lloyd C. *Architects of Illusion: Men and Ideas in American Foreign Policy, 1941–1949.* Chicago: Quadrangle, 1972, 1970.

Graebner, Norman. *Cold War Diplomacy: American Foreign Policy, 1945–1975.* 2d ed. New York: Van Nostrand, 1977.

Heinrichs, Waldo. "American China Policy and the Cold War in Asia: A New Look." In Dorothy Borg and Waldo Heinrichs, eds., *Uncertain Years: Chinese-American Relations, 1947–1950.* New York: Columbia UP, 1980.

Hogan, Michael J. "Corporatism." *Journal of American History* 77 (1990): 153–160.

Kofas, Jon V. *Intervention and Underdevelopment: Greece during the Cold War.* University Park: Pennsylvania State UP, 1989.

Kolko, Joyce, and Gabriel Kolko. *The Limits of Power: The World and United States Foreign Policy, 1945–1954.* New York: Harper and Row, 1972.

Kuisong, Yang. "The Soviet Factor and the CCP's Policy toward the United States in the 1940s." *Chinese Historians* 5 (Spring 1992): 17–34.

Kuniholm, Bruce. *The Origins of the Cold War in the Near East: Great Power Conflict and Diplomacy in Iran, Turkey, and Greece.* Princeton: Princeton UP, 1980.

———. "U.S. Policy in the Near East: The Triumphs and Tribulations of the Truman Administration." In Michael J. Lacy, ed., *The Truman Presidency*, 299–338. Cambridge: Cambridge UP, 1989.

LaFeber, Walter. *America, Russia, and the Cold War, 1945–1966.* New York: Wiley, 1967. 8th ed., New York: McGraw-Hill, 1997.

Lee, Bruce. *Marching Orders: The Untold Story of World War II.* New York: Crown, 1995.

Leffler, Melvyn P. "New Approaches, Old Interpretations, and Prospective Reconfigurations." *Diplomatic History* 19 (Spring 1995): 173–196.

Leffler, Melvyn P., and David S. Painter, eds. *Origins of the Cold War: An International History.* New York: Routledge, 1994.

Lundestad, Geir. *The American Non-Policy towards Eastern Europe, 1943–1947: Universalism in an Area Not of Essential Interest to the United States.* New York: Humanities, 1975.

———. "Empire by Invitation: The United States and Western Europe, 1945–1952." *Journal of Peace Research* 23 (1986): 263–276.

Mark, Eduard. "American Policy toward Eastern Europe and the Origins of the Cold War, 1941–1946: An Alternative Interpretation." *The Journal of American History* 68 (September 1981): 313–336.

Mastny, Vojtech. *Russia's Road to the Cold War: Diplomacy, Warfare, and the Politics of Communism, 1941–1945.* New York: Columbia UP, 1979.

McCormick, Thomas J. *America's Half-Century: United States Foreign Policy in the Cold War.* Baltimore: Johns Hopkins UP, 1989.

McCullough, David. *Truman.* New York: Simon and Schuster, 1992.

McFarland, Stephen L. "A Peripheral View of the Origins of the Cold War: The Crises in Iran, 1941–1947." *Diplomatic History* 4 (1980): 333–351.

Morgenthau, Hans. *In Defense of the National Interest.* New York: Knopf, 1951.

Pollard, Robert. *Economic Security and the Origins of the Cold War, 1945–1950.* New York: Columbia UP, 1985.

Schlesinger, Arthur, Jr. "Origins of the Cold War." *Foreign Affairs* 46 (1947): 22–52.

Sheng, Michael. "The United States, the Chinese Communist Party, and the Soviet Union, 1948–1950: A Reappraisal." *Pacific Historical Review* 62 (1994): 521–536.

Sherry, Michael S. *In the Shadow of War: The United States since the 1930s.* New Haven, CT: Yale UP, 1995.

Sherwin, Martin J. *A World Destroyed: The Atomic Bomb and the Grand Alliance.* New York: Random House, 1975.

Smith, Denis. *The Diplomacy of Fear: Canada and the Cold War, 1941–1948.* Toronto: University of Toronto, 1988.

Stavrakis, Peter J. *Moscow and Greek Communism, 1944–1946.* Ithaca, NY: Cornell UP, 1989.

Stephanson, Anders. "Commentary: Ideology and Neorealist Mirrors." *Diplomatic History* 17 (1993): 285–295.

Strausz-Hupé, Robert, and Stefan T. Possony. *International Relations.* New York: Praeger, 1950.

Taubman, William. *Stalin's American Policy: From Entente to Detente to Cold War.* New York: W. W. Norton, 1982.

Tucker, Nancy Bernkopf. *Patterns in the Dust: Chinese-American Relations and the Recognition Controversy, 1949–1950.* New York: Columbia UP, 1983.

Walker, Samuel J. "The Decision to Use the Bomb: A Historiographical Update." *Diplomatic History* 14 (Winter 1990): 97–114.

Williams, William A. *The Tragedy of American Diplomacy.* New York: Dell, 1972.

Williamson, Samuel R., and Steven L. Rearden. *The Origins of U.S. Nuclear Strategy, 1945–1953.* New York: St. Martin's, 1993.

Woods, Randall B., and Howard Jones. *Dawning of the Cold War: The United States' Quest for Order.* Athens: University of Georgia, 1991.

Zubok, Vladislav, and Konstantin Pleshakov. "Stalin's Inexorable Aggression." In Dennis Merrill and Thomas G. Paterson, eds., *Major Problems in American Foreign Policy.* Vol. 2: *Since 1914,* 284–295. Lexington, MA: D.C. Heath, 1995.

29 War Crimes, International Criminal Law, and the Postwar Trials in Europe and Asia

R. John Pritchard

INTRODUCTION

In addition to the two celebrated international military tribunals held in Nuremberg and Tokyo after the Second World War, tens of thousands of other persons were tried for war crimes in further prosecutions brought by the individual Allied powers after the Second World War.

Most, but by no means all, of these defendants were Germans. In the European theater 5,556 war criminals were tried by Belgium (75), Denmark (80), France (2,107), Luxembourg (68), the Netherlands (204), Norway (80), the United Kingdom (1,085), and the United States (1,857). Others were tried in Europe by Canada. Further war crimes trials were conducted by the Allied and associated powers in Austria, Bulgaria, Czechoslovakia, Ethiopia, Italy, Hungary, Poland, Romania, Yugoslavia, and elsewhere: the statistics in these cases are often unavailable or notoriously unreliable and require further research. The Soviet Union is said to have tried 14,240 in the Soviet Occupation Zone of Germany alone and convicted all except 142 of them by January 1947, but Western scholars have treated these figures with suspicion because it would appear that many of the accused were charged with purely political offenses (particularly anti-Soviet activities).

As many as 5,700 Japanese, Koreans, and Taiwanese were tried in the Far East by Australia, China, France, the Netherlands, the Philippines, the United Kingdom, and the United States for Class B/C offenses against the laws and customs of war. Untold thousands of others were tried in that theater by the Soviet Union: there are no reliable statistics of their number. By far the most numerous postwar prosecutions, however, have been brought by the East and West German governments against their own countrymen, and even after the reunification of Germany those undertakings have continued.

This chapter focuses on available primary source materials and appropriate contexts for considering the postwar trials. Familiarity with the actual records of proceedings is indispensable. Secondary literature surrounding the trials is highly variable in quality and intent. Most of it is impelled by a deep-seated sense of grievance and by a desire to ensure that readers are left in no doubt about the evils committed by those accused of atrocities. There are also many works that analyze particular trials from a critical perspective, generally from the point of view that the trials were procedurally flawed or failed to provide "due process" and were thereby robbed of legitimacy. The bulk of the literature, therefore, should be regarded as commentary, read and considered not as objectively unbiased scholarship but as the product of political, cultural, and often religious points of view that reveal more about the authors than about the proceedings themselves.

Curiously enough, it is not by the quality of the prosecution's case but by the independence, vigor, and perceptiveness (or otherwise) of the defense case that the merit of individual cases is best judged. Above all, the temptation should be avoided to regard judgments by war crimes tribunals as objective or dispassionate in matters of fact or law. The evidence produced by both sides in these adversarial processes deserves to be considered in the light of further historical inquiries into all the circumstances of the particular cases, but the present writer suggests that in his experience the voices of both sides generally deserve to be heard and, with rare exceptions, are authentic.

Courtrooms are dramatic stages, and the sense of occasion that arises within these proceedings is often obscured or distorted by oversimplification in secondary sources that take passages out of context in ways that no one would regard as "fair" or "reasonable" in reports of domestic proceedings. A close study of these proceedings, however, provides real insights into the nature of war and society, their ethical ramifications, historical dimensions, psychological strains, and cultural contexts: a perfectly valid way of learning and anticipating how human beings may react under extreme pressure.

BIBLIOGRAPHIES ON WAR CRIMES AND INTERNATIONAL CRIMINAL LAW

Because the analytical and anecdotal material published on war crimes and war crimes trials of the Second World War is so vast, readers need to consult standard bibliographies for guidance. The best is Tutorow's *War Crimes*. It has significant omissions, imperfections, and inaccuracies, but it is unlikely that these will seriously inconvenience most readers. Tutorow made no attempt, for instance, to consider the substantial literature in Japanese-, Chinese-, or Korean-language sources. Also worthwhile are Lewis' *Uncertain Judgment* and Braham's *The Eichmann Case*. Further bibliographical help is provided by Pritchard's *Tokyo War Crimes Trial*. Ward and Shulman's *The Allied Occupation of Japan* remains indispensable, if dated. Uyehara, *Checklist of Archives in the Japanese Ministry of Foreign Affairs* still fills a gap, as does Young, *Checklist of Microfilm Reproductions of Selected Archives of the Japanese Army, Navy and Other Government Agencies*.

A truly contemporary bibliography is Neumann's 1951 *European War Crimes Trials*. Its virtue remains its excellent indication of the range of material already available by 1945 or that became available while many of the postwar cases were still under way. These trials should be measured by the standards and perceptions of the period in which they occurred. Wolff, *Persecution and Resistance*, is later but has a similar "feel" in relation to source material about the difficulties Jews and anti-Nazi elements faced in Germany and German-occupied territories prior to 1945.

For works on international criminal law see *A Bibliography of International Law* by De Lupis, a barrister who has devoted much of her career to the subject both as an academic and as a practitioner. A new edition of Bassiouni's classic *International Criminal Law* provides a goldmine of updated references. A new edition of his *Crimes against Humanity* has also undergone considerable revision; though lacking a bibliographical section, its footnotes are extensive and much improved. Levie's *Terrorism in War* provides an outstanding introduction to useful reference material. Perhaps the most accessible compendium of the "conventional" laws of war is Schindler and Toman's *The Laws of Armed Conflicts*.

THE UNITED NATIONS WAR CRIMES COMMISSION

The Declaration of St. James in January 1942 formally placed the trial of war criminals on the Allied agenda, leading to the establishment of the United Nations War Crimes Commission (UNWCC) to pool the results of Allied investigations into war crimes and bring their perpetrators to justice. The member governments consisted of the United Kingdom and three of its dominions (Australia, New Zealand, and Canada), India (then still under British rule), ten governments in exile that had fled to the comparative safety of wartime London (Belgium, Czechoslovakia, Denmark, France, Greece, Luxembourg, the Netherlands, Norway, Poland, and Yugoslavia), the Republic of China, and the United States. In this period the "United Nations" denoted nothing more than a wartime coalition of nations committed to hostilities against the European Axis powers and Japan, but it is equally noteworthy that throughout its existence the headquarters of the UNWCC was located in London. While its deliberations were greatly influenced by the United States in particular, the ties that bound the British empire and Commonwealth and the fact that the regular forces loyal to the governments in exile tended to be equipped, clothed, fed, and integrated with the armed forces of the United Kingdom meant that British influence tended to be paramount. This helps explain why the Soviet Union and its dependencies declined to lend support to the commission's foundation and refused to recognize it thereafter. It also explains why the bulk of the publications of the UNWCC were published by His Majesty's Stationery Office in London.

The UNWCC was initially empowered to monitor and coordinate investigations into the evidence of war crimes, to identify perpetrators, and to give advice regarding the existence of prima facie evidence against specific individuals or groups. The particular barbarities of World War II, however, rendered traditional instruments relating to the laws and customs of war inadequate for the prosecution of crimes that now included systematic terrorism, execution of hostages, civilian torture, and myriad other atrocities. As Guptil, custodian of the commission's archives, pointed out in "The Records of the UN War Crimes Commission," as the commission formed opinions about the nature of these crimes and the liability of those responsible, it redefined the concept of war crimes and planned international tribunals different in kind and scope from previous ones. The UNWCC was therefore endowed with a certain degree of technical expertise, but at least from October 1945, if not earlier, it was to be abundantly clear that individual countries would not surrender to the UNWCC the right to determine whom they might or might not try for breaches of the international law of armed conflict. National sovereignty prevailed over international collectivity. In the end, this fatally compromised the authority and relevancy of the UNWCC (and the same result is likely to recur if international lawyers and statesmen succeed in establishing similar institutions in the future).

The commission printed periodical lists of those charged or wanted for interrogation. Two supplemental lists of "key men" served as an incentive for national offices to charge high-ranking Germans. Ultimately, 8,918 charge files were assembled, naming approximately 37,000 Albanian, Bulgarian, German, Hungarian, Italian, Japanese, and Romanian individuals or units involved in war crimes, whose names also appeared in eighty periodical lists distributed to apprehending authorities for purposes of detention and prosecution by member governments in whose territory they had committed their offenses. Priority lists naming particularly heinous criminals emerged in 1947 as a response to the impossible task of apprehending all 20,000 persons listed at the time. In many cases the suspected persons were not nationals of the Axis powers but had committed grave offenses while under German or Japanese military or civil jurisdiction. Nowhere was this clearer than in the Far East, where thousands of Japanese war criminals were actually Korean and Taiwanese nationals, many of whom were camp guards responsible for much of the brutality associated with the notorious Japanese Prisoner of War (POW) and civilian internment. As Flower, who is currently completing what must be regarded as the definitive history of the Burma-Siam Railway, pointed out in "Captors and Captives," guarding some 50,000 POWs who worked on that project initially was entrusted to only forty Japanese officers, eighty-five noncommissioned officers (NCOs), and 1,280 Korean auxiliaries.

Although disengaged from active participation in developing UNWCC policy, a Research Office was an important commission component. Established in May 1944, it produced "Summaries of Information," citing arrest notices from newspapers and providing material for the Nuremberg trial to American and British prosecutorial staffs. Additionally, this office gathered information regarding war crimes legislation, arrests, trials in progress, and commentary into "War Crimes News Digests." While the International Military Tribunals and a variety of military, civilian, occupation, national, and inter-Allied courts tried and sentenced the accused, the commission made arrangements for the examination of their records. During the commission's final days, the research and legal staffs compiled an official history, which reviewed the activities of the commission and the concept of war crimes in general.

The UNWCC's Legal Publications Committee published the commission's *Law Reports of Trials of War Criminals*, with Brand as general editor. The commission intended this fifteen-volume series to be a contribution to the development and codification of this area of international law. Among the most important contributions of this series are its useful essays on different national regulations and practices established by the several Allied powers for the prosecution and punishment of war criminals. For the most part, these are authoritative and remain highly instructive as well as thought-provoking. These *Law Reports* and the United Nations War Crimes Commission's official history are scheduled to be reprinted in the near future, with a short introduction by Pritchard.

The reports on individual cases often do little to capture the nature or complexity of the facts and law at issue. The first fourteen volumes reported on a total of eighty-nine cases. Sixty-one of these were conducted by countries accustomed to common-law traditions, and only twenty-eight cases came from civil or other jurisdictions. No Soviet cases were included nor, more curiously, any Czech, Yugoslav, Belgian, or Luxembourg cases. The trials conducted by the Italians were passed over in silence, too, as were trials conducted by Albania, Bulgaria, Hungary, Greece, and Romania in the Balkans: these trials were a brutal form of housecleaning to settle old political scores. By way of contrast, the Japanese briefly conducted a few token proceedings, but this was seen as merely a ploy to forestall Allied proceedings. The occupation authorities set aside the verdicts, retried the accused, and imposed much heavier penalties upon those convicted. Much the same happened in Germany, notoriously so in the Ardenne massacre case.

The fifteenth volume in the *Law Reports* was a *Digest of Laws and Cases*, with which Brand rounded out the entire work. This provides an overview on the sources of international criminal law, the legal basis of courts' administering international criminal law, the parties to war crimes, the victims of crimes, types and definitions of offenses, permissible and impermissible defenses, court procedures, and sentences. It does not make up for the deficiencies in the reports published in the previous fourteen volumes.

For a time the UNWCC concentrated upon breaches of international criminal law committed in the European theater. Eventually, the Far Eastern Committee, a small group of representatives from governments having an interest in the Pacific theater, recommended the creation of a subcommission to deal with Japanese war criminals and the modification of UNWCC procedures to meet conditions in Asia. Although membership on the subcommission was originally reserved for governments at war with Japan, its scope was later widened. In contrast to summary minutes and associated documents of the main UNWCC and its committees, documentation covering its Far East and Pacific Subcommission is sparse.

The commission expressed periodic concern about the relative independence and meager reportage of its Far Eastern and Pacific Subcommission. Despite minimal direction from London and relative inactivity through mid-1945, however, the subcommission, which was based in faraway Chungking (Chongqing) until the end of the war, when it moved to Nanking (Nanjing), eventually produced two lists of "key men." Meanwhile, Allied war crimes agencies provided Japanese wanted lists to the subcommission for transmission to Allied military commanders engaged in the repatriation of enemy personnel. It printed twenty-six lists of 3,147 Japanese war criminals: 218 were named by the United States, 18 by the Australians, 345 by the French, 43 by the British, and 2,523 by the Chinese.

The individual Allied powers did not feel restricted to limiting their arrest, indictment, trial, and conviction of war criminals to individuals on UNWCC lists. The Australian authorities revealed that by November 1945, 1,045 suspected war criminals had been arrested by the Australian military forces, reaching a peak of 2,219 by June 1946. By the time the UNWCC went out of business in August 1948 that number had fallen to 415.

At the time of the UNWCC's closure, the commission had convicted 2,379 Japanese and 2,857 European war criminals in 1,024 Far Eastern and 969 European cases involving 2,794 and 3,470 suspects, respectively, not counting the Chinese and Soviet trials. These figures, although often cited, were based on incomplete or defective returns; see Levie's *Terrorism in War.*

The national tribunal reports surviving in the records of the UNWCC predominantly concern crimes committed in the name of the Third Reich. The records of the main commission's Far Eastern Committee and a sizable portion of the Far Eastern and Pacific Subcommission's records failed to reach the United Nations Archives. Their whereabouts today, as well as records of several key committees, remain unknown. Given these constraints, it is hardly surprising that the editors who prepared the *Law Reports* experienced difficulties in selecting and highlighting Far Eastern and Pacific cases that were genuinely representative.

Only seventeen of the cases reported in the *Law Reports* concerned trials in the Far Eastern and Pacific theater of the war. In many of the Japanese cases the editors and the commission mixed up the surnames and given names of the accused. The reviews capture little of the nature or complexity of the facts and law in individual cases. The complete proceedings of the Yamashita Tomoyuki case, for instance, consist of 4,063 typescript pages (compressed to 96 pages), and the record of the Honma Masayuki Case weighs in at 3,365 pages (both are available on microfilm from the U.S. National Archives). The Shanghai trials were shorter but still substantially beyond the capacity of the UNWCC editorial team to digest in the limited space allocated to them. The same difficulties are manifest in the UNWCC's official *History of the United Nations War Crimes Commission.*

The Far Eastern trials were not the only ones to be underrepresented in the records and publications of the UN War Crimes Commission. It is particularly regrettable that not one of the Allied war trials of Italian suspected war criminals was reported or even cited in the *Law Reports.* The efforts to digest the Norwegian, Chinese, Dutch, and French proceedings proved troublesome. It was not customary to take official verbatim transcripts in Norwegian trials, and the commission could not obtain copies of transcripts of the Chinese, Dutch, and French proceedings. By contrast the material provided by the United States was far more than could be digested, and much of it was published elsewhere. It is against that background that more recent attempts to develop more systematic compilations on the postwar trials must be measured.

THE INTERNATIONAL MILITARY TRIBUNAL AT NUREMBERG

The full proceedings of the International Military Tribunal (IMT) sitting at Nuremberg commenced on 20 November 1945. In addition to individuals, the tribunal considered whether or not a number of named organizations were criminal. It may be surprising how much attention was given to this rather unconventional aspect of the trial, which entailed findings of guilt by association with far-reaching political and economic effects in all four zones of postwar Germany.

The first English-language official publication of the complete transcripts of the IMT began to appear in July 1946, issued in fortnightly sectional parts as a paperbound, twenty-three-volume work, *The Trial of German Major War Criminals*. His Majesty's Stationery Office (HMSO) also published a *Judgment of the International Military Tribunal*. The tribunal itself published a hardcover edition of its proceedings (with the same lacunae concerning evidence heard behind closed doors) as part of a forty-two-volume series, entitled *Trial of the Major War Criminals before the International Military Tribunal, Nuremberg*. This collection, known as the "Blue Series" after the color of its covers, was printed on highly acidic wood-pulp paper, which is now exceptionally fragile.

The pagination of this Nuremberg edition differs from that of the HMSO edition, and therefore the two sets of finding aids to the HMSO edition are not directly interchangeable. The Nuremberg edition is complete, however, with what is generally the full text of each of the court exhibits, arranged by prosecution or defense document numbers. English-, French-, and German-language exhibits in the collection are published in their original languages. Russian-language exhibits were produced in German and English translations. As only short extracts of the court exhibits tended to be read into the record of the Nuremberg transcripts, these final eighteen volumes are essential for any serious student of the Nuremberg trial. The proceedings were also published in German, French, and a shortened Russian edition.

In addition to the "Blue Series," a further collection, known as the "Red Series," constitutes a main body published by the United States as *Nazi Conspiracy and Aggression*. The first eight volumes include the English-language text of a large number of documents and materials prepared by the British and American Prosecution Divisions for the Nuremberg Major War Crimes Trial, including papers that were not offered or admitted or read in evidence. The recent reproduction on a single CD-ROM disk of both the "Green Series" and the Nuremberg "Subsequent Proceedings" (described later) is greatly welcome, making these materials more accessible to readers.

Of the secondary literature about the Nuremberg IMT, Ginsburg and Kudriavtsev's *The Nuremberg Trial and International Law* is one of the best recent accounts. Conot, *Justice at Nuremberg*, is an in-depth analysis of the origins and preparations for the trial, a summary of the trial itself, a study of the actions of the defendants, and a review of aspects of the history of Nazi Germany that emerged during the proceedings. Smith's *Reaching Judgment at Nuremberg* and *The American Road to Nuremberg* are indispensable. However, the best general introduction is now the Tusas' *The Nurem-*

berg Trial. Like Neave's classic *Nuremberg,* the Tusas' book is also a useful antidote to those who may believe that the Nuremberg IMT was, by and large, prosecuted mainly by the Americans with other participants playing only bit parts.

Other works have focused upon the abnormal psychology of the defendants, such as Persico's *Nuremberg.* On the fiftieth anniversary of Nuremberg a new crop of volumes about the subject appeared, the best of which was a collection of papers published in a commemorative issue of the U.S. Army's *Military Law Review.*

THE INTERNATIONAL MILITARY TRIBUNAL FOR THE FAR EAST

General MacArthur issued the first charter of the International Military Tribunal for the Far East. Composed of eleven members, representing the nations involved in the prosecution, the court met from May 1946 until November 1948, when it rendered judgment, sentencing seven to be hanged, sixteen to life imprisonment, one to twenty years, and one to seven years of imprisonment. The scale and complexity of these proceedings plainly dwarfed those in Nuremberg except on the matter of "criminal organizations," a subject that was to have been reserved for further international proceedings in Tokyo but was, in fact, abandoned.

The official English-language daily typescripts of the proceedings, printed and circulated during the trial, were produced in three slightly different stenciled formats. Due to their length and the prohibitive publication costs, none of the prosecuting countries undertook that task. There was a further difficulty in that the handful of stenciled sets of transcripts scattered around the globe soon were all but unusable without effective indexes and finding aids. Less obviously, every major collection of these records appears to have lacunae, and the original records duplicated on highly acidic paper were subject to rapid disintegration simlar to what afflicted the Nuremberg records.

This deficiency eventually was overcome. The first major breakthrough was a ten-volume collection edited by Nitta, *Kyokutō Kokusai [Stenographic Report],* a finely crafted facsimile reproduction of the official Japanese-language record of the proceedings in open court (but not in chambers). There was already a useful, although somewhat limited, Japanese-language index, *Kyokutō Kokusai Gunji Saiban.* In addition, *Asahi Shinbun* produced *Tôkyô Saiban [The Tokyo Trial].*

In English the dearth of primary materials was even more palpable. The American State Department published a slender *Trial of the Japanese War Criminals* in 1946; it is nothing more than a publication of the indictment. Pal, the Indian member of the tribunal, published his separate opinion as *International Military Tribunal for the Far East.* The full judgment of the

tribunal remained unpublished in its entirety, however, until the last surviving member of the tribunal, Röling, joined with Rüter to produce *The
Tokyo Judgement*, a two-volume work that includes the verbatim text of the
judgment as read in open court and the text of the five separate opinions.

The second major breakthrough took shape as two series conceived and
edited by Pritchard with the assistance of Zaide. The first, *The Tokyo War
Crimes Trial*, appeared in twenty-two volumes. Apart from several introductory essays, including a "Historical Introduction" by Watt, the bulk of
this work consists of an annotated, compact facsimile edition of the official
English-language records of the proceedings in open session and in chambers, altogether approximately 53,000 pages. It preserves the pagination
and format of the original, making no attempt to reset or correct the text.
This series is now being reissued by Pritchard in a new, 110-volume format
including an additional volume of commentary. The second breakthrough, also compiled by Pritchard with Zaide, was a five-volume companion *Comprehensive Index and Guide* of more than 3,500 pages. This, too,
is being updated by Pritchard and will be published in a new, six-volume
format. Both editions supersede all previous indexes and catalogs, including the Japanese *Asahi Shinbunsha Chōsa Kenkyūshitsu* catalog and index
and a better-known, ninety-four-page finding aid compiled by Dull and
Umemura, *The Tokyo Trials*. Pritchard's edition is usable by anyone with
access to archival collections or to his two editions of the trial records.

Quite separately, Wells produced an index devoted to the exhibits of
the Tokyo trial, published under an unwittingly misleading title, *Index to
the Records of the International Military Tribunal for the Far East*. There are
significant differences in approach between this finding aid and those in
Pritchard's collections. Each has its flaws. Nevertheless, they are, in the
main, complementary. Pritchard's *Index and Guide* is far more comprehensive and detailed but makes no attempt to index exhibits not explicitly
mentioned in the proceedings. One difficulty faced by this indexing task
is the large number of very long books, official documents, private diaries,
and newspapers received in evidence and "marked for identification
only." In other instances only excerpts were read into the court transcripts, but the entirety of long documents was admitted in evidence.

The secondary literature on the Tokyo trial is far less voluminous than
its Nuremberg counterpart. Minear's *Victors' Justice* is perhaps the only
book on the subject familiar to most readers new to the subject since the
early 1970s, but Minear was more concerned with the Vietnam War than
with the substance of the Tokyo trial. Until the appearance of Brackman's
Other Nuremberg, there was nothing better in English than Appleman's *Military Tribunals and International Crimes* or Horwitz's extended essay "The
Tokyo Trial." Horwitz was an American assistant prosecutor at the trial;
half a century later his work remains highly informative. Brackman attended the Tokyo trial as a correspondent for *Stars and Stripes*, writing in

a brash style and undiplomatic language favored by American investigative reporters in the 1940s. Brackman outlived all of the members of the tribunal; his account, published posthumously, remained highly critical.

The most recent study, compiled by Cassese, *The Tokyo Trial and Beyond*, is a gloss on the reminiscences of the Dutch member of the tribunal, Röling. It is altogether unsatisfactory, unscholarly, and replete with errors and betrays a level of ignorance about the trial that is quite breathtaking. Ginn's *Sugamo Prison, Tokyo*, by an American participant, is a somewhat simplistic account of those tried and incarcerated, including both Allied POWs whom the Japanese held there and Japanese prisoners sent there by Allied courts. It rather oddly suggests that the "only benefit from conducting War Crimes trials is the psychological moment of restoration it provides for the victors." He concludes that such trials have failed to reduce the later incidence of war crimes, a point of view that only adds to the importance of redoubling continuing efforts to enforce the laws of armed conflict by judicial means.

There is far more about the Tokyo trial in Japanese, but not all of it is well informed or truly scholarly. Shiroyama, *War Criminal: The Life and Death of Hirota Kōki*, is a best-selling, but highly inaccurate and misleading, account of one of the Tokyo trial defendants. For an example of Japanese scholarship at its best, see Kōjima, *Tōkyō Saiban*. Hosoya, Andō, and Onuma edited *Tōkyō Saiban o Tou*, essays read at a major international conference that commemorated Kobayashi's epic, six-hour Japanese feature film *Tōkyō Saiban*, in which the distinguished Japanese motion picture director made extensive use of footage from a U.S. Army Signal Corps film record of the entire Tokyo trial proceedings. Hosoya is the doyen of Japanese historians of the period, and his two coeditors are distinguished Japanese international lawyers. The book was subsequently published in English with the assistance of Minear as *The Tokyo War Crimes Trial*. It remains an outstanding introduction to many of the controversies still surrounding the Tokyo trial. For a good and representative memoir of a prisoner see Kodama's *Sugamo Diary*.

THE QUESTION OF FURTHER INTERNATIONAL PROCEEDINGS AGAINST JAPANESE SUSPECTED MAJOR WAR CRIMINALS

"Crimes against peace," that is, "aggression," was the single defining issue that set the "major" or "Class A" war crimes trials apart from the "Class B/C" trials. The IMT for the Far East found twenty-three of its defendants guilty of that crime, compared to twelve convicted at Nuremberg.

The two other sets of proceedings were the trial of Admiral Toyoda Soemu, a cerebral former chief of the Naval General Staff, and the trial of Lieutenant General Tamura Hiroshi. Strictly speaking, both of these other trials were international in composition, but Americans dominated to such an extent that they are often mistakenly lumped together with the national trials. They bear comparison to the trials established in Germany under the Allied Control Council Law 10. The proceedings of neither trial were published in book form but were stenciled and distributed, with the result that a handful of sets has found its way into research libraries and will reward further study.

THE "SUBSEQUENT PROCEEDINGS" HELD IN GERMANY UNDER CONTROL COUNCIL LAW 10

A passing reference has already been made to the "Subsequent Proceedings" conducted by the Office of the U.S. Chief of Counsel for the Prosecution of Axis Criminality under the Allied Control Council Law 10. These trials were "international" or "German" in that they drew their legitimacy from Germany's unconditional surrender and the four-power condominium exercising executive power over the country. Constitutionally, the Allied powers *were* Germany until they determined otherwise. A large number of trials were conducted by the Soviet Union under the same provisions, but little is known about these cases, and even their number is uncertain.

The American "Subsequent Proceedings" held at Nuremberg in the American Occupational Zone consisted of twelve cases. Altogether these proceedings took place over 1,200 days in court. The typescript transcripts and exhibits consist of more than 330,000 pages stenciled by multilith machines. A number of sets of these copies have survived in various public and private archives scattered across the globe. It was deemed impractical to publish them in their entirety as printed books, but edited extracts were published by the United States as *Trials of War Criminals under Control Council Law 10* in fifteen volumes. Each of the volumes in the series is between 1,200 and 1,600 pages long. The collection, known as the "Green Series," is not fully indexed, but tables of contents are provided for each trial together with lists of court personae, witnesses, and exhibits that enable readers to navigate through the proceedings.

Any list of the secondary literature about the non-IMT Allied trials in Germany must be headed by Taylor's *Anatomy of the Nuremberg Trials*. Later professor at Columbia University Law School, he was a brigadier general and chief of counsel (the chief prosecutor) in overall charge of the twelve U.S. "Subsequent Proceedings." This work is a tour de force. It looks at the foundation of the law of the trials, pretrial stresses and strains, various personalities and policies, the proceedings themselves, and the defendants and provides a mature analysis of the trial results. See also his "Nuremberg Trials." Other recommended works includes Ziemke's *The U.S. Army* in the Occupation of Germany, Wolfe's *Americans as Proconsuls: U.S. Military Government in Germany and Japan,* and Buscher's *The U.S. War Crimes Program in Germany,* all of which address interconnecting themes (from differing perspectives) and are a delight to read.

THE GERMAN NATIONAL WAR CRIMES TRIALS

By far most Europeans indicted for war crimes were Germans charged by East and West Germany. According to the West German minister of justice, by 1965 some 5,025 Germans had been tried by French, British, and American courts; 5,426 had been prosecuted through the German courts. Approximately 70,000 other Germans had been tried abroad, mainly in Eastern Europe. More than 16,000 were tried in East Germany, and more than 87,000 were indicted in West Germany prior to German reunification (though no further action was taken against about three-fourths of these). By sharp contrast and without any hindrance by the Allied powers, Emperor Hirohito applied his royal prerogative of mercy to grant a general pardon to all Japanese war criminals (apart from those sentenced by the Allied powers) with immediate effect from 3 November 1946, with the result that no Japanese war criminal has been subject to trial or conviction by any *Japanese* court since that time. See Pritchard's "The Gift of Clemency."

The best source for studying many of these trials is the impressive, twenty-two-volume *Justiz und NS-Verbrechen [Justice and Nazi Criminals],* edited by Rüter-Ehlermann and Rüter, a remarkable project, not least because it counterbalances the "Anglo-American" common-law case law that figures so strongly within the literature. It also helps dispel the canard that war crimes trials are merely a means to impose "victors' justice" upon a defeated enemy.

There has been severe criticism of many of the early German prosecutions, especially those known as the "Waldheim trials," initiated when the Soviet Union closed its concentration camps, removed 3,432 prisoners to Waldheim Penitentiary, and transferred jurisdiction over them to the East German authorities. The ensuing trials were manifestly harsh and passed draconian sentences upon those convicted. In the aftermath of the trials, the East Germans, like the West Germans, did achieve remarkably well balanced results after painstaking pretrial investigations. One very good introduction to this subject, strongly recommended by the German Federal Ministry of Justice, is Ruckerl, *The Investigation of Nazi Crimes.* It should be read together with De Zayas, *The Wehrmacht War Crimes Bureau.*

Justiz und NS-Verbrechen is the source of choice for serious students of the West German trials. It reviews 616 cases, each one involving a number of defendants and all tried by German courts between the end of the Second World War and 1966. It looks squarely at the nature and pattern of war criminality committed by Germany and associated powers, considers the prevailing circumstances both historically and at the time of the events giving rise to the trials, and examines the sentences imposed by the German courts against the backdrop of the evidence produced by the prosecution and counterarguments put forward by the defense.

A companion work by Rüter-Ehlermann and Rüter provides indexes to names, military units, place-names, and subjects, a compendium of statutory and conventional laws, a handlist to offenses charged, and lists reporting judicial decisions. For constitutional reasons bearing upon statutes of limitations and for reasons of policy, the only war crimes prosecutions conducted by the German authorities since 1956 have been confined to cases involving murder or manslaughter. The previous Allied war crimes trials covered a much broader range of offenses.

THE ALLIED NATIONAL WAR CRIMES TRIALS

Early on there were isolated volumes devoted to the Allied proceedings against European Axis and Japanese war criminals, such as *The People's Verdict*, a commentary on two 1943 trials of Germans hauled before Military Tribunals of the Fourth Ukrainian Front and North Caucasus, and *Materials on the Trial of Former Servicemen of the Japanese Army Charged with Manufacturing and Employing Bacteriological Weapons*, edited extracts from a nineteen-volume transcript of proceedings held in Khabarovsk during 1949, published by the Union of Soviet Socialist Republics. Because these works closely concentrate upon individual "show trials" and were exceptionally politicized, it is difficult to extrapolate wider principles or good practices from them.

THE EXAMPLE OF THE BRITISH WAR CRIMES TRIALS IN THE FAR EAST

The British war crimes trials in the Far East, generally speaking, were more useful as legal precedents than any other trials held following the Second World War. This can be attributed, in part, to the size of the investigative effort (involving over 650 investigators), the self-evident importance of demonstrating through a transparent integrity and evenhandedness of the proceedings that the return of British administrators to Southeast Asia should be counted as a blessing by peoples throughout the region, and, perhaps most of all, the advantages that distance from metropolitan Britain gave to those who had to organize this great endeavor. After careful selection, Pritchard brought together the complete records of 160 of the British trials, involving over 600 defendants, for a ninety-six-volume collection entitled *The British War Crimes Trials in the Far East*. Following an introductory volume, the individual trials are grouped geographically in a series of subseries. There are thirteen volumes on the Burma-Siam Railway; six on Burma, two on Siam (Thailand); nineteen on Malaya; eighteen on Hong Kong; four on the Andaman and Nicobar Islands; ten on the Southwest Pacific Area; two on French Indochina; two on China proper; one on Japan proper; five on Taiwan; one on the Palau Islands, and six concerning war crimes committed on the high seas. Each of these volumes is capable of standing alone, but they dovetail into one another. The final volume, *A Comprehensive Introduction and Guide,* features a guide to the use of the volumes, a general historical introduction, and a set of finding aids. These finding aids, unobtainable elsewhere, cover the trials selected for publication and all other surviving British trials of Japanese war criminals.

The British War Crimes Trials in the Far East incorporates nearly eighty specially commissioned introductory essays, an unrepeatable opportunity to gather together thoughts about these trials from "survivors" on both sides; from participants in these proceedings, including judges, counsel on both sides, and witnesses; from persons who were responsible for Britain's evolving policies in relation to the apprehension and trial of suspected war criminals; from British, Japanese, Australian, American, Canadian, and European academics who have studied the law of armed conflict, the history of the so-called B/C Class trials, or the wider period to which the trials relate; and from those pursuing claims for compensation either on behalf of survivors of Japanese prisoner of war and civilian internment camps or on behalf of convicted war criminals. The contributors represent a broad cross-section of opinion on controversial aspects of the subject. They set the trial records into contexts that will enable readers to come to a balanced, stereoscopic view that is not necessarily the middle road between those who maintain that trials such as these can only produce abuses of law or caricature the facts in issue and those who feel that, with rare exceptions, these particular trials, at least, were conducted with exemplary fairness.

OTHER PUBLICATIONS OF THE RECORDS OF ALLIED WAR CRIMES TRIALS IN THE FAR EAST

In China and Japan, a number of works have been published consisting of extracts of trial records and associated materials. The most important is Chaen's *BC Kyū Senpan Saiban Kankei Shiryō Shūsei [Collected Materials on BC-Class War Crimes Proceedings].* Chaen included statistical tables, though some are less than reliable. Many of the materials are ephemeral in nature but are nonetheless worth recording. His political perspective is far from liberal. The same publishing firm reissued *Jissō no Saiban Senpan [The Facts of the War Crimes Trials],* compiled by the Japan Judicial Affairs Board and reprinted from the 1952 edition published at the height of the Japanese campaign to secure clemency for all war criminals.

THE FURTHER EXAMPLE OF THE ALLIED TRIALS OF ITALIAN WAR CRIMINALS

The terms of the London Conference Agreement ought to have suggested that the Allied powers exerted themselves to bring Italian suspects to trial. Certainly, the terms of the Italian surrender showed that there was such an intent. Despite these indications, several leading authorities have declared that in contrast with proceedings against German and Japanese war criminals, there were no Allied trials against Italians. Bassiouni, for instance, declared in *Crimes against Humanity*, "The UNWCC listed some 750 Italians as accused war criminals, but they were never prosecuted" (82). This misimpression, quite uncontradicted in recent literature, has no doubt been sustained by the fact that the fifteen volumes of the UNWCC's *Law Reports* make no reference to the Italian trials, and neither does the UNWCC's *History of the United Nations War Crimes Commission*. The series of notable war crimes trials published under the editorship of Maxwell-Fyfe also makes no reference to the Italian cases.

In fact, shortly after the Second World War, fifty-one British trials took place on Italian soil. Of these, eleven involved German suspected war criminals and forty Italian defendants. By no means comparable to the number and variety of trials that the British conducted in the Far East, there are sufficient differences between the Italian trials and others to merit the attention of historians and legal practitioners interested in international criminal law.

The general understanding that it was U.S. policy not to proceed against Italian suspects has now been dispelled by fresh archival research. That same research also revealed that members of the Italian armed forces and a number of Italian diplomats were convicted by the Soviet Union. Other Italian servicemen and Italian civilians described as "professional workers" were sentenced by "people's tribunals" or were still being held pending trial by the Albanians as late as 1949. France, Greece, Poland, and Yugoslavia each convicted a number of Italian military war criminals, and an inter-Allied military court in Bologna convicted other Italians. None of this has previously been reported in published literature. To overcome these lacunae, Garwood-Cutler (a member of the Illinois state bar) and Pritchard are producing a new series entitled *The Allied Trials of Suspected Italian War Criminals*, modeled upon Pritchard's *British War Crimes Trials in the Far East*.

MORE RECENT NATIONAL WAR CRIMES TRIALS RELATING TO THE SECOND WORLD WAR

The most significant trial since the immediate aftermath of the war was the trial of Eichmann in Jerusalem during 1961–1962. There are a considerable literature on this highly controversial trial and international disquiet concerning Eichmann's kidnapping by Israeli agents in South America.

The full record of the court proceedings was made available by the Israeli District Court of Jerusalem as *Criminal Case No. 40/61*. The record of Eichmann's appeal to the Israeli Supreme Court and the final judgment of that court were also published. The most important secondary source remains Arendt's classic *Eichmann in Jerusalem*. The attorney general of Israel, Gideon Hausner, chief prosecutor in the Eichmann case, published his account of the trial in German, translated as *Justice in Jerusalem*. Another important commentary is *Eichmann und Komplizen* by the veteran German jurist Kempner, deputy chief prosecutor in the U.S. "Subsequent Proceedings" at Nuremberg. Pearlman's *The Capture and Trial of Adolph Eichmann* and Papadatos' *The Eichmann Trial* are also worth studying.

Subsequently, the cases of Menten in 1977 and 1979, Barbie in 1987, Polyukhovich in 1991, Touvier in 1994, Demjanjuk in 1995, Priebke and Serafinowicz in 1996, Papon in 1997, and others have been featured in the popular press and have been chronicled and analyzed in scholarly submissions published by legal periodicals. The literature of these and later cases continues to evolve, particularly in the aftermath of legislation passed by Australia, Canada, the United Kingdom, and elsewhere following the end of the Cold War, legislation intended to permit the prosecution of suspects who had previously found refuge in Western countries after the collapse of Nazi Germany. These trials since 1989 have generally been unsuccessful, very protracted, and extraordinarily expensive. The reader interested in the issues surrounding them will find their records and the quality of the proceedings deeply disturbing. The better and more illuminating precedents, alas, lie elsewhere, in the immediate postwar trials, and there the scholar may find them in abundance.

BIBLIOGRAPHY

Appleman, John A. *Military Tribunals and International Crimes*. Indianapolis: Bobbs-Merrill, 1954.

Arendt, Hannah. *Eichmann in Jerusalem: A Report on the Banality of Evil*. London: Faber and Faber; New York: Viking/Penguin, 1963; rev., 1979, 1994.

Asahi Shinbun Tōkyō Saiban Kishadan [Asahi Shinbun Tokyo Trial Press Corps]. *Benron-Hanketsu Hen* [The Oral Proceedings and the Judgment]. vol. 1: *Shōsha ga Haisha wo Sabakeru ka* [Did the Victors Gain an Understanding of the Vanquished?]; vol. 2: *Kenji Hen* [The Prosecution's Case]: *Dai Nihon Teikoku no Hanzai* [The Crimes of the Great Japanese Empire]. Tokyo: Kodansha, 1983.

Bassiouni, M. Cherif. *Crimes against Humanity in International Criminal Law*. Dordrecht and Boston: Nijhoff, 1992, 1997.

———, ed. *International Criminal Law*. New York: Practicing Law Institute, 3 vols., 1987; Dobbs Ferry, NY: Transnational, 3 vols., 1997.

Brackman, Arnold C. *The Other Nuremberg: The Untold Story of the Tokyo War Crimes Trial.* New York: Morrow, 1987.

Braham, Randolph L. *The Eichmann Case: A Source Book.* New York: World Federation of Hungarian Jews, 1969.

Brand, George, ed. *Law Reports of the Trials of War Criminals.* 15 vols. London: HMSO, 1947–1949.

Buscher, Frank M. *The U.S. War Crimes Program in Germany, 1946–1955.* Westport, CT: Greenwood, 1989.

Cassese, Antonio, comp. *The Tokyo Trial and Beyond: Reflections of a Peacemonger.* Cambridge: Polity, 1993.

Chaen, Yoshio. *BC-Kyū Senpan Saiban Kankei Shiryō Shûsei [Collected Materials on BC-Class War Crimes Proceedings].* Tokyo: Fuji Shuppan, 1984–1993.

Conot, Robert E. *Justice at Nuremberg.* London: Butler and Tanner, 1983.

De Lupis, Ingrid. *A Bibliography of International Law.* London: Bowker, 1975.

De Zayas, Alfred M. *The Wehrmacht War Crimes Bureau, 1939–1945.* Lincoln: University of Nebraska, 1989.

Dull, Paul Shirley, and Michael Takaaki Umemura. *The Tokyo Trials: A Functional Index to the Proceedings of the International Military Tribunal for the Far East.* Ann Arbor: University of Michigan Center for Japanese Studies, 1957.

Eichmann, Adolf. *In the District Court of Jerusalem. Criminal Case No. 40/61: The Attorney General of the Government of Israel v. Adolf, the Son of Adolf Karl Eichmann.* Washington, DC: Microcard Editions, 1962.

Flower, Sibylla Jane. "Captors and Captives on the Burma-Siam Railway." In Bob Moore and Kent Federowich, eds., *Prisoners of War and their Captors in World War II,* 227–252. Oxford: Berg, 1996.

Garwood-Cutler, Jane L., and R. John Pritchard. *The Allied Trials of Suspected Italian War Criminals, 1945–1947.* 6 vols. Lewiston, NY: Edwin Mellen, in association with the Kempner Collegium, Niagara Falls, NY, 1997–1998.

Ginn, John L. *Sugamo Prison, Tokyo: An Account of the Trial and Sentencing of Japanese Criminals in 1948, by a U.S. Participant.* Jefferson, NC: McFarland, 1992.

Ginsburg, George, and Vladimir N. Kudriavtsev. *The Nuremberg Trial and International Law.* Dordrecht: Nijhoff, 1990.

Guptil, Marilla B. "The Records of the UN War Crimes Commission." In R. John Pritchard, ed., *The British War Crimes Trials in the Far East (1946–1948).* Vol. 43: *British War Crimes Trials concerned with Japanese-Occupied Hong Kong,* Part I: *An Introduction to the Hong Kong Cases.* Lewiston, NY: Kempner Collegium/ Edwin Mellen, (in press).

Hausner, Gideon. *Justice in Jerusalem.* New York: Harper and Row, 1966; London: Nelson, 1967; New York: Herzl, 1977.

Horwitz, Solis Horwitz. "The Tokyo Trial." *International Conciliation,* No. 465 (November 1950): 475–584.

Hosoya Chihiro, Andō Nisuke, and Onuma Yasuaki, eds. *Kokusai Shinpojiumu Tōkyō Saiban o Tou [The Tokyo War Crimes Trial: An International Symposium].* Tokyo: Kodansha, 1984; English edition (with Richard Minear), 1986.

———. *The Trial of the Major War Criminals before the International Military Tribunal, Nuremberg, 14 November 1945–1 October 1946.* 42 vols. Nuremberg: IMT, 1946– 1949 ["The Blue Series"]. Repr. Buffalo, NY: William S. Hein, 1995; and on CD-ROM, Seattle: Aristarchus Knowledge Industries.

International Military Tribunal v. Hermann Göring and 23 Others (1945–1946). Judgment of the International Military Tribunal for the Trial of German Major War Criminals (with the Dissenting Opinion of the Soviet Member) for the Office of H.M. Attorney General, Cmd. 6964, Misc. No. 12. London: HMSO, 1946; reprinted 1966.

————. *The Trial of German Major War Criminals: Proceedings of the International Military Tribunal Sitting at Nuremberg, Germany*. London: HMSO, 21 parts, 1946–1949.

Japan, Judicial Affairs Board. *Jissō no Saiban Senpan [The Facts of the War Crimes Trials]*. Tokyo: Sugamo Homuiin-kai, 1952.

Kempner, Robert M. *Eichmann und Komplizen*. Zurich: Europa, 1961.

Kodama, Yoshio. *Sugamo Diary*. Translated by Fukuda Taro. Tokyo: Radiopress, 1960.

Kōjima, Noboru. *Tōkyō Saiban*. Tokyo: Chūko-Shinshō, 1971.

Kyokutō Kokusai Gunji Saiban: Mokuroku oyobi Sakuin [The Records of the International Military Tribunal for the Far East: Catalogue with Index]. Tokyo: Asahi Shinbunsha Chōsa Kenkyūshitsu [Rising Sun Newspaper Company Research Office], 1953.

Levie, Howard S. *Terrorism in War: The Law of War Crimes*. Dobbs Ferry, NY: Oceana, 1993.

Lewis, John R. *Uncertain Judgment: A Bibliography of War Crimes Trials*. Santa Barbara, CA: ABC-Clio, 1979.

Military Law Review. Vol. 149: *Nuremberg and the Rule of Law: A Fifty-Year Verdict: A Collection of Works Assessing the Legacy of the War Crimes Trials of World War II*. Charlottesville, VA: Judge Advocate General's School, U.S. Army, Summer 1995 [*sic* 1996].

Minear, Richard H. *Victors' Justice: The Tokyo War Crimes Trials*. Princeton: Princeton University, 1971.

Neave, Airey. *Nuremberg: A Personal Record of the Trial of the Major Nazi War Criminals*. London: Hodder and Stoughton, 1978.

Neumann, Inge S. *European War Crimes Trials: A Bibliography*. New York: Carnegie Endowment for International Peace, 1951; Westport, CT: Greenwood, 1978.

Nitta, Mitsuo. *Kyokutō Kokusai Gunji Saiban Hōhan Sokkiroku [Stenographic Report of the Transcripts of the Proceedings of the International Military Tribunal for the Far East]*. Tokyo: O-matsu-dô Shoten, 1968.

Pal, Radhabinod. *International Military Tribunal for the Far East: Dissentient Judgement*. Calcutta: Sanyal, 1953.

Papadatos, Pierre A. *The Eichmann Trial*. New York: Praeger, 1964.

Pearlman, Moshe. *The Capture and Trial of Adolph Eichmann*. London: Weidenfeld and Nicolson, 1963.

The People's Verdict: A Full Report of the Proceedings at the Krasnodar and Kharkov German Atrocities Trials. London and New York: Hutchinson, 1943, 1944.

Persico, Joseph. *Nuremberg: Infamy on Trial*. London: Viking/Penguin, 1994.

Pritchard, R. John. *The British War Crimes Trials in the Far East, 1946–1948*. 95 vols. Lewiston, NY: Edwin Mellen, in association with Robert M. Kempner Collegium, Niagara Falls, NY, and the British Public Record Office, 1997–1998.

————. "The Gift of Clemency following British War Crimes Trials in the Far East, 1946–1948." *Criminal Law Forum* 7:1 (Summer 1996): 15–50.

Pritchard, R. John, with the assistance of Sonia Magbanua Zaide, eds. *The Tokyo War Crimes Trial: The Complete Transcripts of the Proceedings of the International Military Tribunal for the Far East.* 22 vols. London: Garland, in association with the London School of Economics, London, 1981. Currently being updated by R. John Pritchard and issued in a revised format, 6 vols., by Edwin Mellen, Lewiston, NY, in association with Robert M. Kempner Collegium, Niagara Falls, NY, 1997–1998.

———. *The Tokyo War Crimes Trial: The Comprehensive Index and Guide to the Proceedings of the International Military Tribunal for the Far East.* 5 vols. New York and London: Garland and London School of Economics, 1981–1987. Currently being updated by R. John Pritchard, 6 vols., by Edwin Mellen Press, Lewiston, NY, in association with Robert M. Kempner Collegium, Niagara Falls, NY, 1997–1998.

Röling, Bernard Victor Aloysius, and C. F. Rüter. *Tokyo Judgement: The International Military Tribunal for the Far East.* 2 vols. Amsterdam: UP of Amsterdam, 1977, 1978.

Ruckerl, Adalbert. *The Investigation of Nazi Crimes, 1945–1978: A Documentation.* Heidelberg: C. F. Müller, 1979.

Rüter-Ehlermann, Adelheid L., and C. F. Rüter. *Justiz und NS-Verbrechen: Sammlung deutscher Strafurteile wegen Nationalsozialististischer Tötungsverbrechen, 1945–1966: Registerheft zum 1. Band, mit Hilfsmittelteil und Errataliste [Justice and Nazi Criminals: Compilation of German Penal Sentences against National Socialist Homicidal Criminals, 1945–1966: An Index to Volume 1 with Finding Aid and Corrigenda].* Amsterdam: UP of Amsterdam, 1969.

———, eds. *Justiz und NS-Verbrechen Sammlung deutscher Strafurteile wegen Nationalsozialististischer Tötungsverbrechen, 1945–1966 [Justice and Nazi Criminals Compilation of German Penal Sentences against National Socialist Homicidal Criminals, 1945–1966].* Amsterdam: UP of Amsterdam, 1968–1981.

Schindler, Dietrich, and Jirí Toman, eds. *The Laws of Armed Conflicts.* Dordrecht and Boston: Nijhoff, 1981, 1988.

Shiroyama, Saburō. *War Criminal: The Life and Death of Hirota Kōki.* Tokyo: Kodansha, 1977.

Smith, Bradley F. *Reaching Judgment at Nuremberg.* New York: Basic, 1977.

———. *The Road to Nuremberg.* London: A. Deutsch, 1981; also published as *The American Road to Nuremberg: The Documentary Record, 1944–1945.* Palo Alto, CA: Hoover Institution, 1982.

Taylor, Telford. *The Anatomy of the Nuremberg Trials: A Personal Memoir.* New York: Knopf, 1992.

———. *Nuremberg Trials: War Crimes and International Law.* New York: Carnegie Endowment for International Peace, 1949.

Tusa, John, and Ann Tusa. *The Nuremberg Trial.* London: BBC, 1985.

Tutorow, Norman E., with the special assistance of Karen Winnovich. *War Crimes, War Criminals, and War Crimes Trials: An Annotated Bibliography and Source Book.* Westport, CT: Greenwood, 1986.

Union of Soviet Socialist Republics v. Yamada Otozoo and Eleven Others. Materials on the Trial of Former Servicemen of the Japanese Army Charged with Manufacturing and Employing Bacteriological Weapons. Moscow: Foreign Languages Publishing House, 1950.

United Nations War Crimes Commission. *History of the United Nations War Crimes Commission and the Development of the Laws of War.* London: HMSO, 1948.

United States. *Trials of War Criminals before the Nuremberg Military Tribunals under Control Council Law No. 10, Nuremberg, October 1946–April 1949.* 15 vols. Washington, DC: GPO, 1949–1953 ["The Green Series"].

United States, Office of Chief of Counsel for the Prosecution of Axis Criminality. *Nazi Conspiracy and Aggression.* 11 vols. Washington, DC: GPO, 1946–1947 ["The Red Series"]; available in various microform editions.

Uyehara, Cecil H. *Checklist of Archives in the Japanese Ministry of Foreign Affairs, Tokyo, Japan, 1868–1945, Microfilmed for the Library of Congress, 1949–1951.* Washington, DC: Library of Congress, 1954.

Ward, Robert E., and Frank J. Shulman, with the assistance of Nishihara Masashi and Mary Tobin Espey. *The Allied Occupation of Japan, 1945–1952: An Annotated Bibliography of Western Language Materials.* Chicago: American Library Association, 1974.

Wells, Kenneth M. *Index to the Records of the International Military Tribunal for the Far East.* Christchurch, New Zealand: Library of the University of Canterbury, 1983.

Wolfe, Robert, ed. *Americans as Proconsuls: U.S. Military Government in Germany and Japan, 1944–1952.* Carbondale: Southern Illinois UP, 1984.

Wolff, Ilse R. *Persecution and Resistance under the Nazis.* London: Weiner Library, 1960.

Young, John. *Checklist of Microfilm Reproductions of Selected Archives of the Japanese Army, Navy and Other Government Agencies, 1868–1945.* Washington, DC: Georgetown UP, 1959.

Ziemke, Earl F. *The U.S. Army in the Occupation of Germany, 1944–1946.* Washington, DC: GPO, 1975.

Author Index

Western and Eastern (Asian) names are all listed in Western order. A comma is placed after the surname in all cases to avoid confusion.

Subject Index

About the Editor and Contributors

BEN ARNOLD is Associate Professor at Emory University and author of *Music and War: A Research and Information Guide.*

LAWRENCE ARONSEN is Associate Professor of History at the University of Alberta. His publications include *The Origins of the Cold War in Comparative Perspective* (with Martin Kitchen) and a coedited collection, *The North Atlantic Triangle in a Changing World.*

JEFFREY G. BARLOW is a historian at the U.S. Naval Historical Center, Washington, D.C. He is the author of *Revolt of the Admirals: The Fight for Naval Aviation, 1945–1950.*

MICHAEL A. BARNHART, Professor of History at the State University of New York at Stony Brook, authored *Japan Prepares for Total War: The Search for Economic Security, 1919–1941* and *Japan and the World since 1868.* He edited *The Journal of American-East Asian Relations* from 1991 to 1995.

JONATHAN W. BOLTON is Assistant Professor at Auburn University. He has written on British poets in Egypt during the Second World War and is currently working on a study of British midlife autobiography, 1938–1950.

CONRAD C. CRANE is a career army officer and Professor of History at the U.S. Military Academy at West Point.

STEPHEN CURLEY heads the Department of General Academics, Texas A&M University at Galveston. He is the author of *Living on the Edge: Collected Essays on Coastal Texas* and *Celluloid Wars: Film and the American Experience of War,* with Frank Wetta.

JUDITH E. DONESON is currently Visiting Professor of Jewish History at Washington University, St. Louis. She is the author of *The Holocaust in American Film.*

RUTH ELWELL has recently come to academe after years in the publishing industry. She teaches cinema studies at Empire State College in New York City and New Paltz, New York.

BRIAN FOSS is now Associate Professor of Art History at Concordia University, Montreal.

CAROL N. GLUCK is George Sansom Professor of Japanese History at Columbia University. She is author of *Japan's Modern Myths: Ideology in the Late Meiji Period* (1985) and co-editor of *Showa: The Japan of Hirohito* (1992).

WILLIAM B. HAUSER is Professor of History, University of Rochester. His research interests include Japanese social and economic history and cultural images of war.

M. PAUL HOLSINGER, Professor of History at Illinois State University, is the chair for World War II Studies in the Popular Culture Association.

BENJAMIN H. KRISTY is currently the curator of the Cavanaugh Flight Museum in Dallas, Texas.

LOYD E. LEE is Professor of History and Chair of the department at the State University of New York, the College at New Paltz. He is the author of *The Politics of Harmony: Civil Service, Liberalism and Social Reform in Baden, 1800–1850* and *The War Years: A Global History of the Second World War* and editor of *World War II in Europe, Africa, and the Americas, with General Sources: A Handbook of Literature and Research.*

S. P. MACKENZIE, Associate Professor of History at the University of South Carolina, is author of *Politics and Military Morale* and *The Home Guard* and various articles on prisoners of war.

DONALD J. MROZEK, Professor and Chair of the History Department at Kansas State University, is coeditor of *A Guide to the Sources of United States Military History.*

DIEU THI NGUYEN teaches Southeast Asian history at Temple University. She is writing a monograph on *Water, War, and Peace: The Mekong River and the Struggle for Indochina.*

MARK P. PARILLO is now at Kansas State University, where he is currently researching Japanese and U.S. utilization of transportation systems during World War II.

MARK R. PEATTIE, Senior Research Fellow at the Hoover Institution, has taught at Penn State, UCLA, and the University of Massachusetts, Boston. He is author of several works on prewar Japanese imperialism and, with David Evans, of *Kaigun; Strategy, Tactics and Technology in the Imperial Japanese Navy, 1887–1941.*

RICHARD V. PIERARD, Professor of History at Indiana State University, Terre Haute, is editor of *The Revolution of the Candles*, coauthor of *Two Kingdoms: The Church and Culture through the Ages*, and author of numerous essays on conservative religion and politics.

R. JOHN PRITCHARD has edited with commentary the first English-language publication of the Proceedings of the Tokyo War Crimes Trial. He continues to edit and publish on international criminal law and international human rights.

EUGENE L. RASOR, Professor of History, Emory & Henry College in Virginia, has published many bibliographic surveys, including several relating to World War II.

SHIGERU SATO teaches at Newcastle University, Australia. His publications include *War, Nationalism and Peasants.*

GEORG SCHILD is Wissenschaftlicher Mitarbeiter [resident scholar] in the Department of Political Science and Contemporary History at the University of Bonn. He is the author of *Bretton Woods and Dumbarton Oaks* and *Between Ideology and Realpolitik: Woodrow Wilson and the Russian Revolution.*

GERALD L. SITTSER is Associate Professor of Religion and Philosophy at Whitworth College, Spokane, Washington, and author of four books, including *A Grace Disguised* and *A Cautious Patriotism.*

MARK A. STOLER is Professor of History at the University of Vermont. He is the author of *The Politics of the Second Front* and *George C. Marshall: Soldier-Statesman of the American Century.*

WILLIAM M. TSUTSUI is Assistant Professor of History at the University of Kansas. He is the author of *Banking Policy in Japan and Manufacturing Ideology: Scientific Management in Twentieth-Century Japan.*

THOMAS MARVIN WILLIAMSEN is Director of International Programs at Appalachian State University in North Carolina.

ISBN 0-313-29326-0

90000>

EAN

9 780313 293269

HARDCOVER BAR CODE